The Individual Investor's Guide to

COMPUTERIZED

INVESTING

Twelfth Edition 1995

AAII

AMERICAN
ASSOCIATION OF
INDIVIDUAL
INVESTORS®

The American Association of Individual Investors is an independent, not-for-profit corporation formed in 1978 for the purpose of assisting individuals in becoming effective managers of their own assets through programs of education, information and research.

ISBN 0-942641-57-4

Library of Congress Catalog Card Number: 94-79913

Published by the American Association of Individual Investors, Chicago.

Outside distribution by International Publishing Corporation, Chicago.

Data in this *Guide* were gathered from company releases. Factual material is not guaranteed but has been obtained from sources believed to be reliable.

Table of Contents

Preface

This year we publish the 12th annual edition of *The Individual Investor's Guide to Computerized Investing*. The basic purpose of the book is to provide you with information about PCs and investment-related software, services, on-line databases, bulletin boards, and investment special interest groups.

For the 12th edition, we list over 550 software products and over 150 information services. This edition covers a broad array of investment software and services, some new and others well-seasoned. The list changes from year to year as some vendors succeed and others fail. Some vendors' products do not appear simply because they did not respond to repeated requests for information.

In the first chapter, we tell you how to effectively use this *Guide* and offer suggestions on how to find the best investment software or service to meet your needs. Chapter 2 offers an overview of the types of investment programs and services available and what they can and cannot do for you. With this in mind, you can evaluate the programs listed later in the *Guide*. Chapter 3 details the current state of PC hardware and operating systems. Chapters 4 and 5 are the comparison grids for software and data services. Chapters 6 and 7 contain more extensive descriptions of investment software programs and financial information services.

We include several updated appendixes. Appendix I lists bulletin board systems specializing in investments, and Appendix II is a listing of AAII computerized investing special interest groups (SIGs) throughout the country and other computer users groups.

In using the product descriptions and comparison grids, keep in mind that these are based on data provided by the sellers of the products. Some vendors may have a broad definition of what constitutes a particular function. For example, some sellers may feel that their product performs portfolio management if it tracks more than one kind of investment vehicle. We do not have the resources to verify all the vendors' claims, but we make every effort, on the basis of the information we are provided, to categorize products appropriately.

Many people have contributed to the completion of this book. Martha Crawford served as project editor for the *Guide*. Kurt A. Zauke designed the cover of the book. Mark Fister supervised the data collection and assisted in the revision of the book. Michael Gutierrez and Susan Powlick gathered information from companies and updated the product descriptions. Jean Henrich and Carol A. Monk provided copy editing and proofreading services.

We have made every effort to provide a publication that meets your needs and answers the questions you have when you are planning a computer or software purchase. Nevertheless, we are always looking for ways to further improve the *Guide*, and we welcome your suggestions. We hope this year's edition helps you in your investment program.

John Bajkowski
Editor
Computerized Investing

Financial Analyst
AAII
October 1994

1
How To Use This Guide

The personal computer holds great potential as a tool for assisting investors in their investment program. Our goal throughout this *Guide* is to help people realize this potential. This chapter presents information on how to use the book in ways that make sense to you. You may be tempted to skip past this chapter and dive right into the product descriptions in Chapters 6 and 7. That is fine. This book is designed as a reference source; it is not meant to be read cover to cover. But if you want to get the most out of this book, you should read this chapter to understand how the book is organized, what it contains, and how to select and develop a system that is right for you.

BOOK ORGANIZATION

The book is organized into four main sections. Chapters 2 and 3 provide an introductory examination of investment software and financial information services, along with the proper computer hardware required to make use of these programs. Chapters 4 and 5 include reference grids to help locate products by type. Chapters 6 and 7 provide descriptions of software products and information services. Appendix I provides information on bulletin board systems (BBSs) that have an investment focus, and Appendix II lists and describes user groups that focus on computerized investing.

USING THE BOOK

More and more individuals are buying new computers for either the first time or to replace their old computers. If you are planning to purchase a new computer, plan ahead by finding out what software programs you expect to use and what features they will require from your computer.

Chapter 2 provides an overview of investment software and financial information services. It takes the investment software market and breaks it into functional segments from the universal personal finance programs to the more analytical programs such as fundamental analysis systems. While classifying investment software into these functional groups, the chapter discusses what to look for when considering these applications, what things these programs do well and what they do poorly.

Chapter 2 also explores the area of financial information services. Read this chapter to get a feel for the types of data and services available to investors, the different ways you can obtain this data, and the things to look out for when selecting an information service. The chapter's ideas are tied together in its final section: PCs for investment research. Even if you are familiar with investing and investing software, you should find this section a good reminder that PCs are tools that assist you. They should supplement, but not replace, your investment judgment.

Chapter 3 explores the hardware arena as it supports the computerized investing market. The chapter examines the current computer market, describes basic computer components, and looks at how the components fit together in a complete system. It details various systems for users at different levels and explores where you can purchase this equipment. Readers familiar with computers may want to skip the computer basics and concentrate on the sections that discuss current trends.

Those unfamiliar with computers may want to start out at the computer basics section. It presents information on the major system components such as processors, information storage systems, video systems, printers, communications hardware, and operating systems. The discussion of these areas focuses on what each system does, the current options on the market, and what can be gained or lost using different levels of equipment. The interdependence of these components should become apparent as you go through the process of putting together a system that meets the needs of the software you wish to use. Various systems are constructed for entry-level, intermediate, and advanced users.

The last section of Chapter 3 discusses what your options are when it comes to buying equipment, where you should make your purchases given your knowledge, and what to expect in terms of warranties and service from different dealers.

FINDING THE RIGHT PRODUCT FOR YOU

Computer programs offer no new analytical techniques, only the ability to apply existing techniques more rapidly and perhaps more consistently. Anyone who has studied the markets quickly realizes that there are many techniques that can be applied to value the market and securities. Before you can take the next step and select your system, you must focus on what you want your system to accomplish.

Chapter 2 provides a framework for categorizing programs, but if you are not familiar with the capabilities of computerized systems, it would be helpful to page through the listings and descriptions of software programs in Chapter 6 and financial information systems in Chapter 7. Doing so will familiarize you with the diversity of the market—there are products with capabilities and prices that cover a wide spectrum.

When analyzing your situation, you need to examine the tasks you are doing now and may consider doing in the future, the types of securities you plan to hold in your portfolio, and whether you plan to enter your data by hand or rely on a data service.

If you want to see what other individuals are actually doing, there are three good avenues. There are groups that meet on a regular basis to discuss and present approaches to a computerized investment program. These computer special interest groups (SIGs) are a valuable resource that can also be used to get opinions on the pros and cons of various systems when you get to the point of picking a package. Appendix II provides a list of computer SIGs from across the nation. Most are affiliated with the AAII local chapter network, but a listing of other groups or networks is also provided.

If there is no group in your area, or you are just looking for further contacts on the subject, electronic bulletin board systems (BBSs) provide a way for computer users with modems to exchange ideas and even programs. The AAII operates a no-fee BBS based in Chicago. Its number along with a nationwide listing of other BBSs devoted to investing is provided in Appendix I.

Many of the dial-up financial information services, such as CompuServe, America Online, Prodigy, etc., have forums that focus on computer-assisted investing. AAII operates such a forum on America Online.

Once you have a list of tasks for your computerized system to perform, you can use the reference grids in Chapters 4 and 5. In structuring the book, we have provided separate reference grids for software programs and information services. We have further divided the software grids into four sections—financial planning programs, portfolio management programs, technical analysis programs, and a fourth grid that covers fundamental analysis and other specialized functions such as bond analysis. These grids allow you to quickly narrow down your search to those products that match your needs.

INVESTMENT SOFTWARE

The software grids use five broad categories to describe the software—the system required to run the program, the price, the types of securities or assets the program can handle, the types of analysis the program performs, and the sources of electronic data the program can use. The grids provide a page reference for the product description to get more detailed information.

Paging through the software grids, you should be able to narrow down your search to a reasonable number of products that merit further investigation. In examining your list, here are the things you should consider and look for:

- Talk to other users, see what they are using and what they think about your final candidates. A list of local computerized user groups and investment related BBSs can be found in the appendixes.

- Is the price within your budget? Do not make the mistake of thinking that the higher the price, the better the program. There are excellent products at every price range.

- Does the program use a cost-effective data service? If you plan on using a data service to save time from data entry, you may quickly find out that the initial program cost was just a small part of the overall cost of operating the system. Programs vary in data service support. Before you commit to a product, find out how much it will cost to obtain electronic data. Data service prices and information are listed in Chapter 7, but prices do change (up and down) so it is best to call the service directly. Also, services price data access in different ways—flat charge for unlimited access, per minute connect time charges, extra charges for certain data, or a charge per character of information downloaded. Generating comparable costs from different services can take some time.

- Make sure that the program can export its data if needed. The grids indicate whether a program can import and export data and the type of file formats supported. This will allow you to share data among programs and allow you to continue to use the data you have collected should you want to switch programs in a few years.

- Contact the software vendor to request the most recent program information. Investment programs make up a narrow niche and are not readily available in software stores. You will generally need to deal with the vendors directly. Get a demo of the programs you are interested in, even if there is a small fee. Programs differ in their ease of use. Without testing a program, you do not have a way of knowing whether you can or even want to learn how to use the package. And even more importantly, the demo will help to ensure that the program actually does what you want it to do.

- Look at the support policies of the company. Does it offer telephone support, and if so, when is it available? Some vendors charge for providing help. Some may operate a BBS that you can connect to, not only to solve problems but also to get operating tips. Some vendors produce product newsletters that can be a valuable resource for getting the most out of the product. The product listings indicate the availability and type of support given by the company.

- Before you make your purchase, check on the company's return policy. Some software vendors offer full refunds but provide a time limit; others charge a restocking fee or do not refund the postage and handling, while others do not provide any refund. Understand the policy before you buy the product, not after. Vendor return policies are indicated in the product listings in Chapter 6.

- It is best to purchase mail order items with a credit card. If you have problems either receiving the product or getting it to work then you have some recourse or even bargaining power. The Fair Credit Billing Act gives you some power to withhold payment on items purchased if you have made a good faith effort to return an item or have given a seller a reasonable opportunity to correct any problems. With a check, you have little recourse to get your money back once it has been cashed.

FINANCIAL INFORMATION SERVICES

Financial information services supply the electronic data and services used by investors. Like software programs, they vary greatly in scope and purpose. In selecting a service, you need to focus on how it provides data, what information is provided, which systems can use the data, the cost, and even how they determine what to charge for the data. A glance through Chapter 5 should give you an understanding of what is available. In doing this, you may notice that some are strictly raw data providers while others are sources of complete systems including both software and data.

The quickest way to find the data service that meets your needs is to use the financial information services grid in Chapter 5. It presents the type of data each service provides, how it gets the data to you and the functions provided by the service. The grid also contains a page reference so that you can easily read a description of each service and examine the cost structure.

In selecting a data service you should take into account the following factors:

- Take a close look at the features the service offers. Obviously the service should supply the information you want, but a quick look through the grids or product descriptions will show that services vary greatly in breadth and depth. If you are a technician, then you should probably seek a service that specializes in providing historical data for the markets you analyze. You do not want to pay for features that you will never use.

- The data services can vary greatly in how much is charged for access and data. The best way to compare two services is to determine the type of data that you are going to need and compute how much it is going to cost to obtain it. Pricing data is provided along with product descriptions in Chapter 7, but it makes sense to call when you are doing the comparison and request a price schedule directly from the service. They should be able to provide you with an up-to-date and complete pricing guide.

- If you are looking for real-time security data, watch out for exchange fees. Security exchanges charge individuals for access to real-time data. All real-time vendors must collect this fee, but may not mention it in their pricing lists. When looking at real-time quote services, find out if the exchange fee is included.

- Check to see if there is a monthly minimum. Some services require that you spend a certain amount every month or bill you the minimum. If you are an infrequent user, you might be paying for data that you never use.

- Examine how often you plan to use the service. This may dictate which product you select. If you desire a fundamental screening system and plan to run screens frequently, then a service that provides updates on a regular basis at a fixed cost may make sense. However, if you are going to run screens very infrequently, then you may wish to look for an on-line service that provides screening on an as-needed basis and charges you only when you access that feature.

- The information services vary greatly in how they get their product to you. An indication of which transmission methods are available is provided in both the grid and product description page.

- If it is a dial-up service, ask where the closest access number is. The cost balance between two services may change if you have to place a long-distance phone call for one and a local call for the other.

- While demos are less common with information services, some do make demo disks available. Others sell subscription kits that include a few hours of free on-line time to explore the system. Often this free time expires if you do not use it by a specific date, so take advantage of the time while it is available. A few services even provide free trials of their service to get you to try the system.

- If the service charges by the minute, see if there are any software programs available that allow you to construct your data request off-line and then automatically connect, retrieve data, and log off. This will keep time and expenses to a minimum.

- If the service supplies both software and data, check to see if the data can be exported for use in other programs. Some systems are closed.

- If you are looking for a data service to supply data for a specific program, it makes sense to call the program's vendor. They should be able to suggest the best source of data for that program. Some of the more popular programs have their own user groups. The program vendors may be able to put you in touch with these groups to get their opinion.

We hope this *Guide* answers your basic questions and eases the task of investment and portfolio management. Please let us know if you have any suggestions, comments, questions or problems using the book. We make every effort to improve the *Guide* each year.

2
Computerized Investing for Individuals

Personal computers (PCs) continue to drop in price while their power increases. Software is becoming increasingly sophisticated, yet easier to use. On-line databases and information services are growing in depth and breadth of investment information while making the retrieval of this data more affordable and simple. All these developments have brought the capabilities of professional investment analysis home to the individual investor. These powerful tools make it easier for an individual to keep investment records, track portfolio performance, gather investment data, evaluate and select securities, and execute security transactions.

If you are considering buying a PC for investment analysis and management, you must recognize both the costs and the benefits of that decision. Only incremental costs and benefits are relevant—that is, only those costs or benefits that change as a result of buying the PC. For example, if you decide to do all of your investment research and analysis with your computer, you might decide to rely on the services of a discount broker to handle transactions for you, saving commission costs. Those savings would be incremental benefits to you, offsetting the costs of buying the computer and software. If you still need to rely on a full-service broker, you will not realize these savings. Evaluating whether to buy a computer for investment management should be judged by the same criteria as your investments themselves—does this purchase offer greater benefits than its cost? Of course, some of these costs and benefits will be difficult to measure, but you should at least attempt to identify them.

SELECTING INVESTMENT SOFTWARE & FINANCIAL INFORMATION SERVICES

Good quality commercial investment software for some home computer systems is rare while it exists in abundance for other systems. Owners of IBM-compatible PCs (which we will generally refer to as DOS computers) will find a wide selection—literally hundreds of applications are available. The problem here is one of sifting through the choices to find a package that fully meets your needs rather than simply finding something that is available. Investment software for the Apple II line, once the dominant personal computer, has rapidly disappeared. The table on the following page shows the trends in software availability for DOS, Windows, and Macintosh systems.

TYPES OF INVESTMENT SOFTWARE AND SERVICES

Investment software and services generally fall into these categories: financial planning, portfolio management, fundamental stock screening, fundamental techniques of stock valuation, technical screening, technical analysis and charting, on-line financial information services, on-line trading services, disk-based database services, and specialized investment programs.

Financial planning refers to the process of establishing objectives for allocating resources to different classes of assets to meet financial goals. These can range from a simple program to balance your checkbook to a detailed 20-year financial investment and saving plan to meet a number of long-term personal financial goals.

Portfolio management is the process of maintaining records on your investments and analyzing the various characteristics of the portfolio(s), such as performance, allocation of assets, and diversification.

Fundamental stock screening evaluates basic economic, financial, and accounting information in order to select securities that meet specific valuation or performance criteria. Fundamental stock valuation programs apply concepts of security valuation to analyze the worth of a security in relation to its current market value.

Technical analysis is the study of price and volume patterns of a security for the purpose of forecasting the future price behavior of that security. Frequently the information is displayed in graphical form for ease of analysis. Technical screening, like fundamental screening, examines a large universe of securities to select those that match your criteria.

Financial information services and on-line databases provide both historical financial, market, and economic information and current stock market prices and financial news. They may also provide the ability to make transactions on-line. These services may deliver information via modem, FM radio, satellite, or cable TV. Disk-based data services offer the same current fundamental financial data as on-line services as well as historical financial data and price information, but deliver the data by sending a floppy or CD-ROM disk.

Other programs include specialized mathematical applications such

Software for IBM and Macintosh from Previous Editions

	Book Editions		
	1993	1994	1995
DOS Systems—Totals	506*	524	422
Financial Planning	181	153	129
Fundamental Analysis	64	61	54
Technical Analysis.	222	208	148
Portfolio Management	133	112	92
Windows Systems—Totals	na	102	137
Financial Planning	na	42	54
Fundamental Analysis	na	17	24
Technical Analysis	na	32	42
Portfolio Management	na	21	31
Macintosh Systems—Totals	81	81	76
Financial Planning	40	36	28
Fundamental Analysis	14	10	14
Technical Analysis	30	25	20
Portfolio Management	18	20	18

*Includes both DOS and Windows systems from the 1993 edition of this book.

as statistical analysis or linear programming, software for valuing bonds, options, futures, real estate, and "intelligent" software that uses logic or neural networks to make decisions. Many of the programs that investment professionals, economists, and investment consultants use on mainframe computers have now migrated down to personal computers and workstations. While many of these programs are designed primarily for the professional investor, a sophisticated individual with the requisite background and a substantial portfolio might find them useful.

In addition to these broad categories, there are many general purpose programs that can be used for investment analysis. For example, spreadsheet programs such as 1-2-3, Quattro Pro, and Excel are very suitable for users wishing to develop their own analytical models. Many of the on-line financial databases provide software that allows the user to download data directly into their spreadsheets or other analysis programs. For many investors such programs provide all the necessary flexibility and sophistication. *Computerized Investing*, our bimonthly newsletter, offers many investment analysis and portfolio management spreadsheet applications on a regular basis. These spreadsheet templates can also be downloaded from our forum on America Online and our BBS.

One can now duplicate, at home, the in-depth research performed at financial institutions and brokerage houses. Programs that perform sophisticated statistical analysis such as multi-variate regression, moving averages, and time series modeling are available for personal computers at a reasonable cost. Time series analysis is the academic's counterpart to technical analysis. It is used, for example, to forecast interest rate movements, stock market indexes, or other economic variables. Regression analysis is used to estimate or study the relationship among economic or financial variables and might be used to forecast future stock performance. The processing of these more complex analyses can take considerable time without a powerful computer, but it can be done—just plan on taking a break while the system works through a large problem.

Financial Planning and Portfolio Management Software

Nearly 80% of AAII members using a personal computer for investing look to personal finance and portfolio management software to assist them in the investment process. It is easy to see why this category is so popular. Keeping track of your securities, their cost basis, their current value, and their performance can be a time-consuming and tedious process. A computer can automate the process, giving you time to concentrate on your overall investment strategy and security analysis, not to mention your golf game.

Personal finance and portfolio management software comes in many flavors. At one end of the spectrum are the personal finance programs that look at your overall financial picture, while at the other end, are portfolio management programs that help you dissect your portfolio with surgical precision.

The essence of a financial planning system should be one that allows the individual to perform basic home budgeting, to reconcile a personal check register, to examine the tax consequences of different purchase and investment decisions, to flag expenses for tax purposes, to prepare projections of net worth and income for retirement planning purposes, and perhaps to take care of insurance planning and real estate property management. Some investors may not want all these options and can find programs that meet their more specific needs. Others will want a package that can put everything together.

Portfolio management programs should be specifically written to help you monitor your investment portfolio; however, some of these programs may not provide the information you need to evaluate your performance accurately. Many are simply bookkeeping systems whose benefits may be limited. With a good program, however, there are many benefits. Once you have entered the data initially needed to begin using these programs, you may later realize substantial time-savings as future calculations are done by the program. In addition, some programs may allow access to on-line data services to update portfolio values with current price quotations.

What you must remember is that the computer does not make you a better recordkeeper nor will it solve financial problems. If you never save any money, using a computer will not provide for your retirement. If you hate writing down all your expenses for tax purposes, you will like it even less if you have to enter all this data into the computer. The programs, however, may open your eyes to the importance of savings or changing your portfolio's asset allocation to meet your financial goals.

The process of portfolio management should be more than mere recordkeeping; it should permit the analysis of total portfolio wealth allocation. Investors should also be interested in determining insurance needs, cash and security holdings that are appropriate for their lifestyle, financial needs, income, and overall wealth. The focus should be prescriptive programs that can be used for investment analysis.

Even in describing an investor's current situation, there are subtleties that must be dealt with. For instance, most investors' portfolio transactions do not occur at regular, equally spaced intervals. The accurate determination of portfolio performance requires that they be able to deal with transactions as they occur, even if at irregularly spaced intervals. Moreover, withdrawals must be accounted for properly to determine portfolio returns.

Internal rate of return (IRR) is the appropriate value-weighted measure of portfolio return. This is the rate of return, when earned each period, that makes the starting value of your portfolio equal its ending value, with full accounting for cash withdrawals and deposits. This measure can be compared to market returns to determine whether you are earning a sufficient return.

Implicit in the use of the portfolio internal rate of return is the assumption that all investment cash flows are reinvested in the portfolio and earn that rate of return. If you withdraw a cash dividend, it reduces your realized portfolio return because it is not reinvested. Even if you reinvest the dividends, as your realized investment returns change over time, so will your portfolio realized rate of return. Portfolio management software should be able to deal with this and also have the capability of handling not only all your current investments but also any of the investment vehicles you might consider in the future. The portfolio management comparison grid in Chapter 4 indicates if a program provides an IRR calculation.

Most portfolio management programs will prepare Schedules B and D which list interest and dividend income and capital gains and losses. If the program does not actually prepare a tax return, it should be able to group information so that you can do so yourself, or with another program. A final feature that is very useful, especially for investors with large portfolios or for active traders, is the ability to link with an on-line database to obtain current price information for portfolio updating. When used in conjunction with information on the market itself, such as the Standard and Poor's 500 stock index, this can provide the basis for making fundamental portfolio allocation decisions. Some portfolio management programs can even connect to a discount broker to record your transactions, thereby saving even more time for the user.

Fundamental Stock Analysis

Fundamental analysis is the name given to methods of analyzing basic financial, accounting, and economic information and using that information to assess the value of a particular security. This general term covers specific valuation models such as the present value of dividends or price-earnings ratio approaches and screening of databases on some financial variables.

Fundamental Investment Screening

Indeed most (but not all) of the commercially available fundamental investment programs are designed to screen data rather than judge a security's worth on the basis of fundamental valuation principles. There are now a number of programs on the market that will screen a data set of 1,000 to 10,000 companies on any number of fundamental variables. Typically, these programs come with their own data, with the scope of the coverage depending on the database the software uses. Because these "programs" come with their own data sets, which must be periodically updated, fundamental screening systems are listed with the financial information services in this *Guide*.

As an illustration of the screening process, consider an investor who is aware of the published research showing that in the past, smaller market-value companies with low price-to-book ratios have outperformed the market as a whole—even allowing for the risks these companies might pose. The investor could decide to screen the database for companies with a market value of, say, between $20 and $100 million. In addition, the investor might look for those stocks in this group whose price-to-book ratios are low, say below 1.0. The screening program could go through the data rapidly and select those companies meeting these criteria. Of course, once these stocks are selected, the investor must always look further before making any investment. There are many important judgment factors that the computer cannot analyze.

One problem with this technique is that it is possible to establish seemingly reasonable screening criteria that none of the companies in the database satisfy. Without a basic theory that determines the relative importance of your criteria, you cannot adjust your screens to create a list of securities for further analysis. Some of the databases allow users to set the relative importance of different criteria.

A fundamental screening system should give the investor access to a large database and the flexibility to create different criteria for screening—the investor should not be locked into preset criteria. The program should allow the user to transfer these data to other applications, such as a spreadsheet program. Without this latter capability the user cannot do the further analysis essential for effective security selection.

In comparing stock screening services, critical factors include the universe of stocks supported by the database, the depth of stock information, the flexibility of screening software, the frequency of updates, the method of distributing the information, the computer systems it works on, and price.

Fundamental Valuation Techniques

Computers are well suited to fundamental screening but weak when it comes to assisting in fundamental valuation. This is because so much of the valuation rests on your personal growth forecasts of the economy, accompanying industry, and the company itself.

Valuation techniques use fundamental data to assess the worth of a security and judge its desirability as an investment. The basic premise is that investors are generally rational in making investment decisions and valuing the future cash flows of an investment. By determining the risk of the investment relative to some market standard, an investor can estimate the return the security should offer over time. The return compensates for this market risk and is the benchmark for comparison with expected or promised future returns.

One such approach looks at future dividends and their projected growth as the primary determinant of value. All future value, including an estimate of future selling price, is related to these cash flows. Earnings are important indirectly because they generate the cash that can be used for future capital investment and dividend payments. For companies that currently pay no dividends, their future dividend potential is estimated from current earnings and capital investment policies. This approach is valuable for an investor with a long-term time horizon. It emphasizes the cash flows the investor will actually be able to spend or reinvest and focuses on the security's risk and the return that is compensation for taking that risk.

Earnings valuation techniques are similar to the dividend approach but focus on such factors as the interrelationship between reinvested earnings and potential future growth, the profitability of the company relative to sales, and other accounting information. These valuation approaches are related to the dividend valuation model but essentially move the process one step back.

Until recently, the cost of a detailed program of fundamental stock analysis was beyond the means of most individuals. The high cost resulted from the collection of data, a time-consuming and expensive process.

In using and selecting a fundamental valuation program, an investor should consider two main factors—what is the source of data and projections, and which valuation models and techniques are included with the program. Fundamental valuation programs rely on historical balance sheet and income statement data along with estimates of growth in key variables such as earnings and dividends; some programs can access a database to update this information while others require user input. All the programs, however, will require the users to exercise judgment in estimating future growth rates or at least see if the historical growth rates are reasonable estimates of the future. The valuation techniques included with the program will determine the type of data required and the types of companies that can be analyzed by the program.

The software comparison grid covering fundamental analysis programs indicates the number of valuation models provided by the program, whether it can be used for economic forecasting and analysis, and if the program provides financial statement analysis techniques.

Technical Analysis and Screening

The term technical analysis covers a variety of techniques that study relationships between a security's past price and volume movements and patterns to forecast security and market price direction. This analysis is generally best interpreted with the use of graphs, and in many cases the analysis is entirely graphical.

One such approach is to compute a moving average price over time. This is just an average over several time periods—days, weeks, or whatever time period the analyst feels is appropriate. The interval remains constant, but the beginning and ending points move through time and so reflect new information and market conditions. The analyst is not concerned with the reason prices move but simply with the pattern of movements. If the daily price crosses over the moving average line and closes above it, that behavior is regarded as a sign of strength and perhaps signals a buy recommendation. Technical analysis is well suited to the computer because it involves the manipulation of a large amount of data.

Because the essence of technical analysis is price trends, it is essential that these programs provide access to price and volume information. If a program accesses an on-line database, it should capture the data directly. This saves time and money since the user does not have to work through the multiple layers of command menus.

There are a number of programs and data services available that will not only compute the price and/or volume graphs that you want, but they also can log on to an information service, automatically obtain the latest information and update the graphs with that information. To help locate and select the right technical analysis program for you, the software comparison grid detailing technical analysis software indicates the types of charts the program supports, the number of available indicators that the program supports, and whether you can create custom indicators.

More powerful technical analysis programs allow you to test strategies to see how they would have performed in the past; the *Guide's* technical analysis grid also indicates the availability and features surrounding this tool. Some programs will go one step further and actually adjust the rules you are testing to see what would have worked best for you. The availability of this feature is noted in the optimization section of the *Guide's* technical analysis reference grid. To save time, programs can scan a large database of stocks to see which securities, industries or indexes meet your buy or sell criteria. Most of the technical screening programs rely on the user to build a historical database. With the popularity of flat-fee databases increasing, constructing such a database is now much more feasible.

Financial Information Services

These products provide the information investors use in carrying out their investment analyses. This information may be provided via a number of methods including diskette, CD-ROM, modem, direct satellite transmission, or even FM carrier (usually restricted to major metropolitan areas).

From the very earliest days of financial markets, the gathering and processing of information has been crucial and the stock exchanges have used state-of-the-art communications networks. Most of this communication has involved transmitting the latest price quotes to investors, and this remains the focus today. Nevertheless, investors can now obtain detailed and comprehensive information on securities. This includes current and historical financial and market data to aid in their analyses.

Information services provide the necessary information for fundamental and technical analysis and for portfolio management and performance evaluation. Information services may be broadly based networks such as America Online, CompuServe, Dow Jones News/Retrieval (DJN/R), and Prodigy, which can provide information on a variety of topics extending far beyond the investment field. In contrast, some systems may limit themselves to providing information on a specific type of asset, such as futures or options.

If using a modem based service, the investor should ensure that it is possible to access the database with a local phone call. Some of these services provide many databases that are not of interest to investors. To save connect charges, it should be possible to get directly to the relevant database without having to navigate through several layers of command menus. Finally, investors should carefully analyze all the charges that apply to the information they need. Some on-line services have special fees to access certain databases. There may be additional charges for special reports. The service should detail all these charges. Ideally, the service will offer a demonstration package so the potential user can examine firsthand the available information.

A few on-line services and some of the larger commercial banks offer "home banking" services. This allows the individual to pay some bills (those from firms that have an agreement with the bank), transfer funds, get account information, and perform other banking services. More and more of these services are being integrated with personal finance programs that do not require additional entry by users.

In addition, there are some areas of the country where computers can receive information from video text systems. Video text systems are broadly based information services that might include real estate listings, local retail store offerings, home shopping, and other locally useful information. The kinds of services offered are limited only by their imagination and your willingness to pay. So far, local video text services have not been widely used and accepted by consumers.

Some of the on-line databases offer information in graphic form; you can actually receive stock and commodity price charts. You might also receive weather charts. On-line databases generally provide access to information similar to that on the disk-based screening programs. In addition, they provide access to current financial and economic news that may affect a security's value. These databases may also provide price quotes on a delayed basis—or real-time quotes for an extra charge.

For the infrequent trader, there are several less costly ways to acquire this kind of financial information. Many of the financial information services offer current market quotes on a 15- to 20-minute delay at considerably lower cost than real-time quotes. Quotes are available for options, bond, and futures markets, as well as the stock markets. Some companies are providing price information on disk that is already formatted for immediate use in a spreadsheet program.

On-Line Trading Services

Several of these services are linked to a brokerage firm, allowing you to trade securities with your computer while at home. Remember, though, that your order goes to the market through the brokerage's normal channels, so there may be no great time savings over simply calling your broker. These services do not offer access to the exchanges' direct order systems, rather they offer on-line access to a brokerage firm, which then executes the transactions in the normal fashion.

Some of these services offer discounts to investors using them for trading on-line and, of course, offer access to account information so you can check account positions, cash balances, and other relevant data.

Disk and CD-ROM Based Information Services

Financial information services that are distributed on disk—either floppy disk or on CD-ROM—generally contain historical information and a program to screen that data. The information is typically updated periodically by sending out a new data disk. In evaluating such services, it is critical to know how many securities are covered and from what exchanges they are drawn. For example, if you are examining small-cap stocks, the database should extend beyond those securities listed on the New York Stock Exchange.

Specialized Investment Software

As might be expected, there is also a wide variety of software designed for very specific analyses. For almost every type of asset, there are programs used to evaluate its worth. Investors dealing in specialized markets can find programs for the analysis of bonds, options, financial futures, commodities, bond trading strategies, mutual fund tracking, interest rate arbitrage, real estate investment analysis, and more.

For example, there is a generally accepted model, the Black-Scholes model, used to evaluate the worth of options, especially call options. As a consequence, there are a number of programs that can apply that model to evaluate whether option premiums are in line with their theoretical value. Many of these programs also provide the kind of graphs that we associate with technical analysis and can examine a variety of strategies to take advantage of any discrepancy that is found. With the exception of programs that cover broad categories of investment vehicles, such as bonds or mutual funds, these programs will be of use to only a limited number of investors.

PCs FOR INVESTMENT RESEARCH

PCs are excellent tools for investment analysis and financial research and planning. What the computer should allow you to do is spend your time evaluating the results of your research, rather than spending your time on repetitious tasks. The computer can process a lot of information rapidly, it can do numerous iterations testing sensitivity to changes in your fundamental assumptions, and it can display that information in an easily understandable format with graphics.

You should keep in mind, though, that you are relying on the financial expertise of the authors of any software package or service you are using, so carefully check the documentation they provide. If the manual does not explain what the program does and why it does it, you should view the product with some skepticism. The program should tell you more than simply what to do. The advice of the computer is no more relevant than the advice of a human being—after all, it was a human who told the computer what to do in the first place. Remember that almost all investment analysis software is based on observation of past market trends and relationships and some grounding in the theory of valuation. If the past is not a guide to the future, then using a computer will make you no better an investor than you were before. If you do not understand these valuation principles, you cannot be an effective investor with or without a computer.

Perhaps the best strategy is to view your computer as a tool, a little more sophisticated than your pencil and tablet of scratch paper, but the same kind of tool. With this tool and a basic understanding of financial markets, of investment analysis techniques, and of your personal financial objectives, you can be a better investor. With an understanding of the past performance of different investments and of your own needs, you can formulate reasonable financial goals. Then the computer will be a valuable aid in reaching those goals.

3

PC Hardware

THE CURRENT STATE OF THE PC MARKETPLACE

As always, the PC marketplace seems to be in a state of confusion as major software and hardware vendors make conflicting statements as to the superiority of their system versus that of their competitors. As the vendors fight it out, the consumer stands to benefit. Hardware prices continue to drop even as the capabilities increase, and software continues to get more powerful and easier to use.

With the Intel 80486 and Pentium chips (used in IBM-compatible computers) and the Motorola 68040 and Power PC chips (used in the Macintosh), there is sufficient power for most applications. Of greater long-term concern to the consumer are the arguments over the computer's control system, or operating system, and how users interact with it. But as the vendors of these competing operating systems try to talk about their distinct differences, the operating systems look and operate more like each other.

In order to understand these issues and their impact on your buying decisions, you need to know a little about how the market is divided and what role processors and operating systems play in the overall performance of a PC.

The market segmentation is based on both computer hardware (the processor that handles calculations and the "architecture" or "bus" that determines how data is transferred internally) and operating systems (the program that manages the hardware). Either of these hardware or operating system factors could be the predominant force in splitting the market, but originally they worked in tandem. One processor family, the Intel 8088 used in the original IBM PC had one operating system, DOS, and another processor family, the Motorola 68000 used in the Apple Macintosh had another operating system, Mac OS.

Applications software development had to proceed along different lines for each machine, and there was no expectation that the two would ever cross. Nor was there much expectation that different operating systems would be used for any one processor. While some companies tried to insulate users from arcane DOS commands with a "shell" that offered a menu of choices, no one thought that there would be many ways of using the same operating system through different inter-faces—directly via DOS commands, or indirectly through a graphical interface like Windows, or even through input with a "pen-based" system, rather than a keyboard or mouse.

Users face, then, several distinctions in dealing with personal computers. First, there is the fundamental difference between IBM-compatible computers and everything else. We will refer to these machines as IBM PC machines. They all use one of the Intel family of microprocessors, from the 8088 through the Pentium (or increasing number of Intel clone chips), and use an operating system developed by Microsoft and IBM.

The other side of the market includes a variety of hardware and operating systems, but for investors the most important one currently is the Apple Macintosh, which uses one of the Motorola 68000 series of processors and Mac OS.

Once you get beyond hardware and software differences, you have price differences to consider. Machines costing under $2,000 are typically thought of as "home" computers, while more expensive machines are regarded as "office" or "business" computers. Originally, this distinction put both DOS and Mac PCs into the "business" class. Price declines have made machines available in this price range for the home market.

As the price you pay gets higher, so does the usefulness. The more powerful and expensive "home" computers, ranging in price from $1,500 to $2,500, offer the opportunity to completely outfit an investor for detailed investment analysis, including access to on-line databases. You can spend a little more if you insist on better-known brand-name equipment.

A PC system costing $1,500 to $2,500 will satisfy most individuals. For that price you can get a PC with a hard disk, graphics display, modem, and printer. You can expect to pay an additional several hundred dollars for software. This may include communications software, a spreadsheet, a word processor, and investment software. At the high end of the price spectrum, $3,000 to $7,000, you can buy the most sophisticated hardware, complete with superior graphics and printing capabilities, communications, and a large hard disk for data storage.

SOME BASICS FOR NEW (OR SOON-TO-BE NEW) USERS

For most individuals, the process of buying a computer starts with questions about hardware. What is the latest machine available? Who makes the fastest processor I can buy? Which machine will give me the jazziest graphics? Yet even the most sophisticated computer does you little good if there is no software that will run on your machine or take advantage of its capabilities. In fact, you should first evaluate what you want your computer to do, then see what software will do that, and only then should you select the computer system itself.

Another problem for users is that hardware changes have typically outpaced software development. It is quite fair to say that most of today's software was written for machines that have been available for several years. As a consequence, much software does not exploit fully the capabilities of today's hardware. At the current rate of development, it will still be some years before we have software that really utilizes the power of today's most powerful microprocessors. This forces potential buyers to think ahead. You must guess what software might become available later to utilize the capabilities of the newer technology.

Obsolescence will always be a fact of life in the PC market. For an individual investor, however, it should not be a constant concern. Rather, you should concentrate on finding a system that will serve your current needs, has some potential for future expansion, and has a large base of available software. You may not have the fastest computer on your block, but if you can do the analysis you want, you should not care. The standard-setting companies in the market—Apple and IBM—have encouraged outside software development. This should ensure a base for the future, even if your hardware is out-of-date. Given the much slower pace of software development relative to hardware changes, a mid-range PC probably will be technically sufficient for years to come.

In addition, most IBM PC systems can be upgraded with hardware that takes advantage of more advanced technology. For example, you can add the newer graphics boards to older PCs, realizing the benefits of improved display and readability. Newer software that requires more memory may be used by adding memory to the system. Adding a hard disk allows the storage of much more data and may be necessary for some software. And a number of IBM PC computer manufacturers are explicitly offering PCs in which you can upgrade the actual processor. Even Intel is offering replacement processors which are nearly double in speed to the processors they replace.

This is not to say that you will always be able to run the latest software. As microprocessors become more powerful, more powerful software requiring these processors will become available.

DIFFERENCES IN PC HARDWARE

Microcomputer systems vary greatly. To understand the differences, it is helpful to know a little about how a computer processes information.

Computers process information in bits—an on-off (or 0-1) condition indicated by the absence or presence of an electrical charge. These bits are generally processed in chunks known as bytes, each of which is 8 bits. Information is built up from these tiny pieces of data, and the computer processes these bytes of information very rapidly. We usually speak of large multiples of bytes—a kilobyte (abbreviated KB or just K) is 1,024 bytes and a megabyte (abbreviated MB or just M) is 1,024 kilobytes. The part of the computer that processes information is the central processing unit, or CPU.

The speed at which a PC operates is determined by three factors: the number of bits processed simultaneously by the CPU, the number that are transferred in a group from the memory to the processor, and the CPU's clock speed.

Early microcomputers processed and transferred information in 8 bit (or 1 byte) chunks. The latest PCs process and transfer 32 bits of information at once, the same as large minicomputers. The amount of data processed and transferred at once is not the only factor in processing capability. The other significant factor is the clock speed—or how fast the computer's processor deals with instructions. Clock speed is measured in megahertz (MHz) or millions of cycles per second. The faster the cycle time between instructions, the more information the computer can deal with. Early PCs operated at a clock speed of less than 5 MHz; current machines operate at up to 100 MHz; and the next generation of PCs will operate at 150-200 MHz. The faster the clock speed and the more information that is transferred at once, the greater the power of the computer. You should not assume, however, that more advanced processors always operate at the fastest clock speed. One of the trade-offs manufacturers make to lower costs is to offer more advanced processors operating at slower clock speeds.

Nor should you fall into the trap of thinking that a faster CPU will always result in noticeably faster work. For much of the time it is being used, the brains of the computer are in fact idle, waiting for instructions from the user or reading data from or writing it to a disk file. A very significant improvement in processing power will not usually result in the same increase in productivity, unless the supporting hardware is also upgraded. Beyond the choice of processors and clock speed, the most important choices a user will make is to determine information storage capacity and video display capability.

INFORMATION STORAGE

Information is stored in a computer in two ways: volatile and non-volatile media. Volatile media is the RAM memory that stores programs and data currently in use. This memory requires a continuous supply of power and anything stored in it is lost when the computer is turned off or the system is restarted. The second form of media is the non-volatile type. This type of media retains the data stored in it even when the computer is turned off. The most common form of this media is the hard disk drive.

RAM Memory

The memory a computer has and can use is a key consideration and depends, in part, on the CPU. CPUs are physically limited in the amount of memory they can directly address. An 8-bit CPU, such as in older PCs, can only access 64K of memory; a 16-bit CPU, such as the 8088 in the original IBM PCs, can only access 1M of memory using DOS. The 32-bit CPUs, such as the 80386 and 80486, can access 32M of memory, but to remain "compatible" with older DOS systems they act as if 1M is the limit.

IBM-compatible PCs were originally designed to allocate the 1M memory area in a specific way: 640K was allocated to the operating system and program files and the remaining 384K was reserved for hardware files and drivers.

While DOS programs must run within the 640K area of conventional memory, several features allow for flexibility within this limit. First, a program may consist of blocks that can be loaded separately. This allows programs larger than 640K to run in DOS. Then, special memory managers (that follow expanded or extended memory specifications) provide the ability to move data between conventional memory and the area of memory above 1M. This effectively makes the system appear to have direct access to more than 1M of address space when, in fact, it does not.

Most new PCs are equipped with 4M to 8M standard. To take full advantage of the capabilities of these programs, you really need to run programs designed for Windows, OS/2, Windows NT or programs with built-in memory managers. The Macintosh has the ability to address more memory directly.

When a program says that it requires 256K of memory, that means 256K of the conventional memory your computer is available after the operating system and any resident utilities are loaded. Usually, the minimum requirement is exactly that. Many programs can and will make effective use of all available memory. Dealing with the minimum usually means that the program will be frequently transferring program information to and from disk—a time-wasting operation in comparison to the speed with which the CPU works. (Typically, a hard disk will transfer data 1,000 times slower than RAM memory.)

While memory is a relatively cheap addition to your computer, its costs can vary considerably. Nevertheless, the requirements of today's software strongly suggest that investors should install as much memory as their computer can access and use.

Interestingly enough, the ability of the processor to deal with information in memory can exceed the ability of the memory chips to deliver it. The CPU may then insert a pause or "wait state" into its operation. This wait state allows the memory time to retrieve the data before the processor tries to do something with it. Unfortunately, this is wasted time for the processor; it is idle and there is nothing else it can do. The more powerful systems come with a memory cache, a special storage place for recently accessed data that speeds up the processing of information.

Disk Storage

The second type of media in which information is stored is non-volatile memory, generally on either floppy or hard disk drives. These disks store programs and data for transfer to other systems, for sale to consumers, and for a user's permanent files. A floppy disk can store varying amounts of information, depending on the disk itself and the computer with which it is used. The floppy disk on the original IBM PC held 160K, while the newer 3.5" disk can store up to 2.88M, though 1.44M is more typical. The newest Macs can store 1.44M and can read and write data in a format that can be recognized by a PC with a 3.5" disk drive. Unfortunately, disks of the same size are not always interchangeable, though this is less a problem with the 3.5" disks than the 5.25" disks.

The storage capacity of the disk depends on how information is written onto the disk. Data is recorded onto the disk in much the same fashion as music is recorded on an audiocassette tape with magnetic read and write heads that move mechanically over the disk. The disk, unlike the audiocassette tape, must be formatted, or initialized, in order for your computer to read and write data. Formatting simply sets the disk up in the pattern your computer expects to find data. When you write to the disk, the write head realigns the magnetic particles on the disk into a pattern that your computer recognizes as data. The newer disks allow the read/write heads to pack that data more densely. A hard disk works in the same way as a floppy but stores information more densely and is usually not removable or transportable. A typical hard disk that stores 200M is a common minimum size on low-end equipment and 1,000M or more are typical on high-end machines.

VIDEO STANDARDS

The array of video standards in use today is extensive and can be quite confusing. There are different basic configurations, each with different costs. For most individuals, however, there are only a few basic choices you must make as a user. First, you must decide whether or not you want color. Second, you must determine the resolution you want and how much resolution your programs can display. In looking at the quoted resolutions make sure that the manufacturers of both the graphics card and monitor are referring to non-interlaced modes for the various resolutions you plan to work at. Non-interlaced models flicker less than interlaced models. This flickering can lead to headaches and eyestrain even after short periods of use. Finally, examine the refresh rates for the various resolutions: the higher the refresh rate, the lower the flickering. The interaction of these factors will determine how much you will have to spend. The most significant factor impacting on price is whether you want a monochrome or color display. Users planning to work primarily with the Windows platform may also consider graphics accelerator cards, which operate two to three times as fast in Windows as standard video cards.

One of the more obvious changes in PCs over the past several years has been the common acceptance of color displays and the improved resolution those displays can offer. The Mac now supports an array of color displays and resolutions. Along with these improved displays has come a decrease in costs. But resolution in itself is not the whole story. The programs you use must be able to take advantage of the capabilities of your hardware. Spending $500 to $1,000 or more on a new graphics adapter and color display does not make much sense if all the programs you use will still appear exactly the same. Even programs that are only a few years old may not be able to take advantage of what the new hardware can show. While most of the better-known commercial programs will be able to utilize the best currently available resolution, DOS-based investment programs from smaller companies are less likely to do so. In addition, the higher resolution means that screen characters are smaller. This can present difficulties for those people with less than perfect eyesight. Unfortunately, the cost of larger color monitors can be very high, running over $2,000.

Because of memory requirements with graphics adapters, there is a trade-off between the number of colors displayed, the maximum resolution possible, and the speed with which the display is updated. This is a function of memory, since each screen dot occupies a piece of memory and so does each color. The maximum resolution may also depend on whether the display is text (character-based) or graphics. Most display adapters offer different video modes, with the ability to trade off resolution and colors. Each mode specifies the number of colors that can be shown, whether graphics or text can be displayed, and the resolution available.

PRINTER CHOICES

A printer is an essential part of any PC system. Most software can use a wide variety of printers, and many printers can be set up to emulate a standard printer, such as the IBM graphics printer or HP LaserJet, by setting a switch or sending a software code. This means there is a wide range of printer choices.

It is no longer possible to make a simple distinction between "letter quality" and "dot matrix printers." A dot matrix printer operates by striking a series of pins (typically 9 or 24) to print dots in a pattern that creates the impression of a character. The dot matrix printer offers the ability to create graphics output by striking these dots in different patterns.

With the introduction of 24-pin printers, or by over-printing, dot matrix printers can provide output that is virtually as good as a letter-quality printer. For the least cost, a 9-pin printer will handle most jobs. If you want the ability to generate decent looking business correspondence and higher quality printed graphics, a 24-pin printer is appropriate.

The latest printer technology uses a laser beam or LED lights to create letters and graphics in much the same way as a xerographic copier. These laser printers produce letter output that is as good as a typewriter and can print high-quality graphics. While prices of laser printers continue to come down, the initial and continuing costs of operation make this an expense that can be put off by most users.

For a lower initial cost, some manufacturers are offering print quality equivalent to that of a laser printer with a printer that works by spraying a tiny jet of ink onto the page. These ink jet printers can also produce graphics. Ink jet printers are available for both IBM and Macintosh computers and offer a good compromise for most individuals in terms of cost, speed, and quality.

COMMUNICATIONS HARDWARE

A last but important piece of equipment that users should consider is a modem. A modem is a device that transforms computer information so that it can be sent over telephone lines. There have been slow, but steady, changes in the capabilities of communications hardware and programs over the past several years. While the communication process is not necessarily any easier to use or understand, it is faster and less error-prone. In addition, some of the changes have made for faster transmission by using data compression techniques. This increased speed can be misrepresented in advertisements and is a factor for which investors should be on the watch. The faster speed is only possible if the modems on both ends of the link operate the same way. Data compression also makes error detection more critical, and error-checking will offset some of the speed increase from compression.

The basic purpose of a modem is to communicate with the outside world. This part of the world is not only quite large but also potentially quite helpful. You can communicate person-to-person by typing messages to one another; but this is not, and should not be, the major use of a modem. (If you type as fast as most computer users, talking is much faster.)

There are a number of important reasons for having (and using) a modem: connecting with a financial information service to retrieve current price quotes on your investment holdings, tapping into a local bulletin board system (BBS) to get programs or games, logging onto the *Computerized Investing* BBS to download current programs or to get help in the use of a program from the vendor.

Modems can be installed internally or connected externally through a serial port. The speed at which a modem transmits data is measured by its baud rate (bits of data per second). Modems offer a variety of transmission speeds, generally from 300 baud to 28,800 baud.

Today, a 2400-baud modem should be regarded as the low-end for cost-conscious consumers. A 14,400-baud or even 28,800-baud modem is the logical choice for the user looking to satisfy both present and future needs, and most on-line services and BBSs support these speeds. These high-speed modems will also operate at the more prevalent slower speeds.

There are some factors you should consider before purchasing a higher-speed modem. First, the number of services and BBSs that support transmission at 14,400 baud or higher is somewhat limited, though more and more services are offering this support. Second, the speed figures quoted in advertising copy could reflect optimum conditions that might not prevail in practice.

Since modems use telephone lines for communication, they are subject to the same noise problems faced when talking. When talking, noise can be compensated for by repeating a phrase or sentence. Not only must a modem be prepared to do the same thing, it must also be able to detect when an error has occurred. Transmission of digital data like computer programs are even more sensitive to such problems. The difference between saying "I'll meet you on the course tomorrow at 10:00" and receiving "I'll see you on the course tomorrow at 10:00" presents little difficulty. The difference between a program that sends a 0001 and receives a 000F can be disastrous—and that can represent a difference in only one digit out of millions transmitted.

Error correction itself is something users do not generally have to worry about, since communications software takes care of it. Manufacturers, however, have combined error correction with data compression techniques and use this to bolster data transmission speed claims. The important fact to remember is that these transmission protocols work only if both the sending and receiving modems and software support them. Not all BBSs currently support these compression techniques, but fortunately standards now exist. If you are looking at high-speed modems, make sure they support VFast, V.42, V.42*bis*, V.32, V.32*bis* for high speed transmission and compression and V.21, V.22 and V.22*bis* for lower speed transmission.

You should also remember that one way modems compensate for telephone line noise is by reducing transmission speed. This difficulty is more likely with long distance calls and when weather conditions are bad. Improvements in local and long distance networks are reducing the potential for this kind of problem, and the better modems can change speed dynamically as line conditions change. Finally, you must remember the level of usage on the system to which you are connected will affect how rapidly the system can transmit data. The greater the usage, the more time the system must work on other people's requests rather than your own. If you are using the modem for teleconferencing (talking to others on-line), then the modem will transmit only as fast as you can type; it would make sense to call at a lower baud rate if you plan to do this.

To use a modem you will need a communications program. Many modems come bundled with such a program. This program not only tells the computer how to interpret incoming data and to format outgoing data, it also usually provides a number of options to make communications easier. For example, you may be able to automatically dial an on-line database, log in with your assigned password, obtain and display the data you want, and log off without having to enter any of these commands yourself. You may also be able to program the software to redial if it detects a busy signal, and you may instruct it to call automatically at night when rates may be lower. Financial databases often provide specialized communications software to automatically retrieve and download price and other investment information.

DIFFERENCES IN OPERATING SYSTEMS

The software that runs the computer is the operating system. Essentially, the operating system is a "traffic cop." It directs how and when the computer responds to different commands and also handles basic procedures such as copying and naming files or directing files to the printer. While all operating systems perform the same kinds of functions, they are usually incompatible with each other. As a consequence, programs that are written for one kind of system, like the Apple, will not run on an IBM PC, and vice versa. This means that you must take care in selecting a computer and determining whether it will operate the programs you want it to run. Today this means making a choice between IBM PCs and Macintoshes and their respective operating systems. These decisions could become a less important concern in the future, if software companies actually succeed in making a generic operating system. Of course, the other extreme is also possible, with Unix being yet another standard that could intrude into the process.

Originally, the difference between operating systems for the Mac and DOS machines was chiefly distinguished by the "user interface"—that is, the way in which users entered commands. On DOS computers, users typed in commands to be executed; on Macs users moved a mouse pointer to an icon representing a file or program to be executed. With Windows, OS/2, and Windows NT, DOS users now can execute commands in much the same way as Mac users. This process is not always easy, though. The Mac operating system was designed from the beginning as a graphical environment. Consequently, programs that run on the Mac take advantage of this. The DOS operating system was not designed this way. In turn, this means that only programs written explicitly to work under graphic operating environments such as Windows or OS/2 can take advantage of these features.

PUTTING IT ALL TOGETHER

What, then, is an appropriate computer system for an individual investor? How do you, as a potential user, decide what an appropriate investment in computer equipment and software should be? The first, and most important, step is to realistically decide what you want to do. While "professionals" always tell users that this is the logical first step, they seldom offer a means of completing this step. The problem here is not that it is so difficult to determine what you want to do now; rather the problem is determining whether you will be doing anything more complex in the future.

As a guideline, sit down and draw up a list of tasks you want the computer to help you with. You should limit yourself to no more than 10 specific objectives. Trying a greater number can easily require more time than most beginners are willing to spend, and then you can get frustrated because you are not accomplishing all the tasks. In designing these objectives, consider which are the most important and which are the most time-consuming. While doing so, decide whether you are going to rely solely on the computer to perform the task, or whether you are going to replicate what the computer is doing with paper and pencil.

For example, many users start with the idea of using a PC to track their investment portfolios. This means getting current market prices on some regular basis, using those prices to update portfolio values and determining their portfolio rate of return. This is in fact something a computer can do quite readily and automatically. Many investors start by picking up a newspaper, tracking down their holdings, and then writing down the security name or symbol and the price on a piece of paper. This paper record then becomes the source of information to be entered into the portfolio tracking program. This process introduces a second recordkeeping function that may become a source of error but which can also be used to audit the results of the program. More importantly, it means that users are performing manually much of what the computer can do. Doing a job twice can also breed frustration.

For beginners, this redundancy provides a backup should they inadvertently lose data. Nevertheless, the process can be completely automated, and most users quickly get to that point—having their PC dial an on-line service, obtaining the relevant price information, downloading it, and updating security and portfolio values.

Once you've decided what you want to do with the computer, determine whether you are going to design your own analysis or whether you are going to purchase software. For most tasks, purchased software will perform the analysis perfectly well, if not better than you could yourself. In addition, commercial software saves you the necessity of having to reinvent the wheel. Our software listings in Chapter 6 are designed to help you in this process. In particular, you can quickly see what is required to run the software you might purchase. You should also consider buying some program of general use such as a simple word processor and a spreadsheet. As you get more advanced and more comfortable using the computer, you may want to explore additional software packages.

An Entry-Level System

An investor looking for a basic DOS system should plan on one that uses, at least, an 80486DX, 33Mhz processor. IBM PC makers have phased out the 80386 PCs already because the price differential is negligible. The 80486 family of chips started out with the 80486 chip, which is about twice as fast as a comparable 80386. It includes the 80386 instruction set with a few enhancements, a math co-processor, which speeds up high level mathematical calculations, and a memory cache, which speeds up access to slower memory. Intel then came out with the 80486SX, which was the same as the '486DX but without the math co-processor. The basic configuration would include 4M of memory with the possibility of expanding to 16M, a single floppy (with the 3.5" preferred) and a hard drive of at least 200M capacity. The size of most current programs, however, makes 200M a bare minimum; with 340M being a more reasonable alternative. In addition, a printer is essential, with a dot matrix printer offering the cheapest alternative.

Optional upgrades that go beyond the basic system include a modem for communication with on-line services and BBSs. A 14,400-baud modem is the appropriate choice and should not cost more than $150–$300. If you think you will need additional disk capacity, many systems are offered with, or can be configured with, a larger hard drive. 340M would be a reasonable upgrade for a user planning on using Windows and more than one or two major software packages. (Many of the major word processing, spreadsheet, or database programs will use 25M of hard disk storage each. It is surprisingly easy to use up large amounts of disk space before you even realize it!)

Intermediate Systems

While the 486DX can be considered a basic entry-level system, it does not offer as much operating power as does the 80486DX2 or Pentium.

The basic configuration would include 16M of memory, VGA (or Super VGA) graphics, a 14,400-baud modem, and a hard drive of at least 340M capacity. For ease of transferring data, a user could add a second (5.25") floppy drive. If you are planning to use a number of newer, larger programs, upgrading the hard disk to more than 340M makes sense. In addition, as financial data on CD-ROM becomes more available, a CD-ROM drive would be a reasonable addition.

An Advanced System

The advanced user, or someone planning to become advanced, will opt for a Pentium, or RISC-based computer. Systems such as these will have at least 16M, and more reasonably up to 32M, of memory, both 3.5" and 5.25" floppies, a 28,800-baud modem and a hard disk of at least 540M. At the time of this writing, such computers are available through direct mail sources for around $2,000-$3,000; other alternatives can raise the cost as high as $7,500. Additions to this high-end system would include a fax/modem combination board, a larger hard disk drive, and a CD-ROM drive.

Macintosh Systems

The entry-level user would go with a Mac Quadra with 16M of memory, a 14,400-baud modem, and an 350M hard drive. But users who want a little more power would probably want to buy a Performa, which features a more powerful processor—the Power PC.

The advanced user would get a Power PC-based Power Macintosh with 32M of memory, a 500M hard drive, a 14,400-baud or 28,800-baud modem, and a CD-ROM drive.

WHERE TO BUY IT

The final decision a user must make is whether to purchase directly from a mail-order vendor or through a local retail outlet. While many PCs are available only from mail order sources, several large and reliable manufacturers, such as AST and Compaq make machines that are available at retail. In addition, there are a growing number of computer "superstores," such as CompUSA that market PCs. These stores offer convenience as well as discounted prices. They carry a wide range of software as well as hardware, though users should not expect to find many of the specialized investment software packages there.

The trade-offs are basic, though substantial. Most mail order sources are reputable, but just as with a retailer you must consider the possibility that everything will not work as smoothly as you would like. Firms like ARES, Dell Computers, and Gateway 2000 all have good reputations for delivering what they promise and when they promise it. A typical mail order source will charge from 30% to 35% below the manufacturer's suggested list price. Direct mail vendors such as Gateway will offer equipment that may cost 10% to 20% less than a comparable machine through other sources. You must also add shipping and handling charges, but generally you will save the sales tax, if applicable.

The trade-off is that you do not have the retailer to offer direct assistance should something go wrong. You will, however, have direct technical support consisting of telephone technical support as well as on-site service for a limited period. This should take care of simple problems and installation. Beyond that, however, maintenance is the responsibility of the owner. Many vendors are offering on-site service for a year after purchase, and this should cover most potential problems. Again, many of the larger mail order companies have signed agreements with third party concerns to provide continuing maintenance, but these contracts can be quite expensive for the purchaser. You should probably view them in the same light as a maintenance contract for any other major appliance. There are plenty of people in the business, so it must be profitable; but for most of us, it is an option that we will hopefully seldom use. If your computer does not fail within 90 days, it is not likely to do so later. Another factor to consider with direct mail shopping is that most credit card companies offer "buyer protection plans" when you use their cards for a purchase. This offers an additional level of protection for the shopper.

For these reasons, a mail-order source is most appropriate for someone who is comfortable dealing with the details of setting up a machine. These details are really not that difficult—you may have to simply push a switch from one side to the other—but you have to be able to determine which switch must be set and where that switch is located. If the manual provided by the manufacturer is not clear, that may be difficult.

Buying from a retailer may not necessarily mean paying list price. Many retailers will offer a discount on hardware or a package deal with a system purchase that can provide a savings to the consumer. On the other hand, it may be difficult to get a retailer to provide free consultation once you buy the machine. Once again, reputation is the chief concern. The important factor is that you have a local vendor who can (and should) be able to help with any problems.

Talking to people in your area who have purchased from a specific retailer is the best way to gather information. Attend a meeting of the local AAII chapter computer interest group, if there is one in your area. (See Appendix II for a listing.) You can also try the Better Business Bureau or state Department of Consumer Affairs for further details.

4

Investment Software Grids

The software grid is designed to help narrow the wide selection of software products to those that may meet your needs. It focuses on the systems required to operate the software, its cost, the types of assets the program can manipulate, the program's ability to receive data from financial information services and share data with other programs, and the type of functions performed by the program.

The grid contains page references to the full product descriptions in Chapter 6 and a number of abbreviations which are categorized by table headings and explained below:

Systems

Apple II	=	Apple II
DOS	=	PC/MS DOS
Mac	=	Macintosh
OS/2	=	OS/2
Sun	=	Sun Sparc Station
Win	=	Windows
Win NT	=	Windows NT
Unix	=	Unix

Import/Export and Information Services

1-2-3	Lotus 1-2-3
AOL	America Online
ASCII	Text file format
Bon	Bonneville
CIS	CompuServe Information Service
CSI	Commodity Systems, Inc.
CTrac	Compu Trac
DBF	DBase
DDE	Dynamic Data Exchange
Dial	Dial/Data
DIF	Data Interchange Format
DJN/R	Dow Jones News/Retrieval
DTN	Data Transmission Network

GE	GEnie Information Service
IDC	Interactive Data Corp.
PCX	PC Paintbrush
PRN	Lotus 1-2-3 ASCII File
Pro	Prodigy
Meta	MetaStock
QIF	Quicken
QXp	QuoteExpress
Schw	Schwab/Link
Sig	Signal
StSm	StreetSmart
SYLK	Symbolic Link
TC	Telechart 2000
Tick	Tick Data
Tmet	Telemet America
Tscan	Telescan
TTools	Technical Tools
TXF	Tax Exchange Format
XLS	Microsoft Excel
X*P	X*Press

Chart Types

B = Bar
L = Line
P = Point & Figure
E = Equivolume
C = Candlestick
S = Semi-log Scale

Financial Planning Software Grid—Item Descriptions

Financial Goal Setting Given a current financial status and risk tolerance, a saving strategy to meet financial goals is created.

Suggests Asset Allocation Security classes are recommended in accord with a financial strategy.

Budgeting Information entered from checks and credit accounts is categorized and recorded in a budget for financial planning.

Tracks Expenses Expense categories record and display various types of expenditures to provide information about spending patterns.

Cash Flow Report Cash flow statements are generated from budgeting reports to measure the amount of net savings during a period.

Check Printing Checks can be filled out on screen and then printed on special forms, ready to sign. The information is saved so the checkbook is balanced.

Electronic Bill Payment Checks can be sent via the Federal Reserve System of wire transfer.

Net Worth Report All assets and liabilities are accounted for to arrive at net worth.

Tracks Non-Financial Assets Keeps records of real assets such as art, coins, and rugs for consideration in retirement planning.

Insurance Needs Analysis Age, assets, and dependents are considered to arrive at the optimal amount of insurance coverage.

Mortgage Analysis Different mortgage rates and costs are compared to determine the benefit of refinancing.

Tax Planning Periodic tax information is entered and used to generate estimated tax liabilities.

Tax Preparation Tax preparation software interviews the filer to obtain information that is automatically entered on every appropriate form. The forms can be printed and filed with the IRS.

Retirement Planning Specialized retirement planning software focuses on assessing current income and expenses, and determining how much money must be invested to meet retirement goals considering different growth and inflation assumptions.

Financial Calculator Performs basic arithmetic & financial calculations.

Portfolio Management Software Grid—Item Descriptions

Deposit/Withdraw Ability to track the deposit and withdrawal of funds to and from an account.

Buy/Sell Ability to track buy and sell points of individual assets.

Short/Cover Program recognizes the short sales of stocks or related securities as well as the corresponding cover point. The cover point is the price at which securities are bought to cover the short sale.

Margin Allows users to leverage cash accounts to pay for security purchases. Recognizes cash paid for stocks does not necessarily equal price of stocks.

Receive/Deliver Shows transfer of securities from one account to another.

Cash Dividends Calculates and reconciles cash dividends paid on stocks. Useful balances for later calculation of total return in a security or portfolio.

Stock Splits/Stock Dividends Calculates and adjusts number of shares owned when a stock splits the number of shares or pays a stock dividend.

Dividend Reinvestment Calculates number of shares owned when a dividend is reinvested into shares of the underlying stock.

Interest Income Calculates bond coupon payments and money market account interest. Allows user to designate interest income, which can later be separated for tax purposes.

Bond Discount/Premium Program recognizes and accounts for any premiums or discounts paid when purchasing fixed-income securities. Adjusts yield and return figures according to amount of discount or premium.

Commissions/Management Fees Deducts commissions or management fees from appropriate accounts when purchasing assets. When calculating total return of portfolios, you should deduct expenses from returns to accurately depict return figures.

Average Cost Used in computation of mutual fund prices. Since mutual fund shares are not differentiable, all purchased shares are pooled to create an average cost basis.

FIFO Acceptable method for computing basis in security purchases. Assumes first shares purchased are first shares sold.

Specific Lot Most common method for computation of basis. Assumes specific blocks and prices of securities exist and prompts user to choose which block of shares is to be sold when sales take place.

Current Position Displays the current composition of a portfolio.

Holdings by Lot Report displays each specific asset and the price paid for each asset. Will report every purchase price for groups of securities acquired at separate time intervals.

Performance: AIMR Standards The Association of Investment Management and Research has established specific standards for reporting return on assets. This reporting technique must be used by all members of the association.

Performance: From Inception Displays return on assets from the date of creation to ending period.

Performance: Between Any Periods Displays return on assets given a specific beginning and ending period rather than the life of the asset. This report is useful in computing quarterly or yearly returns.

Performance: By Security Displays return figures for individual assets including distributions and dividends to compute total return.

Performance: By Industry Displays return figures for groups of assets. Securities can be grouped by industry or account to measure individual security performance against group performance.

Performance: By Asset Displays performance for an asset taking into account cash flows, interest payments, or other appreciation/depreciation. Allows user to identify over- or underperforming assets.

Performance: By Portfolio Displays return for a selected portfolio.

Performance: Multiple Portfolios Displays overall return figures for a group of multiple portfolios.

Performance: Tax-Adjusted Displays return figure after tax considerations have been applied to gains/losses.

Tax Liability Summary Displays expected tax payments for gains and income incurred for a given period.

Cash Flow Forecast Displays cash flow expected from assets in the portfolio. This report is useful for estimating retirement income. Allows user to structure asset holdings based on future needs.

Custom Reports User is able to create a report with any variable or computation they desire. Allows user to choose specific assets or values to display in reports.

Batch Reporting User is able to automate the generation of one or more reports. This feature is useful for the user that periodically runs the same set of reports.

Technical Analysis Software Grid—Item Descriptions

Chart Types The types of charts that can be plotted, including bar, line, point & figure, equivolume, candlestick and semi-log scale charts.

Max. Charts per Screen The maximum number of charts that can be displayed at the same time on the screen.

Number of Pre-Defined Indicators The number of indicators that are supplied with the software program.

User-Defined Indicators In addition to pre-defined indicators, some programs allow users to write formulas to create new indicators.

Pre-Defined Templates Includes templates for common types of analysis.

User-Defined Templates Allows user to create custom templates.

Batch Chart Printing Charts can be printed one at a time or in groups.

Macro/Script Automation Macros and scripts are recorded keystrokes that speed program operation. Repetitious tasks involving many keystrokes need only be performed once by the user when the macro recorder is on. They can be quickly replayed any number of times thereafter.

Pre-Defined Strategies Includes popular trading strategies.

User-Defined Strategies Allows user to create custom trading strategies.

Total Profit Loss Shows the gross profit or loss of a trading strategy applied to a security or market for a specific period of time.

Return Shows the ratio of profit/loss less fees to initial investment.

Largest Winner/Loser Shows the best and worst trade for a back-tested strategy.

Longest Winning/Losing Run Shows the longest length of time for winning and losing trades.

Percentage Profitable Shows percentage of trades that were profitable.

User-Defined Stops Allows user to set stops for back-testing a strategy.

User-Defined Entry Signals Allows user to set entry signals for back-testing a strategy.

User-Defined Exit Signals Allows user to set exit signals for backtesting a strategy.

Accounts for Commissions Transaction costs are deducted from the profits of trading systems.

Accounts for Slippage The results of orders filled at less than optimal prices are deducted from the profits of trading systems.

Strategy Optimization An adjustment of the parameters of trading rules, such as the periods in a moving average, to see which combination of rules makes the best system.

Max. Criteria per Screen The most criteria that the user can include in one screen.

Number of Screenable Indicators Shows how many pre-defined (and possibly user-defined) indicators can be used in creating criteria for a screening filter.

Fundamental & Other Analysis Software Grid—Item Descriptions

Economic Forecasting Using indicators provided by the government and private organizations to attempt to predict the future behavior of the economy.

Stock Valuation Models Indicates if program includes model(s) for calculating the theoretical value (price) of a stock.

Financial Statement Analysis Assists in examining the data found in a company's financial statement.

No. of Valuation Models Number of different models used to calculate the value of a company's stock.

Bond Analysis Examines characteristics of a bond or portfolio of bonds.

Futures Analysis Examines the characteristics of a future, or a portfolio of futures.

Options Analysis Examines the characteristics of an option, or a portfolio of options.

Real Estate Analysis Examines the financial aspects of various real estate properties.

Spreadsheet A blank work area to organize data, formula, charts, etc.

Simulation/Game An educational program that teaches through simulation of market events.

Statistics A branch of mathematics that deals with the collection, analysis, interpretation, and presentation of numerical data.

Expert System A type of computer software that uses rules, based on the knowledge and experience of an expert in a specific area, to perform the tasks of that expert.

Neural Network A system that attempts to imitate the process by which the nervous system (brain) recognizes patterns.

Financial Planning Software	Page	Systems	Price ($)	AAII Discount (%)	Securities							Import Abilities	Export Abilities
					Stock	Mutual Fund	Bond	Index	Options	Futures	Real Estate		
@ Bonds XL U.S. Series and International Series	322	DOS, Win, Win NT, OS/2, Unix	395-695	15			✓		✓	✓		ASCII, 123, DBF, XLS	ASCII, 123, DBF, XLS
Advanced Total Investor (ATI)	277	DOS, Win	129	23	✓	✓	✓	✓	✓	✓		ASCII, 123, XLS	ASCII, 123, DBF, XLS
@ Exotics XL	323	DOS, Win, Win NT, OS/2, Mac, Unix	695	15	✓			✓	✓	✓		ASCII, 123, DBF, XLS	ASCII, 123, DBF, XLS
Amortizelt!	352	DOS	50	10									
Amortizer Plus	269	DOS, Win	130	10									ASCII, 123
@ nalyst	396	DOS, Win, OS/2, Mac, Unix, Sun Sparc	195-1,495	10	✓		✓	✓	✓	✓	✓		
Andrew Tobias' Tax Cut	311	DOS, Win, Mac	80		✓	✓	✓		✓	✓	✓	ASCII, 123, .TXF, .QIF	
@ Options XL Pro, Premium, and Extended Binomial Series	323	DOS, Win, Win NT, OS/2, Mac, Unix, Sun	395-995	15	✓		✓	✓	✓	✓		ASCII, 123, DBF, XLS	ASCII, 123, DBF, XLS
Asset Allocation Expert	391	DOS	10,000		✓		✓	✓			✓	ASCII, 123, XLS	ASCII, 123, XLS
Asset Allocator	354	DOS	150	15	✓	✓	✓		✓	✓			
BNA Estate Tax Spreadsheet	175	DOS	1,295										
BNA Fixed Asset Management System	175	DOS	995										
BNA Income Tax Spreadsheet with Fifty State Planner	176	DOS	495-890										
BNA Real Estate Investment Spreadsheet	176	DOS	395								✓		
BondCalc	176	DOS, Win, OS/2	2,900				✓					BondScholar, custom formats	ASCII, 123, XLS
Bond Portfolio	172	Win, Mac	25				✓						

Information Services Supported	Financial Planning Tools														
	Financial Goal Setting	Suggests Asset Allocation	Budgeting	Tracks Expenses	Cash Flow Report	Check Printing	Electronic Bill Payment	Net Worth Report	Tracks Non-Financial Assets	Insurance Needs Analysis	Mortgage Analysis	Tax Planning	Tax Preparation	Retirement Planning	Financial Calculator
CIS, DJN/R, Sig, Tmet, Bon, DDE															✓
AOL, CIS, DJN/R, Dial, Pro, GE, Sig, TC, Tscan, FFN													✓		
CIS, DJN/R, Sig, Tmet, Bon, DDE															✓
	✓										✓		✓		✓
													✓		
	✓		✓		✓			✓			✓			✓	✓
CIS													✓		
CIS, DJN/R, Sig, Tmet, Bon, DDE															✓
		✓													
CIS		✓													
	✓											✓			
												✓			
	✓											✓			
	✓				✓							✓			
					✓										✓
															✓

Financial Planning Software	Page	Systems	Price ($)	AAII Discount (%)	Securities							Import Abilities	Export Abilities
					Stock	Mutual Fund	Bond	Index	Options	Futures	Real Estate		
Bond Portfolio Manager	298	DOS, Win, Mac	89	20			✓						ASCII, 123, DBF, XLS
Bond Pricing	173	Win, Mac	15				✓						
Budget Model Analyzer	212	DOS	34	20									
Business Pack	212	DOS	100	20								ASCII	ASCII
CAPTOOL	397	DOS	129	30	✓	✓	✓	✓	✓	✓	✓	ASCII, Pro, Meta, Tscan, QXp, FOX, StSm, AOL	ASCII, 123
CAPTOOL Global Investor	398	DOS	299	30	✓	✓	✓	✓	✓	✓	✓	ASCII, Pro, Meta, Tscan, QXp, FOX, StSm, AOL	ASCII, 123
CAPTOOL Professional Investor	399	DOS	499		✓	✓	✓	✓	✓	✓	✓	ASCII, Pro, SchwabLink 2000, Fidelity, Vanguard, DST Systems, First Trust/Data Lynx, Jack White and Co., Meta, Tscan, QXp, FOX, StSm, AOL	ASCII, 123
CAPTOOL Real Time	399	DOS	189	30	✓	✓	✓	✓	✓	✓	✓	ASCII, Pro, AOL, Meta, FOX, StSm, Tscan	ASCII, 123
CompuServe CD	194	Win	8		✓	✓	✓	✓	✓	✓			ASCII
Crystal Ball	203	Win, Mac	295		✓	✓	✓	✓	✓	✓	✓	123, XLS	123, XLS
CurrencyCast	324	DOS	70		✓	✓	✓	✓	✓	✓	✓	ASCII	ASCII
Debt Analyzer for Windows	281	DOS	25										
DowCast	325	DOS	70		✓	✓	✓	✓	✓	✓	✓	ASCII	ASCII
Easy Money Plus	320	DOS	500		✓	✓	✓				✓		
Econ	202	DOS	50		✓	✓	✓	✓	✓	✓			ASCII
Elderly Tax Planner	321	DOS	100		✓	✓	✓				✓		
Exec-Amort Loan Amortizer Plus	239	DOS	150	10							✓		ASCII
Family Budget	218	DOS	35	20									

Information Services Supported	Financial Goal Setting	Suggests Asset Allocation	Budgeting	Tracks Expenses	Cash Flow Report	Check Printing	Electronic Bill Payment	Net Worth Report	Tracks Non-Financial Assets	Insurance Needs Analysis	Mortgage Analysis	Tax Planning	Tax Preparation	Retirement Planning	Financial Calculator
		✓			✓			✓					✓	✓	
															✓
	✓		✓	✓											
	✓										✓				✓
CIS, DJN/R, Dial, GE, All Quotes												✓	✓		
CIS, DJN/R, Dial, GE, All Quotes												✓	✓		
CIS, DJN/R, Dial, GE												✓	✓		
CIS, DJN/R, Dial, GE, DTN												✓	✓		✓
CIS															
	✓	✓	✓							✓		✓		✓	
DTN		✓													
	✓			✓							✓				✓
DTN	✓	✓													
	✓	✓	✓		✓			✓		✓		✓		✓	
		✓													
	✓	✓			✓							✓		✓	
											✓		✓		✓
				✓									✓		

Financial Planning Software	Page	Systems	Price ($)	AAII Discount (%)	Securities							Import Abilities	Export Abilities
					Stock	Mutual Fund	Bond	Index	Options	Futures	Real Estate		
Fast Cast for Ventures	422	DOS, Win	69	20								ASCII, 123, DBF, XLS	ASCII, 123, DB XLS
Fidelity On-line Xpress	253	DOS	50		✓	✓	✓	✓	✓				ASCII, fixed fie length, Managing Your Money, Taxcut-TXF
Fidelity Retirement Planning Thinkware	254	DOS	15										
Finance 101	184	DOS	39			✓	✓				✓		ASCII
Finance Master	218	DOS	90	20									
Financial Competence	193	Win, Win NT, Mac	99	10								ASCII, 123, XLS	ASCII, 123, XLS
Financial Navigator for DOS	256	DOS	249	10	✓	✓	✓		✓		✓		ASCII, 123, PR .WKI files
Financial Navigator for Windows	256	Win	349	10	✓	✓	✓		✓		✓		ASCII, 123, XLS PRN, WKI files
Financial Needs for Retirement	420	DOS	49										
Financial Pak	267	DOS, Win	150	20	✓	✓							
Financial Planning for Retirement	422	DOS, Win	59	20								ASCII, 123, DBF, XLS	ASCII, 123, DB XLS
Financial Planning TOOLKIT	255	DOS	249	20	✓	✓	✓				✓		123
Financial Statement Cash Flow Forecaster	249	DOS	89	50									ASCII, 123
Financial Toolbox	201	DOS, Win	40	25									
Financial & Interest Calculator	299	DOS, Mac	89	20	✓	✓	✓	✓	✓	✓	✓		
Folioman	246	DOS	89	10	✓	✓	✓	✓	✓		✓	ASCII	ASCII
Folioman+	247	DOS	129	10	✓	✓	✓	✓	✓	✓	✓	ASCII	ASCII
401(k) Forecaster	422	DOS, Win	69	20								ASCII, 123, DBF, XLS	ASCII, 123, DB XLS
FPLAN-KWIK Financial & Retirement Planner	261	DOS	20										

Information Services Supported	Financial Goal Setting	Suggests Asset Allocation	Budgeting	Tracks Expenses	Cash Flow Report	Check Printing	Electronic Bill Payment	Net Worth Report	Tracks Non-Financial Assets	Insurance Needs Analysis	Mortgage Analysis	Tax Planning	Tax Preparation	Retirement Planning	Financial Calculator
	✓			✓	✓				✓				✓		
DJN/R, Tscan, S&P MarketScope									✓				✓		
		✓												✓	
	✓									✓	✓			✓	✓
	✓		✓	✓				✓		✓	✓		✓		✓
					✓										
CIS, DJN/R, Dial, Pro, Navigator Access II			✓	✓	✓	✓		✓	✓						
CIS, DJN/R, Dial, Pro, Navigator Access II			✓	✓	✓	✓		✓	✓						
	✓													✓	
													✓		✓
	✓	✓						✓						✓	
	✓		✓	✓	✓			✓	✓	✓				✓	
			✓		✓										
	✓														
	✓										✓			✓	✓
CIS								✓				✓	✓		✓
CIS								✓				✓	✓		✓
	✓												✓	✓	✓
	✓		✓					✓		✓				✓	

Financial Planning Software	Page	Systems	Price ($)	AAII Discount (%)	Securities: Stock	Mutual Fund	Bond	Index	Options	Futures	Real Estate	Import Abilities	Export Abilities
FPLAN-Personal Financial Planner	261	DOS	35										
FPLAN-Professional Financial Planner	262	DOS	200									Archive files/disks	Archive files/disks
Harvest-Time Retirement Planning Software	197	DOS	50										ASCII, .PIC
How to Write a Business Plan	169	DOS, Mac	125	10							✓		
Investability MoneyMap	294	DOS	20										
Investment Analyst	339	DOS	95	25	✓		✓				✓		
Investment IRR Analysis for Stocks, Bonds & Real Estate	300	DOS, Win, OS/2, Mac	89	20	✓		✓				✓		ASCII, 123, DBF
Investment Master	267	DOS, Win	50	20	✓								
Investor's Accountant	272	DOS	395	25	✓	✓	✓	✓	✓	✓	✓	ASCII	ASCII
The Investor's Edge	238	DOS	49	10	✓	✓	✓				✓		
IRMA	223	DOS	50	20	✓	✓	✓	✓			✓		
Jonathan Pond's Personal Financial Planner	421	DOS, Win	50-60										
Keep Track Of It	223	DOS	50	20									
Kiplinger's Simply Money	196	Win	40			✓	✓	✓	✓	✓	✓	Quicken, BillPay USA	Quicken
Laddering Your Portfolio	423	DOS, Win	45	20								ASCII, 123, DBF, XLS	ASCII, 123, DBF, XLS
Life Insurance Planner	313	DOS	35										
Loan Amortization	424	DOS, Win	39	20								ASCII, 123, DBF, XLS	ASCII, 123, DBF, XLS
Loan Amortization	371	DOS	75	10							✓		
Loan Arranger	224	DOS	30	20									
Loan Master	268	DOS, Win	50	20		✓							
MacInTax Personal 1040	290	Mac	70									ASCII, Quicken, .TXF	Quicken

Information Services Supported	Financial Goal Setting	Suggests Asset Allocation	Budgeting	Tracks Expenses	Cash Flow Report	Check Printing	Electronic Bill Payment	Net Worth Report	Tracks Non-Financial Assets	Insurance Needs Analysis	Mortgage Analysis	Tax Planning	Tax Preparation	Retirement Planning	Financial Calculator
	✓		✓					✓		✓				✓	
	✓		✓					✓		✓				✓	
	✓	✓			✓									✓	✓
	✓														
	✓													✓	✓
	✓			✓	✓							✓			✓
	✓	✓			✓								✓		✓
													✓		✓
CIS, Pro, Tscan								✓	✓			✓	✓		
		✓						✓							✓
	✓												✓		
		✓	✓	✓				✓	✓	✓		✓		✓	✓
				✓				✓	✓						
CIS			✓	✓	✓	✓	✓	✓	✓		✓	✓	✓		✓
														✓	✓
										✓					
											✓				✓
											✓				✓
	✓										✓				
											✓				✓
CIS, GE												✓	✓		

Financial Planning Software	Page	Systems	Price ($)	AAII Discount (%)	Stock	Mutual Fund	Bond	Index	Options	Futures	Real Estate	Import Abilities	Export Abilities
MacMoney	395	Mac	90	25	✓	✓	✓					XLS, CheckFree, Dollars & Sense, Quicken	ASCII
Macro*World Investor	307	DOS	900	28	✓	✓	✓	✓		✓		ASCII	ASCII
Managing Your Money	311	DOS, Win, Mac	80		✓	✓	✓	✓	✓	✓	✓		ASCII, 123
Merit Financial Planner	313	DOS	175	22									
Merit for Managing the Future	314	DOS	199	30									
Microsoft Money	317	Win	30									QIF	QIF, TXF
Microsoft Profit	318	Win	199										
Money	226	DOS	40	20							✓		
MoneyCalc IV	321	DOS	700		✓	✓	✓				✓		
The Money Controller	424	DOS, Win	59	20								ASCII, 123, DBF, XLS	ASCII, 123, DBF, XLS
Money Decisions	226	DOS	130	20	✓	✓	✓	✓			✓		
Money Maker for Windows	359	Win	99	40	✓	✓	✓			✓	✓	✓		ASCII, comma delimited
Mortgage Designer for Windows	307	Win	39	33									
Mortgage Loans—Is it Time to Refinance?	301	DOS, Win, OS/2, Mac	89	20							✓		123, XLS, Works, ClarWorks, AppleWorks
Net Worth Builder	426	DOS, Win	69	20								ASCII, 123, DBF, XLS	ASCII, 123, DBF, XLS
NIS Asset Allocation System	335	DOS	10,000	20		✓		✓					Paradox
OWL Personal Portfolio Manager	346	DOS	55		✓	✓	✓	✓	✓		✓	ASCII	ASCII
Pen Plan	426	DOS, Win	89	20								ASCII, 123, DBF, XLS	ASCII, 123, DBF, XLS
Personal Balance Sheet	229	DOS, Mac	30	20									
Personal Finance Manager	230	DOS, Mac	50	20									

Information Services Supported	Financial Planning Tools														
	Financial Goal Setting	Suggests Asset Allocation	Budgeting	Tracks Expenses	Cash Flow Report	Check Printing	Electronic Bill Payment	Net Worth Report	Tracks Non-Financial Assets	Insurance Needs Analysis	Mortgage Analysis	Tax Planning	Tax Preparation	Retirement Planning	Financial Calculator
	✓		✓	✓	✓	✓	✓	✓						✓	
		✓													
CIS, DJN/R, Pro, Fidelity On-Line Express, BillPay USA, Checkfree	✓	✓	✓	✓	✓	✓	✓	✓	✓	✓	✓	✓	✓	✓	✓
	✓		✓		✓			✓	✓	✓		✓		✓	
	✓			✓				✓	✓			✓		✓	
			✓	✓		✓	✓	✓					✓		✓
			✓	✓	✓	✓		✓	✓						
	✓												✓		
	✓	✓	✓		✓			✓		✓	✓	✓		✓	✓
			✓	✓		✓									
CIS											✓		✓		✓
CIS, Pro	✓										✓			✓	✓
											✓	✓			✓
											✓				
								✓							
	✓	✓													
AOL, CIS, DJN/R, Pro, GE, Farpoint BBS, Just Data (Australia)					✓			✓	✓						
	✓													✓	✓
	✓							✓							
				✓											

Financial Planning Software	Page	Systems	Price ($)	AAII Discount (%)	Securities							Import Abilities	Export Abilities
					Stock	Mutual Fund	Bond	Index	Options	Futures	Real Estate		
Personal Finance Planner	230	DOS	30	20	✓	✓	✓				✓		
Personal Finance System	231	DOS, Mac	40	20									
Personal Real Estate Manager	231	DOS	50	20							✓		
Per%Sense Pro	341	DOS	175		✓	✓	✓	✓	✓	✓			
PFROI	400	DOS	59	30	✓	✓	✓	✓	✓	✓	✓	ASCII, Pro, Meta, Tscan, QXp, FOX, StSm, AOL	ASCII, 123
Portfolio Analyzer	274	DOS	99	25	✓	✓	✓	✓	✓	✓		ASCII	ASCII
Portfolio Management System	340	DOS	150	25	✓	✓							
Portfolio-Pro	352	DOS	70	40	✓	✓							
Portfolio Selection	279	DOS	99			✓	✓	✓	✓	✓		ASCII	ASCII
Portfolio Selection-Professional	280	DOS	595	15	✓	✓	✓	✓	✓	✓	✓	ASCII	ASCII
Portfolio Spreadsheets—Stocks	208	DOS	100		✓	✓							
Portview 2020	233	DOS	80	20	✓	✓	✓	✓	✓	✓	✓		
Profit Planner Plus	426	DOS, Win	99	20								ASCII, 123, DBF	ASCII, 123, DBF
QOS-30	260	Win	2,500	50	✓	✓	✓	✓					
Quant IX Portfolio Evaluator	358	DOS	99		✓	✓	✓		✓		✓	ASCII	ASCII, 123, DBF, DAT, SDF, SYLK
Quant IX Portfolio Manager	359	DOS	59		✓	✓	✓		✓		✓	ASCII	ASCII, 123, DBF
Quicken 4 for Windows	291	Win	40-60			✓	✓	✓	✓	✓	✓	ASCII	ASCII
Quicken 5 for Macintosh	292	Mac	40-50			✓	✓	✓	✓	✓	✓	ASCII	ASCII
Quicken 8 for DOS	292	DOS	40			✓	✓	✓	✓	✓	✓	ASCII	ASCII
Quicken Deluxe 4 for Windows CD-ROM	293	Win	60			✓	✓	✓	✓	✓	✓	ASCII	ASCII
RAMCAP—The Intelligent Asset Allocator	429	DOS	595	17	✓	✓	✓	✓		✓	✓	ASCII	ASCII, PCX
Ratio Evaluator	427	DOS, Win	69	20								ASCII, 123, DBF, XLS	ASCII, 123, DBF, XLS

Information Services Supported	Financial Goal Setting	Suggests Asset Allocation	Budgeting	Tracks Expenses	Cash Flow Report	Check Printing	Electronic Bill Payment	Net Worth Report	Tracks Non-Financial Assets	Insurance Needs Analysis	Mortgage Analysis	Tax Planning	Tax Preparation	Retirement Planning	Financial Calculator
	✓							✓		✓	✓			✓	
				✓											
					✓			✓					✓		
	✓									✓		✓	✓	✓	
CIS, DJN/R, Dial, GE, All Quotes												✓	✓		
CIS, Pro								✓				✓	✓		
												✓	✓		
								✓					✓		
		✓													
		✓													
DJN/R, Sig					✓										
								✓				✓			
	✓		✓	✓	✓										
		✓													
CIS, Pro		✓		✓								✓	✓		
CIS, Pro		✓		✓								✓	✓		
	✓		✓	✓	✓	✓	✓				✓		✓	✓	✓
	✓		✓	✓	✓	✓	✓				✓		✓	✓	✓
	✓		✓	✓	✓	✓	✓				✓		✓	✓	✓
	✓		✓	✓	✓	✓	✓				✓		✓	✓	✓
		✓													
	✓														✓

Financial Planning Software	Page	Systems	Price ($)	AAII Discount (%)	Securities						Real Estate	Import Abilities	Export Abilities
					Stock	Mutual Fund	Bond	Index	Options	Futures			
Real Estate Analyzer	276	DOS, Apple II (ProDOS)	350-395								✓		
Real Property Management II	365	DOS	145-920	15							✓		ASCII
RetirEasy	373	DOS	20										
Retirement Income Forecaster	374	DOS	69	15	✓	✓							ASCII, 123, XLS
Retirement Planner	427	DOS, Win	79	20								ASCII, 123, DBF, XLS	ASCII, 123, DBF, XLS
Retirement Solutions	322	DOS	250										
Retirement Trio	427	DOS, Win	79	20								ASCII, 123, DBF	ASCII, 123, DBF
Rich & Retired	201	DOS, Win	60	25									
Rory Tycoon Portfolio Analyst	188	DOS	149		✓	✓	✓		✓	✓	✓	ASCII, 123	ASCII, 123
Rory Tycoon Portfolio Manager	188	DOS	99		✓	✓	✓		✓	✓	✓		
SolveIt!	353	DOS	90	10	✓	✓	✓				✓		
Sophisticated Investor	320	DOS	195	15	✓	✓		✓				ASCII	ASCII
SPSS for Windows	391	Win	695	call	✓	✓	✓	✓	✓	✓	✓	ASCII, 123, DBF, XLS, ISYLK, SAS, SPSS, SPSS/pct, ODBC	ASCII, 123, DBF, XLS, ISYLK, SAS, SPSS, SPSS/pct, ODBC
Stock Manager	340	DOS	200	25	✓	✓							
Stock Portfolio Allocator	354	DOS	150	15	✓	✓	✓		✓	✓			
StreetSmart	183	Win, Mac	59		✓	✓	✓		✓			StSm	ASCII, 123
Tax Preparer	276	DOS, Apple II (ProDOS)	250-295										
Tax Preparer: Partnership Edition	277	DOS	350										
Ten Steps Pro	314	DOS	175										
Ten Steps to Financial Security	315	DOS	35										
TIP Lease Analysis	165	DOS, Win, Mac	1,000/mo	15							✓	ASCII, 123	ASCII, 123
Total Investor	279	DOS	35		✓	✓	✓	✓	✓			ASCII, 123	ASCII, 123, DBF, Quattro Pro

Information Services Supported	Financial Goal Setting	Suggests Asset Allocation	Budgeting	Tracks Expenses	Cash Flow Report	Check Printing	Electronic Bill Payment	Net Worth Report	Tracks Non-Financial Assets	Insurance Needs Analysis	Mortgage Analysis	Tax Planning	Tax Preparation	Retirement Planning	Financial Calculator
	✓				✓						✓	✓			
			✓	✓	✓	✓							✓		
	✓		✓					✓						✓	
	✓				✓									✓	
	✓													✓	
	✓				✓								✓	✓	
	✓				✓									✓	
														✓	
CIS, DJN/R, Sig								✓							
CIS, DJN/R, Sig								✓							
	✓		✓	✓	✓			✓			✓		✓	✓	
	✓	✓													✓
				✓						✓					
													✓		
CIS		✓													
Schwab host				✓					✓						
												✓	✓		
												✓	✓		
	✓			✓				✓	✓	✓				✓	
	✓			✓				✓	✓	✓				✓	
	✓	✓			✓						✓			✓	
AOL, CIS, DJN/R, Dial, Pro, GE, Sig, TC, Tscan, FFN								✓						✓	

Financial Planning Software	Page	Systems	Price ($)	AAII Discount (%)	Securities							Import Abilities	Export Abilities
					Stock	Mutual Fund	Bond	Index	Options	Futures	Real Estate		
TRADESK	192	DOS	149-299	10	✓			✓		✓			ASCII
TurboTax Personal 1040	294	DOS, Win	70									ASCII, Quicken, Money, .TXF	Quicken
Universal Exotics Add-In	257	DOS, Win, Win NT, OS/2, Mac	224-477	10			✓		✓	✓			
Universal Options Add-In	258	DOS, Win, Win NT, OS/2, Mac	224-477	10			✓		✓	✓			
Universal Swap Add-In	258	DOS, Win, Win NT, OS/2, Mac	749-1,499	10			✓		✓	✓			
Universal Yield Add-In	259	DOS, Win, Win NT, OS/2, Mac	224-477	10			✓		✓	✓			
Universal Zero-Curve Add-In	260	DOS, Win, Win NT, OS/2, Mac	224-477	10			✓		✓	✓			
Wall Street Journal Personal Finance Library	211	Win	40										
WealthBuilder by Money Magazine	369	DOS, Mac	70		✓	✓	✓	✓	✓	✓	✓	Quicken, Managing Your Money	ASCII
Wealth Creator	362	DOS	60	10	✓	✓	✓				✓		ASCII
What'sBest!	303	DOS, Mac	149-4,995									123, XLS	123, XLS
The Yellow Pad	345	DOS	30			✓	✓	✓	✓	✓	✓		

Information Services Supported	Financial Planning Tools														
	Financial Goal Setting	Suggests Asset Allocation	Budgeting	Tracks Expenses	Cash Flow Report	Check Printing	Electronic Bill Payment	Net Worth Report	Tracks Non-Financial Assets	Insurance Needs Analysis	Mortgage Analysis	Tax Planning	Tax Preparation	Retirement Planning	Financial Calculator
CIS, GE												✓	✓		
					✓										✓
					✓										✓
					✓										✓
					✓										✓
					✓										✓
	✓	✓	✓								✓			✓	
	✓	✓	✓	✓				✓	✓	✓	✓	✓	✓	✓	✓
	✓		✓					✓	✓	✓	✓			✓	✓
		✓													
	✓										✓			✓	✓

Portfolio Management Software	Page	Systems	Price ($)	AAII Discount (%)	Stock	Mutual Fund	Bond	Index	Options	Futures	Real Estate	Import Abilities	Export Abilities
Advanced Total Investor (ATI)	277	DOS, Win	129	23	✓	✓	✓	✓	✓	✓		ASCII, 123, XLS	ASCII, 123, DBF, XLS
@nalyst	396	DOS, Win, OS/2, Mac, Unix, Sun Sparc	195-1,495	10	✓		✓	✓	✓	✓	✓		
Asset Allocator	354	DOS	150	15	✓	✓	✓		✓	✓			
Axys Advantage	165	Win	2,900			✓	✓	✓	✓	✓	✓	ASCII	ASCII, 123, XLS
BondCalc	176	DOS, Win, OS/2	2,900				✓					BondScholar, custom formats	ASCII, 123, XLS
Bond Portfolio Manager	298	DOS, Win, Mac	89	20			✓						ASCII, 123, DBF, XLS
Candlestick Forecaster Real Time	286	DOS, OS/2	1,700	5	✓	✓	✓	✓	✓	✓			
CAPTOOL	397	DOS	129	30	✓	✓	✓	✓	✓	✓	✓	ASCII, Pro, Meta, Tscan, QXp, FOX, StSm, AOL	ASCII, 123
CAPTOOL Global Investor	398	DOS	299	30	✓	✓	✓	✓	✓	✓	✓	ASCII, Pro, Meta, Tscan, QXp, FOX, StSm, AOL	ASCII, 123
CAPTOOL Professional Investor	399	DOS	499		✓	✓	✓	✓	✓	✓	✓	ASCII, Pro, SchwabLink 2000, Fidelity, Vanguard, DST Systems, First Trust/Data Lynx, Jack White, Meta, Tscan, QXp, FOX, StSm, AOL	ASCII, 123

Information Services Supported	Deposit/Withdraw	Buy/Sell	Short/Cover	Margin	Receive/Deliver	Cash Dividends	Stock Splits/Stock Dividends	Dividend Reinvestment	Interest Income	Bond Discount/Premium	Commissions/Management Fees	Average Cost	FIFO	Specific Lot	Current Position	Holdings by Lot	Performance: AIMR Standards	Performance: From Inception	Performance: Between Any Periods	Performance: By Security	Performance: By Industry	Performance: By Asset	Performance: By Portfolio	Performance: Multiple Portfolios	Performance: Tax Adjusted	Tax Liability Summary	Cash Flow Forecast	Custom Reports	Batch Reporting
AOL, CIS, DJN/R, Dial, Pro, GE, Sig, TC, Tscan, FFN	✓	✓	✓	✓		✓	✓	✓	✓		✓			✓	✓	✓			✓	✓	✓	✓	✓	✓				✓	
					✓				✓	✓										✓	✓	✓	✓				✓		
CIS																						✓	✓						
Sig, IDC, Schwab, PC Quote, ComStock, DTC		✓	✓	✓		✓	✓			✓	✓	✓	✓	✓			✓	✓		✓	✓	✓					✓	✓	
			✓							✓		✓						✓		✓	✓		✓				✓	✓	
									✓	✓				✓						✓		✓	✓			✓	✓	✓	
Sig		✓	✓																			✓						✓	
CIS, DJN/R, Dial, GE, All Quotes	✓	✓	✓	✓	✓	✓	✓	✓	✓	✓	✓	✓	✓	✓	✓	✓	✓	✓	✓	✓	✓	✓	✓	✓	✓	✓	✓	✓	✓
CIS, DJN/R, Dial, GE, All Quotes	✓	✓	✓	✓	✓	✓	✓	✓	✓	✓	✓	✓	✓	✓	✓	✓	✓	✓	✓	✓	✓	✓	✓	✓	✓	✓	✓	✓	✓
CIS, DJN/R, Dial, GE	✓	✓	✓	✓	✓	✓	✓	✓	✓	✓	✓	✓	✓	✓	✓	✓	✓	✓	✓	✓	✓	✓	✓	✓	✓	✓	✓	✓	✓

Portfolio Management Software	Page	Systems	Price ($)	AAII Discount (%)	Securities							Import Abilities	Export Abilities
					Stock	Mutual Fund	Bond	Index	Options	Futures	Real Estate		
CAPTOOL Real Time	399	DOS	189	30	✓	✓	✓	✓	✓	✓	✓	ASCII, Pro, AOL,Meta, FOX,StSm, Tscan	ASCII, 123
Centerpiece	350	DOS	895		✓	✓	✓	✓	✓		✓	ASCII	ASCII, 123, XLS
Centerpiece Performance Monitor	351	DOS	595		✓	✓	✓	✓	✓		✓	ASCII	ASCII, 123, XLS
Common Stock Decision Aide	419	DOS	49		✓			✓					
Common Stock Selector	421	DOS, Win	59	20	✓							ASCII, 123, DBF, XLS	ASCII, 123, DBF, XLS
Complete Bond Analyzer	299	DOS, Mac	89	20			✓						
Compusec Portfolio Manager	215	Apple II	100	20	✓				✓	✓			
CompuServe CD	194	Win	8		✓	✓	✓	✓	✓	✓			ASCII
CompuServe Research Manager	195	DOS	400-1,000/month		✓	✓	✓	✓	✓			ASCII, 123	ASCII, 123
CompuServe Research Manager for Windows	195	Win	400-1,000/month		✓	✓	✓	✓	✓			ASCII, 123	ASCII, 123
Discover/EN by Telemet	401	Win, OS/2	149/month		✓	✓			✓	✓	✓	ASCII	ASCII, 123, XLS, comma delimited
Discover/OR by Telemet	402	Win, OS/2	330/month		✓	✓	✓	✓	✓	✓	✓	ASCII, 123, XLS, comma delimited	ASCII, 123, XLS, comma delimited
Discover/RE by Telemet	402	Win, OS/2	399		✓	✓			✓	✓	✓	ASCII, 123, XLS	ASCII, 123, XLS
DollarLink	206	DOS	1,300	10	✓	✓			✓	✓	✓	ASCII	ASCII, 123, DBF, XLS, CTrac,Meta, SystemWriter
Enhanced Chartist	380	Mac	1,295	10	✓			✓	✓	✓	✓	ASCII	ASCII

Information Services Supported	Transactions											Basis			Reports														
	Deposit/Withdraw	Buy/Sell	Short/Cover	Margin	Receive/Deliver	Cash Dividends	Stock Splits/Stock Dividends	Dividend Reinvestment	Interest Income	Bond Discount/Premium	Commissions/Management Fees	Average Cost	FIFO	Specific Lot	Current Position	Holdings by Lot	Performance: AIMR Standards	Performance: From Inception	Performance: Between Any Periods	Performance: By Security	Performance: By Industry	Performance: By Asset	Performance: By Portfolio	Performance: Multiple Portfolios	Performance: Tax Adjusted	Tax Liability Summary	Cash Flow Forecast	Custom Reports	Batch Reporting
IS, DJN/R, Dial, GE, DTN	✓	✓	✓	✓	✓	✓	✓	✓	✓	✓	✓	✓	✓	✓	✓	✓	✓	✓	✓	✓	✓	✓	✓	✓	✓	✓	✓	✓	✓
DJN/R, Dial, Sig, DTN, Tmet, Bon, Interactive Data	✓	✓	✓	✓	✓	✓	✓	✓	✓	✓	✓	✓	✓	✓	✓	✓	✓	✓	✓	✓	✓	✓	✓	✓			✓	✓	✓
															✓		✓	✓	✓	✓	✓	✓	✓						✓
		✓																				✓							
		✓																	✓			✓							
DJN/R		✓									✓																		
CIS																													
CIS						✓	✓										✓			✓	✓	✓	✓				✓	✓	
CIS						✓	✓										✓			✓	✓	✓	✓				✓	✓	
Tmet	✓											✓			✓					✓	✓		✓	✓					
Tmet	✓													✓	✓	✓				✓	✓	✓	✓					✓	
Tmet	✓											✓			✓					✓	✓		✓	✓					
Sig, Bon, PC Quote	✓	✓	✓		✓						✓												✓						
Sig, Bon, S&P Constock	✓		✓			✓																							

Portfolio Management Software	Page	Systems	Price ($)	AAII Discount (%)	Securities Stock	Mutual Fund	Bond	Index	Options	Futures	Real Estate	Import Abilities	Export Abilities
Equalizer	183	DOS	59		✓	✓	✓	✓	✓				ASCII, SDF, SYLK
Fidelity On-line Xpress	253	DOS	50		✓	✓	✓	✓	✓				ASCII, fixed field length, Managing Your Money, Taxcut-TXF
Financial Navigator for DOS	256	DOS	249	10	✓	✓	✓		✓		✓		ASCII, 123, PRN, .WKI files
Financial Navigator for Windows	256	Win	349	10	✓	✓	✓		✓		✓		ASCII, 123, XLS, PRN, WKI files
Financial Pak	267	DOS, Win	150	20	✓	✓							
Financial Planning TOOLKIT	255	DOS	249	20	✓	✓	✓			✓			123
Financial & Interest Calculator	299	DOS, Mac	89	20	✓	✓	✓	✓	✓	✓	✓		
FirstAlert	380	DOS, Win, OS/2	200-350/ month		✓	✓	✓	✓	✓	✓		ASCII	ASCII
Folioman	246	DOS	89	10	✓	✓	✓	✓	✓		✓	ASCII	ASCII
Folioman+	247	DOS	129	10	✓	✓	✓	✓	✓	✓	✓	ASCII	ASCII
Fundgraf Supplemental Programs, Disk 1	348	DOS	20	10	✓	✓		✓				123	123
Fund Master TC	407	DOS	289	10	✓	✓	✓	✓				ASCII	ASCII
Fund Pro	408	DOS	789	10	✓	✓	✓	✓				ASCII	ASCII
Individual Stock Investor INSTIN	204	DOS, OS/2	60	10	✓								
Investment IRR Analysis for Stocks, Bonds & Real Estate	300	DOS, Win, OS/2, Mac	89	20	✓		✓				✓		ASCII, 123, DBF

Information Services Supported	Transactions											Basis					Reports												
	Deposit/Withdraw	Buy/Sell	Short/Cover	Margin	Receive/Deliver	Cash Dividends	Stock Splits/Stock Dividends	Dividend Reinvestment	Interest Income	Bond Discount/Premium	Commissions/Management Fees	Average Cost	FIFO	Specific Lot	Current Position	Holdings by Lot	Performance: AIMR Standards	Performance: From Inception	Performance: Between Any Periods	Performance: By Security	Performance: By Industry	Performance: By Asset	Performance: By Portfolio	Performance: Multiple Portfolios	Performance: Tax Adjusted	Tax Liability Summary	Cash Flow Forecast	Custom Reports	Batch Reporting
DJN/R, MarketScope, Company Profile Reports, Schwab Real-Time Quotes		✓	✓	✓		✓	✓		✓		✓			✓	✓				✓				✓						
DJN/R, Tscan, S&P MarketScope		✓	✓	✓		✓	✓		✓	✓	✓			✓		✓			✓	✓	✓	✓	✓					✓	
CIS, DJN/R, Dial, Pro, Navigator Access II	✓	✓	✓	✓	✓	✓	✓	✓	✓	✓	✓	✓	✓	✓	✓	✓		✓	✓	✓	✓	✓	✓	✓		✓	✓	✓	✓
CIS, DJN/R, Dial, Pro, Navigator Access II	✓	✓	✓	✓	✓	✓	✓	✓	✓	✓	✓	✓	✓	✓	✓			✓	✓	✓	✓	✓	✓	✓		✓	✓	✓	✓
		✓										✓																	
		✓	✓																	✓									
																	✓	✓	✓	✓		✓	✓	✓					
Sig, Bon, Knight Ridder, S&P ComStock, PC Quote																			✓	✓	✓		✓	✓					
CIS	✓	✓	✓	✓	✓	✓	✓	✓	✓	✓	✓	✓	✓	✓	✓	✓		✓	✓		✓	✓	✓	✓		✓		✓	✓
CIS	✓	✓	✓	✓	✓	✓	✓	✓	✓	✓				✓	✓	✓	✓	✓		✓	✓	✓	✓		✓		✓	✓	
																			✓	✓			✓						
DJN/R	✓					✓	✓		✓		✓	✓							✓	✓			✓					✓	
DJN/R	✓					✓	✓		✓		✓								✓	✓			✓					✓	
CIS, Pro, Sig	✓		✓			✓													✓	✓	✓		✓					✓	
		✓									✓								✓	✓	✓			✓			✓	✓	✓

Portfolio Management Software	Page	Systems	Price ($)	AAII Discount (%)	Securities							Import Abilities	Export Abilities
					Stock	Mutual Fund	Bond	Index	Options	Futures	Real Estate		
The Investor	423	DOS, Win	129	20	✓	✓	✓		✓	✓	✓	ASCII, 123, DBF, XLS	ASCII, 123, DBF, XLS
Investor's Accountant	272	DOS	395	25	✓	✓	✓	✓	✓	✓	✓	ASCII	ASCII
Investor's Portfolio	384	DOS	795		✓	✓	✓		✓	✓	✓		ASCII
The Investor's Edge	238	DOS	49	10	✓	✓	✓				✓		
IRMA	223	DOS	50	20	✓	✓	✓	✓	✓		✓		
Jonathan Pond's Personal Financial Planner	421	DOS, Win	50-60										
Kiplinger's Simply Money	196	Win	40		✓	✓	✓	✓	✓	✓	✓	Quicken, BillPay USA	Quicken
Macro*World Investor	307	DOS	900	28	✓	✓	✓	✓		✓		ASCII	ASCII
Managing Your Money	311	DOS, Win, Mac	80		✓	✓	✓	✓	✓	✓	✓		ASCII, 123
Market Analyzer Plus for DOS	209	DOS	499	30	✓	✓	✓	✓	✓	✓		ASCII, DIF and SYLK	ASCII, DIF and SYLK
Market Manager Plus for DOS	210	DOS	299	30	✓	✓	✓		✓		✓		ASCII, DIF
Market Manager Plus for Mac	211	Mac	299	30	✓	✓	✓		✓		✓		ASCII
Money Fund Vision	281	DOS, Win	7,975										ASCII, 123, DBF, XLS
Money Maker for Windows	359	Win	99	40	✓	✓	✓		✓	✓	✓		ASCII, comma delimited
Mutual Fund Decision Aide	420	DOS	49			✓		✓					
Mutual Fund Investor	169	DOS	295		✓	✓	✓	✓			✓	ASCII	ASCII
Mutual Fund Manager	204	DOS	49			✓							
NIS Performance Analysis System	336	DOS	16,000	20	✓			✓					Paradox
OWL Personal Portfolio Manager	346	DOS	55		✓	✓	✓	✓	✓		✓	ASCII	ASCII

Portfolio Management Software Grid — feature matrix. Column groups: **Transactions**, **Basis**, **Reports**.

Information Services Supported	Deposit/Withdraw	Buy/Sell	Short/Cover	Margin	Receive/Deliver	Cash Dividends	Stock Splits/Stock Dividends	Dividend Reinvestment	Interest Income	Bond Discount/Premium	Commissions/Management Fees	Average Cost	FIFO	Specific Lot	Current Position	Holdings by Lot	Performance: AIMR Standards	Performance: From Inception	Performance: Between Any Periods	Performance: By Security	Performance: By Industry	Performance: By Asset	Performance: By Portfolio	Performance: Multiple Portfolios	Performance: Tax Adjusted	Tax Liability Summary	Cash Flow Forecast	Custom Reports	Batch Reporting
CIS, DJN/R, Dial, Pro, GE, Sig, TC, Tscan		✓	✓				✓				✓									✓	✓	✓	✓						
CIS, Pro, Tscan	✓	✓	✓	✓		✓	✓	✓	✓	✓	✓	✓	✓	✓	✓	✓	✓	✓	✓	✓	✓	✓	✓	✓	✓			✓	
DJN/R, Dial	✓	✓	✓	✓	✓	✓	✓	✓	✓	✓	✓		✓	✓	✓	✓		✓	✓	✓	✓	✓	✓	✓	✓		✓	✓	✓
		✓	✓			✓	✓	✓	✓	✓								✓	✓	✓			✓	✓					
	✓	✓																											
CIS	✓	✓	✓			✓	✓	✓	✓		✓	✓								✓								✓	
		✓																											
CIS, DJN/R, Pro, Fidelity On-Line Express, BillPay USA, Checkfree		✓	✓			✓	✓		✓	✓	✓									✓	✓	✓	✓					✓	✓
DJN/R	✓	✓	✓			✓	✓	✓	✓		✓		✓	✓	✓				✓	✓	✓		✓					✓	
DJN/R	✓	✓	✓		✓	✓	✓	✓	✓	✓		✓	✓	✓	✓	✓				✓	✓	✓	✓	✓					✓
DJN/R	✓	✓	✓			✓	✓	✓	✓		✓		✓	✓	✓	✓		✓		✓	✓	✓	✓	✓					✓
In house BBS															✓					✓	✓	✓						✓	
CIS, Pro	✓	✓	✓	✓		✓	✓	✓	✓	✓	✓		✓	✓	✓				✓	✓			✓					✓	
																✓						✓							
CIS, Investment Company Data		✓	✓			✓	✓	✓	✓			✓	✓	✓			✓	✓	✓	✓	✓	✓	✓	✓	✓				✓
		✓			✓	✓		✓												✓		✓							
																	✓			✓	✓	✓	✓					✓	
AOL, CIS, DJN/R, Pro, GE, Farpoint BBS, Just Data (Australia)	✓	✓				✓	✓	✓	✓			✓	✓	✓	✓	✓		✓		✓	✓		✓	✓	✓				

Portfolio Management Software	Page	Systems	Price ($)	AAII Discount (%)	Securities							Import Abilities	Export Abilities
					Stock	Mutual Fund	Bond	Index	Options	Futures	Real Estate		
Personal Computer Automatic Investment Management	230	DOS	150	20	✓								
Personal Hotline	417	Mac	595	10	✓	✓	✓	✓	✓	✓		ASCII	ASCII
Personal Portfolio Analyzer	181	DOS	45			✓	✓	✓	✓	✓		ASCII, TC	
Per%Sense	341	DOS	100			✓	✓	✓	✓	✓			
PFROI	400	DOS	59	30	✓	✓	✓	✓	✓	✓	✓	ASCII, Pro, Meta, Tscan, QXp, FOX, StSm, AOL	ASCII, 123
Portfolio Analyzer	274	DOS	99	25	✓	✓	✓	✓	✓	✓		ASCII	ASCII
Portfolio Data Manager	231	DOS	100	20	✓	✓	✓						
Portfolio Decisions	232	DOS	150	20	✓	✓	✓	✓	✓	✓	✓		
Portfolio Management	232	DOS	70	20									
Portfolio Management System	340	DOS	150	25	✓	✓							
Portfolio-Pro	352	DOS	70	40	✓	✓	✓						
Portfolio Spreadsheets	207	DOS	195			✓	✓	✓					
Portfolio Spreadsheets—Bonds	207	DOS	100			✓	✓						
Portfolio Spreadsheets—Stocks	208	DOS	100		✓	✓							
Portfolio Status	233	DOS	30	20	✓	✓	✓		✓	✓	✓		
Portfolio Tracker	362	DOS	75	10	✓	✓	✓					ASCII	ASCII
Portfolio Watcher	318	Mac	150	40	✓	✓						StockWatcher, Wall Street Watcher	ASCII, Picture
Portview 2020	233	DOS	80	20	✓	✓	✓	✓	✓	✓	✓		
Profit Planner Plus	426	DOS, Win	99	20								ASCII, 123, DBF	ASCII, 123, DBF
Prosper-II Mkt	163	DOS	189			✓	✓	✓	✓	✓	✓	ASCII	ASCII
Pulse Portfolio Management System	244	DOS	195	10	✓	✓	✓		✓	✓	✓	ASCII, Meta	ASCII

Information Services Supported	Transactions											Basis			Reports														
	Deposit/Withdraw	Buy/Sell	Short/Cover	Margin	Receive/Deliver	Cash Dividends	Stock Splits/Stock Dividends	Dividend Reinvestment	Interest Income	Bond Discount/Premium	Commissions/Management Fees	Average Cost	FIFO	Specific Lot	Current Position	Holdings by Lot	Performance: AIMR Standards	Performance: From Inception	Performance: Between Any Periods	Performance: By Security	Performance: By Industry	Performance: By Asset	Performance: By Portfolio	Performance: Multiple Portfolios	Performance: Tax Adjusted	Tax Liability Summary	Cash Flow Forecast	Custom Reports	Batch Reporting
		✓													✓				✓				✓					✓	
CIS, DJN/R, Dial, Sig		✓	✓								✓		✓	✓	✓			✓		✓									
		✓					✓	✓				✓	✓	✓	✓	✓		✓	✓	✓			✓	✓			✓		
																		✓	✓	✓		✓	✓						
CIS, DJN/R, Dial, GE, All Quotes	✓	✓	✓	✓	✓	✓	✓	✓	✓	✓	✓	✓	✓	✓	✓	✓	✓	✓	✓	✓	✓	✓	✓			✓	✓	✓	✓
CIS, Pro		✓	✓			✓	✓	✓	✓	✓	✓		✓	✓	✓			✓		✓			✓	✓	✓	✓			
		✓																					✓						
CIS, DJN/R		✓																									✓		
		✓				✓	✓		✓		✓				✓	✓		✓	✓				✓						
		✓				✓	✓		✓	✓				✓		✓		✓	✓				✓	✓	✓				
DJN/R, Sig		✓				✓	✓		✓		✓			✓	✓	✓			✓				✓				✓	✓	
		✓						✓				✓		✓	✓	✓			✓				✓				✓	✓	
DJN/R, Sig		✓				✓	✓					✓		✓					✓				✓				✓	✓	
		✓												✓					✓				✓						
		✓				✓	✓	✓	✓	✓	✓	✓		✓			✓		✓				✓						✓
CIS, DJN/R		✓	✓	✓		✓	✓		✓		✓		✓		✓	✓			✓				✓						
																			✓										
																			✓	✓							✓		
DJN/R, Pro, Sig, DTN, Tmet, XP		✓	✓				✓	✓																					
CIS, DJN/R, Dial, Sig, MarketScan	✓	✓	✓			✓	✓	✓	✓	✓	✓		✓	✓		✓				✓	✓	✓	✓					✓	✓

Portfolio Management Software	Page	Systems	Price ($)	AAII Discount (%)	Stock	Mutual Fund	Bond	Index	Options	Futures	Real Estate	Import Abilities	Export Abilities
Quant IX Portfolio Evaluator	358	DOS	99		✓	✓	✓		✓		✓	ASCII	ASCII, 123, DBF, DAT,SDF, SYLK
Quant IX Portfolio Manager	359	DOS	59		✓	✓	✓		✓		✓	ASCII	ASCII, 123, DBF
Quicken 4 for Windows	291	Win	40-60		✓	✓	✓	✓	✓	✓	✓	ASCII	ASCII
Quicken 5 for Macintosh	292	Mac	40-50		✓	✓	✓	✓	✓	✓	✓	ASCII	ASCII
Quicken 8 for DOS	292	DOS	40		✓	✓	✓	✓	✓	✓	✓	ASCII	ASCII
Quicken Deluxe 4 for Windows CD-ROM	293	Win	60		✓	✓	✓	✓	✓	✓	✓	ASCII	ASCII
Rapid	270	DOS	277	5	✓	✓	✓	✓	✓	✓		ASCII, CSI, TTools, Starquote, Telerate	ASCII
Real Analyzer	365	DOS	95	15							✓		
Real Estate Analyzer	276	DOS, Apple II (ProDOS)	350-395								✓		
Rory Tycoon Portfolio Analyst	188	DOS	149		✓	✓	✓		✓	✓		ASCII, 123	ASCII, 123
Rory Tycoon Portfolio Manager	188	DOS	99		✓	✓	✓		✓	✓			
Smartbroker	184	DOS	95		✓				✓			ASCII	ASCII
SMARTrader	393	DOS, Win	349-450	15	✓	✓	✓	✓	✓	✓	✓	ASCII, 123, XLS, DIF	ASCII, 123, XLS, DIF
SMARTrader Professional	394	DOS	990	15	✓	✓	✓	✓	✓	✓		ASCII, 123, XLS, DIF	ASCII, 123, XLS, DIF
Sophisticated Investor	320	DOS	195	15	✓		✓					ASCII	ASCII
Stock Charting System	182	DOS	50		✓	✓	✓	✓	✓	✓		ASCII	ASCII
Stock Manager	340	DOS	200	25	✓	✓							
Stock Master	268	DOS	50	20	✓	✓							
Stock Master/Stock Plot	236		60	20	✓		✓						
Stock Portfolio	174	Win, Mac	15		✓								
Stock Portfolio Allocator	354	DOS	150	15	✓	✓	✓		✓	✓			
StreetSmart	183	Win	59		✓	✓	✓		✓			StSm	ASCII, 123
Technical Stock Analyst	400	DOS	25		✓	✓	✓	✓			✓	ASCII, 123, DBF, XLS	

Information Services Supported	Deposit/Withdraw	Buy/Sell	Short/Cover	Margin	Receive/Deliver	Cash Dividends	Stock Splits/Stock Dividends	Dividend Reinvestment	Interest Income	Bond Discount/Premium	Commissions/Management Fees	Average Cost	FIFO	Specific Lot	Current Position	Holdings by Lot	Performance: AIMR Standards	Performance: From Inception	Performance: Between Any Periods	Performance: By Security	Performance: By Industry	Performance: By Asset	Performance: By Portfolio	Performance: Multiple Portfolios	Performance: Tax Adjusted	Tax Liability Summary	Cash Flow Forecast	Custom Reports	Batch Reporting
CIS, Pro	✓	✓		✓		✓	✓	✓	✓	✓	✓	✓	✓	✓	✓		✓	✓	✓	✓		✓	✓		✓		✓		✓
CIS, Pro	✓	✓	✓	✓		✓	✓	✓	✓	✓	✓	✓	✓	✓	✓	✓	✓	✓	✓	✓		✓	✓		✓		✓		✓
		✓	✓	✓		✓	✓		✓	✓	✓	✓	✓	✓						✓	✓	✓	✓	✓				✓	
		✓	✓	✓		✓	✓		✓	✓	✓	✓	✓	✓						✓	✓	✓	✓	✓				✓	
		✓	✓	✓		✓	✓		✓	✓	✓	✓	✓	✓						✓	✓	✓	✓	✓				✓	
CRS		✓	✓								✓			✓	✓							✓	✓						
		✓													✓				✓			✓					✓		
																	✓	✓									✓		
CIS, DJN/R, Sig	✓	✓	✓	✓		✓	✓	✓	✓	✓	✓	✓		✓	✓					✓		✓	✓				✓		
CIS, DJN/R, Sig	✓	✓	✓	✓		✓			✓	✓	✓			✓	✓	✓				✓		✓	✓				✓		
DJN/R	✓					✓						✓								✓	✓						✓	✓	
Dial, CSI, Sig, DTN, Tmet, Tick		✓	✓	✓		✓					✓				✓			✓										✓	✓
Dial, CSI, Sig, DTN, Tmet, Tick		✓	✓	✓		✓					✓				✓			✓										✓	✓
																						✓	✓						
		✓					✓	✓				✓	✓		✓					✓	✓		✓						
		✓			✓	✓		✓		✓		✓	✓		✓	✓				✓			✓						
		✓										✓			✓														
		✓										✓			✓					✓			✓						
		✓			✓						✓				✓								✓						
CIS																						✓	✓						
Schwab host		✓	✓	✓		✓	✓		✓	✓	✓	✓	✓		✓					✓		✓	✓					✓	
		✓									✓																		

Portfolio Management Software	Page	Systems	Price ($)	AAII Discount (%)	Securities							Import Abilities	Export Abilities
					Stock	Mutual Fund	Bond	Index	Options	Futures	Real Estate		
Telescan Portfolio Manager (TPM)	404	DOS	395	10	✓	✓	✓	✓	✓		✓		
Tickerwatcher	304	Mac	195-595	10								ASCII, XLS	ASCII, XLS
Total Investor	279	DOS	35		✓	✓	✓	✓	✓			ASCII, 123	ASCII, 123, DBF, Quattro Pro
TRADESK	192	DOS	149-299	10	✓			✓		✓		CSI	ASCII
TradingExpert	168	DOS	996	10	✓	✓		✓	✓			ASCII	ASCII, PRN
Universal Options Add-In	258	DOS, Win, Win NT, OS/2, Mac	224-477	10			✓		✓	✓			
Universal Swap Add-In	258	DOS, Win, Win NT, OS/2, Mac	749-1,499	10			✓		✓	✓			
Universal Yield Add-In	259	DOS, Win, Win NT, OS/2, Mac	224-477	10			✓		✓	✓			
Universal Zero-Curve Add-In	260	DOS, Win, Win NT, OS/2, Mac	224-477	10			✓		✓	✓			
WealthBuilder by Money Magazine	369	DOS, Mac	70		✓	✓	✓	✓	✓	✓	✓	Quicken, Managing Your Money	ASCII

Information Services Supported	Transactions											Basis			Reports														
	Deposit/Withdraw	Buy/Sell	Short/Cover	Margin	Receive/Deliver	Cash Dividends	Stock Splits/Stock Dividends	Dividend Reinvestment	Interest Income	Bond Discount/Premium	Commissions/Management Fees	Average Cost	FIFO	Specific Lot	Current Position	Holdings by Lot	Performance: AIMR Standards	Performance: From Inception	Performance: Between Any Periods	Performance: By Security	Performance: By Industry	Performance: By Asset	Performance: By Portfolio	Performance: Multiple Portfolios	Performance: Tax Adjusted	Tax Liability Summary	Cash Flow Forecast	Custom Reports	Batch Reporting
DJN/R, Tscan	✓	✓	✓	✓	✓	✓	✓	✓	✓	✓	✓	✓	✓	✓	✓	✓			✓	✓	✓	✓	✓	✓		✓		✓	✓
CIS, DJN/R, Dial, Sig, Bon, DTN, XP		✓	✓			✓															✓		✓					✓	
AOL, CIS, DJN/R, Dial, Pro, GE, Sig, TC, Tscan, FFN		✓	✓	✓							✓					✓												✓	
DJN/R, Dial, Sig, Interactive Data, Tscan, PC Quote		✓	✓	✓			✓				✓																		
		✓	✓	✓		✓	✓			✓	✓	✓	✓	✓	✓							✓	✓						

Technical Analysis Software	Page	Systems	Price ($)	AAII Discount (%)	Securities							Import Abilities	Export Abilities
					Stock	Mutual Fund	Bond	Index	Options	Futures	Real Estate		
Advanced G.E.T.	414	DOS	2,750	10	✓	✓	✓	✓	✓	✓		ASCII, Future Source, CSI, Meta, TTools, CTrac, AIQ, Ensi	
Advanced Total Investor (ATI)	277	DOS, Win	129	23	✓	✓	✓	✓	✓	✓		ASCII, 123, XLS	ASCII, 123, DBF, XLS
Alliance 5.0	326	DOS	70	10	✓			✓				ASCII, CSI, Meta, TTools	
Basic Cycle Analysis	263	DOS	450-500	20	✓	✓	✓	✓	✓	✓	✓	ASCII, CTrac, CSI	ASCII
Behold!	297	Mac	995			✓	✓	✓	✓		✓	ASCII, Computrac/M Market analyzer, Trend setter, Futures Truth	ASCII
Buysel	213	DOS	100	20	✓				✓	✓		ASCII	ASCII
Candlestick Forecaster	285	DOS, OS/2	249	5	✓	✓	✓	✓	✓	✓		ASCII, Future Source, Meta	
Candlestick Forecaster Master Edition	286	DOS, OS/2	800	5	✓	✓	✓	✓	✓	✓		ASCII, Future Source, Meta	
Candlestick Forecaster Real Time	286	DOS, OS/2	1,700	5	✓	✓	✓	✓	✓	✓			
CAPTOOL	397	DOS	129	30	✓	✓	✓	✓	✓	✓	✓	ASCII, Pro, Meta, Tscan, QXp, FOX, StSm, AOL	ASCII, 123
CAPTOOL Global Investor	298	DOS	299	30	✓	✓	✓	✓	✓	✓	✓	ASCII, Pro, Meta, Tscan, QXp, FOX, StSm, AOL	ASCII, 123

Information Services Supported	Chart Types	Max. Charts per Screen	Number of Pre-Defined Indicators	User-Defined Indicators	Pre-Defined Templates	User-Defined Templates	Batch Chart Printing	Macro/Script Automation	Pre-Defined Strategies	User-Defined Strategies	Total Profit Loss	Return	Largest Winner/Loser	Longest Winning/Losing Run	Percentage Profitable	User-Defined Stops	User-Defined Entry Signals	User-Defined Exit Signals	Accounts for Commissions	Accounts for Slippage	Strategy Optimization	Max. Criteria per Screen	Number of Screenable Indicators
	B, C, L, S		20	✓			✓																17
AOL, CIS, DJN/R, Dial, Pro, GE, Sig, TC, Tscan, FFN	B, C, E, L, S, P	no limit	41	✓				✓															
	B, L	2	10																				
CSI	B, L, S																						
Dial, MJK	B, C, L, S	1	35	✓		✓	✓	✓	✓	✓	✓	✓	✓	✓	✓	✓	✓	✓	✓	✓	✓	no limit	200
	L																						
DJN/R, Dial, Pro, Sig, DTN, TC	B, C	1	6						✓	✓	✓	✓	✓			✓							
DJN/R, Dial, Pro, Sig, DTN, TC	B, C	1							✓	✓	✓					✓	✓		✓			15+	15+
Sig	B, C	9	1,000						✓	✓	✓					✓						1,000	
CIS, DJN/R, Dial, GE, All Quotes	B, L, S	2																					
CIS, DJN/R, Dial, GE, All Quotes	B, L, S	2																					

Technical Analysis Software	Page	Systems	Price ($)	AAII Discount (%)	Stock	Mutual Fund	Bond	Index	Options	Futures	Real Estate	Import Abilities	Export Abilities
					\multicolumn{7}{c}{Securities}							
CAPTOOL Professional Investor	399	DOS	499		✓	✓	✓	✓	✓	✓	✓	ASCII, Pro, SchwabLink 2000, Fidelity, Vanguard, DST Systems, First Trust/Data Lynx, Jack White and Co., Meta, Tscan, QXp, FOX, StSm, AOL	ASCII, 123
CAPTOOL Real Time	399	DOS	189	30	✓	✓	✓	✓	✓	✓	✓	ASCII, Pro, AOL, Meta, FOX, StSm, Tscan	ASCII, 123
ChartistAlert	379	OS/2	195-280/ month		✓	✓	✓	✓	✓	✓			ASCII, 123
Chartmaster	377	DOS	129	10	✓	✓	✓	✓	✓	✓			ASCII, 123, XLS, Meta Stock
ChartPro	375	DOS	54		✓	✓	✓	✓	✓	✓		ASCII, Most formats	ASCII
Compu/CHART	329	DOS	300	30	✓	✓		✓	✓			ASCII	ASCII
Compu/Chart EGA	215	DOS	300	20	✓								
CompuServe Research Manager	195	DOS	400-1,000/ month		✓	✓	✓	✓	✓			ASCII, 123	ASCII, 123
CompuServe Research Manager for Windows	195	Win	400-1,000/ month		✓	✓	✓	✓	✓			ASCII, 123	ASCII, 123
Connect	284	DOS, Win, Win NT, OS/2	595	10					✓	✓			ASCII, 123, XLS
CSSCO	189	DOS	99					✓	✓	✓		123	

Information Services Supported	Chart Types	Charting							Back-Testing													Screening	
		Max. Charts per Screen	Number of Pre-Defined Indicators	User-Defined Indicators	Pre-Defined Templates	User-Defined Templates	Batch Chart Printing	Macro/Script Automation	Pre-Defined Strategies	User-Defined Strategies	Total Profit Loss	Return	Largest Winner/Loser	Longest Winning/Losing Run	Percentage Profitable	User-Defined Stops	User-Defined Entry Signals	User-Defined Exit Signals	Accounts for Commissions	Accounts for Slippage	Strategy Optimization	Max. Criteria per Screen	Number of Screenable Indicators
CIS, DJN/R, Dial, GE	B, L, S	2																					
CIS, DJN/R, Dial, GE, DTN	B, L, S	2																					
Sig, Bon, Knight Ridder, Reuters, S&P ComStock, PC Quote	B, C, E, L, P	100	100s													✓	✓	✓	✓		✓	no limit	no limit
DTN	B, C	1																					
DJN/R, Pro, GE, Equalizer	B, C, L, P		30																				
Dial, Track Data	B, L, P	9	20																				
Hale	E, L, P																						
CIS	B, C, E, L, S, P																					no limit	no limit
CIS	B, C, E, L, S, P																					no limit	no limit
Dial, DTN	B, C	1																					
	L	4	4								✓						✓	✓	✓				4	4

Technical Analysis Software	Page	Systems	Price ($)	AAII Discount (%)	Securities							Import Abilities	Export Abilities
					Stock	Mutual Fund	Bond	Index	Options	Futures	Real Estate		
CurrencyCast	324	DOS	70		✓	✓	✓	✓	✓	✓	✓	ASCII	ASCII
Data Smoother Semi-Spline/Polynomial Data Smoothing	216	DOS	40-50	20								ASCII	ASCII
Director Utilities for MetaStock Pro—Systems! Volume 1-4	333	DOS	49-139	10	✓	✓				✓		Meta	Meta
Director Utilities for MetaStock Pro—WhatWorks	334	DOS	99	10	✓	✓				✓		Meta	Meta
Discover/EN by Telemet	401	Win, OS/2	149/month			✓	✓		✓	✓	✓	ASCII	ASCII, 123, XLS, comma delimited
Discover/OR by Telemet	402	Win, OS/2	330/month		✓	✓	✓	✓	✓	✓	✓	ASCII, 123, XLS, comma delimited	ASCII, 123, XLS, comma delimited
Discover/RE by Telemet	402	Win, OS/2	399		✓	✓			✓	✓	✓	ASCII, 123, XLS	ASCII, 123, XLS
Discovery	199	DOS	350	15	✓			✓	✓	✓			ASCII, Meta
DollarLink	206	DOS	1,300	10	✓	✓		✓	✓	✓		ASCII	ASCII, 123, DBF, XLS, CTrac, Meta
DowCast	325	DOS	70		✓	✓	✓	✓	✓	✓	✓	ASCII	ASCII
Dow Jones Market Analyzer	209	DOS	349	30	✓	✓	✓	✓	✓				ASCII
Dow Jones/OEX Trading System	415	DOS	147	15						✓		CSI, Tools, CompuTrac	
Dynamic Volume Analysis Charts	428	DOS	100	50	✓			✓	✓	✓			
Enhanced Chartist	380	Mac	1,295	10	✓		✓	✓	✓	✓		ASCII	ASCII
Enhanced Fund Master Optimizer	407	DOS	150	10	✓	✓	✓	✓				Time Trend	
Ensign V	241	DOS	1,295		✓	✓	✓	✓	✓	✓		ASCII, CSI, CTrac	ASCII, CSI, CTrac

Information Services Supported	Chart Types	Max. Charts per Screen	Number of Pre-Defined Indicators	User-Defined Indicators	Pre-Defined Templates	User-Defined Templates	Batch Chart Printing	Macro/Script Automation	Pre-Defined Strategies	User-Defined Strategies	Total Profit Loss	Return	Largest Winner/Loser	Longest Winning/Losing Run	Percentage Profitable	User-Defined Stops	User-Defined Entry Signals	User-Defined Exit Signals	Accounts for Commissions	Accounts for Slippage	Strategy Optimization	Max. Criteria per Screen	Number of Screenable Indicators
DTN	B		5					✓															
	L																						
			40																		✓		
																✓	✓	✓	✓	✓	✓		
Tmet	B, L, S	1																					
Tmet	B, L, S	1	5	✓																			
Tmet	B, L, S	1																					
DTN	B, C, P		60	✓																			
Sig, Bon, PC Quote	B, C, E, L, S, P	496	80	✓			✓												✓		✓		
DTN	B		5																			10	10
DJN/R	B, L, S	1					✓																
Dial, CSI, Sig, DTN, Tick, Compu Trac, MetaStock	B	2	54				✓	✓	✓		✓	✓	✓	✓	✓	✓	✓	✓	✓	✓	✓	50	50
CIS, Dial	B, L	540	6	✓																			
Sig, Bon, S&P Constock	B, C, L, P	40	over 50		✓	✓	✓																
																✓	✓	✓	✓		✓		
Bon	B, C, E, L, P	4	40	✓			✓	✓					✓			✓	✓	✓			✓	5	5

Technical Analysis Software	Page	Systems	Price ($)	AAII Discount (%)	Securities Stock	Mutual Fund	Bond	Index	Options	Futures	Real Estate	Import Abilities	Export Abilities
Epoch Pro	315	DOS	995		✓		✓	✓		✓		ASCII, CTrac, CSI, FutureSource, TTools	
Excalibur	265	Mac	3,400-3,900		✓			✓		✓		ASCII	ASCII
Fibnodes	186	DOS	595	20	✓	✓	✓	✓	✓	✓			
Fidelity On-line Xpress	253	DOS	50		✓	✓	✓	✓	✓				ASCII, fixed field length, Managing your Money, TXF
FirstAlert	380	DOS, Win, OS/2	200-350/ month									ASCII	ASCII
Folioman	246	DOS	89	10	✓	✓	✓	✓	✓		✓	ASCII	ASCII
Folioman+	247	DOS	129	10	✓	✓	✓	✓	✓	✓	✓	ASCII	ASCII
Foreign Exchange Software Package	357	DOS	144	10				✓	✓	✓			
Fourcast	240	DOS, Win	300	20	✓	✓	✓	✓	✓	✓	✓	ASCII, Dial	ASCII
Fourier Analysis Forecaster	220	DOS	100-170	20								ASCII	
Fundgraf	347	DOS	100	10	✓	✓		✓					
Fundgraf Supplemental Programs, Disk 1	348	DOS	20	10	✓	✓		✓				123	123
Fund Master TC	407	DOS	289	10	✓	✓	✓	✓				ASCII	ASCII
Fund Pro	408	DOS	789	10	✓	✓	✓	✓				ASCII	ASCII
Fundwatch	220	DOS	40	20	✓	✓	✓						
Fundwatch Plus	272	DOS, Win	29	25	✓	✓	✓	✓					

| | Charting | | | | | | | | Back-Testing | | | | | | | | | | | | | Screening | |
Information Services Supported	Chart Types	Max. Charts per Screen	Number of Pre-Defined Indicators	User-Defined Indicators	Pre-Defined Templates	User-Defined Templates	Batch Chart Printing	Macro/Script Automation	Pre-Defined Strategies	User-Defined Strategies	Total Profit Loss	Return	Largest Winner/Loser	Longest Winning/Losing Run	Percentage Profitable	User-Defined Stops	User-Defined Entry Signals	User-Defined Exit Signals	Accounts for Commissions	Accounts for Slippage	Strategy Optimization	Max. Criteria per Screen	Number of Screenable Indicators
	B, L			✓																	✓		
	B, C, L, P	1	20	✓									✓				✓	✓	✓	✓	✓	no limit	no limit
			1	✓																		58	58
DJN/R, Tscan, S&P MarketScope	B, C, E, L																						
Sig, Bon, Knight Ridder, S&P ComStock, PC Quote	B, C, E, L, P	100	over 100	✓	✓	✓	✓	✓	✓	✓	✓	✓	✓	✓	✓	✓	✓	✓	✓	✓	✓	6	
CIS	B, L	1	3	✓	✓																		
CIS	B, L	1	3	✓	✓																		
	S																						
Dial	L, S			✓																			
	L		10																				
	L, S	6		✓		✓																	
	L, S	6	1	✓													✓	✓					
DJN/R	L, S	4		✓			✓	✓													✓		
DJN/R	L, S	4		✓			✓	✓													✓		
	L		1																				
	L	no limit	4	✓																			

Technical Analysis Software	Page	Systems	Price ($)	AAII Discount (%)	Stock	Mutual Fund	Bond	Index	Options	Futures	Real Estate	Import Abilities	Export Abilities
Futures Pro	249	Win	595-15,000	call						✓		ASCII	ASCII
GannTrader 2	266	DOS	1,295	25	✓	✓	✓	✓	✓	✓		CTrac, CSI, Meta, Quicktrieve	
Glendale	199	DOS	100		✓			✓	✓	✓			Meta
Hansen-Predict	221	DOS	100	20						✓			
Historical ADL	409	DOS	175					✓					
Hourly DJIA	409	DOS	50					✓					
The Insider	326	DOS	179	10	✓			✓					ASCII
Interactive Multiple Prediction	222	DOS	70	20								ASCII	ASCII
INVESTigator	296	DOS	49	20	✓	✓		✓	✓	✓		ASCII	ASCII
Investing Advisor	222	DOS	50	20	✓	✓		✓			✓		
Investograph Plus, Optimizer	302	DOS	99-399	12	✓	✓	✓	✓	✓	✓		ASCII, CTrac, CSI, Meta	ASCII, CTrac, CSI
The Investor	423	DOS, Win	99	20	✓	✓	✓	✓	✓	✓		ASCII, 123, DBF, XLS	ASCII, 123, DBF, XLS
Investor's Accountant	272	DOS	395	25	✓	✓	✓	✓	✓	✓	✓	ASCII	ASCII
Investor's Advantage	389	DOS	179	50	✓	✓		✓	✓	✓			ASCII
Investor's Advantage for Windows	389	Win	179			✓	✓	✓	✓	✓		ASCII	ASCII
Kiplinger's Simply Money	196	Win	40			✓	✓	✓	✓	✓	✓	Quicken, BillPay USA	Quicken

| Information Services Supported | Charting | | | | | | | | Back-Testing | | | | | | | | | | | | | Screening | |
	Chart Types	Max. Charts per Screen	Number of Pre-Defined Indicators	User-Defined Indicators	Pre-Defined Templates	User-Defined Templates	Batch Chart Printing	Macro/Script Automation	Pre-Defined Strategies	User-Defined Strategies	Total Profit Loss	Return	Largest Winner/Loser	Longest Winning/Losing Run	Percentage Profitable	User-Defined Stops	User-Defined Entry Signals	User-Defined Exit Signals	Accounts for Commissions	Accounts for Slippage	Strategy Optimization	Max. Criteria per Screen	Number of Screenable Indicators
DJN/R, Dial, CSI, Sig, DTN, Bon, Tick, MetaStock, Futures Source, Knight Ridder, Prophet	B	20		✓	✓	✓			✓		✓	✓	✓	✓	✓	✓	✓	✓	✓	✓	✓		
	B	1,000																					
DTN	B, C, L, P																						
				✓																	✓		
Tools for Timing	L, S	1	20																				
Tools for Timing	L	1	6																				
	B, E, L	2	6																				
	L																						
Dial	B, C, L, S, P	3	24			✓		✓														5	10
				✓																			
CIS, DJN/R, Dial, Pro, GE, CSI, Sig, DTN, Tmet, TC, Tick	B, C, E, L, S, P	20	43+	✓	✓	✓	✓	✓	✓	✓	✓	✓	✓	✓	✓	✓	✓	✓	✓	✓	✓	no limit	43+
CIS, DJN/R, Dial, Pro, GE, Sig, TC, Tscan	B, C, E, L, S, P			✓			✓										✓	✓	✓				
CIS, Pro, Tscan	B, C, L, S	no limit																					
Dial	B, L		20																				
Dial	B, C, L		30																				
CIS	B, L	1																					

Technical Analysis Software	Page	Systems	Price ($)	AAII Discount (%)	Stock	Mutual Fund	Bond	Index	Options	Futures	Real Estate	Import Abilities	Export Abilities
Log Scale Comparison	409	DOS	50					✓					
Market Analyzer Plus for DOS	209	DOS	499	30	✓	✓	✓	✓	✓	✓		ASCII, DIF and SYLK	ASCII, DIF and SYLK
Market Analyzer Plus for Mac	210	Mac	349	30	✓	✓	✓	✓	✓	✓		ASCII	ASCII
Market Charter	396	Mac	60	25	✓	✓	✓	✓				ASCII	ASCII
MarketEdge II	382	DOS	39	23	✓	✓		✓				ASCII, 123	ASCII, 123
MarketExpert	116	DOS	249	10				✓				ASCII	ASCII, PRN
Market Master	378	DOS	149-799	10	✓	✓	✓	✓	✓	✓		ASCII, Meta, CSI	
Market Plus (Level 2) /Market Plus (Level 3)	264	DOS	115-145			✓	✓	✓	✓		✓	ASCII, 123, PRN	ASCII
Market Strategist	273	DOS	295	25	✓			✓					ASCII
Market Timer	225	DOS	120	20		✓		✓				ASCII	
Market Timing Utility	278	DOS, Win	59					✓				ASCII, 123, XLS	ASCII, 123, DBF, XLS
MarketWatch	273	DOS, Win	59	25	✓	✓	✓	✓	✓	✓		ASCII	ASCII
Master Chartist	381	DOS	895	6	✓	✓		✓	✓	✓		ASCII	ASCII
McClellan Oscillator Program	264	DOS	350-450	20	✓								ASCII
MegaTech Chart System	376	DOS	175	8.5	✓	✓	✓	✓	✓	✓		ASCII, most formats	ASCII
MESA for Windows	316	Win	350			✓		✓	✓		✓	ASCII, CTrac, CSI, FutureSource, N-squared, TTools	

Information Services Supported	Chart Types	Max. Charts per Screen	Number of Pre-Defined Indicators	User-Defined Indicators	Pre-Defined Templates	User-Defined Templates	Batch Chart Printing	Macro/Script Automation	Pre-Defined Strategies	User-Defined Strategies	Total Profit Loss	Return	Largest Winner/Loser	Longest Winning/Losing Run	Percentage Profitable	User-Defined Stops	User-Defined Entry Signals	User-Defined Exit Signals	Accounts for Commissions	Accounts for Slippage	Strategy Optimization	Max. Criteria per Screen	Number of Screenable Indicators
Tools for Timing	L, S		1																				
DJN/R	B, L, S, P	4	30	✓	✓	✓	✓	✓														8	no limit
DJN/R	B, C, L, S, P	8	60	✓	✓	✓	✓	✓	✓	✓			✓	✓	✓							8	no limit
CIS, GE	B, P		1																				
	L		10																		✓		
Dial, Sig, Interactive Data, PC Quote, DBC MarketWatch	B, C, L		32	✓					✓													32	32
	L	1	4																		✓		
CIS, DJN/R, Dial, Pro, Exchange Access	L		27	✓																			
	B	3	many	✓							✓	✓	✓		✓	✓	✓	✓	✓		✓		
	L																						
AOL, CIS, DJN/R, Dial, Pro, GE, Sig, TC, Tscan, FFN	B, C, E, L, S, P	no limit	13	✓			✓																
CIS, Pro, Tscan	B, C, L, S	no limit	7														✓	✓					
Sig, Bon, CQI, RTS	B, C, L, P	6	50																				
	B, L		2																				
DJN/R, Pro, GE	B, C, L, S, P	16	50+				✓	✓															
	B, L		7																	✓			

Technical Analysis Software	Page	Systems	Price ($)	AAII Discount (%)	Securities Stock	Mutual Fund	Bond	Index	Options	Futures	Real Estate	Import Abilities	Export Abilities
MetaStock	243	DOS	349	10	✓	✓	✓	✓	✓	✓		ASCII, 123	ASCII, 123, PCX
MetaStock RT	244	DOS	495	10	✓	✓	✓	✓	✓	✓		ASCII, 123, CSI, DJMA, CSL	ASCII, 123
Microcomputer Chart Program	225	DOS, Mac	60	20	✓	✓		✓					
Microcomputer Stock Program	226	DOS, Mac	60	20	✓								
MIRAT	410	DOS	250					✓					
Money Fund Vision	281	DOS, Win	7,975										ASCII, 123, DBF, XLS
Money Maker for Windows	359	Win	99	40	✓	✓			✓	✓	✓		ASCII, comma delimited
Mutual Fund Composite Worksheet	424	DOS, Win	90	20	✓	✓	✓	✓				ASCII, 123, DBF, XLS	ASCII, 123, DBF, XLS
Mutual Fund Investor	169	DOS	295			✓	✓	✓	✓		✓	ASCII	ASCII
Mutual Fund Manager	204	DOS	49			✓							
Nature's Pulse	298	DOS, Win, OS/2	1,595	10	✓	✓	✓	✓		✓		ASCII	
Neuralyst for Excel	241	Win, Mac	195	10	✓	✓	✓	✓	✓	✓	✓	ASCII, 123, DBF, XLS	ASCII, 123, DBF, XLS
N-TRAIN	386	DOS, Win, Win NT	747	20	✓	✓	✓	✓	✓	✓	✓	ASCII	ASCII
Option Extension	167	DOS	249	10					✓	✓		ASCII	ASCII
Option Pro	250	Win	795	call					✓	✓		ASCII	ASCII
Option Pro SE (Special Edition)	250	Win	295	call					✓	✓		ASCII	ASCII
OVM/Focus	360	DOS, Win, Mac	399	5	✓			✓	✓	✓		ASCII	ASCII

Information Services Supported	Chart Types	Max. Charts per Screen	Number of Pre-Defined Indicators	User-Defined Indicators	Pre-Defined Templates	User-Defined Templates	Batch Chart Printing	Macro/Script Automation	Pre-Defined Strategies	User-Defined Strategies	Total Profit Loss	Return	Largest Winner/Loser	Longest Winning/Losing Run	Percentage Profitable	User-Defined Stops	User-Defined Entry Signals	User-Defined Exit Signals	Accounts for Commissions	Accounts for Slippage	Strategy Optimization	Max. Criteria per Screen	Number of Screenable Indicators
	B, C, L, S, P	50	75	✓			✓	✓					✓			✓	✓	✓	✓		✓		
Sig	B, C, L, S, P	50	75	✓			✓	✓					✓			✓	✓	✓	✓		✓		
	B, L																						
	L		1																				
Tools for Timing	L		2						✓		✓	✓	✓	✓	✓								
In house BBS	B, L																					120	120
CIS, Pro	L	1	2																				
	L	15																			✓		
CIS, Investment Company Data	L, S		24				✓	✓			✓	✓					✓	✓				5	24
	B, L																						
DJN/R, Dial, CSI, Sig, Bon, TC, Tick	B, C, L, S	1	5	✓	✓																		
																					✓		
				✓																	✓		
DJN/R, Dial, IDC, Tscan	B		32	✓					✓													32	32
Dial, CSI, Sig, DTN, Tick	B	8				✓			✓	✓	✓	✓	✓			✓	✓	✓	✓	✓	✓		
Dial, CSI, Sig, DTN	B	8				✓			✓	✓	✓	✓	✓			✓	✓	✓	✓	✓	✓		
Dial, MarketScan Plus, EMS Telequote	B, L, S	no limit		✓																✓			

Technical Analysis Software	Page	Systems	Price ($)	AAII Discount (%)	Stock	Mutual Fund	Bond	Index	Options	Futures	Real Estate	Import Abilities	Export Abilities
OWL Personal Portfolio Manager	346	DOS	55		✓	✓	✓	✓	✓		✓	ASCII	ASCII
Parity Plus	348	Win	179	10	✓	✓	✓	✓		✓		ASCII, 123, XLS, Meta, CTrac, ChartPro, comma delimited, TC	ASCII, 123, XLS, Meta, CTrac, ChartPro, comma delimited, TC
PC Chart Plus	270	DOS	160	10	✓	✓	✓	✓	✓	✓	✓	ASCII, CSI, Meta, PC Chart	ASCII, Meta, PC Chart
Peerless Intermediate-Term Market Timing Package	404	DOS, Mac	275					✓				ASCII	
Peerless Short-Term Market Timing Package	405	DOS	620									ASCII	
Peerless Stock Market Timing	405	DOS, Mac	275	10	✓	✓		✓	✓	✓			
Personal Analyst	417	Mac	395	10	✓	✓	✓	✓	✓	✓	✓	ASCII	ASCII
Personal Hotline	417	Mac	595	10	✓	✓	✓	✓	✓	✓	✓	ASCII	ASCII
Personal Market Analysis (PMA)	295	DOS	149	10	✓	✓		✓		✓			
Personal Stock Technician (PST)	363	DOS	100	50	✓	✓	✓	✓	✓	✓	✓	ASCII	ASCII
PFROI	400	DOS	59	30	✓	✓	✓	✓	✓	✓	✓	ASCII, Pro, Meta, Tscan, QXp, FOX, StSm, AOL	ASCII, 123
PointsAhead!	388	DOS	149			✓	✓	✓	✓	✓	✓	ASCII, CSI, Meta, CTrac	ASCII
Portfolio Data Manager	231	DOS	100	20	✓	✓	✓						
Portfolio Tracker	362	DOS	75	10	✓	✓	✓					ASCII	ASCII
PowerTrader!	334	Win	595	10	✓	✓				✓		Meta	Meta

Information Services Supported	Chart Types	Max. Charts per Screen	Number of Pre-Defined Indicators	User-Defined Indicators	Pre-Defined Templates	User-Defined Templates	Batch Chart Printing	Macro/Script Automation	Pre-Defined Strategies	User-Defined Strategies	Total Profit Loss	Return	Largest Winner/Loser	Longest Winning/Losing Run	Percentage Profitable	User-Defined Stops	User-Defined Entry Signals	User-Defined Exit Signals	Accounts for Commissions	Accounts for Slippage	Strategy Optimization	Max. Criteria per Screen	Number of Screenable Indicators
AOL, CIS, DJN/R, Pro, GE, Farpoint BBS, Just Data (Australia)	B, L, S	5	8	✓			✓									✓	✓	✓					
	B, C, E, L, P	no limit	50	✓		✓	✓			✓	✓	✓	✓	✓	✓	✓	✓	✓	✓	✓	✓	15	no limit
CIS, Dial, Pro, GE, CSI, TC, All-Quotes	B, C, L, S, P		26																			1	1
DJN/R, Dial	B																						
DJN/R, Dial	B																						
	B			✓																			
Dial	B, C, E, L, P	9	40			✓	✓	✓														1	20
CIS, DJN/R, Dial, Sig	B, C, E, L, S, P	9	40	✓		✓	✓	✓	✓	✓			✓				✓	✓	✓			10	25
	L		no limit	✓			✓																
CIS, DJN/R, Pro, GE	B, L, S		16	✓	✓		✓																
CIS, DJN/R, Dial, GE, All Quotes	B, L, S	1																					
Sig	B, C, E		40	✓																	✓		
	L		5																				
	L	1				✓																	
			40																		✓		

Technical Analysis Software	Page	Systems	Price ($)	AAII Discount (%)	Stock	Mutual Fund	Bond	Index	Options	Futures	Real Estate	Import Abilities	Export Abilities
Professional Analyst	418	Mac	595	10	✓	✓	✓	✓	✓	✓			
Professional Breakout System	327	DOS	385	10	✓	✓	✓	✓	✓	✓		ASCII, CSI, CTrac, Meta	
Prosper-II Mkt	163	DOS	189			✓	✓	✓	✓	✓	✓	ASCII	ASCII
Prosper-II PowerOnline	164	DOS	199			✓	✓	✓	✓	✓	✓	ASCII	ASCII
Put/Call	410	DOS	50						✓				
QTRADER	181	DOS	349	10	✓	✓		✓		✓		ASCII, CSI, CTrac, Meta, TTools	PCX
Quattro Pro	179	DOS, Win	99									ASCII, 123, DBF, Paradox, Reflex	ASCII, 123, DBF, Paradox, Reflex
Quick Charts	393	Win	50	15	✓	✓	✓	✓	✓	✓	✓	ASCII, 123, XLS, DIF	ASCII, 123, XLS, DIF
Quickplot/Quickstudy	191	DOS	89	10	✓			✓		✓		CSI	CSI
QuoteExpress	284	DOS, Win, Win NT, OS/2, PC-MOS	290	10	✓	✓	✓	✓	✓	✓		S&P 500 data base	ASCII, 123
QuoteMaster	394	Mac	395	10	✓	✓	✓	✓	✓	✓		ASCII	ASCII
QuoteMaster Professional	395	Mac	495	15	✓	✓	✓	✓	✓	✓		ASCII	ASCII
Rapid	270	DOS	277	5	✓	✓	✓	✓	✓	✓		ASCII, CSI, TTools	ASCII
Rational Indicators	413	DOS	345-445	10	✓			✓		✓		CTrac, Meta	
RDB Computing Custom Trader	363	DOS	varies			✓	✓	✓	✓	✓	✓	ASCII, CTrac, CSI, Meta	
RDB Programmer Libraries	364	DOS	295-895	5	✓	✓	✓	✓	✓	✓		ASCII	
RDB System Tester	364	DOS	895	5	✓	✓	✓	✓	✓	✓		ASCII	

Information Services Supported	Chart Types	Charting: Max. Charts per Screen	Number of Pre-Defined Indicators	User-Defined Indicators	Pre-Defined Templates	User-Defined Templates	Batch Chart Printing	Macro/Script Automation	Back-Testing: Pre-Defined Strategies	User-Defined Strategies	Total Profit Loss	Return	Largest Winner/Loser	Longest Winning/Losing Run	Percentage Profitable	User-Defined Stops	User-Defined Entry Signals	User-Defined Exit Signals	Accounts for Commissions	Accounts for Slippage	Strategy Optimization	Screening: Max. Criteria per Screen	Number of Screenable Indicators
Sig	B, C, L, P		16																			1	15
	B, L	2	17										✓								✓		
DJN/R, Pro, Sig, DTN, Tmet, XP	B, C, E, L	6	40	✓												✓						na	na
Sig, Tmet	B, E	2	40	✓																		na	na
Tools for Timing	L		10																				
	B, C, L	1	20						✓		✓		✓		✓								
	B, L, S																						
Dial, CSI, Sig, DTN, Tmet, Tick	B, C, E, L, P																					100	100
CSI	B, C	7	24				✓	✓															
Dial, DTN	B, C, L	1	4																				
Sig, Tmet	B, C, L		10																				
Sig, Tmet, Bon	B, C, L		22																				
CRS	B, C, L, S, P	2	25+				✓		✓														
CSI	B, C, L	1	4				✓																
	B, L	5									✓	✓	✓	✓		✓	✓	✓	✓	✓	✓		
	B, L	5		✓																			
	B, L	5		✓				✓			✓	✓	✓	✓		✓	✓	✓	✓	✓	✓	no limit	no limit

Technical Analysis Software	Page	Systems	Price ($)	AAII Discount (%)	Stock	Mutual Fund	Bond	Index	Options	Futures	Real Estate	Import Abilities	Export Abilities
RealTick III	412	Win, Win NT	call		✓	✓	✓	✓	✓	✓		ASCII, TTools	ASCII
Recurrence IV	172	DOS	3,500	5						✓		ASCII	ASCII
Relevance III-Advanced Market Analysis	373	DOS	795	4	✓	✓	✓	✓	✓	✓		CTrac, CSI, Meta	
RiskAlert	381	DOS, OS/2	295/month			✓	✓	✓	✓	✓			ASCII, 123
Rory Tycoon Portfolio Analyst	188	DOS	149		✓	✓	✓		✓	✓		ASCII, 123	ASCII, 123
Smartbroker	184	DOS	95		✓				✓			ASCII	ASCII
SMARTrader	393	DOS, Win	349-450	15	✓	✓	✓	✓	✓	✓	✓	ASCII, 123, XLS, DIF	ASCII, 123, XLS, DIF
SMARTrader Professional	394	DOS	990	15	✓	✓	✓	✓	✓	✓		ASCII, 123, XLS, DIF	ASCII, 123, XLS, DIF
Sophisticated Investor	320	DOS	195	15	✓	✓		✓				ASCII	ASCII
SPSS for Windows	391	Win	695	call	✓	✓	✓	✓	✓	✓		ASCII, 123, DBF, XLS, ISYLK, SAS, SPSS, SPSS/pct, ODBC	ASCII, 123, DBF, XLS, ISYLK, SAS, SPSS, SPSS/pct, ODBC
SPSS/PC+	392	DOS	195									ASCII, 123, DBF, SPSS	ASCII, 123, DBF, SPSS
SPSS/PC+ Trends	392	DOS	395									ASCII, 123, DBF, SPSS	ASCII, 123, DBF, SPSS
Stable—Technical Graphs	430	Win	50	10	✓	✓	✓	✓	✓	✓		ASCII, Meta, CSI, TTools, TC	ASCII
Statistical Analysis and Forecasting Software Package	357	DOS	144	10	✓		✓	✓	✓				
Stockaid 4.0	235	DOS	70	20	✓								

				Charting					Back-Testing													Screening	
Information Services Supported	Chart Types	Max. Charts per Screen	Number of Pre-Defined Indicators	User-Defined Indicators	Pre-Defined Templates	User-Defined Templates	Batch Chart Printing	Macro/Script Automation	Pre-Defined Strategies	User-Defined Strategies	Total Profit Loss	Return	Largest Winner/Loser	Longest Winning/Losing Run	Percentage Profitable	User-Defined Stops	User-Defined Entry Signals	User-Defined Exit Signals	Accounts for Commissions	Accounts for Slippage	Strategy Optimization	Max. Criteria per Screen	Number of Screenable Indicators
Sig, Bon, ComStock, Reuters, PC Quote, Knight Ridder	B, C, L, P	no limit	50	✓			✓																
Sig, Bon, CQG, FutureSource, Tradestation	B		4	✓																		na	na
	B, C, L		40																				
Sig, Bon, Knight Ridder, Reuters, S&P ComStock, PC Quote	B, C, E, L, P	100	100s													✓	✓	✓	✓		✓	no limit	no limit
CIS, DJN/R, Sig	L																						
DJN/R	C, L	5							✓	✓	✓	✓	✓		✓	✓			✓		✓	7	30
Dial, CSI, Sig, DTN, Tmet, Tick	B, C, E, L, P	50	80	✓	✓	✓	✓	✓	✓	✓	✓				✓	✓	✓	✓	✓	✓	✓	100	100
Dial, CSI, Sig, DTN, Tmet, Tick	B, C, E, L, P	50	80	✓	✓	✓	✓	✓	✓	✓	✓	✓	✓		✓	✓	✓	✓	✓	✓	✓	100	100
																					✓	1	4
	B, E, L, S, P				✓	✓	✓	✓															
	B, E, L, S, P																						
	B, L, S																						
	B, L, P	64	20				✓																
	S																						
DJN/R	L, P																						

Technical Analysis Software	Page	Systems	Price ($)	AAII Discount (%)	Stock	Mutual Fund	Bond	Index	Options	Futures	Real Estate	Import Abilities	Export Abilities
								Securities					
Stock Charting System	182	DOS	50		✓	✓	✓	✓	✓	✓		ASCII	ASCII
StockExpert	167	DOS	498	10	✓			✓	✓			ASCII, PRN, Meta	ASCII, PRN, Meta
Stock Graph Maker	332	DOS	60		✓	✓	✓	✓				ASCII, 123	ASCII, 123
Stock Prophet	266	DOS	995	call	✓	✓	✓	✓	✓	✓		ASCII, Computrac, Meta, Tscan	ASCII
Stock Watcher	319	Mac	195	30	✓			✓	✓	✓		ASCII	ASCII, Picture
STOKPLOT	185	DOS	40	10	✓	✓	✓	✓				ASCII	ASCII
StreetSmart	183	Win, Mac	59		✓	✓	✓		✓			StSm	ASCII, 123
SuperCharts	337	Win	195		✓	✓	✓	✓	✓	✓		ASCII, AIQ, CSI, Knight-Ridder, Megatech, Meta Stock, TC, Tick Data	ASCII
Super Tic	200	DOS	100		✓		✓	✓		✓			CSI
Swing Catcher Trading System	416	DOS	497	15						✓		CSI, Tools, CTrac, Meta, Technical	
System Writer 3.0 for Windows	337	Win	call		✓	✓	✓	✓	✓	✓		ASCII, CTrac, CSI, Meta, Tick Data	ASCII
System Writer Plus for DOS	338	DOS	975		✓	✓	✓	✓	✓	✓		ASCII, CTrac, CSI, Meta, Tick Data	ASCII
Take Stock	418	Win, Mac	175	10	✓							NAIC/ S&P data files	
Technical Analysis Charts	397	Apple II	130		✓	✓		✓	✓	✓			
Technical Analysis Scanner	263	DOS	249	15	✓	✓		✓	✓	✓			
Technical Investor	384	DOS	295		✓	✓	✓	✓	✓	✓	✓	ASCII	ASCII

Information Services Supported	Chart Types	Max. Charts per Screen	Number of Pre-Defined Indicators	User-Defined Indicators	Pre-Defined Templates	User-Defined Templates	Batch Chart Printing	Macro/Script Automation	Pre-Defined Strategies	User-Defined Strategies	Total Profit Loss	Return	Largest Winner/Loser	Longest Winning/Losing Run	Percentage Profitable	User-Defined Stops	User-Defined Entry Signals	User-Defined Exit Signals	Accounts for Commissions	Accounts for Slippage	Strategy Optimization	Max. Criteria per Screen	Number of Screenable Indicators
	B, L, S	1																					
DJN/R, Dial, Sig, IDC, PC Quote	B, C, L	no limit	32				✓		✓								✓	✓	✓	✓		32	32
Pro	B																						
	B, L, S	4		✓							✓	✓	✓				✓	✓	✓			✓	
CIS, DJN/R	B, L, S	2	29				✓																
CIS	B, L			✓													✓	✓					
Schwab host	L	no limit																					
Dial, Tscan	B, C, L, S, P	varies	47	✓			✓	✓	✓	✓	✓		✓		✓	✓	✓	✓	✓	✓	✓		
DTN	B, C, L		4																				
Dial, CSI, Sig, DTN, Tick, Compu Trac, MetaStock	B	2	54				✓	✓	✓		✓		✓	✓	✓	✓	✓		✓	✓	✓	✓	60	60
Dial, Tscan	B, C, L, S, P	varies		✓							✓	✓	✓		✓		✓	✓	✓			✓	no limit	
	B, C, L, P			✓							✓	✓	✓		✓		✓	✓	✓			✓	no limit	
	S	1																					
	B, L	sev'l	3	✓			✓	✓															
	L	8	60	✓			✓	✓			✓	✓			✓	✓	✓	✓	✓	✓		no limit	no limit
DJN/R, Dial, TrackData	B, L, S, P	no limit	56	✓	✓	✓	✓	✓															

Technical Analysis Software	Page	Systems	Price ($)	AAII Discount (%)	Securities							Import Abilities	Export Abilities
					Stock	Mutual Fund	Bond	Index	Options	Futures	Real Estate		
Technical Selector	385	DOS	145		✓	✓	✓	✓	✓	✓			ASCII
Technical Stock Analyst	400	DOS	25		✓	✓	✓	✓		✓		ASCII, 123, DBF, XLS	
The Technician	245	DOS	249	15				✓				ASCII	ASCII
TechniFilter Plus	382	DOS	399		✓	✓	✓	✓	✓	✓		ASCII, 123, Meta, CTrac, Market Analyzer, TC, AIQ Trading Expert	ASCII, 123
Telescan Analyzer	403	DOS	99	10	✓	✓	✓	✓	✓	✓			ASCII, 123, XLS
3D for Windows	316	Win	199		✓			✓	✓		✓	ASCII, CTrac, CSI, Future Source, N-Squared, TTools	ASCII
Tickerwatcher	304	Mac	195-595	10								ASCII, XLS	ASCII, XLS
Tiger Multiple Stock Screening & Timing System	406	DOS	995		✓			✓				Meta	ASCII
Timer	411	DOS	350					✓					
Timer Professional	411	DOS	450					✓					
TopVest	385	DOS	3,500		✓	✓	✓	✓	✓	✓	✓	ASCII, Savant	ASCII, Savant
Total Investor	279	DOS	35		✓	✓	✓	✓	✓			ASCII, 123	ASCII, 123, DBF, Quattro Pro
Tracker for Investor's Business Daily	327	DOS	79	10	✓								
Trader's Trainer	328	DOS	139	10	✓			✓	✓	✓			
TradeStation	339	Win	1,895		✓	✓	✓	✓	✓	✓		ASCII, CSI, CTrac, Meta, Tick Data	ASCII

Information Services Supported	Chart Types	Charting							Back-Testing													Screening	
		Max. Charts per Screen	Number of Pre-Defined Indicators	User-Defined Indicators	Pre-Defined Templates	User-Defined Templates	Batch Chart Printing	Macro/Script Automation	Pre-Defined Strategies	User-Defined Strategies	Total Profit Loss	Return	Largest Winner/Loser	Longest Winning/Losing Run	Percentage Profitable	User-Defined Stops	User-Defined Entry Signals	User-Defined Exit Signals	Accounts for Commissions	Accounts for Slippage	Strategy Optimization	Max. Criteria per Screen	Number of Screenable Indicators
																						16	15
	B	1	9	✓																			
EQUIS	B, L, S	36	100	✓												✓	✓	✓					
	B, C, L, P	2	200	✓			✓	✓	✓	✓	✓	✓	✓	✓		✓	✓	✓	✓	✓	✓	no limit	no limit
Tscan	B, C, E, L, S	4	80				✓	✓	✓	✓								✓		✓		
	B		5	✓																			
CIS, DJN/R, Dial, Sig, Bon, DTN, XP	B, C	25																					
DJN/R, CSI, TC	B		20	✓																	✓	5	5
Tools for Timing	L	1	18						✓			✓	✓	✓	✓								
Tools for Timing	L, S	1	26						✓			✓	✓	✓	✓								
CIS, DJN/R, Dial, Sig, TrackData, IDC	B, C, E, L, S, P	9	100+	✓	✓	✓	✓	✓				✓	✓	✓	✓	✓	✓	✓	✓	✓	✓	16	100
AOL, CIS, DJN/R, Dial, Pro, GE, Sig, TC, Tscan, FFN	B, L	2	17					✓															
	B, L	1	10																				
	B	1	10																				
Sig, Bon, S&P ComStock, FutureSource	B, C, L, S, P	varies		✓					✓	✓	✓	✓	✓			✓	✓	✓	✓		✓	no limit	

Technical Analysis Software	Page	Systems	Price ($)	AAII Discount (%)	Stock	Mutual Fund	Bond	Index	Options	Futures	Real Estate	Import Abilities	Export Abilities
TradingExpert	168	DOS	996	10	✓	✓		✓	✓			ASCII	ASCII, PRN
Trading Package	187	DOS	295			✓	✓	✓	✓	✓	✓	CTrac, CIS, CSI, Meta	ASCII
20/20 for DOS	361	DOS	99	5	✓	✓	✓	✓	✓	✓		ASCII	ASCII
20/20 Plus	361	DOS	299	5	✓	✓	✓	✓	✓	✓		ASCII	ASCII
VantagePoint Intermarket Analysis Program	312	DOS	2,450	10	✓			✓	✓		✓	CSI	
Wall Street Watcher	319	Mac	495	20	✓	✓		✓	✓	✓		ASCII	ASCII, Picture
Wave Wise Spreadsheet for Windows	297	Win	150			✓	✓	✓	✓		✓	ASCII, XLS, CTrac, CSI, Symphony, TC	ASCII, XLS
Windows on Wall Street Pro	310	Win	249	25	✓	✓	✓	✓	✓	✓		ASCII, Meta, Computrac	ASCII, Meta

Information Services Supported	Chart Types	Max. Charts per Screen	Number of Pre-Defined Indicators	User-Defined Indicators	Pre-Defined Templates	User-Defined Templates	Batch Chart Printing	Macro/Script Automation	Pre-Defined Strategies	User-Defined Strategies	Total Profit Loss	Return	Largest Winner/Loser	Longest Winning/Losing Run	Percentage Profitable	User-Defined Stops	User-Defined Entry Signals	User-Defined Exit Signals	Accounts for Commissions	Accounts for Slippage	Strategy Optimization	Max. Criteria per Screen	Number of Screenable Indicators
DJN/R, Dial, Sig, IDC, Tscan, PC Quote	B, C, L	1	36	✓			✓		✓							✓	✓	✓	✓			36	36
CSI, Sig, DTN, CIS, CompuTrac	B, C, L	no limit	73	✓			✓															38	73
Dial, MarketScan Plus	B, L, S	million	12																				
Dial, MarketScan Plus and EMS TeleQuote	B, L, S	million	18																				
CSI	B, C																				✓		
CIS, DJN/R	B, L, S, P	2	31				✓	✓															
	B, L, S	12		✓	✓	✓		✓	✓	✓	✓					✓	✓						
CIS, DJN/R, Dial, CSI, TC	B, C, L, S, P	no limit	60-70	✓	✓	✓	✓	✓	✓		✓	✓	✓	✓	✓	✓	✓	✓	✓	✓	✓	no limit	no limit

Fundamental, Other Analysis Software	Page	Systems	Price ($)	AAII Discount (%)	Stock	Mutual Fund	Bond	Index	Options	Futures	Real Estate	Import Abilities	Export Abilities
					Securities								
AAII Fundamental Stock Analysis Disk	168	DOS, Win, Mac	20	25	✓							123	123
@Bonds XL U.S. Series and International Series	322	DOS, Win, Win NT, OS/2, Unix	395-695	15		✓			✓	✓		ASCII, 123, DBF, XLS	ASCII, 123, DBF, XLS
Advanced Business Valuation	248	DOS	295	50	✓								ASCII
Advanced G.E.T.	414	DOS	2,750	10	✓	✓	✓	✓	✓	✓		ASCII, Future Source, CSI, Meta, TTools, CTrac, AIQ, Ensi	
Advanced Total Investor (ATI)	277	DOS, Win	129	23	✓	✓	✓	✓	✓	✓		ASCII, 123, XLS	ASCII, 123, DBF, XLS
@Exotics XL	323	DOS, Win, Win NT, OS/2, Mac, Unix	695	15	✓			✓	✓	✓		ASCII, 123, DBF, XLS	ASCII, 123, DBF, XLS
Amortizelt!	352	DOS	50	10									
@nalyst	396	DOS, Win, OS/2, Mac, Unix, Sun Sparc	195-1,495	10	✓		✓	✓	✓	✓	✓		
@Options XL Pro, Premium, and Extended Binomial Series	323	DOS, Win, Win NT, OS/2, Mac, Unix, Sun	395-995	15	✓		✓	✓	✓	✓		ASCII, 123, DBF, XLS	ASCII, 123, DBF, XLS
Asset Allocator	354	DOS	150	15	✓	✓	✓		✓	✓			
Basic Cycle Analysis	263	DOS	450-500	20	✓	✓	✓	✓	✓	✓	✓	ASCII, CTrac, CSI	ASCII
Binomial Market Model	308	Win	8						✓				
BMW	355	DOS	99	50			✓					ASCII, 123	ASCII, 123

Information Services Supported	Fund'l Analysis				Other Analysis									
	Economic Forecasting	Stock Valuation Models	Financial Statement Analysis	Number of Valuation Models	Bond Analysis	Futures Analysis	Options Analysis	Real Estate Analysis	Spreadsheet	Simulation/Game	Statistics	Expert System	Neural Network	Other
		✓	✓	6										
CIS, DJN/R, Sig, Tmet, Bon, DDE					✓	✓			✓	✓				
		✓	✓					✓						
												✓		
AOL, CIS, DJN/R, Dial, Pro, GE, Sig, TC, Tscan, FFN									✓		✓			
CIS, DJN/R, Sig, Tmet, Bon, DDE						✓	✓		✓	✓				
								✓						
					✓	✓	✓	✓	✓		✓			
CIS, DJN/R, Sig, Tmet, Bon, DDE					✓	✓	✓		✓	✓				
CIS											✓			
CSI											✓			
							✓			✓				
					✓				✓					

Fundamental, Other Analysis Software	Page	Systems	Price ($)	AAII Discount (%)	Stock	Mutual Fund	Bond	Index	Options	Futures	Real Estate	Import Abilities	Export Abilities
BNA Real Estate Investment Spreadsheet	176	DOS	395-595								✓		
BondCalc	176	DOS, Win, OS/2	2,900				✓					BondScholar, custom formats	ASCII, 123, XLS
Bond Portfolio	172	Win, Mac	25				✓						
Bond Portfolio Manager	298	DOS, Win, Mac	89	20			✓						ASCII, 123, DBF, XLS
Bond Pricing	173	Win, Mac	15				✓						
Bonds and Interest Rates Software	356	DOS	144	10	✓	✓	✓	✓	✓	✓	✓		
Bondseye	246	DOS, Win	65				✓					ASCII	ASCII
Bondsheet	341	DOS	95				✓						
BOND$MART	356	DOS	395	75			✓					ASCII, 123	ASCII, 123
Bond-Tech's Bond Calculator	177	DOS	49				✓						
BrainMaker	180	DOS	195		✓	✓	✓	✓	✓	✓	✓	ASCII, 123, DBF, XLS, binary	ASCII
BrainMaker Professional	180	DOS	795		✓	✓	✓	✓	✓	✓	✓	ASCII, 123, DBF, XLS, binary	ASCII, 123, DBF, XLS, binary
Business Pack	212	DOS	100	20								ASCII	ASCII
Buysel	213	DOS	100	20	✓				✓	✓		ASCII	ASCII
Buy-Write Model	329	DOS	50						✓				
Calcugram Stock Options System	213	DOS	100	20					✓	✓			

Information Services Supported	Fund'l Analysis				Other Analysis									
	Economic Forecasting	Stock Valuation Models	Financial Statement Analysis	Number of Valuation Models	Bond Analysis	Futures Analysis	Options Analysis	Real Estate Analysis	Spreadsheet	Simulation/Game	Statistics	Expert System	Neural Network	Other
								✓						
					✓									
					✓				✓					
					✓				✓		✓			
					✓				✓					
	✓		✓		✓	✓		✓			✓			
					✓									
					✓									
					✓									
					✓									
													✓	
CSI													✓	
	✓	✓	✓		✓		✓	✓			✓			
							✓				✓			
							✓							
		✓		1			✓							

Fundamental, Other Analysis Software	Page	Systems	Price ($)	AAII Discount (%)	Securities							Import Abilities	Export Abilities
					Stock	Mutual Fund	Bond	Index	Options	Futures	Real Estate		
Candlestick Forecaster	285	DOS	249	5	✓	✓	✓	✓	✓	✓		ASCII, Future Source, Meta, TTools	
Candlestick Forecaster Master Edition	286	DOS, OS/2	800	5	✓	✓	✓	✓	✓	✓		ASCII, Future Source, Meta, TTools	
Candlestick Forecaster Real Time	286	DOS, OS/2	1,700	5	✓	✓	✓	✓	✓	✓			
CAPTOOL	397	DOS	129	30	✓	✓	✓	✓	✓	✓	✓	ASCII, Pro, Meta, Tscan, QXp, FOX, StSm, AOL	ASCII, 123
CAPTOOL Global Investor	398	DOS	299	30	✓	✓	✓	✓	✓	✓	✓	ASCII, Pro, Meta, Tscan, QXp, FOX, StSm, AOL	ASCII, 123
CAPTOOL Professional Investor	399	DOS	499		✓	✓	✓	✓	✓	✓	✓	ASCII, Pro, SchwabLink 2000, Fidelity, Vanguard, DST Systems, First Trust/Data Lynx, Jack White and Co., Meta, Tscan, QXp, FOX, StSm, AOL	ASCII, 123
CAPTOOL Real Time	399	DOS	189	30	✓	✓	✓	✓	✓	✓	✓	ASCII, Pro, AOL, Meta, FOX, StSm, Tscan	ASCII, 123
Centerpiece	350	DOS	895		✓	✓	✓	✓	✓		✓	ASCII	ASCII, 123, XLS
ChartistAlert	379	OS/2	195-280/ month		✓	✓	✓	✓	✓	✓			123

Information Services Supported	Fund'l Analysis				Other Analysis									
	Economic Forecasting	Stock Valuation Models	Financial Statement Analysis	Number of Valuation Models	Bond Analysis	Futures Analysis	Options Analysis	Real Estate Analysis	Spreadsheet	Simulation/Game	Statistics	Expert System	Neural Network	Other
DJN/R, Dial, Pro, Sig, DTN, TC					✓	✓	✓					✓	✓	
DJN/R, Dial, Pro, Sig, DTN, TC					✓	✓	✓					✓	✓	
Sig					✓	✓	✓					✓	✓	
CIS, DJN/R, Dial, GE, All Quotes	✓	✓			✓									
CIS, DJN/R, Dial, GE, All Quotes	✓	✓	✓		✓									
CIS, DJN/R, Dial, GE	✓	✓	✓		✓									
CIS, DJN/R, Dial, GE, DTN	✓	✓			✓									
DJN/R, Dial, Sig, DTN, Tmet, Bon, Interactive Data					✓									
Sig, Bon, Knight Ridder, Reuters, S&P ComStock, PC Quote						✓	✓					✓	✓	

Fundamental, Other Analysis Software	Page	Systems	Price ($)	AAII Discount (%)	Securities Stock	Mutual Fund	Bond	Index	Options	Futures	Real Estate	Import Abilities	Export Abilities
COMEX, The Game	190	DOS	70						✓	✓			
Commercial/Industrial Real Estate Applications	366	DOS, Win, Mac	150	10							✓		
Commodities and Futures Software Package	357	DOS	144	10				✓	✓	✓			
Common Stock Decision Aide	419	DOS	49		✓			✓					
Common Stock Selector	421	DOS, Win	59	20	✓							ASCII, 123, DBF, XLS	ASCII, 123, DBF, XLS
Comparative Lease Analysis	366	DOS, Win, Mac	295	10									
Complete Bond Analyzer	299	DOS, Mac	89	20			✓						
CompuServe CD	194	Win	8		✓	✓	✓	✓	✓	✓			ASCII
CompuServe Research Manager	195	DOS	400-1,000/month		✓	✓	✓	✓	✓			ASCII, 123	ASCII, 123
CompuServe Research Manager for Windows	195	Win	400-1,000/month		✓	✓	✓	✓	✓			ASCII, 123	ASCII, 123
Covered Options	216	DOS	100	20					✓	✓			
Crystal Ball	203	Win, Mac	295		✓	✓	✓	✓	✓	✓	✓	123, XLS	123, XLS
CSSCO	189	DOS	99					✓	✓	✓		123	
CurrencyCast	324	DOS	70		✓	✓	✓	✓	✓	✓	✓	ASCII	ASCII
Data Smoother Semi-Spline/Polynomial Data Smoothing	216	DOS	40-50	20								ASCII	ASCII
Discover/EN by Telemet	401	Win, OS/2	149/month		✓	✓		✓	✓	✓		ASCII	ASCII, 123, XLS, comma delimited

Information Services Supported	Fund'l Analysis				Other Analysis									Other
	Economic Forecasting	Stock Valuation Models	Financial Statement Analysis	Number of Valuation Models	Bond Analysis	Futures Analysis	Options Analysis	Real Estate Analysis	Spreadsheet	Simulation/Game	Statistics	Expert System	Neural Network	
						✓	✓			✓				
								✓	✓					
	✓					✓	✓				✓			—
	✓	✓							✓					
		✓							✓					—
	✓							✓	✓					
					✓						✓			—
CIS														
CIS		✓	✓	40	✓		✓		✓					—
CIS		✓	✓	40	✓		✓		✓					
						✓								—
	✓								✓	✓	✓			
					✓				✓		✓			—
DTN	✓										✓	✓		
	✓										✓			—
Tmet							✓							

Fundamental, Other Analysis Software	Page	Systems	Price ($)	AAII Discount (%)	Stock	Mutual Fund	Bond	Index	Options	Futures	Real Estate	Import Abilities	Export Abilities
Discover/OR by Telemet	402	Win, OS/2	330/month			✓	✓	✓	✓	✓	✓	ASCII, 123, XLS, comma delimited	ASCII, 123, XLS, comma delimited
Discover/RE by Telemet	402	Win, OS/2	399		✓	✓		✓	✓	✓		ASCII, 123, XLS	ASCII, 123, X▌
DollarLink	206	DOS	1,300	10	✓	✓		✓	✓	✓		ASCII	ASCII, 123, DBF, XLS, CTrac, Meta, SystemWrite▌
DowCast	325	DOS	70		✓	✓	✓	✓	✓	✓	✓	ASCII	ASCII
Dow Jones/ OEX Trading System	415	DOS	147	15						✓		CSI, Tools, CompuTrac	
Dynamic Volume Analysis Charts	428	DOS	100	50	✓			✓	✓	✓			
Easy Money Plus	320	DOS	500		✓	✓	✓			✓			
Econ	202	DOS	50		✓	✓	✓	✓	✓	✓			ASCII
EconPlot	309	DOS	50									BCI Data	
Elderly Tax Planner	321	DOS	100		✓	✓	✓				✓		
Enhanced Chartist	380	Mac	1,295	10	✓		✓	✓	✓	✓		ASCII	ASCII
Enhanced Fund Master Optimizer	407	DOS	150	10	✓	✓	✓	✓				Time Trend	
Ensign V	241	DOS	1,295			✓	✓	✓	✓	✓	✓	ASCII, CSI, CTrac	ASCII, CSI, CT▌
Estamore	217	DOS	100	20									
Excalibur	265	Mac	3,400-3,900		✓			✓		✓		ASCII	ASCII
Exec-Amort Loan Amortizer Plus	239	DOS	150	10							✓		ASCII
Expert Ease Expert System	217	DOS	395	20								ASCII, 123	

Information Services Supported	Fund'l Analysis				Other Analysis									
	Economic Forecasting	Stock Valuation Models	Financial Statement Analysis	Number of Valuation Models	Bond Analysis	Futures Analysis	Options Analysis	Real Estate Analysis	Spreadsheet	Simulation/Game	Statistics	Expert System	Neural Network	Other
Tmet			✓				✓							
Tmet						✓								quote utility
Sig, Bon, PC Quote		✓		1		✓	✓			✓	✓			
DTN											✓	✓		
Dial, CSI, Sig, DTN, Tick, Compu Trac, Meta							✓							
CIS, Dial						✓	✓							
									✓					
	✓													
	✓													
									✓					
Sig, Bon, S&P Comstock					✓	✓	✓							
										✓				
Bon						✓	✓							
								✓						
											✓			
								✓						
											✓	✓		

Fundamental, Other Analysis Software	Page	Systems	Price ($)	AAII Discount (%)	Securities							Import Abilities	Export Abilities
					Stock	Mutual Fund	Bond	Index	Options	Futures	Real Estate		
Expert System Tutorial	218	DOS	30	20									
Expert Trading System	171	Win	varies	10	✓			✓	✓	✓			
Fast Cast for Ventures	422	DOS, Win	69	20								ASCII, 123, DBF, XLS	ASCII, 123, DBF, XLS
Fibnodes	186	DOS	595	20	✓	✓	✓	✓	✓	✓			
Finance 101	184	DOS	39			✓	✓				✓		ASCII
Finance Master	218	DOS	90	20									
Financial Competence	193	Win, Win NT, Mac	99	10								ASCII, 123, XLS	ASCII, 123, XLS
Financial Management System	219	DOS	150	20	✓	✓	✓	✓	✓	✓	✓		
Financial Navigator for DOS	256	DOS	249	10	✓	✓	✓		✓		✓		ASCII, 123, PRN
Financial Navigator for Windows	256	Win	349	10	✓	✓	✓		✓		✓		ASCII, 123, XLS, PRN
Financial Needs for Retirement	420	DOS	49										
Financial Planning for Retirement	422	DOS, Win	59	20								ASCII, 123, DBF, XLS	ASCII, 123, DBF, XLS
Financial Planning TOOLKIT	255	DOS	249	20	✓	✓	✓				✓		123
Financial Statement Analyzer	248	DOS	89	50									ASCII
Financial Statement Cash Flow Forecaster	249	DOS	89	50									ASCII, 123
Financial & Interest Calculator	299	DOS, Mac	89	20	✓	✓	✓	✓	✓	✓	✓		
Fin Val/Finstock	349	DOS	495	40	✓							123	123

Information Services Supported	Fund'l Analysis				Other Analysis									Other
	Economic Forecasting	Stock Valuation Models	Financial Statement Analysis	Number of Valuation Models	Bond Analysis	Futures Analysis	Options Analysis	Real Estate Analysis	Spreadsheet	Simulation/Game	Statistics	Expert System	Neural Network	
											✓	✓		
						✓	✓					✓	✓	
			✓						✓					business forecasting
					✓	✓	✓	✓			✓			
								✓	✓		✓			
								✓						
			✓							✓				instructional program
	✓	✓	1		✓									
CIS, DJN/R, Dial, Pro, Navigator Access II							✓	✓						
CIS, DJN/R, Dial, Pro, Navigator Access II							✓	✓						
									✓					
									✓					
					✓									
			✓											
			✓											
					✓			✓			✓			
CIS, Disclosure, AAII Stock Investor (FINSTOCK)		✓	✓	6					✓					

Fundamental, Other Analysis Software	Page	Systems	Price ($)	AAII Discount (%)	Securities Stock	Mutual Fund	Bond	Index	Options	Futures	Real Estate	Import Abilities	Export Abilities
FirstAlert	380	DOS, Win, OS/2	200-350/ month		✓	✓	✓	✓	✓	✓		ASCII	ASCII
Folioman	246	DOS	89	10	✓	✓	✓	✓	✓		✓	ASCII	ASCII
Folioman+	247	DOS	129	10	✓	✓	✓	✓	✓	✓	✓	ASCII	ASCII
Forecast!	288	DOS, Win	165									123, XLS	123, XLS
The Forecasting Edge	219	DOS	100	20								ASCII, 123, DBF	ASCII, 123, DB
Forecast Pro	179	DOS, Win	595										ASCII, 123, DL
Foreign Exchange Software Package	357	DOS	144	10				✓	✓	✓			
Fortune 500 on Disk	205	DOS, Mac	395		✓							123, XLS	123, XLS
Fourcast	240	DOS, Win	300	20	✓	✓	✓	✓	✓	✓	✓	ASCII, Dial	ASCII
Fourier Analysis Forecaster	220	DOS	100-170	20								ASCII	
401(k) Forecaster	422	DOS, Win	69	20								ASCII, 123, DBF, XLS	ASCII, 123, DBF, XLS
Fundamental Investor	383	DOS	295		✓							ASCII	ASCII
Futures Markets Analyzer	296	DOS	795							✓		ASCII, TTools, CSI, Exchange	
Futures Pro	249	Win	595-15,000	call						✓		ASCII	ASCII
Global Trader Calculator	163	DOS	195	10		✓							
Goldspread Statistical	221	DOS	80	20								ASCII, 123, DBF	ASCII, 123, DB
Hansen-Predict	221	DOS	100	20							✓		

Information Services Supported	Fund'l Analysis				Other Analysis									
	Economic Forecasting	Stock Valuation Models	Financial Statement Analysis	Number of Valuation Models	Bond Analysis	Futures Analysis	Options Analysis	Real Estate Analysis	Spreadsheet	Simulation/Game	Statistics	Expert System	Neural Network	Other
Sig, Bon, Knight Ridder, S&P ComStock, PC Quote						✓	✓		✓		✓	✓		
CIS					✓		✓			✓	✓			
CIS					✓	✓	✓			✓	✓			
									✓		✓			
	✓										✓	✓		
									✓		✓			
	✓					✓								
		✓	✓											
Dial	✓										✓			
											✓			
									✓		✓			
Ford		✓	✓	200										
DJN/R, Dial, CSI, Sig, DTN, Tmet, Genesis, Knight-Ridder, TTools						✓								
DJN/R, Dial, CSI, Sig, DTN, Bon, Tick, Meta, Futures Source, Knight Ridder, Prophet						✓								
					✓									
											✓			
											✓	✓		

Fundamental, Other Analysis Software	Page	Systems	Price ($)	AAII Discount (%)	Stock	Mutual Fund	Bond	Index	Options	Futures	Real Estate	Import Abilities	Export Abilities
Hedgemaster	190	DOS	100						✓	✓			
Historical ADL	409	DOS	175					✓					
Home Appraiser	222	DOS	60	20							✓		
Home Purchase	370	DOS	75	10							✓		
How to Write a Business Plan	169	DOS, Mac	125	10							✓		
Income Property Analysis	370	DOS	75	10							✓		
Individual Stock Investor INSTIN	204	DOS, OS/2	60	10	✓								
Interactive Multiple Prediction	222	DOS	70	20								ASCII	ASCII
Intex Bond Calculations	288	DOS, Win	495-995				✓					123	
Intex CMO Analyst	288	Win	call				✓						
Intex Fixed-Income Subroutines for Bonds, MBSs, CMOs	289	DOS, Mini, Workstation	call		✓		✓		✓	✓			
Intex Mortgage-Backed Calculations	289	DOS, Win	495				✓					123, XLS	
Intex Option Price Calculations	290	DOS, Win	495						✓			123, XLS	
Investment IRR Analysis for Stocks, Bonds & Real Estate	300	DOS, Win, OS/2, Mac	89	20	✓		✓				✓		ASCII, 123, DBF
InvestNow!—Personal	239	DOS	99	50	✓	✓		✓	✓				
InvestNow!—Professional	240	DOS	195	25	✓	✓			✓	✓			
Investograph Plus, Optimizer	302	DOS	99-399	12	✓	✓	✓	✓	✓	✓		ASCII, CTrac, CSI, Meta	ASCII, CTrac, CSI

Information Services Supported	Fund'l Analysis				Other Analysis									
	Economic Forecasting	Stock Valuation Models	Financial Statement Analysis	Number of Valuation Models	Bond Analysis	Futures Analysis	Options Analysis	Real Estate Analysis	Spreadsheet	Simulation/Game	Statistics	Expert System	Neural Network	Other
						✓	✓			✓				
Tools for Timing										✓				
								✓						
								✓						
	✓		✓						✓					
								✓						
CIS, Pro, Sig											✓			
					✓				✓					
					✓				✓					
					✓				✓					
					✓				✓					
							✓		✓					
		✓		3	✓			✓	✓		✓			
						✓	✓				✓			
						✓	✓				✓			
CIS, DJN/R, Dial, Pro, GE, CSI, Sig, DTN, Tmet, TC, Tick					✓	✓	✓				✓	✓		

Fundamental, Other Analysis Software	Page	Systems	Price ($)	AAII Discount (%)	Stock	Mutual Fund	Bond	Index	Options	Futures	Real Estate	Import Abilities	Export Abilities
The Investor	423	DOS, Win	129	20	✓	✓	✓	✓	✓	✓		ASCII, 123, DBF, XLS	ASCII, 123, DBF, XLS
Investor's Accountant	272	DOS	395	25	✓	✓	✓	✓	✓	✓	✓	ASCII	ASCII
Investor's Tool Box	330	DOS	50		✓				✓				
Laddering Your Portfolio	423	DOS, Win	45	20								ASCII, 123, DBF, XLS	ASCII, 123, DBF, XLS
Lease vs. Purchase	424	DOS, Win	69	20								ASCII, 123, DBF, XLS	ASCII, 123, DBF, XLS
Loan Amortization	424	DOS, Win	39	20								ASCII, 123, DBF, XLS	ASCII, 123, DBF, XLS
Loan Amortization	371	DOS	75	10							✓		
Lotus 1-2-3 for OS/2	305	OS/2	495-595									ASCII, DBF	ASCII, DBF
Lotus 1-2-3 Release 4 for DOS	305	DOS	495									ASCII, DBF	ASCII, DBF
Lotus 1-2-3 Release 5 for Windows	306	Win	495									ASCII, DBF	ASCII, DBF
Lotus Improv for Windows	306	Win	495									ASCII, 123	
MacRATS	251	Mac	300									ASCII, 123, DBF	ASCII, 123, DBF
MacRATS 020	252	Mac	400									ASCII, 123, DBF	ASCII, 123, DBF
Macro*World Investor	307	DOS	900	28	✓	✓	✓	✓		✓		ASCII	ASCII
Maintenance Manager	371	DOS	275	10							✓		
Manager's Option	371	DOS	375	10							✓		
Managing Your Money	311	DOS, Win, Mac	80		✓	✓	✓	✓	✓	✓	✓		ASCII, 123
MarketExpert	166	DOS	249	10				✓				ASCII	ASCII, PRN

Information Services Supported	Fund'l Analysis				Other Analysis									
	Economic Forecasting	Stock Valuation Models	Financial Statement Analysis	Number of Valuation Models	Bond Analysis	Futures Analysis	Options Analysis	Real Estate Analysis	Spreadsheet	Simulation/Game	Statistics	Expert System	Neural Network	Other
CIS, DJN/R, Dial, Pro, GE, Sig, TC, Tscan					✓		✓		✓		✓			
CIS, Pro, Tscan					✓									
							✓							
									✓					
							✓							
							✓	✓						
							✓							
					✓				✓		✓			
									✓		✓			
					✓				✓		✓			
									✓		✓			
	✓										✓			
	✓										✓			
	✓	✓	✓	1						✓	✓			
								✓						
								✓						
CIS, DJN/R, Pro, Fidelity On-Line Express, BillPay USA, Checkfree								✓						
Dial, Sig, Interactive Data, PC Quote, DBC MarketWatch												✓		

Fundamental, Other Analysis Software	Page	Systems	Price ($)	AAII Discount (%)	Stock	Mutual Fund	Bond	Index	Options	Futures	Real Estate	Import Abilities	Export Abilities
MarketMaker 1.0 for Windows	287	DOS, Win	29		✓								
Market Strategist	273	DOS	295	25	✓			✓					ASCII
Market Timing Utility	278	DOS, Win	59					✓				ASCII, 123, XLS	ASCII, 123, DBF, XLS
Master Chartist	381	DOS	895	6	✓	✓		✓	✓	✓		ASCII	ASCII
Mathcad 5.0	310	Win, Mac	100									ASCII	ASCII
MBS/ABS Calculator	178	DOS	49				✓						
MetaStock	243	DOS	349	10	✓	✓	✓	✓	✓	✓		ASCII, 123	ASCII, 123, PCX
MetaStock RT	244	DOS	495	10	✓	✓	✓	✓	✓	✓		ASCII, 123, CSI DJMA, CSL	ASCII, 123
Microbj Box Jenkins Forecasting	225	DOS	150	20								ASCII, 123	
Microcomputer Bond Program	225	DOS, Mac	60	20			✓						
Microcomputer Stock Program	226	DOS, Mac	60	20	✓								
Microsoft Excel	317	Win, Mac	339									ASCII, 123, DBF	ASCII, 123, DBF
Money	226	DOS	40	20							✓		
Money Decisions	226	DOS	130	20	✓	✓	✓	✓			✓		
Money Fund Vision	281	DOS, Win	7,975										ASCII, 123, DBF, XLS
Money Maker for Windows	359	Win	99	40	✓	✓	✓		✓	✓	✓		ASCII, comma delimited
Mortgage Loans—Is it Time to Refinance?	301	DOS, Win, OS/2, Mac	89	20							✓		123, Excel, Works, ClarWorks, AppleWorks

Information Services Supported	Fund'l Analysis				Other Analysis									
	Economic Forecasting	Stock Valuation Models	Financial Statement Analysis	Number of Valuation Models	Bond Analysis	Futures Analysis	Options Analysis	Real Estate Analysis	Spreadsheet	Simulation/Game	Statistics	Expert System	Neural Network	Other
		✓	✓											
		✓		many						✓	✓			
AOL, CIS, DJN/R, Dial, Pro, GE, Sig, TC, Tscan, FFN										✓	✓			
Sig, Bon, CQI, RTS						✓								
											✓			
					✓									
							✓				✓			
Sig						✓	✓			✓	✓			
	✓										✓			
					✓									
											✓			
					✓				✓		✓			
								✓						
CIS											✓			
In house BBS									✓		✓			composition analysis
CIS, Pro		✓	✓	3	✓	✓	✓	✓						mutual funds analysis
									✓	✓				

Fundamental, Other Analysis Software	Page	Systems	Price ($)	AAII Discount (%)	Stock	Mutual Fund	Bond	Index	Options	Futures	Real Estate	Import Abilities	Export Abilities
Multivariate Non-Linear Regression and Optimizer	227		100	20								ASCII	ASCII
Multivariate Regression Analysis	227	DOS	60	20								ASCII	ASCII
Mutual Fund Composite Worksheet	424	DOS, Win	90	20	✓	✓	✓	✓				ASCII, 123, DBF, XLS	ASCII, 123, DBF, XLS
Mutual Fund Decision Aide	420	DOS	49			✓		✓					
Mutual Fund Kit	425	DOS, Win	79	20		✓		✓				ASCII, 123, DBF, XLS	ASCII, 123, DBF, XLS
Mutual Fund Selector	425	DOS, Win	59	20		✓						ASCII, 123, DBF, XLS	ASCII, 123, DBF, XLS
NAIC Stock Selection Guide	173	Win, Mac	30		✓								
Nature's Pulse	298	DOS, Win, OS/2	1,595	10	✓	✓	✓	✓		✓		ASCII	
Neuralyst for Excel	241	Win, Mac	195	10	✓	✓	✓	✓	✓	✓	✓	ASCII, 123, DBF, XLS	ASCII, 123, DBF, XLS
Neuralyst Pro for Excel	242	Win, Mac	495	10	✓	✓	✓	✓	✓	✓	✓	ASCII, 123, DBF, XLS	ASCII, 123, DBF, XLS
NIS Asset Allocation System	335	DOS	10,000	20		✓		✓					Paradox
NIS Fixed Income Research Environment	335	DOS	30,000	20			✓						Paradox
NIS Macroeconomic Equity System	336	DOS, Win	12,000-18,000	20	✓			✓					Paradox
NIS Performance Analysis System	336	DOS	16,000	20	✓			✓					Paradox
N-TRAIN	386	DOS, Win, Win NT	747	20	✓	✓	✓	✓	✓	✓	✓	ASCII	ASCII
Nuametrics Econometric Analysis	228	DOS	100	20								ASCII, 123	ASCII
On Schedule	367	DOS, Win, Mac	195	10							✓		

Information Services Supported	Economic Forecasting	Stock Valuation Models	Financial Statement Analysis	Number of Valuation Models	Bond Analysis	Futures Analysis	Options Analysis	Real Estate Analysis	Spreadsheet	Simulation/Game	Statistics	Expert System	Neural Network	Other
											✓			
											✓			
									✓					
									✓		✓			
									✓					
									✓					
		✓	✓	1					✓					
DJN/R, Dial, CSI, Sig, Bon, TC, Tick											✓			
									✓		✓	✓	✓	
									✓		✓	✓	✓	
									✓					
					✓				✓					
	✓	✓							✓					
									✓					
					✓	✓	✓		✓	✓	✓	✓	✓	
	✓								✓					
	✓							✓	✓					

Fundamental, Other Analysis Software	Page	Systems	Price ($)	AAII Discount (%)	Securities							Import Abilities	Export Abilities
					Stock	Mutual Fund	Bond	Index	Options	Futures	Real Estate		
Option Extension	167	DOS	249	10				✓	✓			ASCII	ASCII
Option Master	282	DOS, Mac	89	20					✓				
Option Master for Newton	282	Newton	195	20					✓				
Optionomic Systems	343	DOS, Win, Unix	4,200		✓		✓	✓	✓	✓		ASCII	ASCII
Option Pricing Analysis	342	DOS, Mac	275	25	✓			✓	✓	✓			
Option Pro	250	Win	795	call				✓	✓			ASCII	ASCII
Option Pro SE (Special Edition)	250	Win	295	call				✓	✓			ASCII	ASCII
Option Risk Management	412	Win, Win NT	call		✓			✓	✓	✓			
An Option Valuator/An Option Writer	376	DOS	100	25					✓				
Options-80A: Advanced Stock Option Analyzer	344	DOS, Mac	150	20					✓				
Options Analysis	228	DOS	100	20				✓	✓				
Options and Arbitrage Software Package	357	DOS	144	10	✓		✓	✓	✓	✓			
OptionsCalc	324	DOS	80-100	15					✓				
Options Laboratory	309	Win	130		✓			✓	✓				
Options Made Easy	344	DOS	20						✓				
Options Master for Windows	283	Win	160	20					✓				
Option Strategy Projections	198	DOS	30						✓				
Options Valuation	301	DOS, Mac	89	20	✓		✓	✓	✓	✓	✓		

Information Services Supported	Fund'l Analysis				Other Analysis									
	Economic Forecasting	Stock Valuation Models	Financial Statement Analysis	Number of Valuation Models	Bond Analysis	Futures Analysis	Options Analysis	Real Estate Analysis	Spreadsheet	Simulation/Game	Statistics	Expert System	Neural Network	Other
DJN/R, Dial, IDC, Tscan							✓			✓				
							✓							
							✓							
CIS, Sig, S&P Comstock, Knight-Ridder	✓			2	✓	✓	✓			✓	✓			
DJN/R, Sig							✓							
Dial, CSI, Sig, DTN, Tick							✓							
Dial, CSI, Sig, DTN							✓							
Sig, Bon, ComStock, Reuters, PC Quote, Knight Ridder						✓	✓							
							✓							
							✓							
							✓							
					✓	✓	✓				✓			
						✓	✓							
							✓			✓				
							✓			✓				
							✓							
							✓							
							✓							

Fundamental, Other Analysis Software	Page	Systems	Price ($)	AAII Discount (%)	Securities							Import Abilities	Export Abilities
					Stock	Mutual Fund	Bond	Index	Options	Futures	Real Estate		
OptionVue IV	345	DOS	895						✓	✓		ASCII	ASCII
Option-Warrant Combo	173	Win, Mac	49						✓	✓			
OVM/Focus	360	DOS, Win, Mac	399	5	✓		✓	✓	✓			ASCII	ASCII
Own-Write Model	331	DOS	50		✓			✓					
Parity Plus	348	Win	179	10	✓	✓	✓	✓		✓		ASCII, 123, XLS, Meta, CTrac, ChartPro, comma delimited, TC	ASCII, 123, XLS, Meta, CTrac, ChartPro, comma delimited, TC
PC Regression Multiple Regression	229	DOS	100	20								ASCII, 123, DIF	ASCII
Peerless Intermediate-Term Market Timing Package	404	DOS, Mac	275					✓				ASCII	
Peerless Short-Term Market Timing Package	405	DOS	620									ASCII	
Personal Analyst	417	Mac	395	10	✓	✓	✓	✓	✓	✓		ASCII	ASCII
Personal Hotline	417	Mac	595	10	✓	✓	✓	✓	✓	✓		ASCII	ASCII
Personal Real Estate Manager	231	DOS	50	20							✓		
Personal Stock Technician (PST)	363	DOS	100	50	✓	✓	✓	✓	✓	✓	✓	ASCII	ASCII
PlanEASe Partnership Models	170	DOS	495								✓		
PlanEASe/Windows	171	DOS, Win	995								✓		ASCII, 123
PointsAhead!	388	DOS	149		✓	✓	✓	✓	✓	✓		ASCII, CSI, Meta, CTrac	ASCII

Information Services Supported	Economic Forecasting	Stock Valuation Models	Financial Statement Analysis	Number of Valuation Models	Bond Analysis	Futures Analysis	Options Analysis	Real Estate Analysis	Spreadsheet	Simulation/Game	Statistics	Expert System	Neural Network	Other
DJN/R, Sig, DTN, Tmet, Bon, ComStock, DataVue, DBC/Marketwatch, Tscan						✓	✓							
							✓		✓					
Dial, MarketScan Plus, EMS Telequote							✓							
							✓							
											✓			
											✓			
DJN/R, Dial												✓		
DJN/R, Dial												✓		
Dial							✓							
CIS, DJN/R, Dial, Sig							✓					✓		
								✓						
CIS, DJN/R, Pro, GE											✓			
								✓						
								✓						
Sig					✓	✓					✓			

Fundamental, Other Analysis Software	Page	Systems	Price ($)	AAII Discount (%)	Stock	Mutual Fund	Bond	Index	Options	Futures	Real Estate	Import Abilities	Export Abilities
Portfolio Selection	279	DOS	99		✓	✓	✓	✓	✓	✓		ASCII	ASCII
Portfolio Selection-Professional	280	DOS	595	15	✓	✓	✓	✓	✓	✓	✓	ASCII	ASCII
Portfolio Spreadsheets	207	DOS	195		✓	✓	✓						
Portfolio Spreadsheets—Bonds	207	DOS	100			✓	✓						
Portfolio Spreadsheets—Stocks	208	DOS	100		✓	✓							
Professional Breakout System	327	DOS	385	10	✓	✓	✓	✓	✓	✓		ASCII, CSI, CTrac, Meta	
Profit Planner Plus	426	DOS, Win	99	20								ASCII, 123, DBF	ASCII, 123, DB
Property Listings Comparables	372	DOS	300	10							✓		
Property Management III	367	DOS, Mac	395-1,495								✓		XLS, Foxbase
Property Management PLUS	372	DOS	350	10							✓		
Property Manager	233	DOS	300	20									
Pulse Portfolio Management System	244	DOS	195	10	✓	✓	✓		✓	✓	✓	ASCII, Meta	ASCII
QOS-30	260	Win	2,500	50	✓	✓	✓	✓					
QTRADER	181	DOS	349	10	✓	✓		✓		✓		ASCII, CSI, CTrac, Meta, TTools	PCX
Quant IX Portfolio Evaluator	358	DOS	99		✓	✓	✓		✓		✓	ASCII	ASCII, 123, DBF, DAT, SDF, SYLK
Quattro Pro	179	DOS, Win	99									ASCII, 123, DBF, Paradox, Reflex	ASCII, 123, DBF, Paradox, Reflex
Quick Charts	393	Win	50	15	✓	✓	✓	✓	✓	✓	✓	ASCII, 123, XLS, DIF	ASCII, 123, XLS, DIF

Information Services Supported	Economic Forecasting	Stock Valuation Models	Financial Statement Analysis	Number of Valuation Models	Bond Analysis	Futures Analysis	Options Analysis	Real Estate Analysis	Spreadsheet	Simulation/Game	Statistics	Expert System	Neural Network	Other
											✓			
											✓			
DJN/R, Sig					✓				✓					
					✓				✓					
DJN/R, Sig									✓					
										✓				
	✓		✓					✓	✓					business forecasting
								✓						
								✓						
								✓						
								✓						
CIS, DJN/R, Dial, Sig, MarketScan										✓	✓			
						✓								
CIS, Pro	✓	✓		6										
										✓	✓			
Dial, CSI, Sig, DTN, Tmet, Tick					✓	✓			✓		✓			

Fundamental, Other Analysis Software	Page	Systems	Price ($)	AAII Discount (%)	Securities							Import Abilities	Export Abilities
					Stock	Mutual Fund	Bond	Index	Options	Futures	Real Estate		
RAMCAP—The Intelligent Asset Allocator	429	DOS	595	17	✓	✓	✓	✓		✓	✓	ASCII	ASCII, PCX
Ratios	234	DOS	30	20									
RATS	252	DOS	300	10								ASCII, 123, DBF	ASCII, 123, D
RATS 386	253	DOS	420									ASCII, 123, DBF	ASCII, 123, D
RATS (for UNIX)	252	Unix	varies									ASCII, 123, DBF	ASCII, 123, D
RDB Computing Custom Trader	363	DOS	varies		✓	✓	✓	✓	✓	✓		ASCII, CTrac, CSI, Meta	
RDB System Tester	364	DOS	895	5	✓	✓	✓	✓	✓	✓		ASCII	
Real Analyzer	365	DOS	95	15							✓		
Real Estate Analyzer	276	DOS, Apple II (ProDOS)	350-395								✓		
Real Estate Investment Analysis	368	DOS, Win, Mac	295	10							✓		
Real Estate Partnership Plus	368	DOS, Win, Mac	295	10							✓		
Real Estate Resident Expert	234	DOS	100	20							✓		
Real Property Management II	365	DOS	145-920	15							✓		ASCII
RealTick III	412	Win, Win NT	call		✓	✓	✓	✓	✓	✓		ASCII, TTools	ASCII
REAP PLUS	372	DOS	150	10							✓		
Recurrence IV	172	DOS	3,500	5						✓		ASCII	ASCII
REMS Investor 3000	269	DOS	595	10							✓	123, REMS	ASCII, 123
Resampling Stats	374	DOS, Mac	225	50								ASCII	ASCII

Information Services Supported	Fund'l Analysis				Other Analysis									
	Economic Forecasting	Stock Valuation Models	Financial Statement Analysis	Number of Valuation Models	Bond Analysis	Futures Analysis	Options Analysis	Real Estate Analysis	Spreadsheet	Simulation/Game	Statistics	Expert System	Neural Network	Other
											✓			
			✓											
	✓										✓			
	✓										✓			
	✓										✓			
					✓	✓	✓				✓			
					✓	✓	✓				✓			
								✓						
	✓			7				✓						
									✓	✓				
	✓							✓	✓					
								✓						
								✓						
Sig, Bon, ComStock, Reuters, PC Quote, Knight Ridder					✓	✓	✓		✓	✓				
								✓						
Sig, Bon, CQG, FutureSource, Tradestation						✓						✓		
								✓						
										✓	✓			

Fundamental, Other Analysis Software	Page	Systems	Price ($)	AAII Discount (%)	Securities							Import Abilities	Export Abilities
					Stock	Mutual Fund	Bond	Index	Options	Futures	Real Estate		
Retirement Solutions	322	DOS	250										
Retirement Trio	427	DOS, Win	79	20								ASCII, 123, DBF	ASCII, 123, DB
RiskAlert	381	DOS, OS/2	295/ month		✓	✓	✓	✓	✓	✓			ASCII, 123
Roll Model	331	DOS	45						✓				
Rory Tycoon Options Trader	187	DOS	49						✓				
Rory Tycoon Portfolio Analyst	188	DOS	149		✓	✓	✓		✓	✓		ASCII, 123	ASCII, 123
Rory Tycoon Portfolio Manager	188	DOS	99		✓	✓	✓		✓	✓			
SIBYL/RUNNER Interactive Forecasting	303	Win	495		✓	✓	✓	✓	✓	✓	✓	ASCII, 123	ASCII, 123, DB
Smartbroker	184	DOS	95		✓				✓			ASCII	ASCII
SMARTrader	393	DOS, Win	349-450	15	✓	✓	✓	✓	✓	✓	✓	ASCII, 123, XLS, DIF	ASCII, 123, XLS, DIF
SMARTrader Professional	394	DOS	990	15	✓	✓	✓	✓	✓	✓	✓	ASCII, 123, XLS, DIF	ASCII, 123, XLS, DIF
SolveIt!	353	DOS	90	10	✓	✓	✓				✓		
Sophisticated Investor	320	DOS	195	15	✓	✓			✓			ASCII	ASCII
SORITEC	390	DOS	495										
Spread Maker	332	DOS	50						✓				
SPSS for Windows	391	Win	695	call	✓	✓	✓	✓	✓	✓	✓	ASCII, 123, DBF, XLS, ISYLK, SAS, SPSS, SPSS/pct, ODBC	ASCII, 123, DBF, XLS, ISYLK, SAS, SPSS, SPSS/pct, ODBC
SPSS/PC+	392	DOS	195									ASCII, 123, DBF, SPSS	ASCII, 123, DBF, SPSS
SPSS/PC+ Trends	392	DOS	395									ASCII, 123, DBF, SPSS	ASCII, 123, DBF, SPSS
Statistical Analysis and Forecasting Software Package	357	DOS	144	10	✓		✓	✓	✓	✓			
Statistics Toolbox	428	DOS, Win	50	20								ASCII, 123, DBF, XLS	ASCII, 123, DBF, XLS

Information Services Supported	Fund'l Analysis				Other Analysis									
	Economic Forecasting	Stock Valuation Models	Financial Statement Analysis	Number of Valuation Models	Bond Analysis	Futures Analysis	Options Analysis	Real Estate Analysis	Spreadsheet	Simulation/Game	Statistics	Expert System	Neural Network	Other
									✓					
									✓					
Sig, Bon, Knight Ridder, Reuters, S&P ComStock, PC Quote							✓				✓			
							✓							
CIS, DJN/R, Sig							✓		✓					
CIS, DJN/R, Sig					✓	✓	✓		✓					
CIS, DJN/R, Sig					✓	✓	✓		✓					
	✓										✓			
DJN/R		✓					✓				✓	✓		
Dial, CSI, Sig, DTN, Tmet, Tick					✓	✓	✓		✓		✓			
Dial, CSI, Sig, DTN, Tmet, Tick					✓	✓	✓		✓		✓			
					✓			✓						
										✓	✓	✓		
	✓										✓			
							✓							
											✓			
											✓			
											✓			
	✓					✓					✓			
											✓			

Fundamental, Other Analysis Software	Page	Systems	Price ($)	AAII Discount (%)	Securities							Import Abilities	Export Abilities
					Stock	Mutual Fund	Bond	Index	Options	Futures	Real Estate		
StockExpert	167	DOS	498	10	✓			✓	✓			ASCII, PRN, Meta	ASCII, PRN, Meta
Stock Market Bargains	235	DOS	70	20	✓								
Stock Master/Stock Plot	236	DOS	60	20	✓			✓					
Stock Option Analysis Program	274	DOS	150	10					✓				
Stock Option Calculations and Strategies	198	DOS	40	10					✓				
Stock Option Scanner	275	DOS	150	10					✓				
Stock Portfolio	174	Win, Mac	15		✓								
Stock Prophet	266	DOS	995	call	✓	✓	✓	✓	✓	✓		ASCII, Computrac, Meta, Tscan	ASCII
Stock Valuation	174	Win, Mac	25		✓								
Sto Quest	285	DOS, Win, Win NT, OS/2	199	10	✓							Meta, CTrac	Meta, CTrac
Strategist	343	DOS	4,900-10,700						✓	✓		ASCII	ASCII
Swing Catcher Trading System	416	DOS	497	15						✓		CSI, Tools, CTrac, Meta, Technical	
System Writer 3.0 for Windows	337	Win	call		✓	✓	✓	✓	✓	✓		ASCII, CTrac, CSI, Meta, Tick Data	ASCII
System Writer Plus for DOS	338	DOS	975		✓	✓	✓	✓	✓	✓		ASCII, CTrac, CSI, Meta, Tick Data	ASCII
Take Stock	418	Win, Mac	175	10	✓							NAIC/ S&P data files	
The Technician	245	DOS	249	15				✓				ASCII	ASCII
TechniFilter Plus	382	DOS	399		✓	✓	✓	✓	✓	✓		ASCII, 123, Meta, CTrac, Market Analyzer, TC, AIQ Trading Expert	ASCII, 123

Information Services Supported	Economic Forecasting	Stock Valuation Models	Financial Statement Analysis	Number of Valuation Models	Bond Analysis	Futures Analysis	Options Analysis	Real Estate Analysis	Spreadsheet	Simulation/Game	Statistics	Expert System	Neural Network	Other
			Fund'l Analysis								**Other Analysis**			
DJN/R, Dial, Sig, IDC, PC Quote							✓			✓		✓		
		✓	✓	2										
		✓	✓											
DJN/R, Sig							✓							
							✓							
DJN/R, Sig							✓							
									✓					
													✓	
		✓		5					✓					
Dial, DTN														
Sig, Bon, Knight-Ridder, S&P Comstock		✓		2		✓	✓			✓	✓			
Dial, CSI, Sig, DTN, Tick, Compu Trac, MetaStock												✓		
Dial, Tscan					✓	✓	✓							
					✓	✓	✓							
		✓	✓											
EQUIS											✓			
						✓								

Fundamental, Other Analysis Software	Page	Systems	Price ($)	AAII Discount (%)	Securities							Import Abilities	Export Abilities
					Stock	Mutual Fund	Bond	Index	Options	Futures	Real Estate		
Tech Tutor	327	DOS	50	10									
Telescan Analyzer	403	DOS	99	10	✓	✓	✓	✓	✓	✓			ASCII, 123, XLS
3D for Windows	316	Win	199		✓			✓	✓	✓		ASCII, CTrac, CSI, Future Source, N-Squared, TTools	ASCII
Tickerwatcher	304	Mac	195-595	10								ASCII, XLS	ASCII, XLS
Tiger Multiple Stock Screening & Timing System	406	DOS	995		✓			✓					ASCII
Timer Professional	411	DOS	450					✓					
Time Series/Forecasting	236	DOS	50	20								ASCII, 123	ASCII
TIP Lease Analysis	165	DOS, Win, Mac	1,000/mo	15							✓	ASCII, 123	ASCII, 123
TopVest	385	DOS	3,500		✓	✓	✓	✓	✓	✓	✓	ASCII, Savant	ASCII, Savant
Total Investor	279	DOS	35		✓	✓	✓	✓	✓			ASCII, 123	ASCII, 123, DBF, Quattro Pro
Trader's Money Manager	192	DOS	399	10								ASCII	
Trader's Trainer	328	DOS	139	10	✓			✓	✓	✓			
TradeStation	339	Win	1,895		✓	✓	✓	✓	✓	✓		ASCII, CSI, CTrac, Meta, Tick Data	ASCII
TradingExpert	168	DOS	996	10	✓	✓		✓	✓			ASCII	ASCII, PRN
Trading Package	187	DOS	295		✓	✓	✓	✓	✓	✓		CTrac, CIS, CSI	ASCII
Universal Exotics Add-In	257	DOS, Win, Win NT, OS/2, Mac	224-477	10		✓			✓	✓			

Information Services Supported	Fund'l Analysis				Other Analysis									
	Economic Forecasting	Stock Valuation Models	Financial Statement Analysis	Number of Valuation Models	Bond Analysis	Futures Analysis	Options Analysis	Real Estate Analysis	Spreadsheet	Simulation/Game	Statistics	Expert System	Neural Network	Other
Tscan		✓								✓				
						✓						✓		
BMI, CIS, DJN/R, Dial, Sig, DTN, XP									✓					
Dial, DJN/R, Wordens, MetaStock												✓		
Tools for Timing										✓				
											✓			
								✓		✓				
CIS, DJN/R, Dial, Sig, TrackData, Interactive Data Corporation	✓	✓	✓	800							✓			
AOL, CIS, DJN/R, Dial, Pro, GE, Sig, TC, Tscan, FFN									✓	✓				
CSI										✓	✓			
										✓				
Sig, Bon, S&P ComStock, FutureSource					✓	✓	✓							
DJN/R, Dial, Sig, Interactive Data, Tscan, PC Quote							✓			✓		✓		
CSI, Sig, DTN, CIS, CompuTrac, MetaStock					✓	✓	✓							
					✓	✓	✓		✓	✓	✓			

Fundamental, Other Analysis Software	Page	Systems	Price ($)	AAII Discount (%)	Securities							Import Abilities	Export Abilities
					Stock	Mutual Fund	Bond	Index	Options	Futures	Real Estate		
Universal Options Add-In	258	DOS, Win, Win NT, OS/2, Mac	224-477	10			✓		✓	✓			
Universal Swap Add-In	258	DOS, Win, Win NT, OS/2, Mac	749-1,499	10			✓		✓	✓			
Universal Yield Add-In	259	DOS, Win, Win NT, OS/2, Mac	224-477	10			✓		✓	✓			
Universal Zero-Curve Add-In	260	DOS, Win, Win NT, OS/2, Mac	224-477	10			✓		✓	✓			
VantagePoint Intermarket Analysis Program	312	DOS	2,450	10	✓		✓	✓		✓		CSI	
Vertical Spread Model	333	DOS	55						✓				
Wall Street Trainer	236	DOS	30	20	✓				✓	✓			
Wave Wise Spreadsheet for Windows	297	Win	150			✓	✓	✓	✓		✓	ASCII, XLS, CTrac, CSI, TC2000	ASCII, XLS
WealthBuilder by Money Magazine	369	DOS, Mac	70		✓	✓	✓	✓	✓	✓	✓	Quicken, Managing Your Money	ASCII
Wealth Creator	362	DOS	60	10	✓	✓	✓				✓		ASCII
What'sBest!	303	DOS, Mac	149-4,995									123, XLS	123, XLS
Windows on Wall Street Pro	310	Win	249	25	✓	✓	✓	✓	✓		✓	ASCII, Meta, Computrac	ASCII, Meta
Xtrapolator Time Series Forecasts	237	DOS	130	20								ASCII, 123	ASCII, 123
Yield Curve	428	DOS, Win	35	20								ASCII, 123, DBF, XLS	ASCII, 123, DBF, XLS
Zenterprise Real Estate Investor	237	DOS	70	20							✓		

Information Services Supported	Fund'l Analysis				Other Analysis									
	Economic Forecasting	Stock Valuation Models	Financial Statement Analysis	Number of Valuation Models	Bond Analysis	Futures Analysis	Options Analysis	Real Estate Analysis	Spreadsheet	Simulation/Game	Statistics	Expert System	Neural Network	Other
					✓	✓	✓		✓	✓	✓			
					✓	✓	✓		✓	✓	✓			
					✓	✓	✓		✓	✓	✓			
					✓	✓	✓		✓	✓	✓			
CSI					✓	✓							✓	
							✓							
										✓				
					✓				✓		✓			
										✓				
								✓						
									✓					
CIS, DJN/R, Dial, CSI, TC									✓					
											✓			
									✓					
								✓						

5

Financial Information Services Grid

The Financial Information Services Grid is designed to help you select the service that best meets your needs. The services are presented alphabetically and include the page reference to the full description and price schedule in Chapter 7.

The grid provides the methods by which the data is transferred and information regarding the breadth of coverage through the Number of Securities in Database column. Quote information is divided into security types and indicates if the data is provided on a real-time (RT), delayed (D), or historical (H) basis. If the service provides historical data, the time period for which the data is available is indicated. The grid also indicates the main types of financial data and services provided by each database.

Financial Information Services Grid—Item Description

Modem Information is available via telephone connection using your computer and a modem.

Cable TV Information is available over cable TV lines. Normally user can use their present cable box to translate the information.

FM Information is available through FM airwaves. This setup will require a special receiver.

Satellite Information is broadcast through satellite, which requires down-link equipment and translation hardware. Satellite transmission is normally faster than phone lines.

Diskette Information is available from the service on a floppy disk.

CD-ROM Information is available from service on a CD-ROM disk.

Number of Companies/Securities in Database The total number of companies or securities available through this data provider. Remember there can be multiple securities for a single company.

Domestic Securities: Stock, Index, Bonds, Options, Futures, Mutual

Fund, and Closed-End Fund Quotes (Periods) Quotes are available D (delayed), RT (real-time), or H (historical). If historical data is available, the oldest date of securities is shown.

Foreign Securities: Number of Securities in Database Indicates how many foreign securities are included in the services database.

Foreign Securities: Stock, Index, Bonds, Options, Futures, and Mutual Fund Quotes Shows what type of foreign securities a service covers in its database.

General/Business News Business news is available, including trends and present developments. Also includes non-business-related news.

Economic News/Data Service provides access to economic news. General economic trends such as unemployment, GNP, and inflation figures are available.

Company News Specific company news is available through the service. Companies are normally accessed by name or ticker symbol to speed searches for individual companies.

Financial Statement Data Annual report and other various financial data is available for specific companies. Data includes EPS, net income, and dividend information.

SEC Filings Service provides access to required company filings with the SEC. This data includes 10-K and 10-Q statements. This data also includes insider transactions and holdings.

Analyst Reports Analysts' reports are available that offer professional estimates of company business and prognosis. This information is useful in analyzing the future earnings as compared to other stocks in a particular industry.

Earnings Estimates Earnings estimates are available for specific companies. This data is normally provided by I/B/E/S or Zacks Investment Research, both of which provide consensus estimates.

Charting Price and volume charts are available for viewing or downloading through the service. Some services offer equivolume and histograms in addition to price charts.

Technical Studies/Indicators Technical studies and indicators such as moving averages and relative strength are provided through the service. Some services also provide analysis of charts and discuss indicators and their relevance to price movements

On-Line Brokerage Service offers ability to trade stocks or other securities on-line. Account setup is required with service providers, but many on-line brokers offer discounts and portfolio management functions.

Message/Mail Areas Indicates if a service has an electronic mail/messaging area.

Software Library for Download Shareware or freeware programs are available on-line to download and try out. Downloading a demo of a program is an excellent way to try out a software package before purchasing the full version.

Screening: Fundamental Factors Screening is available on fundamental criteria. For example, to find high income stocks, you would search their universe of stocks for dividend yields over 5% and annual dividends over $1.50.

Screening: Technical Indicators Screening is available based on technical factors. For example, users can search the universe of stocks for companies with high relative strength and a stock price above a 200-day moving average.

Screening: Mutual Funds Screening is available on mutual funds.

Screening: Bonds Screening is available on bonds.

Financial Information Services	Page	Transmission						No. of Cos./Securities in Database	Domestic				
		Modem	Cable TV	FM	Satellite	Diskette	CD-ROM		Stock Quotes (time period)	Index Quotes (time period)	Bond Quotes (time period)	Options Quotes (time period)	Futures Quotes (time period)
AAII Online	436	✓											
All-Quotes	436	✓						100,000+	RT,D,H (100d)	RT,D,H (100d)		RT,D,H (100d)	RT,D,H (100d)
American Venture Capital Exchange	439	✓											
America Online	440	✓							D	D			
BioTech On Disk	492					✓		230					
Bond Buyer Full Text	459	✓									D		
Business Connection	460	✓						2,000,000	H (1y)	H (1y)			
Business DateLine	460	✓											
Business Week Mutual Fund Scoreboard	445					✓		4,000					
CheckFree	449	✓											
CMO/REMIC Pricing Service	506	✓				✓		22,000			D,H		
COMLINE	502						✓						
Compact D/Canada	463						✓	8,000					
Compact D/New Issues	464	✓					✓	15,000					
Compact D/SEC	464	✓					✓	11,000					
Company Screening Service	451	✓						11,000					
CompuServe	451	✓						90,000	D,H (12y)	D,H (12y)	D,H (12y)	D,H (9m)	D,H (12y)
Corporate & Industrial News from Reuters	502						✓						
CSI Data Retrieval Service	449	✓				✓		7,000	H (1962)	H (1928)		H (1982)	H (1949)
Daily Financial Market Research	494	✓							D (end of day)	D (end of day)	D (end of day)	D (end of day)

Mutual Fund Quotes (time period)	Closed-End Quotes (time period)	No. of Securities in Database	Stock Quotes	Index Quotes	Bond Quotes	Options Quotes	Futures Quotes	Mutual Fund Quotes	General/Business News	Economic News/Data	Company News	Financial Statement Data	SEC Filings	Analyst Reports	Earnings Estimates	Charting	Technical Studies/Indicators	On-Line Brokerage	Message/Mail Areas	Software Library for Downloading	Fundamental Indicators	Technical Indicators	Mutual Funds	Bonds
RT,D,H (100d)	RT,D,H (100d)	2,000	✓	✓			✓		✓	✓	✓	✓	✓	✓		✓		✓	✓	✓				
											✓													
D	D								✓	✓	✓	✓						✓	✓	✓				
									✓			✓									✓			
										✓														
									✓		✓	✓	✓	✓				✓			✓		✓	
									✓	✓	✓													
H (monthly to 10 years)																							✓	
																		✓						
									✓		✓													
		8,000										✓	✓	✓							✓			
			✓										✓	✓							✓			
												✓	✓	✓	✓									
												✓				✓					✓			
D,H (12y)	D,H (12y)		✓	✓					✓	✓	✓	✓	✓	✓	✓	✓	✓	✓	✓	✓	✓	✓	✓	
									✓	✓	✓				✓									
H (1986)	H (1987)			✓			✓				✓							✓	✓			✓		
				✓	✓		✓				✓							✓	✓					

Financial Information Services	Page	Transmission						No. of Cos./Securities in Database	Domestic				
		Modem	Cable TV	FM	Satellite	Diskette	CD-ROM		Stock Quotes (time period)	Index Quotes (time period)	Bond Quotes (time period)	Options Quotes (time period)	Futures Quotes (time period)
Daily Pricing Service	506	✓						1,000			H (1975)	H	H
Datadisk Information Services	445					✓		1,000	H (10 years)	H (20 years)			
DATAFEED for AIQ Systems TradingExpert	478	✓				✓		511,000	H (1968)	H (1968)		H (inc)	H (1965)
DATAFEED for MetaStock	479	✓				✓		518,740	H (1968)	H (1968)		H (inc)	H (1965)
Data-Star	455	✓						155,000	D,H	D,H	D,H	D,H	D,H
Delphi	457	✓							D	D	D	D	D
Dial/Data	459	✓						20,000	H (1970)	H (1970)	H (1970)	H (1993)	H (1963)
Dial Up/Historical Data Retriever	478	✓						10,000	H (20yrs)	H (20yrs)			H (20yrs)
Disclosure Data for The Fundamental Investor	501					✓		10,000					
Disclosure SEC Database	465	✓						11,000					
Dividend Reinvestment Plan Stocks	441					✓		1,200	RT				
Dow Daily Close 1960-1991	441					✓				H (1960)			
Dow Industrials	441					✓		1		H (35y)			
Dow Jones Market Monitor	467	✓							D,H (1yr)	D,H (1982)	D,H (1yr)	D,H (1yr)	D,H (1yr)
Dow Jones Market Monitor Plus	467	✓						142,000	D,H (20yrs)	D,H (20yrs)	D,H (20yrs)	D,H (20yrs)	D,H (20yrs)
Dow Jones News/Retrieval	468	✓						150,000+	RT,D,H (20y)	D,H (20y)	D,H (20y)	D,H (up to 90 days from exp.)	D,H (20y)
Dow Jones Total Return Indexes	466					✓				H (5 years)			
Dow Month-by-Month Set	441					✓		4		H (35y)			

Securities		Foreign Securities							Types of Information Provided												Screening			
Mutual Fund Quotes (time period)	Closed-End Quotes (time period)	No. of Securities in Database	Stock Quotes	Index Quotes	Bond Quotes	Options Quotes	Futures Quotes	Mutual Fund Quotes	General/Business News	Economic News/Data	Company News	Financial Statement Data	SEC Filings	Analyst Reports	Earnings Estimates	Charting	Technical Studies/Indicators	On-Line Brokerage	Message/Mail Areas	Software Library for Downloading	Fundamental Indicators	Technical Indicators	Mutual Funds	Bonds
				✓					✓	✓		✓									✓			
H (1982)			✓	✓				✓																
H (1982)			✓	✓			✓	✓																
D,H	D	58,000	✓			✓	✓	✓	✓	✓	✓	✓	✓	✓	✓		✓				✓	✓	✓	✓
D	D								✓	✓	✓			✓					✓	✓				
H (1987)	H (1987)	3,000	✓			✓	✓												✓			✓	✓	✓
H (20yrs)	H (20yrs)																							
												✓												
										✓	✓	✓	✓								✓			
RT																								
D,H (1yr)	D,H (1yr)								✓	✓	✓	✓			✓									
D,H (20yrs)	D,H (20yrs)								✓	✓	✓	✓			✓								✓	
D,H (20y)	D,H (20y)	40,000	✓	✓	✓	✓	✓		✓	✓	✓	✓	✓	✓	✓		✓				✓	✓	✓	✓

Financial Information Services	Page	Modem	Cable TV	FM	Satellite	Diskette	CD-ROM	No. of Cos./Securities in Database	Stock Quotes (time period)	Index Quotes (time period)	Bond Quotes (time period)	Options Quotes (time period)	Futures Quotes (time period)
The DRPdisk	469					✓		1,500					
DTN Wall Street	456		✓		✓			20,000	D	RT	D	D	D
Electronic Bond Fund Report	473	✓						750					
Electronic Futures Trend Analyzer	482	✓						360				H (inc)	H (50y)
Electronic Money Fund Report	473	✓						1,000		D			
Ensign 5	443	✓		✓	✓			110,000	RT,D	RT,D	RT,D	RT,D	RT,D
Equalizer	447	✓							RT,D,H (17y)	RT,D,H (16y)	RT,D,H (16y)	RT,D,H (3m)	RT,D,H (14y)
E*Trade Trading System	470	✓						3,000	RT,D,H (1970)	RT,D,H (1970)		RT,D,H (1993)	D
Fidelity On-Line Xpress (FOX)	471	✓							RT,D,H (1979)	RT,D,H (1979)	RT,D,H (1979)	RT,D,H (1y)	
Final Markets End-of-Day Price Service	482	✓						360				H (inc)	D,H (50y)
Financial Bulletin Board	478	✓											
Findex	502						✓						
First Release	461	✓											
Fixed-Income Pricing Services	507	✓			✓						RT,D,H (1975)	D,H	D,H
Ford Data Base	471	✓				✓		2,680	H (1970)				
Free Financial Network (FFN)	488	✓						10,000	H (3y)	H (1y)			H (1y)
FundScope	438					✓		4,400		H (10y)			
Funds-On-Line	492	✓						308					
FundWatch Online by Money Magazine	452	✓						4,000					
GEnie	472	✓						67,000	RT,D,H (1979)	RT,D,H (1979)	RT,D,H (1979)	RT,D,H (1y)	RT,D,H (1979)
Historical Data	482	✓						360				H	H (50y)
Hourly DJIA	513									H (1986)			
ICC Key Notes	502						✓						

Mutual Fund Quotes (time period)	Closed-End Quotes (time period)	No. of Securities in Database	Stock Quotes	Index Quotes	Bond Quotes	Options Quotes	Futures Quotes	Mutual Fund Quotes	General/Business News	Economic News/Data	Company News	Financial Statement Data	SEC Filings	Analyst Reports	Earnings Estimates	Charting	Technical Studies/Indicators	On-Line Brokerage	Message/Mail Areas	Software Library for Downloading	Fundamental Indicators	Technical Indicators	Mutual Funds	Bonds
																					✓			
D				✓					✓	✓	✓			✓			✓							
									✓	✓							✓						✓	
							✓																	
									✓	✓							✓						✓	
RT,D	RT,D		✓	✓	✓	✓	✓	✓	✓	✓						✓	✓							
RT,D,H (15y)			✓						✓	✓	✓	✓	✓	✓	✓			✓			✓	✓	✓	
RT,D,H (1987)	RT,D,H (1987)								✓		✓			✓					✓	✓				
RT,D,H (1979)	RT,D,H (1979)								✓	✓	✓			✓	✓	✓	✓	✓			✓	✓	✓	
							✓																	
																				✓				
									✓		✓	✓												
									✓	✓	✓			✓										
		3,700	✓									✓									✓			
H (1y)	H (1y)								✓	✓				✓		✓	✓		✓	✓				
H (10y)		400					✓									✓	✓						✓	
D																		✓				✓	✓	
																							✓	
RT,D,H (1979)	RT,D,H (1979)								✓	✓	✓	✓		✓	✓			✓	✓	✓				
							✓																	
			✓						✓		✓			✓										

Financial Information Services	Page	Transmission						No. of Cos./Securities in Database	Domestic				
		Modem	Cable TV	FM	Satellite	Diskette	CD-ROM		Stock Quotes (time period)	Index Quotes (time period)	Bond Quotes (time period)	Options Quotes (time period)	Futures Quotes (time period)
ICDI Mutual Fund Database	480	✓				✓		4,700					
Insider Trading Monitor	446	✓				✓		10,000					
INSTIN 3.0	458	✓	✓	✓		✓		6,500	RT,D,H (10 yr)				
Institutional Brokers' Estimate System (I/B/E/S)	475	✓				✓	✓	4,000					
Investability Mutual Fund Database	480					✓		5,300					
Investext: U.S. Companies	503						✓						
Investment Wizard	494	✓						10,000					
Knight-Ridder End-of-Day News Reports	482	✓						360				H (inc)	H (50y)
Lexis Financial Information Service	486	✓						All U.S. and Can. exchanges	RT,H (15y)	RT,H (15y)	RT,H (15y)		
Lowry's Market Trend Analysis Database on Diskette	483					✓				D,H (1940)			
Market Center	443	✓		✓	✓			110,000	RT,D	RT,D	RT,D	RT,D	RT,D
Market Guide Database	484	✓				✓	✓	6,700	H				
Market Monitor 5	444	✓		✓	✓				RT,D	RT,D	RT,D	RT,D	RT,D
Market NewsAlert	453	✓						10,000					
Market Screen	484							6,700	H (4y)				
Market Screen Online	485	✓						6,700	H (4y)				
Marstat—CSI Data Retrieval Service	450	✓				✓		7,000	H (1962)	H (1928)		H (1982)	H (1949)
Media General Database Service	487	✓				✓	✓	8,000	H (20y)	H (20y)			
Media General Price and Volume History	487					✓		8,000	H (1973)	H (1973)			
Media General Screen & Select	487					✓		8,000					

Securities		Foreign Securities							Types of Information Provided													Screening			
Mutual Fund Quotes (time period)	Closed-End Quotes (time period)	No. of Securities in Database	Stock Quotes	Index Quotes	Bond Quotes	Options Quotes	Futures Quotes	Mutual Fund Quotes	General/Business News	Economic News/Data	Company News	Financial Statement Data	SEC Filings	Analyst Reports	Earnings Estimates	Charting	Technical Studies/Indicators	On-Line Brokerage	Message/Mail Areas	Software Library for Downloading	Fundamental Indicators	Technical Indicators	Mutual Funds	Bonds
D,H (1962)																✓	✓					✓	✓	
			✓								✓	✓									✓			
			✓								✓	✓		✓						✓	✓			
		9,000									✓			✓			✓				✓	✓		
																							✓	
									✓	✓	✓	✓		✓										
		1,000	✓							✓				✓		✓			✓					
									✓	✓														
RT,H (15y)	RT,H (15y)		✓		✓				✓	✓	✓	✓	✓	✓	✓	✓								
																	✓							
RT,D	RT,D		✓	✓	✓	✓	✓	✓	✓	✓	✓					✓	✓							
			✓								✓	✓									✓			
RT,D	RT,D								✓	✓						✓	✓							
											✓	✓	✓	✓	✓									
									✓			✓									✓			
									✓			✓									✓			
H (1986)	H (1987)			✓			✓										✓						✓	
H (5y)	H (5y)											✓					✓				✓	✓	✓	
																	✓					✓		
												✓					✓				✓	✓		

Financial Information Services	Page	Modem	Cable TV	FM	Satellite	Diskette	CD-ROM	No. of Cos./Securities in Database	Stock Quotes (time period)	Index Quotes (time period)	Bond Quotes (time period)	Options Quotes (time period)	Futures Quotes (time period)
Media General Standard Data Diskette	488					✓		8,000					
Micropal	489	✓						5,800					
Momentum	489						✓	8,200	H (5y)				
MoneyCenter	461	✓							D,H (3d)	D,H (3d)	RT,H (3d)	D,H (3d)	D,H (3d)
Money Fund Vision	473	✓						1,000					
MoneyLetter Plus	474	✓											
Morningstar Mutual Funds OnDisc	490						✓	4,000		H (1976)			
Morningstar Mutual Funds OnFloppy	490					✓		3,376		H (15y)			
Mutual Fund Expert—Personal	434					✓		3,500					
Mutual Fund Expert—Pro Plus	435					✓		4,500					
News Real	454	✓		✓					D,H (1979)		D	D	D
OmniNews	453	✓						10,000	RT	RT	RT	RT	
OneSource	493						✓	8,500	H	H	H	H	H
OTC NewsAlert	453	✓						10,000					
PC Quote	495	✓			✓			80,000+	RT	RT	RT	RT	RT
Personal Investing Online Service	504	✓						10,000					
Pocket Quote Pro	508			✓				45,000	RT,D	RT		RT	RT,D
Predicast F&S Index plus Text	503						✓						
Prodigy	496	✓						10,000	D	D	D		
Prophet Data Service	497	✓				✓		10,000	H (1982)	H (1960)			H (1968)
Quarterly Low-Load Mutual Fund Update on Disk	437					✓		1,000					
Quarterly Report on Money Fund Performance	474					✓		1,000		D,H (1q)			

Securities		Foreign Securities							Types of Information Provided													Screening			
Mutual Fund Quotes (time period)	Closed-End Quotes (time period)	No. of Securities in Database	Stock Quotes	Index Quotes	Bond Quotes	Options Quotes	Futures Quotes	Mutual Fund Quotes	General/Business News	Economic News/Data	Company News	Financial Statement Data	SEC Filings	Analyst Reports	Earnings Estimates	Charting	Technical Studies/Indicators	On-Line Brokerage	Message/Mail Areas	Software Library for Downloading	Fundamental Indicators	Technical Indicators	Mutual Funds	Bonds
												✓					✓				✓			
D,H																						✓		
			✓	✓					✓	✓	✓													
H									✓	✓							✓						✓	
									✓	✓						✓	✓		✓				✓	
H (1976)									✓					✓									✓	
H (10y)									✓														✓	
																							✓	
																							✓	
D	D				✓				✓	✓	✓	✓	✓											
D	RT								✓	✓	✓	✓	✓	✓										
H		10,000	✓	✓	✓	✓	✓	✓	✓	✓	✓	✓	✓	✓	✓	✓	✓				✓			
									✓	✓	✓	✓	✓	✓										
D	RT		✓	✓	✓	✓	✓	✓	✓	✓	✓	✓			✓	✓	✓				✓	✓		
									✓	✓	✓	✓							✓					
RT	RT	800	✓								✓													
									✓		✓													
D	D			✓					✓	✓	✓	✓		✓		✓	✓	✓	✓	✓	✓		✓	
		50		✓			✓																	
																							✓	
									✓	✓													✓	

Financial Information Services	Page	Modem	Cable TV	FM	Satellite	Diskette	CD-ROM	No. of Cos./Securities in Database	Stock Quotes (time period)	Index Quotes (time period)	Bond Quotes (time period)	Options Quotes (time period)	Futures Quotes (time period)
QuickWay	498	✓						11,000	RT,D,H (1972)	RT,D,H (1972)		RT,D,H (1972)	RT,D,H (1972)
Quotes and Trading	462	✓							D			D	
Quote.Com	498	✓						25,000	D	D	D	D	D
QuoTrek	454			✓				56,000	RT	RT		RT	RT
Radio Exchange	508			✓	✓			45,000	RT,D	RT		RT	RT
Reuters Money Network	499	✓						20,000	D,H	D,H		D	
Reuters Money Network for Quicken	500	✓						18,500	H	H	H		
S&P 1957-1991 Monthly	442					✓				H (1957)			
S&P ComStock	500	✓			✓			65,000	RT	RT	D	RT	RT
S&P Daily 1953-1991	442					✓				H (1953)			
S&P Daily 1980-1990	442					✓				H (1980)			
S&P Stock Guide Database by DTN	457		✓		✓								
S&P Stock Guide on Disk	505					✓		7,200	H (1971)				
Schwab Brokerage Services on GEnie	447	✓						125,000	RT	RT	RT	RT	
SEC Online	462	✓											
SEC OnLine-10K	503						✓	4,500+					
SEC Online on SilverPlatter	503						✓	4,500					
Securities History Data	481	✓				✓		15,000	H (14y)	H (varies)		H	H (20y)
SEC: Healthcare, Pharmaceuticals & Biotech	504						✓						
Signal	455		✓	✓	✓			65,000	RT,D,H (1978)	RT,D,H (1978)	RT	RT,D	RT,D

Securities		Foreign Securities							Types of Information Provided												Screening			
Mutual Fund Quotes (time period)	Closed-End Quotes (time period)	No. of Securities in Database	Stock Quotes	Index Quotes	Bond Quotes	Options Quotes	Futures Quotes	Mutual Fund Quotes	General/Business News	Economic News/Data	Company News	Financial Statement Data	SEC Filings	Analyst Reports	Earnings Estimates	Charting	Technical Studies/Indicators	On-Line Brokerage	Message/Mail Areas	Software Library for Downloading	Fundamental Indicators	Technical Indicators	Mutual Funds	Bonds
RT,D,H (1972)	RT,D,H (1972)								✓	✓	✓	✓		✓				✓						
																		✓						
D	D	20,000							✓	✓	✓	✓		✓	✓	✓	✓							
D	RT										✓													
RT	RT	800	✓						✓	✓	✓		✓					✓						
D	D,H								✓	✓	✓	✓			✓	✓		✓	✓		✓	✓	✓	
									✓	✓	✓	✓		✓				✓						
D			✓	✓					✓		✓	✓		✓				✓						
									✓		✓			✓										
											✓													
RT																		✓	✓	✓				
											✓	✓												
										✓	✓	✓												
										✓	✓	✓												
H (8y)	H (14y)							✓								✓						✓		
										✓	✓	✓												
D,H (1978)	RT	10-20		✓					✓	✓	✓													

Financial Information Services	Page	Transmission						No. of Cos./Securities in Database	Domestic				
		Modem	Cable TV	FM	Satellite	Diskette	CD-ROM		Stock Quotes (time period)	Index Quotes (time period)	Bond Quotes (time period)	Options Quotes (time period)	Futures Quotes (time period)
Stock Investor	437					✓		8,000	H (5y)				
Stock Market Data	505	✓				✓		10,000	H (1987)	H (1987)			
StockQuoter 2	433	✓		✓					D	D			
StockQuoter RT	433	✓		✓					RT	RT		RT	
Strategic Investor	496	✓											
StreetSmart	448	✓							RT,D,H (17y)	RT,D,H (16y)	RT,D,H (16y)	RT,D,H (3m)	D,H (14y)
Telechart 2000 System	516	✓						10,500	D,H (9y)	D,H (5y)			
Telemet Encore	509			✓	✓			45,000	RT,D	RT		RT	RT,D
Telemet Orion System	509				✓			45,000	RT,D,H (3y)	RT,H (3y)	RT	RT	RT,D
Telescan Analyzer	510	✓						74,000	D,H (20y)	D,H (20y)	D,H (1y)	D,H (20y)	D,H (4y)
Telescan Edge	511	✓						11,000					
Telescan Mutual Fund Edge	511	✓						2,200		D,H (20y)			
Telescan ProSearch 4.0	512	✓						71,600	D,H (20y)	D,H (20y)	D,H (1y)	D,H (20y)	D,H (4y)
Tick-By-Tick Historical Price Data	513	✓				✓		105	H (1989)	H (1982)		H (1977)	H (1977)
Track/On Line	514	✓						20,000	RT,D,H (1970)	RT,D,H (1970)	RT,D,H (1970)	RT,D,H (1993)	RT,D,H (1963)
TradeLine	475	✓				✓		200,000	H (20y)	H (20y)	H (20y)	H (20y)	H (20y)
Tradeline Electronic Stock Guide	476					✓	✓	7,000	H	H			
TradeLine International	477	✓							H (1986)	H (1986)			

Mutual Fund Quotes (time period)	Closed-End Quotes (time period)	No. of Securities in Database	Stock Quotes	Index Quotes	Bond Quotes	Options Quotes	Futures Quotes	Mutual Fund Quotes	General/Business News	Economic News/Data	Company News	Financial Statement Data	SEC Filings	Analyst Reports	Earnings Estimates	Charting	Technical Studies/Indicators	On-Line Brokerage	Message/Mail Areas	Software Library for Downloading	Fundamental Indicators	Technical Indicators	Mutual Funds	Bonds
												✓			✓						✓	✓		
																						✓		
D	D								✓	✓	✓	✓				✓				✓	✓	✓	✓	✓
RT	RT								✓	✓	✓	✓				✓				✓	✓	✓	✓	✓
		6,000										✓			✓									
RT,D,H (15y)			✓						✓	✓	✓	✓	✓	✓	✓				✓		✓	✓	✓	
	D,H (5y)															✓	✓					✓		
RT	RT	800	✓						✓	✓	✓					✓	✓			✓				
RT	RT	800	✓						✓	✓	✓	✓	✓			✓	✓				✓			
D,H (20y)	D,H (20y)	3,000	✓						✓	✓	✓	✓	✓	✓	✓	✓	✓		✓		✓	✓	✓	
									✓		✓	✓	✓		✓	✓	✓				✓	✓	✓	
D,H (20y)									✓	✓	✓	✓	✓		✓	✓	✓		✓		✓	✓	✓	
D,H (20y)	D,H (20y)		✓						✓	✓	✓	✓	✓	✓	✓	✓	✓		✓		✓	✓	✓	
							✓										✓							
H (1987)	H (1987)	3,000	✓			✓	✓		✓	✓	✓	✓	✓	✓	✓									
H (20y)	H (20y)																✓				✓	✓	✓	✓
																✓	✓				✓	✓		
		40,000	✓	✓				✓									✓				✓	✓	✓	

Financial Information Services	Page	Transmission						No. of Cos./Securities in Database	Domestic				
		Modem	Cable TV	FM	Satellite	Diskette	CD-ROM		Stock Quotes (time period)	Index Quotes (time period)	Bond Quotes (time period)	Options Quotes (time period)	Futures Quotes (time period)
Tradeline Pocket Stock Guide	477							6,000	H (1 y)	H (1 y)			
Trader's Spread System (TSS)	507	✓									D,H (6m)	D,H (6m)	D,H (6m)
Treasury Historical Data	507	✓				✓					H (1975)		
TRENDPOINT Data Library	514					✓				H (1928)	H (1961)	H (1985)	H (1985)
TRW Business Credit Profiles	463	✓						2,500,000					
UK Corporations CD	504						✓	3,000					
U.S. Equities OnFloppy	491					✓		6,000	H				
Value/Screen III	515	✓				✓		1,600					
VenCap Data Quest/ Portfolio Companies 1.0	434					✓		varies					
Worldscope EMERGING MARKETS	466	✓				✓	✓						
Worldscope GLOBAL	466	✓				✓	✓	11,000	H (3y)				
X*Press Executive	516		✓		✓			30,000	D	D		D	D
Zacks Consensus Summary Diskette	517					✓		5,000					
Zacks On-Line	517	✓						7,500					

Mutual Fund Quotes (time period)	Closed-End Quotes (time period)	No. of Securities in Database	Stock Quotes	Index Quotes	Bond Quotes	Options Quotes	Futures Quotes	Mutual Fund Quotes	General/Business News	Economic News/Data	Company News	Financial Statement Data	SEC Filings	Analyst Reports	Earnings Estimates	Charting	Technical Studies/Indicators	On-Line Brokerage	Message/Mail Areas	Software Library for Downloading	Fundamental Indicators	Technical Indicators	Mutual Funds	Bonds
																✓	✓				✓	✓		
														✓										
										✓							✓							
											✓	✓												
			✓						✓		✓	✓												
											✓					✓					✓			
											✓				✓						✓	✓		
											✓	✓												
		1,100	✓								✓	✓									✓			
			✓								✓	✓	✓								✓			
D	D		✓	✓	✓	✓	✓	✓	✓	✓	✓	✓	✓		✓	✓								
															✓									
			✓												✓									

Financial Information Services Grid

6

Guide to Investment Software

This chapter is our latest guide to investment software, covering 550 programs. These descriptions are based on information provided by the software publishers and do not represent firsthand knowledge by *Computerized Investing* staff members. We have worked hard to get current information, but the market for investment software is in constant flux. There are frequent modifications to existing software and many price changes. These programs are often produced by small companies— they may not survive; those that do may decide that a new name is more indicative of their current products or may find new distribution channels. When a product name has changed, and/or a product is being distributed by a new vendor, we have indicated the former product name and/or vendor.

In compiling this chapter we have concentrated on financial investment software, but a number of spreadsheet programs, as well as programs for tax planning, real estate analysis, statistical analysis and graphing are included. Also included, as Chapter 4, are the comparison grids which list each software package alphabetically. There are four software grids that cover personal finance programs, portfolio management programs, technical analysis programs, and fundamental analysis programs along with other specialized investment programs. The grids are designed to quickly give you the information necessary to determine what the software does and whether it will work on your computer system.

The product descriptions in this chapter are listed alphabetically by publisher, as many companies publish several programs. The software listing follows the publisher information and each software listing includes the name of the product, its version number, year of last update, number of users, the types of securities the program handles, its function, systems, special software or hardware requirements, price, demo available, AAII discounts, return policy, the technical support provided by the vendors, and a brief description.

To get the most effective use of the *Guide* we suggest that you search through the grids in Chapter 4 and the listing here to identify those products that meet your needs and will operate on your system. After you have a list of products, contact the software manufacturers directly, mentioning that you saw their product(s) listed here, and get their most recent information. Then compare those programs that seem to offer the features you need. Once you have screened the programs for those that provide the functions you need and that fit within your budget, try to see the software work. The manufacturer may offer a demo disk; or investors at the local AAII chapter (listed in Appendix II) may be familiar with the program. You may also try contacting a BBS (listed in Appendix I) and leave a message. Such firsthand information will give you the best evaluation of how you can use the software. Compare the technical support offered by the competing vendors. The support times are Eastern Standard Time, unless otherwise noted.

Finally, many software firms offer discounts to AAII members. These discounts apply to purchases made directly from the software publisher and are not available at retail stores. Those companies offering a member discount are indicated in the product description and software grid. Prices do not include shipping and handling or sales tax where applicable. Before you purchase the product make sure that you understand the vendor's return policy. Many vendors will not refund your money.

ADS ASSOCIATES, INC.

23586 Calabasas Road
Suite 200
Calabasas, CA 91302

(800) 323-4666
(818) 591-2371
fax: (818) 591-2372

GLOBAL TRADER CALCULATOR
Version: 1.2   *Last Updated:* 1989   *No. of Users:* 3,000
Securities: bonds
Functions: bond analysis
Systems: DOS
Price: $195; demo available, $19.95; 10% AAII discount
Return Policy: 30 days
Technical Support: phone hours, 10 am-9 pm, M-F
Description: A software calculator for fixed-income securities—domestic and foreign. Calculates yield to maturity, yield to call, average life, yield to average life, duration, accrued interest, principal amount, total cost/proceeds, next interest amount, simple margin and discount margin in a single keystroke. Defaults to the standard conventions for over 60 security types. User can change variables such as pricing, interest day count, interest payment frequency, sinking fund schedule and face amount. Handles odd coupons. Includes a yield swap analysis function. It also displays the variances of principal amount, yield accrued interest, total proceeds/cost and annual income. Can save and recall over 200 swaps and individual security calculations.

ADVANCED ANALYSIS, INC.

48408 Red Run Drive
Canton, MI 48187

(804) 745-8008
fax: (313) 981-4680

PROSPER-II MKT
Version: 5.0   *Last Updated:* 1994   *No. of Users:* 275
Securities: stocks, bonds, futures, mutual funds, indexes, options
Functions: portfolio management, technical analysis
Systems: DOS
Special Requirements: Radio Exchange, Signal, X*Press, Prodigy, Telescan
Price: $189
Return Policy: 30 days; $30 restocking fee

Technical Support: phone hours, 9 am-11 pm, M-F

Description: A technical analysis program for trading stocks, futures, options and indexes. User can analyze daily and weekly quote data for up to 27,500 issues. Program has more than 40 indicators and tools for presenting signals of price reversals, trends, volume accumulation or distribution. Indicators include percentage, spread, value, Bollinger Bands, Commodity Channel Index, K%D, RSI, ROC, directional movement, stops, MACD, MAOSC, moving average, AAI Index, compare, group, volume, EquiVolume, on-balance volume, volume accumulation, Crocker's Method, Carpino's Method, etc. Tools include cycle finding, channel charting, bar chart zooming, profitability testing, etc. Program performs automatic search for stocks that meet user's criteria. Autosave updates quote data automatically without intervention. Other utility functions allow for data management. Program performs on-line analysis with Radio Exchange or Signal; access to a variety of data services: Telescan, Dow Jones News/Retrieval, MetaStock Data Files, and all other ASCII files.

PROSPER-II POWERONLINE

Version: 6.0   *Last Updated:* 1994   *No. of Users:* 280

Securities: stocks, bonds, futures, mutual funds, indexes, options

Functions: technical analysis

Systems: DOS

Special Requirements: Radio Exchange or Signal, math co-processor recommended

Price: $199

Return Policy: 30 days; $30 restocking fee

Technical Support: phone hours, 9 am-11 pm, M-F

Description: An on-line intraday technical analysis program that works with Radio Exchange or Signal analyzing quote data at cycles less than 20 seconds. Designed to deal with the volatility of the market. Converts Radio Exchange or Signal from quote broadcasting to on-line decision making. Program helps identify market reversal points. Analyzes up to 30 tickers for 3 days' data of futures, indexes, options and stocks. Program has 3 modes: Quote listing mode lists quotes as they are gathered. Value mode lists value of holdings as a function of the latest quote. Analysis mode presents the instantaneous analysis results for various indicators including price, volume, RSI, K%D, m-K%D, MACD, price channels, percentage of movement, spread between any 2 tickers, etc.

ADVENT SOFTWARE, INC.

301 Brannan Street   (800) 648-7005
San Francisco, CA 94107   (415) 543-7696
                                                 fax: (415) 543-5070

AXYS ADVANTAGE
Version: 1.1   *Last Updated:* na   *No. of Users:* 50
Securities: stocks, bonds, futures, mutual funds, indexes, options, real
    estate
Functions: portfolio management
Systems: Windows
Special Requirements: 386+
Price: $2,900; demo available, none
Technical Support: phone hours, 9 am-8 pm, M-F; fee for tech sup-
    port—1st year free, renewable
Description: A Windows-based portfolio management system tailored
to meet the specific needs of smaller money management firms and financial planners. Offers portfolio accounting, decision support, and
flexible reporting. Allows users to produce presentation quality reports with a choice of fonts and formats. Reports can be run in real-
time, as of any time period, for individual or groups of portfolios.
Graphics can be easily created with an integrated link to Excel. Other
features include: over 60 reports to support investment decision making, client communication, billing, etc.; accurate performance measurement; an integrated interface with Interactive Data Corp for electronically downloading security prices, descriptive information and
corporate actions; also includes integrated interface with Charles
Schwab for electronically downloading transaction information, and
for reconciling positions and cash balances.

AFFILIATED COMPUTER SERVICES, INC.

525 Market Street   (800) 627-1969
Suite 1400   (415) 267-0330
San Francisco, CA 94105   fax: (415) 267-0333

TIP LEASE ANALYSIS
Version: 24   *Last Updated:* 1993   *No. of Users:* 350
Securities: real estate

Functions: financial planning, real estate analysis, simulation/game
Systems: DOS, Windows, Mac
Special Requirements: modem & phone line
Price: $1,000/month; demo available; 15% AAII discount
Return Policy: 14 days
Technical Support: phone hours, 24 hours; newsletter
Description: An on-line lease and investment analysis software product used by leasing companies, banks, and other financial services firms. TIP prices and structures equipment, real estate, fleet, and other leases. A linear lease analysis product that will solve for a profitability measure specified by the user, while optimizing all other aspects of the transaction. The program uses English commands to enable new users to describe and solve transactions. Provides the user with complete tax, accounting, cash, yield, IRS, and casualty and termination reports.

AIQ INC.

(formerly AIQ Systems, Inc.)

916 Southwood Blvd.   (800) 332-2999
P.O. Drawer 7530   (702) 831-2999
Incline Village, NV 89450   fax: (702) 831-6784

MARKETEXPERT
Version: 4.0   *Last Updated:* 1993   *No. of Users:* na
Securities: indexes
Functions: technical analysis, expert system
Systems: DOS
Price: $249; demo available, $44; 10% AAII discount
Return Policy: 45 days
Technical Support: phone hours, 10:30 am-7:30 pm, M-F; newsletter
Description: Helps determine direction the stock market will move. Combines 20 pieces of daily market data and 32 technical analysis indicators to form a fact base. An inference procedure then combines fact base with a rule base (containing 400 decision rules derived by technical analysis experts) to arrive at an expert rating that tells the user when and in which direction the stock market will move in the short to intermediate term. Graphically displays pricing activity of the DJIA, NYSE, and the SPX; 24 technical indicators display a technical study of the market. Built-in communication interface allows updating from variety of data services.

OPTION EXTENSION
Version: 3.0   *Last Updated:* 1993   *No. of Users:* na
Securities: indexes, options
Functions: technical analysis, options analysis, simulation/game
Systems: DOS
Price: $249; demo available, $44; 10% AAII discount
Return Policy: 45 days
Technical Support: phone hours, 10:30 am-7:30 pm, M-F; newsletter
Description: Uses expert systems to interpret technical indicators to generate optimum short-term buy and sell signals. An indicated value (forecast) is then calculated. Black-Scholes analytics and strategy selection models are then applied to equity and index options, suggesting which strategy, position and number of contracts to buy or sell. Profit manager provides mechanical stop levels for closing positions based on user-defined risk tolerance level. The knowledge base allows user to see why the buy or sell ws developed; 24 technical indicators are graphically displayed and may be adjusted for detailed analysis. Communications built-in for automatic data retrieval form a variety of data services.

STOCKEXPERT
Version: 4.00   *Last Updated:* 1993   *No. of Users:* na
Securities: stocks, indexes, options
Functions: technical analysis, options analysis, simulation/game, expert system
Systems: DOS
Price: $498; demo available, $44; 10% AAII discount
Return Policy: 45 days
Technical Support: phone hours, 10:30 am-7:30 pm, M-F; newsletter
Description: Uses dozens of technical indicators to compute an expert rating for every stock in its database, then prints reports listing those stocks with the day's highest expert ratings both upside and downside. Next, profit manager can help protect both principal and profits by setting user stop-loss parameters. Stock plots display a 7-month period of market action for every stock allowing a graphical study of price, performance, and the concurrent behavior of technical indicators. Prints price activity and technical indicators for up to 1 year. Expert rating can be displayed for any stock on any market date allowing "what if" simulations. Automatically updates prices via modem.

TRADINGEXPERT
Version: 2.5   *Last Updated:* 1994   *No. of Users:* na
Securities: stocks, mutual funds, indexes, options
Functions: portfolio management, technical analysis, options analysis, simulation/game, expert system
Systems: DOS
Special Requirements: DOS 3.3+, 12M free disk space, 2400 baud modem, math co-processor recommended
Price: $996; demo available, $44; 10% AAII discount
Return Policy: 45 days
Technical Support: phone hours, 10:30 am-7:30 pm, M-F; newsletter
Description: A stock market timing system. Helps users determine when and in which direction markets, sectors, groups, or stocks will move in the short to intermediate term. Using both the expert system and quantitative analysis, it combines over 485 rules and 34 technical indicators with 17 pieces of daily stock and market data to provide user with charts, reports, and expert ratings. Program tracks and graphically displays an unlimited number of indexes, sectors, groups, and stocks, along with 32 technical indicators for each on a daily or weekly basis. Data is automatically updated via modem.

AMERICAN ASSOCIATION OF INDIVIDUAL INVESTORS

625 N. Michigan Avenue   (312) 280-0170
Suite 1900   fax: (312) 280-1625
Chicago, IL 60611

AAII FUNDAMENTAL STOCK ANALYSIS DISK
Version: 2.0   *Last Updated:* 1994   *No. of Users:* na
Securities: stocks
Functions: fundamental analysis
Systems: DOS, Windows, Mac
Special Requirements: spreadsheet program
Price: $20; 25% AAII discount
Return Policy: 30 days
Technical Support: BBS support
Description: Offers spreadsheet templates for financial statement analysis using financial ratios, common size income statements and balance sheets, and DuPont analysis. Also presents worksheets offering various stock valuation models and techniques such as the P/E

relative model, dividend discount model, Graham earnings multiplier, variable growth model, price-to-sales ratio, and price-to-book ratio. Requires spreadsheet program capable of reading and working with Lotus 1-2-3 files.

AMERICAN INSTITUTE OF SMALL BUSINESS

7515 Wayzata Boulevard (800) 328-2906
Minneapolis, MN 55426 (612) 545-7001
fax: (617) 505-7020

HOW TO WRITE A BUSINESS PLAN
Version: 1.51   *Last Updated:* 1994   *No. of Users:* 10,000+
Securities: real estate, company acquisitions
Functions: financial planning, fundamental analysis, spreadsheet
Systems: DOS, Mac
Price: $125; demo available; 10% AAII discount
Return Policy: 14 days
Technical Support: phone hours. 7:30 am - 3:00 pm, M-F
Description: Allows user to prepare a complete business plan including the narrative and financial documentation. Provides menu of choices for each section of the business plan covering all elements of any business plan. Provides the summary, marketing plans, production plans, research and development, personnel, advertising schedules, key management, industry information, company structure, business advisors and funding sources. Prepares all financials and spreadsheets including balance sheets, profit and loss, and cash flow statements for three years or more. Utilizes word processing and accounting software packages.

AMERICAN RIVER SOFTWARE

1523 Kingsford Drive (916) 483-1600
Carmichael, CA 95608

MUTUAL FUND INVESTOR
Version: 5.3   *Last Updated:* 1993   *No. of Users:* 1,500
Securities: stocks, bonds, mutual funds, indexes, real estate
Functions: portfolio management, technical analysis,
Systems: DOS

Price: $295; demo available, $10
Return Policy: all sales final
Technical Support: phone hours, 11:30 am-8 pm, M-F
Description: Enables close performance monitoring of up to 104 funds and other securities, in addition to performing portfolio management functions. Several thousand client portfolios may be tracked (32,000 transactions per client) with reporting of current portfolio value, share balance, internal rate of return, FIFO and average cost basis, profit/loss reports, as well as cross referencing of open accounts to portfolios. Reports may be generated for one or any family of portfolios. Program charts daily and weekly adjusted prices over time, displays moving averages and relative strength and computes total return performances, volatility, momentum and buy/sell signals between any two user-chosen dates. Allows comparisons between buy and hold versus switching strategies. Graphs and reports can be printed on laser or dot matrix printers, and may also be exported to other graphics programs. Data may be entered either manually or automatically via modem from CompuServe or Investment Company Data. Example portfolios and free data are supplied for 30 funds and indexes. Program performs sorting and screening criteria on over 4,400 mutual funds from monthly updated data disks supplied by Investment Company Data.

ANALYTIC ASSOCIATES

4817 Browndeer Lane   (800) 959-3273
Rolling Hills Estates, CA 90274   (310) 541-0418

PLANEASE PARTNERSHIP MODELS
Version: 4.0   *Last Updated:* 1994   *No. of Users:* 1,000
Securities: real estate
Functions: real estate analysis
Systems: DOS
Price: $495; demo available, free
Return Policy: 30 days
Technical Support: toll-free number; phone hours, 11 am-7 pm, M-F; newsletter; fee for tech support—$95
Description: Adds partnership analysis capability to planEASe, enabling you to take any property projected with planEASe and easily

convert the analysis into a limited partnership forecast with final reports and graphs suitable for investor presentation. In addition to all the capabilities of planEASe itself, these models allow as many partnership fees as needed, allow for separate allocation of tax and cash benefits, and handle working capital, preferred returns and staged investments.

PLANEASE/WINDOWS

Version: 4.0   *Last Updated:* 1994   *No. of Users:* 1,000+
Securities: real estate
Functions: real estate analysis
Systems: DOS, Windows
Price: $995; demo available, free
Return Policy: 30 days
Technical Support: toll-free number; phone hours, 11 am-7 pm, M-F; newsletter; fee for tech support—$95
Description: Enables the financial analysis and cash flow projection of any income-producing property (apartments, offices, shopping centers, etc.), including development projects. Internal rates of return, financial management rates of return and net present values are computed before and after taxes. The system features sensitivity analysis with a printed graph of results, and Monte Carlo risk analysis with a printed histogram of results. All reports and graphs may be directed to the Windows clipboard and pasted into your favorite Windows word processor and/or spreadsheet for further processing. PlanEASe has been revised for all current tax provisions, and provides many choices for handling depreciation and passive losses.

APPLIED ARTIFICIAL INTELLIGENCE CORPORATION

1446 S. Highway 327   (803) 667-1986
Box 25
Florence, SC 29506

EXPERT TRADING SYSTEM

Version: na   *Last Updated:* 1994   *No. of Users:* na
Securities: stocks, futures, indexes, options
Functions: futures analysis, options analysis, expert system, neural network
Systems: Windows

Price: varies with customizing and consulting; 10% AAII discount
Return Policy: all sales final
Description: Expert Trading System (ETS) uses applied artificial intelligence techniques to attempt to beat the market. The ETS trades in securities, futures, and/or options.

AVCO FINANCIAL, CORP.

8 Grigg Street
Suite 3
Greenwich, CT 06830

(203) 661-7381
fax: (203) 869-0253

RECURRENCE IV
Version: 4   *Last Updated:* 1994   *No. of Users:* 283
Securities: futures
Functions: technical analysis, futures analysis, expert system
Systems: DOS
Special Requirements: Real-time data
Price: $3,500; 5% AAII discount
Return Policy: all sales final
Technical Support: phone hours, 8 am-5 pm, M-F
Description: A real-time day trading system designed as an add-on product for traders who use only the currency markets, with no overnight exposure. Consists of three components: an artificial intelligence program; a pattern recognition program; and an automated program that monitors the markets and signals specific entries, exits, and stops when key patterns develop.

BAARNS PUBLISHING

(formerly Heizer Software)

1150 Sepulveda Blvd.
Suite D
Mission Hill, CA 91345

(800) 377-9235
(818) 837-1441

BOND PORTFOLIO
Version: 1.0   *Last Updated:* na   *No. of Users:* na
Securities: bonds
Functions: financial planning, bond analysis, spreadsheet
Systems: Windows, Mac

Special Requirements: Excel
Price: $25; demo available, $2
Return Policy: all sales final
Technical Support: phone hours, 12 pm-8 pm, M-F
Description: Calculates duration, modified duration, duration based on periods, volatility and yields including current yield, yield to maturity and yield to first call. An entire bond portfolio may be tracked. Provides a summary that calculates the totals and averages based on the whole portfolio. Requires Excel.

BOND PRICING
Version: 1.0   *Last Updated:* na   *No. of Users:* na
Securities: bonds
Functions: financial planning, bond analysis, spreadsheet
Systems: Windows, Mac
Special Requirements: Excel or Works
Price: $15; demo available, $2
Return Policy: all sales final
Technical Support: phone hours, 12 pm-8 pm, M-F
Description: Calculates current yield and yield to maturity from standard bond price, coupon and maturity data. Calculates price required to meet user-defined yield criteria to call date and maturity. Requires Excel or Works.

NAIC STOCK SELECTION GUIDE
Version: 1.0   *Last Updated:* na   *No. of Users:* na
Securities: stocks
Functions: fundamental analysis, spreadsheet
Systems: Windows, Mac
Special Requirements: Excel or Works
Price: $30; demo available, $2
Return Policy: all sales final
Technical Support: phone hours, 12 pm-8 pm, M-F
Description: Duplicates NAIC's standard Stock Selection Guide and performs all the calculations required to arrive at a buy/hold/sell recommendation.

OPTION-WARRANT COMBO
Version: 1.0   *Last Updated:* na   *No. of Users:* na
Securities: futures, options
Functions: options analysis, spreadsheet

Systems: Windows, Mac
Special Requirements: Excel
Price: $49; demo available, $2
Return Policy: all sales final
Technical Support: phone hours, 12 pm-8 pm, M-F
Description: Combines 2 programs: Option-Warrant Analyzer calculates theoretical values of up to 6 options and warrants. Can be used to find the most under- or over-valued option of any stock. Option-Warrant Analyzer (Black-Scholes) calculates theoretical values of up to 6 options and warrants. Requires Excel.

STOCK PORTFOLIO

Version: 1.0   *Last Updated:* na   *No. of Users:* na
Securities: stocks
Functions: portfolio management, spreadsheet
Systems: Windows, Mac
Special Requirements: Excel or Works
Price: $15; demo available, $2
Return Policy: all sales final
Technical Support: phone hours, 12 pm-8 pm, M-F
Description: Fulfills routine trading record needs for investors in common and preferred stocks. Records buy/sell dates and prices, commissions, dividends, overall portfolio performance statistics, etc. Handles partial sales, short sales and long- and short-term holding periods. Requires Excel or Works.

STOCK VALUATION

Version: 1.0   *Last Updated:* na   *No. of Users:* na
Securities: stocks
Functions: fundamental analysis, spreadsheet
Systems: Windows, Mac
Special Requirements: Excel
Price: $25; demo available, $2
Return Policy: all sales final
Technical Support: phone hours, 12 pm-8 pm, M-F
Description: Uses 5 methods to compute a stock's theoretical price to determine whether the stock is over- or under-valued. Includes a stock split/stock dividend adjusting template. Growth rate and expected return are also calculated. Requires Excel.

BNA SOFTWARE

1231 25th Street, N.W.   (800) 424-2938
Suite 3-200   (202) 452-4453
Washington, DC 20037   fax: (202) 452-7547

BNA ESTATE TAX SPREADSHEET
Version: 94.1   *Last Updated:* 1994   *No. of Users:* na
Functions: financial planning
Systems: DOS
Special Requirements: 520K memory
Price: $1,295 single user version; $1,945 network version; demo available, free
Return Policy: all sales final
Technical Support: toll-free number; phone hours, 9 am-5 pm, M-F
Description: An estate planning system that simultaneously calculates three family estate plans or six plans for a single decedent. It computes federal and state estate and inheritance taxes for all 50 states and Washington, D.C. It also performs many sophisticated computations including interrelated residue calculations for marital and charitable deductions, GST, Section 6166 interrelated interest calculations, charitable trusts, gift tax computations, GRITS, GRATS, GRUTS, and more. An estate tax summary and liquidity analysis are among the program's reports.

BNA FIXED ASSET MANAGEMENT SYSTEM
Version: 94.1   *Last Updated:* 1994   *No. of Users:* na
Functions: financial planning
Systems: DOS
Price: $995 single user version; $1,495 network version; demo available, free
Return Policy: all sales final
Technical Support: toll-free number; phone hours, 9 am-5 pm, M-F
Description: Calculates depreciation expense for book, federal, and state reporting, including AMT, ACE, and earnings and profits depreciation. Supports 32 depreciation methods and handles up to 20,000 assets for each company. Performs automatic calculations, including Section 179 expense and application of company limit, and determination and enforcement of the mid-quarter convention. Has complete set of tax and asset management reports.

BNA INCOME TAX SPREADSHEET WITH FIFTY STATE PLANNER

Version: 94.1   *Last Updated:* 1994   *No. of Users:* na

Functions: financial planning

Systems: DOS

Price: single user versions: $890, federal only $495; network versions: $1,335, federal only $750; demo available, free

Return Policy: all sales final

Technical Support: toll-free number; phone hours, 9 am-5 pm, M-F

Description: Calculates federal and state income taxes for individuals from 1987 on, provides projections for 10 years or cases, handles input from K-1s and 1099s with complete audit trail. The optional Fifty State Planner handles taxes for all 50 states, the District of Columbia and New York City. Automatically handles complex tax limitations and phase-outs. Includes complete set of over 60 reports.

BNA REAL ESTATE INVESTMENT SPREADSHEET

Version: 90.1   *Last Updated:* 1990   *No. of Users:* na

Securities: real estate

Functions: financial planning, real estate analysis

Systems: DOS

Price: $395 single user version, $595 network version; demo available

Technical Support: toll-free number; phone hours, 9 am-5 pm, M-F

Description: Computes yearly cash flows and rates of return for up to a 40-year period. Automatically computes many calculations, including depreciation, loan amortization, taxes, and rates of return. Has complete set of reports, including income statement, balance sheet, and statement of cash flows.

BONDCALC CORPORATION

(formerly BondCalc, Corp)

295 Greenwich Street   (212) 587-0097
Apt. 3B   fax: (212) 587-9142
New York, NY 10007-1050

BONDCALC

Version: 1.3B   *Last Updated:* 1994   *No. of Users:* 24

Securities: bonds

Functions: financial planning, portfolio management, bond analysis

Systems: DOS, Windows, OS/2

Special Requirements: 386+, 4M RAM, math coprocessor
Price: $2,900 and up; demo available, $50
Return Policy: all sales final
Technical Support: phone hours, 8 am-7 pm, 7 days; fee for tech support—1st yr included; 20% of price thereafter
Description: A pricing and analytical system that constructs the cash flows for all types of fixed-income securities with aftertax, leveraging and multi-currency capabilities. Specializes in private placements, commercial mortgages, bank loans, esoteric high-yield securities, municipals, emerging market debt, convertibles and other corporate securities. Equity portion of convertibles is valued using artificial intelligence techniques for range of stock growth rates. Portfolios have all cash flows for projections and precise calculations. BondCalc performs OAS pricing (using calibrated binomial trees), swap analysis, matrix pricing, zero spot curve pricing and other valuation techniques. Uses implied forward yield curve or 2-dimensional interest rate forecasts to value make-whole calls, swaps and horizon analysis work-outs. Output consists of: results returned to screen, over 100 preset analytical graphs and reports and a report and graph writer with over 200 columns to choose from and a single security report writer with over 50 statistics for each call date. All output is publication quality and can be imported into spreadsheets.

BOND-TECH, INC.

P.O. Box 192 (513) 836-3991
Englewood, OH 45322 fax: (513) 836-1497

BOND-TECH'S BOND CALCULATOR
Version: na   *Last Updated:* na   *No. of Users:* na
Securities: bonds
Functions: bond analysis
Systems: DOS
Price: $49 ($75 with MBS/ABS Calculator)
Return Policy: all sales final
Technical Support: phone hours, 9 am-5 pm, M-F
Description: Analytical tool for comparing the relative value of securities of completely different types (e.g. notes, bonds, money market instruments). User inputs the defining characteristics of a security and the system computes various values for the security: dollar price (in decimal & 32nds), yield, discount rate, discount basis equivalent, bond

equivalent, CD equivalent yield, semiannual equivalent yield, breakeven overnight finance rate, yield value of 1/32 or 1/2, dollar value of 1 basis point, duration, modified duration, adjusted modified duration, convexity, aftertax yield, taxable coupon equivalent, yield with reinvestment, and future value per million. Other system capabilities include computing horizontal returns and modifying standard security conventions. Allows multiple databases for storage of security information for subsequent additional analysis, on-line help system, tutorial, and mouse support.

MBS/ABS CALCULATOR
Version: na   *Last Updated:* na   *No. of Users:* na
Securities: bonds, mortgage-backed securities, asset-backed securities
Functions: bond analysis
Systems: DOS
Price: $49 ($75 with Bond Calculator)
Return Policy: all sales final
Technical Support: phone hours, 9 am-5 pm, M-F
Description: Analytical tool for comparing the value of different MBS/ABS securities. Allows maintenance of history of each security. Outstanding principal for up to 13 consecutive periods is stored with the security record in the form of factors. Each factor indicates the portion of original principal remaining to be paid on the associated factor date. System computations for evaluation of the securities: paydown per million per period, average paydown per million per period, cumulative prepayment speed, interim prepayment speed, dollar price, MBS/ABS yield, semiannual equivalent yield, breakeven overnight financing rate, duration, modified duration, weighted average life (yrs), extension factored par, extension principal, extension interest, and extension total. Allows multiple databases for storage of security information. Comprehensive help system, tutorial, and mouse support provided.

BORLAND INTERNATIONAL

1800 Green Hills Road   (800) 321-4566
P.O. Box 660001   (408) 461-9122
Scotts Valley, CA 95067-0001   fax: (408) 439-9119

QUATTRO PRO
Version: 6.0   *Last Updated:* 1994   *No. of Users:* 2.5 mil.
Functions: technical analysis, spreadsheet, statistics
Systems: DOS, Windows
Price: $99; demo available
Return Policy: 90 days
Technical Support: phone hours, 6 am-5 pm, M-F; BBS support
Description: A spreadsheet program combining built-in push-button power with new intelligent graphs. Offers advanced spreadsheet analysis tools, network support and database access. Can access features and functions from the built-in SpeedBar. Has publishing and presentation capabilities and is compatible with Lotus 1-2-3.

BUSINESS FORECAST SYSTEMS

68 Leonard Street   (617) 484-5050
Belmont, MA 02178   fax: (617) 484-9219

FORECAST PRO
Version: 1.15   *Last Updated:* 1994   *No. of Users:* na
Functions: spreadsheet, statistics
Systems: DOS, Windows
Price: $595; demo available
Return Policy: 30 days
Technical Support: BBS support; newsletter
Description: A complete stand-alone forecasting system designed for the business person. Uses artificial intelligence and methodology for forecasting accuracy. Contains the methods found most effective for business data (Exponential Smoothing Models, Box-Jenkins and Dynamic Regression). A built-in expert system analyzes user's data and recommends the appropriate technique. Provides automatic fitting routines and guidance making the need for a background in statistics unnecessary.

CALIFORNIA SCIENTIFIC SOFTWARE

10024 Newton Road   (800) 284-8112
Nevada City, CA 95959   (916) 478-9041
                     fax: (916) 478-9042

BRAINMAKER

Version: 3.1   *Last Updated:* 1993   *No. of Users:* 16,000

Securities: stocks, bonds, futures, mutual funds, indexes, options, real estate

Functions: neural network

Systems: DOS

Price: $195

Return Policy: 30 days

Technical Support: phone hours, 8 am-5:30 pm, M-F; BBS support

Description: A complete software system for designing, building, training, testing and running neural networks that parallel computers modeled after the human brain, combining the brain's ability to analyze and learn with the computer's ability to process data quickly and accurately. Includes NetMaker, a network generation and data manipulation program with spreadsheet style display, which has the ability to perform complex arithmetic operations on user's data and build network description and training files automatically. Data may be read from Lotus, dBase, ASCII and Excel files. Support for graphics post-processing of network results is provided. Fact files may be connected together to create very large databases.

BRAINMAKER PROFESSIONAL

Version: 3.1   *Last Updated:* 1993   *No. of Users:* 3,750

Securities: stocks, bonds, futures, mutual funds, indexes, options, real estate

Functions: neural network

Systems: DOS

Price: $795

Return Policy: 30 days

Technical Support: phone hours, 8 am-5:30 pm, M-F; BBS support

Description: Professional version of BrainMaker neural network development system includes automatic and semi-automatic development tools for network optimization. Supports over 25,000 independent variables, graphics output, high-speed Binary and Hypersonic training. Includes runtime license and source code sufficient to run trained neural network on any platform. Optional accelerator system allows for faster training. Network will run up to 41.3 million connections per second.

CARIBOU CODEWORKS

HCR 3 Box 71   (218) 663-7118
Lutsen, MN 55612

QTRADER
Version: 2.5   *Last Updated:* 1994   *No. of Users:* na
Securities: stocks, futures, mutual funds, indexes
Functions: technical analysis, futures analysis
Systems: DOS
Price: $349; demo available, free; 10% AAII discount
Return Policy: all sales final
Description: Produces high-resolution, full-color charts for the graphical analysis of futures and stocks. Over 20 indicators plus precision line drawing tools. The current trend and reversal price, current position, projected highs and lows, high/low breakout points and stops are all displayed on screen with the bar chart and indicators. Supports virtually all printers and will save charts to disk as .PCX files. CSI and Compu Trac compatible. Has pulldown menu system, dialog boxes, and mouse support.

CHARLES L. PACK

25303 La Loma Drive   (415) 949-0887
Los Altos Hills, CA 94022-4542

PERSONAL PORTFOLIO ANALYZER
Version: 3.4   *Last Updated:* 1994   *No. of Users:* na
Securities: stocks, bonds, futures, mutual funds, indexes, options
Functions: portfolio management
Systems: DOS
Price: $44.95
Return Policy: 90 days
Technical Support: phone hours, 11 am-8 pm, M-F; newsletter
Description: Performs record keeping, numerical analysis and reporting on existing portfolios of stocks, bonds, mutual funds, cash and other security types. Combines multiple portfolios and displays or prints 9 detailed and 15 summary reports. Calculates portfolio allocation by security type, by industry or fund category, and by brokerage firm or investment objective. Also calculates realized and unrealized

gains/losses, holding periods, yield, total return (ROI), portfolio beta, and relative strength vs. any fund or index. Reports include tax information (Schedule D), ROI and gain/loss since purchase and between two dates, expected income and taxability analysis, and maturity schedule. Security prices can be entered manually or imported from an external ASCII file. The program keeps beginning and ending quotes for any single date range. Reinvested dividends are treated as share purchases, and individual tax lots are accounted for. Security sales may be applied on a FIFO or LIFO basis or applied to a particular purchase lot; when necessary a purchase lot is automatically split. The program handles stock splits and fund distributions. It is menu-driven, includes both context-sensitive on-line help and a printed manual, and is designed for ease of use by individuals and small fund managers.

STOCK CHARTING SYSTEM
Version: 3.2 **Last Updated:** 1992 **No. of Users:** na
Securities: stocks, bonds, futures, mutual funds, indexes, options
Functions: portfolio management, technical analysis
Systems: DOS
Price: $49.95
Return Policy: 90 days
Technical Support: phone hours, 11 am-8 pm, M-F; newsletter
Description: Integrated system performs both technical analysis and portfolio management. Graphics features include high/low/close chart (line graph for funds) with up to 3 moving averages and optional trading band. A volume histogram, on-balance volume, or 1 of 6 different oscillators are optional. Also available is a full-screen relative strength chart on which the price action of any security may be compared to any other security used as a base. Current or historical data can be entered manually or imported from external ASCII files, allowing the user to obtain information from almost any database service (using an external spreadsheet or communications program). Portfolio manager handles any number of portfolios consisting of bonds, stocks, funds or other security types. Individual tax lots are segregated and up to 5 portfolios may be combined in reports designed to monitor portfolio performance and include gain/loss, holding period, beta, annual appreciation (IRR), total return and asset allocation. Security prices are from the stock charts. Program is menu-driven with both context-sensitive on-line help screens and printed manual.

CHARLES SCHWAB & COMPANY, INC.

101 Montgomery Street   (800) 334-4455
Department S   (415) 627-7000
San Francisco, CA 94104   fax: (415) 403-5503

EQUALIZER
Version: 2.4   *Last Updated:* 1993   *No. of Users:* na
Securities: stocks, bonds, mutual funds, indexes, options
Functions: portfolio management
Systems: DOS
Price: $59; on-line fees additional
Return Policy: 30 days
Technical Support: toll-free number; phone hours, 9 am-11 pm, M-F
Description: Users can trade a wide variety of securities from their personal computers for speed, privacy, control and convenience; get real-time quotes when needed; access DJN/R and S&P's MarketScope to get investment information and to see what many of Wall Street's leading independent analysts are saying; read current and historical investment news about companies; keep in touch with stories that affect the market; evaluate market trends and review technical and fundamental data; screen for and monitor stocks; manage portfolio with automatic updating; and track hypothetical portfolios. Also, users have instant access to Schwab account information and can export data for use by other programs.

STREETSMART
Version: 1.0C   *Last Updated:* 1994   *No. of Users:* na
Securities: stocks, bonds, mutual funds, options
Functions: financial planning, portfolio management, technical analysis
Systems: Windows
Special Requirements: Windows 3.1
Price: $59; demo available, free
Return Policy: 30 days
Technical Support: toll-free number; phone hours, 9 am-11 pm, M-F
Description: Provides real-time market data access to quotes, analysis and news on a wide range of financial instruments. Offers securities monitoring capabilities—multiple pages with up to 540 instruments per page, 5 presentation formats, various sorting methods, color trend indicator, page-specific tickers and baskets, audible and visual limit

alerts; option analytics; charting, including moving average, envelope, RSI and oscillator studies with user-defined parameters and a 1-year database on NYSE, Amex, and Nasdaq NMS stocks, and on U.S. futures and indexes; fundamental data; news—Dow Jones scrolling headlines, news and news retrieval with keyword search and news alert capabilities; symbol guide; a 5-day, real-time and sales feature covering all U.S. and European equities and U.S. futures and indexes; programmable screen formats and hot keys.

CHARLTON WOOLARD

17280 Anna
Southfield, MI 48075

(810) 557-3766

FINANCE 101
Version: 2.4   *Last Updated:* 1994   *No. of Users:* 1,500
Securities: bonds, mutual funds, real estate
Functions: financial planning, real estate analysis, spreadsheet, statistics
Systems: DOS
Price: $39; demo available, $5
Return Policy: all sales final
Description: Covers detailed loan amortizations and refinancing, insurance, buy vs. lease analysis, savings and withdrawal planning, break-even analysis, real estate, present and future value calculations, cash flow, investment analysis and more. Includes menu-driven financial calculations and a dictionary of real estate terms.

SMARTBROKER
Version: 2.0   *Last Updated:* 1994   *No. of Users:* na
Securities: stocks, options
Functions: portfolio management, fundamental analysis, technical analysis, options analysis, statistics, expert system
Systems: DOS
Price: $95; demo available, $20
Return Policy: all sales final
Description: Stock and options analysis program. Downloads up to 4,000 stocks from the Dow Jones News Service, keeps price and volume trend data, performs analyses, recommends which stocks/options to play, and tracks its own recommendations over time. Also downloads news headlines of the stocks it recommends. Produces top-

20 summary tables of performing and non-performing stocks from those being tracked. Informs user as to when they should buy/sell specific stocks.

CLARKS RIDGE ASSOCIATES

R.D. 3 Box 134
Leesburg, VA 22075

(703) 882-3476

STOKPLOT
Version: 6   *Last Updated:* 1992   *No. of Users:* na
Securities: stocks, bonds, mutual funds, indexes
Functions: technical analysis
Systems: DOS
Special Requirements: not compatible with MS DOS 6.xx. DR DOS and MS DOS 3.xx to 5.xx is satisfactory.
Price: $40; 10% AAII discount
Return Policy: 30 days
Technical Support: phone hours, 9 am-3 pm, M-F
Description: Provides tools for analyzing the price history of an investment vehicle. 1-, 2- and 5-year plots are presented with high, low, close, and relative volume, providing access to numerical values for any entry. Long- and short-interval moving averages are plotted on the graphical display. Additional curves parallel the moving average to show percentages above/below the moving average. User may select the intervals for the moving averages (the defaults are 30 weeks and 5 weeks) and the percentage values (default is 10%). The period (end date) to be plotted is also selectable by the user (default is the most recent 52, 104, or 260 weeks). The auto correlation function can be used to indicate a period characteristic in the price history if present. Another section plots normalized closing price history with the Dow Jones industrial average for a one-year period. Utilities are provided to adjust for splits, convert CompuServe to STOKPLOT file format and invoke the user choices indicated above. Buy/sell indicators are based on user-selected criteria. Portfolios can be constructed and their history plotted. New candidates can be evaluated by covariance with existing portfolios.

COAST INVESTMENT SOFTWARE, INC.

358 Avenida Milano　　　　　　　　　　　　　　　(813) 346-3801
Sarasota, FL 34242-1517　　　　　　　　　　　fax: (813) 346-3901

CAPTURE

Version: 1.5　　　　　　*Last Updated:* 1994　　　　　*No. of Users:* na
Securities: stocks, bonds, futures, mutual funds, indexes, options
Functions: quote utility
Systems: DOS
Price: $99
Return Policy: all sales final
Technical Support: phone hours, 9 am-5 pm, M-F
Description: Accesses Signal and develops a library of intraday data files to be used for technical analysis by the Coast Investment Software trading package as well as a variety of vendor software. Provides an inexpensive method of building a comprehensive intraday database.

FIBNODES

Version: 4.07　　　　　　*Last Updated:* 1994　　　　　*No. of Users:* na
Securities: stocks, bonds, futures, mutual funds, indexes, options
Functions: technical analysis, bond analysis, futures analysis, options
　　analysis, real estate analysis, statistics
Systems: DOS
Price: $595; 20% AAII discount
Return Policy: all sales final
Technical Support: phone hours, 9 am-5 pm, M-F
Description: A computerized Fibonacci retracement and objective calculator specially designed for intraday trading and position trading where accurate stop placement and targeted profit objectives are needed. Calculates the two major nodes or up to 58 combined nodes per market swing; recalculates up to 58 nodes within 10 seconds of a new market high or low; analyzes market moves, like those in the S&P, into recognizable, tradable pieces; calculates profit objectives; highlights user selected nodes for recognition and indicates areas for proper stop placement. Manual includes specific examples. Contains automatic 32nd conversion for Treasury bonds and Treasury notes.

LOTUP

Version: 2.34　　　　　　*Last Updated:* 1994　　　　　*No. of Users:* na
Securities: stocks, bonds, futures, mutual funds, indexes, options

Functions: quote utility
Systems: DOS
Price: $99
Return Policy: all sales final
Technical Support: phone hours, 9 am-5 pm, M-F
Description: Downloads a variety of daily historical quotes from Signal to build a database for use with the Coast Investment Software trading package. Historical database created by Lotup can be converted to a variety of useful formats by using data conversion utility software currently available from other vendors.

TRADING PACKAGE
Version: 6.31   *Last Updated:* 1994   *No. of Users:* na
Securities: stocks, bonds, futures, mutual funds, indexes, options
Functions: technical analysis, bond analysis, futures analysis, options analysis
Systems: DOS
Price: $295; demo available, free
Return Policy: all sales final
Technical Support: phone hours, 9 am-5 pm, M-F
Description: A trading and market research tool that allows user to speculate using the Coast Investment Software (CIS) method or to select an alternative method that reflects individual objectives and needs. Provides end-of-day/intraday signals. Includes: bar chart capability of high, low, and close with manual or automatic scale selection; RSI, stochastics, MACD, trendlines, and Hurst cycle projection capability. A variety of moving average studies, including time-displaced moving averages, can graphically display the "key of the day" alone or in combination with the CIS proprietary, intermediate- and long-term trend indicators. Variable detrended oscillator study filters high-risk trades; proprietary CIS Oscillator Predictor Study indicates which price changes will produce overbought and oversold conditions in the market place. Includes database management capabilities.

COHERENT SOFTWARE SYSTEMS

1012 Elk Grove Avenue   (310) 452-1175
Venice, CA 90291

RORY TYCOON OPTIONS TRADER
Version: 1.00   *Last Updated:* 1992   *No. of Users:* na

Securities: options
Functions: options analysis, spreadsheet
Systems: DOS
Price: $49
Return Policy: all sales final
Technical Support: phone hours, 3 pm-8 pm, M-F
Description: Spreadsheet template that retrieves quotations and analyzes over 50 possible option trades. User enters a stock symbol and up to 3 contract months; system automatically retrieves the current stock price from an electronic quote service, constructs appropriate option symbols and retrieves quotations for a variety of trading strategies suited to the current stock price. Quotes are displayed in a table that may be used for manual data entry if no electronic service is available. The table of quotes is merged into risk/reward formulas that evaluate the trading strategies. One-page reports are printed through a menu. Includes interface to DJN/R, CompuServe, and Signal.

RORY TYCOON PORTFOLIO ANALYST
Version: 1.08   *Last Updated:* 1991   *No. of Users:* na
Securities: stocks, bonds, futures, mutual funds, options
Functions: financial planning, portfolio management, technical analysis, bond analysis, futures analysis, options analysis, spreadsheet
Systems: DOS
Price: $149
Return Policy: all sales final
Technical Support: phone hours, 3 pm-8 pm, M-F
Description: Real-time and historical charting with portfolio management spreadsheet template. Historical charts include price, volume, momentum, and moving averages of any duration. Charts may be viewed on screen or as high-resolution printouts. Dimensions of printed charts are variable up to full-page size for inclusion in reports. Signal users may chart price, volume, momentum and block trading in real time. Program will continuously display market price and volume for up to 90 securities on a text display while cycling through a list of constantly updated charts on a graphics monitor. Includes interfaces to DJN/R and CompuServe for automatic quote retrieval.

RORY TYCOON PORTFOLIO MANAGER
Version: 1.08   *Last Updated:* 1991   *No. of Users:* na
Securities: stocks, bonds, futures, mutual funds, options

Functions: financial planning, portfolio management, bond analysis, futures analysis, options analysis, spreadsheet
Systems: DOS
Price: advanced, $99
Return Policy: all sales final
Technical Support: phone hours, 3 pm-8 pm, M-F
Description: Spreadsheet template that organizes, tracks and reports on up to 2,500 investments in stocks, bonds, options, cash accounts, CDs, precious metals, mutual funds, futures contracts, and IRA, Keogh and employee profit sharing plans. Calculates net worth, profit/loss, yield to maturity, asset distribution, margin value, margin requirement, brokerage commissions, imputed interest, bond amortization and book value, and annual income projections for covered call and naked put options. Calculations are displayed for individual investments, investment categories or the whole portfolio. Able to generate 19 printed reports, including short- and long-term Schedule D reports. Quotations may be imported from services such as Signal.

COMFUTURE SOFTWARE SYSTEMS

10555 Paces Avenue   (704) 841-4026
Apartment 411
Matthews, NC 28105-2712

CSSCO
Version: 2.1   *Last Updated:* 1993   *No. of Users:* 230
Securities: futures, indexes, options
Functions: technical analysis, futures analysis, spreadsheet, statistics
Systems: DOS
Price: $99; demo available, $19
Return Policy: all sales final
Technical Support: phone hours, 8 am-8 pm, 7 days
Description: A cyclical oscillator trading system that generates buy, sell, hold and wait signals for commodities and totals profit/loss for trades. Indicators include moving averages, relative strength index, smoothed stochastics and a combined indicator. Open, high, low and close data can be input manually or from preformatted files. Values for stops, profit percentages and contract roll can also be input.

COMMODITY EXCHANGE, INC.

4 World Trade Center
Room 6404
New York, NY 10048

(800) 333-2900
(212) 938-7921
fax: (212) 938-2660

COMEX, THE GAME

Version: na   *Last Updated:* 1989   *No. of Users:* na
Securities: futures, options
Functions: futures analysis, options analysis, simulation/game
Systems: DOS
Price: $69.95
Technical Support: phone hours, 9 am-5 pm, M-F
Description: A simulation of the gold and silver marketplace that teaches the basics of options and futures trading. User enters several opening parameters, then tests trading acumen in a computer-generated, 180-day market environment. Includes extensive options and futures price data; price history charts; automatic calculation of margin requirements, net debit/credit and downside/upside break-even points; profit and loss graphs; and a news ticker relating next-day price movements.

HEDGEMASTER

Version: 1.15   *Last Updated:* 1991   *No. of Users:* na
Securities: futures, options
Functions: futures analysis, options analysis, simulation/game
Systems: DOS
Price: $99.95
Technical Support: phone hours, 9 am-5 pm, M-F
Description: Simulates the trading and hedging environment of a professional trader using the physical, forward, futures, and options markets. Allows user to enter positions and trades for the different forms of metals owned, namely bullion inventories, forward commitments, futures, options, and consignments. Through use of historical data, user can try different strategies and simulate the profit and loss outcome— "what if" situations.

COMMODITY SYSTEMS, INC. (CSI)

200 W. Palmetto Park Road　　　　　　　　(800) 274-4727
Boca Raton, FL 33432, USA　　　　　　　　(407) 392-8663
　　　　　　　　　　　　　　　　　　fax: (407) 392-1379

QUICKPLOT/QUICKSTUDY
Version: 4.05　　　　*Last Updated:* 1993　　　*No. of Users:* 800
Securities: stocks, futures, indexes
Functions: technical analysis
Systems: DOS
Price: $89; demo available, $5; 10% AAII discount
Return Policy: 15 days
Technical Support: phone hours, 8 am-11:30 pm, M-F; 9 am-1 pm, Sat;
　　newsletter
Description: Designed for use with Commodity Systems, Inc. Data Retrieval Service. Creates graphic displays and numeric output of daily prices, volume and open interest activity in the futures and stock markets. Provides wide variety of technical studies including: stochastics, moving averages with data shifts and bands, commodity channel index, momentum, spreads, ratios, on-balance and non-seasonal volume, trendlines, William's %R and moving average convergence/divergence. Provides 3 proprietary studies: Probable Direction Index (PDI) to determine the probable market direction; CSI-Trend to determine if market is in trending or trading (scalping) position; and CSI Stop to project tomorrow's high, low, and close as well as protective stops. Requires user to purchase CSI format data or manually input through CSI's Quicktrieve software system.

QUICKTRIEVE/TRADE DATA MANAGER
Version: IBM 4.05　　　*Last Updated:* 1993　　　*No. of Users:* 4,000+
Securities: stocks, futures, mutual funds, indexes, options
Functions: quote utility
Systems: DOS, Mac
Price: $59; 10% AAII discount
Return Policy: 30 days; $15 restocking fee
Technical Support: phone hours, 8 am-11:30 pm, M-F; 9 am-1 pm, Sat;
　　newsletter
Description: A downloading system that can: retrieve daily prices for the current date and for any of the previous 9 weeks; deliver electronic error corrections as required; accept electronic portfolio changes and

orders as well as questions and messages concerning user's account; convert data formats between Commodity Systems, Inc., MetaStock, ASCII and Compu Trac, and prepare weekly or monthly data files; compute stock split adjustments and rewrite historical files; and de-compress historical data supplied by diskette. The PC version provides alerts for each trading day of the current calendar year showing dates for economic and other government announcements regarding the markets and evaluates the integrity of user's data files by checking for errors and omissions. This version also corrects improperly created files from other sources as well as accepts, processes, and delivers historical data.

TRADER'S MONEY MANAGER
Version: 2.1   **Last Updated:** 1993   **No. of Users:** 40+
Functions: simulation/game, statistics
Systems: DOS
Special Requirements: Math co-processor recommended
Price: $399; demo available, $15; 10% AAII discount
Technical Support: phone hours, 8 am-11:30 pm, M-F; 9 am-1 pm, Sat; newsletter
Description: Trader's Money Manager analyzes the track record of any trading system and computes the probability of reaching a goal with limited capital. It also determines the required capital for trading a system and rates candidate system for selection. To enhance results from a successful system, it tells you when to increases or decrease market exposure, thus, maximizing downstream profits. The program uses a Monte Carlo simulation to synthesize actual trading experience. A user-supplied record of simulated or actual profits and losses and your system's parameter consumption count as the major inputs.

TRADESK
Version: 2.0   **Last Updated:** 1992   **No. of Users:** 100+
Securities: stocks, futures, indexes
Functions: financial planning, portfolio management
Systems: DOS
Special Requirements: 4M free disk space, math co-processor recommended
Price: $149 CSI daily user or $299 unrestricted use; demo available, $22; 10% AAII discount
Return Policy: 30 days; $22 restocking fee

Technical Support: phone hours, 8 am-11:30 pm, M-F; 9 am-1 pm, Sat; newsletter

Description: Keeps an unlimited number of trading accounts in balance, keeps track of all open orders, takes daily notes on both accounts and individual contracts and lets user review all interrelated data in a variety of report formats. Acts as a Personal Information Manager optimized for a commodity trader. Program is configured in separate modules: Manages open and closed trades for an unlimited number of trading accounts, maintains contract specifications for an unlimited number of contracts or issues and employs a text editor to keep daily notes for each trading account and contract.

COMPETENCE SOFTWARE

RRI Box 24   (603) 435-5098
Jct. Rts. 28 & 107   fax: (603) 435-7869
Pittsfield, NH 03263, USA

FINANCIAL COMPETENCE
Version: 1.5   *Last Updated:* 1994   *No. of Users:* 10,000
Functions: financial planning, fundamental analysis, simulation/game, instructional program
Systems: Windows, Windows NT, Mac
Special Requirements: 4M RAM; 14M free disk space
Price: $99/package; site licenses available; 10% AAII discount
Return Policy: 30 days
Technical Support: phone hours, 8:30 am-7 pm, M-F
Description: Financial Competence is a 7-lesson, self-paced course on how to understand and use business financial statements. The course is personalized with user's name, company, industry, product, market and actual financial results. Users are walked through the course step-by-step and construct their own statements (income statement, balance sheet, and cash flow statement) as they move through the lessons. Later lessons instruct the user on the relationship of the statements, use of major financial ratios, what banks and investors look for, how to construct alternate cash flow statements starting with net income, major methods of costing sales and inventory, and outside factors to consider when reviewing a company's financial performance. Upon completion of the lessons, the user's data can be exported to a spreadsheet or word processing package for printing finished financial state-

ments.

INVESTMENT COMPETENCE
Version: 1.0   *Last Updated:* 1994   *No. of Users:* na
Functions: instructional
Systems: Windows, Mac
Special Requirements: 4M RAM; 14M free disk space
Price: $99/package; site licenses available; 10% AAII discount
Return Policy: 30 days
Technical Support: phone hours, 8:30 am-7:00 pm
Description: Investment Competence is a 7-lesson, self-paced multi-media tutorial training the user on the basics of investing. The tutorial covers investing basics on various investment vehicles including real estate, commodities, money markets, collectibles, etc., in addition to covering topics such as stock and bond markets, measuring performance, and managing a portfolio.

COMPUSERVE, INC.

120 Broadway	(800) 543-4616
Suite 3330	(212) 227-3881
New York, NY 10271	fax: (212) 227-7194

COMPUSERVE CD
Version: na   *Last Updated:* na   *No. of Users:* na
Securities: stocks, bonds, futures, mutual funds, indexes, options
Functions: financial planning, portfolio management, fundamental analysis
Systems: Windows
Special Requirements: 4M RAM, CompuServe account, modem
Price: $7.95
Technical Support: toll-free number; phone hours, 8 am-5 pm, M-F
Description: CompuServe CD, a multi-media extension of the CompuServe Information Service, is now available on a Windows compatible CD-ROM. Products on the disk are designed to help save users time and connect charges, such as the on-disk version of File Finder that searches and downloads programs stored in CompuServe forum libraries. The disk is currently organized into six departments. Technology and Trends includes sample software, functional software, and commercial demos. The Entertainment section includes previews of

films and albums, reviews, games, and more. Home & Leisure focuses on family hobbies, travel, and leisurely pursuits. Shopping provides a window on CompuServe's electronic mall, and Personal Enterprise emphasizes productivity in the workplace, financial planning, and small business entrepreneuring.

COMPUSERVE RESEARCH MANAGER
Version: 2.0   *Last Updated:* 1994   *No. of Users:* na
Securities: stocks, bonds, mutual funds, indexes, options
Functions: portfolio management, fundamental analysis, technical analysis, bond analysis, options analysis, spreadsheet
Systems: DOS
Special Requirements: modem, spreadsheet
Price: $400-$1,000/mo. depending on what databases are accessed; demo available, free
Return Policy: all sales final
Technical Support: toll-free number; phone hours, 8 am-5 pm, M-F; BBS support; newsletter
Description: Offers access to a collection of databases, including over 190,000 North American securities; 90,000 international securities; and the Disclosure, Zacks, Compustat, and I/B/E/S databases. Once data is downloaded, more than 40 standard templates provide worksheets for immediate use. Lets user modify standard templates, design custom templates using the template builder, or have CompuServe develop templates to suit any spreadsheet model.

COMPUSERVE RESEARCH MANAGER FOR WINDOWS
Version: 3.0   *Last Updated:* 1993   *No. of Users:* na
Securities: stocks, bonds, mutual funds, indexes, options
Functions: portfolio management, fundamental analysis, technical analysis, bond analysis, options analysis, spreadsheet
Systems: Windows
Special Requirements: modem, Windows compatible spreadsheet
Price: $400-$1,000/mo. depending on what databases are accessed; demo available, free
Return Policy: all sales final
Technical Support: toll-free number; phone hours, 8 am-5 pm, M-F; BBS support; newsletter
Description: Acts as a single interface between on-line financial databases and the Windows versions of spreadsheet programs such as Lotus 1-2-3, Quattro Pro, and Excel. Measures a company's relative

strength by comparing investments within the same industry, comparing against indexes, and evaluating investments using standard or proprietary financial ratios. Offers access to a collection of databases, including over 190,000 North American securities; 90,000 international securities; and the Disclosure, Zacks, COMPU.S.TAT, and I/B/E/S databases. Once data is downloaded, more than 40 standard templates provide worksheets for immediate use. Lets user define custom models and save them as a template for future use.

COMPUTER ASSOCIATES INTERNATIONAL, INC.

One Computer Associates Plaza   (800) 225-5224
Islandia, NY 11788   (516) 342-5224
       fax: (516) 342-5734

KIPLINGER'S SIMPLY MONEY
Version: 2.0   *Last Updated:* 1994   *No. of Users:* 1,000,000+
Securities: stocks, bonds, futures, mutual funds, indexes, options, real estate
Functions: financial planning, portfolio management, technical analysis
Systems: Windows
Price: $39.95; $14.95 for upgrade
Technical Support: toll-free number; phone hours, 8 am-11 pm, M-F; BBS support; newsletter
Description: Financial management software package. Tracks checking, savings, credit card, cash, mortgage, loan asset, liability, investment and payroll accounts, and tax-free accounts. Also tracks financial moves on a nearly unlimited number of accounts and offers recommendations on each. Reminds user when repetitive payments or planned actions are due. Creates budgets based on past income and spending patterns. Prints checks or works with BillPay U.S.A. Links to spreadsheets and databases via DDE. Contains over 30 graphs and 50 specialized reports. Imports and exports Quicken files. Calculates amortization information for mortgage and loans. Tracks net value of home and improvements. Uses tax categories and reports based on IRS forms; exports via .TXF files to other tax programs. Analyzes and charts performance against a specified goal for each investment. Includes integrated on-line stock price updates. Also provides for small business support, including such factors as income, cash flow, balance

sheets, accounts receivable, and payroll. Compatible with Windows 3.1 and higher.

COMPUTER LAB

12 Sunset Way   (800) 397-1456
Suite A112   (702) 433-2695
Henderson, NV 89014   fax: (702) 433-2698

HARVEST-TIME RETIREMENT PLANNING SOFTWARE

Version: 4.0   *Last Updated:* 1994   *No. of Users:* 1,000
Functions: financial planning
Systems: DOS
Price: $49.95
Return Policy: 30 days
Technical Support: toll-free number; phone hours, 10 am-9 pm, M-F
Description: User enters retirement goals plus current assets, planned savings and projected average return for each of these 4 investment categories: taxable, tax-free, qualified tax-deferred and non-qualified tax deferred. Program automatically calculates taxes and any penalties on distributions plus all age-related adjustments to Social Security. Savings and investment strategy are evaluated in terms of retirement goals. Unique year-by-year retirement cash flow model projects annual requirements to meet inflation-adjusted living expenses, calculates taxes due each year, then withdraws funds in most tax-advantageous way. This feature accounts for wide variations in taxes from year to year during retirement and assures that adequate funds are calculated to pay these taxes and support lifestyle goals. Designed for those approaching retirement or already retired as well as for those planning retirement. Full-color graphs on screen show results, detailed year-by-year numbers available on screen and through printer. Effect of changing any entry can be graphed instantly, enabling user to quickly test options and conduct detailed analysis to develop a plan tailored to his or her goals, resources, preferences, and risk tolerance.

COMPU-VEST SOFTWARE

545 Fairview Avenue   (708) 469-4437
Glen Ellyn, IL 60137

OPTION STRATEGY PROJECTIONS
Version: 2.0   *Last Updated:* 1992   *No. of Users:* 650
Securities: options
Functions: options analysis
Systems: DOS
Price: $30 postpaid, $35 outside N. America
Return Policy: all sales final
Technical Support: phone hours, 10 am-4 pm, M-F
Description: Allows user to project profit or loss for an option strategy at a user specified closeout date. Calculates and displays the "fair market" option prices at a specified closeout date for a range of possible prices for the underlying stock and reports the profit/loss for the individual options in the strategy and for the overall strategy. The option values are calculated using the Black-Scholes model. The program recognizes and identifies over 90 different option strategies, including puts and/or calls with or without a long or short stock position. Other features include: a routine to check entries and correct errors or change input without starting over again; the ability to change closeout date for a strategy to analyze different situations; user can establish a file with pertinent data for a strategy to be able to call up the data later and use it to calculate final profit/loss at accurate closeout prices. All buy and sell calculations include a typical deep discount broker's commissions. Includes a manual on disk.

STOCK OPTION CALCULATIONS AND STRATEGIES
Version: 5.0   *Last Updated:* 1990   *No. of Users:* 1,150
Securities: options
Functions: options analysis
Systems: DOS
Price: $40 postpaid, $50 outside N. America; demo available, $10; 10% AAII discount
Return Policy: all sales final
Technical Support: phone hours, 10 am-4 pm, M-F
Description: Nine menu-driven programs. Identifies over 90 different put and/or call strategies with or without stock positions and projects profit/loss and break-even points. User can calculate fair market prices of options and hedge ratios (Black-Scholes); calculate days to option expiration and volatility by recent price history or implied volatility; project option prices and reward/risk ratio at the end of a specified holding period; calculate the probability a stock will be above or below a range of future prices; establish and maintain files of

prices and other market action data; keep record of mutual fund investments; calculate simple, exponential and weighted moving averages of file data; choose discount or full-service broker's commissions. All buy and sell calculations include commissions.

CYBER-SCAN, INC.

3601 Pulaski Road N.E.   (612) 682-4150
Buffalo, MN 55313

DISCOVERY
Version: na   *Last Updated:* na   *No. of Users:* na
Securities: stocks, futures, indexes, options
Functions: technical analysis
Systems: DOS
Price: $350; demo available; 15% AAII discount
Return Policy: all sales final
Technical Support: phone hours, 9 am-5 pm, M-F; BBS support
Description: Charts futures, stocks, and options. Consists of technical tools to fully analyze trades. Contains more than 60 technical studies including bar charts, moving averages, RSI, stochastics, MACD, point and figure charts, CCI, spreads, and stop systems. Can update each day and accumulate historical price data with no limit to size and number of files. Features data update using DTN Monitor, step-by-step tutoring on audio tapes, detailed written documentation, complete auto-run capability, and on-line help screens.

GLENDALE
Version: na   *Last Updated:* na   *No. of Users:* na
Securities: stocks, futures, indexes, options
Functions: technical analysis, quote utility
Systems: DOS
Price: $100
Return Policy: all sales final
Technical Support: phone hours, 9 am-5 pm, M-F; BBS support
Description: A utility package to transfer and use information from DTN's delayed quote system. Functions include: the ability to print information from a DTN terminal to user's printer; manually update and maintain historical data files; update historical data files, directly posting from user's DTN terminal; and view data files with a bar or point and figure charting program. Stocks, indexes or futures contracts

may be tracked. Starter data included.

QUOTE COMMANDER
Version: na   *Last Updated:* na   *No. of Users:* na
Securities: stocks, bonds
Functions: quote utility
Systems: DOS
Special Requirements: 1M expanded memory
Price: $99.95
Return Policy: all sales final
Technical Support: phone hours, 9 am-5 pm, M-F; BBS support
Description: Collects and displays unlimited stock and bond prices. Features include: listed quotes by symbol (up to 2,500 each) and 36 lists; random quote—any of 17,000 quotes by symbol; notifies user if instrument trades at specific level for up to 20 issues; automatic export of data in ASCII, MetaStock or CSI formats at specified time for use with other analysis programs. Program makes available all quotes on DTN that can be accessed by randomly entering the ticker symbol.

SUPER TIC
Version: na   *Last Updated:* na   *No. of Users:* na
Securities: stocks, bonds, futures, indexes
Functions: technical analysis, quote utility
Systems: DOS
Special Requirements: 1M expanded memory
Price: $99.95
Return Policy: all sales final
Technical Support: phone hours, 9 am-5 pm, M-F; BBS support
Description: Produces modified CSI file with intraday data using Data Transmission Network as the source. Integrates with Discovery for charting capability. Bars selectable from 5 to 120 minutes.

DATA CRUNCH SOFTWARE

1431 Lincoln Drive   (317) 776-1832
P.O. Box 293
Noblesville, IN 46060

DC DOWNLOADER
Version: na   *Last Updated:* na   *No. of Users:* na

Securities: stocks
Functions: downloading utility
Systems: Windows
Price: $255 (demo cost can be applied to the purchase); demo available, $30; 10% AAII discount
Return Policy: all sales final
Description: DC Downloader is an automated multiple directory downloader specifically designed by investors to download stock data from Dial/Data and maintain a MetaStock compatible split database. Stock data may be automatically split or unsplit by the discretion of the user. Another utility feature available within DCD is an ASCII data dump to the screen, printer, or a data file. The stock copy feature will copy or append selected stock from a source directory to a destination directory.

DATATECH SOFTWARE

6360 Flank Drive
Harrisburg, PA 17112

(717) 652-4344
fax: (717) 652-3222

FINANCIAL TOOLBOX
Version: 1.0   *Last Updated:* 1993   *No. of Users:* na
Functions: financial planning
Systems: DOS, Windows
Price: $39.95; 25% AAII discount
Return Policy: 30 days
Technical Support: phone hours, 8:30 am-5 pm, M-F
Description: A complete set of tools to solve everyday financial questions. Includes loan calculations with amortization chart, savings calculations, goal planner, payment comparison grid, rent vs. buy, mortgage refinancing comparison, home inventory, and personal records tracking.

RICH & RETIRED
Version: 1.1   *Last Updated:* 1993   *No. of Users:* na
Functions: financial planning
Systems: DOS, Windows
Price: $59.95; demo available, free; 25% AAII discount
Return Policy: 30 days
Technical Support: phone hours, 8:30 am-5 pm, M-F
Description: Helps set and meet retirement goals. Contains dozens of

retirement specific features including IRAs, 401(k)s, Social Security estimates, life expectancy calculations, reverse mortgages and more. User can see the effect of different interest, tax, or inflation rates. Can also plan future asset purchases. Develops "what if" scenarios. Able to import data from Quicken or Managing Your Money. Includes on-line help.

DATA TRANSMISSION NETWORK, CORP.

9110 W. Dodge Road   (800) 485-4000
Suite 200   (402) 390-2328
Omaha, NE 68114   fax: (402) 390-9690

DTN PORT
Version: 3.4   *Last Updated:* 1994   *No. of Users:* na
Securities: stocks, bonds, futures, mutual funds, indexes
Functions: quote utility
Systems: DOS
Price: $225 plus subscription fees for DTN Wall Street; demo available
Technical Support: BBS support
Description: Allows all the electronically-updated quotes from DTN Wall Street to be passed through the serial communications port on the DTN receiver. Provides approximately 20,000 NYSE, AMEX, and Nasdaq quotes. DTN Wall Street subscribers can store, view, or translate quote data that is passed through the DTN serial port interface. Designed to capture, manage, and store quote information using background data capture. Status of a single quote can be viewed by entering the trading symbol. The only limitation to the number of quotes users can "capture" is the available memory of their computers. Also stores quotes on hard-disk for a permanent record or for import into other compatible programs.

DC ECONOMETRICS

1001-A East Harmony #349
Fort Collins, CO 80525

ECON
Version: 2.0   *Last Updated:* 1994   *No. of Users:* 600+
Securities: stocks, bonds, futures, mutual funds, indexes, options

Functions: financial planning, fundamental analysis
Systems: DOS
Price: $49.95
Return Policy: 30 days
Description: Econometric models forecast S&P 500, T-bond and T-bill interest rates, zero-coupon bonds, inflation, and gold prices. Statistically optimized forecasts given for 3, 6, and 12 months in the future. Once a month the user enters 9 numbers: S&P 500 close, prime rate, T-bond rate, T-bill rate, CPI, unemployment percentage, S&P 500 dividend yield, S&P 500 P/E ratio, and gold. An asset allocation routine tells how much of each asset to hold with four strategies from conservative to aggressive. Futures and options are recommended for very aggressive traders. The models were derived by linear regression using 30 years of data from 1963 to 1993. The fit to this data is R=.90 for the S&P 500 12-month forecast.

DECISIONEERING, INC.

1526 Spruce Street
Boulder, CO 80302

(800) 289-2550
(303) 449-5177
fax: (303) 449-1442

CRYSTAL BALL
Version: 3.0.2   *Last Updated:* 1994   *No. of Users:* 5,000
Securities: stocks, bonds, futures, mutual funds, indexes, options, real estate
Functions: financial planning, fundamental analysis, spreadsheet, simulation/game, statistics
Systems: Windows, Mac
Price: $295; demo available
Return Policy: 30 days
Technical Support: toll-free number; phone hours, 8 am-6 pm, M-F; newsletter
Description: A forecasting and risk analysis program. Uses Monte Carlo simulation to forecast all statistically possible results for a given situation. Has graphic reporting format and a confidence level so the user can determine the likelihood of any event.

DENVER DATA, INC.

9785 Maroon Circle   (303) 790-7327
Meridian One Suite 340
Englewood, CO 80112

MUTUAL FUND MANAGER
Version: 2.0   *Last Updated:* 1990   *No. of Users:* na
Securities: mutual funds
Functions: portfolio management, technical analysis
Systems: DOS
Price: $49; demo available, $5
Return Policy: 90 days
Technical Support: phone hours, 11 am-6:30 pm, M-F
Description: User can monitor the status and performance of any size mutual fund or money market portfolio. Maintains an annual record of fund transactions including all purchases, redemptions and distributions. Produces 3 performance reports including a weekly report offering weekly gain or loss, current net asset values and percentage of change for each fund and the total portfolio comparing the performance with leading market indexes. Fund track and performance summary permit user to examine moving averages over any time period, from 1 to 52 weeks. Report also generates an exclusive beta-predicted performance feature that compares current and historical fund performance. Portfolio distribution analysis report displays the percentage of net asset value by each fund and fund type in a portfolio and calculates composite beta for the portfolio. Records money market accounts and calculates, displays and prints weekly interest earnings. Generates bar graph or line graph performance charts. Line graph feature may be adjusted to show moving averages.

DESIGN CREATIONS

PO Box 948   (800) 933-5910
Twain Harte, CA 95383   (209) 532-8413
                         fax: (209) 532-1545

INDIVIDUAL STOCK INVESTOR INSTIN
Version: 3.0   *Last Updated:* 1994   *No. of Users:* 850
Securities: stocks

Functions: portfolio management, fundamental analysis
Systems: DOS, OS/2
Special Requirements: 3M free disk space
Price: $59.95; 10% AAII discount
Return Policy: 30 days
Technical Support: phone hours, 9 am-5 pm, M-F; newsletter
Description: Contains 10 directories and 58 databases designed to perform portfolio management and fundamental research and analysis, create model portfolios, keep permanent transactions records, customize reports for each database, and create strategies and scenarios. Interactive with CompuServe, Prodigy, and Signal. Teaches user to search for financial data and information, assimilate what has been learned into an organizational format for immediate and future use, perform research and analysis and focus on the decision-making process.

DISCLOSURE, INC.

5161 River Road
Bethesda, MD 20816

(800) 945-3647
(301) 951-1300
fax: (301) 718-2343

FORTUNE 500 ON DISK
Version: na   *Last Updated:* na   *No. of Users:* na
Securities: stocks
Functions: fundamental analysis
Systems: DOS, Mac
Special Requirements: 4M RAM—Mac version
Price: $395
Technical Support: toll-free number; phone hours, 8:30 am-6:00 pm, M-F; 10:00 am-2:00 pm, Sat.
Description: A PC-based information tool offering access to financial and other information on the Fortune 500 and Fortune service 500 companies. Included are descriptions of key business activities; complete two-year financial statements; five-year summaries of sales, net income, and earnings per share; annual financial ratios; and listings of subsidiaries. It also includes the ability to retrieve and rank companies by financial performance, location, company size, and other criteria. Company listings include names, titles, and remuneration of top executives and directors. The software also provides the ability to gener-

ate mailing labels from the existing companies. Data can be sorted and displayed in a variety of ways and can be downloaded to spreadsheets and other software packages. Available on diskette or CD-ROM for both Macintosh and IBM compatible systems.

DOLLARLINK SOFTWARE

1407 Douglass Street	845-8445
San Francisco, CA 94131	(415) 641-0721
	fax: (415) 282-8486

DOLLARLINK
Version: 5.0   *Last Updated:* 1994   *No. of Users:* na
Securities: stocks, futures, mutual funds, indexes, options
Functions: portfolio management, fundamental analysis, technical analysis, futures analysis, options analysis, simulation/game, statistics
Systems: DOS
Special Requirements: 386+
Price: $1,300 or $100/month rental; lease to buy available; demo available, $50; 10% AAII discount
Return Policy: all sales final
Technical Support: phone hours, 12 pm-8 pm, M-F; newsletter; fee for tech support—$300/year after 1st year
Description: Real-time technical analysis program for stocks, indexes, options and commodities. Uses Signal, BMI, or PC Quote data feeds, and tracks up to 1,000 symbols. Charts over 80 intraday and historical studies in up to 496 windows on any portfolio symbol at any time. Zoom and draw trendlines, bands and channels, Fibonacci and Gann levels, etc. Data can be imported and exported. Built-in programmable keyboard macros eliminate repetitive keystroking. User-created custom indexes updated automatically and can be charted. Auto-pilot modes automate start-ups, shutdowns, data management and keyboard macros. Studies can be customized; alerts can be generated based on user's logic. Dual monitors supported. Real-time portfolio management module included. Offers a theoretical real-time option pricing model and strategies. Automatically keeps track of 20,000 active options and computes accurate market-implied volatilities.

DONALD H. KRAFT & ASSOCIATES

9325 Kenneth Avenue   (708) 673-0597
Skokie, IL 60076   fax: (708) 673-0597

PORTFOLIO SPREADSHEETS
Version: na   *Last Updated:* 1993   *No. of Users:* na
Securities: stocks, bonds, mutual funds
Functions: portfolio management, bond analysis, spreadsheet
Systems: DOS
Special Requirements: Lotus 1-2-3 release 2.4 or later
Price: $195; demo available, $5
Return Policy: all sales final
Technical Support: phone hours, 10 am-7 pm, M-F
Description: A package of 6 automated Lotus 1-2-3 spreadsheets enabling users to manage an unlimited number of portfolios of stocks, bonds, mutual funds, and options, and to calculate net worth and distribution of assets. Includes Portfolio Spreadsheets-Stocks, Portfolio Spreadsheets-Bonds, as well as 4 other spreadsheets to keep track of net worth, evaluate bond yield to maturity, calculate annualized ROI for writing covered calls and tracking stocks. User is guided by specially designed menus and can select many predesigned printed reports and charts to help manage portfolios.

PORTFOLIO SPREADSHEETS—BONDS
Version: na   *Last Updated:* 1993   *No. of Users:* na
Securities: bonds, mutual funds
Functions: portfolio management, bond analysis, spreadsheet
Systems: DOS
Special Requirements: Lotus 1-2-3 release 2.4 or later
Price: $100; demo available, $5
Return Policy: all sales final
Technical Support: phone hours, 10 am-7 pm, M-F
Description: An automated Lotus 1-2-3 spreadsheet enabling users to manage an unlimited number of portfolios of bonds and bond mutual funds. Users select from 12 predesigned printed reports to help manage bond portfolios. Features include: recordkeeping; ability to arrange bond portfolios into any desired sequence (e.g., unrealized gain/loss, maturity date, early call date, current yield) before viewing and printing reports; scheduling interest income; posting interest and return of principal as received; recording CU.S.IP number, where each

security is kept, how interest is paid (coupon, check, broker), and who owns the security; reporting Schedule D information; helping user plan bond purchases with ladder of maturities report; separate summary reports for government, tax-free and corporate bonds and displaying in color with proportionally-spaced type fonts. Users can modify the spreadsheet. Includes manual.

PORTFOLIO SPREADSHEETS—STOCKS
Version: na   *Last Updated:* 1993   *No. of Users:* na
Securities: stocks, mutual funds
Functions: financial planning, portfolio management, spreadsheet
Systems: DOS
Special Requirements: Lotus 1-2-3 release 2.4 or later
Price: $100; demo available, $5
Return Policy: all sales final
Technical Support: phone hours, 10 am-7 pm, M-F
Description: An automated Lotus 1-2-3 spreadsheet enabling users to manage an unlimited number of portfolios of stocks and stock mutual funds. Users select from 9 predesigned printed reports and 8 charts to help manage portfolios. Features include: recordkeeping; ability to arrange stock portfolios into any desired sequence (e.g. unrealized gain/loss, current yield, stock name) before viewing and printing reports; calculating portfolio diversification by stock and industry group; scheduling all dividend income; posting dividends as received; recording where each security is kept, how dividends are paid (check, broker), and who owns the security; displaying charts depicting portfolio's performance; alerting for price objectives; comparing performance with market indicator; calculating compound rate of growth for each stock and reporting Schedule D information. Includes columns for estimated EPS, P/E, and beta. Displays in color with proportionally spaced type fonts. Users can modify the spreadsheet. Current prices are typed or downloaded from DJN/R or Signal. Theoretical portfolios are also tracked.

DOW JONES & COMPANY, INC.

P.O. Box 300   (800) 815-5100
Princeton, NJ 08543   (609) 520-4641
                              fax: (609) 520-4660

DOW JONES MARKET ANALYZER

Version: 2.2   *Last Updated:* 1994   *No. of Users:* na

Securities: stocks, bonds, mutual funds, indexes, options
Functions: technical analysis
Systems: DOS
Special Requirements: Hayes Smart modem or compatible
Price: $349; demo available, $7.75; 30% AAII discount
Return Policy: 30 days; $20 restocking fee
Technical Support: phone hours, 9 am-9 pm, M-F
Description: Collects historical price and volume data for stocks, bonds, Treasury issues, options, mutual funds, and market indexes from Dow Jones. Off-line, constructs charts that reveal underlying trends for individual stocks and the market as a whole. Charts include bar, comparison and relative strength. Analysis features include moving averages, support/resistance lines and volume indicators. The auto-run capability allows users to program and save for subsequent use a sequence of charting and analysis commands that can be automatically applied to user-selected stocks.

DOW JONES SPREADSHEET LINK

Version: 2.04   *Last Updated:* 1994   *No. of Users:* na

Securities: stocks, bonds, futures, mutual funds, indexes, options
Functions: communications
Systems: DOS
Special Requirements: Lotus 1-2-3 v.2.3 or later or Microsoft Excel v.3.0 or later or Quattro Pro v.4.0 or later.
Price: $149; demo available, $7.75; 30% AAII discount
Return Policy: 30 days; $20 restocking fee
Technical Support: phone hours, 9 am-9 pm, M-F
Description: Enables users of Lotus 1-2-3, Quattro Pro, or Microsoft Excel to access information from DJN/R and automatically transfer it to their spreadsheet for analysis. Program uses personalized templates to collect current and historical quotes, Dow Jones averages and other market indexes, commodities, bonds, Treasury issues, mutual funds, stock options, fundamental data, earnings forecasts and more. Also provides access to all DJN/R databases, automated retrieval of news stories and headlines and automatic retrieval sessions.

MARKET ANALYZER PLUS FOR DOS

Version: 2.07   *Last Updated:* 1989   *No. of Users:* na

Securities: stocks, bonds, futures, mutual funds, indexes, options

Functions: portfolio management, technical analysis
Systems: DOS
Special Requirements: Hayes modem or compatible
Price: $499; demo available, $7.75; 30% AAII discount
Return Policy: 30 days; $20 restocking fee
Technical Support: phone hours, 9 am-9 pm, M-F
Description: Collects historical quotes for stocks, bonds, Treasury issues, options, mutual funds, market indexes and commodities from DJN/R. Creates bar, comparison, relative strength, and point and figure charts. Analysis tools include moving average convergence-divergence, commodity channel index, William's %R, directional movement, Wilder relative strength, scale changes, trendlines, moving averages, support/resistance lines and stochastics which can be used as is or modified for personalized analysis. The technical screening reports compare current price volume to past activity and point out stocks with the greatest profit potential. Manages up to 800 portfolios.

MARKET ANALYZER PLUS FOR MAC
Version: 2.07   *Last Updated:* 1991   *No. of Users:* na
Securities: stocks, bonds, futures, mutual funds, indexes, options
Functions: technical analysis
Systems: Mac
Special Requirements: Hayes modem or compatible
Price: $349; demo available, $7.75; 30% AAII discount
Return Policy: 30 days; $20 restocking fee
Technical Support: phone hours, 9 am-9 pm, M-F
Description: Collects historical quotes for stocks, bonds, Treasury issues, options, mutual funds, market indexes, and commodities from DJN/R. Creates bar, comparison, relative strength, point and figure, and candlestick charts. Analysis tools include moving average convergence-divergence, commodity channel index, William's %R, directional movement, Wilder relative strength, scale changes, trendlines, moving averages, support/resistance lines and stochastics which can be used as is or modified for personalized analysis. The technical screening reports compare current price volume to past activity and point out stocks with the greatest profit potential.

MARKET MANAGER PLUS FOR DOS
Version: 3.02   *Last Updated:* 1990   *No. of Users:* na
Securities: stocks, bonds, mutual funds, options, real estate
Functions: portfolio management

Systems: DOS
Special Requirements: Hayes modem or compatible
Price: $299; demo available, $7.75; 30% AAII discount
Return Policy: 30 days; $20 restocking fee
Technical Support: phone hours, 9 am-9 pm, M-F
Description: A portfolio management program that values holdings with current prices for stocks, bonds, options, mutual funds, and Treasury issues from DJN/R. Monitors dividends, tracks broker commissions, and generates a variety of reports including holdings, realized gain/loss and security and cash transactions. Alert reports include option expirations and bond maturity. Also allows for hypothetical portfolios, contains a calendar for tracking of daily financial activity, updates selected portfolios and saves security data in a format for subsequent analysis in user's spreadsheet.

MARKET MANAGER PLUS FOR MAC

Version: 3.02   *Last Updated:* 1988   *No. of Users:* na
Securities: stocks, bonds, mutual funds, options, real estate
Functions: portfolio management
Systems: Mac
Special Requirements: Hayes modem or compatible
Price: $299; demo available, $7.75; 30% AAII discount
Return Policy: 30 days; $20 restocking fee
Technical Support: phone hours, 9 am-9 pm, M-F
Description: A portfolio management program that values holdings with current prices for stocks, bonds, options, mutual funds, and Treasury issues from DJN/R. Monitors dividends, tracks broker commissions, and generates a variety of reports including holdings, realized gain/loss and security and cash transactions. Alert reports include option expirations and bond maturity. Also allows for hypothetical portfolios, contains a calendar for tracking of daily financial activity, updates selected portfolios and saves security data in a format for subsequent analysis in user's spreadsheet.

WALL STREET JOURNAL PERSONAL FINANCE LIBRARY

Version: 1.0   *Last Updated:* 1994   *No. of Users:* na
Functions: financial planning
Systems: Windows
Price: $39.95
Return Policy: all sales final
Technical Support: phone hours, 9 am-7 pm, M-F

Description: The Wall Street Journal Personal Finance Library is a Windows based software program that contains 18 articles from The Wall Street Journal's "Your Money Matters" column and 13 corresponding, interactive worksheets that give you possible solutions and strategies tailored to your specific situation. Topics range from investment strategies for building a portfolio, buying a home, refinancing your mortgage, paying down debt, putting your kids through college and planning for retirement.

DYNACOMP, INC.

The Dynacomp Office Building   (800) 828-6772
178 Phillips Road   (716) 265-4040
Webster, NY 14580

BUDGET MODEL ANALYZER
Version: na   *Last Updated:* na   *No. of Users:* na
Functions: financial planning
Systems: DOS
Price: $33.95; 20% AAII discount
Return Policy: 30 days; 25% restocking fee
Technical Support: phone hours, 9 am-5 pm, M-F
Description: Provides a picture of overall cash flow. User provides a list of all income and expenses. Each income and expense must be specified as per day, work day, week, 2 weeks, month, quarter or year. Program can then expand the list into a complete matrix that shows each item in the list expressed in each of the period specifications. Shows the results of all income and expenses. Produces a bar graph giving a graphical representation of user's budget.

BUSINESS PACK
Version: na   *Last Updated:* 1993   *No. of Users:* na
Functions: financial planning, fundamental analysis, bond analysis, options analysis, real estate analysis, statistics
Systems: DOS
Price: $99.95; 20% AAII discount
Return Policy: 30 days; 25% restocking fee
Technical Support: phone hours, 9 am-5 pm, M-F
Description: A collection of 100 ready-to-run programs for various business calculations including: break-even analysis; checkbook main-

tenance; mortgage amortization table; rate of return on investment with variable/constant inflows; effective interest rate of a loan; value of a bond; Black-Scholes options analysis, alpha and beta variables computations for a stock; conditional profit tables; future price estimation with inflation; mailing list system; 3 methods for repayment of loans; arbitrage computations; loan amount a borrower can afford; stock market portfolio storage-valuation program; etc. All programs can be customized.

BUYSEL

Version: na   *Last Updated:* na   *No. of Users:* na
Securities: stocks, futures, options
Functions: technical analysis, options analysis, statistics
Systems: DOS
Price: $99.95; 20% AAII discount
Return Policy: 30 days; 25% restocking fee
Technical Support: phone hours, 9 am-5 pm, M-F
Description: Analyzes stocks, commodities, and options. Contains 4 distinct trading methods and money management systems that produce explicit buy/sell transaction signals; Black-Scholes call option model over any time period for a common stock; and statistical correlation computation between several stocks or commodities. Closing price charts are automatically scaled. Price data entry and validation on a daily basis or quick approximation of long periods of real price data.

CALCUGRAM STOCK OPTIONS SYSTEM

Version: na   *Last Updated:* na   *No. of Users:* na
Securities: futures, options
Functions: fundamental analysis, options analysis
Systems: DOS
Price: $99.95; 20% AAII discount
Return Policy: 30 days; 25% restocking fee
Technical Support: phone hours, 9 am-5 pm, M-F
Description: Guides in the selection and combination of options. The daily follow-up program lets the user know when to close out at best advantage. The pricing model used is based on modern portfolio theory. The first program in the software package computes normal (theoretical) values, differences from actual prices and implied volatilities for the options on a stock. The main program, Options Hedging, examines the prospects of spreads and combinations. Because option

prices fluctuate around the normal values, the profit in any hedge position varies from day to day. A third program lets the investor follow the progress on a daily basis.

COINDATA
Version: na   *Last Updated:* 1993   *No. of Users:* na
Functions: coin collection valuation
Systems: DOS
Price: $39.95; Coindata and Stampdata, $69.95; 20% AAII discount
Return Policy: 30 days; 25% restocking fee
Technical Support: phone hours, 9 am-5 pm, M-F
Description: Records various characteristics that describes user's collections, searches for coins having particular characteristics, computes totals, and prints in several formats. Up to 300 coin records can be cataloged on a single-sided disk (800 on a double-sided diskette). Collection size is unlimited if using a dual-drive system.

COINS
Version: na   *Last Updated:* 1993   *No. of Users:* na
Functions: coin collection valuation
Systems: DOS
Price: $49.95; 20% AAII discount
Return Policy: 30 days; 25% restocking fee
Technical Support: phone hours, 9 am-5 pm, M-F
Description: Enables user to catalog an entire coin collection and obtain several reports that serve for personal investment information. Contains a built-in standard coin file, 1,600 common U.S. coin descriptions, and the latest market value for most grades providing an automatic means for tracking the value of a user's collection. Annual update disks are available.

COLLECTORS PARADISE
Version: na   *Last Updated:* 1993   *No. of Users:* na
Functions: collection valuation
Systems: DOS, Commodore C-64
Price: $29.95; 20% AAII discount
Return Policy: 30 days; 25% restocking fee
Technical Support: phone hours, 9 am-5 pm, M-F
Description: Keeps a complete inventory of all coins, stamps, and rare collectibles. Quickly adjusts the current value of items to keep insurance and personal records up-to-date. Add, delete, or change items

while scrolling through inventory looking at up to 11 items per screen.

COMPU/CHART EGA
Version: na *Last Updated:* na *No. of Users:* na
Securities: stocks
Functions: technical analysis
Systems: DOS
Price: $299.95; 20% AAII discount
Return Policy: 30 days; 25% restocking fee
Technical Support: phone hours, 9 am-5 pm, M-F
Description: Applicable to both short-term and long-term trading. Data is downloaded by modem (via the Hale System/Track service). Historical market files can hold from 7 months (daily) to 33 months (weekly) of data on any of the stocks, indexes, or funds followed. Features include display of user's last trade on chart, user alerts when trade-target has been reached, ex-dividend dates, where user left off in the last session, etc. Charts include: moving average, price/volume, oscillator, point and figure, comparison, and a multi-chart scanner to check portfolio after an update (9 charts per screen). Other features include: interday monitor with dynamic bar, back scan, last trade slider on chart, last trade status report, percentage below maximum display, price factoring, and automatic data retrieval.

COMPUSEC PORTFOLIO MANAGER
Version: na *Last Updated:* na *No. of Users:* na
Securities: stocks, futures, mutual funds, options
Functions: portfolio management
Systems: Apple II
Price: $99.95; 20% AAII discount
Return Policy: 30 days; 25% restocking fee
Technical Support: phone hours, 9 am-5 pm, M-F
Description: Ranks stocks in a portfolio by showing which should be reduced, eliminated, or increased. Calculates, for any stock, the compound growth rate between the earnings per share for an earlier time period and earnings per share for a later time period. Calculates the payback period. Shows daily volume, records date and time when quotes were retrieved, and shows unrealized gains and losses with subtotals and an analogous breakdown for realized capital gains and losses. Shows the number of securities held, the total number of shares held, and the average cost per share for total holdings security as well as average cost per share for each separate holding. Program can also

download quotes by telephone when using a modem and DJN/R.

COVERED OPTIONS
Version: na   *Last Updated:* na   *No. of Users:* na
Securities: futures, options
Functions: options analysis
Systems: DOS
Price: $99.95; 20% AAII discount
Return Policy: 30 days; 25% restocking fee
Technical Support: phone hours, 9 am-5 pm, M-F
Description: Emphasizes options "covered" by owned securities but includes use of uncovered positions. Allows users to evaluate the options on a stock so they can select the highest value for sale or cheapest value for purchase. The annualized option gain is computed to show a position effectiveness. Program gives both graphical and tabular representations of what will happen to the gain as the stock price changes for any future date. Computes probability that the stock will remain within a profitable range. Provides a printed report of the gains or losses in the stock (bond) and the option and the present annualized option yield.

CREDIT RATING BOOSTER
Version: na   *Last Updated:* na   *No. of Users:* na
Functions: credit report
Systems: DOS
Price: $29.95; 20% AAII discount
Return Policy: 30 days; 25% restocking fee
Technical Support: phone hours, 9 am-5 pm, M-F
Description: Provides a printout or full-screen display of user's up-to-date credit history in a format for presentation to a loan officer.

DATA SMOOTHER SEMI-SPLINE/POLYNOMIAL DATA SMOOTHING
Version: na   *Last Updated:* 1993   *No. of Users:* na
Functions: fundamental analysis, technical analysis, statistics
Systems: DOS
Price: $39.95-$49.95; 20% AAII discount
Return Policy: 30 days; 25% restocking fee
Technical Support: phone hours, 9 am-5 pm, M-F
Description: Smooths out day-to-day stock market fluctuations to better see the overall market behavior. Also useful for sales, business, sci-

entific data and in situations which no overall functional form is apparent.

DECISION ANALYSIS
Version: na   *Last Updated:* 1993   *No. of Users:* na
Functions: decision analysis
Systems: DOS
Price: $39.95; 20% AAII discount
Return Policy: 30 days; 25% restocking fee
Technical Support: phone hours, 9 am-5 pm, M-F
Description: Organizes choices and the factors involved to help the user make better decisions. Lets user define choices and criteria and supply ratings. Analyzes ratings to show how each choice compares with the others and presents analysis in comparison tables.

ESTAMORE
Version: na   *Last Updated:* 1993   *No. of Users:* na
Functions: real estate analysis
Systems: DOS
Price: $99.95; 20% AAII discount
Return Policy: 30 days; 25% restocking fee
Technical Support: phone hours, 9 am-5 pm, M-F
Description: Cost estimator for single family residences. Starts from the concept level, with refinement as desired. Values for specified parameters are stored for use in future estimates. Can be used as a sales tool for real estate agents in helping clients understand the value of their selection and the effect of specific requirements. Contractors can quickly provide ball park estimates and refine them for bids. Lenders, insurance agents, and appraisers can establish values for existing (replacement value) and new houses. User can choose the level of detail desired. Prints summary reports or detailed breakdown reports by category (detail sheets).

EXPERT EASE EXPERT SYSTEM
Version: na   *Last Updated:* na   *No. of Users:* na
Functions: statistics, expert system
Systems: DOS
Price: $395; 20% AAII discount
Return Policy: 30 days; 25% restocking fee
Technical Support: phone hours, 9 am-5 pm, M-F
Description: A sophisticated decision-tree analysis tool that creates an

expert system of a user's own design incorporating their specialized knowledge. Once the expert system is created, a non-expert can use it without re-programming to obtain the same result or decision that the program designer would have reached. Creates a decision tree based on rules it derives from user's examples, automatically eliminating redundancies and alerting to any inconsistencies. Text can be added in user's words to fit the people who use the expert system, which can be expanded, modified or refined at any time.

EXPERT SYSTEM TUTORIAL

Version: na   *Last Updated:* na   *No. of Users:* na
Functions: statistics, expert system
Systems: DOS
Price: $29.95; 20% AAII discount
Return Policy: 30 days; 25% restocking fee
Technical Support: phone hours, 9 am-5 pm, M-F
Description: Provides a way to examine expert systems to see if the procedure is applicable to user's situation.

FAMILY BUDGET

Version: na   *Last Updated:* na   *No. of Users:* na
Functions: financial planning
Systems: DOS
Price: $34.95; 20% AAII discount
Return Policy: 30 days; 25% restocking fee
Technical Support: phone hours, 9 am-5 pm, M-F
Description: A 2-part electronic home data recordkeeping program. Part 1, budget, is used to record expenditures, both cash and credit, and income on a daily basis for 1 calendar year. Three categories are used to record tax-deductible items, namely interest and taxes, medical expenses and charitable donations. Part 2, charge accounts, provides a continuous record of all credit card transactions. Provides options for hardcopy printout.

FINANCE MASTER

Version: na   *Last Updated:* na   *No. of Users:* na
Functions: financial planning, real estate analysis
Systems: DOS
Price: $89.95; 20% AAII discount
Return Policy: 30 days; 25% restocking fee
Technical Support: phone hours, 9 am-5 pm, M-F

Description: A menu-driven personal finance system, with on-line help screens, pop-up calculator, and data windows. Requires no accounting knowledge. The program remembers periodic expenses, maintains check registers, prints checks, keeps records of cash, savings accounts, credit cards (with transaction records) and sets up budget with comparisons (e.g., bar charts) showing budgeted and actual expenses. Financial calculations performed include those involved in loan payments and amortization (fixed/adjustable), savings plans and accumulation schedules, retirement (e.g., annuities) and college planning, mortgage refinancing/home equity loan analysis and buy, lease, rent decisions. The program also manages financial assets and investments, including stocks, bonds, mutual funds, personal assets and obligations; displays financial analyses and results with plots and charts; computes life insurance needs based on user's personal situation; prepares personal financial and net worth statement; and allows automatic or manual expense allocation to multiple categories. Reports and data listings may be printed or saved to disk. Password protection available.

FINANCIAL MANAGEMENT SYSTEM
Version: na   *Last Updated:* na   *No. of Users:* na
Securities: stocks, bonds, futures, mutual funds, indexes, options, real estate
Functions: fundamental analysis, bond analysis
Systems: DOS
Price: $149.95; 20% AAII discount
Return Policy: 30 days; 25% restocking fee
Technical Support: phone hours, 9 am-5 pm, M-F
Description: Menu-driven set of coordinated sub-programs. Topics include: financial ratios (liquidity, leverage, activity, profitability), Du-Pont analysis, break-even analysis, lease-buy decision, net present value, rates of return, profitability index, inventory model, capital budgeting under uncertainty, and refunding a bond.

THE FORECASTING EDGE
Version: na   *Last Updated:* 1993   *No. of Users:* na
Functions: statistics, expert system
Systems: DOS
Price: $99.95; 20% AAII discount
Return Policy: 30 days; 25% restocking fee
Technical Support: phone hours, 9 am-5 pm, M-F

Description: A menu-driven package that applies Box-Jenkins time series forecasting method. Analysis is well-suited to data with a cyclical component, such as sales, the stock market, and similar seasonal processes. Aimed at users having little technical knowledge of forecasting theory. Designed as an "expert system" to automatically make most of the choices for the user, and to display the results in a simple, graphical format.

FOURIER ANALYSIS FORECASTER
Version: na   *Last Updated:* na   *No. of Users:* na
Functions: technical analysis, statistics
Systems: DOS
Price: from $99.95 to $169.95; 20% AAII discount
Return Policy: 30 days; 25% restocking fee
Technical Support: phone hours, 9 am-5 pm, M-F
Description: A software package for the study of data containing cyclical components. The program lets the user access the techniques of Fourier analysis in determining the periods of underlying cycles without having to understand the math involved. Data is entered from the keyboard or from a disk file and can be, saved, added, edited, deleted, etc. Analyzed data can be broken down into 2 general components: an underlying trend, and a multi-cyclic pattern. The types of trends that can be fitted are: polynomial (linear, quadratic, or cubic) in time (T) or inverse time (1/T) trends; exponentially increasing/decreasing trends (single and double exponential); logarithmic trends. A typical use includes stock and commodity cycle identification and forecasting. Comes in math co-processor versions, with a speed increase of 6 to 7 times faster than the non-coprocessor versions.

FUNDWATCH
Version: na   *Last Updated:* na   *No. of Users:* na
Securities: stocks, bonds, mutual funds
Functions: technical analysis
Systems: DOS
Price: $39.95; 20% AAII discount
Return Policy: 30 days; 25% restocking fee
Technical Support: phone hours, 9 am-5 pm, M-F
Description: Simplifies evaluation and comparison of various common investments, including mutual funds, stocks, bonds, and many commodities. Calculates yields, evaluates trends with moving averages, creates comparative graphs, provides direct comparisons with

interest-earning investments and maintains basic portfolio information.

GOLDSPREAD STATISTICAL

Version: na   *Last Updated:* 1993   *No. of Users:* na
Functions: statistics
Systems: DOS
Price: $79.95; 20% AAII discount
Return Policy: 30 days; 25% restocking fee
Technical Support: phone hours, 9 am-5 pm, M-F
Description: An integrated system with spreadsheet, data management, and statistical features. Can read and write Lotus 1-2-3 files, includes all Lotus functions and is upward compatible with Lotus commands. Macros are also a superset of the corresponding Lotus macros. 29 common statistical functions are available including pdfs, cdfs, and their inverses (Poisson, normal, binomial, Chi-squared, T, and F). Statistical tests include ANOVA (one-way, two-way, randomized complete block), descriptive statistics (mean, median, standard deviation, skewness, kurtosis, etc.), frequency tables and polygons, hypothesis testing (T, Z, F), non-parametric testing (Spearman, Chi-square, sign, contigency, Wilcoxon, Kruskal-Wallis, Mann-Whitney, runs, etc.), and rank order.

HANSEN-PREDICT

Version: na   *Last Updated:* na   *No. of Users:* na
Securities: real estate
Functions: technical analysis, statistics, expert system
Systems: DOS
Price: $99.95; 20% AAII discount
Return Policy: 30 days; 25% restocking fee
Technical Support: phone hours, 9 am-5 pm, M-F
Description: A self-learning, general purpose expert system. Predicts the future outcomes of situations based on the information available at that time. Program defines the input variables (e.g., symptoms, financial indications, soil conditions) and the possible outcomes (e.g., possible diseases, harvest values for various crops). Examines relationships between variables and outcomes and refines its understandings of the situation. Deals with ambiguous and underdefined situations in a statistical manner predicting the most likely outcome or decision. Can also treat clearly discontinuous variables.

HOME APPRAISER

Version: na   *Last Updated:* na   *No. of Users:* na
Securities: real estate
Functions: real estate analysis
Systems: DOS
Price: $59.95; 20% AAII discount
Return Policy: 30 days; 25% restocking fee
Technical Support: phone hours, 9 am-5 pm, M-F
Description: Estimates potential market value of real property. Allows user to approximate effects of various physical, economic, and territorial factors with impact on the overall value of the property. User supplies selected information about the house (or condo), and the computer provides a depreciated value and a bottom-line estimate of projected market value.

INTERACTIVE MULTIPLE PREDICTION

Version: na   *Last Updated:* na   *No. of Users:* na
Functions: technical analysis, statistics
Systems: DOS
Price: $69.95; 20% AAII discount
Return Policy: 30 days; 25% restocking fee
Technical Support: phone hours, 9 am-5 pm, M-F
Description: A multiple linear regression package that handles up to 1,000 samples (data points) with 79 independent variables. Calculates the multiple regression coefficients, beta weights, R, R-squared, along with the usual standard error estimates (sigma, chi-square, residuals, etc.) Includes: provisions for cross-validation studies—may be run with odd, even or all rows. Choice of full (all variables) or stepwise forward multiple regression, and user can determine combination of variables (up to 10) that produce the highest R-squared and lowest standard error of the estimate. A statistical test determines which univariate transformation is likely to be the most productive. A sweep-search option computes the R-squared for a selected group of predictors ignoring all others to discover which predictor has the biggest impact on R-squared. Most intermediate results are displayed on the screen for user to follow the steps in the procedures. Options enable user to retrieve all initial, intermediate and final data/results for archival purposes.

INVESTING ADVISOR

Version: na   *Last Updated:* na   *No. of Users:* na
Securities: stocks, mutual funds, indexes, real estate

Functions: technical analysis
Systems: DOS
Price: $49.95; 20% AAII discount
Return Policy: 30 days; 25% restocking fee
Technical Support: phone hours, 9 am-5 pm, M-F
Description: Helps user make unemotional decisions about buying and selling investments. Incorporates a means of timing the purchase and sale of investments based on a price-trend analysis and on buy/sell rules. Includes the ability to track both long- and short-term trends to pick best strategy. User can initialize database, add or delete investments, calculate the action to take, and adjust the database for splits of the investment.

IRMA
Version: na   *Last Updated:* na   *No. of Users:* na
Securities: stocks, bonds, mutual funds, indexes, options, real estate
Functions: financial planning, portfolio management
Systems: DOS
Price: $49.95; 20% AAII discount
Return Policy: 30 days; 25% restocking fee
Technical Support: phone hours, 9 am-5 pm, M-F
Description: Records and tracks investment information. Pertinent data for a diversified portfolio of up to 90 different investments are entered. Handles common and preferred stocks, bonds, deposit accounts, funds, partnerships, options and taxable and non-taxable investments. Varied presentations of user's data support decision-making in 3 areas: financial, tax, and investment planning.

KEEP TRACK OF IT
Version: na   *Last Updated:* na   *No. of Users:* na
Functions: financial planning
Systems: DOS
Price: $49.95; 20% AAII discount
Return Policy: 30 days; 25% restocking fee
Technical Support: phone hours, 9 am-5 pm, M-F
Description: Budget program that organizes finances and prints out a monthly net-worth statement showing all assets and liabilities. Presents a monthly report of income and expenditures by category or generates year-to-date report.

LINEAR PROGRAMMER MINIMAX
Version: na   *Last Updated:* 1993   *No. of Users:* na
Functions: asset/investment optimization
Systems: DOS
Price: $69.95; 20% AAII discount
Return Policy: 30 days; 25% restocking fee
Technical Support: phone hours, 9 am-5 pm, M-F
Description: A more powerful version of Linear Programmer that can treat over- and under-constrained problems, maximize an objective function, and solve simultaneous linear equations.

LOAN ARRANGER
Version: na   *Last Updated:* na   *No. of Users:* na
Functions: financial planning, loan analysis
Systems: DOS
Price: $29.95; 20% AAII discount
Return Policy: 30 days; 25% restocking fee
Technical Support: phone hours, 9 am-5 pm, M-F
Description: Tracks up to 25 personal loans, such as a home mortgage, automobile, education, and home improvement. User can: monitor the remaining balance of each loan, the number of payments left, and the date of the final payment; see and print reports on the current status of all obligations and on year-to-date payments for each; print complete or partial amortization tables for each loan; and combine various terms (principal, interest rates, and number of payments) to compare monthly payments and the total interest paid.

MARKET FORECASTER
Version: na   *Last Updated:* na   *No. of Users:* na
Securities: stocks, mutual funds, indexes
Functions: market timing
Systems: DOS
Price: $199.95; 20% AAII discount
Return Policy: 30 days; 25% restocking fee
Technical Support: phone hours, 9 am-5 pm, M-F
Description: Attempts to predict the magnitude and direction of stock market movements over the next 2 to 4 months. Suggests when to buy stocks, mutual funds, or options, or when to retreat. Features include: the ability to play "what if" games; an audio signal when it is time to take action; a self-checker to assure the right forecast; and an encrypted forecast and other recorded information available by phone.

MARKET TIMER
Version: na   *Last Updated:* na   *No. of Users:* na
Securities: mutual funds, indexes
Functions: technical analysis, market timing
Systems: DOS
Price: $119.95; 20% AAII discount
Return Policy: 30 days; 25% restocking fee
Technical Support: phone hours, 9 am-5 pm, M-F
Description: Provides the necessary buy and sell signals based on a trend analysis of the Value Line composite index. Generates buy and sell equity market switch signals; allows performance testing of different market trend sensitivities on past data; includes a daily 10-year history of the Value Line composite index; maintains a list of the mutual funds the user is invested in; updatable from daily newspapers; and displays charts with trendlines for any selected time period.

MICROBJ BOX JENKINS FORECASTING
Version: na   *Last Updated:* 1993   *No. of Users:* na
Functions: fundamental analysis, statistics
Systems: DOS
Price: $149.95; 20% AAII discount
Return Policy: 30 days; 25% restocking fee
Technical Support: phone hours, 9 am-5 pm, M-F
Description: A time series forecasting system based on the Box-Jenkins methodology. Does not require programming experience. User can proceed through the data manipulation, analysis, graphics, and forecasting modules by using simple commands.

MICROCOMPUTER BOND PROGRAM
Version: na   *Last Updated:* na   *No. of Users:* na
Securities: bonds
Functions: bond analysis
Systems: DOS, Mac
Price: $59.95; 20% AAII discount
Return Policy: 30 days; 25% restocking fee
Technical Support: phone hours, 9 am-5 pm, M-F
Description: Estimates prices and yields of fixed-income securities under a broad range of assumptions. Makes estimates about the future.

MICROCOMPUTER CHART PROGRAM
Version: na   *Last Updated:* na   *No. of Users:* na

Securities: stocks, mutual funds, indexes
Functions: technical analysis
Systems: DOS, Mac
Price: $59.95; 20% AAII discount
Return Policy: 30 days; 25% restocking fee
Technical Support: phone hours, 9 am-5 pm, M-F
Description: Features price charts, volume bar charts, smoothed volume lines, up to 3 overlays, smoothed velocity (price change) line and on-balance volume using percentage price change.

MICROCOMPUTER STOCK PROGRAM
Version: na   *Last Updated:* na   *No. of Users:* na
Securities: stocks
Functions: technical analysis, statistics
Systems: DOS, Mac
Price: $59.95; 20% AAII discount
Return Policy: 30 days; 25% restocking fee
Technical Support: phone hours, 9 am-5 pm, M-F
Description: Gives buy and sell timing signals based on auto-regressive price trend analysis. Data required: weekly prices (high, low, close) and volume.

MONEY
Version: na   *Last Updated:* na   *No. of Users:* na
Securities: real estate
Functions: financial planning, real estate analysis
Systems: DOS
Price: $39.95; 20% AAII discount
Return Policy: 30 days; 25% restocking fee
Technical Support: phone hours, 9 am-5 pm, M-F
Description: Features interest and depreciation calculations as well as analysis of real estate sales and short-term loans.

MONEY DECISIONS
Version: na   *Last Updated:* na   *No. of Users:* na
Securities: stocks, bonds, mutual funds, indexes, real estate
Functions: financial planning, statistics
Systems: DOS
Price: $129.95; 20% AAII discount
Return Policy: 30 days; 25% restocking fee
Technical Support: phone hours, 9 am-5 pm, M-F

Description: Consists of 70 interactive problem-solving programs for investments, loans, business management, forecasting and graphics. A communications interface is provided along with 1 free hour of connect time to CompuServe.

MULTIVARIATE NON-LINEAR REGRESSION AND OPTIMIZER

Version: na   *Last Updated:* 1993   *No. of Users:* na
Functions: statistics
Systems:
Price: $99.95; 20% AAII discount
Return Policy: 30 days; 25% restocking fee
Technical Support: phone hours, 9 am-5 pm, M-F
Description: Allows user to apply regression and optimization to multi-dimensional non-linear problems. Also permits non-linear programming with a non-linear objective function. Non-linear constraint equations can be entered using the constraint editor. Constraints can include functions, multi-line statements and logical expressions. Fitting functions, objective functions, and constraints are all created using the MNLRO editor. Syntax used follows rules of BASIC. All standard functions are available (SIN, COS, SQR, LOG, power, etc.). All entries can be saved to disk files. Regresses up to 10 unknown coefficients for a data set of up to 10 dimensions by 300 data points. Can also locate the minimum and maximum for functions of up to 10 variables.

MULTIVARIATE REGRESSION ANALYSIS

Version: na   *Last Updated:* na   *No. of Users:* na
Functions: statistics
Systems: DOS
Price: $59.95; 20% AAII discount
Return Policy: 30 days; 25% restocking fee
Technical Support: phone hours, 9 am-5 pm, M-F
Description: A statistics package that complements Multilinear Regression (MLR). Along with the standard data editing, variable removal, etc., capabilities also include: reverse step-wise regression; up to 54 named variables (9,999 observations for 6 variables); tables of means, standard deviations, correlation coefficients, partial correlation coefficients; minimum, maximum, skewness and kurtosis for each variable. Does correlation eliminations (by calculating coefficients for cross terms, squares, cubes. Also includes calculated regression coefficients, beta coefficients, F ratios, R-squared; binary-to-decimal correction, (to avoid single/double precision data file loading problems);

double-precision square-root routine; correlation matrix inversion to reduce error and matrix inversion test for poorly conditioned data. Has inverse diagonal display; residual analysis with Durbin-Watson D; one-sided U statistics; scatterplot of residuals vs. dependent variable; plot of residual distribution compared with normal distribution; chi-square statistic; and probability plot of residuals (should be a straight line).

NUAMETRICS ECONOMETRIC ANALYSIS
Version: na   *Last Updated:* na   *No. of Users:* na
Functions: fundamental analysis, statistics
Systems: DOS
Price: $99.95; 20% AAII discount
Return Policy: 30 days; 25% restocking fee
Technical Support: phone hours, 9 am-5 pm, M-F
Description: Menu-driven economic analysis program. Uses single and multiple regression techniques for statistical analysis and forecasting. Features data management, seasonal adjustments and plotting in high resolution graphics. Uses VisiCalc and Lotus data files. Has menu options including creating, updating or deleting files, regression analysis, general statistics and residual analysis.

OPTIMIZER LINEAR PROGRAMMER
Version: na   *Last Updated:* na   *No. of Users:* na
Functions: linear programming
Systems: DOS
Price: $99.95
Return Policy: 30 days; 25% restocking fee
Technical Support: phone hours, 9 am-5 pm, M-F
Description: A disk-based linear programming system. Does not require knowledge of higher mathematics. Program can be used to solve problems in: production scheduling, personnel assignment, product buying, product pricing and personal finance. Also provides sensitivity analysis, including the shadow price (dual variable), range of resources over which the shadow prices are valid, slack quantities (helpful in further improving efficiency or costs), and stability (how sensitive the solution is to the objective function coefficients). Includes a manual containing tutorial information and examples.

OPTIONS ANALYSIS
Version: na   *Last Updated:* na   *No. of Users:* na

Securities: futures, options
Functions: options analysis
Systems: DOS
Price: $99.95; 20% AAII discount
Return Policy: 30 days; 25% restocking fee
Technical Support: phone hours, 9 am-5 pm, M-F
Description: Using the Black-Scholes formula, program determines the value of put and call options as a function of both stock price and time to expiration.

PC REGRESSION MULTIPLE REGRESSION

Version: na   *Last Updated:* na   *No. of Users:* na
Functions: statistics
Systems: DOS
Price: $99.95; 20% AAII discount
Return Policy: 30 days; 25% restocking fee
Technical Support: phone hours, 9 am-5 pm, M-F
Description: A statistical analysis tool that includes data file handling, transformation and selection capabilities. Reads data files created by PC Statistician and PC ANOVA, as well as standard DIF and ASCII files. Multiple regression function can treat up to 37 named variables, with simultaneous or stepwise forward and backward regression choices. The solution includes a complete ANOVA table, along with regression weights, t-test and p-values, partial R-squared, standard errors and predicted/residual scores. Missing data is allowed. The correlation module provides correlation and variance-covariance matrices, along with descriptive statistics and multiple and partial correlation. Twenty data transformations are available, including lead and lag for time series analysis, moving averages and exponential smoothing. User can create x-y plots directly from data files and perform interactive curve fitting. Plots can be saved to disk and printed.

PERSONAL BALANCE SHEET

Version: na   *Last Updated:* na   *No. of Users:* na
Functions: financial planning
Systems: DOS, Mac
Price: $29.95; 20% AAII discount
Return Policy: 30 days; 25% restocking fee
Technical Support: phone hours, 9 am-5 pm, M-F
Description: User creates a statement of financial position. Calculates total assets (cash, accounts receivable, stocks, bonds, real property,

etc.) and liabilities; includes debt/worth, current and acid test ratios. User can forecast changes in net worth based on changes in investments and liabilities.

PERSONAL COMPUTER AUTOMATIC INVESTMENT MANAGEMENT

Version: na   *Last Updated:* na   *No. of Users:* na
Securities: stocks
Functions: portfolio management
Systems: DOS
Price: $149.95; 20% AAII discount
Return Policy: 30 days; 25% restocking fee
Technical Support: phone hours, 9 am-5 pm, M-F
Description: Based on a concept developed by Robert Lichello in his book, "How to Make $1,000,000 Automatically." Enables user to create and maintain data files containing company/corporation name, number of shares, cash and interest earned. Calculates stock value, portfolio value, buy/sell, market orders and return on investment (ROI). Maintains current and historical records of all transactions for evaluation of investment performance.

PERSONAL FINANCE MANAGER

Version: na   *Last Updated:* na   *No. of Users:* na
Functions: financial planning
Systems: DOS, Mac
Price: $49.95; 20% AAII discount
Return Policy: 30 days; 25% restocking fee
Technical Support: phone hours, 9 am-5 pm, M-F
Description: Includes all features of Dynacomp's Personal Finance System plus several more for users with more complicated and extensive financial records. Up to 4 savings accounts and 4 checking accounts can be simultaneously maintained with the balance in each account automatically displayed in the menu mode. A cash account is included. Program can sort, search, and merge.

PERSONAL FINANCE PLANNER

Version: na   *Last Updated:* na   *No. of Users:* na
Securities: stocks, bonds, mutual funds, real estate
Functions: financial planning
Systems: DOS
Price: $29.95; 20% AAII discount

Return Policy: 30 days; 25% restocking fee
Technical Support: phone hours, 9 am-5 pm, M-F
Description: Prepares personal balance sheets, income statements and detailed financial analyses. Provides insurance, real estate, stocks, bonds, mutual funds and IRA analyses and projections. Facilitates the performance of complex "what if" projections to depict the long-term effects of changes in saving and spending patterns. Helps pinpoint problem areas and opportunities. Projections can be made for retirement or for any other time period.

PERSONAL FINANCE SYSTEM
Version: na   *Last Updated:* na   *No. of Users:* na
Functions: financial planning
Systems: DOS, Mac
Price: $39.95; 20% AAII discount
Return Policy: 30 days; 25% restocking fee
Technical Support: phone hours, 9 am-5 pm, M-F
Description: Keeps track of all tax-deductible items, bank deposits, monthly charges, cash payments, etc. Will automatically deduct any check fees if desired. Does financial summaries for any category on a per item, monthly or yearly basis. Will print the results in detail or summary form, access the printer and plot the results on a monthly bar graph.

PERSONAL REAL ESTATE MANAGER
Version: na   *Last Updated:* na   *No. of Users:* na
Securities: real estate
Functions: financial planning, real estate analysis
Systems: DOS
Price: $49.95; 20% AAII discount
Return Policy: 30 days; 25% restocking fee
Technical Support: phone hours, 9 am-5 pm, M-F
Description: A recordkeeping system for up to 10 properties. Organizes and automates the accounting tasks of the part-time landlord keeping track of all expenses by category, rent, security deposits and basic tenant information. Year-to-date summaries and status reports on profitability, cash flow and asset/liability/net worth are available.

PORTFOLIO DATA MANAGER
Version: na   *Last Updated:* na   *No. of Users:* na
Securities: stocks, bonds, mutual funds

Functions: portfolio management, technical analysis
Systems: DOS
Price: $99.95; 20% AAII discount
Return Policy: 30 days; 25% restocking fee
Technical Support: phone hours, 9 am-5 pm, M-F
Description: Records and monitors portfolio performance: stocks, bonds, mutual funds, CDs, cash, etc. Features include: recordkeeping of specific tax year files; monitoring portfolio performance as a whole; technical analysis including trendlines, moving averages, momentum rate of change curves, acceleration curves and relative strength graphs; and special data fields for other numeric information (e.g., P/E ratios, dividends, S&P ratings, etc.). User enters values directly from newspaper, including fractions and decimal prices. Saves up to 10 years for any security.

PORTFOLIO DECISIONS
Version: na   *Last Updated:* na   *No. of Users:* na
Securities: stocks, bonds, futures, mutual funds, indexes, options, real estate
Functions: portfolio management
Systems: DOS
Price: $149.95; 20% AAII discount
Return Policy: 30 days; 25% restocking fee
Technical Support: phone hours, 9 am-5 pm, M-F
Description: Helps organize, record, and evaluate investments. Program can communicate with DJN/R or CompuServe, allowing immediate updates of market prices, access to other CompuServe facilities and automatic daily updating of user's portfolio. Reports include: tax return interest report, dividend report, capital gains/losses report, portfolio activity detail summary, ticker reports, and monthly income forecast.

PORTFOLIO MANAGEMENT
Version: na   *Last Updated:* na   *No. of Users:* na
Functions: portfolio management
Systems: DOS
Price: $69.95; 20% AAII discount
Return Policy: 30 days; 25% restocking fee
Technical Support: phone hours, 9 am-5 pm, M-F
Description: User defines own investment categories for portfolio management. Has file sorting and plotting capabilities.

PORTFOLIO STATUS

Version: na   *Last Updated:* na   *No. of Users:* na
Securities: stocks, bonds, futures, mutual funds, indexes, options
Functions: portfolio management
Systems: DOS
Price: $29.95; 20% AAII discount
Return Policy: 30 days; 25% restocking fee
Technical Support: phone hours, 9 am-5 pm, M-F
Description: Generates analysis of security portfolios. User enters the name of each security, ticker symbol, number of shares, purchase date, and cost. To generate an analysis of the portfolio, the user enters the price of each security and the program computes the current market value, profit or loss, percent profit, days since purchase, and then computes totals.

PORTVIEW 2020

Version: na   *Last Updated:* na   *No. of Users:* na
Securities: stocks, bonds, futures, mutual funds, indexes, options, real estate
Functions: financial planning, portfolio management
Systems: DOS
Price: $79.95; 20% AAII discount
Return Policy: 30 days; 25% restocking fee
Technical Support: phone hours, 9 am-5 pm, M-F
Description: Combines recordkeeping, tax planning and investment analysis. Computes ROI for any investment—stocks, bonds, mutual funds, real estate, commodities, partnerships, options, etc.—with optional adjustments for taxes and inflation. Report for any list of holdings includes investment history, price history, net worth on any date and performance between any 2 dates.

PROPERTY MANAGER

Version: na   *Last Updated:* 1993   *No. of Users:* na
Functions: real estate analysis
Systems: DOS
Price: $299.95; 20% AAII discount
Return Policy: 30 days; 25% restocking fee
Technical Support: phone hours, 9 am-5 pm, M-F
Description: Integrated system that covers all facets of rental property management. Exceeds recommended minimum for computerized property management systems as established by the Institute of Real

Estate Management. Tenant record for each unit includes current and past occupant, along with related information, such as monthly rent, amount due, security deposits being held in escrow, move-in date, lease expiration date, mailing address, etc. Cash receipts are entered directly from user's bank deposit slip with all updating of the tenant's accounts and general ledger taken care of automatically.

RATIOS
Version: na   *Last Updated:* na   *No. of Users:* na
Functions: fundamental analysis
Systems: DOS
Price: $29.95; 20% AAII discount
Return Policy: 30 days; 25% restocking fee
Technical Support: phone hours, 9 am-5 pm, M-F
Description: Computes various financial ratios given certain financial data. Includes: net operating margin, ROA, ROE, current ratio, quick ratio, debt ratio, inventory turnover, times interest earned, fixed charges, coverage, funded debt to working capital, net working capital turnover and earnings per share.

REAL ESTATE RESIDENT EXPERT
Version: na   *Last Updated:* na   *No. of Users:* na
Securities: real estate
Functions: real estate analysis
Systems: DOS
Price: $99.95; 20% AAII discount
Return Policy: 30 days; 25% restocking fee
Technical Support: phone hours, 9 am-5 pm, M-F
Description: Analyzes single-family homes and fully estimates the factors that affect their value. Guides users through the decision-making process by asking questions regarding the type and condition of the foundation, faucets, sewer lines, electrical service, siding, insulation, heating, etc. Grades conditions on a scale of 1 to 10 and records and analyzes input.

STAMPDATA
Version: na   *Last Updated:* 1993   *No. of Users:* na
Functions: stamp collection valuation
Systems: DOS
Price: $39.95; both Coindata and Stampdata, $69.95; 20% AAII discount
Return Policy: 30 days; 25% restocking fee

Technical Support: phone hours, 9 am-5 pm, M-F
Description: Records various characteristics that describe user's stamp collections, searches for stamps having particular characteristics, computes totals, and prints in several formats.

STAMPS
Version: na   *Last Updated:* 1993   *No. of Users:* na
Functions: stamp collection valuation
Systems: DOS
Price: $49.95; 20% AAII discount
Return Policy: 30 days; 25% restocking fee
Technical Support: phone hours, 9 am-5 pm, M-F
Description: Covers all U.S. stamps indexed by the Scott Catalogue Numbers. Maintains a want list complete with prices. Records the date and price of new purchases. Calculates percentage profit of sales.

STOCKAID 4.0
Version: na   *Last Updated:* na   *No. of Users:* na
Securities: stocks
Functions: technical analysis
Systems: DOS
Price: $69.95; 20% AAII discount
Return Policy: 30 days; 25% restocking fee
Technical Support: phone hours, 9 am-5 pm, M-F
Description: Has enhanced graphics as well as the ability to automatically retrieve data from the DJN/R. Lets user maintain, view, and study the history and performance of up to 64 NYSE stocks on the same disk. Many graphical displays illustrate stock actions, trends, and indicators.

STOCK MARKET BARGAINS
Version: na   *Last Updated:* na   *No. of Users:* na
Securities: stocks
Functions: fundamental analysis
Systems: DOS
Price: $69.95; 20% AAII discount
Return Policy: 30 days; 25% restocking fee
Technical Support: phone hours, 9 am-5 pm, M-F
Description: Provides 2 tests for finding undervalued stocks: the Graham approach and a parameter test of price/earnings ratio, ratio of assets to liabilities, change in earnings per share, number of institutional

investors and current earnings per share. User can display and/or print all stocks satisfying tests 1 and 2, display complete data on file about any given stock, add new stocks for analysis at any time and update stocks already in data files.

STOCK MASTER/STOCK PLOT
Version: na   *Last Updated:* na   *No. of Users:* na
Securities: stocks, indexes
Functions: portfolio management, fundamental analysis
Systems:
Price: $59.95; 20% AAII discount
Return Policy: 30 days; 25% restocking fee
Technical Support: phone hours, 9 am-5 pm, M-F
Description: Helps record fiscal data, record stock transactions, and track price action on companies user selects. User may maintain records for up to 30 stocks; store 10 years of fiscal data for each stock and historical price data; maintain up to 8 portfolio files composed of any combination and any number of shares of the stocks tracked; record up to 20 buy/sell transactions for each of the stocks; calculate trailing P/E ratios for any stock with at least 4 quarters of earnings data entered; display the value of any of the portfolios maintained using the most recently entered price for each stock; plot the historical value of any portfolio as a percent of the first value plotted.

TIME SERIES/FORECASTING
Version: na   *Last Updated:* na   *No. of Users:* na
Functions: statistics
Systems: DOS
Price: $49.95; 20% AAII discount
Return Policy: 30 days; 25% restocking fee
Technical Support: phone hours, 9 am-5 pm, M-F
Description: A menu-driven package consisting of several programs for data file creation, editing, and analysis. Files may be examined using one of 3 trend models: linear, quadratic, or exponential. Detrended and detrended/deseasonalized data files can be set up while running the time series analysis and then tested using the autocorrelation routine.

WALL STREET TRAINER
Version: na   *Last Updated:* na   *No. of Users:* na
Securities: stocks, futures, options

Functions: simulation/game
Systems: DOS
Price: $29.95; 20% AAII discount
Return Policy: 30 days; 25% restocking fee
Technical Support: phone hours, 9 am-5 pm, M-F
Description: Simulates fast action, long or short trading in the stock and futures markets; 8 different types of put and call options may be traded on low margins. 1-2 users may compete. Users may choose to buy on price dips and sell on rallies or follow an extended bullish or bearish move that could get bigger or melt away. Teaches how to use optional real-world, automatic stop-loss orders to prevent large losses should the market move against user and how to use optional automatic take-profit orders.

XTRAPOLATOR TIME SERIES FORECASTS
Version: na   *Last Updated:* na   *No. of Users:* na
Functions: statistics
Systems: DOS
Price: $129.95; 20% AAII discount
Return Policy: 30 days; 25% restocking fee
Technical Support: phone hours, 9 am-5 pm, M-F
Description: A menu-driven multipurpose forecasting system. Features include: data management, forecast methods, automatic best-fit curve selector, and plotting in high-resolution graphics. Uses VisiCalc and Lotus data files. Includes selection of the forecast horizon, listing the historical plus forecast data, and the fitted values plus forecast. User may save the listings to a file and seasonally adjust data and forecast by a ratio to moving average method.

ZENTERPRISE REAL ESTATE INVESTOR
Version: na   *Last Updated:* na   *No. of Users:* na
Securities: real estate
Functions: real estate analysis
Systems: DOS
Price: $69.95; 20% AAII discount
Return Policy: 30 days; 25% restocking fee
Technical Support: phone hours, 9 am-5 pm, M-F
Description: User can calculate profitability of investment in real estate; compare the potential gains from different properties under various scenarios; change assumptions such as appreciation rate, depreciation term, rental income, maintenance expenses, etc; compute the

monthly before- and aftertax cash flows and the aftertax rate of return; and calculate the price in order to meet a chosen profitability goal. Each screen shows the financial projections for any 5-year period.

EDCO SOFTWARE CONCEPTS

75 Van Tassel Lane   (510) 254-7601
Orinda, CA 94563

THE INVESTOR'S EDGE
Version: 4.0   *Last Updated:* 1994   *No. of Users:* na
Securities: stocks, bonds, mutual funds, real estate
Functions: financial planning, portfolio management
Systems: DOS
Price: $49; 10% AAII discount
Return Policy: 30 days; $10 restocking fee
Technical Support: phone hours, 11:30 am-8:30 pm
Description: Handles 200 accounts of stocks, mutual funds, bonds, fixed dollar denominated, and appreciable dollar denominated investments (handles 396 investments per account). Provides a general notepad and a notepad for each account. Provides automatic assignment of investment file names. Records all investment transactions. Provides for automatic reinvestment of earnings. Screens and prints individual investment reports, portfolio reports with various breakdowns, asset allocation report, net worth statement, and others. Individual investment reports include a header of general information followed by a transaction section and a footer showing present price, present value, and gain or loss. Graphically presents risk balance in portfolio. Computes IRR of investments and portfolio. Updates price for all accounts from price register. Includes a calculator. Provides supplementary programs for bond duration calculation, loan amortization, six interest rate programs, and graphic presentation of stock prices versus the running average. Menus are of toggle down type. Contains a tutorial account and on screen guidelines. User's manual included.

ELECTROSONICS, INC.

36380 Garfield   (800) 858-8448
Suite 1   (810) 791-0770
Clinton Township, MI 48035   fax: (810) 791-3010

EXEC-AMORT LOAN AMORTIZER PLUS

Version: 2.05   *Last Updated:* 1989   *No. of Users:* na

Securities: real estate

Functions: financial planning, real estate analysis

Systems: DOS

Price: $149.95; demo available, $5 plus $5 shipping; 10% AAII discount

Return Policy: 60 days

Technical Support: phone hours, 9 am-5 pm, M-F; fee for tech support—$79.95

Description: Has loan amortization schedules with APRs. Includes fixed-rate and ARMs plus APRs with points and fees per U.S. regulation Z, balloon payments, prepaid interest calculations, solve for unknown, yields/IRR, present value and future value. Has 11 ways to schedule payments including biweekly; 6 ways to calculate payments; 360, 365, or 365/360 day interest calculations; 5 ways to schedule extra payments, credit and odd period interest calculations. Includes in-context help screens, calendar or fiscal-year reporting and optional report titles and comment section. Schedules loans to $100 trillion.

EMERGING MARKET TECHNOLOGIES, INC.

1230 Johnson Ferry Road   (404) 973-2300
Suite D10   fax: (404) 973-3003
Marietta, GA 30068

INVESTNOW!—PERSONAL

Version: 2.07   *Last Updated:* 1993   *No. of Users:* 3,000

Securities: stocks, mutual funds, indexes, options

Functions: futures analysis, options analysis, simulation/game

Systems: DOS

Price: $99; demo available, $49; 50% AAII discount

Return Policy: all sales final

Technical Support: phone hours, 9 am-5 pm, M-F; newsletter; fee for tech support—call

Description: A memory-resident program that determines a stock's return from its dividends and realized/unrealized profit or loss. Users can input actual brokerage fees or have the program provide "typical" commission rates on trades. Computes simple and annual returns on investments and applies applicable necessary margin requirements. The only option window included is covered calls.

INVESTNOW!—PROFESSIONAL

Version: 2.07   *Last Updated:* 1993   *No. of Users:* 3,500
Securities: stocks, futures, mutual funds, options
Functions: futures analysis, options analysis, simulation/game
Systems: DOS
Price: $195; 25% AAII discount
Return Policy: all sales final
Technical Support: phone hours, 9 am-5 pm, M-F; newsletter; fee for tech support—call
Description: A memory-resident program that analyzes the buying of calls and puts, the writing of naked and covered calls, and the writing of naked puts. Determines a stock's return from its dividends and realized/unrealized profit or loss. Users can input actual brokerage fees or have the program provide typical commission rates on trades. Computes simple and annual returns on investments and applies applicable necessary margin requirements.

ENGINEERING MANAGEMENT CONSULTANTS

P.O. Box 12518   (904) 668-0635
Tallahassee, FL 32317-2518

FOURCAST

Version: na   *Last Updated:* 1993   *No. of Users:* 500
Securities: stocks, bonds, futures, mutual funds, indexes, options, real estate
Functions: fundamental analysis, technical analysis, statistics
Systems: DOS, Windows
Price: $300; demo available, $5; 20% AAII discount
Return Policy: 30 days
Technical Support: phone hours, 9 am-4 pm, M-F
Description: A program for the analysis of multiple time series. Analyzes cycles, then combines and forecasts them to provide an indicator of change of direction. Features include: a user-oriented editor, interactive input, modem input, chronological data entry, easy updating, data transformations, high resolution graphics, forecasts over user-defined time periods, color graphics, keyboard macros, communications capability and the ability to read files in the Dial/Data format.

ENSIGN SOFTWARE

2641 Shannon Court
Idaho Falls, ID 83404

(800) 255-7374
(208) 524-0755
fax: (208) 525-8781

ENSIGN V
Version: 5.0   *Last Updated:* 1992   *No. of Users:* 1,000
Securities: stocks, bonds, futures, mutual funds, indexes, options
Functions: technical analysis, futures analysis, options analysis
Systems: DOS
Price: $1,295; demo available
Return Policy: all sales final
Technical Support: toll-free number; phone hours, 8 am-5 pm, M-F; fee
  for tech support—$10/month
Description: Plots real-time, intraday, and historical charts using the
Bonneville market information data stream. Technical analysis tools
include stochastics, relative strength index, moving averages, momentum, oscillator, Keltner Channel, directional movement index, volatility stop, parabolic stop, Fibonacci time and price, volume, open-inter-
est, swing lines, Gann angles and draw lines. Chart types are 1 to 600
minutes per bar, daily, weekly, and monthly. Other features include
hard copy printed charts, color, single key operation, backtesting, user
symbols and formulas.

EPIC SYSTEMS, CORP.

P.O. Box 277
Sierra Madre, CA 91025-0277

(818) 355-2988
fax: (818) 355-6162

NEURALYST FOR EXCEL
Version: 1.3   *Last Updated:* 1993   *No. of Users:* 1,000+
Securities: stocks, bonds, futures, mutual funds, indexes, options, real
  estate
Functions: technical analysis, spreadsheet, statistics, expert system,
  neural network
Systems: Windows, Mac
Special Requirements: Excel
Price: $195; 10% AAII discount
Return Policy: 30 days; shipping & handling restocking fee

Technical Support: phone hours, 12 pm-8 pm, M-F
Description: Provides neural network analysis capability for numeric data series. Data can be stock prices, indexes, option prices, futures, valuation data, macroeconomic data, etc., in any combination. Program will learn from historical examples and identify patterns and relationships that may lead to successful predictions for future data. All Excel functions, macros and charts remain accessible for data pre- and post-processing. Includes a supplemental Traders Macro Library that facilitates the inclusion of a number of popular technical analysis indicators (moving averages, oscillators, momentum, RSI, stochastics, etc.) for the user's analysis.

NEURALYST PRO FOR EXCEL
Version: 1.0   *Last Updated:* 1994   *No. of Users:* 100+
Securities: stocks, bonds, futures, mutual funds, indexes, options, real estate
Functions: spreadsheet, statistics, expert system, neural network
Systems: Windows, Mac
Price: $495; 10% AAII discount
Return Policy: 30 days; shipping & handling restocking fee
Technical Support: phone hours, 12 pm-8 pm, M-F
Description: Provides high performance neural network analysis capability for numeric data series. Neuralyst Pro is an extended version of Neuralyst with many powerful enhancements, including: genetic training, accelerated training, multiple neural network paradigms and more. Data can be stock prices, indexes, option prices, futures valuation data, macroeconomic data, etc., in any combination. Neuralyst Pro will learn from historical examples and identify patterns and relationships that may lead to successful predictions for future data. All Excel functions, macros, and charts remain accessible for data pre- and post-processing. Includes a supplemental trader's macro library that facilitates the inclusion of a number of popular technical analysis indicators (moving averages, oscillators, momentum, RSI, stochastics, etc.) for the user's analysis.

EQUIS INTERNATIONAL

3950 South 700 E.   (800) 882-3040
Suite 100   (801) 265-8886
Salt Lake City, UT 84107   fax: (801) 265-3999

THE DOWNLOADER

Version: 3.5 *Last Updated:* 1994 *No. of Users:* na
Securities: stocks, bonds, futures, mutual funds, indexes, options
Functions: utility software
Systems: DOS
Special Requirements: modem
Price: $99; Dial/Data specific version $49; Signal specific version, $49;
  CompuServe specific version, $49
Return Policy: 60 days
Technical Support: phone hours, 10 am-7 pm, M-F; BBS support; news-
  letter
Description: Stock market data collection program for historical and
end-of-day price quotes to be used with MetaStock or compatible pro-
grams. Accesses five different data vendors to collect stock, bond,
commodity, index, options, and mutual fund information. Collect data
needed from CompuServe, Dial/Data, DJN/R, Market Scan or Signal.
Features include 1200-, 2400-, or 9600-baud rate, unattended operation, complete mouse support and a graphical user interface with dialog boxes, auto-dial and redial, simple-to-create keyboard macros for
complete program automation, custom modem configurations and a
built-in telephone directory for vendor numbers.

METASTOCK

Version: 4.5 *Last Updated:* 1994 *No. of Users:* 30,000
Securities: stocks, bonds, futures, mutual funds, indexes, options
Functions: technical analysis, options analysis, statistics
Systems: DOS
Price: $349; demo available, $5; 10% AAII discount
Return Policy: 60 days
Technical Support: phone hours, 10 am-7 pm, M-F; BBS support; newsletter
Description: Studies the relationships between securities' price movement, past price, and volume. Includes more than 75 pre-programmed
technical indicators to analyze stocks, bonds, commodities, futures, indexes, mutual funds, or options. Contains over 75 math and statistical
functions for creating custom indicators and formulas. Has graphical
interface with full mouse support. Can display up to 50 charts simultaneously for comparison of securities, indexes, and studies with up to
1,000 days, weeks, or months of data. Smart Charts remembers all of
the details of each chart created. Page layouts let user group any number of charts together for future reference. Prints high-resolution

charts. Learn-as-you-plot mode allows user to study the data, make trading decisions, and then advance that chart one day at a time to simulate real trading. Has system tester with automatic optimization to backtest and fine-tune trading strategies. Compatible with more than 60 national and international data services. With additional software, such as EQUIS International's The DownLoader, users can automatically collect daily, weekly, and monthly price quotes.

METASTOCK RT
Version: 4.0 *Last Updated:* 1993 *No. of Users:* na
Securities: stocks, bonds, futures, mutual funds, indexes, options
Functions: technical analysis, futures analysis, options analysis, simulation/game, statistics
Systems: DOS
Special Requirements: 2M expanded memory; math co-processor recommended
Price: $495; demo available, $5; 10% AAII discount
Return Policy: 60 days
Technical Support: phone hours, 10 am-7 pm, M-F; BBS support; newsletter
Description: Provides all of MetaStock's features and capabilities in real-time. Users can track securities in any time period: tick charts, 1-, 2- and 5-minute bars, and more. Automatically updates and recalculates all charts, formulas and indicators in real-time as new price information is received. The Most Actives screen lets users see the top gainers, losers, and volume on the NYSE, OTC, and among stock options. Lets users set their own price and volume alert levels. The customizable quote table helps users track price and volume information for over 500 different securities. Provides up-to-the-minute prices on more than 55,000 securities from nearly any market through the DBC Signal datafeed.

PULSE PORTFOLIO MANAGEMENT SYSTEM
Version: 1.1 *Last Updated:* 1991 *No. of Users:* 3,600
Securities: stocks, bonds, futures, mutual funds, options, real estate
Functions: portfolio management, simulation/game, statistics
Systems: DOS
Price: $195; demo available, trial version $49; 10% AAII discount
Return Policy: 60 days
Technical Support: phone hours, 10 am-7 pm, M-F; BBS support; newsletter

Description: Tracks stocks, options, bonds, futures, mutual funds, money market accounts, CDs, mortgages, collectibles, Treasury bills, real estate, zeros, and precious metals. Offers complete accounting for cash and cash equivalent accounts, automatic reinvestment of dividends and distributions, splits, margin, short sales and tax lots. Has more than 80 pre-programmed calculations including accrued interest, annualized return, beta, yield, yield to call, yield to maturity, cost tax basis, liquidation value and estimated income. Monthly events calendar lets user see important investment activities at a glance with a pop-up detailed report of day's events including dividends expected, maturities, expirations, future income, and transactions. Reports include holdings, diversification, fixed income, realized gains/losses, income received, expenses paid, portfolios summary, price alerts. All can be customized spreadsheet-like into hundreds of combinations. User can update portfolios manually or automatically retrieve current price data from Signal, CompuServe, DJN/R, Dial/Data, Market Scan, ASCII files or MetaStock. Supports international date/numeric formats and securities quoted in foreign currencies.

THE TECHNICIAN

Version: 5.2   *Last Updated:* 1991   *No. of Users:* 4,500
Securities: indexes
Functions: technical analysis, statistics
Systems: DOS
Price: $249; modem updating service $120/year; demo available, $5; 15% AAII discount
Return Policy: 60 days
Technical Support: phone hours, 10 am-7 pm, M-F; BBS support; newsletter
Description: Graphics-oriented program that analyzes the stock market to anticipate price changes. Offers more than 100 specialized indicators and studies that chart momentum, sentiment, monetary and relative strength conditions of the market. Offers composite indicators and formulas to enable users to custom design their own indicators. Contains more than 14 years of daily historical data. Includes daily stock and index averages, STIX, TRIN, short- and long-term interest rates, precious metals and foreign currencies. Users can manually update data or use an on-line database. Each chart can display up to 1,000 days of data, and as many as 36 high-resolution charts can be displayed on the screen simultaneously. Users can test their trading systems and define conditions that generate buy/sell signals. The pro-

gram then displays buy/sell arrows on the chart and shows the amount of money that would be made or lost.

ERGO, INC.

1419 Wyant Road   (800) 772-6637
Santa Barbara, CA 93108   (805) 969-9366

BONDSEYE
Version: 2.1   *Last Updated:* 1986   *No. of Users:* na
Securities: bonds
Functions: bond analysis
Systems: DOS, Windows
Price: $65
Return Policy: all sales final
Technical Support: phone hours, 12 pm-8 pm, M-F
Description: A bond and money market instrument calculator. Functions provided are yield to maturity/call, price from yield, yield with external reinvestment rates, swap analysis, duration, accrued interest, dollar extensions, T-bill discount rate/pricing, equivalent bond yield, net present value, future value, sum of coupons, interest-on-interest, accretion schedules, convertible bond analysis, effective par rates, crossover yield/price and calendar functions. Analyzes odd first/second coupons, long/short accrued interest periods, redemption of principal after last coupon, premium amortization and unusual pay frequencies. Issue types include corporate, municipal, and T-bonds, Treasury bills, CDs, repos, the bankers' acceptances, commercial paper and money market funds.

E-SENTIAL SOFTWARE

P.O. Box 41705   (213) 257-2524
Los Angeles, CA 90041

FOLIOMAN
Version: 2.0   *Last Updated:* 1994   *No. of Users:* na
Securities: stocks, bonds, mutual funds, indexes, options, real estate, collectibles

Functions: financial planning, portfolio management, technical analysis, bond analysis, options analysis, simulation/game, statistics
Systems: DOS
Price: $89; demo available, $5 toward purchase; 10% AAII discount
Return Policy: all sales final
Technical Support: phone hours, 12 pm-8 pm, M-F
Description: FolioMan is a portfolio manager with pulldown menus, mouse, and scrollable multi-windows. Data can be entered for stocks, bonds, mutual funds, options, dividends, interest, reinvestments, capital gains and other aspects of investing. An unlimited number of portfolios may be tracked. Investments may be viewed, evaluated, graphed, and compared via a variety of available reports. Each view contains information such as realized and unrealized gains or losses, internal and total rate of return, annualized rate of return, asset allocation, price histories, price alerts, investment income and expense, tax reports, and more. All of the views are available for a single portfolio or a group of portfolios, as well as for a single issue or a group of issues. Investment performance can be compared to your choice of market indexes. All of the reports and graphs are printable. FolioMan has a built-in communications program that automatically downloads current prices from CompuServe. FolioMan can also import prices from a number of sources, including Prodigy, FFN, Dial/Data, and other ASCII (Text based) Supercharts, TC2000, Investor's FastTrack, and Megatech charting programs. Prices may also be updated manually.

FOLIOMAN+
Version: 2.0   *Last Updated:* 1994   *No. of Users:* na
Securities: stocks, bonds, futures, mutual funds, indexes, options, real estate, collectibles
Functions: financial planning, portfolio management, technical analysis, bond analysis, futures analysis, options analysis, simulation/game, statistics
Systems: DOS
Price: $129; demo available, $5 toward purchase; 10% AAII discount
Return Policy: all sales final
Technical Support: phone hours, 12 pm-8 pm, M-F
Description: Portfolio manager includes pulldown menus, mouse and scrollable multi-windows. Data entry for stocks, bonds, mutual funds, options, futures, dividends, interest, reinvestments, capital gains and other aspects of investing. Can track an unlimited number of portfo-

lios and view, rate, and compare investments in 40 ways. Each view contains information such as realized and unrealized gains or losses, internal and total rate of return, annualized rate of return, asset allocation, price histories, price alerts, investment income and expense, tax reports, and more. All views are available for a single portfolio or group of portfolios or a single issue or a group of issues. Compares investment performance to market indexes such as Dow Jones, S&P 500, etc. All of the reports and graphs are printable. FolioMan has a built-in communications program that automatically downloads current prices from CompuServe. FolioMan can also import prices from a number of sources, including Prodigy, FFN, Dial/Data and any other ASCII (text-based) source. Your can also directly import current prices from MetaStock, Surpercharts, TC2000, Investor's FastTrack, and Megatech charting programs. Prices may also be updated manually.

ESSENTIALSOFTWARE, CORP.

1126 South 70th Street   (414) 475-3450
Suite 422A   fax: (414) 475-3578
West Allis, WI 53214

ADVANCED BUSINESS VALUATION
Version: 3.3   *Last Updated:* 1994   *No. of Users:* na
Securities: stocks
Functions: fundamental analysis, real estate analysis
Systems: DOS
Price: $295; demo available, $15; 50% AAII discount
Return Policy: 30 days
Technical Support: phone hours, 10 am-5 pm, M-F; fee for tech support—$25/year or hourly
Description: System for determining the value of a business for buy/sell purposes, stock offerings, etc. Performs financial statement analysis and forecasting with 3-dimensional graphics and a variety of valuation techniques. The program also provides a report writer which generates an overview report of valuation results.

FINANCIAL STATEMENT ANALYZER
Version: 3.0   *Last Updated:* 1994   *No. of Users:* na
Functions: fundamental analysis
Systems: DOS

Price: $89; 50% AAII discount
Return Policy: 30 days
Technical Support: phone hours, 10 am-5 pm, M-F; fee for tech support—$25/year or hourly
Description: Produces 79 business/financial ratios. Evaluates liquidity, profitability, efficiency, solvency, and investment potential. Includes ratio explanations. Calculates dollar and percent variances between alternatives. Results graphically illustrated. Allows user to add footnotes, disclaimers, headings, and comparable industry ratios.

FINANCIAL STATEMENT CASH FLOW FORECASTER
Version: 1.05   *Last Updated:* 1994   *No. of Users:* na
Functions: financial planning, fundamental analysis
Systems: DOS
Price: $89; 50% AAII discount
Return Policy: 30 days
Technical Support: phone hours, 10 am-5 pm, M-F; fee for tech support—$25/year or hourly
Description: Creates financial statements in user-defined formats. Includes aging schedules, subworksheets and accumulation of values. Creates relationships between accounts and performs analyses for up to 60 periods. Instant access provided to 60 ratios and pre-defined or user-defined graphs.

ESSEX TRADING COMPANY, LTD.

24 W. 500 Maple Avenue   (800) 726-2140
Suite 108   (708) 416-3530
Naperville, IL 60540   fax: (708) 416-3558

FUTURES PRO
Version: 22   *Last Updated:* 1994   *No. of Users:* na
Securities: futures
Functions: technical analysis, futures analysis
Systems: Windows
Special Requirements: Windows 3.1+; Hayes compatible modem
Price: $595-$15,000 depending on number of markets/logics enabled; call for AAII discount
Return Policy: all sales final

Technical Support: phone hours, 9 am-6 pm, M-F; BBS support; newsletter

Description: Futures Pro is an end-of-day Windows-based trading system giving its user daily trading recommendations for all markets enabled within the user-customized portfolio. The trading logic for the
system is fully disclosed to the user. You will receive specific entry and
exit prices, as well as intraday stop and reversal prices on up to 53 of
the world's futures markets. In addition to those markets activated
within your portfolio, 15 years of actual daily price data is included for
all futures markets at no additional charge. Additional market cover-
ages can be added to your Futures Pro at any time. They can either be
sent via overnight delivery or downloaded directly from Essex's proprietary Traders' Lounge BBS. You may choose any or all trading models covering short-, medium-, or long-term holding periods (3-45 day
average). Parameter sets can be changed to fit personal trading style;
Futures Pro generates its disciplined trading signals based upon chosen variables.

OPTION PRO
Version: 1.2   *Last Updated:* 1994   *No. of Users:* na
Securities: indexes, options
Functions: technical analysis, options analysis
Systems: Windows
Special Requirements: Windows 3.1+
Price: $795; call for AAII discount
Return Policy: all sales final
Technical Support: phone hours, 9 am-6 pm, M-F; BBS support; news-
letter

Description: Option Pro gives specific buy and sell, entry and exit recommendations for the world's largest index product—the OEX, using
only end-of-day data. Signals are generated from any of five trading
models. Four models (momentum, relative strengh, volatility, and
TRIN) suggest the purchase of either puts or calls. Each model may
identify a different OEX series to enter. The trades are monitored on a
daily basis, and position flattening occurs automatically before time
decay begins to affect profitability. The sell premium model recommends the simultaneous selling of puts and calls to take advantage of
time erosion. The trading logic is fully disclosed to the user.

OPTION PRO SE (SPECIAL EDITION)
Version: 1.2   *Last Updated:* 1994   *No. of Users:* na

Securities: indexes, options
Functions: technical analysis, options analysis
Systems: Windows
Special Requirements: Windows 3.1+
Price: $295; call for AAII discount
Return Policy: all sales final
Technical Support: phone hours, 9 am-6 pm M-F; BBS support; news-
    letter
Description: Option Pro SE includes evaluation tools for both equities
and index options using tick-by-tick, delayed, or end-of-day data.
Over- and undervalued options in the Static evaluation routine can be
identified with either the Black-Scholes or binomial pricing models. A
pop-up window automatically calculates series volatility and "Greek"
variables. The Dynamic Evaluation routine graphs your options portfolio (including hedges), to plan in advance for changes in volatility,
interest rates, and underlying price or to see the effects of time decay
on positions. The Options Pro SE also contains "what-if" capabilities
in its TradeFinder routine. Based on user's future scenario of any equity or index, and trading strategies, TradeFinder interfaces with the
other internal routines and lists in ranked order up to 50 best trades.
The OEX Daily Trading Signal Module can be added to the SE at any
time. It presents specific end-of-day OEX buy/sell entry and exit signals. The trades recommended are generated from any of five trading
models. The logic behind this module is fully disclosed to the user.

ESTIMA

1800 Sherman Avenue   (800) 822-8038
Suite 301   (708) 864-8772
Evanston, IL 60201   fax: (708) 864-6221

MACRATS
Version: 4.0   *Last Updated:* 1992   *No. of Users:* na
Functions: fundamental analysis, statistics
Systems: Mac
Price: $300; demo available, $40
Return Policy: all sales final
Technical Support: phone hours, 11 am-7 pm, M-F; BBS support; news-
    letter
Description: A tool for analysis of time series data. Combines all of the

most commonly used forecasting techniques: Box-Jenkins (ARIMA), exponential smoothing, vector autoregressions, and spectral analysis with time series graphics. Also includes full econometrics and regression capabilities, complete structured programming language (IF-ELSE, DO, WHILE, etc.), and matrix language. Has special support for daily and weekly data, and data with multiple observations per day.

MACRATS 020
Version: 4.0   *Last Updated:* 1992   *No. of Users:* na
Functions: fundamental analysis, statistics
Systems: Mac
Price: $400; demo available, $40
Return Policy: all sales final
Technical Support: phone hours, 11 am-7 pm, M-F; BBS support; newsletter
Description: A tool for analysis of time series data. Combines all of the most commonly used forecasting techniques: Box-Jenkins (ARIMA), exponential smoothing, vector autoregressions, and spectral analysis with time series graphics. Also includes full econometrics and regression capabilities, complete structured programming language (IF-ELSE, DO, WHILE, etc.), and matrix language. Has special support for daily and weekly data, and data with multiple observations per day.

RATS
Version: 4.0   *Last Updated:* 1992   *No. of Users:* na
Functions: fundamental analysis, statistics
Systems: DOS
Price: $300; demo available, $40; 10% AAII discount
Return Policy: all sales final
Technical Support: phone hours, 11 am-7 pm, M-F; BBS support; newsletter
Description: A tool for analysis of time series data. Combines all of the most commonly used forecasting techniques: Box-Jenkins (ARIMA), exponential smoothing, vector autoregressions, and spectral analysis with time series graphics. Also includes full econometrics and regression capabilities, complete structured programming language (IF-ELSE, DO, WHILE, etc.), and matrix language. Has special support for daily and weekly data, and data with multiple observations per day.

RATS (FOR UNIX)
Version: 4.0   *Last Updated:* 1992   *No. of Users:* na

Functions: fundamental analysis, statistics,
Systems: Unix
Special Requirements: ANSI C compatible compiler
Price: call
Return Policy: all sales final
Technical Support: BBS support; newsletter
Description: A tool for analysis of time series data. Combines all of the most commonly used forecasting techniques: Box-Jenkins (ARIMA), exponential smoothing, vector autoregressions, and spectral analysis, with time series graphics. Also includes full econometrics and regression capabilities, complete structured programming language (IF-ELSE, DO, WHILE, etc.), and matrix language. Has special support for daily and weekly data, and data with multiple observations per data.

RATS 386
Version: 4.0   *Last Updated:* 1992   *No. of Users:* na
Functions: fundamental analysis, statistics
Systems: DOS
Special Requirements: 386+
Price: $420; demo available, $40
Return Policy: all sales final
Technical Support: phone hours, 11 am-7 pm, M-F; BBS support; newsletter
Description: A tool for analysis of time series data. Combines all of the most commonly used forecasting techniques: Box-Jenkins (ARIMA), exponential smoothing, vector autoregressions, and spectral analysis with time series graphics. Also includes full econometrics and regression capabilities, complete structured programming language (IF-ELSE, DO, WHILE, etc.), and matrix language. Has special support for daily and weekly data, and data with multiple observations per day.

FIDELITY INVESTMENTS

82 Devonshire Street   (800) 544-0246
R20A   fax: (617) 728-7257
Boston, MA 02190

FIDELITY ON-LINE XPRESS
Version: 2.1   *Last Updated:* 1993   *No. of Users:* na
Securities: stocks, bonds, mutual funds, indexes, options

Functions: financial planning, portfolio management, technical analysis

Systems: DOS

Special Requirements: modem, Fidelity brokerage or mutual fund account

Price: $49.95; demo available

Return Policy: 30 days

Technical Support: toll-free number; phone hours, 8 am-11:30 pm, M-Sat.

Description: With FOX the customer can trade and get real time quotes (quick or expanded) on common and preferred stocks listed on the New York Stock Exchange, American Stock Exchange, all regional exchanges and Nasdaq, options on all listed and Nasdaq stocks and most major indexes and lastly on all mutual funds available through FundsNetwork. FundsNetwork includes 1,500 funds from nearly 100 fund companies, and over 200 no-transaction fee funds from Benham, Berger, Evergreen, Founders, Janus, Neuberger & Berman, SteinRoe, and Strong. In addition, customers can get automatic updates of brokerage and mutual fund account balances, monitor the performances of these investments, download detailed account transaction data including check and credit card transactions for U.S.A. customers, track asset by tax lot, obtain capital gains reports, prepare information in schedule D format and export data to other programs for further analysis. Research can be conducted using the news and analysis services of Telescan, DJN/R and S&P MarketScope. Through these optional services, customers can receive in-depth company news, historical quotes, investment screening, graphics capabilities and more.

FIDELITY RETIREMENT PLANNING THINKWARE

Version: 1.0   *Last Updated:* 1994   *No. of Users:* 20,000

Functions: financial planning

Systems: DOS

Special Requirements: 5M free disk space

Price: $15 plus $2.50 shipping & handling

Return Policy: 30 days

Technical Support: toll-free number; phone hours, 24 hours

Description: Helps lay the foundation for user's retirement plan. The interactive program starts with an overview of key concepts such as: saving for retirement, inflation, compounding, tax deferral and dollar-cost averaging, the cost of delaying, diversification, and asset allocation. The program is designed for investors just getting started on retirement planning as well as those who are well on their way. The user guide, with simple step-by-step instructions, makes it easy to install and use.

FINANCIAL DATA CENTER

(formerly Financial Data, Corp.)

P.O. Box 1332   (215) 527-5216
Bryn Mawr, PA 19010   fax: (215) 527-5226

FINANCIAL PLANNING TOOLKIT
Version: 4.0   *Last Updated:* 1994   *No. of Users:* 6,000
Securities: stocks, bonds, mutual funds, real estate
Functions: financial planning, portfolio management, bond analysis
Systems: DOS
Price: $249; 20% AAII discount
Return Policy: 30 days
Technical Support: phone hours, 9 am-5 pm, M-F; fee for tech support—$70/year optional
Description: A menu-driven stand-alone collection of 49 templates. Enter personal data and these templates perform calculations in 7 major areas. Investments template determines the performance of stocks, bonds, T-bills and stock rights. Inflation template examines the effects of inflation on capital, assets, income, investments, IRAs and college savings plans. Real Estate template computes mortgage payments, amortization, refinancing and holding period returns. Insurance template calculates life insurance, net costs, death benefits and rates of return. Budgeting generates reports on income and expenses, dividend and interest income and monthly cash flow. Net Worth template determines current and projected net worth. Financial Goals template evaluates financial position in light of goals, including educational funding and retirement.

FINANCIAL NAVIGATOR INTERNATIONAL

254 Polaris Avenue   (800) 468-3636
Mountain View, CA 94043   (415) 962-0300
                                                       fax: (415) 962-0730

FINANCIAL NAVIGATOR FOR DOS

Version: 5.2   *Last Updated:* 1993   *No. of Users:* na

Securities: stocks, bonds, mutual funds, options, real estate, user-defined

Functions: financial planning, portfolio management, options analysis, real estate analysis

Systems: DOS

Price: $249; demo available, $10; 10% AAII discount

Return Policy: 30 days; restocking fee varies

Technical Support: phone hours, 11 am-8 pm, M-F; newsletter; fee for technical support—per incident

Description: Provides financial management for users with complex financial situations—investors with marketable securities, owners of real estate or oil and gas interests, trusts, non-profits, and estates, and business owners filing Schedule C. Combines double-entry bookkeeping with a simple method of data entry. Handles multiple businesses, cash flow planning and multiple equity accounts. Provides a full audit trail, summarizes information for income tax preparation and tracks investments. Produces over 60 different reports, including balance sheets, income statements, and tax summaries. Handles 2,500 accounts, 10,000 payees/payors and account balances up to $2 billion. Tracks executive stock options and working interest. Includes a cost-basis balance sheet and securities portfolio analysis. Version 5.2 is a DOS application that is fully capable of running under the MS Windows environment and features a graphical user interface with full mouse support, pulldown menus, pop-up lists and dialog boxes.

FINANCIAL NAVIGATOR FOR WINDOWS

Version: 6.0   *Last Updated:* 1994   *No. of Users:* na

Securities: stocks, bonds, mutual funds, options, real estate

Functions: financial planning, portfolio management, options analysis, real estate analysis

Systems: Windows

Price: $349; 10% AAII discount

Return Policy: 30 days; restocking fee varies

Technical Support: phone hours, 11 am-8 pm, M-F; newsletter; fee for technical support—per incident

Description: Provides financial management for users with complex financial situations—-investors with marketable securities, owners of real estate or oil and gas interests, trusts, non-profits, and estates, and business owners filing Schedule C. Combines double-entry bookkeeping with a simple method of data entry. Handles multiple businesses, cash flow planning and multiple equity accounts. Provides a full audit trail, summarizes information for income tax preparation and tracks investments. Produces over 60 different reports, including balance sheets, income statements and tax summaries. Handles 2,500 accounts, 10,000 payees/payors and account balances up to $2 billion. Tracks executive stock options and working interest. Includes a cost-basis balance sheet and securities portfolio analysis. Version 6.0 is a Windows application that is fully capable of running under the MS Windows environment and features a graphical user interface with full mouse support, pulldown menus, pop-up lists, and dialog boxes.

NAVIGATOR ACCESS II
Version: 2.0   *Last Updated:* 1992   *No. of Users:* na
Securities: stocks, bonds, mutual funds, options
Functions: quote utility
Systems: DOS, Windows
Price: $199 (which includes ProComm)
Return Policy: 30 days; restocking fee varies
Technical Support: phone hours, 11 am-8 pm, M-F; newsletter; fee for
   technical support—per incident
Description: Enables user to automatically obtain current and historical marketable securities prices for quick updating of portfolios. Allows access to a variety of on-line pricing services including: CompuServe, Dial/Data, DJN/R, Interactive Data, and Prodigy. Able to download over 60,000 common and preferred stocks, warrants, mutual funds, corporate bonds, municipal bonds, and traded options using Interactive Data on-line services. Can be used in conjunction with Financial Navigator or as a stand-alone program.

FINANCIAL SYSTEMS SOFTWARE (FSS), LTD.

(formerly Financial Infotec U.K., Ltd.)
2 London Wall Bldgs.   (44-71) 628-4200
London Wall
LondonEC2M-5PP, UK

UNIVERSAL EXOTICS ADD-IN
Version: 2.3   *Last Updated:* 1993   *No. of Users:* na
Securities: bonds, futures, options

Functions: financial planning, portfolio management, bond analysis, futures analysis, options analysis, spreadsheet, simulation/game, statistics

Systems: DOS, Windows, Windows NT, OS/2, Mac

Price: $223.50-$477; demo available, free (full working version); 10% AAII discount

Return Policy: 30 days

Description: Calculates exotic option prices and sensitivities using both a flexible proprietary Monte Carlo simulation algorithm and closed form solutions. Exotic options handled include average price (Asian), barrier (knock-out and knock-ins), compound, contingent, ladder and lookback options on bonds, commodities, currencies, futures, and shares (including constant dividend streams and discrete dividend payments). Either individual or portfolios of options are handled.

UNIVERSAL OPTIONS ADD-IN

Version: 6.0   *Last Updated:* 1993   *No. of Users:* na

Securities: bonds, futures, options

Functions: financial planning, portfolio management, bond analysis, futures analysis, options analysis, spreadsheet, simulation/game, statistics

Systems: DOS, Windows, Windows NT, OS/2, Mac

Price: $223.50-$477; demo available, free (full working version); 10% AAII discount

Return Policy: 30 days

Description: Calculates option prices using the Black, Black-Scholes, Garman-Kolhagen and the Cox-Rubenstein models for European and American style options. It handles options on bonds, commodities, currencies, futures, and shares (including constant dividend streams and discrete dividend payments). Calculates implied volatilities and sensitivities, such as delta, gamma, fugit, kappa, rho, and theta2. Also contains cumulative normal function that enables the production of pricing matrix, risk return profiles and implied volatility analysis for either individual or portfolios of options.

UNIVERSAL SWAP ADD-IN

Version: 6.5   *Last Updated:* 1993   *No. of Users:* na

Securities: bonds, futures, options

Functions: financial planning, portfolio management, bond analysis, futures analysis, options analysis, spreadsheet, simulation/game, statistics

Systems: DOS, Windows, Windows NT, OS/2, Mac

Price: $749.25-$1,498.50; demo available, free (full working version); 10% AAII discount

Return Policy: 30 days

Description: Multi-currency interest rate swap add-in. Builds a term structure of interest rates and a volatility curve for each currency being monitored using a flexible curve fitting algorithm. Functions include swap, FRA, IRG, cap, collar, floor, zero-curve and discount factor functions which gives maximum flexibility to quantify both standard and non-standard transactions. Ability to check prices being quoted by the counterparty. Multi-currency portfolios of swaps, FRAs, IRGs, caps, collars, and floors are continuously marked to market.

UNIVERSAL YIELD ADD-IN

Version: 2.21   *Last Updated:* 1993   *No. of Users:* na

Securities: bonds, futures, options

Functions: financial planning, portfolio management, bond analysis, futures analysis, options analysis, spreadsheet, simulation/game, statistics

Systems: DOS, Windows, Windows NT, OS/2, Mac

Price: $223.50-$477; demo available, free (full working version); 10% AAII discount

Return Policy: 30 days

Description: A yield calculator that handles international fixed-income products including MTNs, deferred, long or short first coupon bonds as well as bonds callable between coupon dates. Works out standard AIBD yields (both annual and semiannual), hedges (even when instruments have a different number of payments per annum), repos, money market yields on all instuments (which can be compared directly with Libor), duration and convexity. Holidays and weekends are taken into account for bonds in their final coupon period. Can set up international fixed-income portfolios, with yield, duration, and convexity analysis using spreadsheets. Has a cash flow analyzer for swaps, projects, loans, and esoteric instruments. Provides ability to construct risk/return profiles on arbitrage trades as well as models of bond futures and provides flexible trading system. Yields can be calculated for Australian bonds, JGBs, Swedish money market instruments, UK glits, U.S. bills, U.S. treasuries, Yankees, etc.

UNIVERSAL ZERO-CURVE ADD-IN
Version: 2.0   *Last Updated:* 1993   *No. of Users:* na
Securities: bonds, futures, options
Functions: financial planning, portfolio management, bond analysis, futures analysis, options analysis, spreadsheet, simulation/game, statistics
Systems: DOS, Windows, Windows NT, OS/2, Mac
Price: $223.50-$477; demo available, free (full working version); 10% AAII discount
Return Policy: 30 days
Description: Analyzes multiple cash flows against one or more zero-curves. Contains an interpolating lookup function (straight line or cubic splinning) which has a wide variety of uses, including calculating forward FX rates, swap rates and forward commodity rates. Zero-curves are entered by the user or calculated using the Universal Swap Add-in. Can co-exist with the Universal Exotics, Options, Swap and Yield Add-ins, providing the ability to create complex models combining bonds, bond futures, options, and swaps.

FINANCIOMETRICS, INC.

P.O. Box 1788   (510) 254-9338
Lafayette, CA 94549   fax: (510) 254-2932

QOS-30
Version: 2.0   *Last Updated:* 1993   *No. of Users:* na
Securities: stocks, bonds, mutual funds, indexes
Functions: financial planning, statistics
Systems: Windows
Special Requirements: MicroSoft Excel 4.0
Price: $2,500 first year, $1,250 every year after; demo available, $50; 50% AAII discount
Return Policy: all sales final
Technical Support: phone hours, 12 pm-3 pm, M-F
Description: Quadratic optimization system for optimal allocation among asset categories, mutual funds, and individual assets. Trades off risk versus expected return based on information supplied by the user to arrive at the optimal portfolio holding. Limited to 30 portfolio holdings. Uses fast algorithm that takes advantage of the structure of portfolio optimization problems to achieve an increase in optimization speed, when compared with a general purpose quadratic program-

ming algorithm. Features: upper and lower bounds on individual portfolio holdings; linear equality and inequality constraints on portfolio attributes (such as portfolio beta) and on asset groups (such as industry or country holdings); transactions costs that can vary with transaction size; and turnover constraint. Also allows risk-free assets and performs quadratic and linear optimization.

FIRST FINANCIAL SOFTWARE

P.O. Box 592967   (800) 736-4920
Orlando, FL 32859-2967   (407) 855-5561

FPLAN-KWIK FINANCIAL & RETIREMENT PLANNER
Version: 1.0   *Last Updated:* 1994   *No. of Users:* na
Functions: financial planning
Systems: DOS
Special Requirements: mouse recommended
Price: $20; demo available, $10
Return Policy: all sales final
Technical Support: phone hours, 24 hrs—messages
Description: Designed to complement other basic financial programs that only track current income and expenses, by determining longer range financial goals and how to modify current income/expenses for maximum efficiency. Analysis available on budgeting, net worth, economic assumptions, education funding, retirement planning, capital needs, estate preservation, and income protection. An on-screen tutorial with printable check-list, on-screen help and printable subject data guides are available to help individuals through the program with a minimum of learning required. When completed with the analysis user can print a customized personal summary report.

FPLAN-PERSONAL FINANCIAL PLANNER
Version: 5.0   *Last Updated:* 1994   *No. of Users:* na
Functions: financial planning
Systems: DOS
Special Requirements: mouse recommended
Price: $35; demo available, $10
Return Policy: all sales final
Technical Support: toll-free number; phone hours, 24 hrs—messages
Description: Designed to complement other basic financial programs by determining longer range financial goals and how to modify cur-

rent income/expenses for maximum efficiency. An on-screen tutorial with printable check-list, on-screen help and printable module data guides are available to help individuals through the program with a minimum of learning required. When completed with an analysis, the user can view and/or print a customized personal report relative to the planning module being used.

FPLAN-PROFESSIONAL FINANCIAL PLANNER
Version: 5.0   *Last Updated:* 1994   *No. of Users:* na
Functions: financial planning
Systems: DOS
Price: $200; demo available, $15
Return Policy: 30 days; $20 restocking fee
Technical Support: toll-free number; phone hours, 24 hrs—messages; fee for tech support—$125
Description: Designed for financial planning professionals to develop and monitor comprehensive financial planning issues for their prospects and clients. An on-screen tutorial with printable check-list, on-screen help and printable module data guides are available to help individuals through the program with a minimum of learning required. When completed with an analysis user can view and/or print a customized report relative to all or just the planning module desired.

FLEXSOFT

7172 Regional Street   (510) 829-9733
#276   fax: (510) 829-9733
Dublin, CA 94568

PERSONAL TICKER TAPE
Version: 3.0   *Last Updated:* 1994   *No. of Users:* 300
Securities: stocks, bonds, futures, mutual funds, indexes, options
Functions: quote utility
Systems: DOS
Special Requirements: Modem
Price: $79; demo available, free; 10% AAII discount
Return Policy: all sales final
Technical Support: phone hours, 11 am-8 pm, M-F; BBS support
Description: Downloads daily closing quotes from CompuServe, GEnie, Dial Data, and DJN/R. Directly updates MetaStock, Megatech and

ASCII format data files and contains a historical data maintenance facility to modify these files. Generates "color coded" daily update screens, highlighted symbols whose volume and/or price has changed by specified percentage amounts. Also generates a file containing a summary report for all symbols processed.

TECHNICAL ANALYSIS SCANNER

Version: 5.37   *Last Updated:* 1994   *No. of Users:* 600
Securities: stocks, futures, mutual funds, indexes, options
Functions: technical analysis
Systems: DOS
Price: $249; demo available, $5; 15% AAII discount
Return Policy: all sales final
Technical Support: phone hours, 11 am-8 pm, M-F; BBS support
Description: Scans, screens, and analyzes stocks, commodities, mutual funds, or market indexes. Using the 60+ built-in technical indicators, user can compare values against other indicators or values, make decisions based on the results of those comparisons and create specialized reports. Confirms profitability of trading system. Keeps track of the days that securities were bought, sold, or stopped out of positions, tabulating results on a daily basis or in a report that tells how the system performed.

FOUNDATION FOR THE STUDY OF CYCLES

900 West Valley Road   (800) 477-0741
Suite 502   (610) 995-2120
Wayne, PA 19087   fax: (610) 995-2130

BASIC CYCLE ANALYSIS

Version: na   *Last Updated:* na   *No. of Users:* na
Securities: stocks, bonds, futures, mutual funds, indexes, options, real estate
Functions: technical analysis, statistics
Systems: DOS
Price: $450 for foundation members; $500 for non-members; 20% AAII discount
Return Policy: 30 days
Technical Support: phone hours, 1 pm-7 pm, M-F
Description: Designed to do a complete cycle analysis of a time series.

Consists of routines to find and statistically test cycles. Requires no technical skill or statistical expertise. All internal parameters can be customized by advanced users.

MCCLELLAN OSCILLATOR PROGRAM
Version: na   *Last Updated:* na   *No. of Users:* na
Securities: stocks
Functions: technical analysis
Systems: DOS
Price: $350 for foundation members; $450 for non-members; 20% AAII
  discount
Return Policy: 30 days
Technical Support: phone hours, 1 pm-7 pm, M-F
Description: Consists of stock market timing tools. Graphically presents both the oscillator and summation index in issues and volume. Comes with integrated graphics and has a complete data entry routine. From four years to as little as months of data can be viewed on the screen at one time. User can scroll through the entire database without reloading. Includes more than 30 years of stock market and issue data and nearly 20 years of volume data.

F2S ENTERPRISES

P.O. Box 1011   (713) 471-7998
LaPorte, TX 77572-1011   fax: (713) 471-7220

MARKET PLUS (LEVEL 2) / MARKET PLUS (LEVEL 3)
Version: 2.1   *Last Updated:* 1993   *No. of Users:* na
Securities: stocks, bonds, futures, mutual funds, indexes
Functions: technical analysis
Systems: DOS
Price: $115 (level 2) / $145 (level 3); demo available, $8
Return Policy: all sales final
Technical Support: phone hours, 6 pm-10 pm, M-F
Description: Contains over 3 dozen technical indicators and trendline tools. Technical charting tools include: simple-weighted-exponential moving averages, Wilders RSI, Williams %R, moving average convergence/divergence (MACD), Bollinger bands, cone index, Fibonacci studies, Andrews method, filter zones, trading bands, Flex-PLOT and Multi-PLOT for unlimited custom exponential moving averages with user-defined shifts (displacement) and color presentation and direct

graphic comparison of any two securities. Investor Defined Studies (IDS) are also available for access at any time. Other features include: multiple investments per file, custom performance sorting, report generation, stock split/dividend adjustments, price editing and file backup.

FUTURES TRUTH CO.

815 Hillside Road   (704) 697-0273
Hendersonville, NC 28739   fax: (704) 692-7375

EXCALIBUR
Version: 1.16   *Last Updated:* 1993   *No. of Users:* <100
Securities: stocks, futures, indexes
Functions: technical analysis, statistics
Systems: Mac
Price: $3,400 includes daily and tick-by-tick data; $3,900 includes additional tick data; demo available
Return Policy: 30 days; $200 restocking fee
Technical Support: phone hours, 8 am-5 pm, M-F; fee for tech support—100 free hours; negotiable thereafter
Description: User can test stock or commodity trading system in 3 steps: 1) modify Fortran code, usually no more than 20 lines using the bundled QUED/M text editor by Paragon Concepts, Inc.; 2) compile and execute code using the included MacFortran/020 compiler by Absoft; 3) review the reports and analysis of the completed run by scanning the color charts to verify buy and sell points. Test how any system would have performed over the last 20 years. Reports are generated automatically and detail statistical information, trade-by-trade reports, time-of-trade analysis, entry and exit filter analysis, daily equity curve, user-defined money management schemes, worst trades analysis, pyramid schemes and more. All popular technical indicators are given and can be reprogrammed with the included source code. No knowledge of Fortran required. Advanced programmers can add codes indefinitely to customize all features. $3,400 version includes daily data on 23 major commodities and 10 stocks, most starting before 1970, and over 6 years of 5-minute bar data for S&Ps, bonds, and Swiss francs. Complete tick data and pyramiding capability. $3,900 version includes all of the above plus tick data for an additional 32 markets.

FUTURE WAVE SOFTWARE

1330 S. Gertruda Avenue   (310) 540-5373
Redondo Beach, CA 90277   fax: (310) 540-5373

STOCK PROPHET
Version: 1.5   *Last Updated:* 1994   *No. of Users:* na
Securities: stocks, bonds, futures, mutual funds, indexes, options
Functions: technical analysis, neural network
Systems: DOS
Price: $995; contact vendor for AAII discount
Return Policy: all sales final
Description: Stock Prophet is applicable to futures, stocks, mutual funds, bonds and the overall market. It provides the preprocesssing and post-processing required to operate the BrainMaker neural network learning program. Over 30 common indicators and some unique indicators are available for preprocessing. In addition, it allows the analyst to conveniently select multiple appropriate financial indicators and intermarket factors for prediction of market price trends. The neural network model combines the selected multiple indicators into a single clear indication of the future price trend used as the buy/sell indicator. Stock Prophet allows the indicator to be easily tested for profitability.

GANNSOFT PUBLISHING CO.

11670 Riverbend Drive   (509) 548-5990
Leavenworth, WA 98826-9353   fax: (509) 548-4679

GANNTRADER 2
Version: 2.0   *Last Updated:* 1994   *No. of Users:* 850
Securities: stocks, bonds, futures, mutual funds, indexes, options
Functions: technical analysis
Systems: DOS
Special Requirements: mouse recommended
Price: $1,295; demo available, $10; 25% AAII discount
Return Policy: 30 days
Technical Support: phone hours, 11 am-8 pm, M-F; fee for tech support—$100/year optional maintanence update
Description: Program plots price charts with angles, squares and plan-

ets; and plots angles from highs, lows, 360-degree angles or user-selected. Analyzes up to 5 Gann squares at a time from any price and time point; plots planets, aspects, averages, MOF, CE Average, etc., and calculates support and resistance points, Square of 9 as well as Hexagon chart positions.

G.C.P.I.

P.O. Box 790   (906) 226-7600
Dept. #50-E
Marquette, MI 49855

FINANCIAL PAK
Version: 3.0   *Last Updated:* 1987   *No. of Users:* 150
Securities: stocks, mutual funds
Functions: financial planning, portfolio management
Systems: DOS, Windows
Price: $149.95; 20% AAII discount
Return Policy: 30 days; 15% restocking fee
Technical Support: phone hours, 8 am-5 pm, M-F
Description: Three separate menu-driven programs that deal with stock investments, amortization schedules, lump-sum and annuity investments. The stock market investment aid reports stock and mutual fund buy and sell information based on an average-cost basis with an emphasis on obtaining consistent returns. The loan program provides amortization schedules and loan summaries for all types of loans, including zero-interest and balloon loans. The third program provides information about lump-sum and annuity investments. Handles periodic savings plans, mutual funds, and IRA accounts.

INVESTMENT MASTER
Version: 2.0   *Last Updated:* 1987   *No. of Users:* 150
Securities: mutual funds
Functions: financial planning
Systems: DOS, Windows
Price: $49.95; 20% AAII discount
Return Policy: 30 days; 15% restocking fee
Technical Support: phone hours, 8 am-5 pm, M-F
Description: Provides an investment summary that lists all the input and calculated parameters for investments. Investment summaries

can be output to display screen, printer or disk file. Solves for any unknown investment parameters. Can handle a deposit or withdrawal type of annuity or a lump-sum investment. Useful in obtaining answers about periodic savings deposit plans, mutual funds and IRA accounts.

LOAN MASTER
Version: 3.2   *Last Updated:* 1987   *No. of Users:* 200
Securities: bonds
Functions: financial planning
Systems: DOS, Windows
Price: $49.95; 20% AAII discount
Return Policy: 30 days; 15% restocking fee
Technical Support: phone hours, 8 am-5 pm, M-F
Description: Provides loan amortization schedules and loan summaries for all types of loan situations including zero-interest and balloon contracts. Users can obtain results based on each payment or summarized on an annual basis. Annual amortization schedule is useful for tax purposes and for analyzing home and auto loans.

STOCK MASTER
Version: 2.0   *Last Updated:* 1987   *No. of Users:* 150
Securities: stocks, mutual funds
Functions: portfolio management
Systems: DOS
Price: $49.95; 20% AAII discount
Return Policy: 30 days; 15% restocking fee
Technical Support: phone hours, 8 am-5 pm, M-F
Description: Designed for user who needs buy/sell advice with an emphasis on consistent returns. Can be used on a periodic basis to obtain timely buy/sell instructions on stocks and mutual funds. Completely menu-driven with options for adding a transaction, listing the transaction log and checking any account status.

GOOD SOFTWARE, CORP.

4125 Keller Springs Road   (800) 925-5700
Suite 156   (214) 713-6370
Dallas, TX 75244   fax: (214) 713-6308

AMORTIZER PLUS

Version: 3.01/4.0 Win   *Last Updated:* 1994   *No. of Users:* 25,000
Functions: financial planning
Systems: DOS, Windows
Price: $129.95; 10% AAII discount
Return Policy: 30 days
Technical Support: phone hours, 9:30 am-6:30 pm, M-F
Description: A menu-driven loan amortization tool. When user enters any 3 of 4 variables (original amount, interest rate, number of periods or payment amount) program automatically calculates the 4th. The override feature allows all 4 variables to be entered when all information is known. User can print detailed or summary amortization schedules with 3 lines for comments or change the variables to perform "what if" scenarios. Accommodates variable phase loans—adjustable rate, graduated payments, negative amortization, interest-only and multiple balloons—and calculates APR and wrap notes. Includes annual, semiannual, quarterly, monthly, biweekly and exact-day interest compounding periods; accomodates Rule of 78s, fixed-principal and principal-only loans, payments in advance (leases) and other loan conditions.

REMS INVESTOR 3000

Version: 5.01   *Last Updated:* 1992   *No. of Users:* 8,000
Securities: real estate
Functions: real estate analysis
Systems: DOS
Price: $595; 10% AAII discount
Return Policy: 30 days
Technical Support: phone hours, 9:30 am-6:30 pm, M-F
Description: Real estate financial analysis and reporting program for existing or proposed projects. Forecasts the cash flows from the acquisition, financing, development, operation and sale up to 25 years in the future. Accepts and reports up to 10 of 11 financing vehicles or ground leases; uses APOD (Annual Property Operating Data) format to detail operating income and expenses to project cash flows including NOI; provides for 10 individual or group partnerships allowing for active and passive income, losses allowed and ordinary and capital gains tax rates; handles extensive depreciation and amortized expenses; provides multiple methods of specifying the property sale amount (CAP rate, appreciation, specified price); evaluates lease versus buy, exchanges and installment sales; reports key financial ratios (IRR, FMRR,

ROI, ROE, NPV and wealth accumulation). Reports can be exported to a file and imported into a wordprocessor or spreadsheet for further analysis or customization. Program will accept data from REMS Lessor or from Lotus 1-2-3 and similar spreadsheets.

GREENSTONE SOFTWARE, INC.

14 Sapphire Cres.   (905) 840-5252
Brampton, Ontario L6Z 4C9, Canada

RAPID
Version: 4.02   *Last Updated:* 1992   *No. of Users:* na
Securities: stocks, bonds, futures, mutual funds, indexes, options
Functions: portfolio management, technical analysis
Systems: DOS
Price: $277; demo available, $5; 5% AAII discount
Return Policy: all sales final
Technical Support: phone hours, 9 am-9 pm, M-Sat.
Description: Produces graphs of stocks and commodities and provides all of the latest tools, including Bollinger Bands and Japanese candlesticks plus a number of proprietary indicators such as Look Ahead Price Bar, Projected Standard Deviation Bands, Searson Chinese Charts and more. A new feature allows user to enter trades and track portfolio graphically. Also, can now read Tech Tools and CSI data. A downloader is included.

GURU SYSTEMS, LTD.

3873 Airport Way   (604) 299-1010
Box 9754   fax: (604) 299-1099
Bellingham, WA 98227

PC CHART PLUS
Version: 3.1   *Last Updated:* 1993   *No. of Users:* na
Securities: stocks, bonds, futures, mutual funds, indexes, options
Functions: technical analysis
Systems: DOS
Price: $160; demo available, $5; 10% AAII discount
Return Policy: all sales final

Technical Support: phone hours, 12 pm-8 pm, M-F; BBS support; newsletter; fee for tech support—first year free

Description: An integrated technical analysis program that combines charting, database and telecommunications capabilities. Generates stock charts and standard technical indicators such as moving averages, relative strength and RSI. Built-in telecommunications capabilities can be used to download historical, end-of-day, intraday and real-time prices from All-Quotes, CompuServe, Dial/Data and GEnie. Supports PC Chart, ASCII, CSI and MetaStock data formats and up to 800 files in one subdirectory. Technical indicators include: bar charts, OI, volume, candlesticks, RSI, moving averages, parabolic system, directional movement index, logarithmic plot, point and figure, stochastics, daily/weekly/monthly charts, money flow index, relative strength, volatility, alpha-beta, trendlines, speed lines, Fibonacci retracements, guru, market guru, and A/D indicators. All technical indicators are fully adjustable.

QUOTE TRANSLATOR

Version: 1.2   *Last Updated:* 1993   *No. of Users:* na

Securities: stocks, bonds, futures, mutual funds, indexes, options

Functions: quote utility

Systems: DOS

Price: $99; demo available, $5; 10% AAII discount

Return Policy: all sales final

Technical Support: phone hours, 12 pm-8 pm, M-F; BBS support; newsletter; fee for tech support—first year free

Description: A data conversion and archival program that can be used to convert various data formats such as Apex, ASCII, CSI, MetaStock, PC Chart, Prodigy and TeleChart text files to other formats. Can also be used to append and split files by calendar years and to create continuous commodity futures contracts. Program can be modified to meet particular needs.

HAMILTON SOFTWARE, INC.

6432 E. Mineral Place   (800) 733-9607
Englewood, CO 80112   (303) 795-5572

FUNDWATCH PLUS

Version: 2.0   *Last Updated:* 1992   *No. of Users:* 5,000
Securities: stocks, bonds, mutual funds, indexes
Functions: technical analysis
Systems: DOS, Windows
Price: $29; 25% AAII discount
Return Policy: all sales final
Technical Support: phone hours, 8 am-5 pm, M-F
Description: Simplifies evaluation and comparison of various investments including mutual funds, stocks, money markets, and market indexes. Allows user to evaluate such investments without requiring a modem or on-line service. Annualizes total returns including proceeds from dividends and distributions, evaluates market trends, analyzes volatility, and provides comprehensive investment comparisons. Graphics include superimposed investment performance, moving averages, and relative strength. Share prices are manually entered on a weekly or longer basis and combined with dividends and distributions to reveal total investment performance.

INVESTOR'S ACCOUNTANT

Version: 3.0   *Last Updated:* 1993   *No. of Users:* 100
Securities: stocks, bonds, futures, mutual funds, indexes, options, real estate
Functions: financial planning, portfolio management, technical analysis, bond analysis
Systems: DOS
Price: $395; demo available, $5; 25% AAII discount
Return Policy: all sales final
Technical Support: phone hours, 8 am-5 pm, M-F
Description: Portfolio maintenance and analysis program that handles multiple portfolios and any investment type. Reports (for individual or grouped portfolios) include internal rate of return (both before and after taxes); time-weighted portfolio rate of return; current or historical portfolio status with association of assets by type, industry, and country; gain/loss between any two points in time; gain/loss from inception (both before and after taxes); tax liability year-to-date; attachments to Schedule B & D; foreign tax; projected income; income reconciliation; and detailed transaction listings. Reported status includes accrued bond interest. Converts foreign denominated securities to local currency on reports. Can update prices either manually or by importing from a downloaded ASCII file, and can export files to spread-

sheets. Provides for entry of distributions, mergers, and stock splits across all portfolios. Sales may be reported using FIFO, specific ID or average cost. Bond analysis includes calculation of imputed interest, premium amortization, and yield to maturity both before and after taxes. Alerts user on prices, dividends, expirations, percentage gain/loss and holdings going long term within user-entered parameters. Includes all of HSI's MarketWatch features for tracking and graphing individual securities. Pop-up windows provide entry codes, security symbols, portfolio IDs and calculator with paste option. Facilitates reporting according to AIMR standards.

MARKET STRATEGIST
Version: 1.0   *Last Updated:* 1993   *No. of Users:* 100
Securities: stocks, indexes
Functions: fundamental analysis, technical analysis, simulation/game, statistics
Systems: DOS
Price: $295; demo available, $5; 25% AAII discount
Return Policy: all sales final
Technical Support: phone hours, 8 am-5 pm, M-F
Description: A back-testing system including 7 years of S&P 100 index historical stock market data that enables user to develop and test, under actual trading conditions, a set of rules or a system for stock trading. Complete database and menu-driven software enable custom development and testing of both technical and fundamental trading criteria. Chronological simulation handles stock splits, earnings, commissions and margin costs; enables stock comparison with market indexes and industry groups. Trading system performance is plotted graphically along with the S&P 500 index. A series of reports include: industry group summaries, stock-trade plots, yearly summaries and performance and trade details. Can plot 100 stocks separately.

MARKETWATCH
Version: 2.0   *Last Updated:* 1993   *No. of Users:* 500
Securities: stocks, bonds, futures, mutual funds, indexes, options
Functions: technical analysis
Systems: DOS, Windows
Price: $59; demo available, $5; 25% AAII discount
Return Policy: all sales final
Technical Support: phone hours, 8 am-5 pm, M-F
Description: Evaluates and compares investments including mutual

funds, stocks, options, commodities, money markets and market indexes. Either manual or automatic price volume entry from any ASCII source. Annualizes yields including proceeds from earnings and distributions; evaluates price movement and price trends; graphs performance of multiple securities along with moving averages and/or volumes, high/low/close/volume and candlesticks; reveals performance of individual portfolios and provides investment comparisons. Accommodates an unlimited number of securities for which share prices (and optional volumes) are updated according to any time interval(s) and are combined with earnings and distributions to reveal total investment performance.

PORTFOLIO ANALYZER
Version: 3.1   *Last Updated:* 1993   *No. of Users:* 3,000
Securities: stocks, bonds, futures, mutual funds, indexes, options
Functions: financial planning, portfolio management
Systems: DOS
Price: $99; demo available, $5; 25% AAII discount
Return Policy: all sales final
Technical Support: phone hours, 8 am-5 pm, M-F
Description: Investment portfolio maintenance and analysis program. Reports include (by security or security type within portfolio or portfolio groups): security internal rate of return both before and after estimated taxes, portfolio status with asset allocation by security type, gain/loss, tax liability, interest yields, income and attachments to IRS Schedules B and D. Accommodates virtually unlimited number of portfolios, securities and transactions. Alerts on prices. Can update prices with downloaded ASCII file. Includes calculator with paste option. Provides for global entry of distributions, mergers and stock splits. Sales may be reported using FIFO or specific ID. All investment types, including options and futures contracts, are accommodated. Automatic pop-up information windows eliminate need to memorize entry codes, portfolio ID or security symbols.

H & H SCIENTIFIC

13507 Pendleton Street   (301) 292-2958
Fort Washington, MD 20744

STOCK OPTION ANALYSIS PROGRAM
Version: na   *Last Updated:* 1993   *No. of Users:* 350

Securities: options
Functions: options analysis
Systems: DOS
Price: $150; demo available, $35; 10% AAII discount
Return Policy: all sales final
Technical Support: phone hours, 9 am-5 pm, M-F
Description: The expected profit/loss on transactions involving up to five different options can be calculated and graphed for any time until the options expire. Suited for doing "what if" calculations for complicated stock option positions. Stock and option prices can be obtained from Dow Jones, DBC Signal or entered manually. Calendar spreads, vertical spreads, straddles, butterfly spreads, covered and single option positions can be analyzed as current positions or future holdings. Begins by calculating the standard deviation of the stock price from the volatility. The program calculates the neutral hedge ratio for each option and the market-implied volatility and the user specifies which volatility to use. The prices of the stock are then calculated, and the user specifies the volatility to use. The prices of the stock are then calculated for 3 standard deviations on either side of the mean. Within this range the price of each option and the proceeds, including commission costs, for closing that option transaction are calculated. The net gain/loss is then calculated assuming that the stock closes at that price. Three commission schedules are provided and these can be modified or new ones created.

STOCK OPTION SCANNER
Version: na   *Last Updated:* 1993   *No. of Users:* 200-250
Securities: options
Functions: options analysis
Systems: DOS
Price: $150; demo available, $35; 10% AAII discount
Return Policy: all sales final
Technical Support: phone hours, 9 am-5 pm, M-F
Description: Scans up to 4,000 stock options (downloaded from Dow Jones, DBC Signal or entered manually) and ranks the top 50 and bottom 50 options (or option positions) according to the statistically expected rate of return. Horizontal spreads, vertical spreads, straddles, and neutral hedges can be ranked. Two methods are provided for determining over/under priced options. The first is based on the ratio of the market-assigned volatility to the historical volatility. The second is based on the theortical option price and the actual price. The ranking

can be based on either the ratio of the prices or on the absolute price difference. Neutral hedges are ranked based on holding 100 shares of stock and selling the number of calls determined by the inverse hedge ratio. The rate of return is calculated as the net profit divided by the product of the value of the stock (plus any additional margin required) multiplied by the time until the option expires. Can run unattended analyses for up to 5 preselected scans with the printout collected at a later time.

HOWARDSOFT

1224 Prospect Street   (800) 822-4829
Suite 150   (619) 454-0121
La Jolla, CA 92037   fax: (619) 454-7559

REAL ESTATE ANALYZER
Version: 3rd   *Last Updated:* 1988   *No. of Users:* na
Securities: real estate
Functions: financial planning, portfolio management, fundamental analysis, real estate analysis
Systems: DOS, Apple II (ProDOS)
Special Requirements: IBM version requires GW-BASIC or BASICA
Price: Apple $350; IBM $395; demo available, $15
Return Policy: all sales final
Technical Support: phone hours, 11:30 am-7:30 pm, M-F; newsletter
Description: Analyzes real estate investment opportunities. Compares properties, creative financing, tax consequences, depreciation, cash flow and more. Projects investment results with 30-year tables of pre-tax and aftertax cash flow and 7 measures of return on investment. Features 10 loans and 50 leases, built-in tax laws, menu-driven control, monthly precision, flexible inflation modeling and "what if" planning. Provides an investment guide, examples and on-screen help keys.

TAX PREPARER
Version: 1994   *Last Updated:* 1994   *No. of Users:* 23,000+
Functions: financial planning
Systems: DOS, Apple II (ProDOS)
Price: Apple $250 (annual updates $99); IBM $295 (annual updates $99)
Return Policy: all sales final
Technical Support: phone hours, 11:00 am-7:30 pm, M-F; newsletter

Description: Automates preparation of tax returns by looking up numbers in tables and performing the arithmetic, then automatically completing and computing numerous IRS worksheets. Performs the math for the simple and complex returns. Transfers hundreds of numbers back and forth among forms and recalculates the entire return as often as necessary. Handles unlimited recordkeeping and unlimited number of stocks, bonds, rentals, accounts and depreciated assets. Gives "what if" capabilities with tax laws built-in past the current year and hundreds of pages of line-by-line detail so that users see what the software is doing and can handle unusual exceptions. Has built-in depreciation calculations, automated handling of passive loss rules and IRS-accepted printouts on dot-matrix or laser printers.

TAX PREPARER: PARTNERSHIP EDITION
Version: 1994   *Last Updated:* 1994   *No. of Users:* na
Functions: financial planning
Systems: DOS
Price: $350, annual update $165
Return Policy: all sales final
Technical Support: phone hours, 11:00 am-7:30 pm, M-F; newsletter
Description: Has all the features of Tax Preparer: Federal Edition, plus helps plan tax strategies, keep tax records and prepare IRS-accepted partnership returns. Distribution worksheet handles complex partnership arrangements and automatically creates all the partners' K-1s. All of the A.C.R.S. tables and depreciation calculations are built-in and automatic.

HUGHES FINANCIAL SERVICES

P.O. Box 1244   (603) 598-4676
Nashua, NH 03061-1244   fax: (603) 598-4676

ADVANCED TOTAL INVESTOR (ATI)
Version: 3.1   *Last Updated:* 1994   *No. of Users:* 1,250
Securities: stocks, bonds, futures, mutual funds, indexes, options
Functions: financial planning, portfolio management, technical analysis, spreadsheet, statistics
Systems: DOS, Windows
Special Requirements: Lotus 1-2-3 v.2.0 or higher, Lotus 1-2-3 for Windows, Quattro Pro, Quattro Pro SE, Excel
Price: $129; 23% AAII discount

Return Policy: 30 days; $10 restocking fee

Technical Support: phone hours, 9 am-6 pm, M-F; BBS support; newsletter

Description: Builds upon Total Investor's basic features. All report and analysis graphs can be edited using the Lotus WYSIWYG add-in or Quattro Pro's Annotate function. Allows user to add trendlines, text, arrows and draw freehand on all plots. The template adapts to the spreadsheet in use to optimize graphics and other features. High resolution charts zoom in on any segment of a security's price history. Can graphically display portfolio allocation (stocks, bonds, cash, etc.), calculate portfolio returns and identify price alerts. A cash management ledger allows user to track and report on dividends, distributions, checking and similar securities and the entire portfolio. Includes all of Total Investor's basic features plus: charts—line/bar, candlestick, equivolume, P&F, linear/log, and open/open interest; spreads; trends—Bollinger bands, trendlines, parabolic and directional movement (+DI, -DI, DX, ADX, ADXR); oscillators—CCI, MACD, stochastics, and William's %R; volume—Chaiken A/D, Chaiken oscillator, PVT and volume oscillator. A special version of ATI is now available for Excel and Quattro Pro V5 for Windows and DOS.

MARKET TIMING UTILITY

Version: 1.0   *Last Updated:* 1993   *No. of Users:* 150

Securities: indexes

Functions: technical analysis, spreadsheet, statistics

Systems: DOS, Windows

Special Requirements: Lotus 1-2-3 v.2.0 or higher, Lotus 1-2-3 for Windows, Quattro Pro, Quattro Pro SE, Excel (requires ATI purchase)

Price: $59

Return Policy: 30 days; $10 restocking fee

Technical Support: phone hours, 9 am-6 pm, M-F; BBS support; newsletter

Description: A spreadsheet template that works with Advanced Total Investor. The template calculates and displays many popular indicators used to trade the market index. Features 13 indicators including McClellan Oscillator, Summation Index, A/D ratio, A/D line, A/D differential, STIX, breadth thrust, TRIN, smoothed TRIN, open TRIN, cumulative volume and U/D volume ratio. By working as an add-in, all the analytical, graphical, and other tools in ATI are available to the user. One year of data for NYSE advances, NYSE declines, up volume and down volume is included with the program. Data can be updated from data sources such as Prodigy, Signal, and CompuServe using HFS data link products.

TOTAL INVESTOR

Version: 2.1   *Last Updated:* 1993   *No. of Users:* 3,100

Securities: stocks, bonds, mutual funds, indexes, options

Functions: financial planning, portfolio management, technical analysis, spreadsheet, statistics

Systems: DOS

Special Requirements: Lotus 1-2-3 v.2.0 or higher, Quattro Pro, or Quattro Pro SE. Requires Quattro Pro V4 or earlier.

Price: $35 registration fee—program is shareware; demo available

Return Policy: all sales final

Technical Support: phone hours, 9 am-6 pm, M-F; BBS support; newsletter

Description: An integrated portfolio management and technical analysis template for use with Lotus 1-2-3. Tracks securities and transactions, charts stocks, and helps make trading decisions based on technical indicators. Maintains both current quotes for user's portfolio and historical quotes for charting and analysis. A manual data-entry mode is supported so that both price and volume quotes can be entered directly from a newspaper's financial section. All data is sorted in Lotus compatible files. Also works with all major on-line quote services with separate data link templates available from HFS. Indicators covered include: charts—plot price, volume, all data or zoom; volume—accumulation, on-balance, positive, negative and ease of movement; relative strength—security versus DJIA or other issues and Wilder RSI; moving averages—simple or exponential; and oscillators—momentum.

HULME MATHEMATICS

3701 General Patch, N.E.   (800) 223-7204
Albuquerque, NM 87111   (505) 298-7204

PORTFOLIO SELECTION

Version: 1.2   *Last Updated:* 1993   *No. of Users:* na

Securities: stocks, bonds, futures, mutual funds, indexes, options

Functions: financial planning, statistics

Systems: DOS
Price: $99; demo available, $9
Return Policy: all sales final
Technical Support: phone hours, 11 am-7 pm, M-F
Description: Uses the Markowitz mean-variance model to help users decide how much of each security to buy. The user supplies past prices and dividends or interest for each security under consideration, and the program computes efficient portfolios (minimum-risk mixtures of the securities) over the entire range of possible expected returns. The user can then choose a level of return and risk that is comfortable and see what portion of the total investment should be allocated to each security. The program is menu-driven. Each portfolio may have up to 61 observations on up to 100 securities. A math co-processor is optional. An alternative is to supply expected returns and covariances instead of past prices and dividends or interest.

PORTFOLIO SELECTION-PROFESSIONAL
Version: 1.0   *Last Updated:* 1994   *No. of Users:* na
Securities: stocks, bonds, futures, mutual funds, indexes, options, real estate, any asset with historical data
Functions: financial planning, statistics
Systems: DOS
Special Requirements: Math co-processor
Price: $595; demo available, free; 15% AAII discount
Return Policy: all sales final
Technical Support: toll-free number; phone hours, 11 am-7 pm
Description: Uses a constrained version of the Markowitz mean-variance model to compute the efficient frontier. Along with all the features of the original Portfolio Selection, this professional version allows the user to specify constraints in the form of simple bounds and/or general linear equations or inequalities. This 32-bit application requires a math co-processor and uses color to display graphical user interfaces with highlighted menus under either keyboard or mouse control. The user has a choice of three forms of input: historical prices and dividends (or interest), expected returns, standard deviations and correlations, and expected returns and covariances, which may be entered through the keyboard in full-screen editing mode or through an ASCII file. In addition to the numerical displays of individual efficient portfolios, it is possible to display the entire efficient frontier graphically as well as to output coordinates of the frontier to an ASCII file for plotting elsewhere.

IBC/DONOGHUE, INC.

290 Eliot Street   (800) 343-5413
P.O. Box 9104   (508) 881-2800
Ashland, MA 01721-9104   fax: (508) 881-0982

MONEY FUND VISION
Version: 4   *Last Updated:* 1994   *No. of Users:* na
Securities: money funds
Functions: portfolio management, technical analysis, spreadsheet, statistics, composition analysis
Systems: DOS, Windows
Special Requirements: 386+, 570K memory, modem
Price: $7,975 introductory price $9,975 renewal price; demo available, free
Technical Support: phone hours, 9 am-5 pm, M-F
Description: Allows user to monitor and compare their portfolio's performance to other specified money markets. Creates money fund data searches using pulldown and pop-up menus to replace macro computer instructions. Fund type, portfolio composition, compound yields, expense ratios, asset size, and number of shareholders are examples of the information ready to download via PC or LAN. Also provides graphs and charts displaying market trends, expert commentary and past feature articles from Money Fund Report and IBC/Donoghue's monthly Money Market Insight, as well as new money fund data not previously available from any other source, including the percentage of each portfolio that matures in 7 days.

INSIGHT SOFTWARE SOLUTIONS

P.O. Box 354   (801) 295-1890
Bountiful, UT 84011

DEBT ANALYZER FOR WINDOWS
Version: na   *Last Updated:* na   *No. of Users:* na
Functions: financial planning
Systems: DOS
Price: $25
Description: This Windows-based financial application is used to help reduce and eliminate debt. The program is designed to take all current

debt information and project a possible solution for eliminating that debt. The user ranks their debts in order of priority. Monthly payments are then made to each of their debts and after one debt is paid off, that payment is applied to the highest priority debt. Several options are available for accelerating and optimizing your debt elimination, such as using minimum payments, applying extra payments, and selecting one of nine predefined priority methods. The Debt Analyzer also allows the user to create loan consolidation schedules and will calculate the amount of money saved by doing so. It also includes the ability to specify the term or payment of the loan (the sum of all debt payments may also be used as the consolidated loan payment). Interest rates may be entered as a daily, monthly, APR, or annual effective rate.

INSTITUTE FOR OPTIONS RESEARCH, INC.

P.O. Box 6586
Lake Tahoe, NV 89449

(800) 334-0854 x840
(702) 588-3590
fax: (702) 588-8481

OPTION MASTER
Version: 4.09   *Last Updated:* 1990   *No. of Users:* 1,000
Securities: options
Functions: options analysis
Systems: DOS, Mac
Price: $89 plus $8 handling fee; 20% AAII discount
Return Policy: 30 days; 30% restocking fee
Technical Support: phone hours, 11 am-8 pm, M-F
Description: Measures the theoretical value of an option. Will also give the probability of profit when buying, writing or entering an option strategy. With a few computer-prompted entries, user can determine the fair value of options on any stock, index or commodity. Does not require access to database or information service. All information can be obtained from the options listing in any major newspaper.

OPTION MASTER FOR NEWTON
Version: na   *Last Updated:* 1994   *No. of Users:* na
Securities: options
Functions: options analysis
Systems: Newton
Price: $195 plus $8 shipping & handling; 20% AAII discount

Return Policy: 30 days; 30% restocking fee
Description: Option Master for Newton has all the features of Option Master for Windows. Runs option calculations on any stock, index or commodity option to determine their fair value, or the probability of profit on any option strategy. Also calculates delta, gamma, vega, and theta. A palm-sized computer user can carry around. User writes one number, taps a few times on the screen with pen, and prices any option, or determines the probability of profit of any option strategy.

OPTIONS MASTER FOR WINDOWS

Version: 1.2   *Last Updated:* 1992   *No. of Users:* 500
Securities: options
Functions: options analysis
Systems: Windows
Price: $159.95 plus $8 shipping & handling; includes free $79 pricing video; 20% AAII discount
Return Policy: 30 days; 30% restocking fee
Technical Support: phone hours, 11 am-8 pm, M-F
Description: Based on computer-simulated options trading, uses option pricing formulas available to determine the fair price of an option and calculates the probability of profit. Enables user to determine the fair value of options on any stock, index, or commodity. Does not require access to database or information service. All information can be obtained from the options listing in any major newspaper. Calculates implied volatility, delta, gamma, vega & theta.

INTEGRATED FINANCIAL SOLUTIONS, INC.

1049 S.W. Baseline   (800) 729-5037
Suite B-200   (503) 640-5303
Hillsboro, OR 97123   fax: (503) 648-9528

CANADIAN QUOTES MODULE FOR QUOTE EXPRESS

Version: na   *Last Updated:* na   *No. of Users:* na
Functions:
Systems: DOS
Special Requirements: Quote Express and subscription to DTN
Price: $95
Technical Support: toll-free number
Description: A module for QuoteExpress that enables the collection of

5,000 new Canadian quotes carried on Data Transmission Network. DTN's Canadian Quotes covers trading on the four exchanges—Alberta, Montreal, Toronto, and Vancouver. Prices are reported in Canadian dollars indicated by a "#" prefix. If desired, QuoteExpress can automatically convert Canadian currency to U.S. currency based on the current exchange rate.

CONNECT
Version: 2.0   *Last Updated:* 1994   *No. of Users:* na
Securities: futures, options
Functions: technical analysis
Systems: DOS, Windows, Windows NT, OS/2
Price: $595; 10% AAII discount
Return Policy: all sales final
Technical Support: toll-free number; phone hours, 11 am-8 pm M-F; BBS support
Description: Gathers DTN data on futures, commodity and commodities opitons, DTN News, On-Line Symbol Index, graphing/charting, and makes it available on an intraday as well as end-of-day basis. Pop-up quotes and alarms track high, low and volume, while DTN News is stored on the hard drive for viewing or output to a printer or text editor. Ease of use is supported by short cut keys and on-line help. Unlimited list building and management. Once lists are built by symbol, user can sort and rank them for analysis. Data can be collected for use with Connect, as well as downloaded into over 190 analysis, spreadsheet, or portfolio management software programs. Also provides a user-defined ticker that scrolls across the lower screen, displayed latest prices.

QUOTEEXPRESS
Version: 4.2   *Last Updated:* 1994   *No. of Users:* na
Securities: stocks, bonds, futures, mutual funds, indexes, options
Functions: technical analysis, quote utility
Systems: DOS, Windows, Windows NT, OS/2, PC-MOS
Special Requirements: DTN
Price: $290; demo available, $44—30 day trial; 10% AAII discount
Return Policy: all sales final
Technical Support: toll-free number; phone hours, 11 am-8 pm, M-F; BBS support
Description: Financial software that acts as an investment analysis and management system by interfacing DTN Wall Street with the user's

computer. Quotes on stocks, bonds, mutual funds, index, futures and market indicators are gathered and distributed into more than 100 packages. Instantly, accesses the last price of any issue broadcast on DTN and updates users analysis databases. Collects data in the background with only 35K of RAM, storing it on the hard disk and leaving the computer available for charting, analysis or corrrespondence. Alarms monitor-sensitive issues or user can start a ticker that scrolls prices on closely-watched issues across the screen. Features: "hot" switches that jump directly into charting and analysis programs, such as MetaStock or CompuTrac; imports lists or portfolios from external programs without re-keying ability to set daily data or choose intraday data with intervals ranging from 1 to 60 minutes. Graphing module includes live updates on intraday charts of up to 2,000 intervals. Has a data pointer, Japanese candlesticks, 3 types of moving averages and multiple trendlines.

STO QUEST

Version: na   *Last Updated:* 1994   *No. of Users:* na
Securities: stocks
Functions: fundamental analysis
Systems: DOS, Windows, Windows NT, OS/2
Price: $199; 10% AAII discount
Return Policy: all sales final
Technical Support: toll-free number; phone hours, 11 am-8 pm; BBS support
Description: Use industry group ranking to locate best investment opportunities. Program prepares Metastock or ASCII files and QuoteExpress screen lists for collecting data on over 6,000 stocks separated by industry group. The user can then rank the companies in each industry by performance for making trading decisions. Also, the user can add individual stocks to any grouping.

INTERNATIONAL PACIFIC TRADING COMPANY

1050 Calle Cordillera   (800) 444-9993
#105   (714) 498-4009
San Clemente, CA 92672-6240   fax: (714) 498-5263

CANDLESTICK FORECASTER

Version: 2.0   *Last Updated:* 1993   *No. of Users:* 1,000+

Securities: stocks, bonds, futures, mutual funds, indexes, options
Functions: technical analysis, bond analysis, futures analysis, options
    analysis, expert system, neural network
Systems: DOS
Price: $249; demo available, $15; 5% AAII discount
Return Policy: 30 days; 15% restocking fee
Technical Support: phone hours, 11 am-8 pm, M-F; BBS support; news-
    letter
Description: Provides a window environment that graphically dis-
plays candlestick charts, interprets over 700 patterns, issues buy/sell
signals and gives information about candlestick patterns it finds using
proprietary artificial intelligence, neural networking structures and
pattern recognition systems.

CANDLESTICK FORECASTER MASTER EDITION
Version: 4.2   *Last Updated:* 1994   *No. of Users:* 1,000+
Securities: stocks, bonds, futures, mutual funds, indexes, options
Functions: technical analysis, bond analysis, futures analysis, options
    analysis, expert system, neural network
Systems: DOS, OS/2
Price: $800; demo available, $15; 5% AAII discount
Return Policy: 30 days; 15% restocking fee
Technical Support: phone hours, 11 am-8 pm, M-F; newsletter
Description: The Master Edition is an extended candlestick trading
program that recognizes over 1,000 patterns and encompasses the use
of standard western technical studies and neural networking to issue
market-sensitive text messages that identify each pattern found. Program will issue buy/sell signals and show configuration, continuation, confluence and combination patterns. Features include: candle
watch, candle vision, custom pages and trendlines.

CANDLESTICK FORECASTER REAL TIME
Version: 5.2   *Last Updated:* 1994   *No. of Users:* 300+
Securities: stocks, bonds, futures, mutual funds, indexes, options
Functions: portfolio management, technical analysis, bond analysis,
    futures analysis, options analysis, statistics, expert system
Systems: DOS, OS/2
Special Requirements: 386+
Price: $1,700; 5% AAII discount
Return Policy: 30 days; $20 restocking fee

Technical Support: phone hours, 11 am-8 pm, M-F; fee for tech support—$400

Description: The Real Time is an extended real-time candlestick trading program that recognizes over 1,000 patterns and encompasses the use of standard western technical studies and neural networking to issue market-sensitive text messages that identify each pattern found. Program will issue buy/sell signals and show configuration, continuation, confluence and combination patterns. Features include: candle watch, candle vision, custom pages and trendlines.

INTERNATIONAL SOFTWARE SYSTEMS

1832 Dauphin St.   (205) 478-8637
Mobile, AL 36606

MARKETMAKER 1.0 FOR WINDOWS
Version: 1.1   *Last Updated:* 1994   *No. of Users:* na
Securities: stocks
Functions: fundamental analysis
Systems: DOS, Windows
Price: $29
Description: Users enter historical data from company reports using a spreadsheet-like format to build a database of stocks for fundamental analysis. At least two periods of data are required (out of five) and the maximum number of companies that can be simultaneously analyzed is 100. MarketMaker can project future earnings per share and share price based on past performance. It also calculates the financial stability, average sales growth, debt ratio, current growth in earnings per share, average growth in earnings per share, current and previous returns on shareholders' equity, current and previous aftertax returns on sales, dividends per share, yields based on high and low share prices for the period, average price-earnings ratio, and relative strength. A report feature, story section (to record personal experience of stock), and graphing feature (graphs sales per share and aftertax income per share versus time) are included. The program also features what-if analysis capability.

INTEX SOLUTIONS, INC.

35 Highland Circle   (617) 449-6222
Needham, MA 02194   fax: (617) 444-2318

FORECAST!
Version: na   *Last Updated:* 1994   *No. of Users:* na
Functions: spreadsheet, statistics
Systems: DOS, Windows
Special Requirements: Lotus 1-2-3 or Excel
Price: $165
Return Policy: 30 days
Description: Includes a variety of time series models such as trend analysis (linear, exponential, hyperbolic and S-curve), moving averages, exponential smoothing, decomposition analysis and seasonal adjusted forecasts. Offers multiple regression models and a statistical analysis module, including histograms. Up to 300 observations and up to 10 variables may be entered simultaneously; the program will forecast up to 52 periods into the future. Data may be loaded from an existing worksheet or from the Windows clipboard.

INTEX BOND CALCULATIONS
Version: 2.4   *Last Updated:* 1994   *No. of Users:* na
Securities: bonds
Functions: bond analysis, spreadsheet
Systems: DOS, Windows
Special Requirements: Lotus 1-2-3, Excel
Price: $495 basic, $795 advanced, $995 int'l version; demo available, contact vendor
Return Policy: 30-60 days; restocking fee
Technical Support: phone hours, 8 am-6 pm, M-F; newsletter
Description: An add-in program that lets user compute yield, price, duration and more within Lotus 1-2-3 or Excel. Provides SIA-compliant calculations for bills, notes and bonds. Functions can be added to spreadsheet or database with a single keystroke.

INTEX CMO ANALYST
Version: 2.0   *Last Updated:* 1994   *No. of Users:* na
Securities: bonds
Functions: bond analysis, spreadsheet
Systems: Windows

Special Requirements: Lotus 1-2-3 for Windows, Excel
Price: call for pricing information
Return Policy: 30 days
Technical Support: phone hours, 8 am-6 pm, M-F; newsletter
Description: An add-in to Microsoft Excel and Lotus 1-2-3 for Windows that is designed to analyze and manage CMOs. Analyze a single tranche or an entire portfolio. All key CMO calculations are provided, including price, yield and WAL. A wide variety of advanced features are offered such as vector analysis and forwarding settlement. Includes Intex's database of over 1,000 deals—more than 20,000 bonds. Includes monthly pay down factors for all seasoned deals along with models for newly-issued deals. Prints, graphs, analyzes deals, or automatically generates a cash flow report of an entire life of a bond.

INTEX FIXED-INCOME SUBROUTINES FOR BONDS, MBSS, CMOS

Version: 2.1   *Last Updated:* na   *No. of Users:* na
Securities: stocks, bonds, futures, options
Functions: bond analysis, spreadsheet
Systems: DOS, Mini, Workstation
Price: call for pricing information
Return Policy: all sales final
Technical Support: phone hours, 8 am-6 pm, M-F
Description: Program provides all key calculations for every type of bond, MBS or CMO instrument. Provides over 36 different calculations including yield, duration, convexity and accrued interest. On-going development process assures compatibility with the industry's newest instruments. Subroutines are written in "C"—user can select subroutines for the PC, workstation or mainframe environments.

INTEX MORTGAGE-BACKED CALCULATIONS

Version: 2.1   *Last Updated:* 1993   *No. of Users:* na
Securities: bonds
Functions: bond analysis, spreadsheet
Systems: DOS, Windows
Special Requirements: Lotus 1-2-3, Excel
Price: $495 and up; demo available, contact vendor
Return Policy: 30 days; restocking fee
Technical Support: phone hours, 8 am-6 pm, M-F; newsletter
Description: A mortgage-backed security (MBS) analysis program that computes all key calculations, factoring in considerations such as pre-

payment rates, delay days and service costs. Functions are entered into spreadsheet or database with a few commands. Three different versions: basic offers a CPR prepayment model; advanced provides CPR, PSA and FHA models and support for ARMs; excess servicing provides added calculations for institutions that issue MBS instruments.

INTEX OPTION PRICE CALCULATIONS
Version: 2.1   *Last Updated:* 1994   *No. of Users:* na
Securities: options
Functions: options analysis, spreadsheet
Systems: DOS, Windows
Special Requirements: Lotus 1-2-3, Excel
Price: $495; demo available, contact vendor
Return Policy: 30 days; restocking fee
Technical Support: newsletter
Description: Three common pricing models are provided for computing options on bonds as well as equities (stocks, commodities, futures and currencies). Models include Black-Scholes, binomial and "down and out." Both puts and calls are supported, as well as American and European methods. All the "Greek" sensitivity ratios (delta, gamma, theta, vega, rho and psi) are included for additional analysis, along with essential volatility and implied volatility functions. Runs as an add-in with Lotus 1-2-3 or Excel.

INTUIT INC.

155 Linfield Ave   (800) 964-1040
P.O. Box 3014   (415) 322-0573
Menlo Park, CA 94026

MACINTAX PERSONAL 1040
Version: 11.0   *Last Updated:* 1993   *No. of Users:* 185,000
Functions: financial planning
Systems: Mac
Special Requirements: Macintosh Plus or higher; 2M RAM; System 6.0.5 or greater
Price: $69.95, $29.95 renewal
Return Policy: 30 days
Technical Support: toll-free number; phone hours, 10:30 am-8 pm, M-F; BBS support; newsletter

Description: Displays over 100 forms and schedules in their exact form on screen. Tax calculations are performed automatically, and since all forms, schedules and worksheets are linked, they are updated every time a change is made. User double-clicks the mouse on any line to get complete IRS instructions. All printouts are exact replicas and can be filed with the IRS. Text files from spreadsheets, databases and accounting programs, such as Quicken, MacMoney, Managing Your Money, and Personal Tax Analyst, can be directly imported into MacInTax. State programs can be purchased separately.

QUICKEN 4 FOR WINDOWS
Version: 4.0   *Last Updated:* 1994   *No. of Users:* na
Securities: stocks, bonds, futures, mutual funds, indexes, options, real estate
Functions: financial planning, portfolio management
Systems: Windows
Special Requirements: 386+, Windows 3.1, 3M RAM, 8M hard disk space (12M for deluxe version)
Price: $39.99; $59.99 deluxe version
Return Policy: 60 days
Technical Support: toll-free number; phone hours, 9 am-5 pm, M-F
Description: Personal and small business financial organization program. Bills module prints checks, categorizes all spending, and contains functions for electronic bill payment. Investments module tracks stocks, bonds, mutual funds, etc. Produces performance graphs/reports, reports capital gains, and includes an investment calculator. Tracks all credit card spending, computes principal/interest on loans, accounts for fixed/variable interest rates, develops payments schedules, contains loan and refinance calculator, and keeps track of all forms of bank accounts including checking, savings, and cash. Contains module for tax recordkeeping, links to tax software, and has tax schedule reports. Computes value of user's home and important possessions. Creates budget spreadsheets, budget vs. actual reports and graphs, and provides retirement and college planning. Also prints reports on cash flow, income and expenses, category detail, budgets, net worth and more. Customize any report with subtotaling, filtering, and sorting options. Deluxe version includes home inventory and net worth tracking function, a tax guidebook and tax link assistant, plus the tradeline electronic stock guide that provides historical stock price information and Quicken quotes that provide current stock prices.

QUICKEN 5 FOR MACINTOSH

Version: 5.0   *Last Updated:* 1994   *No. of Users:* na

Securities: stocks, bonds, futures, mutual funds, indexes, options, real estate

Functions: financial planning, portfolio management

Systems: Mac

Special Requirements: 4M RAM for System 7 or higher

Price: $39.95 street price; $49.95 direct from Intuit

Return Policy: 60 days

Technical Support: toll-free number; phone hours, 9 am-5 pm, M-F

Description: Personal and small business financial organization program. Bills module prints checks, categorizes all spending, and contains functions for electronic bill payment. Investments module tracks stocks, bonds, mutual funds, etc. Also produces performance graphs/reports, reports capital gains, and includes an investment calculator. Tracks all credit card spending, computes principal/interest on loans, accounts for fixed/variable interest rates, develops payments schedules, contains loan and refinance calculator, and keeps track of all forms of bank accounts including checking, savings, and cash. Also contains module for tax recordkeeping, links to tax software, and has tax schedule reports. Computes value of user's home and important possessions. Creates budget spreadsheets, budget vs. actual reports and graphs, and provides retirement and college planning. Also prints reports on cash flow, income and expenses, category detail, budgets, net worth and more. Customizes any report with subtotaling, filtering, and sorting options. New features include the iconbar, improved bank account reconciliation, question-based help screens, enhanced quickfill, quick report, comparison reports, financial forecasts, and improved tax planning.

QUICKEN 8 FOR DOS

Version: 8.0   *Last Updated:* 1994   *No. of Users:* na

Securities: stocks, bonds, futures, mutual funds, indexes, options, real estate

Functions: financial planning, portfolio management

Systems: DOS

Special Requirements: 386+, 2.7M hard disk space

Price: $39.95

Return Policy: 60 days

Technical Support: toll-free number; phone hours, 9 am-5 pm, M-F

Description: Personal and small business financial organization program. Bills module prints checks, categorizes all spending, and contains functions for electronic bill payment. Investments module tracks stocks, bonds, mutual funds, etc. Produces performance graphs/reports, reports capital gains, and includes an investment calculator. Tracks all credit card spending, computes principal/interest on loans, accounts for fixed/variable interest rates, develops payments schedules, contains loan and refinance calculator, and keeps track of all forms of bank accounts including checking, savings, and cash. Contains module for tax recordkeeping, links to tax software, and has tax schedule reports. Computes value of user's home and important possessions. Creates budget spreadsheets, budget vs. actual reports and graphs, and provides retirement and college planning. Also prints reports on cash flow, income and expenses, category details, budgets, net worth and more. Customizes any report with subtotaling, filtering, and sorting options. New version includes improved tax planner, global find and replace, plus Quicken quotes.

QUICKEN DELUXE 4 FOR WINDOWS CD-ROM

Version: 4.0   *Last Updated:* 1994   *No. of Users:* na
Securities: stocks, bonds, futures, mutual funds, indexes, options, real estate
Functions: financial planning, portfolio management
Systems: Windows
Special Requirements: 486+, 8M RAM, 12M hard disk space
Price: $59.99
Return Policy: 60 days
Technical Support: toll-free number; phone hours, 9 am-5 pm, M-F
Description: Personal and small business financial organization program. Bills module prints checks, categorizes all spending, and contains functions for electronic bill payment. Investments module tracks stocks, bonds, mutual funds, etc. Produces performance graphs/reports, reports capital gains, and includes an investment calculator. Tracks all credit card spending, computes principal/interest on loans, accounts for fixed/variable interest rates, develops payments schedules, contains loan and refinance calculator, and keeps track of all forms of bank accounts including checking, savings, and cash. Contains module for tax recordkeeping, links to tax software, and has tax schedule reports. Computes value of user's home and important possessions. Creates budget spreadsheets, budget vs. actual reports and graphs, and provides retirement and college planning. Also prints reports on cash flow, income and expenses, category detail, budgets, net

worth and more. Customizes any report with subtotaling, filtering, and sorting options. Includes interactive advice section, multi-media library, mutual fund selector, tax guidebook, plus all the other features offered in the deluxe version on floppy.

TURBOTAX PERSONAL 1040
Version: 11.0   *Last Updated:* 1993   *No. of Users:* 680,000
Functions: financial planning
Systems: DOS, Windows
Special Requirements: Windows 3.1+, 4M RAM, 10M free disk space
Price: $69.95, $29.95 renewal
Return Policy: 30 days
Technical Support: phone hours, 10:30 am-8 pm M-F; BBS support; newsletter
Description: Provides tax preparation, planning and recordkeeping. Inputs are similar to a spreadsheet with full-screen IRS forms. Menu-driven commands and on-line help are available. Computations are done for over 100 forms, schedules and worksheets. The package provides on-line IRS instructions, a quick-link forms finder for the user, tax forms printed to IRS specifications and a data examiner to check for omissions in the tax return. Companion programs for preparing state taxes are available and sold separately.

INVESTABILITY CORPORATION

P.O. Box 43307   (502) 722-5700
Louisville, KY 40253

INVESTABILITY MONEYMAP
Version: na   *Last Updated:* na   *No. of Users:* na
Functions: financial planning
Systems: DOS
Price: $20
Return Policy: 30 days; $3 restocking fee
Technical Support: phone hours, 9 am-5 pm, M-F
Description: Users specify inflation rates, projected investment returns, portfolio sizes or income/contribution streams, frequency of cash flows, and time periods. The output—on-screen or printed with ability to produce personalized headings—shows projected contribution/income amounts and portfolio balances for each cash flow date, providing an investment/retirement schedule that can act as a bench-

mark for actual investment or retirement programs. Format lets user specify target goals in present-day dollars, then produces the resulting schedule incorporating inflation adjustments. Also calculates present value, future value and payment amounts on a time-value-of-money basis.

INVESTMENT SOFTWARE

543 CR 312   (303) 884-4130
Ignacio, CO 81137

PERSONAL MARKET ANALYSIS (PMA)
Version: 4.0   *Last Updated:* 1992   *No. of Users:* na
Securities: stocks, futures, mutual funds, indexes
Functions: technical analysis
Systems: DOS
Price: $149; 10% AAII discount
Return Policy: 30 days
Technical Support: phone hours, 10 am-7 pm, M-F
Description: Calculates, charts and stores values of technical indicators. Predefined and user-defined indicators available. The manual discusses the predefined indicators and furnishes descriptions and set-up instructions for a variety of other indicators including: moving average, loose convergence-divergence, relative strength index, momentum or rate-of-change indicators, stochastic oscillators, volume indicators (NVI, OBV, PVT, and DVT), parabolic time/price system and directional movement indicator. Additional features: simple indicators can be combined and manipulated to produce other derivative indicators; input data can be charted to the same time scale and on the same chart as personal indicators; expanded charting capabilities—up to 3 curves per chart, charts any 12 consecutive-month period, automatic chart scaling, insertion of flags to indicate significant points, addition of lines to indicate trends, bounds, etc., automatic printing of pre-selected chart groups, menu-driven.

INVESTMENT TECHNOLOGY

5104 Utah Street   (903) 455-3255
Greenville, TX 75402

INVESTIGATOR *(formerly Investigator+)*
Version: 1.2   *Last Updated:* 1993   *No. of Users:* 100
Securities: stocks, futures, mutual funds, indexes, options
Functions: technical analysis
Systems: DOS
Price: $49; demo available, $10; 20% AAII discount
Return Policy: all sales final
Technical Support: phone hours, 24 hours
Description: A charting, technical analysis and data management program for stocks, options, indexes, mutual funds or commodities. Uses accepted technical indicators developed by contributors in the technical analysis field. Maintains up to 1,000 days or weeks of data for 1,000 different issues (500 daily and 500 weekly). Data updates and creation can be manual or fully automatic using "XACCESS" download software with Dial/Data. Multiple chart formats are available with a large selection of technical indicators. A screening system allows selection based on up to 5 criteria from a choice of 10 screening methods.

INVESTMENT TOOLS, INC.

P.O. Box 9816   (702) 851-1157
Reno, NV 89507-9816

FUTURES MARKETS ANALYZER
Version: 4.0   *Last Updated:* 1994   *No. of Users:* na
Securities: futures
Functions: futures analysis
Systems: DOS
Price: $795/yr.; demo available, $9 shipping & handling
Return Policy: all sales final
Technical Support: phone hours, 12 pm-3 pm, M-F
Description: Monitors 39 futures contracts including stock index futures, currencies, meats, grains, metals, CRB index, crude oil, heating oil, cotton, sugar, coffee and cocoa. User inputs daily high, low and closing prices; generates a report giving buy/sell signal, entry price, exit price and stop for 39 futures contracts. Optimizes parameters automatically at the time of change of contract month. Will accept manual data input or ASCII file. Accepts daily quote file from Technical Tools, CSI and Genesis Data Services, Signal, Radio Exchange, DTN Wall Street, Dial/Data, DJN/R and Knight-Ridder. Will import data from historical data files in CSI, MetaStock, or CompuTrac format.

INVESTOR'S TECHNICAL SERVICES

P.O. Box 164075   (512) 328-8000
Austin, TX 78716   fax: (512) 328-3078

BEHOLD!
Version: 2.1   *Last Updated:* 1994   *No. of Users:* 200
Securities: stocks, bonds, futures, mutual funds, indexes
Functions: technical analysis
Systems: Mac
Price: $995; $395 for 3 mo., manual-$50; demo available, free
Return Policy: all sales final
Technical Support: phone hours, 9 am-5 pm, M-F; BBS support
Description: Technical analysis program that features backtesting and optimizing of technical trading systems for a variety of securities. Testing may utilize data for a single security or a portfolio of securities. Strategies are written in English are support intermarket analysis. Daily trading supported through automation macros and autodetermination of indicated market positions for a portfolio of securities. Real-time trading is supported by link to TickerWatcher.

JEROME TECHNOLOGY, INC.

P.O. Box 403   (908) 369-7503
Raritan, NJ 08869   fax: (908) 369-5993

WAVE WISE SPREADSHEET FOR WINDOWS
Version: 6.0   *Last Updated:* 1994   *No. of Users:* na
Securities: stocks, bonds, futures, mutual funds, indexes
Functions: technical analysis, bond analysis, spreadsheet, statistics
Systems: Windows
Price: $150; demo available, $20
Return Policy: all sales final
Technical Support: phone hours, 8:30 am-6 pm, M-F
Description: Combines a traditional spreadsheet with the graphics capabilities of stock market charting packages. Provides formula construction capabilities to make custom indicators and studies. Formulas can be automatically applied to the entire column for fast computations. Performs Elliot Wave analysis, cycle analysis, Fibonacci Retracements, and "what if" analysis using built-in technical analysis and sta-

tistics functions. Includes line and bar charts, full zoom capability and chart overlay/split screen capability.

KASANJIAN RESEARCH

P.O. Box 4608   (909) 337-0816
Blue Jay, CA 92317   fax: (909) 337-8388

NATURE'S PULSE
Version: 4.0   *Last Updated:* 1993   *No. of Users:* na
Securities: stocks, bonds, futures, mutual funds, indexes
Functions: technical analysis, expert system
Systems: DOS, Windows, OS/2
Price: $1,595; demo available, free; 10% AAII discount
Return Policy: all sales final
Technical Support: phone hours, 10:30 am-7:30 pm, M-F; BBS support; newsletter; fee for tech support—varies
Description: A change-in-trend forecasting system that also forecasts likely support and resistance levels. Includes a time and price analysis toolkit. By using pre-defined ratio files, future changes in trend can be determined. Over 250,000 calculations are possible. Uses all combinations of dates, cycles, price levels and ratios to project time and price clusters. The program reads all major data formats. The automode function allows automatic analysis with forecasts.

LARRY ROSEN CO.

7008 Springdale Road   (502) 228-4343
Louisville, KY 40241   fax: (502) 228-4782

BOND PORTFOLIO MANAGER
Version: 94.1   *Last Updated:* 1994   *No. of Users:* 256
Securities: bonds
Functions: financial planning, portfolio management, bond analysis, spreadsheet, statistics
Systems: DOS, Windows, Mac
Special Requirements: spreadsheet program
Price: $89; 20% AAII discount
Return Policy: all sales final
Technical Support: phone hours, 9 am-5 pm, M-F

Description: Keeps track of the market value of each bond and the entire portfolio (priced to the lesser value of yield to call or maturity); the month and day that each interest payment is due (as interest is received or coupons are clipped receipts can be checked off on the list for that month of receivables expected; also interest receipts can be balanced by month throughout the year); and unrealized gain or loss for each bond, ranked in order of magnitude from the largest loss to largest gain. Calculations are made using taxable basis adjusted for amortization to determine which bonds to consider selling or swapping to create a tax loss. Evaluates and reports portfolios by credit worthiness of the bond issuer (e.g., 25% of portfolio is rated AAA, etc.) and date of maturity, call or put, (e.g., 18% of the portfolio matures or is expected to be called in 1998). Features housekeeping information such as bond location, serial number, whether registered or coupon, purchasing broker, call and put dates in chronological order. User enters 10 interest rates from the current yield curve and current date and the software then makes all the calculations including market value of each bond. Calculates duration and convexity for both individual bonds and entire portfolio.

COMPLETE BOND ANALYZER
Version: 94.1   *Last Updated:* 1994   *No. of Users:* 1,873
Securities: bonds
Functions: portfolio management, bond analysis, statistics
Systems: DOS, Mac
Price: $89; 20% AAII discount
Return Policy: all sales final
Technical Support: phone hours, 9 am-5 pm, M-F
Description: Calculates bond yield to maturity given price and price given yield to maturity. Also calculates yield to call, accrued interest at purchase or sale, duration and revised duration, theoretical spot rates, etc. Results are computed for taxables or tax-exempts, for 360- or 365-day years, and for government, agency, conventional or zero-coupon bonds.

FINANCIAL & INTEREST CALCULATOR
Version: 94.1   *Last Updated:* 1994   *No. of Users:* 2,234
Securities: stocks, bonds, futures, mutual funds, indexes, options, real estate
Functions: financial planning, portfolio management, bond analysis, real estate analysis, statistics

Systems: DOS, Mac
Price: $89; 20% AAII discount
Return Policy: all sales final
Technical Support: phone hours, 9 am-5 pm, M-F
Description: User can perform studies including: internal rate of return for retirement plans including multiple cash flows within the same or different years; loan amortization schedules; variable rate mortgage loan amortization schedules; mortgage points—how they effect the true cost of a loan; future value of a single or a series of investments—how much an investment today or a series of equal investments are worth in the future with growth at a stated interest rate; present value of a single future payment—the discounted value today of money due in the future; present value of an annuity—the discounted value today of a series of future equal periodic payments; internal rate of return given a series of cash flows; and supercompounding—finds either the amount to invest to accumulate a stated sum in the future or the future value, assuming the investment amount is increased each year by a stated amount.

INVESTMENT IRR ANALYSIS FOR STOCKS, BONDS & REAL ESTATE

Version: 94.2   *Last Updated:* 1994   *No. of Users:* 1,778
Securities: stocks, bonds, real estate
Functions: financial planning, portfolio management, fundamental analysis, bond analysis, real estate analysis, spreadsheet, statistics
Systems: DOS, Windows, OS/2, Mac
Special Requirements: spreadsheet program
Price: $89; 20% AAII discount
Return Policy: all sales final
Technical Support: phone hours, 9 am-5 pm, M-F
Description: Calculates the internal rate of return (after taxes) for existing or proposed investments at any desired interest rate for reinvestment of cash flows, as well as with zero reinvestment. User can compute and display a complete year-by-year (up to 40 years) detailed cash flow analysis. Annual income details, interest, expenses, principal, pretax and aftertax cash flows can be printed. Requires a spreadsheet program. Allows a direct comparison of projected investment results between both investments of the same type (e.g. stocks) and different types (e.g. stocks vs. real estate or bonds.)

MORTGAGE LOANS—IS IT TIME TO REFINANCE?
Version: 94.1   *Last Updated:* 1994   *No. of Users:* 435
Securities: real estate
Functions: financial planning, real estate analysis, spreadsheet
Systems: DOS, Windows, OS/2, Mac
Special Requirements: spreadsheet program
Price: $89; 20% AAII discount
Return Policy: all sales final
Technical Support: phone hours, 9 am-5 pm, M-F
Description: Determines whether or not to refinance a loan by considering: the interplay between the old and new interest rate; the costs to obtain the new loan; appraisal; up-front fees to the lender—points; origination fees; number of years remaining on the old loan compared to the number of years over which the new loan is repayable; the length of time the borrower is likely to keep the new loan (before selling); the amount of the new loan; and pay-off penalties, if any on both the old and new loans, etc. Applies time value of money concepts to help the borrower select the best path. Determines the net present value resulting form refinancing the loan. Works with Lotus 1-2-3, Excel, Works, ClarisWorks and AppleWorks.

OPTIONS VALUATION
Version: 94.1   *Last Updated:* 1994   *No. of Users:* 276
Securities: options
Functions: options analysis
Systems: DOS, Mac
Price: $89; 20% AAII discount
Return Policy: all sales final
Technical Support: phone hours, 9 am-5 pm, M-F
Description: Computes options values for stocks, European bond embedded options and American bond embedded options. Additional programs calculate time spread or elapsed time; average weighted life; Macaulay duration; and modified duration. Calculate option values given volatility, or volatility given the price of the option. Also calculates historical volatility if price history is supplied.

LIBERTY RESEARCH CORPORATION

1250 Capital of Texas Highway (800) 827-0090
Bldg. 2, Suite 304 (512) 329-2762
Austin, TX 78746 fax: (512) 329-2588

INVESTOGRAPH PLUS, OPTIMIZER
Version: 2.1 *Last Updated:* 1992 *No. of Users:* na
Securities: stocks, bonds, futures, mutual funds, indexes, options
Functions: technical analysis, bond analysis, futures analysis, options analysis, simulation/game, statistics
Systems: DOS
Price: IVT $399.99; Optimizer $99; demo available, $19.95; 12.5% AAII discount
Return Policy: 30 days; $75 restocking fee
Technical Support: phone hours, 10 am-6 pm, M-F; newsletter
Description: A technical analysis program that includes: arithmetic and exponential moving averages, arithmetic average cycle extraction, on-balance volume, negative volume index, open interest, volume, RSI, stochastic, directional movement index, commodity channel index, MACD, moving average envelopes, trendlines, point and figure charting, equivolume charting, momentum oscillator relative strength charts, and spread charts. Proprietary functions include: moving average that minimizes lag in calculated values, least squares cycle extraction, cumulative ease-of-movement study, least squares momentum, automatic least squares channel drawing, spread oscillation, Formula X, Formula Y, Formula H oscillators, six preprogrammed trading systems, filtering trading system, buy/sell signals with user-defined studies, envelope edge predictions, "what-if" technical studies, price predictions with probability tables, trend-adjusted options fair prices, statistically calculated trend finder, and Fibonacci levels within trend channels. Has menus and prompts, on-line help messages, and auto-processing capability. Also includes interface to user-written programs for trading simulations and oscillator calculations.

LINCOLN SYSTEMS, CORP.

P.O. Box 391 (508) 692-3910
Westford, MA 01886

SIBYL/RUNNER INTERACTIVE FORECASTING
Version: 6.01   *Last Updated:* 1994   *No. of Users:* 550
Securities: stocks, bonds, futures, mutual funds, indexes, options, real estate
Functions: fundamental analysis, statistics
Systems: Windows
Price: $495; demo available, free
Return Policy: 30 days
Technical Support: phone hours, 9 am-5 pm, M-F
Description: Sibyl advises methods suitable for user's data, selecting from 19 recognized time-series methods. Summarizes statistics for each selection. Complete statistics: 10 aggregate error measures displayed, actual/forecast graphics ex-post and ex-ante forecast statistics. Sends forecasts to Lotus software for spreadsheet use.

LINDO SYSTEMS, INC.

1415 N. Dayton
Chicago, IL 60622

(800) 441-2378
(312) 871-2524
fax: (312) 871-1777

WHAT'SBEST!
Version: 2.0   *Last Updated:* 1993   *No. of Users:* na
Functions: financial planning, spreadsheet
Systems: DOS, Mac
Special Requirements: Spreadsheet program
Price: 400 variables $149; 1,500 variables $695; 4,000 variables $995; 16,000 variables $2,995; 32,000 variables $4,995; demo available, free
Return Policy: 60 days
Technical Support: phone hours, 10 am-6 pm, M-F; newsletter
Description: Add-in for Lotus spreadsheet. Finds answers that maximize profit and minimize cost on a variety of applications such as portfolio allocation and debt defeasance. Personal version, up to 400 variables; commercial version, up to 1,500 varibles; professional version, up to 4,000 variables; industrial version, up to 16,000 variables; extended version, up to 32,000 variables.

LINN SOFTWARE, INC.

8641 Pleasant Hill Road   (404) 929-8802
Lithonia, GA 30058   fax: (404) 929-8802

TICKERWATCHER
Version: 7.0   *Last Updated:* 1994   *No. of Users:* 5,000+
Functions: portfolio management, technical analysis, spreadsheet
Systems: Mac
Special Requirements: 4M RAM, Apple system 6.07 or above
Price: $195, $295, $395, $595 depending on version selected; 10% AAII
   discount
Return Policy: 60 days
Description: Provides Macintosh user with real-time or delayed quote
monitoring, portfolio management, and daily charts on ticker sym-
bols. Intraday data collection and intraday color charting features are
provided. Handles all security types—stocks, futures, options, etc.
Provides price, volume and news alerts on any ticker. Unlimited number of quote pages can be organized in any sequence. Can handle 255
priced portfolios. Performs historical monitoring and charting of portfolio values. Chart types: bar, candlestick, volume. Each chart includes
5 moving averages. Includes multi-window chart slide show feature.
Exports closing or historical data to spreadsheets and other applications. Daily auto-update of Compu Trac/M or Hotline history files.
Real-time data link for Excel spreadsheets. Tracks industry groups
with Industry Monitor's predefined lists. TickerWatcher Studies is a library of technical indicator chart types added to TickerWatcher. It contains the Wilder's RSI, MACD, Lane's Slow Stochastic D, Avg. Directional Movement Index, Commodity Channel Index, ARMS Ease of
Movement, Chicago Floor Trading Pivotal Point, Rate of Change. TickerWatcher supports the S&P Sock Guide (DTN edition), and Canadian
stock quotations (DTN, BMI, InGenius). TickerWatcher tracks stocks
and commodities.

LOTUS DEVELOPMENT CORPORATION

55 Cambridge Parkway   (800) 343-5414
Cambridge, MA 02142   (617) 577-8500
                                               fax: (617) 661-0024

LOTUS 1-2-3 FOR OS/2
Version: 2.0   *Last Updated:* 1993   *No. of Users:* na
Functions: bond analysis, spreadsheet, statistics
Systems: OS/2
Price: $495 for standard edition, $595 for network server edition
Return Policy: all sales final
Technical Support: phone hours, 24 hours M-F; fee for tech support—3
    months free, $99/year
Description: A graphical version of Lotus 1-2-3 designed for OS/2.
Presentation Manager provides full user interface, including WYSI-
WYG display, full mouse support, windowing, pulldown menus and
dialog boxes, enhanced graphing, and presentation-quality output.
Has previews and palettes in dialog boxes plus Graph Gallery for pre-
viewing and selecting graphs and charts. Includes advanced spreadsheet features such as 3-D worksheets, file linking, direct access to external data sources through DataLens, and network support. Also has
solver and goal-seeking technology for answering "what if" problems.

LOTUS 1-2-3 RELEASE 4 FOR DOS
Version: 4   *Last Updated:* 1994   *No. of Users:* na
Functions: spreadsheet, statistics
Systems: DOS
Price: $495
Return Policy: all sales final
Technical Support: phone hours, 24 hours M-F
Description: Offers 3-D multi-page worksheets to organize, consoli-
date and compare information and WYSIWYG screen display and
presentation-quality output. Includes spreadsheet auditing tools for
documenting and tracking formulas and computations, and a file
viewer, based on Lotus Magellan technology, for browsing, retrieving
or linking to Lotus 1-2-3 files located on disk. Supports multi-files in
memory. Provides Solver, a goal-seeking tool that solves problems defined in the spreadsheet environment, access to external data via
DataLens and extended, expanded and virtual memory support for
building larger spreadsheets. Provides graphic and drawing enhance-

ments also found in release 2.4, including wrapping text around graphics and placing and displaying an unlimited number of "live" graphs anywhere in the worksheet. Offers 8,192 rows, 256 columns and 256 pages of worksheet space and background recalculation and undo.

LOTUS 1-2-3 RELEASE 5 FOR WINDOWS
Version: 5   *Last Updated:* 1994   *No. of Users:* na
Functions: bond analysis, spreadsheet, statistics
Systems: Windows
Special Requirements: 3M RAM
Price: $495
Return Policy: all sales final
Technical Support: phone hours, 24 hours M-F
Description: Lotus 1-2-3 release for users running Windows 3.0+ operating system environments. Features include SmartIcons, 3D spreadsheets, version manager, data query assistant, intelligent charting, and the Lotus Classic menu.

LOTUS IMPROV FOR WINDOWS
Version: 2.1   *Last Updated:* 1993   *No. of Users:* na
Functions: spreadsheet, statistics
Systems: Windows
Price: $495
Return Policy: 90 days
Technical Support: phone hours, 12 hours M-F; newsletter
Description: A spreadsheet program that allows users to view information dynamically at the click of a mouse, use English formulas instead of numerical syntax and create presentations using data, text, graphics, images and sound. Allows users to view and compare data in different ways, without manually rebuilding the spreadsheet. Data can be viewed or arranged to compare data relationships; summarized data can be expanded to show detail; or information can be hidden for clarity. Automatically and immediately displays the worksheet to reflect the new arrangement, without recalculation or re-entry of formulas or data. Features multi-dimensional structure that supports a robust spreadsheet design, so that users can display, arrange and manipulate up to 12 categories of data with a worksheet at one time.

MACRO*WORLD RESEARCH, CORP.

4265 Brownsboro Road   (800) 841-5398
Suite 170   (910) 759-0600
Winston-Salem, NC 27106-3429   fax: (910) 759-0636

MACRO*WORLD INVESTOR
Version: na   *Last Updated:* na   *No. of Users:* 500
Securities: stocks, bonds, futures, mutual funds, indexes
Functions: financial planning, portfolio management, fundamental analysis, simulation/game, statistics
Systems: DOS
Price: $899.95; $399.95/year for update; 28% AAII discount
Return Policy: 30 days
Technical Support: phone hours, 9 am-5 pm, M-F
Description: Forecasting and investment analysis to provide projected rates of return, degree of risk, buy/hold/sell signals for user-specified portfolios, optimal risk/return mix for buy recommendations, simulations of past results and forecasts of fundamental performance (earnings, book value, dividends, economic values and ratios). Features summary reports covering short-term outlook, turning points and exceptions; forecast ranges, confidence levels and recession periods; and custom portfolio optimizations. Equipped with 5-10 years of stock price data on all companies the user subscribes to with 10-25 years of data available for over 120 U.S. and international business and financial indicators including Canada, Japan, Germany and the U.K. Exchanges history and forecasts with other systems to allow users to include additional data. Update service provides new data, historical revisions, bulletins and telephone support.

MAEDAE ENTERPRISES

5430 Murr Road   (719) 683-3860
Peyton, CO 80831

MORTGAGE DESIGNER FOR WINDOWS
Version: 2.2   *Last Updated:* 1994   *No. of Users:* 250+
Functions: financial planning
Systems: Windows
Special Requirements: Windows 3.0 or higher

Price: $39 plus $5 shipping & handling; demo available, free; 33% AAII discount

Return Policy: all sales final

Technical Support: phone hours, 8 am-5 pm, M-Sat.

Description: Mortgage Designer is a personal finance program that includes functions for "what if," loan amortization, tax adjustable payments, PIII, cost of mortgage, mortgage database, breakeven analysis for refinancing, plus much more. Includes a color toolbar, 3D dialogs and built-in help.

MANTIC SOFTWARE CORPORATION

1523 Country Club Road   (800) 730-2919
Fort Collins, CO 80524   (303) 224-1615

BINOMIAL MARKET MODEL

Version: A.08   *Last Updated:* 1994   *No. of Users:* na

Securities: options

Functions: options analysis, simulation/game

Systems: Windows

Special Requirements: Windows 3.1 and mouse

Price: $7.50

Return Policy: all sales final

Technical Support: phone hours, 10 am-7 pm, M-F

Description: Uses simulation, interactive graphics and integrated hypertext instructional material to teach about volatility and the statistics of stock price movements. The program simulates price movements using the Binomial Model, a technique used to calculated the "fair value" of American-style stock and index options. Topics explored include the definition of volatility and how to calculate it; how the Binomial Model works, the statistical probability of trends in price data: estimating the expected range of future price movements; how to create a probability weighted "map" of future stock prices; assumptions inherent in option price calculations: and how the value of an option is derived from the price map. The program graphs simulated price movements over time, with long- and-short-term moving averages; calculates volatility and plots price distributions, graphs the probability of "price runs" of various lengths: show the expected range and probability fo future stock prices; draws the future price map; and calculates option values, illustrating each step on the price map. Simulated price streams can be written to an ASCII text file.

OPTIONS LABORATORY
Version: na   *Last Updated:* 1993   *No. of Users:* na
Securities: stocks, indexes, options
Functions: options analysis, simulation/game
Systems: Windows
Special Requirements: Mouse & Windows 3.1
Price: $129.95
Return Policy: 30 days
Technical Support: phone hours, 10 am-7 pm, M-F
Description: An interactive, graphical learning software package using real or simulated prices to teach and explore options strategies. Comes with a customized texbook. Evaluates, tracks, and adjusts any option position. Teaches option basics and classic strategies. Covers conservative and speculative techniques, emphasizing the use of analytical tools for risk management. Analyses of individual options and the overall position are displayed graphically. Models any strategy with up to four different European or American options and the underlying security. It predicts value and payoff; share equivalent risk; probability weighted performance; early exercise threshold prices; dividend effects; and time evolution. In Advance Mode, the Trade Sheet tracks actual trades and changing positions.

MARASYS, INC.

2615 N. 4th Street, #755   (800) 879-2934
Coeur d'Alene, ID 83814   (208) 772-2308
                                      fax: (208) 772-2308

ECONPLOT
Version: 1.0   *Last Updated:* 1994   *No. of Users:* 50
Functions: fundamental analysis
Systems: DOS
Price: $49.95
Return Policy: all sales final
Technical Support: phone hours, 11 am-7 pm, M-F
Description: Plots the 4-year business cycle indicators from Public Brand Software. Of the 250 indicators, user can plot up to 15 indicators per window with 1 or 2 windows per screen, each indicator being plotted in a different color. Up to 15 indicators can be grouped together for easier access. Separate or common scales can be used per window.

MARKETARTS, INC.

P.O. Box 850922   (214) 235-9594
Richardson, TX 75085-0922   fax: (214) 783-6798

WINDOWS ON WALL STREET PRO
Version: 2.1   *Last Updated:* 1993   *No. of Users:* na
Securities: stocks, bonds, futures, mutual funds, indexes, options
Functions: technical analysis, spreadsheet
Systems: Windows
Price: $249, $149 retail version; demo available, free; 25% AAII discount
Technical Support: phone hours, 10 am-6 pm, M-F; BBS support
Description: A technical analysis research tool that enables the user to enter, chart, track, and analyze investment data on stocks, bonds, options, mutual funds, commodities, and many other forms of investments for buy and sell opportunities. It includes technical analysis tools, a built-in end-of-day downloading system, a comprehensive online information service system, a personal investment assistant to schedule events for unattended operation, a profitability and system tester that generates buy and sell profitability reports, indicator libraries, and a custom formula builder. Files may be imported with full compatibility from Compu Trac, MetaStock, TC-2000, AIQ, and CSI. Professional version includes Smartscan+ which enables user to scan, screen and monitor securities based on price and volume changes, trading signals, customized alerts, or users select securities.

MATHSOFT, INC.

101 Main Street   (800) 628-4223
Cambridge, MA 02142-1519   (617) 577-1017
                                            fax: (617) 577-8829

MATHCAD 5.0
Version: 5.0   *Last Updated:* 1994   *No. of Users:* 500,000
Functions: statistics
Systems: Windows, Mac
Special Requirements: Mac Plus, SE or II with 2M RAM math coprocessor; Windows
Price: $99.95; demo available

Return Policy: all sales final
Technical Support: phone hours, 9 am-5 pm, M-F
Description: Includes electronic handbook for access to standard formulas, constants, geometry, symbolic calculations for computer algebra, and other features. Includes pulldown menus, mouse point-and-click capabilities, context-sensitive help, and extended memory support. Serves as an on-line reference library for problem-solving information. Includes hundreds of formulas, constants, and diagrams. Also lets user do symbolic calculations with a simple menu pick. Live document interface allows user to calculate interactively on a PC as if working on a scratchpad or white board. Equations are automatically formatted. Built-in functions include numeric and symbolic integration, differentiation, FFTs, spline fits, and a range of statistical and transcendental functions. Also provides complex number support, solutions of simultaneous equations, matrix operations and 2-D and 3-D plotting.

MECA SOFTWARE, INC.

55 Walls Drive   (203) 256-5000
Fairfield, CT 06430-5139   fax: (203) 255-6300

ANDREW TOBIAS' TAX CUT
Version: na   *Last Updated:* 1993   *No. of Users:* na
Securities: stocks, bonds, futures, mutual funds, options, real estate
Functions: financial planning
Systems: DOS, Windows, Mac
Price: $79.95
Return Policy: 30 days
Technical Support: phone hours, 9 am-6 pm, M-F; after Feb. 7 days/week; BBS support
Description: Complete step-by-step tax preparation. Guides user through entire return. Interview automatically figures what to ask, explains how to answer each question, then fills out the forms. Audits return to make sure it's correct and every deduction has been taken. Every calculation is guaranteed accurate. If user is penalized because of a miscalculation made by TaxCut, MECA pays the penalty.

MANAGING YOUR MONEY
Version: na   *Last Updated:* 1993   *No. of Users:* na
Securities: stocks, bonds, futures, mutual funds, indexes, options, real estate

Functions: financial planning, portfolio management, real estate analysis

Systems: DOS, Windows, Mac

Price: $79.95

Return Policy: 30 days

Technical Support: phone hours, 9 am-6 pm, M-F, 9 am-3 pm, Sat.; BBS support; newsletter; fee for tech support—90 days free, then $49.95 for PlusPlan

Description: Financial organizer that contains 6 different modules to help in managing user's finances. Banking and bill paying module organizes all bank accounts and pays user's bills. Also tracks income and expenses by budget category, balances user's checkbook, reconciles user's accounts, and prints checks. Insurance planning module estimates insurance needs, tracks policies, and sorts and organizes vital records. The investments module organizes and tracks all user's investments, prints reports and graphs, and includes an asset allocation module. Includes data links to Fidelity On-Line Xpress and Prodigy's PC Financial Network. Net worth module tracks assets, liabilities, and net worth history. Includes new debt reduction feature. Financial analysis module helps plan for retirement, children's college costs, and other financial goals. Also analyzes how much home user can afford, whether to refinance mortgage, and if it is better to buy or lease your next car. Program also includes a module to track small business finances, including accounts payable and receivable with aging, profit and loss, cash flow forecasting, variable fiscal years, invoicing, balance sheets, and business tax schedules C, E, and F.

MENDELSOHN ENTERPRISES, INC.

(formerly Predictive Technologies Group)

25941 Apple Blossom Lane
Wesley Chapel, FL 33544

732-5407
(813) 973-0496
fax: (813) 973-2700

VANTAGEPOINT INTERMARKET ANALYSIS PROGRAM
(formerly VantagePoint Neural Trading System)

Version: 2.5   *Last Updated:* 1993   *No. of Users:* na

Securities: stocks, bonds, futures, indexes, currencies

Functions: technical analysis, bond analysis, futures analysis, neural network

Systems: DOS

Special Requirements: mouse recommended
Price: $2,450 for 1st market; $1,450 for 2nd; additional discounts on other markets; 10% AAII discount
Return Policy: all sales final
Technical Support: phone hours, 9 am-5 pm, M-F
Description: Alerts user to the intermarket relationships that are responsible for influencing price movements in today's financial markets. Utilizes a series of neural networks to find hidden patterns and relationships between related financial markets and the particular market that you are trading. VantagePoint's user customizable charts allow you to visualize its information graphically. Predictions are presented in a one-page daily report. VantagePoint quantifies the direction and strength of the market for the next day. Available for the Treasury bonds, S&P 500 index, Swiss franc, Deutsche mark, Japanese yen, and Eurodollar. Telephone support includes trading and technical support.

MERIT SOFTWARE CONCEPTS, INC.

P.O. Box 771966　　　　　　　　　　　　　(800) 880-8228
Houston, TX 77215-1966　　　　　　　　　(713) 782-9974
　　　　　　　　　　　　　　　　　　fax: (713) 782-3731

LIFE INSURANCE PLANNER
Version: 6.4　　　　　*Last Updated:* 1993　　　　*No. of Users:* na
Functions: financial planning
Systems: DOS
Price: $35
Return Policy: all sales final
Technical Support: phone hours, 8 am-5 pm, M-F
Description: Analyzes last expense needs, special fund needs (such as mortgage, estate taxes, education of children) and on-going needs for income, taking into account your current investment portfolio, Social Security benefits and spousal employment.

MERIT FINANCIAL PLANNER
Version: 4.0　　　　　*Last Updated:* 1994　　　　*No. of Users:* na
Functions: financial planning
Systems: DOS
Special Requirements: 5M of free disk space

Price: $175; demo available, $5; 22% AAII discount
Return Policy: all sales final
Technical Support: toll-free number; phone hours, 8 am-5 pm, M-F
Description: User can enter financial information, such as checking account, account number, balance, interest rate, taxation, stock position, purchase date, purchase price, dividend rate, current price, taxation and Merit calculates annualized rates of return on a pretax and after-tax basis. Current cash flow with income is detailed in 20+ categories for deductions and government payments and expenses categorized in 50+ areas, with the ability to add new listings. Social Security at retirement is calculated with Merit projecting a present and future value calculations. Names and addresses of all professional advisers. Merit then prints reports, financial statements, tax planning guide and action plan to provide you with an up-to-date financial "to do" list.

MERIT FOR MANAGING THE FUTURE
Version: 3.03   *Last Updated:* 1993   *No. of Users:* 1,200
Functions: financial planning
Systems: DOS
Price: $199; demo available, $5; 30% AAII discount
Return Policy: all sales final
Technical Support: phone hours, 8 am-5 pm, M-F
Description: Financial planning program designed to help individuals develop successful strategies for achieving financial independence and retirement. Organize and monitor complex financial records, with data entered on income, benefits, retirement plans, Social Security, assets, liabilities, rates of return, and expenses. Creates goals and planning strategies using data. Calculates retirement needs, future value of current investments and amount needed to be saved each year to reach goals. Can change assumptions to follow changes in financial conditions. Prints several types of financial reports, including tables and graphs.

TEN STEPS PRO
Version: 6.4   *Last Updated:* na   *No. of Users:* na
Functions: financial planning
Systems: DOS
Price: $175
Return Policy: all sales final
Description: Professional version of Ten Steps to Financial Security. Multi-user program includes a time billing system. Enter personal fi-

nancial information, set retirement goals and develop strategies for achieving financial security. The 10 steps are: goals, life expectancy, expenses, rate of return, inflation, taxes, funding, sources, strategies, and action steps. Teacher uses the value of designing investment strategies to be consistant with their goals. Designed to be a cost-efficient and effective tool for providing financial planning to individuals.

TEN STEPS TO FINANCIAL SECURITY

Version: 6.4 *Last Updated:* 1993 *No. of Users:* 1,100
Functions: financial planning
Systems: DOS
Price: $35
Return Policy: all sales final
Technical Support: phone hours, 8 am-5 pm, M-F
Description: Enter personal financial information, set retirement goals and develop strategies for achieving financial security. The 10 steps are: goals, life expectancy, expenses, rate of return, inflation, taxes, funding, sources, strategies, action steps. Teaches user the value of designing investment strategies to be consistent with their goals. Designed to be a cost efficient and effective tool for providing financial planning to individuals.

MESA

P.O. Box 1801 (800) 633-6372
Goleta, CA 93116 (805) 969-6478
fax: (805) 969-1358

EPOCH PRO

Version: na *Last Updated:* 1990 *No. of Users:* na
Securities: stocks, bonds, futures, indexes
Functions: technical analysis
Systems: DOS
Special Requirements: Math co-processor recommended
Price: $995; demo available
Return Policy: all sales final
Technical Support: phone hours, 9 pm-1 am, M-F; BBS support
Description: Program for mechanical trading based on short-term cycles. Features a 3-D chart of profitability versus 2 trading parameters, allowing the parameters to be positioned in the most robust region

with minimum sensitivity to market variations. Approach is different from conventional optimization. Buy/sell signals are derived from a leading indicator. Explicit stop/loss values are given to protect profits and to signal a position reversal. Trading record can be back-tested over any selected span of time.

MESA FOR WINDOWS
Version: 4   *Last Updated:* 1992   *No. of Users:* 700
Securities: stocks, bonds, futures, indexes
Functions: technical analysis
Systems: Windows
Special Requirements: Math co-processor recommended
Price: $350; demo available
Return Policy: all sales final
Technical Support: phone hours, 9 pm-1 am, M-F; BBS support
Description: Measures short-term market cycles; uses the same maximum entropy technique used in seismic exploration and in missile defense systems. Measured cycles are recombined to form a prediction based on their continuation. The dominant cycle is plotted as a time graph below a conventional bar chart. The measured cycles are also displayed as a spectrograph for a complete picture of cycle activity. Trend modes and cycle modes are identified by the price action relative to an instantaneous trendline computed using a cycle filter. Display includes the proprietary band pass indicator, which is tuned day-by-day by the measured cycle length.

3D FOR WINDOWS
Version: na   *Last Updated:* 1990   *No. of Users:* 150
Securities: stocks, bonds, futures, indexes
Functions: technical analysis, futures analysis, expert system
Systems: Windows
Special Requirements: Math co-processor recommended
Price: $199; demo available
Return Policy: all sales final
Technical Support: phone hours, 9 pm-1 am, M-F; BBS support
Description: Plots the profitability of 7 indicators as a 3-dimensional surface. Allows selection of the best indicator to use due to changing market conditions. User can establish the most robust combination of indicator parameters by locating the parameter intersection at the smoothest part of the 3-D surface. The smooth surface means that the profitability has the least sensitivity to market variations. User adapts

indicator to market with the most robust set of parameters. Program does not perform optimization, user takes what the market gives. Trades resulting from the selected parameters can be viewed on a bar chart display. The 7 indicators are: stochastics, RSI, MACD, double moving average, parabolic stop and reverse, band pass, and CCI.

MICROSOFT CORPORATION

One Microsoft Way
Redmond, WA 98052

(800) 426-9400
(206) 882-8080
fax: (206) 936-7329

MICROSOFT EXCEL
Version: 5   *Last Updated:* 1993   *No. of Users:* 5 million
Functions: bond analysis, spreadsheet, statistics
Systems: Windows, Mac
Price: $339
Return Policy: all sales final
Technical Support: phone hours, 9 am-9 pm, M-F; BBS support; newsletter
Description: Full-featured, integrated spreadsheet, database and charting program based on a graphical interface. Macintosh version operates under system 6.0.2 or later; IBM version runs under Microsoft Windows. Spreadsheet features include linking multiple spreadsheets, minimal recalculation that recalculates only spreadsheet formulas affected by a change, background recalculation that recalculates only when the user is not entering data, 131 built-in functions, the ability to create new functions and an extensive macro language. Includes 6 basic chart types: area, bar, column, line, pie and scatter, which can be combined to produce over 50 charts including a high, low, close bar chart. Other charting features include a logarithmic scale, arrows and free-floating text.

MICROSOFT MONEY
Version: 3.0   *Last Updated:* 1993   *No. of Users:* na
Functions: financial planning
Systems: Windows
Price: $29.95; demo available
Return Policy: all sales final
Technical Support: phone hours, 9 am-9 pm, M-F; BBS support

Description: A personal financial management program. Loan Tracking tracks all types of loan transactions and balances, and creates amortization schedules so that user can obtain reports on balances and interest payments at any time. Charting plots all financial data to give users a snapshot of their finances. Transaction Coaches provide on-line guides that help users with first-time transaction entries. Automatic Budgeting automatically creates budgets based on previous spending trends.

MICROSOFT PROFIT
Version: 2.0   *Last Updated:* 1991   *No. of Users:* na
Functions: financial planning
Systems: Windows
Price: $199; demo available
Return Policy: all sales final
Technical Support: toll-free number; phone hours, 9 am-9 pm, M-F;
    BBS support; fee for tech support—$2/minute
Description: A business management and accounting program for a small business that does not require prior accounting knowledge. Features include transactions drawer in which all invoices, purchase orders, checks, and other commonly-used forms can be found; cardfile drawer in which all of the company's records are stored; 6 accounting reports and 30 business management reports; profit signs drawer in which users can get a quick visual snapshot of their company's performance via charts and graphs; and accounting journals and ledgers that conform with generally accepted accounting principles.

MICRO TRADING SOFTWARE, INC.

Box 175   (203) 762-7820
Wilton, CT 06897

PORTFOLIO WATCHER
Version: 1.25   *Last Updated:* 1993   *No. of Users:* na
Securities: stocks, bonds, mutual funds
Functions: portfolio management
Systems: Mac
Price: $149.95; demo available; 40% AAII discount
Return Policy: all sales final
Technical Support: phone hours, 9 am-5 pm, M-F; newsletter
Description: Provides complete recordkeeping of investment portfo-

lio. Records stock, bond, mutual fund and cash transactions. Reports such as portfolio valuation, open position and dividends received can be displayed on the screen or printed. Handles an unlimited number of portfolios and integrates with Wall Street Watcher and Stock Watcher.

STOCK WATCHER
Version: 3.0   *Last Updated:* 1993   *No. of Users:* na
Securities: stocks, futures, mutual funds, indexes, options
Functions: technical analysis
Systems: Mac
Price: $195; demo available; 30% AAII discount
Return Policy: all sales final
Technical Support: phone hours, 9 am-5 pm, M-F; newsletter
Description: Analyzes stocks, commodities, mutual funds and market indexes. Features include cycle and trendline analysis; high resolution graphics; rapid generation of graphs and summary reports; 4 graph sizes that display any of the dozens of built-in technical indicators such as stochastics, MACD, moving averages, oscillators, on-balance volume, advance/decline line, relative strength and TRIN. Automatic current-day and historical quote retrieval from CompuServe and DJN/R.

WALL STREET WATCHER
Version: 4.0   *Last Updated:* 1993   *No. of Users:* na
Securities: stocks, futures, mutual funds, indexes, options
Functions: technical analysis
Systems: Mac
Price: $495; demo available; 20% AAII discount
Return Policy: all sales final
Technical Support: phone hours, 9 am-5 pm, M-F; newsletter
Description: Charts over 20 indicators such as simple, weighted and exponential moving averages with percent bands of high, low or closing prices; moving averages of volume; Wilder's relative strength index; stochastics; Granville's on-balance volume; MACD, rate of change/momentum and moving average oscillators; William's %R; TRIN (Arm's index); advance/decline lines; cumulative advance/decline lines; McClellan summation index and oscillator; moving average of new highs/new lows differential; and point and figure charting. Five technical indicators on each of 3 separate windows can be plotted at once. Price swings can be measured in terms of price, time and per-

cent retracement. Time cycles can be marked and projected using Fibonacci and Gann time periods. Includes a macro language to automate chart preparations. Daily and historical stock and commodity quotes can be automatically retrieved from DJN/R and CompuServe.

MILLER ASSOCIATES

P.O. Box 4361   (702) 831-0429
Incline Village, NV 89450

SOPHISTICATED INVESTOR
Version: 2.0   *Last Updated:* 1993   *No. of Users:* na
Securities: stocks, mutual funds, indexes
Functions: financial planning, portfolio management, technical analysis, simulation/game, statistics, expert system
Systems: DOS
Special Requirements: Lotus 1-2-3 recommended
Price: $195; $75 for upgrade; demo available, $5; 15% AAII discount
Return Policy: 30 days; $25 restocking fee
Technical Support: phone hours, 12 pm-7 pm, M-F
Description: Optimizes stock portfolios for maximum return and minimum risk based upon a version of Markowitz's Modern Portfolio Analysis. Features full statistical correlation of a portfolio with the S&P 500, complete with alpha and beta computations, standard error of estimate and correlation coefficient determinations. Linear optimization allows users to make portfolios consistent with their stock risk and return constraints. Allows "what if" analysis. Handles portfolios of up to 50 stocks. TSI/1 for computers with no graphics capability. TSI/2 for computers with graphics.

MONEY TREE SOFTWARE

1753 Wooded Knolls Drive   (503) 929-2140
Suite 200   fax: (503) 929-2787
Philomath, OR 97370

EASY MONEY PLUS
Version: 1.0   *Last Updated:* 1994   *No. of Users:* 950
Securities: stocks, bonds, mutual funds, real estate
Functions: financial planning, spreadsheet

Systems: DOS
Special Requirements: Lotus 1-2-3
Price: $500; annual updates $200; 45-day rental $25; demo available
Return Policy: all sales final
Technical Support: phone hours, 11 am-8 pm, M-F; fee for tech support—$200
Description: Addresses the changing needs of the personal financial planning market of the late 1990s. Features quick data entry, and easy to understand reports, charts, graphs and diagrams. A 30-page report covers all items needed for a comprehensive plan including a life cycle asset allocation section, retirement and insurance planning, income tax, estate tax, budget, education funding and more.

ELDERLY TAX PLANNER
Version: 4   *Last Updated:* 1994   *No. of Users:* 2,000
Securities: stocks, bonds, mutual funds, real estate
Functions: financial planning, spreadsheet
Systems: DOS
Special Requirements: Lotus 1-2-3 or Quattro Pro
Price: $100; annual updates $25; demo available
Return Policy: all sales final
Technical Support: phone hours, 11 am-8 pm, M-F; fee for tech support—$25
Description: Computes income taxes and determines the taxable portion of Social Security benefits and the effect of moving savings or investments into tax-free municipal funds or tax-deferred annuities; shows the resulting tax savings and the effect on spendable income and capital.

MONEYCALC IV
Version: 4   *Last Updated:* 1994   *No. of Users:* 2,100
Securities: stocks, bonds, mutual funds, real estate
Functions: financial planning
Systems: DOS
Special Requirements: Lotus 1-2-3 or Quattro Pro
Price: $700; annual updates $350; demo available
Return Policy: all sales final
Technical Support: phone hours, 11 am-8 pm, M-F; newsletter; fee for tech support—$350
Description: A system for financial planning. The 50 programs may be used as separate report modules or interfaced with the Client Data

Module for client data input. Includes all 1986 tax reform act tax features, multiple year projections of taxes, net worth, cash flow, estate plans, retirement, survivor and disability needs, etc.

RETIREMENT SOLUTIONS

Version: 4   *Last Updated:* 1994   *No. of Users:* 600
Functions: financial planning, spreadsheet
Systems: DOS
Special Requirements: Lotus 1-2-3 or Quattro Pro
Price: $250; annual update, $75; demo available
Return Policy: all sales final
Technical Support: phone hours, 11 am-8 pm, M-F; fee for tech support—$75
Description: Collection of 9 programs covering retirement planning. Calculates all taxes due on a qualified plan distribution (regular tax, 5- and 10-year average, IRA rollover) and projects benefits before- and aftertax through life expectancy. Includes principal report, lump-sum distribution, computes minimum distribution requirements, and early and excess distribution tax penalties.

MONTGOMERY INVESTMENT TECHNOLOGY

(formerly Montgomery Investment Group)

P.O. Box 508   (610) 688-2508
Wayne, PA 19087-0508   fax: (610) 688-5084

@BONDS XL U.S. SERIES AND INTERNATIONAL SERIES

(formerly @Bonds ProSeries and Premium Series)
Version: 4.0   *Last Updated:* 1994   *No. of Users:* na
Securities: bonds, futures, options
Functions: financial planning, bond analysis, futures analysis, spreadsheet, simulation/game
Systems: DOS, Windows, Windows NT, OS/2, Unix
Special Requirements: Lotus 1-2-3, Excel
Price: U.S. series $395; international series $695 single user license; demo available, $49.95; 15% AAII discount
Return Policy: 30 days; 25% restocking fee
Technical Support: phone hours, 9 am-5 pm, M-F; fee for tech support—15%
Description: A Lotus 1-2-3 and Excel add-in. Allows users to calculate bond-related statistics including yields, prices, duration, modified du-

ration, etc. Fixed-income instruments that can be evaluated are U.S. Treasuries, notes, corporates, munis, zeros, etc. Custom templates can be created to employ quantitative techniques such as horizon, market timing, rolling yield curve, portfolio optimization and more. Can evaluate odd first-coupon and callable bonds.

@EXOTICS XL *(formerly Exotics and @Exotics)*
Version: 4   *Last Updated:* 1994   *No. of Users:* na
Securities: stocks, futures, indexes, options
Functions: financial planning, futures analysis, options analysis, spreadsheet, simulation/game
Systems: DOS, Windows, Windows NT, OS/2, Mac, Unix
Special Requirements: Excel, Lotus
Price: $695 and up; demo available, $173; 15% AAII discount
Return Policy: 90 days; 25% restocking fee
Technical Support: phone hours, 9 am-5 pm, M-F; fee for tech support—15%
Description: An Excel and Lotus program that provides user with models for evaluating "Exotic" options (also known as second generation options). The models available include average price, lookback, knockout, average strike, option-on-option (compound) and spreads. The type of contracts evaluated include options on foreign exchange, commodities, energy, agriculture, metals, futures and more. The functions calculate theoretical value risk sensitivities (delta, gamma, etc.) and implied volatility. Expert template and macro design services for foreign exchange, agriculture and energy market applications are also offered.

@OPTIONS XL PRO, PREMIUM, AND EXTENDED BINOMIAL SERIES
Version: 4   *Last Updated:* 1994   *No. of Users:* na
Securities: stocks, bonds, futures, indexes, options
Functions: financial planning, bond analysis, futures analysis, options analysis, spreadsheet, simulation/game
Systems: DOS, Windows, Windows NT, OS/2, Mac, Unix, Sun
Special Requirements: Lotus 1-2-3, Excel
Price: pro series $395; premium series $695; extended binomial series $995; demo available, $49.95; 15% AAII discount
Return Policy: 30 days; 25% restocking fee
Technical Support: phone hours, 9 am-5 pm, M-F; fee for tech support—15%

Description: A Lotus 1-2-3 and Excel add-in. Allows users to calculate theoretical options prices, implied volatilities and sensitivity values such as delta, gamma and theta directly within spreadsheets. A choice of 10 options pricing models is available including: Binomial (Cox-Ross-Rubinstein), Euro dollar, Indexes, Leaps, Garmon-Kohlhagen, Black, Pseudo-American, Black-Scholes, Modified Black-Scholes and Adesi-Whaley (Quadratic). Enables analysis on any underlying asset: stocks, bonds, futures, indexes, commodities, foreign exchange and more. The base product is not a Lotus macro or template but a collection of functions that extends the capabilities of Lotus specifically for option trading and analysis. Works as a program within a program and has real-time capabilities.

OPTIONSCALC
Version: 2.0   *Last Updated:* 1994   *No. of Users:* na
Securities: options
Functions: futures analysis, options analysis
Systems: DOS
Price: Black-Scholes series $79.95; binomial series $99.95; 15% AAII
   discount
Return Policy: all sales final
Technical Support: phone hours, 9 am-5 pm, M-F
Description: Designed to price options using two pricing models: Binomial or Black-Scholes. Two versions are available. Values "Executive Stock Options" in accordance with the guidelines established by FASB and the SEC. Black-Scholes Series evaluates futures, FX and commodity options, European style options, and options with "smooth" cash flows or dividends. Binomial Series evaluates exchange-traded stock options and LEAPs, American style options, options with "discrete" cash flows or dividends, and long-dated options.

NETWORK SERVICES GROUP

(formerly UltraVision\USA)

1095 Market Street, Suite 514   (415) 863-8407
San Francisco, CA 94103-1628   fax: (415) 255-9392

CURRENCYCAST
Version: 4.01   *Last Updated:* 1994   *No. of Users:* na
Securities: stocks, bonds, futures, mutual funds, indexes, options, real
   estate

Functions: financial planning, fundamental analysis, technical analysis, statistics, expert system
Systems: DOS
Price: $69.95/year (includes quarterly updates); demo available, free
Return Policy: all sales final
Technical Support: phone hours, 10 am-6 pm, M-F
Description: Designed to forecast European Economic Community exchange rates for 1 day, 1 week and 1 month in advance. Included for analysis are closing values for gold, British pound, Canadian dollar, Swiss franc, Japanese yen, German mark and ECU in terms of the U.S. dollar. On-line help, data input, charting, forecasting and inference engine are all included. Data input allows the manual input of data; an alternative is to import ASCII data into the database. The charting feature displays the forecasted values against the actual values for one trading month. Historical, forecasted, random walk, 5-day average and 20-day averages are displayed. The inference engine takes the statistical model and utilizes a rule-based system to present trading rules in English. Demo available from Channel 1\BBS.

DOWCAST
Version: 4.01   *Last Updated:* 1994   *No. of Users:* na
Securities: stocks, bonds, futures, mutual funds, indexes, options, real estate
Functions: financial planning, technical analysis, statistics, expert system
Systems: DOS
Price: $69.95 (includes quarterly updates); demo available, free
Return Policy: all sales final
Technical Support: phone hours, 10 am-6 pm, M-F; BBS support
Description: An expert system designed to forecast the closing of the Dow Jones industrials, S&P 500, T-bills, silver, and the Japanese yen. Has six functions: on-line manual; charting; inference engine; data input; forecasting; and knowledge base. Forecasts values for 1-, 5-, and 22-days, plus 1 year closings. Includes knowledge base/inference engine for tracking existing investments. Internet access available.

NEW HIGH CO.

RD #2   (800) 643-8950
Riverhead, NY 11901   (516) 722-5407
                              fax: (516) 722-5409

ALLIANCE 5.0
Version: 5.0   *Last Updated:* na   *No. of Users:* na
Securities: stocks, indexes
Functions: technical analysis
Systems: DOS
Price: $69.95; 10% AAII discount
Return Policy: all sales final
Technical Support: phone hours, 9 am-5 pm, M-F
Description: A daily charting program that combines many issues and charts them as a group. Various technical analysis studies can then be performed on the group as a whole or on individual issues in the group. Various groups can be charted against each other or against the market as a whole.

THE INSIDER
Version: 1.0   *Last Updated:* na   *No. of Users:* na
Securities: stocks, indexes
Functions: technical analysis
Systems: DOS
Price: $179; 10% AAII discount
Return Policy: all sales final
Technical Support: phone hours, 9 am-5 pm, M-F
Description: Real-time program that studies Signal's trade-by-trade volume to reveal the components of a stock's trading pattern. Charts equivolume, TRIN, open TRIN, PVI, NVI, OBV and more.

IT'S ALIVE
Version: na   *Last Updated:* na   *No. of Users:* na
Securities: stocks, bonds, futures, mutual funds, indexes, options
Functions: quote data utility
Systems: DOS
Price: $195; demo available; 10% AAII discount
Return Policy: 7 days; shipping restocking fee
Technical Support: phone hours, 9 am-5 pm, M-F
Description: Allows use of existing, daily-based charting software for real-time, on-line, intraday charting and technical analysis. Captures data coming from Signal receiver. Automatically stores all the securities from Signal portfolio in 5-, 15-, 30- and 60-minute files. Capture occurs in background, leaving computer free to run most other software in the foreground. Runs technical analysis programs such as Compu Trac, MetaStock or Byte Research's Professional Breakout System for

intraday charting.

PROFESSIONAL BREAKOUT SYSTEM
Version: 3.11   *Last Updated:* na   *No. of Users:* na
Securities: stocks, bonds, futures, mutual funds, indexes, options
Functions: technical analysis, simulation/game
Systems: DOS
Price: $385; demo available; 10% AAII discount
Return Policy: 30 days; shipping restocking fee
Technical Support: phone hours, 9 am-5 pm, M-F
Description: Gives entry and exit signals for stocks, futures, options and indexes. Provides full graphic charting, as well as a proven mechanical trading method. Uses volatility breakout system with charting and technical analysis features to filter and confirm the trades indicated by the mechanical portion of the system. Directly reads any data in CSI, Compu Trac, MetaStock or ASCII formats. Free downloading software is supplied. Features: historical profitability testing of the built-in volatility system, plus testing of user-defined trading systems or ideas. No programming is required to test any system. Walking-forward testing for real-time results. Includes 17 technical indicators and 4 trading reports. Allows high resolution, color charting, and 3-D graphics to spot parameters and optimizable stops.

TECH TUTOR
Version: 1.0   *Last Updated:* na   *No. of Users:* na
Functions: simulation/game
Systems: DOS
Price: $49.95; 10% AAII discount
Return Policy: all sales final
Technical Support: phone hours, 9 am-5 pm, M-F
Description: Technical analysis tutorial. Includes subjects such as: chart construction, support and resistance, trendlines, channels, price gaps, major reversals, patterns, price objectives, continuation patterns, volume and open interest, moving averages, oscillators, point and figure charting, Elliot wave theory, cycles and more. Visualizes concepts that are difficult to understand when explained in a book. Charts are shown and analyzed on the screen. Covers material for everyone from beginner to seasoned trader.

TRACKER FOR INVESTOR'S BUSINESS DAILY
Version: 2.0   *Last Updated:* na   *No. of Users:* na

Securities: stocks
Functions: technical analysis
Systems: DOS
Price: $79; 10% AAII discount
Return Policy: all sales final
Technical Support: phone hours, 9 am-5 pm, M-F
Description: Allows investor to build a database and chart stocks that are highlighted in different categories in Investor's Business Daily.

TRADER'S TRAINER

Version: 1.2   *Last Updated:* na   *No. of Users:* na
Securities: stocks, futures, indexes, options
Functions: technical analysis, simulation/game
Systems: DOS
Price: $139; 10% AAII discount
Return Policy: all sales final
Technical Support: phone hours, 9 am-5 pm, M-F; newsletter
Description: Tests and trains user by replaying actual data exactly as it happened on a given day. Lets beginner and experienced investors pit their skills against past stock, option and commodity markets. Allows trader to speed up the day's trading and start and stop the action at any time. Contains powerful analytical tools as well as an automated system for entering and exiting trades. A sophisticated accounting system calculates the value of the trader's portfolio in real-time.

NEWTEK INDUSTRIES

P.O. Box 46116   (213) 874-6669
Los Angeles, CA 90046

COMMISSION COMPARISONS

Version: 1.4   *Last Updated:* 1993   *No. of Users:* na
Securities: stocks, bonds, options
Functions: commission comparisons
Systems: DOS
Price: $39.95
Return Policy: all sales final
Technical Support: phone hours, 12 am-8 pm, M-F
Description: Shows how 15 selected discount brokerages and 1 full-service brokerage compare in commission costs for any transaction in stocks, options or bonds. The number of shares, contracts or bonds and

prices are entered, and each brokerage commission is calculated and sorted by cost. Displays the vital statistics of the brokerage of choice, including toll-free phone numbers, nationwide offices and special trading requirements, if any.

COMPU/CHART
Version: 1.3　　　　　*Last Updated:* 1994　　　　　*No. of Users:* na
Securities: stocks, mutual funds, indexes, options
Functions: technical analysis
Systems: DOS
Special Requirements: modem
Price: $299.95; demo available, $7; 30% AAII discount
Return Policy: 30 days; $100 restocking fee
Technical Support: phone hours, 12 am-8 pm, M-F
Description: Program uses high-resolution color graphics to display charts and indicators. Charts include the scanner, displaying 9 different markets per screen; the oscillator-scan, displaying 5 different oscillator windows per market; moving averages, which allow the juxtaposition of detailed oscillators; price-volume charting and exponential-average divergence with the moving averages chart in a choice of time frames and status report. Stochastics (with user-assigned periods), moving up/down volume ratio, channel lines, back-scanner, intraday monitor, dynamic bar indicator, immediate update report, adaptable format and use of high-resolution color to distinguish trends and patterns allow user to tailor analysis time to the market situation. Intraday monitor creates a "Dynamic bar" or historical chart showing current trading action during market hours on the historical chart. Quotes can be typed or downloaded from Prodigy. Adds ASCII historical report files for each equity and a "priority list" of equities that have made significant moves as reported during update routine. Equities can be added to Priority List manually, as well. The list can be referred to from the primary charting module, helping to prioritize analysis time.

NICHE SOFTWARE PRODUCTS

P.O. Box 3574　　　　　　　　　　　　　　　　　(703) 368-8372
Manassas, VA 22110

BUY-WRITE MODEL
Version: 1.2　　　　　*Last Updated:* 1993　　　　　*No. of Users:* na

Securities: options
Functions: options analysis
Systems: DOS
Price: $50
Return Policy: all sales final
Technical Support: phone hours, 9 am-4 pm, M-F
Description: Calculates exercise probabilities/return potentials for simultaneous equity buy-call sell. Determines which options yield best return at lowest risk and how sale of options might compare to holding the stock. Calculates fair value of options to detect if overpriced or underpriced and probability of call exercise. Shows rate of return if exercised and new basis if not. Prints texts and graphs. Graphs show profit as a function of stock, compares buying and holding, shows improvement in break-even point/loss protection. "Profitability graph" created by running B&S model for option price data points covering the probable range of stock movement statistically expected during option period. Full documentation and help are included.

INVESTOR'S TOOL BOX
Version: 1.0   *Last Updated:* 1993   *No. of Users:* na
Securities: stocks, options
Functions: options analysis
Systems: DOS
Price: $50
Return Policy: all sales final
Technical Support: phone hours, 9 am-4 pm, M-F
Description: A collection of functions for the stock investor and the options trader. Includes ten main functions: Symbol finds OTC options (updateable) and expire dates. Theta graphically shows daily decay of time value. Delta gives implied volatility, days to expire, theoretical minimum and maximum and delta for option. Fair, given the volatility of the stock, shows the fair price for puts and calls, expiration date, and number of days to expiration. Results show your round-trip stock results, figures commissions, margin costs, profit and ROI. Neutral calculates ratios for delta neutral spreads. Uses either true volatility (gives fair options value) or calculates implied volatility. Repair determines remedial action necessary to rebalance a delta neutral spread. Blend nets out your position (including the calculation of commissions) if you average up or down. Taxes calculates taxable vs. non-taxable returns for any tax bracket. IRS is designed for option traders: input all opening and closing transactions and it maintains database of

trades, trade results, prints positions, and does an end-year roll over of all open positions to the next year.

OWN-WRITE MODEL
Version: 1.1 *Last Updated:* 1993 *No. of Users:* na
Securities: stocks, options
Functions: options analysis
Systems: DOS
Price: $50
Return Policy: all sales final
Technical Support: phone hours, 9 am-4 pm, M-F
Description: Calculates exercise probabilities/return potentials for stock covered call writing. Screens for fair option price, expected return, and exercise probability. Determines which options yield best return at lowest risk, how sale of options might compare to holding stock, and probability of exercise. Shows rate of return if exercised and new basis if not. Rapidly tests potential positions. Prints texts and graphs. Graphs show profit as a function of stock, shows improvement in break-even point and protection afforded by call sale. "Profitability graph" created by running B&S model for option price data points covering the probable range of stock movement statistically expected during option period. Probability of position above strike is displayed. Full documentation and help are included.

ROLL MODEL
Version: 1.1 *Last Updated:* 1993 *No. of Users:* na
Securities: options
Functions: options analysis
Systems: DOS
Price: $45
Return Policy: all sales final
Technical Support: phone hours, 9 am-4 pm, M-F
Description: Provides data and calculations necessary to analyze alternative actions possible when short call options are near expiration and are in-the-money (may be rolled to a higher strike and/or a later expiration date, brought back, or allowed to be exercised). Allows user to enter current position and selected prospective positions. Performs all calculations necessary to determine best course of action. Determines current unrealized gain position, position if exercise is allowed, and position if user elects to "buy back" and cover short option. Evaluates the roll-up, roll-out, or roll-up/out alternatives selected. Computes

commissions, presents results in matrix format and provides an "instant analysis." Prints detailed reports. Assists in initial selection of opportunities for covered call writing. Analyzes current basis and unrealized gain position, and the impact of these on your cover basis, cash flows and new prospective net unrealized gain position. Full documentation and help.

SPREAD MAKER
Version: 2.4   *Last Updated:* 1993   *No. of Users:* na
Securities: options
Functions: options analysis
Systems: DOS
Price: $50
Return Policy: all sales final
Technical Support: phone hours, 9 am-4 pm, M-F
Description: Evaluates vertical, horizontal and diagonal call spread investment candidates. Assists in selection of potential spread positions and calculates the change in basis for original long position if such a spread is established. Shows probable outcomes of positions based on expectation of stock price at expiration dates. Analyzes potential outcomes and prints out available alternative actions and their net results. All analysis output may be printed for comparison, study and retention. Full documentation and help are included.

STOCK GRAPH MAKER
Version: 1.3   *Last Updated:* 1993   *No. of Users:* na
Securities: stocks, bonds, mutual funds, indexes
Functions: technical analysis
Systems: DOS
Special Requirements: 1M expanded RAM
Price: $60
Return Policy: all sales final
Technical Support: phone hours, 9 am-4 pm, M-F
Description: Creates/maintains database of historical stock prices and volumes. Graphs on demand or sequentially. Spreadsheet compatibility allows data preparation, update and further analysis. Spreadsheet is not required. Graphs closing prices, high/low/close and volume. Detects trends, resistance and support levels. Captures graphs for printing. Allows annotation of graphs with notes such as dividend dates, split dates, or portfolio holdings. Automatically updates database via Prodigy through QuoteTrack. Data collected as text from

other on-line sources may be manipulated to serve as inputs. Conversion functions allow use of word processor or editor to create inputs and/or to modify database. Allows manual inputs for quick corrections. Entire database can be viewed and edited on-line. Prints detailed catalog report and detailed data on any stock in database. Full documentation and help are included.

VERTICAL SPREAD MODEL
Version: 1.1   *Last Updated:* 1993   *No. of Users:* na
Securities: options
Functions: options analysis
Systems: DOS
Price: $55
Return Policy: all sales final
Technical Support: phone hours, 9 am-4 pm, M-F
Description: Shows theoretical curves for option prices as stock prices vary. Depicts probable position value at any simulated future time within contract period. Nets probable values of position after consideration of Time value wasting and Hedge ratio based on probable movement as a function of the changing stock value. Shows expected expiration results. "Profitability graph" created by running Black & Scholes model for option price data points covering the probable range of stock movement statistically expected during option period. Probability of position being at or above the break-even point is displayed. "What-if?" selection allows querying position at any simulated date within contract period.

NIRVANA SYSTEMS

3415 Greystone Drive   (800) 880-0338
Suite 205   (512) 345-2545
Austin, TX 78731   fax: (512) 345-2592

DIRECTOR UTILITIES FOR METASTOCK PRO—SYSTEMS!
VOLUME 1-4
Version: na   *Last Updated:* 1992   *No. of Users:* 1,200
Securities: stocks, futures, mutual funds
Functions: technical analysis
Systems: DOS
Price: $49 each, $139 for all 4; 10% AAII discount

Return Policy: all sales final
Technical Support: phone hours, 1 pm-6 pm, M-F
Description: Has 40 predefined trading systems for MetaStock (20) with optimization parameters defined, and the same 20 systems with default parameters for use with AutoStock and WhatWorks, or by itself with MetaStock.

DIRECTOR UTILITIES FOR METASTOCK PRO—WHATWORKS

Version: 2.2   *Last Updated:* 1992   *No. of Users:* 1,200
Securities: stocks, futures, mutual funds
Functions: technical analysis
Systems: DOS
Price: $99; 10% AAII discount
Return Policy: all sales final
Technical Support: phone hours, 1 pm-6 pm, M-F
Description: A utility for MetaStock Professional version 2.0 and higher that will automatically test a list of systems and find the most profitable for each security in one or more of the data subdirectories.

POWERTRADER!

Version: na   *Last Updated:* 1992   *No. of Users:* 1,200
Securities: stocks, futures, mutual funds
Functions: technical analysis
Systems: Windows
Price: $595; 10% AAII discount
Technical Support: phone hours, 1 pm-6 pm, M-F; newsletter
Description: PowerTrader directly reads four formats: MetaStock, Worden Bros., AIQ, CSI, and ASCII with no import tasks to perform. The Focus List sorts opportunities based on user's criteria. The voting line feature is a single trading signal summary. The program provides automatic trendline and divergence trading systems, cycle analysis, and candlestick, and volume confirmations. The PowerTrader charts have several features including group overlay plots and automatic chart pattern marking. Using lab mode and trading game simulator, user can practice before risking real capital. PowerTrader also has a built-in portfolio and an adviser to assist with managing your trades.

NORTHFIELD INFORMATION SERVICES, INC.

184 High Street
5th Floor
Boston, MA 02110-3001

(800) 262-6085
(617) 451-2222
fax: (617) 451-2122

NIS ASSET ALLOCATION SYSTEM
Version: 4.13   *Last Updated:* 1994   *No. of Users:* 8
Securities: mutual funds, indexes
Functions: financial planning, statistics
Systems: DOS
Price: $10,000/year; demo available; 20% AAII discount
Return Policy: all sales final
Technical Support: phone hours, 9 am-5 pm, M-F; newsletter
Description: Deals with long-term asset allocation. Uses an exclusive optimization algorithm to find the most suitable asset mix giving appropriate consideration to user-defined constraints such as level of risk tolerance, time horizon and minimum yield. Provides a variety of output displays including detailed graphics of the efficient frontier, enabling users to see the impact of the optimization. Included are performance measurements, wealth projections and actuarial studies. Users choose from more than 24 asset classes from which historical and current data is supplied on monthly data diskettes, which may be overridden. Long-range forecasts for the return and volatility of each asset class is published in a client newsletter. Includes database covering more than 2,500 indexes and mutual funds containing monthly data back to 1962.

NIS FIXED INCOME RESEARCH ENVIRONMENT
Version: na   *Last Updated:* na   *No. of Users:* 5
Securities: bonds
Functions: bond analysis, statistics
Systems: DOS
Price: $30,000; 20% AAII discount
Return Policy: all sales final
Technical Support: phone hours, 9 am-5 pm, M-F; newsletter; fee for tech support—$6,000
Description: Provides portfolio analytic and reporting tools. Helps determine and evaluate the tactical and strategic investment decisions that will conform to the portfolio objectives, monitor, evaluate and modify fixed-income portfolios. Composed of 3 integrated elements; a

"what if" capability that lets user model alternative yield environments and portfolio strategies; a specialized reporting system for fixed income portfolios that allows user to automate custom-designed portfolio reports; and a data integrator that links users accounting system, external sources of pricing data and an issue-descriptive database into a single resource. Performs option adjusted spreads (OAS) calculations over 18,000 issues.

NIS MACROECONOMIC EQUITY SYSTEM
Version: 1.1   *Last Updated:* 1990   *No. of Users:* 15
Securities: stocks, indexes
Functions: fundamental analysis, statistics
Systems: DOS, Windows
Price: $12,000/year—DOS; $18,000/year—Windows; demo available; 20% AAII discount
Technical Support: phone hours, 9 am-5 pm, M-F; newsletter
Description: A combination of software and proprietary data. Assists in stock portfolio management from a macro-economic point of view. Over 4,500 stocks have been analyzed to establish relationships between changes in the economy and individual stock performance. Program provides: database showing how sensitive specific stocks are to economic events (i.e., changes in inflation, interest rates, industrial production); stock-picking tool (stocks can be ranked by forecast performance in the user's own scenario of future economic conditions); an optimizer, constructing portfolios from user selected stocks to maximize the forecast return while minimizing risk; decomposes risk into factors to show the types of risk a portfolio is susceptible to. Supports multiple economic scenarios and contains its own portfolio accounting system so that calculations can be applied to actual portfolios. Can download portfolio accounting data from software such as the Advent Professional Portfolio.

NIS PERFORMANCE ANALYSIS SYSTEM
Version: na   *Last Updated:* na   *No. of Users:* 4
Securities: stocks, indexes
Functions: portfolio management, statistics
Systems: DOS
Price: $16,000; 20% AAII discount
Return Policy: all sales final
Technical Support: phone hours, 9 am-5 pm, M-F; newsletter
Description: Provides an explanation of equity portfolio performance

by characterizing a portfolio and its benchmark index on beta, 11 fundamental factors and distribution among 55 industry groups. The impact on relative returns of each aspect of existing differences may be identified. Identifies the separate impact of market timing, "style" characteristics, industry selection and stock selection. Can be used to monitor and pinpoint the strengths and weaknesses of the decision process, audit compliance with policies and improve central control of a multi-manager scheme.

OMEGA RESEARCH, INC.

Omega Research Building
9200 Sunset Drive
Miami, FL 33173-3266

(800) 556-2022
(305) 270-1095
fax: (305) 270-8919

SUPERCHARTS
Version: 2.1   *Last Updated:* 1994   *No. of Users:* 13,000
Securities: stocks, bonds, futures, mutual funds, indexes, options
Functions: technical analysis
Systems: Windows
Special Requirements: Windows 3.1, 4M RAM
Price: $195
Return Policy: 30 days
Technical Support: phone hours, 9 am-6 pm, M-F; BBS support
Description: A charting and technical analysis program for Windows. No limit to number of technical indicators that can be overlaid on any chart. 43 years of daily data can be displayed on a single chart, and customized pages can be saved after trendlines, indicators and text have been added. Users can create multi-data chart windows containing up to 50 different data files simultaneously, facilitating comparison of securities. Includes pre-written technical indicators and over 150 built-in functions for use in formulas. Also contains a downloader and DataManager for downloading price and fundamental data.

SYSTEM WRITER 3.0 FOR WINDOWS
Version: 3.0   *Last Updated:* 1994   *No. of Users:* na
Securities: stocks, bonds, futures, mutual funds, indexes, options
Functions: technical analysis, bond analysis, futures analysis, options
    analysis
Systems: Windows

Special Requirements: Windows 3.1

Price: call for pricing; demo available

Return Policy: 30 days

Technical Support: phone hours, 9 am-6 pm, M-F; BBS support; newsletter

Description: Technical analysis program lets user historically test and optimize any trading system without programming knowledge. Users describe the buy/sell rules of any trading systems they wish to test historically. Program takes user's instructions and converts them into actual machine code. Next, it runs a historical simulation using any desired data and prepares a series of detailed reports revealing exactly how user's system performed over the last 5, 10, and 20 years. Includes charting features that enable graphic evaluation of any system's historical performance. Then, with the press of one key, a bar chart of the test data appears. Overlayed with color-coded arrows pinpointing user system's buy and sell points. Press one more key and a graph appears in a second window at the bottom of the screen with a graph revealing the day-to-day account balance for the entire test period.

SYSTEM WRITER PLUS FOR DOS

Version: 2.18   **Last Updated:** 1991   **No. of Users:** 4,000+

Securities: stocks, bonds, futures, mutual funds, indexes, options

Functions: technical analysis, bond analysis, futures analysis, options analysis

Systems: DOS

Price: $975; demo available

Return Policy: 30 days; $45 restocking fee

Technical Support: phone hours, 9 am-6 pm, M-F; BBS support

Description: Technical analysis program lets user historically test and optimize any trading system without programming knowledge. Users describe the buy/sell rules of any trading systems they wish to test historically. Program takes user's instructions and converts them into actual machine code. Next, it runs a historical simulation using any desired data and prepares a series of detailed reports revealing exactly how user's system performed over the last 5, 10, and 20 years. Includes charting features that enable graphic evaluation of any system's historical performance. Once a simulation has been performed, simply press 1 key and a bar chart of the test data appears. Overlayed with color-coded arrows pinpointing user system's buy and sell points. Press 1 more key and a graph appears in a 2nd window at the bottom of the screen with a graph revealing the day-to-day account balance for the entire test period.

TRADESTATION

Version: 3.5   *Last Updated:* 1994   *No. of Users:* 3,000+

Securities: stocks, bonds, futures, mutual funds, indexes, options
Functions: technical analysis, bond analysis, futures analysis, options analysis
Systems: Windows
Special Requirements: 486+, Windows 3.1, 4M RAM, online datafeed
Price: $1,895; demo available
Return Policy: 30 days
Technical Support: phone hours, 9 am-6 pm, M-F; BBS support; newsletter; fee for tech support—$495
Description: Technical analysis program that allows users to automate, track and back-test any trading strategy in real-time or historically, on dozens of markets simultaneously, without programming knowledge. Users describe their custom buy/sell rules which can then be applied to data charts for any desired markets. In real-time, pro gram monitors these markets, on a tick-by-tick basis, instantly generating audio/visual alarms when buy/sell opportunities based on user's criteria occurs. Exact market orders to be placed or cancelled are then generated. Tracks open position profit/loss of a trade on a tick-by-tick basis and allows users to chart custom indicators and formulas historically and in real-time. Historical back-testing of systems generates detailed performance reports for the period tested. Charting features allow unlimited amounts of technical studies (built-in or custom) and tools to be overlayed and enable graphic evaluation of any system's performance. Color coded arrows overlay on charts to pinpoint every buy/sell point for a specified strategy over the tested period.

OMNI SOFTWARE SYSTEMS, INC.

702 N Ernest   (219) 924-3522
Griffith, IN 46319

INVESTMENT ANALYST

Version: 4.2   *Last Updated:* 1988   *No. of Users:* 2,000
Securities: stocks, bonds, real estate
Functions: financial planning
Systems: DOS
Price: $95; demo available, $35; 25% AAII discount

Return Policy: all sales final

Technical Support: phone hours, 9:30 am-5:30 pm, M-F

Description: Analyzes potential investments, considering inflation or deflation, various depreciation methods, cash flow, tax rates, financing and possible future sales price. Printed statements forecast results of a present or contemplated investment, including internal rate of return, variable expense items, net gain or loss after taxes, amortization calculations, cash flow analysis and depreciation using several alternatives.

PORTFOLIO MANAGEMENT SYSTEM

Version: 6.0   *Last Updated:* 1988   *No. of Users:* 1,200+

Securities: stocks, mutual funds

Functions: financial planning, portfolio management

Systems: DOS

Price: $150; demo available, $35; 25% AAII discount

Return Policy: all sales final

Technical Support: phone hours, 9:30 am-5:30 pm, M-F

Description: Portfolio management system for up to 100 stocks. Produces reports and schedules for reporting dividends and gains or losses. Tracks dividend due dates, dividends received or reinvested, and additional purchases of the same stock; calculates long- and short-term gains and losses.

STOCK MANAGER

Version: na   *Last Updated:* 1988   *No. of Users:* 2,000

Securities: stocks, mutual funds

Functions: financial planning, portfolio management

Systems: DOS

Price: $200; demo available, $35; 25% AAII discount

Return Policy: all sales final

Technical Support: phone hours, 9:30 am-5:30 pm, M-F

Description: Meets recordkeeping needs of individuals requiring sophisticated accounting and reporting capabilities. Keeps portfolio data; produces over 10 separate reports from over 25 different items of information kept on each stock in the file. Long- and short-term gains and losses are automatically calculated, and the necessary forms for tax returns are prepared at the end of the year. All stocks sold during the year are deleted for the next year's portfolio. Special reports include the valuation of the portfolio at current market prices and reports for Schedules B and D of the IRS 1040 form.

ONES & ZEROS

708 W. Mt. Airy Avenue
Philadelphia, PA 19119

(215) 248-1010
fax: (215) 248-1010

BONDSHEET
Version: 3.0   *Last Updated:* 1993   *No. of Users:* 1,000
Securities: bonds
Functions: bond analysis
Systems: DOS
Price: $95; demo available
Return Policy: 30 days
Technical Support: toll-free number; phone hours, 8 am-8 pm, M-F
Description: A bond calculator. Computes yield to maturity, yield to call and current yield, before or after tax. Computes price from any of these yields. Smart swap analysis tells if it pays to trade one bond for another after all taxes and commissions have been considered. Supports Monroe-compatible standard yields and "true" yields, with no standard approximations. Has contextual help facility.

PER%SENSE
Version: 2.2   *Last Updated:* 1994   *No. of Users:* 10,000
Securities: stocks, bonds, futures, mutual funds, indexes, options
Functions: portfolio management
Systems: DOS
Price: $99.95; demo available
Return Policy: 30 days
Technical Support: toll-free number; phone hours, 8 am-8 pm, M-F
Description: A financial calculation tool. Includes modules for loan analysis, passbook savings and mortgage comparison. Analyzes IRRs for complex investments. Includes COLA-stepped payments and calculates the present value of any payment stream. Contextual, hypertext help facility and on-screen examples included.

PER%SENSE PRO
Version: 2.2   *Last Updated:* 1994   *No. of Users:* 1,000
Securities: stocks, bonds, futures, mutual funds, indexes, options
Functions: financial planning
Systems: DOS
Price: $175; demo available
Return Policy: 30 days

Technical Support: toll-free number; phone hours, 8 am-8 pm, M-F
Description: Includes all the functions of Per%Sense and IPA, plus tax interest and actuarial analysis, math co-processor support and scrolling windows for unlimited data entry. Actuarial analysis merges actuarial tables with financial calculations to determine what the real rate of return of an annuity is and how a life insurance policy compares as an investment to a CD or bond. Tax Interest computes interest on back taxes where the interest rates change over time, and other present and future value calculations with changing interest rates. Includes contextual and hypertextual help facility along with on-screen examples.

OPA SOFTWARE

P.O. Box 90658
Los Angeles, CA 90009

(310) 545-3716

OPTION PRICING ANALYSIS

Version: 4.0   *Last Updated:* 1993   *No. of Users:* 2,500
Securities: stocks, futures, indexes, options
Functions: options analysis
Systems: DOS, Mac
Special Requirements: Modem
Price: $275, $25 upgrade; demo available, $25; 25% AAII discount
Return Policy: 30 days
Technical Support: phone hours, 10 am-10 pm, M-F
Description: Provides user with easily interpreted data screens. Features include: stock, index, futures and options prices via a modified Black-Scholes model; automatically selects best option and options strategy; determines CBOE margin costs; projects profits and losses for straddles, combinations and spreads; evaluates basic option strategies via an "expert system"; provides hedge ratios, deltas and omegas; determines option sensitivity to time changes; graphs option prices for changes in the issue price and time; calculates expiration times and dates; downloads market prices and volumes.

OPTIONOMICS CORPORATION

2835 E. 3300 South
Suite 200
Salt Lake City, UT 84109

(800) 255-3374
(801) 466-2111
fax: (801) 466-7320

OPTIONOMIC SYSTEMS

Version: na   *Last Updated:* 1991   *No. of Users:* na

Securities: stocks, bonds, futures, indexes, options

Functions: fundamental analysis, bond analysis, futures analysis, options analysis, simulation/game, statistics

Systems: DOS, Windows, Unix

Price: $4,200/year; demo available

Return Policy: all sales final

Technical Support: phone hours, 9:30 am-6 pm, M-F

Description: A real-time options tool for analyzing strategies and risk management on commodity futures and stock index. Features include: real-time data quote system that interfaces with Signal to show current price changes; real-time option analysis that shows how implied volatility, delta, gamma, vega and theta change with the market in addition to alpha range management for each option analyzed; strategy/simulation programs that answer "what if" option questions (positions can be input from scratch, or read from a file); and data management and output utilities that can be used to plot a variety of graphs including the ability to plot implied volatility. The system can produce matrix for selected options showing arrays of strike prices for changing levels of price and implied volatility and print daily option summaries

STRATEGIST

Version: na   *Last Updated:* 1994   *No. of Users:* na

Securities: futures, options

Functions: fundamental analysis, futures analysis, options analysis, simulation/game, statistics

Systems: DOS

Price: $4,900-$10,700/year; demo available

Return Policy: all sales final

Technical Support: phone hours, 9:30 am-6 pm, M-F

Description: Real-time risk analysis software lets the user consolidate portfolios that include over-the-counter options and forwards along with listed futures and options. The user is then given a real-time view of the markets impact on delta, gamma, vega and theta for any integrated portfolio and trades. Unlimited capability to answer "what if" scenarios for any aspect of the portfolio and integrates graphic and tabular profit/loss risk reports for options, futures and OTC trades. This analysis can be set for any time horizon and include any scenario. Also includes pulldown menus with clipboard and highlight features that provide easy access and manuevering of trades.

OPTIONS-80

P.O. Box 471
Concord, MA 01742

(508) 369-1589

OPTIONS-80A: ADVANCED STOCK OPTION ANALYZER
Version: 3.0   *Last Updated:* 1993   *No. of Users:* 350
Securities: options
Functions: options analysis
Systems: DOS, Mac
Price: $150 plus $3 shipping and handling; demo available, $10; 20%
   AAII discount
Return Policy: 30 days
Technical Support: phone hours, evenings
Description: Analyzes calls, covered writes, puts and spreads for the
purpose of maximizing return from stock options. Performs Black-
Scholes modeling and calculates market-implied volatility; plots an-
nualized yield against the price action of the underlying stock and ac-
counts for future payments, as well as transaction costs and the time
value of money. Will produce on-screen or printed tables and comparative charts. Guides user to optimum strategy.

OPTIONVUE SYSTEMS INTERNATIONAL, INC.

175 E. Hawthorn Parkway
Suite 180
Vernon Hills, IL 60061

(800) 733-6610
(708) 816-6610
fax: (708) 816-6647

OPTIONS MADE EASY
Version: na   *Last Updated:* 1990   *No. of Users:* 2,100
Securities: options
Functions: options analysis, simulation/game
Systems: DOS
Price: $19.95
Return Policy: all sales final
Technical Support: phone hours, 10 am-6 pm, M-F
Description: An options tutorial. Provides a basic introduction to the
vocabulary and basic strategies for trading options.

OPTIONVUE IV

Version: 1.66   *Last Updated:* 1994   *No. of Users:* 3,000

Securities: futures, options

Functions: futures analysis, options analysis

Systems: DOS

Price: $895; demo available, $44

Return Policy: all sales final

Technical Support: phone hours, 10 am-6 pm, M-F; BBS support; news-letter

Description: For the private investor trading options on stocks, indexes, currencies, bonds and commodities. Results of investment simulation and "what if" analyses are presented in both graph and tabular forms. Can generate specific buy and sell recommendations based on a price forecast for the underlying security and the amount of money to be invested. Fair values, implied volatility, delta, time delay and other parameters are displayed for each option as well as for the trader's existing and contemplated total position. The pricing model, a dividend-adjusted Black-Scholes formula, is also adjusted for the possibility of early exercise. Features include volatility tracking, trade commission schedules, a perpetual expiration calendar, margin requirements, function key customization and the ability to handle convertible securities and warrants. The communication module supports automatic data capture from DJN/R, DataVue, Signal, ComStock, Telescan, DBC/Market Watch and Radio Exchange.

ORINDA SOFTWARE CORPORATION

P.O. Box 1789   (510) 254-3503
Orinda, CA 94563   fax: (510) 254-7811

THE YELLOW PAD

Version: 1.4   *Last Updated:* 1994   *No. of Users:* 200+

Securities: stocks, bonds, futures, mutual funds, indexes, options, real estate

Functions: financial planning

Systems: DOS

Special Requirements: 5M free disk space

Price: $29.95 plus $5 shipping & handling; California residents add sales tax; demo available, $7.50

Return Policy: 30 days

Technical Support: phone hours, 11 am-8 pm, M-F

Description: An MS DOS-level financial calculator designed to project "what-if" scenarios into the future. Users enter starting investment amounts, additions or withdrawals, interest or dividend rates, projected growth, estimated taxes, expected inflation, amortization directives, years to compute, etc. The Yellow Pad computes and displays projected compounded growth and income for each year of the computation. The Yellow Pad promotes understanding of the long term effect of inflation adjusted compound growth and income.

OTTO-WILLIAMS, LTD.

P.O. Box 794   (301) 306-0409
Lanham, MD 20703-0794

OWL PERSONAL PORTFOLIO MANAGER
Version: 5.0   *Last Updated:* 1994   *No. of Users:* 800
Securities: stocks, bonds, mutual funds, indexes, options, real estate
Functions: financial planning, portfolio management, technical analysis
Systems: DOS
Price: $55; companion program—Owl Portfolio Price Loader, $15; demo available, $10
Return Policy: 30 days; $10 restocking fee
Technical Support: phone hours, 8 am-4 pm, M-F; BBS support; newsletter
Description: Portfolio management and technical analysis program. Tracks stocks, bonds, mutual funds, cash accounts, other assets, liabilities, dividends, interest and capital gains in up to 500 portfolios. Report generator customizes 15 reports to include any combination of portfolios so that separate portfolios can be defined for IRAs, 401(k)s, children's college funds, what-if analyses, etc. Reports include net worth, capital gains, unrealized gains, dividends, interest, performance analysis, present position, and more. Charts for technical analysis may be plotted for periods of 1 to 3 years. Technical indicators include: moving averages, polynomial trend analysis; on-balance volume; and stochastic oscillators. Wilder's and net worth can also be plotted for any combination of portfolios. A companion program is available to import price quotes downloaded from America Online, CompuServe, Prodigy, DJN/R, GEnie and others.

PARSONS SOFTWARE

1230 W. 6th Street　　　　　　　　　　　　　　　(303) 669-3744
Loveland, CO 80537

FUNDGRAF
Version: 3.1　　　　　*Last Updated:* 1992　　　　*No. of Users:* na
Securities: stocks, mutual funds, indexes
Functions: technical analysis
Systems: DOS
Price: $100; additional data disks, $20; demo available, $10; 10% AAII
　　discount
Return Policy: 30 days; $15 restocking fee
Technical Support: phone hours, 12 pm-8 pm, M-F
Description: Finds and graphs the best-performing mutual funds for
any period up to 260 weeks. Plots price action and calculates moving
averages (simple or exponential). Allows different mutual funds to be
superimposed on semi-log price scales for direct comparison of performance for any period. Dividends, capital gains distributions or
splits are taken into account in graphs and in calculating the percentage change between time periods. Data (daily or weekly) can be entered manually and erroneous data corrected. Includes 4 years of
weekly data for 32 no-load mutual funds. Additional disks with 32
funds each are available. Calculates relative strength ratings for all
funds. Buy and sell signals are generated based on either crossover or
trend change.

FUNDGRAF DOWNLOADER
Version: 2.0　　　　　*Last Updated:* 1994　　　　*No. of Users:* na
Securities: stocks, bonds, mutual funds, indexes
Functions: quote utility
Systems: DOS
Price: $25; 10% AAII discount
Return Policy: all sales final
Technical Support: phone hours, 12 pm-8 pm, M-F
Description: A supplemental disk for use in downloading data from
CompuServe database. Current data is downloaded from Com-
puServe's Basic Quote Section, which requires no fee other than the
normal monthly basic CompuServe charge. Sample scripts for auto-
matic downloading using ProComm communication package (DOS
version) furnished. Program converts downloaded data to Fundgraf

data format for use in Fundgraf programs.

FUNDGRAF SUPPLEMENTAL PROGRAMS, DISK 1
Version: 1.0   *Last Updated:* 1989   *No. of Users:* na
Securities: stocks, mutual funds, indexes
Functions: portfolio management, technical analysis
Systems: DOS
Price: $20; 10% AAII discount
Return Policy: all sales final
Technical Support: phone hours, 12 pm-8 pm, M-F
Description: Contains 4 Fundgraf programs. Make-PRN and Add-PRN move data between the Fundgraf data files and a spreadsheet program (i.e., Lotus 1-2-3, Quattro Pro) or similar programs. Data from other sources can then be added with Add-PRN. From a Fundgraf data disk, data can be imported to a spreadsheet with Make-PRN. Check-dat checks dividends, prices and percent changes for any 2 consecutive weeks or days. Test-SIG calculates the growth of a $1,000 initial investment made in any or all of the funds assuming that (1) the funds are sold every time the price goes below the moving average and then bought every time the price goes above the moving average, and (2) the cash is invested at a fixed interest rate while out of the market. User selects the lengths for 2 moving averages and the fixed interest rate. For comparison, it calculates the value of $1,000 at a fixed interest rate and the value of the fund if bought and held throughout the period. Results show how effective the selected moving average signal was during the period. Reports number of purchases made during period.

PARTECH SOFTWARE SYSTEMS

2 Bryant Street   (415) 546-9316
Suite 200   fax: (415) 546-9319
San Francisco, CA 94105

PARITY PLUS
Version: 1.5   *Last Updated:* 1993   *No. of Users:* na
Securities: stocks, bonds, futures, mutual funds, indexes
Functions: technical analysis, statistics
Systems: Windows
Special Requirements: Windows, 4M RAM, mouse
Price: $179; demo available; 10% AAII discount

Return Policy: all sales final
Technical Support: phone hours, 11:30 am-8 pm, M-F; BBS support
Description: A stock charting and technical analysis program for Windows 3.X. Includes more than 50 indicators and provides support for complex user-defined formulas up to 500 characters long. Chart types include high/low/close bar chart, Japanese candlesticks, 12 types of point and figure charts, Arms equivolume charts, Crocker type charts, horizontal bar charts of days at price and volume at price, line charts and histograms. Each chart can include up to 9 indicators and 11 panes. Panes can be stacked or overlaid and maintain independent scales. Multiple indicators can be plotted in a single pane. Charts can contain up to 8,100 data points for each indicator. Two stocks can be in memory simultaneously permitting spread and relative strength charting. User can define an unlimited number of chart types and configurations, and up to 30 charts can be displayed simultaneously to draw trendlines, Fibonacci Arcs and channel lines on any chart. Interface allows charting of groups of stocks, batches of studies, or a cluster of charts in a predefined screen layout. Includes on-line help. Profit testing and optimization tools let user test trading strategies against all the securities in a group; summarize results for an entire group or examine summary and transaction details for every security in the group. Has scanning and filtering features. Parity's chart, profit test and scan definitions can be exported to a file and shared between users. Fully compatible with MetaStock, Compu Trac, ChartPro, MegaTech, TeleChart 2000, and comma delimited ASCII data files. Price data can be imported from, or exported to, text files, Excel and Lotus 1-2-3. Also permits import of non-price data.

PC SOLUTIONS, INC.

104-40 Queens Boulevard
Forest Hills, NY 11375

(718) 275-7930

FIN VAL/FINSTOCK *(formerly Plan Version 2.1)*
Version: 2.1   *Last Updated:* 1993   *No. of Users:* na
Securities: stocks
Functions: fundamental analysis, spreadsheet
Systems: DOS
Price: $495; demo available, $20 (applies toward purchase); 40% AAII discount
Return Policy: 30 days

Technical Support: phone hours, 9 am-10 pm, 7 days; fee for tech support—free first year

Description: Provides forecast earnings, cash flows and share prices using a comprehensive set of analytical tools. Includes reports and graphs displaying historical and forecast income statements, balance sheets, cash flows and ratio analysis. A discounted cash flow valuation exhibit displays 150 values using 6 methods (P/E ratio, book value, cash flow to perpetuity, Graham, EBIT multiples) over a range of terminal value assumptions and discount rates. Investor rate of return analysis depicts forecast share prices and investment returns based on forecast earnings and projected P/E multiples. Ratio analyses include executive summaries, profitability and common size reports. User can enter historical income statements and balance sheets (minimum 1 year) or download information from a financial database for input to the model. PC Solutions will provide, free of charge to Finval purchases, a comparative analysis model, FINSTOCK, which compares financial and market data from the AAII Stock Investor database.

PERFORMANCE TECHNOLOGIES, INC.

4814 Old Wake Forest Road
Raleigh, NC 27609

(800) 528-9595
(919) 876-3555
fax: (919) 876-2187

CENTERPIECE

Version: 3.2   ***Last Updated:*** 1994   ***No. of Users:*** 1,400

Securities: stocks, bonds, mutual funds, indexes, options, real estate, limited partnerships, annuities

Functions: portfolio management, bond analysis

Systems: DOS

Price: $895 professional system; $150 FNN Signal interface; $150 Charles Schwab & Co. interface; demo available, $25

Return Policy: all sales final

Technical Support: toll-free number; phone hours, 9 am-5 pm, M-F; newsletter; fee for tech support—$150 (includes upgrades)

Description: Reports include summaries by position, performance, unrealized gains and losses by trade lot, realized gains and losses, income received and a projection of monthly income and principal redemptions. Bond analysis provides standard bond computations. Global reports include a master list of holdings, cross reference by security and bond maturity and option expiration schedules. Performance and analytical measures include time-weighted rate of return, total return, current yield, unrealized gain or loss, yield to maturity, yield to call, duration, after tax yield and taxable equivalent. Accounting functions include deposits, withdrawals, global income posting, automatic reinvestment lots for mutual funds, return of principal, accrued interest, splits and automatic cash, money fund and margin accounting. Sell transactions may be matched to specific buy lots. Market prices may be updated manually or via modem. Program handles stocks, bonds, mortgage-backed securities, options, mutual funds, CDs, T-bills, commercial paper and money market funds. User-defined security type is appropriate for limited partnerships and annuities. Users may optionally define subgroups or sectors for each security type. Provides asset allocation weightings by position, sector and security type. A real-time interface with Signal is available. Includes client billing for fee-based advisers.

CENTERPIECE PERFORMANCE MONITOR

Version: 2.0 *Last Updated:* 1994 *No. of Users:* 200

Securities: stocks, bonds, mutual funds, indexes, options, real estate, limited partnerships, annuities

Functions: portfolio management

Systems: DOS

Special Requirements: Centerpiece

Price: $595; demo available

Return Policy: all sales final

Technical Support: toll-free number; phone hours, 9 am-5 pm, M-F; newsletter; fee for tech support—$150 (includes upgrades)

Description: Provides performance measurement and reporting by total portfolio, asset class or individual security using BAI-prescribed methods (exact method or linked internal rate of return method with monthly valuations and exact timing of capital flows). Allows comparisons with multiple market indexes and the construction of properly weighted composite returns. Facilitates compliance with AIMR performance presentation standards.

PERSONAL MICRO SERVICES

2702 Turnberry Road
St. Charles, IL 60174

(708) 513-0297
fax: (708) 513-0298

PORTFOLIO-PRO

Version: na   *Last Updated:* na   *No. of Users:* 350
Securities: stocks, bonds, mutual funds, precious metals
Functions: financial planning, portfolio management
Systems: DOS
Price: $69.95; 40% AAII discount
Return Policy: 14 days; $5 restocking fee
Technical Support: phone hours, 10 am-6 pm, M-F
Description: Tracks stocks, bonds, precious metals, IRAs and other security instruments. All functions are menu-driven, allowing the user to create portfolios, update prices, record dividends and interest and make other data entries. Program generates a current portfolio position, IRS Schedule D (gains and losses), Schedule B (interest and dividend income), closed-out positions (reported in sequence by sales date for 1- or multiple-year period) and an investment summary (total realized/unrealized gains/losses). Records complete history of investment activity for each portfolio. Computes holding period and annualized return and months held for each security. Recalculates data for stock splits and handles multiple portfolios.

PINE GROVE SOFTWARE

23 Flower Hill Drive   (800) 242-9192
Suite 1600   (609) 730-1430
Trenton, NJ 08638   fax: (609) 730-1530

AMORTIZEIT!

Version: 2.0   *Last Updated:* 1994   *No. of Users:* 6,000+
Functions: financial planning, real estate analysis
Systems: DOS
Special Requirements: 512K memory
Price: $50 ($5 shipping); demo available, $5; 10% AAII discount
Return Policy: 60 days
Technical Support: toll-free number; phone hours, 8 am-9 pm, M-F; BBS support
Description: Amortization program supports 8 payment and compounding periods, Rule of 78s, U.S. rule, interest only loans, fixed principal loans and normal loans. Payments can be in advance or in arrears. Random or scheduled extra payments can be applied to reduce the principal balance. Calculates the interest saved as a result of extra

payments. The interest due can be calculated for any number of days or between any 2 dates. User can set any payment amount for a loan and can calculate the remaining balance.

SOLVEIT!
Version: 4.3   *Last Updated:* 1993   *No. of Users:* 10,000+
Securities: stocks, bonds, mutual funds, real estate
Functions: financial planning, bond analysis, real estate analysis
Systems: DOS
Price: $90; demo available, $5; 10% AAII discount
Return Policy: 60 days
Technical Support: phone hours, 8 am-10 pm, M-F; BBS support
Description: Program includes: future value of a deposit, future value of a series, present value and time to double, present value of a series, net present value, uneven cash flow, interest due, time to withdrawal of funds, required payment needed for a future sum, interest rate earned, equivalent interest rate, purchasing power and inflation, loan calculator, amortization table, remaining balance of a loan after any payment, balloon payment, accelerated payments, depreciation routines, (MACRs, ACRs), gross profit margin of series, break-even point, economic order quantity, net worth statement, affordable house price, second mortgage, rental income property analysis, budget cash flow, weighted average, calendar math, and bond values and yields with inflation factor.

PISCES SOFTWARE

P.O. Box 579-9171   (312) 281-7916
Chicago, IL 60613   fax: (312) 281-7916

PISCES METASTOCK EXPORT UTILITY
Version: 1.0   *Last Updated:* 1993   *No. of Users:* 150
Securities: stocks, bonds, futures, mutual funds, indexes, options
Functions: quote utility
Systems: DOS
Special Requirements: MetaStock
Price: $75; 10% AAII discount
Return Policy: all sales final
Technical Support: phone hours, 9 am-5 pm, M-F
Description: Exports data to chart programs, spreadsheets, or to other MetaStock Directories. Exports data from any MetaStock chart direc-

tory to any other directory. All export formats are under user's control and include volume conversion. Creates ASCII or PRN files. Exports last day or records since a specified date. Formats fields with fractions, decimals, justified or padded, and exports selected fields. Delimits fields with commas, spaces or columns of text. Exports from daily to weekly or monthly files. Volume manipulation: Volx10 or Volx100, also Vol/10 Vol/100. Exports from MetaStock to MetaStock. Encloses fields in quotes. Program is menu driven and batch file controlled.

PORTFOLIO SOFTWARE

14 Lincoln Avenue   (617) 328-8248
Quincy, MA 02170

ASSET ALLOCATOR
Version: 1.0   *Last Updated:* 1994   *No. of Users:* na
Securities: stocks, bonds, futures, mutual funds, options
Functions: financial planning, portfolio management, statistics
Systems: DOS
Price: $150; 15% AAII discount
Return Policy: 30 days
Technical Support: phone hours, 9 am-6 pm, M-F
Description: Applies Markowitz algorithm to portfolio selection. Shows how to allocate funds among assets in a portfolio to minimize risk and maximize a return. Can compare user-generated allocations with corresponding efficient allocations having the same return to compare risk levels. Allows user to view the efficient frontier on a spreadsheet corner by corner over the range of efficient returns. Program comes in versions with closing prices and dividends, or rates of return as a database. Asset Allocator is also available in a version that uses rates of return, standard deviations and correlation coefficients among asset pairs as a database. User should specify desired database when ordering. Files can be created, updated and edited through the keyboard, converted from CompuServe files, or created on any spreadsheet program such as Lotus 1-2-3 or Excel. Linear constraints can be written against any asset or group of assets. Program can handle any size portfolio depending on memory capacity of computer being used.

STOCK PORTFOLIO ALLOCATOR
Version: 2.0   *Last Updated:* 1994   *No. of Users:* 50+

Securities: stocks, bonds, futures, mutual funds, options
Functions: financial planning, portfolio management, allocation
Systems: DOS
Price: $150; 15% AAII discount
Return Policy: 30 days
Technical Support: phone hours, 9 am-6 pm, M-F
Description: Applies Markowitz algorithm to portfolio selection. Shows how to allocate funds among securities in a portfolio to minimize risk and maximize return. Can compare user-generated allocations with corresponding efficient allocations having the same return to compare risk levels. Allows one to view the efficient frontier on a spreadsheet corner-by-corner over the range of efficient returns. Program comes in versions with closing prices and dividends, or rates of return as a database. User should specify desired database when ordering. Files can be created, updated, and edited through the keyboard, converted form Compuserve files, or created on any spreadsheet program such as Lotus 1-2-3 or Excel. Linear constraints can be written against any security or group of securities. Program can handle any size portfolio depending on memory capacity of computer being used.

PORTSIDE MARKET

10926 Adare Drive   (703) 425-2275
Fairfax, VA 22032

BMW
Version: 1.0   *Last Updated:* na   *No. of Users:* 250
Securities: bonds
Functions: bond analysis, spreadsheet
Systems: DOS
Special Requirements: Lotus 1-2-3
Price: $99; demo available, $10; 50% AAII discount
Return Policy: 90 days
Description: A collection of Lotus 1-2-3 and Symphony macros that work together to form a bond analysis system. Uses a window to display the cell values of settlement date, maturity date, coupon, price, yield, date issued, call date and call price. The window is hidden by pressing a zoom key. Does not interfere with user's spreadsheet layout. Bond data is given wherever the cursor is positioned.

BOND$MART

Version: 2.1   *Last Updated:* 1989   *No. of Users:* na

Securities: bonds

Functions: bond analysis

Systems: DOS

Special Requirements: Lotus 1-2-3

Price: $395; demo available, $10; 75% AAII discount

Return Policy: 90 days

Description: Handles calculations for government, corporate, agency or municipal bonds and notes; interest at maturity notes and CDs; T-bills or discount securities; zero-coupon bonds; short/long odd lot first coupon bonds; Eurobonds; Japanese discount notes. Calculations include yield to maturity and/or call, before or after taxes; current yield; CD equivalent yield; Macaulay duration and horizon duration; price volatility; reinvestment rate-to-yield; discount rate-to-price and others. Uses the Security Industry Association (SIA) standard as a default for bond calculations, but user may set own parameters. Includes a spreadsheet interface for data transfer to a Lotus 1-2-3 spreadsheet for further analysis.

PROGRAMMED PRESS

599 Arnold Road   (516) 599-6527

West Hempstead, NY 11552-3918   fax: (516) 599-6527

BONDS AND INTEREST RATES SOFTWARE

Version: 2.0   *Last Updated:* 1994   *No. of Users:* 7,000

Securities: stocks, bonds, futures, mutual funds, indexes, options, real estate

Functions: fundamental analysis, bond analysis, futures analysis, real estate analysis, statistics

Systems: DOS

Price: $144; 10% AAII discount

Return Policy: all sales final

Technical Support: phone hours, 9 am-5 pm, M-F

Description: Contains 16 interactive programs for forecasting and evaluating price, risk and return on fixed-income securities such as bonds, mortgages and T-bills. Present value of annuities and lump sums can also be calculated.

COMMODITIES AND FUTURES SOFTWARE PACKAGE
Version: 2.0   *Last Updated:* 1994   *No. of Users:* 6,000
Securities: futures, indexes, options
Functions: fundamental analysis, futures analysis, options analysis, statistics
Systems: DOS
Price: $144; 10% AAII discount
Return Policy: all sales final
Technical Support: phone hours, 9 am-5 pm, M-F
Description: Has 13 interactive programs for forecasting price, risk and return on futures contracts. Contracts include commodities, stock index futures, soybean spreads and arbitrage using options (reverse conversion or conversion of options).

FOREIGN EXCHANGE SOFTWARE PACKAGE
Version: 2.0   *Last Updated:* 1994   *No. of Users:* 5,000
Securities: futures, indexes, options, currencies
Functions: fundamental analysis, technical analysis, futures analysis
Systems: DOS
Price: $144; 10% AAII discount
Return Policy: all sales final
Technical Support: phone hours, 9 am-5 pm, M-F
Description: Contains 11 interactive programs for analyzing and forecasting exchange rates for foreign currencies.

OPTIONS AND ARBITRAGE SOFTWARE PACKAGE
Version: 2.0   *Last Updated:* 1994   *No. of Users:* 8,000
Securities: stocks, futures, indexes, options
Functions: bond analysis, futures analysis, options analysis, statistics
Systems: DOS
Price: $144 plus shipping; 10% AAII discount
Return Policy: all sales final
Technical Support: phone hours, 9 am-5 pm, M-F
Description: Options and Arbitrage Software Package Has 6 option valuation models: Black-Scholes, Stoll-Parkinson, Bookbinder, empirical put and call models, stock index futures and arbitrage analysis.

STATISTICAL ANALYSIS AND FORECASTING SOFTWARE PACKAGE
Version: 2.0   *Last Updated:* 1993   *No. of Users:* 7,000
Securities: stocks, bonds, futures, indexes, options

Functions: fundamental analysis, technical analysis, futures analysis, statistics
Systems: DOS
Price: $144 plus shipping; 10% AAII discount
Return Policy: all sales final
Technical Support: phone hours, 9 am-5 pm, M-F
Description: Has 20 interactive programs covering the various types of averages, variation, moving averages, exponential smoothing for forecasting, seasonal variation, trends, growth rates, time series decomposition, multiple correlation and regression.

QUANT IX SOFTWARE

5900 N. Port Washington Road
Suite 142
Milwaukee, WI 53217

(800) 247-6354
(414) 961-0669
fax: (414) 961-2121

QUANT IX PORTFOLIO EVALUATOR
Version: 5.0   *Last Updated:* 1993   *No. of Users:* na
Securities: stocks, bonds, mutual funds, options, real estate
Functions: financial planning, portfolio management, fundamental analysis
Systems: DOS
Price: $99; demo available, $2.50
Return Policy: 30 days
Technical Support: phone hours, 9 am-5 pm, M-F; BBS support
Description: Consists of 2 independent programs combined. Portfolio manager features: single or multiple portfolio management for stocks, bonds, mutual funds, government issues, cash items, etc., total accounting, automatic pricing through either CompuServe or Prodigy. Reports show market values, investment income, gains and losses (realized and unrealized), commissions, transactions between 2 dates, percentage returns, percentage of asset type and portfolio totals and income tax information. Security analysis features: fundamental ratio analysis, 6 security valuation models, diversification analysis, "what if" testing and portfolio and security risk assessments. Also has built-in communications with on-line help. Other features include high/low price alerts, maturity report, mutual fund objectives classification and batch processing. BBS: (414) 961-2592

QUANT IX PORTFOLIO MANAGER

Version: 5.0   *Last Updated:* 1993   *No. of Users:* na

Securities: stocks, bonds, mutual funds, options, real estate
Functions: financial planning, portfolio management
Systems: DOS
Price: $59; demo available, $2.50
Return Policy: 30 days
Technical Support: phone hours, 9 am-5 pm, M-F; BBS support
Description: Portfolio manager features: single or multiple portfolio management for stocks, bonds, mutual funds, government issues, cash items, etc., total accounting, automatic pricing through either CompuServe or Prodigy. Reports show market values, investment income, gains and losses (realized and unrealized), commissions, transactions between 2 dates, percentage returns, percentage of asset type and portfolio totals and income tax information. Built-in communication with on-line help. High/low price alerts, maturity reports, mutual fund objective, classifications, batch processing, BBS (414) 961-2592.

Q-WEST ASSOCIATES

13223 Black Mountain Road   (800) 618-6618
#1-410   (619) 484-6648
San Diego, CA 92129   fax: (619) 484-8606

MONEY MAKER FOR WINDOWS

Version: 2.0   *Last Updated:* 1994   *No. of Users:* 2,000

Securities: stocks, bonds, futures, mutual funds, options, real estate
Functions: financial planning, portfolio management, fundamental analysis, technical analysis, bond analysis, futures analysis, options analysis, real estate analysis, mutual funds analysis
Systems: Windows
Special Requirements: Windows 3.1+, mouse or modem recommended
Price: $99; 40% AAII discount
Return Policy: 30 days; $15 restocking fee
Technical Support: phone hours, 9 am-5 pm, M-F
Description: Three programs in one (Money Maker Analyzer, Money Maker Portfolio & Money Maker Chart) featuring investment analysis, portfolio management tools and charting utilities for technical analysis. Money Maker Analyzer is an integrated tool that covers the basic analysis of stocks, options, bonds, mutual funds, futures, real estate

and more. It uses charts and tables to make investment concepts easy to understand. Money Maker Portfolio is a bookkeeping tool that tracks all daily transactions of investments in stocks, options, mutual funds, futures, bonds and cash accounts. Automatically downloads the price updates for all security types in your portfolio through CompuServe. It also can import security prices for Prodigy's Quote Track. Money Maker Portfolio provides 12 types of reports including average cost, short- or long-term capital gains, ordinary income, price history, performance report with annualized rate of return or rate of return between any periods, and so on. It supports short position, margin, margin interest, splits, dividend reinvestment, password protection, etc. It even includes new 3-D charting features for price histories and performance. The Money Maker Chart is a charting program that can automatically download the price histories for your selections of the security through CompuServe. It covers several pre-defined indicators to help you analyze technical behavior of the security.

RADIX RESEARCH LIMITED

P.O. Box 91181   (604) 926-5308
West Vancouver, BC V7V 3N6, Canada   fax: (604) 925-2607

OVM/FOCUS
Version: 4.1   *Last Updated:* 1993   *No. of Users:* 2,800+
Securities: stocks, bonds, indexes, options
Functions: technical analysis, options analysis
Systems: DOS, Windows, Mac
Price: $399 (Canadian); demo available, $5; 5% AAII discount
Return Policy: all sales final
Technical Support: phone hours, 11 am-9 pm, M-F; newsletter
Description: An option trading package. Includes: valuation models and volatility screening, charting package with recursive indicators; a multi-source downloader; universal import/export facility and universal option position worksheet with full graphical display. Can calculate and chart historical composite implied volatility; historical volatility scanning and calculation using the Parkinson Extreme volatility method. The valuation matrix screen has up to 72 valuations per asset and all the derivatives including probability and implied volatility. The graphics worksheet reduces the most complex position to a single profit/loss curve over user-specified parameters together with equivalent share position plotting. Position editing is fully supported.

The built-in downloader and Universal ASCII Import/Export Manager give user total control over the data. Multiple directory support together with backup and restore for unlimited data capacity. Includes database of information on North American optionable assets together with historical implied volatility data on the OEX.

20/20 FOR DOS

Version: 1.10   *Last Updated:* 1993   *No. of Users:* 2,500+

Securities: stocks, bonds, futures, mutual funds, indexes, options
Functions: technical analysis
Systems: DOS
Price: $99; demo available, $5; 5% AAII discount
Return Policy: all sales final
Technical Support: phone hours, 11 am-9 pm, M-F; newsletter
Description: Full-featured, graphical analysis software package using third generation computer techniques. Contains DataLink, an integrated downloader for retrieval of historical and closing price data. Other features include: pulldown menus, hot-keys, pick-lists and context-sensitive on-screen help manual. Contains all popular indicators plus SmartCursor and big-system features such as AutoScale and Compression to graph from 1 to 12 years of data on the screen or printer. Supports most printers including lasers with custom chart capability in printouts. Comes complete with 6 years of data for indexes.

20/20 PLUS

Version: 1.6   *Last Updated:* 1993   *No. of Users:* 2,500+

Securities: stocks, bonds, futures, mutual funds, indexes, options
Functions: technical analysis
Systems: DOS
Price: $299 (Canadian); demo available, $5; 5% AAII discount
Return Policy: all sales final
Technical Support: phone hours, 11 am-9 pm, M-F
Description: Includes all features found in 20/20 plus the McClellan oscillator for index trading using indexes such as the OEX or S&P 500. Implements the full Sherman McClellan oscillator and summation index and color-coded buy and sell signals. The price is $299 in Canadian dollars but is adjusted each day according to the U.S/Canadian exchange rate. Updated to include Bollinger bands DMI and trailing reverse.

RAM TECHNOLOGIES, INC.

964 Westport Crescent
Unit 14
Mississauga, Ontario L5T-1S3, Canada

(905) 795-9222
fax: (905) 795-9223

PORTFOLIO TRACKER

Version: 2.0   *Last Updated:* 1994   *No. of Users:* 500
Securities: stocks, bonds, mutual funds
Functions: portfolio management, technical analysis
Systems: DOS
Price: $450 professional version: $74.95 personal use version; demo
     available; 10% AAII discount
Return Policy: all sales final
Technical Support: phone hours, 9 am-5 pm, M-F
Description: Portfolio tracking program. Produces various reports on
current value and performance of different types of investments.
Maintains personal data and transaction history for all accounts. Calculates annualized (time-weighted) returns on investments. Keeps
track of total assets under management. Records commissions and
service fees. Produces asset allocation graphs. Handles multi-currency
accounts. Globally updates product prices, dividends, stock splits and
currencies. Tracks life insurance policies and maturity dates for CIGs,
term deposits, bonds, T-bills, etc. Interfaces with other software such
as BellCharts, Wealth Creator and Compulife. Export/import information in Wealth Creator format or ASCII comma delimited format.

WEALTH CREATOR

Version: 5.01   *Last Updated:* 1994   *No. of Users:* 1,200
Securities: stocks, bonds, mutual funds, real estate
Functions: financial planning, real estate analysis
Systems: DOS
Price: $199 professional version: $59.95 personal use version; demo
     available; 10% AAII discount
Return Policy: all sales final
Technical Support: phone hours, 9 am-5 pm, M-F
Description: Contains over 45 different financial calculations such as
present and future values, net worth, budgeting, life and disability in-
surance, college education planner, retirement planner bond calcula-
tions, and loan and mortgage schedules. Can also produce 10 different
pie charts, line graphs and bar charts.

RAZORLOGIC SYSTEMS

P.O. Box 112
Kneeland, CA 95549

(800) 500-0444
(707) 668-4054
fax: (707) 668-4055

PERSONAL STOCK TECHNICIAN (PST)

Version: 1.01   *Last Updated:* 1992   *No. of Users:* na

Securities: stocks, bonds, futures, mutual funds, indexes, options, real estate

Functions: technical analysis, statistics

Systems: DOS

Price: $99.50; demo available, $15; 50% AAII discount

Return Policy: 30 days

Technical Support: BBS support

Description: A stock market technical analysis and tracking program designed to support short- or long-term portfolio decision-making. Alerts user to buy or sell opportunities, gathers and analyzes current or past price and volume data using a wide range of common and advanced indicators; calculates and plots oscillators, moving averages, momentum rate-of-change, support-resistance, on-balance volume, relative strength indicators (RSI), stochastics and more. Compatible with online services: Dow Jones News, CompuServe, FFN, GEnie, Prodigy, MetaStock.

RDB COMPUTING, INC.

8910 N. Kenton Avenue
Skokie, IL 60076

(708) 982-1910

RDB COMPUTING CUSTOM TRADER

Version: 2.0   *Last Updated:* 1994   *No. of Users:* na

Securities: stocks, bonds, futures, mutual funds, indexes, options

Functions: technical analysis, bond analysis, futures analysis, options analysis, statistics

Systems: DOS

Price: varies; demo available, $5

Return Policy: all sales final

Technical Support: phone hours, 11 am-7 pm, M-F

Description: Provides a foundation upon which to build technical analysis programs. Includes setup screens, charts, and system performance statistics. Supports various data formats. Can be enhanced and modified by RDB Computing on a custom programming basis to provide new technical analysis indicators, charts, and trading systems.

RDB PROGRAMMER LIBRARIES

Version: 3.0   *Last Updated:* 1994   *No. of Users:* na

Securities: stocks, bonds, futures, mutual funds, indexes, options

Functions: technical analysis

Systems: DOS

Price: $295 C-language data access; $895 C-language charting; $495 compiled libraries (data access plus charting); demo available, $25; 5% AAII discount

Return Policy: all sales final

Technical Support: phone hours, 11 am-7 pm, M-F

Description: Libraries for adding data file access and technical charting to your technical analysis program. Available both as C language source code and as compiled libraries accessible from QuickBASIC, C, or any other programming language. Data file access library provides support for reading ASCII, CompuTrac, CSI, or MetaStock format data files. Charting library supports up to 5 charts per screen, bar charts, indicator charts overlaying bar charts, buy/sell arrows, intraday equity curve, complete control over bar indicator colors, and zoom feature.

RDB SYSTEM TESTER

Version: 3.0   *Last Updated:* 1994   *No. of Users:* na

Securities: stocks, bonds, futures, mutual funds, indexes, options

Functions: technical analysis, bond analysis, futures analysis, options analysis, statistics

Systems: DOS

Price: $895; demo available, $25; 5% AAII discount

Return Policy: all sales final

Technical Support: phone hours, 11 am-7 pm, M-F

Description: Trading system shell program for historical testing and daily trade signal generation of technical analysis tools and trading systems. Targeted toward the more technical user willing to learn QuickBASIC or C language programming (or a trader able to hire a programmer). Trading rules are written by the user in either QuickBASIC or C language. Testing of most trading systems involves modification of one or two subroutines in a sample source code program. Allows additional customizing by the user if necessary. Includes support for ASCII, CompuTrac, CSI and MetaStock format data files as well as manual data updates. Contains setup screens for entering system specific parameters (can be customized by user). Includes up to 5 charts per screen containing bars, indicators (can be customized by user), buy/sell arrows, intraday equity curve, complete control over bar and indicator color and zoom feature. Also has 2 pages of system performance statistics, trades summary, and bar-by-bar intermediate calculations report (can be customized by user). User interaction takes place via windows, menus and fill-in-the-blank forms.

REAL-COMP, INC.

P.O. Box 1210   (408) 996-1160
Cupertino, CA 95015

REAL ANALYZER
Version: 3.0   *Last Updated:* 1992   *No. of Users:* na
Securities: real estate
Functions: portfolio management, real estate analysis
Systems: DOS
Price: $95; demo available, $45; 15% AAII discount
Return Policy: 30 days
Technical Support: phone hours, 11 am-8 pm, M-F; newsletter
Description: Helps users decide when to buy, sell or exchange their home or income property by projecting cash flow, profitability and return on investment before and after taxes. User can compare properties, evaluate alternative financing, structure loans and compare renting with owning. Includes ability to compose a title page, a partial first-year analysis and formatted reports.

REAL PROPERTY MANAGEMENT II
Version: 1.7   *Last Updated:* 1993   *No. of Users:* na
Securities: real estate
Functions: financial planning, real estate analysis
Systems: DOS
Price: $145 to $920; demo available, $45; 15% AAII discount
Return Policy: 30 days
Technical Support: phone hours, 11 am-8 pm, M-F; newsletter
Description: For property managers and owners. Records and budgets 12 months of income, expense, profit, cash flow and bank balance for properties such as apartments, offices, condominium associations, etc.

Reports balance due by unit and lost revenue, maintains tenant files and compares "actuals" to "budget" by account, unit and month. Generates formatted reports customized for both the owner and the accountant. Checks may be printed by the Check Writer and Vendor file. Tenant invoicing, 1099 form writer, disbursement sort by unit/account/vendor, macro reporting, exporting, metering and cost allocation modules are optional.

REALDATA, INC.

78 N. Main Street
South Norwalk, CT 06854

(800) 899-6060
(203) 838-2670
fax: (203) 852-9083

COMMERCIAL/INDUSTRIAL REAL ESTATE APPLICATIONS
Version: 3.0   *Last Updated:* 1992   *No. of Users:* 2,800
Securities: real estate
Functions: real estate analysis, spreadsheet
Systems: DOS, Windows, Mac
Special Requirements: for DOS: Lotus 1-2-3; for Macintosh, Windows: Excel
Price: $150; 10% AAII discount
Return Policy: all sales final
Technical Support: phone hours, 9 am-5:30 pm, M-F; newsletter
Description: Project Cost Analysis produces a budget that a lender can evaluate as part of the developer's request for financing. Gives an overview of the proposed project and summarizes the costs of land, construction, design and engineering, financing, development and leasing. Automatically derives the maximum loan a project will support and calculates the income needed to produce a required rate of return. Evaluates the income and expenses for the lease-up period and analyzes the first year of operation. It also projects the possible resale at the end of the first year.

COMPARATIVE LEASE ANALYSIS
Version: 1.0   *Last Updated:* 1993   *No. of Users:* na
Functions: fundamental analysis, real estate analysis, spreadsheet
Systems: DOS, Windows, Mac
Special Requirements: for DOS: Lotus 1-2-3; for Macintosh, Windows: Excel

Price: $295; 10% AAII discount
Return Policy: all sales final
Technical Support: phone hours, 9 am-5:30 pm, M-F
Description: Compares up to six different leases with varying provisions for CPIs, pass-throughs, build-outs and other considerations. "What if" feature provides a lease negotiation simulation. Includes detailed and summary reports.

ON SCHEDULE
Version: 2.0   *Last Updated:* 1988   *No. of Users:* 1,500
Securities: real estate
Functions: fundamental analysis, real estate analysis, spreadsheet
Systems: DOS, Windows, Mac
Special Requirements: for DOS: Lotus 1-2-3; for Macintosh, Windows: Excel
Price: $195; 10% AAII discount
Technical Support: phone hours, 9 am-5:30 pm, M-F; newsletter
Description: Helps produce a month-by-month plan for drawing, using and repaying a development loan. Predicts and manages numerous inflows and outflows of cash for homes in the final, intermediate and beginning phase of construction, each with different cash requirements. While drawing down funds, user may be writing contracts on units soon to close, collecting the proceeds of sales written several months ago and applying some of these proceeds to reduce outstanding loan balance.

PROPERTY MANAGEMENT III
Version: 1.2   *Last Updated:* 1990   *No. of Users:* na
Securities: real estate
Functions: real estate analysis
Systems: DOS, Mac
Price: $395 to $1,495; demo available, $45
Return Policy: all sales final
Technical Support: phone hours, 9 am-5:30 pm, M-F; newsletter
Description: Features property, unit and lease profiles; accounts receivable; accounts payable; lease abstracts (or complete leases can be stored on disk for every tenant); automatic billing of monthly rent, 3 other user-defined recurring charges and unlimited non-recurring charges; open-item, accrual-based accounting, with transaction detail retained for past months; detailed tenant statements, with aging and automated collection letters; complete payables system with cash

management and discount scheduling; automatic posting and payment of recurring monthly expenses, such as mortgage payments; cash requirements report, check printing and vendor 1099s; tenant's share of CAM charges automatically transferred posted from AP to tenant's account; integrated general ledger that updates immediately as AR and AP transactions are posted; up-to-date financial statements available to print at any time and sample chart of accounts provided on disk. Each property can have a different chart of accounts; user can copy COA set-up from the sample or from an existing property to a new property. Each property can have a different fiscal year. Repair/work order tracking keeps tabs on repairs requested, in progress and completed. Pop-up lists find GL account number, property ID, lease number—almost anything that is stored in list form—without leaving or losing user's place on the screen.

REAL ESTATE INVESTMENT ANALYSIS
Version: 8.0   *Last Updated:* 1994   *No. of Users:* 7,500
Securities: real estate
Functions: real estate analysis, spreadsheet
Systems: DOS, Windows, Mac
Special Requirements: for DOS: Lotus 1-2-3; for Macintosh, Windows: Excel, Lotus v.4
Price: $295; 10% AAII discount
Return Policy: all sales final
Technical Support: phone hours, 9 am-5:30 pm, M-F; newsletter
Description: Templates provide 10-year sensitivity analysis for income-producing real estate, analyze income and expense, print an amortization schedule, calculate internal rates of return, and develop an annual operating statement. Lease analysis is included. An 8-page business plan summarizes all the detailed supporting reports about the purchase, financing, resale, taxes and operation of any income-producing property. The plan is formatted for presentation to the bank or partners. Tax-change upgrades are provided at a very nominal cost.

REAL ESTATE PARTNERSHIP PLUS
Version: 1.0   *Last Updated:* 1990   *No. of Users:* 300
Securities: real estate
Functions: fundamental analysis, real estate analysis, spreadsheet
Systems: DOS, Windows, Mac
Special Requirements: for DOS: Lotus 1-2-3; for Macintosh, Windows: Excel

Price: $295; 10% AAII discount
Return Policy: all sales final
Technical Support: phone hours, 9 am-5:30 pm, M-F; newsletter
Description: Includes 4 applications. The partnership model begins as property analysis. Instead of examining the federal tax ramifications for an individual investor, REPP allows user to enter a series of assumptions about how to allocate income, cash flows and sale proceeds to the limited and general partners. Allows user to specify a preferred return for the limited partners. Program then generates a detailed, summarized property analysis and produces a partnership analysis that shows how the benefits of the partnership should be allocated to each class of partner year-by-year and how the partner's capital accounts can be expected to progress each year. Finally, it produces an overview report, with comparison of performance of invested funds to other vehicles, such as CDs, T-bills, etc.

REALITY TECHNOLOGIES, INC.

2200 Renaissance Boulevard
King of Prussia, PA 19406

(800) 346-2024
(215) 277-7600
fax: (215) 278-6115

WEALTHBUILDER BY MONEY MAGAZINE
Version: 4.0/3.0 Mac   *Last Updated:* 1994   *No. of Users:* na
Securities: stocks, bonds, futures, mutual funds, indexes, options, real estate
Functions: financial planning, portfolio management, simulation/game
Systems: DOS, Mac
Price: $69.99
Return Policy: 30 days
Technical Support: phone hours, 8:30 am-11:30 pm, M-F, 9:30 am-5 pm Sat.; BBS support; newsletter
Description: Helps user take stock of current financial situation and plan financial future. User enters information about present financial position, including asset holdings, income and expenses; then outlines each financial objective such as home purchase, education or retirement. Program computes what user needs to budget on an annual basis and recommends an optimal asset allocation for each objective based on the portfolio theory. User can sort, filter and graph database

of over 3,000 mutual funds, 5,000 stocks, 6,000 bonds and 4,000 CDs and money markets to evaluate specific investment opportunities. The program compares user's projected assets at current level of budgeting and investment to the level of assets necessary to reach goals. Will print a recommended action plan, detailing the next financial steps. Helps with tax, insurance and estate planning and allows "what if" analysis. User can change any information or assumption to see the impact on overall financial picture. Includes Reality's Smart Investor Network by Money Magazine, an on-line personal investing service that gives users access to on-line research databases, quotes, tradings, personalized clipping service, investment alerts, historical pricing charts, automatic portfolio updates and more.

REALTY SOFTWARE COMPANY

P.O. Box 4285
Park City, UT 84060

(801) 649-6149

HOME PURCHASE
Version: na   *Last Updated:* 1987   *No. of Users:* 800
Securities: real estate
Functions: real estate analysis
Systems: DOS
Price: $75; 10% AAII discount
Return Policy: all sales final
Technical Support: phone hours, 11 am-8 pm, M-F
Description: Analyzes the effects of insurance, property taxes, utility expenses, interest rates, closing costs, debt service and the buyer's tax bracket on the total cash necessary for purchase and the total monthly payment. Calculations include leverage achieved, loan-to-value ratio and return on investment.

INCOME PROPERTY ANALYSIS
Version: na   *Last Updated:* 1988   *No. of Users:* 950
Securities: real estate
Functions: real estate analysis
Systems: DOS
Price: $75; 10% AAII discount
Return Policy: all sales final
Technical Support: phone hours, 11 am-8 pm, M-F
Description: Supplies financial analysis of almost any income-produc-

ing property. Up to 4 loans may be entered along with rents, vacancy factor, insurance, taxes, repairs, etc.

LOAN AMORTIZATION
Version: na   *Last Updated:* 1989   *No. of Users:* 1,000
Securities: real estate
Functions: financial planning, real estate analysis
Systems: DOS
Price: $75; 10% AAII discount
Return Policy: all sales final
Technical Support: phone hours, 11 am-8 pm, M-F
Description: Amortizes loan payments. Calculates automatically or on a fixed payment basis, displaying a schedule of loan payments (including dates), payment number, payment amount, principal, interest and loan balance.

MAINTENANCE MANAGER
Version: na   *Last Updated:* 1992   *No. of Users:* na
Securities: real estate
Functions: real estate analysis
Systems: DOS
Price: $275 single user; $475 multi version; demo available, $25; 10% AAII discount
Return Policy: all sales final
Description: Keeps track of maintenance records on almost any kind of property. System can track all maintenance requests and provide lists of requests in 4 major categories including all requests, active requests, completed request and inactive requests.

MANAGER'S OPTION
Version: na   *Last Updated:* 1992   *No. of Users:* 1,000
Securities: real estate
Functions: real estate analysis
Systems: DOS
Price: $375; demo available, $25; 10% AAII discount
Return Policy: all sales final
Technical Support: phone hours, 11 am-8 pm, M-F
Description: Accounting functions include owner/building information, management fees, balance sheets, checks to owners, 1099 forms, tenant deposit interest, lists of owners and owner account balance.

PROPERTY LISTINGS COMPARABLES

Version: na   *Last Updated:* 1992   *No. of Users:* 500
Securities: real estate
Functions: real estate analysis
Systems: DOS
Price: $300; demo available, $25; 10% AAII discount
Return Policy: all sales final
Technical Support: phone hours, 11 am-8 pm, M-F
Description: Maintains real estate listings and comparable sold properties. Includes a comprehensive screening capability for selecting properties. Property information is entered and updated by filling in a form on the computer screen. Selections of properties on file can be made using various criteria such as minimum and maximum price, number of bedrooms and baths, heat type and city. Performance selections can be made based on a maximum gross factor, a maximum price per square foot of improvements and a minimum cash flow requirement.

PROPERTY MANAGEMENT PLUS

Version: na   *Last Updated:* 1994   *No. of Users:* 4,000
Securities: real estate
Functions: real estate analysis
Systems: DOS
Price: $350; demo available, $25; 10% AAII discount
Return Policy: all sales final
Technical Support: phone hours, 11 am-8 pm, M-F
Description: Handles both residential and commercial properties for 1 or many owners. Features include tenant information, late rent report, vacancy report, expired lease report, automatic late charge, rent statements, bank reconciliation, graph income and expenses, ledger detail, operating statements, income detail report, expense detail report, check printing, rent receipts, bank deposit slips and a word processor.

REAP PLUS

Version: na   *Last Updated:* 1991   *No. of Users:* 500
Securities: real estate
Functions: real estate analysis
Systems: DOS
Price: $150; 10% AAII discount
Return Policy: all sales final
Technical Support: phone hours, 11 am-8 pm, M-F

Description: Provides instant analysis of any real estate investment including internal rate of return calculations. Features include a 5-year forecast projection of rents, vacancy factors, operating expenses, debt service, depreciation and appreciation. Shows before- and aftertax cash flows for each year. Functions as a 5-year spreadsheet for tax-sheltered real estate investments without requiring any additional software.

RED CAT SYSTEMS, INC.

P.O. Box 399   (800) 374-9165
Concord, MA 01742

RETIREASY
Version: 1.02   *Last Updated:* 1993   *No. of Users:* na
Functions: financial planning
Systems: DOS
Price: $20 plus $5 shipping
Return Policy: 30 days
Technical Support: newsletter
Description: A retirement planning system to help develop, reach, and maintain retirement goals. Has 350+ page retirement planning guidebook (purchased separately from software). Determines how much money is needed to retire in comfort, how long money will last, the effect of inflation on retirement finances, the role of Social Security, if user's pension is enough, the effects taxes have on retirement, how user can save for retirement, ways user can invest retirement savings, how much insurance is needed, and how to plan an estate. Allows user to track progress toward retirement goals. Encourages testing of "what if" plans by allowing user to test potential changes to plans. No additional software needed.

RELEVANCE III, INC.

4741 Trousdale Drive   (615) 333-2005
Suite One   fax: (615) 834-5688
Nashville, TN 37220

RELEVANCE III-ADVANCED MARKET ANALYSIS
Version: 2.4   *Last Updated:* 1993   *No. of Users:* 500

Securities: stocks, bonds, futures, mutual funds, indexes, options
Functions: technical analysis
Systems: DOS
Price: $795; 4% AAII discount
Return Policy: all sales final
Technical Support: phone hours, 10:30 am-5:30 pm, M-F; newsletter
Description: Scan 1 to 50 or more markets each night with professional trading methods to filter out and trade the opportunities. Select trading methods including Gann, Andrews, Elliott, Fibonacci, Wyckoff, etc. Other features include moving averages, stochastics, Wilder's RSI, directional movement, commodity channel index, MACD, William's %R, accumulation distribution index, ultimate oscillator, day-by-day simulation mode, risk reward analysis, candlesticks, time/price studies and 9 pages of trading plans for each market.

RESAMPLING STATS

612 N. Jackson   (703) 522-2713
Arlington, VA 22201   fax: (703) 522-5846

RESAMPLING STATS
Version: 3   *Last Updated:* 1992   *No. of Users:* na
Functions: simulation/game, statistics
Systems: DOS, Mac
Price: $225; 50% AAII discount
Return Policy: 30 days
Technical Support: phone hours, 9 am-5 pm, M-F
Description: Program for applied everyday problems in statistics and probability. Handles new statistics of resampling. Has no formulas or tables. Handles all problems with numerical simulation experiments. Recent work in mathematical statistics on the bootstrap and related methods provides a theoretical foundation. Program commands mimic the physical operations in conducting Monte Carlo trials with "urns" or random numbers; for example, "shuffle" randomizes a set of elements.

RETIREMENT INCOME FORECASTER

32 Bruce Avenue   (508) 842-8154
Shrewsbury, MA 01545-3002

RETIREMENT INCOME FORECASTER

Version: 1.2   *Last Updated:* 1994   *No. of Users:* na
Securities: bonds, mutual funds
Functions: financial planning
Systems: DOS
Price: $69; demo available, $16; 15% AAII discount
Return Policy: 30 days
Technical Support: phone hours, 8 am-5 pm, M-F
Description: A financial analyzer displayed in cash-flow format to visualize year-to-year forecast of investing for retirement and withdrawing income from a future retirement fund. Displays year-to-year financial details. Software includes the IRS Life Expectancy Tables and offers several ways to structure a retirement income plan. The IRS minimum distribution method and a standard annuity method are available; as well as a "structure your own plan" method. All can be printed in year-to-year format. Final results can be exported to a spreadsheet file for graphing. Earnings can be expressed as either a single, average rate or at varing annual rates that the user can enter. For example, the past experience of the S&P 500 for each of the past 24 years could be entered.

RET-TECH SOFTWARE, INC.

151 Deer Lane   (708) 382-3903
Barrington, IL 60010   fax: (708) 382-3906

CHARTPRO

Version: 1.07   *Last Updated:* 1991   *No. of Users:* 1,000+
Securities: stocks, bonds, futures, mutual funds, indexes, options
Functions: technical analysis
Systems: DOS
Price: $54
Return Policy: all sales final
Technical Support: phone hours, 10 am-6 pm, M-F; BBS support
Description: Creates daily, weekly and monthly high/low/close bar charts using high resolution color graphics. Menu-driven, the master version permits the user to calculate many technical studies including: simple, exponential, displaced and volume-weighted moving averages; parabolic time/price; on-balance volume, relative strength, momentum and point and figure charts; support/resistance study, Fibonacci fans, line oscillator, directional movement indicator, commodity

cycle index, William's %R, moving average envelope, directional movement index, MACD, CCI, accumulation/distribution index, fast/slow stochastics, Gann fans, Fibonacci support/resistance lines, Bollinger bands, candle charts, McClellan oscillator and more. Also included with the master version are a program for manual data entry and programs for accessing the DJN/R for automatic quote retrieval and automatic entry into the ChartPro files. Supports Prodigy, GEnie and other sources. Documentation is included for all routines.

MEGATECH CHART SYSTEM
Version: 2.03   *Last Updated:* 1993   *No. of Users:* 3,000+
Securities: stocks, bonds, futures, mutual funds, indexes, options
Functions: technical analysis
Systems: DOS
Price: $175; demo available, $5; $15 AAII discount
Return Policy: all sales final
Technical Support: phone hours, 10 am-6 pm, M-F; BBS support
Description: Uses unlimited banks of 30 pre-programmable, 1-key recall screens with up to 16 charts per screen. Charts may include technical studies such as various moving averages, point and figure, candle charts, stochastics, Arms index, McClellan oscillator, trendlines, fans, angles, parallel lines, money flow, open interest, spreads, multiple-tissue overlay, MACD, CCI, relative strength, oscillators, DMI, parabolic time/price and others. Additional features include customizable screens, zoom up/down, chart scroll, "Tech on Tech," notepads for each issue and true autoprint. Support for Prodigy is included; others are available on request. MegaTech supports over 300 specific printers including postscript and color. Create custom indexes, portfolios and multi-issue spreads. Flexible ASCII text import and export.

REVENGE SOFTWARE

P.O. Box 1073   (516) 271-9556
Huntington, NY 11743

AN OPTION VALUATOR/AN OPTION WRITER
Version: na   *Last Updated:* na   *No. of Users:* na
Securities: options
Functions: options analysis
Systems: DOS

Price: $99.95; demo available, $10; 25% AAII discount
Return Policy: 30 days; $25 restocking fee
Technical Support: phone hours, 8 am-4 pm, M-F
Description: A package for evaluating stock options. Consists of 2 interactive programs, An Option Valuator and An Option Writer, enabling the user to analyze options. An Option Valuator uses the Black-Scholes equations to predict the future fair market value of a call or put option and calculate option volatility and hedge ratios. An Option Writer evaluates covered option writing strategies, computes and displays total investment, maximum profit, maximum percent profit, total investment cost, number of days to option expiration, percent investment yield, annualized investment yield, yield if option exercised, break-even stock price and total profit. Special features include graph displays, an options calendar giving the complete expiration date when only the month and year are entered and an option editor permitting the user to modify any option parameter so that the effect of the change on other parameters may be observed.

RJT SYSTEMS

1049 SW Baseline   (800) 729-5037
Suite B-200   (503) 640-5303
Hillsboro, OR 97123   fax: (503) 693-7487

CHARTMASTER
Version: 6.2   *Last Updated:* 1994   *No. of Users:* na
Securities: stocks, bonds, futures, mutual funds, indexes, options
Functions: technical analysis
Systems: DOS
Price: $129; 10% AAII discount
Return Policy: all sales final
Technical Support: toll-free number; phone hours, 11 am-8 pm, M-F;
    BBS support; fee for tech support—optional
Description: Binds together DTN data with user's computer. Price and text data from DTN is downloaded to Chartmaster, where it can be exported into other investment programs, or plotted in full color charts. These graphs include basic analytical tools such as; candlesticks, trendlines, and simple and weighted moving averages. It also includes all the capabilites of DataLink.

DATALINK

Version: 6.2   *Last Updated:* 1994   *No. of Users:* na

Securities: stocks, bonds, futures, mutual funds, indexes, options
Functions: downloading
Systems: DOS
Price: $89; 10% AAII discount
Return Policy: all sales final
Technical Support: toll-free number; phone hours, 11 am-8 pm, M-F; BBS support; fee for tech support—optional
Description: Use low cost data and news with Lotus, MetaStock, CompuTrac, OptionVue and over 100 other technical, portfolio, forecasting and client management systems. Program transfers stock, futures, index, market indicator and option prices into end-of-day analysis and portfolio programs eliminating data-entry errors. All pages, whether prices or news, can be printed on a parallel printer, stored on diskette or edited in a word processor or desktop publisher. Charting module also available.

ELECTRONIC SYMBOL INDEX

Version: 4.2   *Last Updated:* 1994   *No. of Users:* na

Securities: stocks, bonds, mutual funds, indexes
Functions: ticker utility
Systems: DOS
Price: $49; 10% AAII discount
Return Policy: all sales final
Technical Support: toll-free number; phone hours, 1 pm-10 pm, M-F; BBS support; fee for tech support—optional
Description: Performs searches for ticker symbols by company name (or first few characters of). User can electronically update new issues as they become available on the market using DTN Wall Street and Datalink or can manually edit the listings. The cross-reference database contains over 15,000 stocks, bonds and mutual funds.

RMC

(formerly Ingenious Technologies Corporation)

Box 60842   (408) 773-8715
Sunnyvale, CA 94088-0842

MARKET MASTER

Version: 4.53   *Last Updated:* 1994   *No. of Users:* na

Securities: stocks, bonds, futures, mutual funds, indexes, options
Functions: technical analysis
Systems: DOS
Price: $149 to $799; demo available, $49; 10% AAII discount
Return Policy: all sales final
Technical Support: phone hours, 12 pm-6 pm, M-F
Description: Forecasting software that creates leading indicators to forecast the direction, magnitude and target of future price movement for any number of stocks, futures contracts and market indexes, foreign stocks and futures exchanges. Has 2 major components: quantitative pattern analysis and error detection and learning (it automatically detects any past inaccuracy and continues to refine its analyses to make future forecasts more accurate). The 2 are combined and the resulting forecasts are automatically displayed graphically after data entry. Four versions: Regular Market Master (E2), with indicators 1 and 2 for end-of-day analysis; Market Master Plus (E4), with indicators 1 through 4 for end-of-day analysis; and Market Master Ultra (4), with indicators 1 through 4 for intraday analyses and end-of-day analysis.

ROBERTS-SLADE, INC.

619 N. 500 West
Provo, UT 84601

(800) 433-4276
(801) 375-6850
fax: (801) 373-2775

CHARTISTALERT
Version: na   *Last Updated:* na   *No. of Users:* na
Securities: stocks, bonds, futures, mutual funds, indexes, options
Functions: technical analysis, futures analysis, options analysis, statistics, expert system
Systems: OS/2
Price: $195-$280/month; demo available
Return Policy: all sales final
Technical Support: phone hours, 9 am-5 pm, M-F; BBS support; newsletter
Description: General features are quotes, news, portfolio management, advanced charting, technical analysis, historical data, trendlines, and more. This new module will give users the ability to create their own formulas and custom studies. Alerts and alarms can also be set and triggered based on any user criteria. Provides the ability to com-

pletely automate your trading system. Editor is designed with simple commands for user with average technical skills.

ENHANCED CHARTIST

Version: 3.2   *Last Updated:* 1994   *No. of Users:* na

Securities: stocks, bonds, futures, indexes, options

Functions: portfolio management, technical analysis, bond analysis, futures analysis, options analysis

Systems: Mac

Special Requirements: MAC II series or better; 4M RAM, 40M free hard disk space

Price: $1,295 plus $295/year; demo available; 10% AAII discount

Return Policy: all sales final

Technical Support: phone hours, 9 am-6 pm, M-F; fee for tech support—$295

Description: Offers a complete line of technical and charting analysis tools on stocks, futures, options, and indexes. Enhanced Chartist features real-time quote manipulation on 1,500 symbols; provides options analysis, including volatilities and theoreticals; portfolio management; historical data (tick, intraday, daily, weekly, and monthly); advanced technical analysis; trendline analysis (Gann, Fibonacci, etc.); custom displays on each monitor; hot key recall on user-defiened screens; charting tools (zoom, tabular status, etc.) and more.

FIRSTALERT

Version: 2.91   *Last Updated:* 1994   *No. of Users:* 300

Functions: portfolio management, technical analysis, futures analysis, options analysis, spreadsheet, expert system

Systems: DOS, Windows, OS/2

Special Requirements: 486-66, 16M RAM, 300M free disk space

Price: $200-$350 monthly; demo available

Return Policy: all sales final

Technical Support: phone hours, 9 am-7 pm, M-F; BBS support; newsletter

Description: FirstAlert software series is a technical analysis and advanced options analytics program. FirstAlert is designed in three separate modules. ChartistAlert comprises about 75% of FirstAlert, providing quotes, news, portfolio management, advanced charting, technical analysis, historical data, trend lines, and more. RiskAlert is designed for the advanced options trader, featuring on-line price volatility, theorical charts, volatility skews, average implied and implied volatility, theoretical PnL charting, position and strategy testing. SignalAlert allows the user to automate his/her trading system. Features include stock filtering and group management techniques, multiple criteria alert processing, alerts on technical and custom studies, back testing, optimization and custom programmability. Other features of the FirstAlert series include the ability to run DOS and Windows applications alongside FirstAlert.

MASTER CHARTIST
Version: 2.67b   *Last Updated:* na   *No. of Users:* na
Securities: stocks, futures, mutual funds, indexes, options
Functions: technical analysis, options analysis
Systems: DOS
Price: $895; demo available; 6% AAII discount
Technical Support: phone hours, 10 hours daily; newsletter; fee for tech support—$295
Description: Has multiple windows, unique point and click interface and high resolution graphics. Supports several data vendors and can track and chart commodities, options and stocks. More than 50 technical indicators are available with options analysis and advanced trendline analysis. Run one monitor for quotes and one for charts.

RISKALERT
Version: na   *Last Updated:* na   *No. of Users:* na
Securities: stocks, bonds, futures, mutual funds, indexes, options
Functions: technical analysis, options analysis, statistics
Systems: DOS, OS/2
Price: $295/month; demo available
Return Policy: all sales final
Technical Support: phone hours, 9 am-5 pm, M-F; BBS support
Description: Designed for the advanced options trader. Features include several option models, advanced "what if" analysis on time, price and volatility, value sheets, matrix reports, historical and implied volatility charts, theoretical PnL charting, position and strategy testing, and more.

RTR SOFTWARE, INC.

19 W. Hargett Street   (919) 829-0786
Suite 204   fax: (919) 829-0891
Raleigh, NC 27601

TECHNIFILTER PLUS
Version: 7.1.5   *Last Updated:* 1993   *No. of Users:* na
Securities: stocks, bonds, futures, mutual funds, indexes, options
Functions: technical analysis, futures analysis
Systems: DOS
Special Requirements: DOS 5.0 or higher
Price: $399
Return Policy: 30 days; $25 restocking fee
Technical Support: phone hours, 9 am-6 pm, M-F; newsletter
Description: Historically tests buy/sell strategies on real data and filters through thousands of issues to identify specified patterns. There are 35 sample reports, more than 185 formulas and 20 ready-to-use strategy tests. Built-in reports and formulas include 45 formulas that pick out candlestick patterns and popular indicators. All reports, formulas and tests can be modified and saved for later use, or users can devise their own. Report features include multi-layered filtering, scoring for "best and worst" issues and exporting. Testing features include the ability to vary up to 5 groups of different parameters to see which variation would have been the most profitable and to test whole directories at once. There are 3 testing methodologies: one for stocks, one for futures and one that simulates percentage trading. Users can screen and test current and historical point and figure patterns, chart indicators and trading strategies, and automate routine tasks. Works with data produced by Dow Jones and Market Analyzer Plus, Equis International's MetaStock Telechart 2000, Savant's The Technical Investor, Compu Trac, Inmark's Market Maker and AIQ Trading Expert.

SASI SOFTWARE, CORP.

P.O. Box 457   (503) 625-5384
Sherwood, OR 97140

MARKETEDGE II
Version: 1.0   *Last Updated:* 1993   *No. of Users:* 100+

Securities: stocks, mutual funds, indexes
Functions: technical analysis
Systems: DOS
Price: $39; 23% AAII discount
Return Policy: 30 days
Technical Support: phone hours, 6 pm-10 pm, M-F; newsletter
Description: A market timing package that focuses on timing of the overall market to identify major tops and bottoms. Market breadth data (advances, declines, volume) is integrated into a Master Breadth Index. Other indicators featured include stochastics, relative strength index and Bollinger bands. Features include pop-up menus, on-screen help windows and full-color graphs.

SAVANT SOFTWARE, INC.

120 Bedford Center Road   (800) 231-9900
Bedford, NH 03110   (603) 471-0400
                                              fax: (603) 472-5981

ENHANCED COMMUNICATIONS
Version: 1.01   *Last Updated:* 1992   *No. of Users:* na
Securities: stocks, bonds, futures, mutual funds, indexes, options
Functions: quote utility
Systems: DOS
Price: $245; demo available, $29
Return Policy: 30 days
Technical Support: phone hours, 9 am-5 pm, M-F
Description: Communications program for users of Savant's Fundamental Investor, Investor's Portfolio and Technical Investor. Retrieves prices from Signal, TrackData and DJN/R. Includes: data validation, data insertion, timed retrieval, symbol aliasing for different databases, custom log-on/log-off procedures, script files and macro procedures.

FUNDAMENTAL INVESTOR
Version: 1.8   *Last Updated:* 1991   *No. of Users:* na
Securities: stocks
Functions: fundamental analysis
Systems: DOS
Price: $295; demo available, $29
Return Policy: 30 days

Technical Support: phone hours, 9 am-5 pm, M-F

Description: Provides fundamental analysis, communications and fundamental screening. Allows storage of over 300 data items with data available on more than 10,000 companies. Data can be entered and edited manually, from subscription disks, or automatically by modem. User can screen all securities in the database greater than, less than or equal to each parameter; sort stocks on a single parameter (before or after screening); calculate financial ratios from basic financial information (using spreadsheet-like functions); sort stocks based on a group of user-specified parameters. Allows automatic retrieval of fundamental data from Ford Investor Services.

INVESTOR'S PORTFOLIO

Version: 1.29   *Last Updated:* 1992   *No. of Users:* na

Securities: stocks, bonds, futures, mutual funds, options, real estate

Functions: portfolio management

Systems: DOS

Price: $795 standard version, $995 international version; demo available, $29

Return Policy: 30 days

Technical Support: phone hours, 9 am-5 pm, M-F

Description: Tracks a virtually unlimited number of portfolio accounts, calculating market value, evaluating the performance, adjusting for splits and distributions, and generating reports. Handles all different types of investments, including: long or short positions in stocks, mutual funds, put and call options, CDs, zero-coupon bonds, Treasury issues, commodities, mortgage-backed securities, warrants, etc. Allows user to segregate investments in accounts and to group securities within an account. Other features include automatic reinvestment of income, open order tracking, and more. Reporting section calculates annualized compound total return, after-tax performance, risk-adjusted rate of return, and unrealized gains and losses. Other reports show capital gains, trading performance, position status, dividend and interest income, expenses, security cross reference and industry sector analysis. Over 30 user-modifiable reports available.

TECHNICAL INVESTOR

Version: 2.82   *Last Updated:* 1991   *No. of Users:* na

Securities: stocks, bonds, futures, mutual funds, indexes, options, real estate

Functions: technical analysis

Systems: DOS
Price: $295; demo available, $29
Return Policy: 30 days
Technical Support: phone hours, 9 am-5 pm, M-F
Description: Combines charting, communications and technical database programs; fully integrates with the other Savant investor products, all of which can be accessed from one screen. The database stores daily high/low with close/volume information for up to 2,500 securities, with up to 40 years daily data for a security. Charts include price and volume bars; high, low and close price lines; point and figure charts; positive/negative volume indicators; relative strength and others. Plot multiple stocks on the same window or use the multiple-window feature to compare charts for different securities side by side. The communications package updates prices automatically from Track-Data or DJN/R, providing current quotes or up to 10 years of historical data on stocks, commodities, market indexes, etc. Most securities are handled automatically; any type of security may be entered manually.

TECHNICAL SELECTOR

Version: 1.2   *Last Updated:* 1990   *No. of Users:* na
Securities: stocks, bonds, futures, mutual funds, indexes, options
Functions: technical analysis
Systems: DOS
Price: $145; demo available, $29
Return Policy: 30 days
Technical Support: phone hours, 9 am-5 pm, M-F
Description: Security filter program for Savant's Technical Investor. Analyzes studies to select stocks, mutual funds, options, etc., that exhibit bullish or bearish tendencies or breakouts. Includes relative strength index, stochastics, moving average crossovers, volume accumulation and moving average convergence/divergence. Filters the data on several studies, prints statistical and filter reports and creates lists of securities that pass each filter.

TOPVEST

Version: 1.3   *Last Updated:* 1992   *No. of Users:* na
Securities: stocks, bonds, futures, mutual funds, indexes, options, real estate
Functions: fundamental analysis, technical analysis, statistics
Systems: DOS

Special Requirements: 386+, 4M RAM
Price: $3,500; demo available, $95
Return Policy: 30 days
Technical Support: phone hours, 9 am-5 pm, M-F; newsletter; fee for tech support—$500 after first year
Description: Workstation software for technical and fundamental analysis of stocks and other securities. Handles 12,000 securities per data directory with up to 32,000 days, weeks or months of price/volume history and up to 800 fundamental items per security. Includes over 100 built-in technical indicators including moving averages, RSI, stochastics, MACD, candlesticks, point and figure, equivolume, Fourier and adaptive filtering. User equations and studies allow the creation of new indicators and trading systems that can be back-tested and optimized. User can use own fundamental valuation systems to screen on undervalued companies and can download prices (open, high, low, close, volume and open interest) from TrackData, CompuServe, IDC, Signal or DJN/R. Data validation allows automatic correction of errors and retrieval of missing data. Fundamental data covering over 10,000 companies is supplied on disk on an annual subscription basis. Macros allow complete automation, including loops, conditional branching, variables and keyboard entry. A configurable user interface includes pulldown menus, dialog boxes, function keys and command line entry.

SCIENTIFIC CONSULTANT SERVICES, INC.

20 Stagecoach Road (516) 696-3333
Selden, NY 11784 fax: (516) 696-3333

N-TRAIN
Version: 1.1   *Last Updated:* 1993   *No. of Users:* 15
Securities: stocks, bonds, futures, mutual funds, indexes, options, real estate
Functions: technical analysis, bond analysis, futures analysis, options analysis, spreadsheet, simulation/game, statistics, expert system, neural network
Systems: DOS, Windows, Windows NT
Special Requirements: 386+, math coprocessor recommended
Price: $747; 20% AAII discount
Return Policy: all sales final
Technical Support: phone hours, 2 pm-7 pm, M-F

Description: A neural network system that can be used in both technical (price and volume) and fundamental (earnings, interest rate, etc.) analysis of any security or financial instrument. Capacity limited only by memory and disk size. Has double-precision math, and the user has full control over transfer functions, learning rules, etc. Program for users who plan to develop neural trading systems.

SERENSON CONSULTING SERVICE

P.O. Box 266   (203) 283-8111
Thomaston, CT 06787

QUOTE COLLECTOR
Version: na   *Last Updated:* 1992   *No. of Users:* 100+
Securities: stocks, mutual funds, indexes, options
Functions: quote utility
Systems: DOS
Special Requirements: X*Press
Price: varies; demo available, via X*Press feed; 10% AAII discount; 20% restocking fee
Technical Support: phone hours, after 5 pm, M-F
Description: Uses the X*Press information to collect stock quotes for building a historical database. It is designed to run as an unattended collection process. The program will output data compatible with a variety of technical analysis programs; MetaStock, Compu Trac, NSQ, Prosper II plus, FundMaster, AIQ Stock Expert, OptionExpert, Viking, Stoktrak, MarketMaster. It also produces DBF, DIF and ASCII file formats.

SMALL INVESTOR'S SOFTWARE COMPANY

138 Ocean Avenue   (800) 829-9368
Amityville, NY 11701   (516) 789-9368

INFOLINK
Version: 1.0   *Last Updated:* 1992   *No. of Users:* na
Securities: stocks, bonds, futures, mutual funds, indexes, options
Functions: transfer utility
Systems: DOS

Special Requirements: serial port and DTN service
Price: $22.95
Return Policy: 30 days
Technical Support: phone hours, 10 am-6 pm, M-F; BBS support
Description: A transfer utility program for DTN users only. Establishes a link between DTN and computer's hard drive allowing the saving of all information DTN beams off the satellite. Enables user to edit, cut, paste, transfer, move, search, capture, import, crop, rearrange, and print all data. Enables use of parallel printer. For networks, saves the cost of purchasing numerous DTN units. Allows user to create historical files of quotes, and also the news of the day every day.

POINTSAHEAD!
Version: 2.01   *Last Updated:* 1992   *No. of Users:* na
Securities: stocks, bonds, futures, mutual funds, indexes, options
Functions: technical analysis, bond analysis, futures analysis, statistics
Systems: DOS
Price: $149; demo available, free-online
Return Policy: 30 days
Technical Support: phone hours, 9 am-6 pm, M-F; BBS support; news-
    letter
Description: A charting and technical analysis program. Provides Japanese candlestick, equivolume, and bar charting; 40 technical and statistical indicators to be used on futures, stocks, indexes, options, options on futures, mutual funds and money market funds. Provides data management, collection and editing. Collects data on all ticker symbols. Converts numbers into graphs and profit-spotting trends. Cursor control identifies historical data, statistics and price levels. Creates weekly charts from daily charts. Displays 3 graphs simultaneously. Features moving averages including exponential, median, simple or weighted; net real price change, midpoint to midpoint of daily trading ranges; past price action for each weekday; update charts with current prices throughout the trading day; user-defined colors, graph size, hot keys and multiple directories; and utilities to remove duplicate data, remove last entry, insert data, backup data and delete data.

SOFTWARE ADVANTAGE CONSULTING CORPORATION

38442 Gail
Clinton Township, MI 48036

(800) 729-2431
(313) 463-4995

INVESTOR'S ADVANTAGE

Version: 2.21   *Last Updated:* 1992   *No. of Users:* 600

Securities: stocks, futures, mutual funds, indexes, options

Functions: technical analysis

Systems: DOS

Price: $179; 50% AAII discount

Return Policy: 30 days; 10% restocking fee

Technical Support: phone hours, 8 am-7 pm, M-F

Description: Analysis tool for stock selection and market timing. Charts stocks, mutual funds, market indexes, commodities and options in 640 x 200 resolution color. Individual equity studies include high/low/close, relative strength, volume, moving averages (3 durations per issue), stochastics, Wilder's RSI, momentum, sine waves (for cycle analysis), trendlines and more. Individual charts include readout of high/low/close and volume. General market barometers include DJIA, NYSE composite, advance/declines, put/call ratio, odd lot/short ratio, overbought/oversold ratio, new high/new lows, specialist short ratio and the 20 most active indicators. Zoom feature available on all charts. Relative strength report sorts stocks, strongest to weakest, to help identify best performers. Market entries and exits can be timed using market barometers. Other reports include the monthly percentage change report. Data can be exported for spreadsheet use.

INVESTOR'S ADVANTAGE FOR WINDOWS

Version: 4.0   *Last Updated:* 1993   *No. of Users:* 100

Securities: stocks, bonds, futures, mutual funds, indexes, options

Functions: technical analysis

Systems: Windows

Price: $179

Return Policy: 30 days; 10% restocking fee

Technical Support: phone hours, 8 am-7 pm, M-F

Description: Windows-based analysis tool for stock selection and market timing. Multiple moveable and sizeable charts of stocks, mutual funds, market indexes, commodities and options. Individual equity studies include high/low/close, Japanese candlesticks, volume, relative strength, on-balance volume, moving averages (9 variable settings for advanced, centered, simple and exponential), stochastics, MACD, Wilder's RSI and DMI, momentum, open interest, trendline drawing and more. General market barometers include DJIA, NYSE composite, advance/declines, put/call ratio, odd-lot short ratio, overbought/oversold ratio, McClellan oscillator, summation index, traders index, 15 most active (daily), 20 most active (weekly), specialist short ratio, and new highs/new lows. A moving readout of barometer values is accessible from the keyboard. Zoom feature on all charts. Reports include a relative strength ranking report, moving average breakout report, overbought/oversold report (using stochastics) and the monthly percentage and portfolio valuation data export for spreadsheet use. Automatic downloading of quotes from Dial/Data (downloading software is included). On-line context-sensitive help is built-in.

SORITES GROUP, INC.

P.O. Box 2939
Springfield, VA 22152

(703) 569-1400
fax: (703) 569-1424

SORITEC
Version: 6.6   *Last Updated:* 1993   *No. of Users:* 800
Functions: fundamental analysis, statistics
Systems: DOS
Price: $495; demo available, $25
Return Policy: all sales final
Technical Support: phone hours, 9 am-5 pm, M-F; fee for tech support—$95
Description: A problem-oriented 4th-generation language. Selected system features: econometrics, simulation, forecasting, statistics, mathematics, data entry and manipulation. Used for time series and cross sectional analysis. Applications include economic research and policy analysis; sales forecasting and market research; stock, bond and commodity price forecasting; public utility load and rate analysis; laboratory research; production and cost function estimation and Monte Carlo simulation.

SPONSOR-SOFTWARE SYSTEMS, INC.

860 Fifth Avenue
New York, NY 10021

(212) 724-7535
fax: (212) 580-9703

ASSET ALLOCATION EXPERT
Version: 5.0   *Last Updated:* 1994   *No. of Users:* 100
Securities: stocks, bonds, indexes, real estate
Functions: financial planning
Systems: DOS
Price: $10,000/year; demo available
Return Policy: all sales final
Technical Support: phone hours, 24 hours, 7 days; newsletter
Description: Optimization system generates efficient portfolios for up to 14 asset classes for up to 20 years. Uses Nobel prize-winning methodology as well as downside risk techniques. Features include databases of capital market indexes, full statistical capabilities, and an interactive graphic module.

SPSS, INC.

444 N. Michigan Avenue
Suite 3300
Chicago, IL 60611

(800) 543-6609
(312) 329-3500
fax: (312) 329-3668

SPSS FOR WINDOWS
Version: 6.1   *Last Updated:* 1994   *No. of Users:* 200,000
Securities: stocks, bonds, futures, mutual funds, indexes, options
Functions: financial planning, technical analysis, statistics
Systems: Windows
Special Requirements: Windows 3.0, 4M RAM
Price: $695; demo available; call for AAII discount
Return Policy: 60 days
Technical Support: toll-free number; phone hours, 10 am-6 pm, M-F; BBS support; newsletter
Description: A package for data entry, statistical analysis, data and file management, charting and reporting. Statistical procedures include cross tabulations, descriptive statistics, exploratory data analysis, correlations, ANOVA, frequency counts, means, regression, non-parametric tests and t-tests. Includes over 50 integrated business and analytical

charts that can be generated automatically through user analysis or built independently. Charts are object-oriented and editable. Supports DDE and OLE and file formats for Excel, Lotus 1-2-3, dBASE, SAS, ASCII, SYLK, Oracle and SQL Server and is 100% Windows compatible—user can specify analytical options through menus and dialog boxes. Add-on modules for specialized tasks include: SPSS Professional Statistics, SPSS Advanced Statistics, SPSS Tables, SPSS Trends, SPSS Categories, SPSS CHAID, and SPSS LISREL 7.

SPSS/PC+

Version: 4.1   **Last Updated:** 1991   **No. of Users:** 200,000
Functions: technical analysis, statistics
Systems: DOS
Price: $195; demo available
Return Policy: 30 days
Technical Support: phone hours, 10 am-6 pm, M-F; BBS support; newsletter
Description: An interactive, menu-driven data management, analysis and presentation software package that features automatic error-checking, extensive on-line help and the ability to read and write ASCII files for the exchange of data with other microcomputer packages. Includes a split-screen editor as well as a communications protocol for transferring files between micro and mainframe computers. Statistical routines range from simple descriptive measures and cross-tabulation tables to regression analyses, including logistic. Data management facilities allow for selecting, sorting and weighting cases, merging multiple files, data aggregation and creating new variables. A complete report writer produces custom formatted reports with the user having control over titles, margins and the calculation of summary statistics. The system handles files of up to 500 variables and an unlimited number of cases, and it includes Graph-in-the-Box from New England Software.

SPSS/PC+ TRENDS

Version: 4.0   **Last Updated:** 1990   **No. of Users:** 200,000
Functions: technical analysis, statistics
Systems: DOS
Price: $395; demo available
Return Policy: 30 days
Technical Support: phone hours, 10 am-6 pm, M-F; BBS support; newsletter

Description: Analysis tools include 2-stage least squares and weighted least squares regression, uni- and bivariate spectral analysis and Box-Jenkins analysis based upon ARIMA algorithms. Also contains more than a dozen smoothing models, curve-fitting and 3 autoregressive models. User can compare fits among alternative models as well as save and reuse models. Validation and forecasting periods can be changed and modified, and missing values can be correctly estimated with the latest statistical algorithms.

STRATAGEM SOFTWARE INTERNATIONAL, INC.

520 Transcontinental Dr.   (800) 779-7353
Suite B   (504) 885-7353
Metairie, LA 70001   fax: (504) 885-7292

QUICK CHARTS
Version: 1.8   *Last Updated:* na   *No. of Users:* na
Securities: stocks, bonds, futures, mutual funds, indexes, options, real estate
Functions: technical analysis, bond analysis, futures analysis, spreadsheet, statistics
Systems: Windows
Price: $50; demo available, free; 15% AAII discount
Technical Support: phone hours, 9 am-5:30 pm, M-F; newsletter; fee for tech support—$300 (optional)
Description: QuickCharts is a simple chart drawing program directed toward the beginner as a learning tool. Displays several bar/volume charts on the screen at one time.

SMARTRADER
Version: na   *Last Updated:* na   *No. of Users:* na
Securities: stocks, bonds, futures, mutual funds, indexes, options, real estate
Functions: portfolio management, technical analysis, bond analysis, futures analysis, options analysis, spreadsheet, statistics
Systems: DOS, Windows
Price: $349-Windows version; $450-DOS version; demo available, free; 15% AAII discount
Technical Support: phone hours, 9 am-5:30 pm, M-F; newsletter; fee for tech support—$300 (optional)

Description: A technical analysis program for the experienced technician. Based on a spreadsheet, user can load multiple data issues and studies, create custom formulas and perform historical backtesting of trading systems. Includes many charting features. Studies can be overlayed on barcharts or other studies. Spreadsheet data may be displayed with charts on screen. A vertical chart cursor can be turned on in all charts at the same time. Scrolls all charts in synchronization (spreadsheet also if displayed). Includes QuickCharts.

SMARTRADER PROFESSIONAL
Version: na   *Last Updated:* na   *No. of Users:* na
Securities: stocks, bonds, futures, mutual funds, indexes, options
Functions: portfolio management, technical analysis, bond analysis, futures analysis, options analysis, spreadsheet, statistics
Systems: DOS
Price: $990; demo available, free; 15% AAII discount
Technical Support: phone hours, 9 am-5:30 pm, M-F; newsletter; fee for tech support—$300 (optional)
Description: Capable of testing somewhat more complex trading scenarios than regular version. Has ability to create complex custom calculations. Includes automation interface, using schedules and tasks, allows the trader to run an automated system. Includes SMARTrader (DOS).

STRATEGIC PLANNING SYSTEMS, INC.

1409 Kuehner Dr. #1174   (800) 488-5898
Simi, CA 93063   (805) 522-8979
                                                    fax: (805) 522-9687

QUOTEMASTER
Version: 1.9   *Last Updated:* 1992   *No. of Users:* na
Securities: stocks, bonds, futures, mutual funds, indexes, options
Functions: technical analysis, quote utility
Systems: Mac
Price: $395; demo available; 10% AAII discount
Return Policy: 15 trial days
Technical Support: phone hours, 1 pm-7 pm, M-F
Description: Monitors all major U.S. financial markets in real-time. Accesses information for all major stock and commodity exchanges. Cov-

ers futures, options, Nasdaq securities, mutual funds and money market funds. Supports security data sent over FM airwaves by Signal and Telemet America. User is able to constantly monitor 1,250 securities at 1 time from an available choice of 40,000 securities. Securities may be grouped in individual window with no limit to the number of securities allowed per window. Program produces intraday and inter-day charts on any security.

QUOTEMASTER PROFESSIONAL
Version: 1.92   *Last Updated:* 1992   *No. of Users:* na
Securities: stocks, bonds, futures, mutual funds, indexes, options
Functions: technical analysis
Systems: Mac
Price: $495; demo available, free; 15% AAII discount
Return Policy: 15 trial days
Technical Support: phone hours, 1 pm-7 pm, M-F
Description: Includes all the features of QuoteMaster, plus intraday charts that can be set up from tick-by-tick up to 60 minutes. User can draw trendlines, zoom in or out on charts to set grid lines and high/low/close intervals. User can double-click mouse on any chart to track and display chart values on the bottom of the screen. Chart types include: MACD, envelopes, %R, RSI, volume accumulation, volume accumulation oscillator, linear regression, trading bands, accumulation-distribution, on-balance volume and momentum.

SURVIVOR SOFTWARE LIMITED

11222 La Cienega Boulevard   (310) 410-9527
Suite 450   fax: (310) 338-1406
Inglewood, CA 90304

MACMONEY
Version: 4.0   *Last Updated:* 1993   *No. of Users:* 60,000
Securities: stocks, bonds, mutual funds
Functions: financial planning
Systems: Mac
Price: $89.95; demo available, $5; 25% AAII discount
Return Policy: 30 days; $5 restocking fee
Technical Support: phone hours, 12 pm-5 pm, M-F; newsletter
Description: Allows user to track expenditures and income by enter-

ing bank, cash and credit card transactions. Enter as many as 30,000 transactions each year in up to 6,000 categories. Reports include net worth (personal balance sheet), net income (income and expenses), cash flow, major expenses and tax categories.

MARKET CHARTER
Version: 1.1   *Last Updated:* na   *No. of Users:* na
Securities: stocks, bonds, mutual funds, indexes
Functions: technical analysis
Systems: Mac
Special Requirements: Hypercard 1.2.5 or higher
Price: $59.95; demo available, $5; 25% AAII discount
Return Policy: 30 days
Technical Support: phone hours, 12 pm-5 pm, M-F; newsletter
Description: Stock charting and technical analysis. Price/value histories of stocks, mutual funds, market indexes and/or other market information are maintained and charted on a weekly basis. A moving average for weekly closing prices is also calculated for each chart.

TECH HACKERS, INC.

50 Broad Street   (212) 344-9500
New York, NY 10004   fax: (212) 344-9519

@NALYST
Version: 2.0   *Last Updated:* 1993   *No. of Users:* 10,000+
Securities: stocks, bonds, futures, indexes, options, real estate
Functions: financial planning, portfolio management, bond analysis, futures analysis, options analysis, real estate analysis, spreadsheet, statistics
Systems: DOS, Windows, OS/2, Mac, Unix, Sun Sparc
Special Requirements: Lotus 1-2-3, Symphony, Excel 2.1+, or Applix
Price: $195 to $1,495; 10% AAII discount
Return Policy: 30 days; shipping restocking fee
Technical Support: phone hours, 9 am-5 pm, M-F
Description: Provides 150 new add-in @ functions for Lotus 1-2-3, Symphony, Applix and Microsoft Excel. Functions perform industry-standard security calculations such as yield to maturity of a bond, theta of an option or the implied PSA of a GNMA. Securities handled include Treasury, agency, municipal, corporate bonds and international, bills, CDs, options and mortgage-backed securities. Performs

generalized cash flow analysis, and date and business day arithmetic. Functions integrate into any worksheet and recalculate automatically like built-in functions.

TECHNICAL ANALYSIS, INC.

4757 California Avenue SW
Seattle, WA 98116-4499

(800) 832-4642
(206) 938-0570
fax: (206) 938-1307

TECHNICAL ANALYSIS CHARTS
Version: 2.0   *Last Updated:* 1989   *No. of Users:* na
Securities: stocks, futures, mutual funds, indexes, options
Functions: technical analysis
Systems: Apple II
Price: $129.95
Return Policy: all sales final
Description: Charts, displays and prints any indicator or sequence of data that fits in a standard CSI/Compu Trac or Dow Jones Market Analyzer format. Gives user ability to create stock/commodity charts with the Apple II. Pulldown menus allow access to all commands with either the keyboard or mouse and let user instantly customize the look of trading charts. Can plot raw market data or the results of technical analyses. Acts as a convenient "switcher" between DOS 3.3 and Pro-DOS operating systems. Includes one subroutine for reading market data from disk into memory and another that performs technical analysis studies.

TECHSERVE, INC.

P.O. Box 9
Issaquah, WA 98027

(800) 826-8082
(206) 865-0249
fax: (206) 746-7712

CAPTOOL
Version: 4.5   *Last Updated:* 1994   *No. of Users:* na
Securities: stocks, bonds, futures, mutual funds, indexes, options, real estate, user-defined
Functions: financial planning, portfolio management, fundamental analysis, technical analysis, bond analysis

Systems: DOS
Price: $129; 30% AAII discount
Return Policy: 45 days
Technical Support: phone hours, 11 am-8 pm, M-F; BBS support
Description: Investment manager that combines portfolio manager with stock and bond evaluators, batch processing of multiple portfolios and client management. Tracks investment cost bases (5 tax lot methods), computes portfolio and security ROI before/after taxes, generates over 20 portfolio reports including client statement and graphics. Stock evaluation is performed by financial ratio screening and a risk-adjusted discounted internal cash flow calculation. Bond evaluation includes yield to call, yield to maturity, and bond swap comparison including swap NPV. Prices may be downloaded from DJN/R, CompuServe, GEnie, Dial/Data, All Quotes and others. Imports prices from many sources such as Prodigy, America Online, MetaStock, Telescan, Telechart 2000, Quote Express, Fidelity Online Express, StreetSmart, and MegaTech. Graphs price open/high/low/close/volume with moving average for technical evaluation. Also plots user-specified macroeconomic indicators. Numerous help screens and 380-page manual included. Complies with AIMR standards.

CAPTOOL GLOBAL INVESTOR

Version: 4.5   *Last Updated:* 1994   *No. of Users:* na
Securities: stocks, bonds, futures, mutual funds, indexes, options, real estate, user-defined
Functions: financial planning, portfolio management, fundamental analysis, technical analysis, bond analysis
Systems: DOS
Price: $299; 30% AAII discount
Return Policy: 45 days
Technical Support: phone hours, 11 am-8 pm, M-F; BBS support
Description: International, multi-currency version of CAPTOOL. Permits securities denominated in different currencies to co-exist in a common portfolio. Currency exchange rate records hold up to 10 user-defined currencies plus a portfolio-based currency. Also features a fund accounting module for management of pooled investments such as investment club, pension or trust fund. Customizable report headers and labels permit user translation into non-English reports. Supports international date and decimal formats. Optional 132-column display on most VGA displays. Utilizes math co-processors. Supports

HP500 series color printers. Complies with AIMR standards.

CAPTOOL PROFESSIONAL INVESTOR

Version: 4.5   *Last Updated:* 1994   *No. of Users:* na

Securities: stocks, bonds, futures, mutual funds, indexes, options, real estate, user-defined

Functions: financial planning, portfolio management, fundamental analysis, technical analysis, bond analysis

Systems: DOS

Special Requirements: 386+

Price: $499, $200 annual license fee; demo available, $29

Return Policy: 45 days

Technical Support: phone hours, 11 am-8 pm, M-F; BBS support; fee for tech support—$200 (see above)

Description: Complete portfolio management package with client management features for the professional investor. Contains enhanced batch processing tools such as a Trade Blotter with Broker/Dealer file imports and a Block Trader. On-line communication available with Schwab, Fidelity, Vanguard, DST Systems, First Trust/DataLynx, Jack White and Co., Bear Sterns, Prudential, and others. Includes the CAP-TOOL Global Investor program. Also includes allocation driven block trades, automatic reconciliation with Broker/Dealer files, management fee calculation and billing, credit and debit interest calculations on cash balances, color graphics printing and client-specific customizable reports. Complies with AIMR standards.

CAPTOOL REAL TIME

Version: 4.5   *Last Updated:* 1994   *No. of Users:* na

Securities: stocks, bonds, futures, mutual funds, indexes, options, real estate, user defined

Functions: financial planning, portfolio management, fundamental analysis, technical analysis, bond analysis

Systems: DOS

Special Requirements: DTN subscription; Quote Express

Price: $189; 30% AAII discount

Return Policy: 45 days

Technical Support: phone hours, 11 am-8 pm, M-F; BBS support

Description: CAPTOOL Real Time incorporates all of the portfolio management features of the regular CAPTOOL portfolio software, plus has the capability to automatically refresh current portfolio valuations from near real-time data feeds provided by DTN. DTN subscription and Quote Express software required in order to activate CAPTOOL Real Time features.

PFROI

Version: 6.0   *Last Updated:* 1994   *No. of Users:* 5,000+

Securities: stocks, bonds, futures, mutual funds, indexes, options, real estate

Functions: financial planning, portfolio management, technical analysis

Systems: DOS

Price: $59; 30% AAII discount

Return Policy: 45 days

Technical Support: phone hours, 11 am-8 pm, M-F; BBS support

Description: Portfolio manager that tracks investment cost bases (5 tax lot methods) and computes portfolio and security ROI (IRR method, both time- and dollar-weighted variations) both before and after estimated taxes. Generates over 20 reports with output to screen, text and Lotus-compatible WKS files or to printer. Estimated taxes are computed with user-configurable tax rates. Features include valuation and allocation graphics, beta computation and price downloading from DJN/R, CompuServe, GEnie, Dial/Data, All Quotes and others. Handles most security types (stocks, bonds, mutual funds, zero-coupon bonds, options, etc.) and transactions including mutual fund reinvestment, fractional shares, splits, shorts, return of capital, etc. Handles multiple portfolios with no limit on number of securities per portfolio.

TECHSOFT, INC.

768 Walker Road, Suite 294   (703) 759-3847
Great Falls, VA 22066

TECHNICAL STOCK ANALYST

Version: 2.2   *Last Updated:* 1994   *No. of Users:* na

Securities: stocks, bonds, futures, mutual funds, indexes, commodities

Functions: portfolio management, technical analysis

Systems: DOS

Price: $24.95 plus shipping ($2.50 U.S./Can./Mex.; $4 foreign)

Return Policy: all sales final

Technical Support: phone hours, 9 am-5 pm, M-F; fee for tech support—1 month free

Description: Technical analysis program. By using 9 technical indicators (including moving averages, relative strength, on balance volume, stochastics, etc.) user can spot buy and sell signals on securities. Trend-lines can be drawn with a mouse and one of the moving averages can be defined by the user. Charts allow either a short-term (7 mos. of daily or 2.7 yrs. of weekly data) or long-term graph (14 mos. of daily or 5.4 yrs. of weekly data) to be viewed. Portfolio manager allows unlimited portfolios to be kept. Each portfolio keeps track of securities and their buy/sell price, commissions, number of shares, and bought/sold dates. When graphing portfolios, the percentage change in price and capital gained or lost is also shown and updated after every new stock price entry. Stock prices can be entered manually, or read in stock AS-CII files from many different quote services. Five sample stocks are also included with a year's worth of back data for analysis.

TELEMET AMERICA, INC.

325 First Street
Alexandria, VA 22314

(800) 368-2078
(703) 548-2042

DISCOVER/EN BY TELEMET
Version: 3.12   *Last Updated:* 1993   *No. of Users:* 400
Securities: stocks, futures, mutual funds, indexes, options
Functions: portfolio management, technical analysis, options analysis
Systems: Windows, OS/2
Special Requirements: mouse, or PM and mouse
Price: $149/month; demo available, free
Return Policy: 25 days
Technical Support: toll-free number; phone hours, 8:30 am-5:30 pm, M-F; newsletter
Description: Real-time stock, option, index, fund, and futures prices are available linked by FM radio data channel for Telemet Encore system. Software uses the "Microsoft Windows" or Presentation Manager OS/2 to offer charts, headline news and quotes on the computer screen. It charts intraday and end-of-day prices. Price and volume alerts, news alerts, 99 custom market watch pages (with 30 stocks per page) and Dow Jones Headlines are part of software. All prices can be "exported" to other PC applications with a file export utility. Telemet Encore also features a link to the Microsoft Excel and Lotus Windows spreadsheets.

DISCOVER/OR BY TELEMET

Version: 3.7   *Last Updated:* 1994   *No. of Users:* 400+

Securities: stocks, bonds, futures, mutual funds, indexes, options

Functions: portfolio management, fundamental analysis, technical analysis, options analysis

Systems: Windows, OS/2

Special Requirements: Mouse, or PM and mouse

Price: $330/month; demo available, free

Return Policy: 25 days

Technical Support: phone hours, 8:30 am-5:30 pm, M-F; newsletter

Description: Real-time stock, option, index, fund, and futures prices are available linked by data channel form Telemet Orion system. Software uses the "Microsoft Windows" or Presentation Manager OS/2 to offer charts, headline and full text news and quotes on the computer screen. It charts intraday and end-of-day prices. Product includes 3-year chart history on all U.S. equities and 150 indexes. Price and volume alerts, news alerts, 250 custom market watch pages (with up to 600 stocks per page) and Dow Jones News are part of software. All prices can be "exported" to other PC applications with a file export utility. Telemet Discovery/OR also features a link to the Microsoft Excel and the Lotus Windows spreadsheets.

DISCOVER/RE BY TELEMET

Version: 3.12   *Last Updated:* 1993   *No. of Users:* 2,000

Securities: stocks, futures, mutual funds, indexes, options

Functions: portfolio management, technical analysis, options analysis, quote utility

Systems: Windows, OS/2

Special Requirements: mouse, or PM and mouse

Price: $399; demo available, free

Return Policy: 25 days

Technical Support: toll-free number; phone hours, 8:30 am-5:30 pm, M-F; newsletter

Description: User can follow the market in real-time. Uses Microsoft Windows, updated continuously on-screen, to provide high resolution graphs and windows with high/low/last quotes on the computer screen at the same time. Supports the DDE interface in other Windows programs (e.g., user can "hot link" to Microsoft Excel spreadsheet).

TELESCAN, INC.

10550 Richmond Avenue   (800) 324-8246
Suite 250   (713) 952-1060
Houston, TX 77042   fax: (713) 952-7138

MUTUAL FUND SEARCH

Version: 1.0   *Last Updated:* 1992   *No. of Users:* 5,000+
Securities: mutual funds
Functions: mutual fund analysis
Systems: DOS
Price: $100; 10% AAII discount
Return Policy: 30 days
Technical Support: toll-free number; phone hours, 7 am-12 am, M-F; 9 am-6 pm weekends; newsletter
Description: Mutual Fund Search, used in conjunction with Telescan Analyzer, lets user sort through more than 1,800 mutual funds in 24 categories. Using a selective screening process to find mutual funds that meet their objectives, investors may search for mutual funds in four different general headings—equity funds, fixed-income funds, money market funds, and municipal bond funds. Eighty different criteria may be used to define the investor's objectives, including purchase requirements, consistency characteristics, performance characteristics and portfolio composition.

TELESCAN ANALYZER

Version: 3.08   *Last Updated:* 1994   *No. of Users:* 100,000+
Securities: stocks, bonds, futures, mutual funds, indexes, options
Functions: fundamental analysis, technical analysis
Systems: DOS
Price: $99; 10% AAII discount
Return Policy: 30 days
Technical Support: phone hours, 7 am-12 am, M-F; 9am-6pm weekends; newsletter; fee for tech support—$50
Description: Combination software program and on-line database that allows user to perform technical and fundamental analysis on more than 80,000 stocks (NYSE, Amex, Nasdaq, and Canadian exchanges), mutual funds, industry groups, options and market indexes. Updated approximately every 15 minutes. Information dates back 20 years. Users can access more than 80 popular technical and fundamental indicators; read and plot insider trading information; access quarterly

earnings reports and Zack's Estimate Service of analysts' projections for future earnings; read late-breaking and historical news, company fact sheets and money-making investment newsletters; view intraday graphs, and up to 4 graphs on a single screen; and use profit tester and stock optimizer to test buy/sell signals of technical indicators and find optimal parameters. Access to S&P MarketScope, Morningstar, MarketGuide Reports, and SEC Online.

TELESCAN PORTFOLIO MANAGER (TPM)

Version: 3.0   *Last Updated:* 1993   *No. of Users:* 1,500
Securities: stocks, bonds, mutual funds, indexes, options, real estate
Functions: portfolio management
Systems: DOS
Price: $395; demo available, $10; 10% AAII discount
Return Policy: 30 days
Technical Support: phone hours, 7 am-12 am, M-F; 9 am-6 pm weekends; newsletter
Description: A portfolio management program that tracks the purchase and sale of stocks, options, mutual funds, corporate bonds, tax-free bonds, government bonds and T-bills. Automatically maintains a cash account and retains a permanent history of sold securities for tax accounting including dates of trades, lots, cost basis, sale price, commissions and profit or loss. Reports include: statements of accounts, asset allocations, values of individual portfolios, dividend and interest transactions and tax summaries formulated to match IRS requirements. Report can be prepared simultaneously for one, several or all portfolios. Offers: unlimited portfolios, easy corrections on prices and commissions, fraction converter, bond calculator, option builder, on-screen alerts signaling when goals and risk levels are met and new highs or lows are obtained and password security protection. Downloads from Telescan or DJN/R.

TIGER INVESTMENT SOFTWARE

P.O. Box 9491   (619) 459-8577
San Diego, CA 92169

PEERLESS INTERMEDIATE-TERM MARKET TIMING PACKAGE

Version: 1994   *Last Updated:* 1994   *No. of Users:* 1,400
Securities: indexes

Functions: technical analysis, expert system
Systems: DOS, Mac
Price: $275 (includes a 3-month subscription to Peerless Forecasts); demo available, $10
Return Policy: 15 days
Technical Support: phone hours, 9 am-3 pm, M-F; BBS support; newsletter; fee for tech support—$200
Description: The 200-page manual tracks and explains buy/sell signals between 1969-1992. Both major and minor (shorter-term) signals appear automatically. Five years of back-data is provided. Daily hand-updating can be performed.

PEERLESS SHORT-TERM MARKET TIMING PACKAGE
Version: 1994   *Last Updated:* 1994   *No. of Users:* 500
Functions: technical analysis, expert system
Systems: DOS
Price: $620 (includes a 3-month subscription to Peerless Forecasts); demo available, $10
Return Policy: all sales final
Technical Support: phone hours, 9 am-3 pm, M-F; BBS support; newsletter
Description: Back-tested to 1972, the 200-page manual shows how a handful of the best technical tools reliably call short-term (one week to one month) DJIA, OPX, S&P and Nasdaq market tops and bottoms. Time-proven, original, and powerful hourly intraday trading techniques are also discussed. The best hourly moving average, band width, and momentum indicators are presented in comprehensive detail covering the last four years. The IBM-compatible programs automatically generate arrows on graphs warning of impending short-term reversals. The hourly program tells exactly what level of the DJIA must reach the next hourly momentum indicator. The necessary back data is provided in the package. Gives automatic buy and sell signals on indexes.

PEERLESS STOCK MARKET TIMING
Version: 1994   *Last Updated:* 1994   *No. of Users:* 1,200
Securities: stocks, futures, mutual funds, indexes, options
Functions: technical analysis
Systems: DOS, Mac
Price: $275 plus $100 for back data (1969-1991); 10% AAII discount
Return Policy: all sales final

Technical Support: phone hours, 9 am-3 pm, M-F; BBS support; newsletter; fee for tech support—$200

Description: Predicts the general market's likely short- and intermediate-term direction and magnitude of moves. Automatic "signal-arrows" pinpoint key reversal points. Helps time the purchase and sale of mutual funds and index options/futures as well as individual stocks at critical market junctures. Users get all the daily DJIA, breadth and volume data back to 1969 to replicate the major Peerless buy and sell signals. Users employ a Help Table to learn the past reliability and significance of each of the 6 different major buy and sell signals. Users may also plot short-term volume, breadth and momentum indicators using their choice of moving averages and price bands.

TIGER MULTIPLE STOCK SCREENING & TIMING SYSTEM

Version: 1994   *Last Updated:* 1994   *No. of Users:* 700

Securities: stocks, indexes

Functions: technical analysis, expert system

Systems: DOS

Special Requirements: 386+

Price: $995 (includes a 6-month subscription to Peerless Forecasts and hot line); demo available, $10

Return Policy: all sales final

Technical Support: phone hours, 9 am-3 pm, M-F; BBS support; newsletter; fee for tech support—$200

Description: Five hundred individual stocks are updated nightly and ranked for relative strength, price versus volume divergences, and consistent long-term accumulation as measured by proprietary intraday volume formula. A composite power ranking of 500 stocks is then created. Users may replicate thru back-testing. A short-term timing scan is run against the top and bottom stocks, and final sets of printed recommendations appear as the most bullish or bearish. Graphs of these stocks, or any others, are then printed with automatic arrowed short-term buy and sell signals. Stocks with significant divergences, unusual volume, price and relative strength breakouts, trendbreaks, or stochastic buy and sell signals are flagged and graphed with highlighting buy and sell arrows. Users may plot daily and weekly charts, adjust moving averages and price bands and experiment with over 20 different indicators. Includes its own verification and optimization programs as well as historical daily data on 500 stocks.

TIME TREND SOFTWARE

337 Boston Road
Billerica, MA 01821

(508) 250-3866
fax: (508) 250-3877

DATA RETRIEVER
Version: 6.0   *Last Updated:* 1989   *No. of Users:* 2,800
Securities: stocks, bonds, futures, mutual funds, indexes, options
Functions: data collection
Systems: DOS
Price: $45; 10% AAII discount
Return Policy: 45 days
Technical Support: phone hours, 9 am-5 pm, M-F
Description: Communications software, used to download data from Dial/Data. Historical data as well as the current closes can be retrieved on mutual funds, stocks, indexes, futures and dividends for mutual funds. Adjustments for dividends are automatically made to your mutual fund data.

ENHANCED FUND MASTER OPTIMIZER
Version: 6.0   *Last Updated:* 1989   *No. of Users:* 500
Securities: stocks, bonds, mutual funds, indexes
Functions: technical analysis, simulation/game
Systems: DOS
Price: $150; 10% AAII discount
Return Policy: 45 days
Technical Support: phone hours, 9 am-5 pm, M-F
Description: A simulation module that runs in conjunction with Fund Master TC or Fund Pro. Analyzes results and gives parameters for best performance of various trading strategies. Indicators include moving average or exponential average, crossover, double average crossover, overbought/oversold simulations and MACDTM, stop losses, buy and sell filters.

FUND MASTER TC
Version: 6.0   *Last Updated:* 1990   *No. of Users:* 3,500
Securities: stocks, bonds, mutual funds, indexes
Functions: portfolio management, technical analysis
Systems: DOS
Price: $289; demo available, $5; 10% AAII discount
Return Policy: 45 days

Technical Support: phone hours, 9 am-5 pm, M-F; fee for tech support—$90

Description: Integrated technical analysis with portfolio management for mutual funds, stock indicators, full-featured charting capabilities of moving averages, exponential averages, trendlines and channels, trading bands, overlay capabilities, relative strength charting. Select best-performing funds using momentum ranking. Rank funds using user-defined equation in groups of funds you specify. Build your own database 1000 funds, 7 1/2 years of daily data, each. Automatic adjustment of dividends. Communicaton capabilities for automatic updating.

FUND PRO

Version: 1.0   *Last Updated:* na   *No. of Users:* 200

Securities: stocks, bonds, mutual funds, indexes

Functions: portfolio management, technical analysis

Systems: DOS

Price: $789; 10% AAII discount

Return Policy: 45 days

Technical Support: phone hours, 9 am-5 pm, M-F; fee for tech support—$90

Description: Portfolio management with technical analysis for mutual funds, stocks and indicators. Fund Pro is designed to manage 1,000 client accounts. It will produce user-defined reports. Compare your performance to the performance of a market index of your choosing. View reports that determine total funds under management. Custom client billing, quarterly, semiannually or annually, with percent levels for charging commissions. Global utilities for buying and selling funds in all portfolios. Charting capabilities of moving averages, exponential averages, trendlines and channels, trading bands, overlay capabilities, relative strength charting. Select best-performing funds using momentum ranking. Rank funds using user-defined equations in groups of funds you specify. Build your own database, 1,000 funds, 7 1/2 years of daily data each. Automatic adjustment of dividends. Communication capabilities for automatic updating.

TOOLS FOR TIMING

11345 Highway 7   (800) 325-1344
#499   (612) 939-0076
Minnetonka, MN 55305   fax: (612) 938-1275

HISTORICAL ADL

Version: 2.5   *Last Updated:* 1994   *No. of Users:* 282
Securities: indexes
Functions: technical analysis, simulation/game
Systems: DOS
Special Requirements: will not work with Hercules
Price: $175
Return Policy: 60 days
Technical Support: toll-free number; phone hours, 8:30 am-4 pm, M-F
Description: User can plot the DJIA, S&P 500, DJ20 bonds, advance-decline line, new high indicator, new low indicator, and a selection of popular momentum indicators. Graphs can show as few as 5 trades to as many as your computer's memory will allow. Includes data from October 1, 1928 to the day prior to shipping.

HOURLY DJIA

Version: 1.50   *Last Updated:* 1994   *No. of Users:* 434
Securities: indexes
Functions: technical analysis
Systems: DOS
Special Requirements: will not work with Hercules
Price: $50
Return Policy: 60 days
Technical Support: toll-free number; phone hours, 8:30 am-4 pm, M-F
Description: Shows the DJIA on an hourly basis along with the last hour indicator and several popular momentum indicators calculated from hourly parameters. Indicators provided: last-hour indicator, trading bands, Bollinger bands, relative strength index, stochastics and MACD. Includes data from July 1, 1986 to the day prior to shipping.

LOG SCALE COMPARISON

Version: 1.50   *Last Updated:* 1994   *No. of Users:* 436
Securities: indexes
Functions: technical analysis

Systems: DOS
Special Requirements: will not work with Hercules
Price: $50
Return Policy: 60 days
Technical Support: toll-free number; phone hours, 8:30 am-4 pm, M-F
Description: Each index is placed on its own log scale starting at the same point on the left side of the screen. The log of any number changes by the same amount when the number is doubled, so indexes on their log scales show their relative performance. The program allows users to view any period greater than 9 trading days and to select which indexes to view. Data is included to the day prior to the shipping date. Starting dates vary with the indexes: DJIA, S&P 500, DJT, DJU—1/1/1968; NYSE composite—9/1/1970; ASE and OTC composites—1/3/1972; OEX—1/1/76.

MIRAT

Version: 1.50   *Last Updated:* 1994   *No. of Users:* 744
Securities: indexes
Functions: technical analysis
Systems: DOS
Special Requirements: will not work with Hercules
Price: $250; demo available, $25
Return Policy: 60 days
Technical Support: toll-free number; phone hours, 8:30 am-4 pm, M-F
Description: A mechanical trading system based on the theory that the market moves in cycles defined by peaks in the number of new lows. Uses only 2 indicators, new low and advance decline line. Includes data from January 1, 1978 to the day prior to shipping.

PUT/CALL

Version: 1.50   *Last Updated:* 1994   *No. of Users:* 448
Securities: options
Functions: technical analysis
Systems: DOS
Special Requirements: will not work with Hercules
Price: $50
Return Policy: 60 days
Technical Support: toll-free number; phone hours, 8:30 am-4 pm, M-F
Description: Program graphically expresses 7 different relationships of OEX put, call, volume and open interest. Indicators provided: put/call ratio, Hines ratio, put/call volume with put/call open interest,

put/call volume as a percentage of put/call open interest, put/call volume as a percentage of put/call open interest smoothed, put open interest subtracted from call/open interest, DJIA and OEX. Includes data from mid-1984 to the day prior to shipping.

TIMER

Version: 3.50   *Last Updated:* 1994   *No. of Users:* 444
Securities: indexes
Functions: technical analysis
Systems: DOS
Special Requirements: will not work with Hercules
Price: $350; demo available, $25
Return Policy: 60 days
Technical Support: toll-free number; phone hours, 8:30 am-4 pm, M-F
Description: System breaks market activity into cycles defined by peaks in the new low indicator. There have been 24 complete cycles since the beginning of 1978 averaging about 130 trading days. The 7 primary indicators are designed to enable user to pick the tops and bottoms of these cycles. Shows indicators and demonstrates when they are most effective. Each cycle is isolated and shown in its entirety, its beginning and its top, along with the appropriate indicators at each stage. Annual survey with captioned graphs shows how the indicators worked throughout each year from 1978 to the present. Includes data from January 1, 1978 to the day prior to shipping. Timer also includes MIRAT.

TIMER PROFESSIONAL

Version: 2.50   *Last Updated:* 1994   *No. of Users:* 473
Securities: indexes
Functions: technical analysis, simulation/game
Systems: DOS
Special Requirements: will not work with Hercules
Price: $450
Return Policy: 60 days
Technical Support: toll-free number; phone hours, 8:30 am-4 pm, M-F
Description: Provides all the features of Timer and includes a log scale comparison of all indexes of all 3 U.S. markets. Also includes MIRAT. The system breaks market activity into cycles defined by peaks in the number of new lows.

TOWNSEND ANALYTICS, LTD.

100 S. Wacker Drive (800) 827-0141
Suite 1506 (312) 621-0141
Chicago, IL 60606 fax: (312) 621-0487

OPTION RISK MANAGEMENT
Version: 5.0 *Last Updated:* 1994 *No. of Users:* na
Securities: stocks, futures, indexes, options
Functions: futures analysis, options analysis
Systems: Windows, Windows NT
Special Requirements: Windows 3.1, math co-processor
Price: contact vendor
Technical Support: toll-free number; phone hours, 10 am-6 pm, M-F;
  BBS support; newsletter
Description: An option portfolio analysis program implemented un-
der Microsoft Windows and Windows NT Computes measures of risk
and return for option positions and option spreads; results of the
analyses are presented in tables and graphs. Users control parameters
for interest rates, volatilities, volatility skew, vega range and market
movement range. Analyzes all types of spreads and calculates profit
and loss, premium value and technical measures of risk. Premiums
and futures or stock prices can be entered manually or automatically
via several real-time quote services.

REALTICK III
Version: 5.1 *Last Updated:* 1994 *No. of Users:* na
Securities: stocks, bonds, futures, mutual funds, indexes, options
Functions: technical analysis, bond analysis, futures analysis, options
  analysis, spreadsheet, statistics
Systems: Windows, Windows NT,
Special Requirements: Windows 3.1; Windows NT; T/Port card
Price: contact vendor; demo available
Technical Support: toll-free number; phone hours, 10 am-6 pm, M-F;
  BBS support; newsletter
Description: A real-time graphics program for stocks, futures, indexes,
options and other instruments implemented under Microsoft Win-
dows and Windows NT for multi-tasking and a live link to Microsoft
Excel. Database maintenance is provided by a separate data server,
Townsend's TA-SRV which is included. Displays intraday and daily
charts, technical studies, Market Profile, tables, news, and quote

screens in separate windows on multiple programmable pages. Pages can be recalled with hot keys. Does not limit the number of windows per page, number of pages or number of symbols user can follow. Technical studies can be overlaid on bar charts and parameters and can include a number of moving averages, stochastics, market profiles, channels and oscillators. Trendlines are also available. User-defined synthetics can be created in Microsoft Excel and updated. Position analysis, option theoreticals, and other features are available.

TA-SRV
Version: 5   *Last Updated:* 1994   *No. of Users:* na
Securities: stocks, bonds, futures, mutual funds, indexes, options
Functions: quote utility
Systems: Windows, Windows NT
Special Requirements: T/Port card
Price: contact vendor; demo available
Technical Support: toll-free number; phone hours, 10 am-6 pm, M-F;
    BBS support; newsletter
Description: A real-time data server implemented under Microsoft Windows and Windows NT for multi-tasking. The server is the basis of Townsend Analytics' real-time trading station. TA-SRV is included with RealTick III and Option Risk Management but is also available as a stand-alone program. Provides live or historical quotes in any time interval including tick data to Windows applications such as Microsoft Excel through the Dynamic Data Exchange protocol. Communicates with application programs and builds a database of tick data, daily data and 15-minute bar data from live quotes for a large number of futures contracts, stocks, indexes, options and other instruments. Data archiving and aging features are available. Supports data from Signal, S&P CompStock, Reuters, PC Quote, Bonneville, Knight Ridder, Reuters and others. The TAL Toolkit is available for writing C or Visual Basic programs to interface to TA-SRV.

TRADER'S INSIGHT, INC.

8 Renwick Avenue   (516) 423-2413
Huntington, NY 11743-3052

RATIONAL INDICATORS
Version: 3.0   *Last Updated:* 1992   *No. of Users:* 60
Securities: stocks, futures, indexes

Functions: technical analysis

Systems: DOS

Price: $345; $445 with candlestick charting; demo available, $20; 10% AAII discount

Return Policy: all sales final

Technical Support: phone hours, 9 am-5 pm, M-F

Description: Charts prices employing the Random Walk Index described in Technical Analysis of Stocks and Commodities, "Of Trends and Random Walks," 2/91. Decides if stock/future is trending or moving randomly. Program shows a price chart on the top 1/2 of the screen, either in bars or candles with indicators below. User can page back 1 screen at a time or jump to a future date. No arbitrary choices are made by the user (as in choosing moving average length). Candle charts include automatic pattern recognition and pattern labelling.

TRADING TECHNIQUES, INC.

677 W. Turkey Foot Lake Road

Akron, OH 44319

(216) 645-0077

fax: (216) 645-1230

ADVANCED G.E.T.

Version: 5.5   *Last Updated:* 1994   *No. of Users:* na

Securities: stocks, bonds, futures, mutual funds, indexes, options

Functions: technical analysis, expert system

Systems: DOS

Special Requirements: mouse required

Price: $2,750; demo available; 10% AAII discount

Return Policy: all sales final

Technical Support: phone hours, 8 am-5:30 pm, M-F; BBS support

Description: Designed for all markets using Gann and Elliot techniques. Works on daily data in many standard formats. The major feature is its ability to provide 3 degree Elliot wave counts automatically without any user assistance. Also provides Gann angles, potential change in trend dates, Fibonacci calculations, auto price projections for each market swing and many other proprietary indicators. Provides unattended printing routines and has an automatic trade search routine. Has a built-in training mode. Seasonals on stocks as well as commodities. Joseph Trend index.

TRAX SOFTWORKS, INC.

5840 Uplander Way   (800) 367-8729
Culver City, CA 90230   (310) 649-5800
                                                 fax: (310) 649-6200

CYPRESS
Version: 2.3b   *Last Updated:* 1994   *No. of Users:* 1000+
Securities: stocks, bonds, futures, mutual funds, indexes, options
Systems: Windows
Price: $179
Return Policy: 30 days
Technical Support: toll-free number; phone hours, 10 am-4 pm. M-F
Description: Cypress is a Windows-based interface to Dow Jones
News/Retrieval. Cypress offers push buttons and pulldown menus to
facilitate gathering of financial data and news. Features include pulldown menus; user-customizable toolbar buttons for simplifying common queries; buttons to replace typed commands and menus; a capture facility for retrieving information for later review and formatting;
selection of communication parameters through a dialog box; a log-on
and log-off buttons that automatically dial, supply your password,
and disconnect. Cypress offers enhanced text search functionality, including expanded search criteria, choice of scan or full-text retrieval,
and a list of past searches. Improved clipping file support, support for
popular modem pools, selection of multiple stories in Wires and multiple Wires codes offer increased functionality. Selection of stocks from
multiple portfolios, and on-screen timer showing time connected to
Dow Jones and access to today's Wall Street Journal stories.

TREND INDEX COMPANY

2809 E. Hamilton, #117   (715) 833-1234
Eau Claire, WI 54701   fax: (715) 833-8040

DOW JONES/OEX TRADING SYSTEM
Version: 2.82   *Last Updated:* 1994   *No. of Users:* 120
Securities: futures
Functions: technical analysis, options analysis
Systems: DOS
Price: $147; demo available, $10; 15% AAII discount

Return Policy: all sales final

Technical Support: phone hours, 10 am-6 pm, M-F; BBS support; newsletter

Description: Full-featured trading system for trading OEX or S&P options and 34 individual stocks. Automatic analysis of 54 indicators based on recent price relationships. Each indicator is assigned a point weighting factor based on its validity. Cumulative total of all indicators is used as a set-up for the signals. Actual buy/sell signals are generated based on the indicators' total point value combined with pattern recognition parameter and cycle techniques. Monitoring the market during the day is not required. The entire trade—including the trade entry order, specific target price and stop-loss price—can be given to a broker at one time and before the market opens. Each trade entry signal is at market on opening and can be placed as one complete order. Data files can be updated manually with the utility editor updating program, featuring semiautomatic menu-prompted entry, with a built-in calendar for automatic day and date entries.

SWING CATCHER TRADING SYSTEM

Version: 3.01   *Last Updated:* 1994   *No. of Users:* 300

Securities: futures

Functions: technical analysis, bond analysis, futures analysis, expert system

Systems: DOS

Price: $497; demo available, $20; 15% AAII discount

Return Policy: all sales final

Technical Support: phone hours, 10 am-6 pm, M-F; BBS support; newsletter

Description: Full-featured trading system for trading 35 futures markets. Automatic analysis of 54 indicators based on recent price relationships. Each indicator is assigned a point weighting factor based on its validity. Cumulative total of all indicators is used as a set-up for the signals. Actual buy/sell signals are generated based on the indicators' total point value combined with pattern recognition parameter and cycle techniques. Monitoring the market during the day is not required. The entire trade—including the trade entry order, specific target price and stop-loss price—can be given to a broker at one time and before the market opens. Each trade entry signal is at market on opening and can be placed as one complete order. Data files can be updated manually with the utility editor updating program, featuring semiautomatic menu-prompted entry, with a built-in calendar for automatic day and date entries.

TRENDSETTER SOFTWARE

P.O. Box 6481
Santa Ana, CA 92706

(800) 825-1852
(714) 547-5005
fax: (714) 547-5063

PERSONAL ANALYST
Version: 2.0   *Last Updated:* 1994   *No. of Users:* 1,500
Securities: stocks, bonds, futures, mutual funds, indexes, options
Functions: technical analysis, options analysis
Systems: Mac
Special Requirements: 2M RAM
Price: $395; 10% AAII discount
Return Policy: 30 days
Technical Support: toll-free number; phone hours, 10 am-7 pm, M-F
Description: A market analysis program. Charts bar, Japanese candle, point and figure and line on demand. Daily, weekly and monthly charts are all created from the same data. Custom layouts with up to 9 charts per layout and 16 indicators per chart. Able to shift from one layout to another. Employs the Macintosh interface. User can scroll through portfolio, ranked and sorted by a variety of factors and resize, zoom, tile and stack windows and indicators with pulldown menu.

PERSONAL HOTLINE
Version: 6.8   *Last Updated:* 1994   *No. of Users:* 1,500
Securities: stocks, bonds, futures, mutual funds, indexes, options
Functions: portfolio management, technical analysis, options analysis, expert system
Systems: Mac
Special Requirements: 2M RAM
Price: $595; 10% AAII discount
Return Policy: 30 days
Technical Support: phone hours, 10 am-7 pm, M-F
Description: Expert model lets user discern which charts need closer examination and, when the time to take action nears, delivers all of the charting and analysis features of Personal Analyst. Based on channel identification and chart pattern recognition. Model makes recommendations on when to buy, sell and place stop-losses. Tracks its own trad-

ing results, trailing stops and moving objectives as market conditions change.

PROFESSIONAL ANALYST
Version: 3.1   *Last Updated:* 1994   *No. of Users:* 1,500
Securities: stocks, bonds, futures, mutual funds, indexes, options
Functions: technical analysis
Systems: Mac
Special Requirements: 2M RAM
Price: $595; 10% AAII discount
Return Policy: 30 days
Technical Support: phone hours, 10 am-7 pm, M-F
Description: This upgrade of Trendsetter Software's Mac-based intraday financial markets analysis program features several new and improved features. Using the Signal headline news service capability, users may view data at the bottom of the screen, and/or in full-screen display mode. The auto operation feature automatically loads symbols when the market opens and saves data at market close. The news alert function informs the user of previous high/low percentage, previous close percentage and personal trade tracking. Newly added is a graphical representation of alert levels on all charts, plus default alert choices including Neil Weintraub's pivot point system. A charting feature allows users to create their own intraday tick, bar, or candle charts. Pro Analyst 3.0 also allows users to save their custom charting options for combinations of basic (bar, line, candlestick) and 23 secondary technical analyses (stochastics, RSI, DMI, etc.) including new line, arc, and fan with Gann and Fibonacci. Five new technical analysis tools are contained in Pro Analyst 3.0, including fast stochastics, speed resistance lines, Andrew's pitchfork (Trident), on-balance volume, and volume accumulation.

TRIPLE-I

19221 E. Oakmont Drive   (305) 829-2892
Miami, Fl 33015   fax: (305) 289-5121

TAKE STOCK
Version: 2.0   *Last Updated:* 1993   *No. of Users:* 400
Securities: stocks
Functions: fundamental analysis, technical analysis
Systems: Windows, Mac

Special Requirements: 4M RAM; Excel 3 or 4 for Mac, Excel 4.0 for Windows
Price: $175; 10% AAII discount
Return Policy: 30 days; $15 restocking fee
Technical Support: phone hours, 9 am-5 pm, M-F
Description: Provides a number of criteria for analyzing a company's balance sheet and operating dynamics. It analyzes the historical multiples, not only to determine if a stock is a good value but, if not, at what price it would be. Provides a plain language summary of reasons to buy and items to check. Comparison features permit the comparative analysis of up to 5 stocks. The "challenge tree" provides a 5-year analysis of the consequence of selling one position to buy another (including the impact of taxes and commissions). Grades portfolio on the basis of the dollar-weighted percentage that is at or above the ideal in more than 30 different parameters. Provides tools to determine exactly what stock or stocks should be bought and/or sold to improve that grade.

V.A. DENSLOW & ASSOCIATES

4151 Woodland Avenue
Western Springs, IL 60558

(708) 246-3365
fax: (708) 246-3365

COMMON STOCK DECISION AIDE
Version: 1.0   *Last Updated:* 1990   *No. of Users:* na
Securities: stocks, indexes
Functions: portfolio management, fundamental analysis, spreadsheet
Systems: DOS
Special Requirements: Lotus 1-2-3, 2.01+
Price: $49
Technical Support: phone hours, 10 am-12 am, M-F
Description: Calculates aftertax (0%, 15%, 28%) compounded returns of common stocks from each of up to 12 past years to the present and returns each year including dividend credits. Calculates earnings growth rates, dividend yields, price/earnings ratio ranges, projected current year high and low price/share and compounded returns on user's investment. Shows growth characteristics, volatility and yields. Comparison with returns of DJIA and S&P 500 is provided. Buy/sell/hold decisions can be based on firm data. Printouts allow study and comparisons, and graphing can be done.

FINANCIAL NEEDS FOR RETIREMENT

Version: 2.0   _Last Updated:_ 1994   _No. of Users:_ na
Functions: financial planning, spreadsheet
Systems: DOS
Special Requirements: Lotus 1-2-3, 2.01+
Price: $49
Return Policy: 20 days
Technical Support: phone hours, 10 am-12 am M-F
Description: Users can project their financial outlook over a 25-year period by entering personal information such as taxable and non-taxable assets, average percent return, incomes from various sources including Social Security, pension, IRA, SEP, Keogh, annuity plans, tax rates, living expenses, inflation rates and personal tax exemptions. Of the 23 rows of automatic calculations, the main result to watch is when or if user's assets begin to deplete and later disappear. "What if" trials show the effects of working longer, adjusting lifestyle, improving investments, making gifts, etc. Program can cover both pre- and post-retirement years. Future lump changes in assets or medical needs can be included, as well as variable post-retirement earnings.

MUTUAL FUND DECISION AIDE

Version: 1.0   _Last Updated:_ 1990   _No. of Users:_ na
Securities: mutual funds, indexes
Functions: portfolio management, spreadsheet, statistics
Systems: DOS
Special Requirements: Lotus 1-2-3, 2.01+
Price: $49
Return Policy: 20 days
Technical Support: phone hours, 10 am-12 am, M-F
Description: Evaluates fund performance using available data. Calculates average annual compounded returns and total returns from each of up to 12 past years to the current date, after-load fee and after 0%, 15% and 28% taxes. Gives total return and distribution yield for each year on same basis. Adjusts data to today's values for realistic comparisons between funds at an identical time. Growth rates, volatility, trends in performance for recent years and effects of taxes and various load fees can be observed. User can rank funds on any desired criteria and make better decisions on suitability, consistency and profit potential. Compounded annual return on individual investments can be calculated over exact days held. Comparison with returns of DJIA and S&P 500 is provided. Printouts allow study and comparison, and

graphing can be done. Input data is readily available from prospectuses.

VERTIGO DEVELOPMENT GROUP

58 Charles Street   (617) 225-2065
Cambridge, MA 02141

JONATHAN POND'S PERSONAL FINANCIAL PLANNER
Version: na   *Last Updated:* 1994   *No. of Users:* na
Functions: financial planning, portfolio management
Systems: DOS, Windows
Special Requirements: 4M RAM
Price: CD, $59.95; floppy disk, $49.95
Description: The program steps users through the process of building a portfolio of financial investments to meet their lifetime goals. It provides insight on investment strategies such as tax planning, retirement budgeting, and other financial topics. It assesses your financial picture through a series of interactive quizzes, tests and active information pages, then recommends a customized reading plan based on your needs. It also examines your insurance needs to reduce your personal risk, and focuses on budgeting to create a customized spending and borrowing plan. Another section reviews tax minimization planning, and how you can accumulate wealth by using your home as an investment. A final section contains a retirement and an estate planner. CD version includes video clips with personal tips from Mr. Pond.

VILLAGE SOFTWARE, INC.

186 Lincoln Street   (800) 724-9332
Boston, MA 02111   (617) 695-9332
                                                 fax: (617) 695-1935

COMMON STOCK SELECTOR
Version: na   *Last Updated:* 1993   *No. of Users:* 100
Securities: stocks
Functions: portfolio management, fundamental analysis, spreadsheet
Systems: DOS, Windows
Special Requirements: spreadsheet program
Price: $59; 20% AAII discount

Return Policy: 30 days
Technical Support: toll-free number; phone hours, 9 am-6 pm, M-F
Description: Shows earnings growth rates, price/earnings ratio ranges, projected high/low prices per share, and compounded returns. Compares stock performance with the DJIA and S&P 500. Make your buy/sell/hold decisions based on real comparative data.

FAST CAST FOR VENTURES
Version: 2   *Last Updated:* 1994   *No. of Users:* 100
Functions: financial planning, fundamental analysis, spreadsheet, business forecasting
Systems: DOS, Windows
Special Requirements: spreadsheet program
Price: $69; 20% AAII discount
Return Policy: 30 days
Technical Support: toll-free number; phone hours, 9 am-6 pm, M-F
Description: Automatically prepares statements on a monthly, quarterly, or yearly basis. Projects pro forma balance sheets, income statements and cash flow statements. Also allows user to produce up to 13 supporting schedules and graphs financial data.

FINANCIAL PLANNING FOR RETIREMENT
Version: 2.0   *Last Updated:* 1991   *No. of Users:* 150
Functions: financial planning, spreadsheet
Systems: DOS, Windows
Special Requirements: spreadsheet program
Price: $59; 20% AAII discount
Return Policy: 30 days
Technical Support: toll-free number; phone hours, 9 am-6 pm, M-F
Description: Project year-by-year financial status over 25 years into retirement. Using personal information such as income from various sources, personal tax rates, current living needs and expected inflation, user can track their income and worth of assets over the years. Using "what-if" scenarios, user can see where a financial course will take them.

401(K) FORECASTER
Version: 2.3   *Last Updated:* 1994   *No. of Users:* na
Functions: financial planning, spreadsheet, expert system
Systems: DOS, Windows
Special Requirements: spreadsheet program

Price: $69; 20% AAII discount
Return Policy: 30 days
Technical Support: toll-free number; phone hours, 9 am-6 pm, M-F
Description: Prepares personalized projection of contributions, accumulations, tax savings, and retirement income. Helps user understand the real trade-offs between high and low contributions. Includes all logic for federal tax calculations and adds state tax and employer matching capabilities.

THE INVESTOR
Version: 3.5   *Last Updated:* 1994   *No. of Users:* na
Securities: stocks, bonds, futures, mutual funds, indexes, options
Functions: portfolio management, technical analysis, bond analysis, options analysis, spreadsheet, statistics
Systems: DOS, Windows
Special Requirements: spreadsheet program
Price: $129; 20% AAII discount
Return Policy: 30 days days; shipping & handling restocking fee
Technical Support: toll-free number; phone hours, 9 am-6 pm, M-F
Description: Portfolio management and technical analysis system. Tracks and manages your security transactions, and gives you information you need to make trade decisions from the indicators which are supported (including Bollinger band, parabolic and directional movement, various oscillators, stochastics, Williams %R, Chaiken, etc.) A series of price alerts will warn you automatically if your trade criteria are met. Charting module graphically displays your portfolio allocation, and can zoom into any period in a security's price history. Manual data is supported and you can import data from every major eletronic data source through the use of the Datalink add-ins (available separately).

LADDERING YOUR PORTFOLIO
Version: na   *Last Updated:* 1993   *No. of Users:* 100
Functions: financial planning, spreadsheet
Systems: DOS, Windows
Special Requirements: spreadsheet program
Price: $45; 20% AAII discount
Return Policy: 30 days
Technical Support: toll-free number; phone hours, 9 am-6 pm, M-F
Description: Helps maximize returns on investments by determining average yields and terms to help build a portfolio of short- and long-

term funds and certificates.

LEASE VS. PURCHASE
Version: 2   *Last Updated:* 1994   *No. of Users:* na
Functions: real estate analysis
Systems: DOS, Windows
Special Requirements: spreadsheet program
Price: $69; 20% AAII discount
Return Policy: 30 days
Technical Support: toll-free number; phone hours, 9 am-6 pm, M-F
Description: Analyzes information to make a lease vs. purchase decision. Handles different depreciaton methods, maintenance options, lease buy-out scenarios, and more. It can handle up to 72 periods—months or years.

LOAN AMORTIZATION
Version: na   *Last Updated:* 1993   *No. of Users:* 100
Functions: financial planning, real estate analysis, spreadsheet
Systems: DOS, Windows
Special Requirements: spreadsheet program
Price: $39; 20% AAII discount
Return Policy: 30 days
Technical Support: toll-free number; phone hours, 9 am-6 pm, M-F
Description: Calculates an amortizaton table and allows for variable payments, refinancing, and unscheduled principal payments.

THE MONEY CONTROLLER
Version: 1   *Last Updated:* 1994   *No. of Users:* na
Functions: financial planning
Systems: DOS, Windows
Special Requirements: spreadsheet program
Price: $59; 20% AAII discount
Return Policy: 30 days
Technical Support: toll-free number; phone hours, 9 am-6 pm, M-F
Description: Control your personal finances with this integrated, checking and budgeting tool. It creates over a dozen savings and payment schedules, and writes checks on your laser printer. Money Controller works from within your spreadsheet.

MUTUAL FUND COMPOSITE WORKSHEET
Version: 1.25   *Last Updated:* 1993   *No. of Users:* 100+

Securities: stocks, bonds, mutual funds, indexes
Functions: technical analysis, spreadsheet
Systems: DOS, Windows
Special Requirements: spreadsheet program
Price: $90; 20% AAII discount
Return Policy: 30 days
Technical Support: toll-free number; phone hours, 9 am-6 pm, M-F
Description: A Lotus 1-2-3 template designed to calculate switch signals for growth mutual funds. The signals are based on 39-week moving averages of the DJIA, DJTA and a composite of 5 mutual funds. The template is completely menu-driven by Lotus macros. User enters Friday closing prices and the template will display a sell or buy signal based on a fully-explained trading plan. Graphs of price and moving averages and relative strengths are displayed. The template contains about 2 years of historical prices. Historical data is adjusted automatically.

MUTUAL FUND KIT
Version: 1   *Last Updated:* 1994   *No. of Users:* na
Functions: spreadsheet
Systems: DOS, Windows
Special Requirements: spreadsheet program
Price: $79; 20% AAII discount
Return Policy: 30 days
Technical Support: toll-free number; phone hours, 9 am-6 pm, M-F
Description: Load fees, tax rates, and comparisons with standard measures are all calculated. The Mutual Fund Kit can also help to create a buy-and-sell plan for your funds.

MUTUAL FUND SELECTOR
Version: na   *Last Updated:* 1993   *No. of Users:* 100+
Securities: mutual funds
Functions: spreadsheet
Systems: DOS, Windows
Special Requirements: spreadsheet program
Price: $59; 20% AAII discount
Return Policy: 30 days
Technical Support: toll-free number; phone hours, 9 am-6 pm, M-F
Description: Calculates aftertax, after-load fee, and compound returns allowing user to compare funds with each other and with standard measures such as the DJIA and the S&P 500. Compare growth charac-

teristics, volatility, trends, tax and load fee effects.

NET WORTH BUILDER

Version: 2   *Last Updated:* 1994   *No. of Users:* na
Functions: financial planning
Systems: DOS, Windows
Special Requirements: spreadsheet program
Price: $69; 20% AAII discount
Return Policy: 30 days
Technical Support: toll-free number; phone hours, 9 am-6 pm, M-F
Description: Assists in organizing all your financial facts for mortgage applications, investment plans and more. Net Worth Builder helps you construct 15 different personal asset and liability schedules, and one, unified net worth statement.

PEN PLAN

Version: 1.1   *Last Updated:* 1993   *No. of Users:* 100
Functions: financial planning
Systems: DOS, Windows
Special Requirements: spreadsheet program
Price: $89; 20% AAII discount
Return Policy: 30 days
Technical Support: toll-free number; phone hours, 9 am-6 pm, M-F
Description: A comprehensive pension plan and retirement toolkit. Five modules targeted at key aspects of retirement planning work together to help user make retirement planning decisions. Compute the taxes on various lump-sum and distributions from IRAs and pensions and compare them to various rollover options. Calculates the effects of excise tax and other factors such as changing life expectancy.

PROFIT PLANNER PLUS

Version: 2.5   *Last Updated:* 1992   *No. of Users:* 2,000
Functions: financial planning, portfolio management, fundamental analysis, real estate analysis, spreadsheet, business forecasting
Systems: DOS, Windows
Special Requirements: spreadsheet program
Price: $99; 20% AAII discount
Return Policy: 30 days
Technical Support: toll-free number; phone hours, 9 am-6 pm, M-F
Description: Build full sets of financial statements for business plan, operations forecast, or business acquisition. Analyzes up to 12 years of

historical information and creates projections. Able to create business plans with mixed time units (months for year 1, followed by quarters for up to 25 subsequent years). Generates all the standard pro-forma financial tables in detail, summary, or percentage formats. Includes point-and-shoot graphics capability, and full spreadsheet publishing.

RATIO EVALUATOR
Version: 2   *Last Updated:* 1994   *No. of Users:* na
Functions: financial planning
Systems: DOS, Windows
Special Requirements: spreadsheet program
Price: $69; 20% AAII discount
Return Policy: 30 days
Technical Support: toll-free number; phone hours, 9 am-6 pm, M-F
Description: Ratio Evaluator calculates over 25 key financial ratios. Computes and tracks changes in ratios over several accounting periods. Manually enter the key financial data into the sheet- or link ratio evaluator to Fast-Cast for Ventures for automatic calculation. Ratio Evaluator produces reports with graphs.

RETIREMENT PLANNER
Version: 1   *Last Updated:* 1994   *No. of Users:* na
Functions: financial planning
Systems: DOS, Windows
Special Requirements: spreadsheet program
Price: $79; 20% AAII discount
Return Policy: 30 days
Technical Support: toll-free number; phone hours, 9 am-6 pm, M-F
Description: Retirement Planner covers IRAs, retirement cash flow, income source planning and more. It helps user organize and predict living needs, personal tax liabilities, effects of inflation, and the worth of assets over time.

RETIREMENT TRIO
Version: na   *Last Updated:* 1993   *No. of Users:* 100
Functions: financial planning, spreadsheet
Systems: DOS, Windows
Special Requirements: spreadsheet program
Price: $79; 20% AAII discount
Return Policy: 30 days
Technical Support: toll-free number; phone hours, 9 am-6 pm, M-F

Description: Provides 3 planning tools covering issues on IRAs, planning for retirement income sources and understanding the overall effects of cash flow planning.

STATISTICS TOOLBOX
Version: na   *Last Updated:* 1994   *No. of Users:* na
Functions: statistics
Systems: DOS, Windows
Special Requirements: spreadsheet program
Price: $49.94; 20% AAII discount
Return Policy: 30 days
Technical Support: toll-free number; phone hours, 9 am-6 pm, M-F
Description: Designed as both a warning aid and a general purpose statistical tool, the Statistics Toolbox performs regression analysis, forecasting, and demographic analysis.

YIELD CURVE
Version: na   *Last Updated:* 1993   *No. of Users:* 100+
Functions: spreadsheet
Systems: DOS, Windows
Special Requirements: spreadsheet program
Price: $35; 20% AAII discount
Return Policy: 30 days
Technical Support: toll-free number; phone hours, 9 am-6 pm, M-F
Description: Constructs yield curve using quotations from the daily paper or any other financial publication.

VOLUME DYNAMICS, INC.

3536 Swallow Drive   (407) 259-5751
Melbourne, FL 32935

DYNAMIC VOLUME ANALYSIS CHARTS
Version: VD9   *Last Updated:* 1994   *No. of Users:* 400+
Securities: stocks, futures, indexes, options
Functions: technical analysis, futures analysis, options analysis
Systems: DOS
Special Requirements: modem optional
Price: $99.50; demo available, $5; 50% AAII discount
Return Policy: all sales final
Technical Support: phone hours, 9 am-9 pm, M-F

Description: Technical analysis package for use in the purchase and sale of stocks, commodities and indexes. Based on a momentum theory using cumulative volume as a measure of market supply and demand forces. A primary chart co-plots price and the cumulative volume line so that their relative movements are clear, plots the 200-day and the 50-day price moving average, and any "n"-day moving average and daily volume bars. Auxiliary chart plots the cumulative volume line and an up/down volume factor and can be used to study the market momentum to confirm oversold and overbought points and to forecast price trends. Provides rules to determine buy and sell points and (past) charts of stocks, indexes and commodities showing points. Analysis program summarizes all 6 technical factors and flags stock that has a rise in volume on any day exceeding 2 times the average daily volume.

WILSON ASSOCIATES

21241 Ventura Boulevard
Suite 173
Woodland Hills, CA 91364

(800) 480-3888
(818) 999-0015
fax: (818) 715-1767

RAMCAP—THE INTELLIGENT ASSET ALLOCATOR
Version: 6.0   *Last Updated:* 1993   *No. of Users:* 950
Securities: stocks, bonds, futures, mutual funds, indexes, real estate
Functions: financial planning, statistics
Systems: DOS
Price: $595; demo available, $6.95; 17% AAII discount
Return Policy: all sales final
Technical Support: phone support; BBS support; newsletter; fee for tech support—$339/year for updates
Description: An optimizing tool that finds the best mix of asset classes for an investment portfolio. Considers 123 asset classes in its optimization routine, including real estate, leasing and foreign stocks and bonds. The optimizing routine is set by the user. Pulldown menus help minimize training time. Finds the portfolio mix with the least amount of risk at any level of expected return or the best returns available at any level of risk using the asset classes selected by the user. Uses historical data for risk, return and co-variance that provides the basis for building optimal portfolios. Includes graphics. BBS: (303) 753-0392.

WINTERRA SOFTWARE GROUP

P.O. Box 4106   (303) 470-6323
Highlands Ranch, CO 80126   fax: (303) 470-6323

STABLE—TECHNICAL GRAPHS
Version: 2.0   *Last Updated:* 1994   *No. of Users:* na
Securities: stocks, bonds, futures, mutual funds, indexes, options
Functions: technical analysis
Systems: Windows
Special Requirements: Windows 3.1+; 4M RAM recommended
Price: $49.95; demo available, $5; 10% AAII discount
Return Policy: 60 days
Technical Support: phone hours, 8 pm-11 pm, M-F; BBS support
Description: A stock market/technical analysis program written for the user who has existing, or access to, historical financial data. Combines popular technical analysis along with the graphical capabilities of Windows 3.0/3.1, to display and print indicator studies used in analyzing any stock, bond, commodity, mutual fund, index or option. As many as 64 security charts can be created for individual or comparative analysis and study. A chart "slider" allows direct comparison of important indicator events across all graphics in a chart. Technical analysis charts can also be printed to an attached printer. Advanced Dynamic Data Exchange (DDE) capabilities have been built to support real-time chart updating, and to allow "remote" display control over any chart. Additional program features include desktop chart management, pop-up menus for performing frequently-used graphing tasks, functional toolbar, on-line help, and user-selectable colors. Imports CSI, MetaStock, Technical Tools TC2000, and ASCII formatted data files.

7

Guide to Financial Information Services

In this chapter we describe financial databases and financial information services. These descriptions are based on information provided by the publishers and the listing is alphabetical by company name.

Each listing includes the name of the publisher, the service name, how the service is transmitted, the type of data provided, systems required to use the service, pricing information, and a brief description of the service.

The method used to provide data varies among vendors. Some send disks to subscribers while others provide on-line modem or even satellite access. The method in which the service is provided is indicated through the transmission description. Before subscribing to a service, evaluate how frequently your investment strategy changes and how often you need to update your portfolio and select a service accordingly. You may need to subscribe to more than one service if, for instance, you require inexpensive historical quotes and diverse analytical data.

Once you have decided on a service, send or call for the most recent information and compare pricing against similar services. This may be a difficult task, as different services price differently. Some charge by the minute for connect time, but not beyond that; others may have an initial fee and a charge for each report generated. Response times may also vary among systems. All of these factors will affect your ultimate cost. The cost structure for these services is divided into four possible fees—start-up, access, current quote, and historical quotes. Not all services will levy all four types of fees and only those that apply are indicated. Start-up fees refer to any cost associated with initiating a subscription with service. Access fees refer to any costs associated with getting the main data or services or the quotes. If the service levies an extra charge for current or historical quotes, these fees are indicated in the current or historical quote fee section.

ADVANCED WIRELESS, INC.

435 Indio Way   733-8398
Sunnyvale, CA 94086   (408) 735-8833
                                            fax: (408) 733-5888

STOCKQUOTER 2

Provides: general/business news, economic news/data, company
news, financial statement data, charting, software library for downloading, fundamental stock screening, technical screening, mutual
fund screening, stock quotes, index quotes, mutual fund quotes,
closed-end fund quotes

Transmission: cable TV, satellite

Start-Up Fees: included in subscription fee

Access Fees: $24.95/month

Computer Systems: DOS, Win, Win NT, OS/2

Description: Subscription service that provides continuous intraday
delayed price quotations for NYSE, Amex, and Nasdaq listed securities, mutual funds, money market funds, limited partnerships and
ADRs throughout the trading day and end-of-day closing data continuously until the market reopens. All major indexes are supplied as
well. The Online Wireless decoder card plugs into a PC and the
StockQuoter 2 software does the rest. These are supplied free as part
to the initial subscription fee. The decoder card is connected to a
broadcast TV antenna, cable TV cable or satellite dish to receive continuous intraday updates of up to 1,000 stocks, funds or indexes
specified in the portfolio window, or obtain spot prices on over 16,000
items in the database by typing that item's symbol. News from three
major wire services is also continuously available. Data provided for
stocks is: previous, open, high, low, tick, volume, and change. Daily
tracking files may be written at any time and are compatible with most
popular technical analysis or portfolio management programs. User-
definable filters or alarms can be set for stocks with news, a specified
price move, and many other parameters.

STOCKQUOTER RT

Provides: general/business news, economic news/data, company
news, financial statement data, charting, software library for downloading, fundamental stock screening, technical screening, mutual
fund screening, stock quotes, index quotes, options quotes, mutual
fund quotes, closed-end fund quotes

Transmission: cable TV, satellite
Start-Up Fees: included in the subscription fee
Access Fees: $195/month
Current Quote Fees: exchange fees
Computer Systems: DOS, Win, Win NT, OS/2
Description: Subscription service that provides all of the benefits and features of StockQuoter 2, but in real-time. StockQuoter RT includes options and futures as well.

AI RESEARCH CORPORATION

2003 Saint Julien Court
Mountain View, CA 94043

(415) 852-9140
fax: (415) 852-9522

VENCAP DATA QUEST//PORTFOLIO COMPANIES 1.0
Provides: company news, financial statement data
Transmission: diskette
Start-Up Fees: $59.95
Access Fees: call vendor
AAII Discount: 10%; applies to start-up fees
Computer Systems: DOS
System Requirements: 512K memory
Description: A stand-alone computerized database directory of private companies financed by venture capital firms. Majority of these private companies are recent IPOs or potential IPO candidates.

ALEXANDER STEELE SYSTEMS TECHNOLOGIES, INC.

12021 Wilshire Boulevard
Suite 340
Los Angeles, CA 90025

(800) 237-8400 x796
(310) 478-4213
fax: (310) 479-4131

MUTUAL FUND EXPERT—PERSONAL
Provides: mutual fund screening
Transmission: diskette
Access Fees: monthly updates: $185/year; quarterly updates: $95/year
Computer Systems: DOS
Description: Provides over 100 pieces of information on over 3,500 mutual funds. Data on 34 market indexes is also provided for comparison. Screening/filtering process allows users to create and display a

temporary database consisting of only those mutual funds that meet the specified conditions. All reports can be applied to filtered groups of funds or the whole universe. Reports consist of: current fund ranking showing the absolute and decile rank for a single fund within most fields of the database; averages showing the average value for all meaningful fields; short-term performance containing the latest monthly and latest 1, 2, 3, and 4 quarters performance; long-term performance containing annualized and total performance data for the last 3, 5, and 10 years and annual performance for each year since 1984; risk and statistics containing various risk and statistical performance measures; screening including data on loads, expenses, asset size, cash position, turnover rate, ticker, minimum initial and subsequent purchases, and the availability of telephone switching; directory of contact information; and long-term market index reports on 34 market indexes.

MUTUAL FUND EXPERT—PRO PLUS
Provides: mutual fund screening
Transmission: diskette
Access Fees: monthly updates: $599/year; quarterly updates: $399/year
Computer Systems: DOS
Description: Provides over 114 pieces of information on over 4,500 mutual funds. Data on 61 market indexes is also provided for comparison. Screening/filtering process allows users to create and display a temporary database consisting of only those mutual funds that meet the specified conditions. All reports can be applied to filtered groups of funds or the whole universe. Reports consist of: current fund ranking showing the absolute and decile rank for a single fund within most fields of the database; averages showing the average value for all meaningful fields; short-term performance containing the latest monthly and latest 1, 2, 3, and 4 quarters performance; long-term performance containing annualized and total performance data for the last 3, 5, 10, 15, and 20 years and annual performance for each year since 1974; risk and statistics containing various risk and statistical performance measures covering the last 3-, 5-, and 10-year periods; screening including data on loads, expenses, asset size, cash position, turnover rate, ticker, minimum initial and subsequent purchases, and the availability of telephone switching; directory of contact information; and long-term market index reports on 61 market indexes.

ALL-QUOTES, INC.

40 Exchange Place   (800) 888-7559
Suite 1500   (212) 425-5030
New York, NY 10005   fax: (212) 425-6895

ALL-QUOTES

Provides: general/business news, economic news/data, company news, financial statement data, SEC filings, analyst reports, charting, on-line brokerage, stock quotes, index quotes, options quotes, futures quotes, mutual fund quotes, closed-end fund quotes

Transmission: modem

Start-Up Fees: $195 to $500

Access Fees: $0.39/minute or $200/month

Current Quote Fees: $0.39/minute or $200/month

Computer Systems: DOS, Mac

Description: Maintains and operates a financial and business information database and markets on-line financial information services. Includes real-time and delayed stock, option and commodity trading data from exchanges. Financial and business news from UPI, Business Wire, PR Wire, Pan Pacific News Network, DPA and other sources are provided as part of a premium service. The interbank foreign exchange quotations are up to the second and provided 24 hours a day.

AMERICAN ASSOCIATION OF INDIVIDUAL INVESTORS

625 N. Michigan Avenue   (312) 280-0170
Suite 1900   fax: (312) 280-1625
Chicago, IL 60611

AAII ONLINE

Provides: message/mail areas, software library for downloading

Transmission: modem

Access Fees: part of America Online, $9.95/month for 5 hours, $3.50/hr each additional hour

Description: AAII Online provides a categorical listing of past articles appearing in the AAII Journal and Computerized Investing publications. A message board provides topical discussions on a variety of investment-related subjects. Over 200 programs are available for download from the software library. A Reference Library lists data produced by AAII including: a dividend reinvestment plan guide, an annual discount broker survey, a guide to investment information, an investment glossary, Stock Investor database screens updated monthly, and sentiment and asset allocation survey results. The AAII Online area also provides a means for communicating and ordering products from AAII. The AAII Online area is available only through America Online, keyword AAII.

QUARTERLY LOW-LOAD MUTUAL FUND UPDATE ON DISK
Provides: mutual fund screening
Transmission: diskette
Access Fees: $50/year for quarterly updates for non-members; $39/year for quarterly updates for members
AAII Discount: 22%
Computer Systems: DOS, Mac
Description: Quarterly updated program and newsletter contains 100 variables for 1,000 no-load and low-load mutual funds. This menu-driven program is capable of ranking and screening for funds that match your personal selection criteria. Return data provided by the program includes quarterly returns for the last year compounded annually; returns for the last year, 3 years, 5 years, and 10 years; annual returns for each of the last 10 years, and returns over the last bull and bear markets. Additional information provided by the program includes expense ratio, portfolio turnover, portfolio manager and tenure, portfolio composition summary along with information regarding special objectives. Return comparison and ranking against funds with the same investment category are also provided. Risk measures include standard deviation, an investment objective risk index, betas for equity funds and average maturity figures for bond funds. Fund contact information is included as well as all fees and expenses related to investment in the fund. Contains all performance and risk data on 40 indexes and averages. Subscription includes the quarterly newsletter, which provides commentary on market and mutual fund developments in addition to reporting mutual fund performance.

STOCK INVESTOR
Provides: financial statement data, earnings estimates, fundamental stock screening, technical screening, stock quotes
Transmission: diskette
Access Fees: $99/year for AAII members; $150 for non-members
Computer Systems: DOS, Win

System Requirements: 386+; 3M RAM; 25M free disk space

Description: Quarterly updated program containing fundamental financial data on over 8,000 publicly traded companies listed on the NYSE, Amex, Nasdaq national market and Nasdaq small-cap market. Includes complete information on 200 industry groups. Program allows users to look up, analyze, and screen for companies meeting specific criteria on over 250 variables. Includes consensus earnings estimates from I/B/E/S. Fundamental data provided by Media General. Income statement data supplied by system includes eight quarters of earnings and dividend data, five years of revenue, cost, cash flow, earnings, and dividend figures. Balance sheet data covers three years of operations. Provides over twenty ratios and growth rates and users can create twenty custom variables. Includes price data covering the last five years. Valuations provide a quick snapshot of prices supported by current market multiples and growth rates. Includes detailed information on company dividend reinvestment plans (DRP). Screening function enables searches for companies meeting up to 30 criteria on any data field. Portfolios can be created and users can print out predefined or custom reports. Allows data to be exported to a number of popular file formats.

AMERICAN RIVER SOFTWARE

1523 Kingsford Drive   (916) 483-1600
Carmichael, CA 95608

FUNDSCOPE

Provides: charting, technical studies/indicators, mutual fund screening, index quotes, mutual fund quotes

Transmission: diskette

Access Fees: $25/single update, $100/year for quarterly updates, $300/year for monthly updates

Computer Systems: DOS

Description: Screening and ranking program and database that encompasses over 4,400 equity and bond funds as well as several popular market indexes such as Dow Jones industrials, transportations, utilities, bonds and the S&P 500. Allows user to search quickly through its database, sort by any of several fields of information, and display total return performance graphs over time for all the funds and indexes in the database. It can also display the graph of any mutual fund dating from 10 years ago to the current month along with numerous tables, reports and analyses, all of which can be printed. Data includes fund contact information, inception date, investment minimums, telephone exchange availability, loads, fund objective, assets, asset growth, cash position, expense rate, 12b-1 status, beta, yield, portfolio turnover, average maturity, and return and rankings for 1 month, 3 months, year-to-date, 1 year, 3 years, 5 years, and 10 years. Closing net asset values and distributions for the current month are also provided and may be exported. (ASCII format).

AMERICAN VENTURE CAPITAL EXCHANGE

621 SW Adler, Suite 415   (800) 292-1993
Portland, OR 97205   (503) 221-9981
                                             fax: (503) 221-9987

AMERICAN VENTURE CAPITAL EXCHANGE
Provides: company news
Transmission: modem
Start-Up Fees: $95/year for Ventures Seeking Capital database; $395/year for Ventures Seeking Capital database and Mergers & Acquisitions database.
AAII Discount: 50%; applies to start-up fees
Computer Systems: any computer, modem, communications software
Description: This is a service for S.E.C.-defined accredited investors. Accredited investors are those with a high net worth or those who are professional investors. Database lists the executive summaries of early stage companies that are seeking capital to start or expand their companies. Investors view a summary of the business plan on-line and can then call the principals of the company to get the full business plan if they are interested. Companies are generally looking for between $100,000 and $2,000,000 to start or expand their business. As of August 1994, over 250 such companies were listed. Merger & Acquisition database lists one-paragraph descriptions for middle market companies for sale and offers of buyers who are seeking companies; calls/faxes/mails in to receive the seller or buyer, phone and address.

AMERICA ONLINE

8619 Westwood Center Drive
Vienna, VA 22182

(800) 827-6364
(703) 448-8700
fax: (703) 883-1509

AMERICA ONLINE

Provides: general/business news, economic news/data, company news, financial statement data, on-line brokerage, message/mail areas, software library for downloading, stock quotes, index quotes, mutual fund quotes, closed-end fund quotes

Transmission: modem

Access Fees: $9.95/month (includes 5 free hours/month); $3.5/hour; free 30-day trial (10 free hours)

Computer Systems: DOS, Win, Mac

Description: Provides: business and financial news by NewsGrid (compiled from UPI, Business Wire, PR Newswire and several international wire services); market news (updated daily after market close); NYSE, Amex, Nasdaq, advances, declines, volume, Dow Jones indexes, price change high, low; S&P Index; Options Index put volume, call volume, ratio; most active issues; percentage gains and losses; and news on bonds, commodities, OTC, currency. Prices updated continuously during market hours, 20-minute delayed, provided by StockLink. Automated portfolio management (portfolio is directly tied to on-line broker); all transactions are automatically reflected in portfolio. Displays quantity of shares, date bought, age, basis, current price, change, and present value. Displays cash or margin account; portfolio summary shows long- and short-term unrealized capital gains or losses; shows asset quantity, dividend/interest, current income and estimated annual income from dividends; and automatically keeps tax records for current and previous years. With "Shadow" portfolio user can maintain a portfolio, indicating sales and purchases, even if user does not trade on-line. Option and Stock Watch features offered by StockLink allow user to monitor and learn of price changes on specific stocks and options during trading hours. Tracks any stock or option on U.S. exchanges. Also offers stock trading, investor's network (investment advice), investing contests, and small/home business resource.

BAARNS PUBLISHING

(formerly Heizer Software)

1150 Sepulveda Blvd.   (800) 377-9235
Suite D   (818) 837-1441
Mission Hill, CA 91345

DIVIDEND REINVESTMENT PLAN STOCKS
Provides: stock quotes, mutual fund quotes
Transmission: diskette
Start-Up Fees: $40 full address; $25 without address; $19.50 printout
Computer Systems: Win, Mac
System Requirements: Works or Execl
Description: A database of companies with dividend reinvestment plans for over 1,200 stocks. Investing guidelines for DRPs are in text format.

DOW DAILY CLOSE 1960-1991
Provides: index quotes
Transmission: diskette
Start-Up Fees: program $59; annual updates $12
Computer Systems: Win, Win NT, Mac
System Requirements: Excel or Works
Description: For analysis of market movements or historical prices or to backtest trading systems. Daily closing averages for the Dow Jones industrials, utilities and transportation averages for the last 32 years.

DOW INDUSTRIALS
Provides: index quotes
Transmission: diskette
Start-Up Fees: $12
Computer Systems: Win, Win NT, Mac
System Requirements: Excel or Works
Description: Provides monthly stock price averages for the Dow Jones industrials. Provides monthly averages from 1951 through 1990. Information is supplied in a database format.

DOW MONTH-BY-MONTH SET
Provides: index quotes
Transmission: diskette

Start-Up Fees: $25
Computer Systems: Win, Win NT, Mac
System Requirements: Excel or Works
Description: Provides monthly averages of Dow Jones industrial, transportation, utility and composite averages for the last 35 years. Supplied in database format.

S&P 1957-1991 MONTHLY

Provides: index quotes
Transmission: diskette
Start-Up Fees: $12
Computer Systems: Win, Win NT, Mac
System Requirements: Excel or Works
Description: Provides monthly averages of the S&P stock price index going back to 1957. Supplied in database format.

S&P DAILY 1953-1991

Provides: index quotes
Transmission: diskette
Start-Up Fees: $99
Computer Systems: Win, Win NT, Mac
System Requirements: Excel or Works
Description: Provides daily prices for the S&P 500 stock price index going back to 1953. Supplied in a database format.

S&P DAILY 1980-1990

Provides: index quotes
Transmission: diskette
Start-Up Fees: $39
Computer Systems: Win, Win NT, Mac
System Requirements: Excel or Works
Description: Provides daily closing prices for the S&P composite. Includes prices for every trading day from 1/1/80 to 12/31/90. Includes monthly S&P dividend yields and monthly T-bill rates. Supplied in a database format.

BMI

3 Triad Center   (800) 255-7374
Suite 100   (801) 532-3400
Salt Lake City, UT 84180-1201   fax: (801) 532-3202

ENSIGN 5

Provides: general/business news, economic news/data, charting, technical studies/indicators, stock quotes, index quotes, bond quotes, options quotes, futures quotes, mutual fund quotes, closed-end fund quotes

Transmission: modem, FM, satellite

Start-Up Fees: $697 level 1 software; $1,295 full package; $597 satellite hardware; $597 FM; $125 for user installation; $397 for BMI installation

Access Fees: $10/month

Current Quote Fees: $227/month for stocks and commodities plus exchange fees

Computer Systems: DOS

System Requirements: RS-232 serial port; graphics printer recommended

Description: Real-time technical analysis program that allows investors to follow over 80,000 stocks, commodities, options, mutual funds, and indexes. Features include: an equity table that allows investors to follow their portfolio's profits and losses; a top-20 list that pulls up the most active stocks and commodities by volume, percentage up and down, and best yield percentage for the day; an instant quote page that allows investors to view all transmitted information on a particular symbol; and ability to program trading strategies and backtest them. Chart types include bar, equivolume, Japanese candlestick, line, market profile, point and figure, percentage and tick. Technical studies include accumulation/distribution, Bollinger bands, commodity channel index, directional movement index, envelopes, exponential averages, Keltner channel, William's %R, momentum, on balance volume, open interest, MACD, parabolic stop, relative strength index, moving averages, stochastics, trailing stop, trendlines, Fibonacci, Gann, and swing lines. Time and sales feature enables investors to verify buy and sell orders.

MARKET CENTER

Provides: general/business news, economic news/data, company news, charting, technical studies/indicators, stock quotes, index quotes, bond quotes, options quotes, futures quotes, mutual fund quotes, closed-end fund quotes

Transmission: modem, FM, satellite

Start-Up Fees: $397 for software; $597 for satellite hardware; $397 FM hardware; $125 for installation

Access Fees: $10/month
Current Quote Fees: $227/month for real-time quotes plus exchange fees, $49/month for delayed futures quotes
Computer Systems: DOS
System Requirements: RS-232 serial port, 2M RAM
Description: Features a super quote page that allows trader to view all symbol information transmitted by BMI; a display of the last eight ticks; volume, price and news alerts; business and financial graphs; ability to transfer data to other programs using ASCII; and a built-in portfolio manager. Tick-by-tick updates are available on the programmable scrolling Ticker Tape. Technical analysis charts are available for tick, 5-, 15-, 30-, and 60-minute, daily, weekly, and monthly formats. Available technical studies include: relative strength index, momentum, moving average, oscillator and stochastics. Performs cross rate analysis with built-in spreadsheet. Time and sales feature allows investors to track and verify their buy and sell orders. Automatic option chaining shows all options for an underlying contract or symbol.

MARKET MONITOR 5

Provides: general/business news, economic news/data, charting, technical studies/indicators, stock quotes, index quotes, bond quotes, options quotes, futures quotes, mutual fund quotes, closed-end fund quotes
Transmission: modem, FM, satellite
Start-Up Fees: $1,797
Current Quote Fees: $227/month plus exchange
Computer Systems: DOS
Description: A complete turn-key trading system. Features: a super quote page that allows trader to view all symbol information transmitted by BMI; a display of the last eight ticks; volume, price and news alerts; detailed weather maps and business and financial graphs; and a built-in portfolio manager. Tick-by-tick updates are available on the programmable scrolling Ticker Tape. Technical analysis charts are available for tick, 5-, 15-, 30-, and 60-minute, daily, weekly, and monthly formats. Available technical studies include: relative strength index, momentum, moving average, oscillator and stochastics. Performs cross rate analysis with built-in spreadsheet. Time and sales feature allows investors to track and verify their buy and sell orders. Automatic option chaining shows all options for an underlying contract or symbol.

BUSINESS WEEK MUTUAL FUND SCOREBOARD

P.O. Box 1597   (800) 553-3575
Fort Lee, NJ 07024   (201) 461-7921
                                                fax: (201) 461-9808

BUSINESS WEEK MUTUAL FUND SCOREBOARD
Provides: mutual fund screening, mutual fund quotes
Transmission: diskette
Access Fees: equity or fixed-income funds only—$224.95/year for
    monthly updates or $149.95/year for quarterly updates; equity and
    fixed-income funds—$299/year for monthly updates or
    $224.95/year for quarterly updates
Computer Systems: DOS
Description: Self-contained screening and database tool for 1,950 equity and 2,050 fixed-income mutual funds. Allows user to search and
rank funds meeting specific investment needs and objectives using
multiple search and sort criteria on over 25 information fields. Data is
updated monthly or quarterly and includes fund name, ticker, telephone, size, fees, objective, last 3-month, 12-month, 5-year and 10-year
performance figures, portfolio data, average weighted maturity in
years, risk level, Business Week rating, Morningstar rating, comparison to Standard & Poor's averages, beta and footnotes. Provides
monthly average total return for past 12 months and annual total returns for past ten years.

CAMBRIDGE PLANNING & ANALYTICS, INC.

55 Wheeler Street   (800) 328-3475
P.O. Box 276   (617) 576-6465
Cambridge, MA 02138   fax: (617) 354-7295

DATADISK INFORMATION SERVICES
Provides: economic news/data, financial statement data, fundamental
    stock screening, stock quotes, index quotes
Transmission: diskette
Start-Up Fees: $200
Access Fees: $695 financial; $595 economic; $495 equities; $395 produc-
    tion, consumer or retail
Current Quote Fees: $495 equities with monthly updates

Historical Quote Fees: $495 equities with monthly updates
Computer Systems: DOS, Win
System Requirements: Graphics printer
Description: Economic, financial and business databases with software for analysis and presentation. Has 6 databases: general economic, financial, equities (stock prices, earnings and yields), production, consumer and retail, with thousands of series covering historical and current data. Data service is updated monthly and contains the most recently available published information. Data can be presented in tabular form or graphically and can be directed to the screen, printer or file. Equities service includes screening capabilities across companies. Data conversions on time series include: frequency conversions, moving averages, periodic rates of change, index values and rates of return, lead and lag operations, and correlation and regression analysis.

CDA/INVESTNET

3265 Meridian Parkway	(800) 243-2324
Suite 130	(305) 384-1500
Ft. Lauderdale, FL 33331	fax: (305) 384-1540

INSIDER TRADING MONITOR

Provides: company news, SEC filings, fundamental stock screening
Transmission: modem, diskette
Start-Up Fees: $50
Access Fees: $1/minute ($35/month minimum)
Computer Systems: any computer, modem, communications software
Description: A database of all securities transactions of officers, directors and major shareholders of all publicly held corporations required to file under the Securities Act of 1934. Tracks securities by watch list and provides summary and ranking reports by list or portfolio. Over 10,000 U.S. securities are tracked including those on the pink sheets; over 30,000 transactions are added to the database monthly. Includes companies listed on the Toronto Stock Exchange. Transactions are updated within 24 hours of release by the SEC. Tracks all Form 144 (intention to sell) filings daily. Also available through DJN/R and DTN.

CHARLES SCHWAB & COMPANY, INC.

101 Montgomery Street	(800) 334-4455
Department S	(415) 627-7000
San Francisco, CA 94104	fax: (415) 403-5503

EQUALIZER

Provides: general/business news, economic news/data, company news, financial statement data, SEC filings, analyst reports, earnings estimates, on-line brokerage, fundamental stock screening, technical screening, mutual fund screening, stock quotes, index quotes, bond quotes, options quotes, futures quotes, mutual fund quotes

Transmission: modem

Start-Up Fees: $69

Current Quote Fees: free within limits, otherwise $1.45/minute prime; $0.35/minute non-prime

Computer Systems: DOS

Description: Combines on-line trading, information access and portfolio management. Schwab account members can receive the same real-time quotes, account information and on-line trading available through the Schwab Brokerage Services on GEnie. Access to other data services is provided including DJN/R and S&P MarketScope.

SCHWAB BROKERAGE SERVICES ON GENIE

Provides: on-line brokerage, message/mail areas, software library for downloading, stock quotes, index quotes, bond quotes, options quotes, mutual fund quotes

Transmission: modem

Access Fees: $4.95/month

Current Quote Fees: free of charge within limits, otherwise $1.45/minute prime; $0.35/minute non-prime

Computer Systems: any computer, modem, communications software

Description: Automated system accessible through the GEnie information service (General Electric's Network for Information Exchange). Offers on-line order entry for stocks, options, mutual funds and listed bonds; order changes and cancels and order status viewing. All executed trades through the service receive an additional 10% commission discount off Schwab's normal rate. Account Summary module offers access to daily updated Schwab Account cash, margin and equity balances; summaries of all positions held at Schwab including security symbols, company descriptions and quantities held long or short; and electronically delivered trade confirmations. Real-Time Quotes module offers access to up-to-the-minute quotes on a wide variety of securities and includes data on last trade prices, net change, daily volume, option open interest, dividend amounts, stock split information, price/earnings ratio, yield, earnings per share and 52-week high/low figures. Major market indicators are also retrievable. Schwab's Investors' RoundTable area offers an electronic investment bulletin board, a real-time conference area for on-line chatting on investment topics and a software library with investment resources and programs for downloading.

STREETSMART

Provides: general/business news, economic news/data, company news, financial statement data, SEC filings, analyst reports, earnings estimates, on-line brokerage, fundamental stock screening, technical screening, mutual fund screening, stock quotes, index quotes, bond quotes, options quotes, futures quotes, mutual fund quotes

Transmission: modem

Start-Up Fees: $59

Current Quote Fees: Free within limits, otherwise $1.45/minute prime; $0.35/minute non-prime

Computer Systems: Win

Description: Provides real-time market data access to quotes, analysis and news on a wide range of financial instruments. Offers securities monitoring capabilities—multiple pages with up to 540 instruments per page, 5 presentation formats, various sorting methods, color trend indicator, page-specific tickers and baskets, audible and visual limit alerts; option analytics; charting, including moving average, envelope, RSI and oscillator studies with user-defined parameters and a 1-year database on NYSE, Amex and Nasdaq NMS stocks and on U.S. futures and indexes; fundamental data; news—Dow Jones scrolling headlines, news and news retrieval with keyword search and news alert capabilities; symbol guide; a 5-day, real-time and sales feature covering all U.S. and European equities and U.S. futures and indexes; programmable screen formats and hot keys.

CHECKFREE CORP.

8275 N. High Street
Columbus, OH 43235-1497

(800) 882-5280
(614) 898-6000
fax: (614) 898-6177

CHECKFREE
Provides: on-line brokerage
Transmission: modem
Start-Up Fees: $29.95
Access Fees: $9.95/month for 20 transactions; $3.50/10 over 20
AAII Discount: 33%; applies to start-up fees
Computer Systems: DOS, Mac
Description: A nationwide electronic bill payment system using a PC and a modem. Pays bills and handles all routine recordkeeping without check, stamps or paperwork. Works with any financial institution in the U.S., and handles all interaction with user's bank and merchants. The user signs up for service and enters required information in the software—merchants to be paid, amount of payment and date of payment. Upon command the software automatically transmits payment information to the CheckFree processing center where user's payments are processed through the Federal Reserve System.

COMMODITY SYSTEMS, INC. (CSI)

200 W. Palmetto Park Road
Boca Raton, FL 33432, USA

(800) 274-4727
(407) 392-8663
fax: (407) 392-1379

CSI DATA RETRIEVAL SERVICE
Provides: economic news/data, charting, technical studies/indicators, technical screening, stock quotes, index quotes, options quotes, futures quotes, mutual fund quotes, closed-end fund quotes
Transmission: modem, diskette, magnetic tape
Start-Up Fees: $59
Current Quote Fees: $11/month and up
Historical Quote Fees: $0.20/month for stock data, futures contract data and for each strike price, put or call (U.S.); $0.30/month for non-U.S. items
AAII Discount: 10%; applies to start-up fees

Computer Systems: DOS, Mac

System Requirements: 640K memory, 4M free disk space, Hayes-Compatible modem

Description: Offers daily updates and historical data on all U.S. stocks, mutual funds, all U.S. futures, foreign futures, futures options, stock index options and cash markets. Subscribers receive: Quicktrieve/Quickmanager and Quickplot/Quickstudy to download, manage graphically review and analyze the market information. Current technical indicators include: average of 2 or more fields, call/put ratio, commodity channel index, CSI stop, CSI intermarket relative movement, MACD, non-seasonal volume, on-balance volume, PDI, relative strength index, single field detrend, spread/ratio of 2 volatility systems, William's %R and Williams' accumulation/distribution.

MARSTAT—CSI DATA RETRIEVAL SERVICE

Provides: technical studies/indicators, technical screening, stock quotes, index quotes, options quotes, futures quotes, mutual fund quotes, closed-end fund quotes

Transmission: modem, diskette, magnetic tape

Start-Up Fees: $59; includes downloader, data management, and graphics software

Current Quote Fees: $11/month and up

Historical Quote Fees: from $0.10/month for U.S. market data and from $0.20/month for non-U.S. market data

AAII Discount: 10%; applies to start-up fees

Computer Systems: DOS, Mac

System Requirements: 640K memory, 4M free disk space, Hayes-Compatible modem

Description: Includes end-of-day and historical coverage of all U.S. and most overseas futures and cash markets plus the Amex, the entire NYSE, Nasdaq, mutual funds, options, indexes and money markets. QuickTrieve and QuickManager software included. QuickTrieve interacts with CSI's market statistics database to capture historical as well as daily data that is tailored to each individual portfolio. QuickManager maintains data files and provides flexibility in data management. Supports data format as well as conversion to ASCII and other formats. Included are seasonal indexes going back to the beginning of most popularly traded commodities or as early as 1949. Also includes Perpetual Contract data—contracts that arrange years of futures price history into a single continuous time series.

COMPUSERVE, INC.

5000 Arlington Ctr Blvd
Columbus, OH 43220

(800) 848-8199
(614) 529-1349

COMPANY SCREENING SERVICE

Provides: financial statement data, earnings estimates, fundamental stock screening

Transmission: modem

Access Fees: $15/hr

Computer Systems: any computer, modem, communications software

Description: Fundamental stock analysis service. Includes I/B/E/S earnings estimates, current and quick ratios, long term debt/equity, P/E ratio, P/sales ratio, P/EPS growth, yield, price position, price volitility, ROA, ROE, EPS, sales, net income, market value, total assets, book value, cash flow, and % ownership by insiders and institutions. Data provided by Disclosure, S&P, I/B/E/S and others. Also provides brief company descriptions and industry groupings based on SIC.

COMPUSERVE

Provides: general/business news, economic news/data, company news, financial statement data, SEC filings, analyst reports, earnings estimates, charting, technical studies/indicators, on-line brokerage, message/mail areas, software library for downloading, fundamental stock screening, technical screening, mutual fund screening, stock quotes, index quotes, bond quotes, options quotes, futures quotes, mutual fund quotes, closed-end fund quotes

Transmission: modem

Start-Up Fees: free introductory membership and $15 usage credit for AAII members

Access Fees: basic service pricing: $8.95/month for unlimited basic service, $8.00/hour at 1200- and 2400-baud and $16.00/hour for 9600-baud access for extended services; alternative pricing program includes $2.50/month for account maintenance, $12.80/hour at 1200- and 2400-baud and $22.80/hour at 9600-baud

Current Quote Fees: free with basic service plan; $0.015/quote with alternative pricing plan

Historical Quote Fees: $0.05/quote, 25% discount with executive option; $0.01/quote for Metastock quote club membership which costs $9.95/month

Computer Systems: any computer, modem, communications software
Description: Offers over 1,700 products and services. Basic Quotes provides 20-minute delayed price and volume data on thousands of stocks, options, market indicators, closed-end funds and exchange rates. End-of-day quotes available for open-end mutual funds, bonds and commodities. MicroQuote II provides over 12 years of pricing history on over 160,000 publicly traded securities plus 20 years of dividend distribution data. Money magazine's FundWatch On-line includes performance information and details on over 1,900 mutual funds. Detailed company reports and earnings estimates are provided by such sources as S&P, Value Line, Disclosure and Institutional Brokers Estimate System (I/B/E/S). Members can discuss investment opportunities in the Investors Forum, where on-line support is also provided for popular software products. Several databases provide details on international companies. Global Report, a business and financial information service from Citibank, is on-line, as well as 3 brokers available 24 hours a day. Interfaces are available that support the transfer of information to microcomputer software packages. Other services: MMS International (provides daily analysis of the markets) and RateGram (reports the highest yielding federally insured CD rates). Financial services included with the basic service plan: current quotes, FundWatch On-line by Money Magazine, an issue/symbol reference and a mortgage calculator.

FUNDWATCH ONLINE BY MONEY MAGAZINE

Provides: mutual fund screening
Transmission: modem
Access Fees: part of basic service priced at $8.95/month for unlimited
   basic service
AAII Discount: free intro, $15 usage credit; applies to start-up fees
Computer Systems: any computer, modem, communications software
Description: Mutual fund database for screening and reporting on over 4,000 funds. Allows you to screen on numerous criteria to find the best-performing funds with the lowest expense rates. Detailed reports show how any of the funds have performed in the current month, current year, and over 1, 3, 5, and 10 year time spans, as well as the fees and expenses and a contact phone number.

COMTEX SCIENTIFIC CORP.

4900 Seminary Rd. #800   (800) 624-5089
Alexandria, VA 22311-1811   (203) 358-0007
fax: (203) 358-0236

MARKET NEWSALERT

Provides: general/business news, economic news/data, company
news, financial statement data, SEC filings, analyst reports
Transmission: modem
Start-Up Fees: varies
Computer Systems: any computer, modem, communications software
Description: Provides news and background information on NYSE,
Amex, Nasdaq and pink sheet companies, SEC filings, press releases
and stock offerings. News is available by company and industry as
well as the type of business activity (e.g., mergers, joint ventures, new
product introductions).

OMNINEWS

Provides: general/business news, economic news/data, company
news, financial statement data, SEC filings, analyst reports, stock
quotes, index quotes, bond quotes, options quotes, mutual fund
quotes, closed-end fund quotes
Transmission: modem
Start-Up Fees: varies
Computer Systems: any computer, modem, communications software
Description: Information compiled from the inputs of over 12 major
international newswires, the NASD, the SEC and other specialized
sources. Provides real-time coverage of corporate, political, economic
and market developments as well as the SEC filings for over 15,000
publicly traded companies. Can be customized and is available as a
real-time broadcast, a batched feed, a turn-key system or via electronic
mail.

OTC NEWSALERT

Provides: general/business news, economic news/data, company
news, financial statement data, SEC filings, analyst reports
Transmission: modem
Start-Up Fees: varies
Computer Systems: any computer, modem, communications software
Description: An up-to-the-minute news service that covers over 11,000

Nasdaq and pink sheet companies updated continuously. Contains late-breaking news about earnings, new products, joint ventures, SEC filings, IPOs and more. Includes unique pink sheet ticker symbol. All news saved in a database for 180 days.

DATA BROADCASTING CORPORATION

1900 S. Norfolk Street (800) 367-4670
San Mateo, CA 94403 (415) 571-1800
fax: (415) 571-8507

NEWS REAL

Provides: general/business news, economic news/data, company news, financial statement data, SEC filings, stock quotes, bond quotes, options quotes, futures quotes, mutual fund quotes, closed-end fund quotes
Transmission: modem, FM
Start-Up Fees: $49
Access Fees: $11.95/month database fee plus on-line DJN/R charges
Computer Systems: DOS
Description: An electronic news manager that delivers customized business and financial news. Downloads from DJN/R articles or stock market quotes in user-chosen categories. Accesses stories from DJN/R, selected stories from the Wall Street Journal and Barron's as recent as a few seconds and as far back as 90 days. Accesses more than 55 Dow Jones databases including articles from the Washington Post, Forbes, Fortune, Money, Inc., Financial World and over 150 regional business journals since 1985. Gives access to Dun and Bradstreet Financial Records on more than 750,000 companies and more than 4,700 company profiles from Standard and Poor's. Compatible with Signal which offers real-time delayed or end-of-day quotes for over 65,000 stocks, options, futures, indexes and funds.

QUOTREK

Provides: company news, stock quotes, index quotes, options quotes, futures quotes, mutual fund quotes, closed-end fund quotes
Transmission: FM
Start-Up Fees: $295
Current Quote Fees: $70/month plus surcharges of $3-$88/exchange
System Requirements: No computer needed
Description: A hand-held portable receiver. Provides real-time quotes

in over 40 major cities. Monitors over 65,000 issues on the major stock, options and futures exchanges plus the Dow Jones News Headlines and Alerts service and over 90 key indexes. A 90-character LCD display shows last sale, net change, high and low, previous day's close and total volume. A built-in battery lasts 8 hours on a single charge.

SIGNAL

Provides: general/business news, economic news/data, company news, stock quotes, index quotes, bond quotes, options quotes, futures quotes, mutual fund quotes, closed-end fund quotes

Transmission: cable TV, FM, satellite

Start-Up Fees: $595 for Signal enhanced receiver and software; $695 for full-capture Signal Plus receiver and software

Current Quote Fees: $160/month plus exchange fees of $3-$88/exchange (for Signal enhanced receiver); $180/month plus exchange fees of $3-$88/exchange for Signal Plus reciever.

Computer Systems: DOS, Win, Mac

Description: A combination hardware and software package that delivers real-time market quotes to a personal computer. Data is also available on a delayed or end-of-day basis. A special FM receiver captures stock data from FM radio subchannels broadcast in major metropolitan areas or nationwide if used with an equatorial satellite. Data is also available via cable. User can view information 3 ways: detail, summary, and alert (set by the user). Depending on the exchange accessed, display pages contain the following information: last trade or bid, net change from the previous close or net change, today's volume, today's high and low trades and time of the last trade. Works with over 100 different analytical software packages. Historical data is also available. Equity, mutual funds, indexes, and indicators for the NYSE, Amex, Nasdaq, U.S. regional, Toronto, and Montreal exchanges. Historical data goes back to 1978 in daily, weekly or monthly time periods and is available on 360K or 1.2 M diskettes in ASCII, Lotus 1-2-3 or MetaStock file formats. Also available are open interest, exchange-listed, exchange-traded and Dow Jones News Alerts, and intraday Dow Jones News headlines.

DATA-STAR

One Commerce Square	(800) 221-7754
Suite 1010	(215) 587-4400
Philadelphia, PA 19103	fax: (215) 587-2147

DATA-STAR

Provides: general/business news, economic news/data, company news, financial statement data, SEC filings, analyst reports, earnings estimates, technical studies/indicators, message/mail areas, software library for downloading, fundamental stock screening, technical screening, mutual fund screening, bond screening, stock quotes, index quotes, bond quotes, options quotes, futures quotes, mutual fund quotes, closed-end fund quotes

Transmission: modem

Access Fees: varies from database to database plus $11/hour access fee

Historical Quote Fees: from $2.02

Computer Systems: any computer, modem, communications software

Description: Contains over 300 international business databases that provide access to company intelligence and brokerage reports. Selections vary from ABC Europe to Who Owns Whom. Supplies company directories, SEC reports, detailed annual balance sheets, competitive analysis, market research and industry trends. Users can look for citations in full-text formats or in management and production lists to organize their corporate and sales forecasting. Frost & Sullivan market research, a full-text database, contains in-depth, proprietary industrial accounts and statistics. Company directory databases focus on stocks, subsidiaries and shareholders, as well as on annual reports. Disclosure provides investors with sources of financial information on public companies that trade their stock on the U.S. exchanges. INVESTEXT, Extel Card and the Canadian Financial Database are other major sources of international business intelligence, as is Tradeline.

DATA TRANSMISSION NETWORK CORP.

9110 W. Dodge Road (800) 485-4000
Suite 200 (402) 390-2328
Omaha, NE 68114 fax: (402) 390-9690

DTN WALL STREET

Provides: general/business news, economic news/data, company news, analyst reports, technical studies/indicators, stock quotes, index quotes, bond quotes, options quotes, futures quotes, mutual fund quotes

Transmission: cable TV, satellite

Start-Up Fees: $295

Current Quote Fees: $41.95/month for quarterly billing

Computer Systems: DOS, Mac
Description: Electronic video service provides quotes for stocks, bonds, mutual funds and futures plus financial news and information. Stock, bond and fund quotes are delayed 15 minutes, and futures are delayed 10 to 30 minutes. Information is transmitted by KU-band and C-band satellite signals or cable TV in selected areas. All equipment is provided including programmable receiver, video monitor, KU-band satellite dish or cable splitter. A serial port is provided for the connection of a personal computer. Supports many analytical and portfolio management software programs.

S&P STOCK GUIDE DATABASE BY DTN

Provides: general/business news, financial statement data, earnings estimates
Transmission: cable TV, satellite
Access Fees: $18/month, plus $8/month for access to S&P Stock Guide database
Computer Systems: DOS, Mac
System Requirements: Subscription to DTN Wall Street
Description: This new elective service is offered through DTN Wall Street where subscribers may download the full S&P Stock Guide database to their personal computers. The database contains fundamental research data on companies traded on the New York, American, and Nasdaq exchanges. The data includes company descriptions, earnings history, SIC codes, S&P categories, rankings, balance sheets, capitalizations, dividend yields, rates and history, institutional holdings, latest prices, historical ranges, trading volume history and sales history. The database is updated weekly and is transmitted three times a week.

DELPHI

1030 Massachusetts Avenue
Cambridge, MA 02138
(800) 695-4005
(617) 491-3393
fax: (617) 491-6642

DELPHI

Provides: general/business news, economic news/data, company news, analyst reports, message/mail areas, software library for downloading, stock quotes, index quotes, bond quotes, options quotes, futures quotes, mutual fund quotes, closed-end fund quotes

Transmission: modem, via Internet: Telenet to Delphi.com
Access Fees: 10/4 plan—$10/month includes 4 hours, $4/hour thereafter; 20/20 plan—$20/month includes 20 hours, $1.80/hour thereafter
Computer Systems: any computer, modem, communications software
Description: Offers a range of services including quotes and market analysis, CD rates, futures information, portfolio analysis, stock and market analysis, press release wires (Business Wire and PR Newswire) and software shopping. Translation service is also available, as is UPI news. Now offers full Internet access, including file transfer (FTP), remote log-on (Telenet), and worldwide electronic mail.

DESIGN CREATIONS

18701 Tiffeni Drive, Suite G	(800) 933-5910
Box 948	(209) 586-2082
Twain Harte, CA 95383	fax: (209) 586-2145

INSTIN 3.0

Provides: company news, financial statement data, earnings estimates, software library for downloading, fundamental stock screening, stock quotes
Transmission: modem, cable TV, FM, diskette
Start-Up Fees: $99.95
Historical Quote Fees: $139.95 S&P Stock Guide on Disk annual subscription fee
AAII Discount: 5%; applies to start-up fees
Computer Systems: DOS, OS/2
System Requirements: DOS 3.1 or higher, OS/2 2.0 or higher, 20M hard disk space
Description: INSTIN is a stand-alone or interactive portfolio management program that now contains the S&P Stock Guide on Disk. A free copy is included with initial purchase. Stock quotes can be obtained through CompuServe, Prodigy or Signal. User can create model portfolios, maintain current portfolios, keep permanent transaction records, create custom reports, maintain buy and sell lists, record dividends, track stocks, export information to spreadsheets, perform fundamental research and analysis, plus many other functions.

DIAL/DATA DIVISION OF GLOBAL MARKET INFORMATION

(formerly Dial/Data)

56 Pine Street
New York, NY 10005

(800) 275-5544
(212) 248-0300
fax: (212) 248-9162

DIAL/DATA

Provides: technical studies/indicators, fundamental stock screening, technical screening, mutual fund screening, stock quotes, index quotes, bond quotes, options quotes, futures quotes, mutual fund quotes, closed-end fund quotes

Transmission: modem

Start-Up Fees: $35

Current Quote Fees: $0.01 to $0.035/issue/day; flat fee plans available starting at $35/month for stocks and indexes

Historical Quote Fees: $0.01 to $0.035/issue/day; flat fee plans available starting at $35/month for stocks and indexes

Min. Usage per Month: $15

Computer Systems: any computer, modem, communications software

Description: Supplies daily or historical price data for indexes, stocks, futures, options, mutual funds, bonds, government issues, money markets and stock dividends. All U.S., Canadian and European exchanges are covered. Users can select daily, weekly or monthly frequencies for retrieval. Data sets for stocks include open, high, low, close and volume. Data sets for futures include open, high, low, close, volume and open interest. Technical data is available from 1970 for all original S&P issues. Stock splits and dividends are reported the evening they occur. The service is available through ADP AutoNet, SprintNet, or CompuServe's Data Network via modem.

DIALOG INFORMATION SERVICES, INC.

3460 Hillview Avenue
Palo Alto, CA 94304

(800) 334-2564
(415) 858-3785
fax: (415) 858-7069

BOND BUYER FULL TEXT

Provides: economic news/data, bond quotes

Transmission: modem
Start-Up Fees: $295 for access to entire DIALOG service
Access Fees: $2.50/minute
Computer Systems: any computer, modem, communications software
Description: Corresponds to the print publication, The Bond Buyer, and the weekly publication, Credit Markets, that specialize in the fixed-income investment market. Provides daily coverage of government and Treasury securities, financial futures, corporate bonds and mortgage securities. Includes coverage of U.S. congressional actions, worldwide monetary and fiscal policies and regulatory changes relating to the bond industry. Also lists planned bond issues, bond calls and redemptions and results of bond sales.

BUSINESS CONNECTION
Provides: general/business news, company news, financial statement data, SEC filings, analyst reports, on-line brokerage, fundamental stock screening, mutual fund screening, stock quotes, index quotes
Transmission: modem
Start-Up Fees: $295 for access to entire DIALOG service
Access Fees: varies
Computer Systems: any computer, modem, communications software
Description: Menu-driven, application-oriented service that offers on-line access to data on over two million public and private companies worldwide. Searchers select the type of information they seek from menus and the service automatically selects the applicable database and retrieves the data. Databases on the service include Dun and Bradstreet, Standard & Poor's, Moody's and Disclosure. Five application sections are available: corporate intelligence provides detailed information on companies; financial screening enables searchers to identify companies based on their financial characteristics; products and markets provide detailed information about a specific product or industry; sales prospecting aides searchers in locating new clients or customers; travel planning allows users to plan and book trips.

BUSINESS DATELINE
Provides: general/business news, economic news/data, company news
Transmission: modem
Start-Up Fees: $295 for access to entire DIALOG service
Access Fees: $2.30/minute
Computer Systems: any computer, modem, communications software

Description: Contains full text of articles from regional business publications from throughout the U.S. and Canada. Also includes Crain's News Service publications, nine daily newspapers and BusinessWire. Articles cover regional business activities and trends, as well as information about small companies, new start-ups, family owned and closely held firms, including their products or services and the executives who run the companies.

FIRST RELEASE
Provides: general/business news, economic news/data, company news, analyst reports
Transmission: modem
Start-Up Fees: $295 for access to entire DIALOG service
Access Fees: $1.60/minute
Computer Systems: any computer, modem, communications software
Description: Provides access to the latest news from four major news wire databases updated within 15 minutes of transmission over the wire. BusinessWire delivers timely news stories that are simultaneously distributed to over 700 news media and more than 100 institutions and firms in the investment community. Knight-Ridder/Tribune, Business News provides the complete text of news stories on worldwide financial and commodity markets and the events that move them. Financial coverage centers on credit markets, foreign exchange, mortgage-backed securities and financial futures, as well as banking, economic news and corporate earnings. Commodity coverage includes both cash and futures market analysis. Weather information is available from Global Weather services, Knight-Ridder's weather forecasting center. Reports on the expected impact that government policy will have on the financial and commodity markets are available. PR Newswire contains the complete text of business/financial news releases. Reuters contains the full text of news releases from the Reuter Business Report, which provides breaking news and market commentaries as well as fast follow-up analysis. Reuter Library Service is the source of world news.

MONEYCENTER
Provides: general/business news, economic news/data, company news, stock quotes, index quotes, bond quotes, options quotes, futures quotes
Transmission: modem
Start-Up Fees: $295 for access to entire DIALOG service

Access Fees: $2.00/minute
Computer Systems: any computer, modem, communications software
Description: Includes financial information of three kinds: news, quotes and fixed pages. News provides coverage of broad domestic and international events that influence markets, gathered from world-wide news bureaus. Quotes are real-time, except for delayed bids and offers on government securities. Covers a wide assortment of other money-market instruments, fixed-income and mortgage-backed securities. Fixed pages are single screens of information on a variety of topics including credit markets, mortgage-backed securities, economic indicators, energy prices and more. Information can be searched via a menu or using standard program commands.

QUOTES AND TRADING
Provides: on-line brokerage, stock quotes, options quotes
Transmission: modem
Start-Up Fees: $295 for access to entire DIALOG service
Access Fees: $0.60/minute
Computer Systems: any computer, modem, communications software
Description: Provides 20-minute delayed stock and options quotes from the NYSE and Amex, Nasdaq and the four major options exchanges. Order entry allows the purchase or sale of any stock or option listed in the Wall Street Journal. Up to 75 portfolios can be set up with the value of the portfolio's securities updated to reflect current market prices. Service can also track portfolio gains and losses and project the dividend income. Tax records maintained on the service can include securities, stocks, options, mutual funds and bonds, and can reflect all stocks and options transactions. Quantitative tools to evaluate stock option transactions are also available.

SEC ONLINE
Provides: financial statement data, SEC filings
Transmission: modem
Start-Up Fees: $295 for access to entire DIALOG service
Access Fees: $1.40/minute
Computer Systems: any computer, modem, communications software
Description: Full-text database of reports filed by public companies with the SEC. Includes all companies on the New York and American Stock Exchanges plus over 2,000 Nasdaq National Market companies. Contains the actual, unedited text of 10-Ks, 10-Qs, 20-Fs, annual reports and proxy statements, including any amendments to them.

Provides the following documents as filed with the SEC: annual report (not required to be filed with the SEC), Form 20-F (official annual report filed by non-U.S. registrants 6 months after the fiscal year-end), Form 10-K (official annual report file filed by U.S. public companies 90 days after fical year-end), Form 10-Q (official quarterly report filed 45 days after the close of each quarter) and proxy statement (official report/notification to shareholders of shareholder meetings and issues to be voted upon).

TRW BUSINESS CREDIT PROFILES
Provides: company news, financial statement data
Transmission: modem
Start-Up Fees: $295 for access to entire DIALOG service
Access Fees: $1.80/minute
Computer Systems: any computer, modem, communications software
Description: Contains payment history, bankruptcy, tax and legal history, UCC filings, banking relationships, Standard Industrial Classification (SIC) codes, sales ranges and more. Contains about 2,500,000 companies including 10,000 public company records that have financial information provided by S&P. Represents commercial as well as industrial establishments from all product areas, as identified by 1987 SIC codes. Records contain at least two of the following elements: identifying information, bank data, supplemental data, key facts data, S&P data, government data, or trade data. A small percentage contain information on bankruptcies, tax liens and judgements.

DISCLOSURE, INC.

5161 River Road
Bethesda, MD 20816

(800) 945-3647
(301) 951-1300
fax: (301) 718-2343

COMPACT D/CANADA
Provides: financial statement data, SEC filings, analyst reports, fundamental stock screening
Transmission: CD-ROM
Access Fees: $4,500/year with monthly updates, commercial; $3,600/year with monthly updates, non-profit
Computer Systems: DOS, Mac
System Requirements: CD-ROM
Description: Offers unlimited access on CD-ROM to facts and figures

on more than 8,000 public, private, and crown companies in all 10 Canadian provinces. Uses either Easy Menu Mode or Dialog commands for data searching and display. Retrieved data can be displayed, printed and transferred to disk or downloaded to spreadsheets and other software packages. Organized into 3 main sections: resume section, including the company name, address, CUSIP, business rankings, corporate status (e.g., public or private), holding company information, legal counsel and date of latest annual financial information; Financial section, containing annual financials for up to 5 years, including income statements, balance sheets (assets/liabilities), and key ratios; and the Summary section, containing quarterly financials included for sales, income, dividends, outstanding shares and earnings per share. A filings list, president's letter, ownership information, company officers, and merger and acquisition data are included in the text section. Over 100 search variables are available.

COMPACT D/NEW ISSUES *(formerly Compact D/'33)*
Provides: SEC filings, analyst reports, fundamental stock screening
Transmission: modem, CD-ROM
Access Fees: $5,800/year commercial; $4,500/year non-profit
Computer Systems: DOS, Mac
System Requirements: CD-ROM, modem
Description: Provides access to 1933 Act Registrations and Prospectuses data; issue-by-issue securities information for SEC reporting companies that consists of material extracted from Registration Statements and prospectuses filed with the SEC. Coverage of transactions includes those reported in 1933 Act Registration Statements filed on Forms S-1, S-2, S-3, S-4, S-8, S-18, F-1, F-2, F-3, F-4, pre- and post-effective amendments, final prospectus and supplements. Each disk contains: key-word searchable full text sections for controlled-vocabulary searching; over 12 preformatted display options; the capability to customize display and report formats; and mailing labels and lists of registrant companies, agents and legal counsel.

COMPACT D/SEC
Provides: financial statement data, SEC filings, analyst reports, earnings estimates, fundamental stock screening
Transmission: modem, CD-ROM
Access Fees: $5,800/year commercial; $4,500/year non-profit
Computer Systems: DOS, Mac

System Requirements: CD-ROM for direct subscriptions; modem for active service

Description: Offers corporate information on 11,000 public companies whose securities are traded on the NYSE, Amex, Nasdaq and OTC. Abstracted from the documents filed with the SEC. Contains over 250 database search variables. Also contains the Zacks Investment Database of Wall Street Estimates with research and analysis covering more that 4,000 companies. Each disk contains: complete profiles of 11,000 public companies; annual (7-year comparative) balance sheets and income statements; annual cash flow statements (up to 3 years); quarterly financial reports (up to 6 years and including a calculated 4th quarter); 5-year summary and 5-year growth rates for net income, sales and EPS; officer/director names, titles, ages and salaries (for top 6 officers); president's letter, management discussion, auditors report and footnotes to the financials; ratios and price/earnings data; corporate earnings estimates; all subsidiaries; abstracts of extraordinary events; a listing of documents filed with the SEC; listing of exhibits filed with 10-Ks, 10-Qs, 8-Ks; Registrations Statements and ownership profiles. Contains detailed stock ownership information for companies extracted from documents filed with the SEC by corporate insiders, 5 percent owners and institutional owners. Information includes company name, exchange, ticker symbol, SIC codes, outstanding shares, stockholder names, number of most recent shares traded, total number of shares held and date of latest filing. On-line access is available through ADP Brokerage Information Services, Attorney Liability Assurance Society, CompuServe Executive Financial Information Services, Data-Star, Dialog Information Services, Dow Jones News/Retrieval, IDD Plus, Global Information Technologies, M.A.I.D., Mead Data Central, OCLC, Quotron Systems, Inc., Sandpoint, and Savant Investor Services.

DISCLOSURE SEC DATABASE *(formerly Disclosure Database)*

Provides: financial statement data, SEC filings, analyst reports, earnings estimates, fundamental stock screening

Transmission: modem

Access Fees: varies depending on vendor

Computer Systems: any computer, modem, communications software

Description: A file of business and financial information of about 11,000 public companies in the United States. Compiled from documents filed with the U.S. Securities and Exchange Commission, the SEC Database includes both current and historical financial data, including: company profile; annual and quarterly balance sheets, annual and quarterly income statements; annual cash flow statements; price/earning data; annual ratios; management information; and as-reported financial data.

WORLDSCOPE EMERGING MARKETS
Provides: company news, financial statement data, fundamental stock screening
Transmission: modem, diskette, CD-ROM
Access Fees: call
Computer Systems: DOS, Mac
Description: Provides fundamental data on over 1,100 companies in developing market regions. Data elements include: company profiles; financial statements; ratios (annual averages); market data (current and historical); annotated news headlines; company specific accounting practices identified; company/country listing; and exchange rates.

WORLDSCOPE GLOBAL *(formerly Disclosure/Worldscope)*
Provides: company news, financial statement data, SEC filings, fundamental stock screening, stock quotes
Transmission: modem, diskette, CD-ROM, magnetic tape, cartridge, fax
Access Fees: commercial—$8,500/year with monthly updates; non-profit—$5,200/year with monthly updates
Computer Systems: DOS, Mac
Description: Gives user access to current comprehensive and comparative financial management and market information on more than 11,000 companies in over 40 countries (includes those with the largest capital markets worldwide and 24 industries. Data elements include: company profiles; financial statements; ratios (annual & five-year averages); market data (current and historical); annotated news headlines; company specific accounting practices identified; company/country listing; and exchange rates.

DOW JONES INFORMATION SERVICES

P.O. Box 300   (800) 445-9454
Princeton, NJ 08543-0300   fax: (609) 520-7765

DOW JONES TOTAL RETURN INDEXES
Provides: index quotes

Transmission: diskette
Start-Up Fees: $300/one time set, $425/quarterly updates
Description: Contains 5 years worth of daily total return data for the Dow Jones equity market index, as well as cumulative returns for the Dow Jones industrial, utilities, and 65 composite averages. Also includes data for the industry group you select, as well as 5 years worth of cumulative total return data for your company. Disks delivered just after the close of your company's fiscal year. Quarterly updates available. Information importable into spreadsheet and database programs.

DOW JONES MARKET MONITOR

P.O. Box 300   (800) 815-5100
Princeton, NJ 08543-0300   fax: (609) 520-4660

DOW JONES MARKET MONITOR

Provides: general/business news, economic news/data, company news, financial statement data, earnings estimates, stock quotes, index quotes, bond quotes, options quotes, futures quotes, mutual fund quotes, closed-end fund quotes
Transmission: modem
Access Fees: $29.95/month for 8 hours of access from 7:01 pm to 6:00 am, M-F and all day weekends and certain holidays. Additional access charged at $.06/minute.
Current Quote Fees: included in monthly fee
Historical Quote Fees: included in monthly fee
Computer Systems: any computer, modem, communications software
Description: Dow Jones Market Monitor offers news, quotes, forecasts and analyses. Moving news from five Dow Jones newswires; articles from The Wall Street Journal and other publications important to investors; a years worth of daily mutual fund quotes; security snapshots, including earnings per share, P/E ratio, yield and more; weekly stock quotes, back two years; hard-to-find international news; and abstracts of analysts' research reports.

DOW JONES MARKET MONITOR PLUS

Provides: general/business news, economic news/data, company news, financial statement data, earnings estimates, technical screening, stock quotes, index quotes, bond quotes, options quotes, futures quotes, mutual fund quotes, closed-end fund quotes

Transmission: modem

Access Fees: $69.95/month for 8 hours of access to Dow Jones Market Monitor, plus 5 hours access to TAP, securities information for Tradeline

Current Quote Fees: included in monthly fee

Historical Quote Fees: included in monthly fee

Computer Systems: any computer, modem, communications software

Description: Offers historical pricing on equities, bonds, options, mutual funds and indexes traded on more than 17 North American exchanges. Screening capabilities search all 142,000 securities to identify those that match investors' specifications. Dividend history information provided on splits, cash dividends, cash equivalents, stock distributions and interest payments, plus total return information and tax-related dividend details. Capital change reports include prices adjusted for stock splits and other capital changes; can also show process on an unadjusted basis. Beta analysis reports include comparisons of price movements of individual stock against the stock market as a whole. Analytical profit/loss reports show "what if" strategies, using hypothical investment to compare performances of up to 800 securities. Security snapshots show an overview of hard-to-find performance data. Also provides all the news, quotes, forecasts and analyses previously only available on Dow Jones Market Monitor.

DOW JONES NEWS/RETRIEVAL

P.O. Box 300   (800) 522-3567x119
Princton, NJ 08540   (609) 452-1511
                                                     fax: (609) 520-4660

DOW JONES NEWS/RETRIEVAL

Provides: general/business news, economic news/data, company news, financial statement data, SEC filings, analyst reports, earnings estimates, technical studies/indicators, fundamental stock screening, technical screening, mutual fund screening, bond screening, stock quotes, index quotes, bond quotes, options quotes, futures quotes, mutual fund quotes, closed-end fund quotes

Transmission: modem

Start-Up Fees: $29.95 (includes 3 free hours); $19.95 annual subsequently

Access Fees: $1.50 per 1,000 characters of information; some special fees apply to certain databases

Computer Systems: any computer, modem, communications software
Description: Contains a broad selection of business and financial information composed of more than 60 on-line services. Users can receive real-time or delayed quotes from all major exchanges. Historical quotes dating back to 1979 are available for stocks, indexes, mutual funds and futures. Historical quotes on options date back 1 year. Includes more than 1,700 international, national and regional publications including exclusive access to the text of the Dow Jones Newswires, The Wall Street Journal and Barron's, plus same day access to full text New York Times news service and LA Times. Financial and investment services include excerpts from SEC records on more than 10,000 companies, financial information and company profiles from S&P research reports from Business Research Corp., consensus earnings forecasts from Zack's, fundamental corporate financial and market performance data from Media General and Money Market Service's weekly economic and foreign exchange survey.

DRPSOFT

P.O. Box 169   (508) 987-1962
Oxford, MA 01540

THE DRPDISK
Provides: fundamental stock screening
Transmission: diskette
Start-Up Fees: $36
AAII Discount: 11%; applies to start-up fees, access fees
Computer Systems: DOS
Description: Provides a complete listing of available dividend reinvestment plans. Lists 900 common stocks by name, symbol, industry, state, address, phone, exchange, cash limits, fees, discounts, price, dividend and yield. Program notes stocks which have split or paid a stock dividend within the past 12 months, or that have raised dividends for at least 10 years consecutively. Also notes companies available through direct initial purchase or from NAIC, First Share or Moneypaper. Program includes many sorting and printing macros to allow user to focus on selected criteria, such as yield, industry, cash limits, etc. Automatically prints inquiry letters and labels for requesting a prospectus, annual report, etc. Additional files list approximately 330 funds, REITS and limited partnerships, two dozen Canadian stocks, all 65 Dow stocks and more. Features pulldown menus and

pop-up macro menus. Prices file lists last 12 months, as well as price on Jan. 1 of 1990, 1991, 1992, and 1993. Also sorts by percentage change. Allows users to view graph of any DRP stock vs. the average DRP stock. Subscriptions available to purchases of an original DRPdisk.

E*TRADE SECURITIES, INC.

480 California Avenue
1st Floor
Palo Alto, CA 94306

(800) 786-2575
(415) 326-2700
fax: (415) 324-3578

E*TRADE TRADING SYSTEM

Provides: general/business news, company news, analyst reports, on-line brokerage, message/mail areas, stock quotes, index quotes, options quotes, futures quotes, mutual fund quotes, closed-end fund quotes

Transmission: modem, E*Trade Securities, America Online, CompuServe, or GTE Mainstreet

Access Fees: $0.27/minute anytime; 12 minutes of free time credited towards connect time charges for each executed trade

Current Quote Fees: $30/month real-time quotes per the exchanges; 15 minute delayed quotes are part of the standard E*Trade System's connect time charges

Historical Quote Fees: $0.04/each day's quotes (in addition to standard connect time charges) which includes the high, low, close, and volume

Computer Systems: any computer, modem, communications software

Description: Menu-driven trading system featuring PC or Tele*Master touch-tone trading, 24 hours a day, real-time news alerts and quotes, place and review orders, instant updating of portfolios, portfolio and tax record management, Black-Scholes options analysis, and free checking in user's choice of money market funds. Tracks over 100 securities at a time. Prices of securities include the current high, low, bid, ask, bid size, volume, dividend, yield and EPS. This data can be downloaded into other software programs as well. Will also alert an investor to any late-breaking news on a particular security. Commission rates for stocks are $25 per trade for any number of shares of OTC stocks at any price. For listed security orders greater than 5,000 shares add on addition 3/4 cent per share for the entire order. Day trade rates are $20 each way subject to same per share charges. Option rates are $20 plus

$1.75/contract, with a $29 minimum.

FIDELITY INVESTMENTS

82 Devonshire Street   (800) 544-0246
R20A   fax: (617) 728-7257
Boston, MA 02190

FIDELITY ON-LINE XPRESS (FOX)
Provides: general/business news, economic news/data, company
    news, analyst reports, earnings estimates, charting, technical stud-
    ies/indicators, on-line brokerage, fundamental stock screening,
    technical screening, mutual fund screening, stock quotes, index
    quotes, bond quotes, options quotes, mutual fund quotes, closed-
    end fund quotes
Transmission: modem
Start-Up Fees: $49.95 plus $5 shipping
Current Quote Fees: free, subject to Fidelity quote policy
Historical Quote Fees: varies
Computer Systems: DOS
System Requirements: 3M free RAM; Fidelity account required (mf or
    brokerage)
Description: A personal money management package. Users can place
brokerage orders; get real-time quotes on stocks, listed corporate
bonds, mutual funds, options and market indicators; access real-time
research, news and screening services from DJN/R, Telescan and
Standard & Poor's. Users can also track status of all investments, customize reports to track portfolio performance and keep records of
important tax information by tracking assets by tax lots and analyzing
capital gains. Utilizes pulldown menus, windows-like interface,
mouse support and help screens.

FORD INVESTOR SERVICES

11722 Sorrento Valley Road   (619) 755-1327
San Diego, CA 92121   fax: (619) 455-6316

FORD DATA BASE
Provides: financial statement data, fundamental stock screening, stock
    quotes

Transmission: modem, diskette

Access Fees: $350/month monthly updates; $450/month biweekly updates; $700/month weekly updates; or $96/hour on-line access

Computer Systems: DOS

Description: Screening service and database. Covers 2,680 companies
with 93 fundamental data items on each company. Provides standard
financial information including normal earnings, quality ratings, and
independently derived earnings and dividend growth rates. Includes
same fundamental data on 3,700 international stocks. Two proprietary
indicators—price/value ratio and an earnings trend parameter—are
provided to help identify undervalued common stocks. Allows users
to screen and rank stocks; create, maintain, and analyze a portfolio;
perform sector and industry analyses; and compute portfolio data averages and S&P 500 averages.

GE INFORMATION SERVICES

401 N. Washington Street   (800) 638-9636
Rockville, MD 20850   (301) 340-4442
                                                 fax: (301) 340-4433

GENIE

Provides: general/business news, economic news/data, company
   news, financial statement data, analyst reports, earnings estimates,
   on-line brokerage, message/mail areas, software library for downloading, stock quotes, index quotes, bond quotes, options quotes,
   futures quotes, mutual fund quotes, closed-end fund quotes

Transmission: modem

Access Fees: $8.95/month flat fee access for basic service, includes 4
   hours, each additional hour $3; $9.50/hour prime-time surcharge;
   $6/hour 9600 baud surcharge

Computer Systems: any computer, modem, communications software

Description: Provides access to a broad range of topics through a 3-
tiered pricing structure. With GEnie*Basic, users have access to over
100 services such as RoundTables, where ideas can be exchanged with
other members; closing stock and mutual fund prices; news, weather
and sports; Grolier's Encyclopedia; electronic mail; shopping; games
and entertainment. For a non-prime hourly rate, users have access to
GEnie Value services such as libraries of files, real-time conferences,
security quotes with a portfolio tracking feature, newswire services
and additional on-line games. GEnie professional service provides ac-

cess to additional fee services such as security objective services, registered investment advisers, newsletters, on-line brokerage through Charles Schwab and access to DJN/R.

IBC/DONOGHUE, INC.

290 Eliot Street

P.O. Box 9104

Ashland, MA 01721-9104

(800) 343-5413

(508) 881-2800

fax: (508) 881-0982

ELECTRONIC BOND FUND REPORT

Provides: general/business news, economic news/data, technical studies/indicators, mutual fund screening

Transmission: modem

Start-Up Fees: $1,995/year

Computer Systems: any computer, modem, communications software

Description: Allows subscribers to electronically download the complete Bond Fund Report database in a spreadsheet format. Supplies statistical information contained in the printed version of Bond Fund Report. Additionally, it allows users to write their own macros for customized analysis to meet special needs. LAN price quotes are available from an account executive.

ELECTRONIC MONEY FUND REPORT

Provides: general/business news, economic news/data, technical studies/indicators, mutual fund screening, index quotes

Transmission: modem

Start-Up Fees: $2,195/year

Computer Systems: any computer, modem, communications software

Description: Allows subscribers access to electronically download the complete bond fund report database in as spreadsheet format. Supplies statistical information contained in the printed version of the bond fund report. Additionally, it allows users to write their own macros for customized analysis to meet special needs. LAN price quotes are available from an account executive.

MONEY FUND VISION

Provides: general/business news, economic news/data, technical studies/indicators, mutual fund screening, mutual fund quotes

Transmission: modem

Start-Up Fees: $9,995/year

Computer Systems: any computer, modem, communications software
Description: Direct-link money fund data service that can be down-loaded weekly to personal computers or LANs. Vision's data retrieval tools connect with the Money Fund Report database. Permits users to create customized reports without writing macro instructions. Vision provides five years of historical money fund data to allow users to compare current market conditions to past industry trends. LAN price quotes are available from an account executive.

MONEYLETTER PLUS
Provides: general/business news, economic news/data, charting, technical studies/indicators, message/mail areas, mutual fund screening
Transmission: modem
Start-Up Fees: $50 for 12/hrs. or 6 months
Computer Systems: any computer, modem, communications software
Description: MoneyLetter Plus is an on-line, continuously updated version of Donoghue's MoneyLetter, which may be accessed at any time with modem-equipped personal computers. Provides all information printed in Donoghue's MoneyLetter. Also includes Hotline reports, past stories, individual fund profiles and performance data. Contains information published in the Bond Fund Advisor and investing background information from IBC/Donoghue's Mutual Funds Almanac and IBC/Donoghue's Mutual Funds Directory.

QUARTERLY REPORT ON MONEY FUND PERFORMANCE
Provides: general/business news, economic news/data, mutual fund screening, index quotes
Transmission: diskette
Start-Up Fees: $825/yr.
Computer Systems: DOS, Win, Win NT
System Requirements: Lotus 1-2-3
Description: Lists charged and incurred expense ratios of more than 1,000 taxable and tax-free funds, broken into the same categories as Money Fund Report for 3 months and for the quarter. Quarterly gross and net total returns and assets for each fund are listed. Includes top-performing funds by both gross and net total return for six categories. Commentary and analysis of the data are also included. Available on disk in both spreadsheet and database formats. Disk format allows for manipulation of data and includes quarterly historical data.

I/B/E/S, INC.

345 Hudson Street   (212) 243-3335
New York, NY 10014   fax: (212) 727-1386

INSTITUTIONAL BROKERS' ESTIMATE SYSTEM (I/B/E/S)

Provides: financial statement data, earnings estimates, technical studies/indicators, fundamental stock screening, technical screening
Transmission: modem, diskette, CD-ROM
Access Fees: varies depending upon source
Computer Systems: any computer, modem, communications software
System Requirements: CompuServe account
Description: Tracks, organizes, and disseminates data relating to earnings forecasts and the consensus derived from these forecasts for more than 4,000 publicly traded U.S. companies, 400 Canadian corporations and more than 9,000 publicly traded companies in 37 other countries. Data includes annual and quarterly earnings and long-term growth estimates. Separate databases are maintained for U.S., Canadian, and international companies. Available through a daily PC-based product (I/B/E/S Express), custom and standard printed reports, as well as other microcomputer-based systems. Data for the U.S. service is collected from more than 2,500 securities analysts employed by 170 participating institutional brokerage and research firms worldwide; for the Canadian service, from 21 participating firms; and for the international service, from more than 400 investment research departments in Europe, Australia, the Pacific Rim, and other emerging markets. Data is also available through over 30 electronic redistributors including OneSource, IDC, DAIS, Factset Data Systems, Inc., Vestek, BARRA, Bloomberg, Bridge, Quotron and Shark. Data is provided on tape for mainframes and on-line bulletin board services.

IDD INFORMATION SERVICES

Two World Trade Center, 18th Floor   (212) 323-9107
New York, NY 10048   fax: (212) 912-1457

TRADELINE *(formerly Tradeline North America)*

Provides: technical studies/indicators, fundamental stock screening, technical screening, mutual fund screening, bond screening, stock quotes, index quotes, bond quotes, options quotes, futures quotes, mutual fund quotes, closed-end fund quotes

Transmission: modem, diskette
Access Fees: varies
Historical Quote Fees: varies
Computer Systems: any computer, modem, communications software
Description: Provides financial information for company analysis, price/performance analysis, technical analysis, industry/geographic evaluation, client reporting and much more. Updated daily, provides security information for 17 majors North American exchanges as well as over-the-counter issues, equities, bonds, options, and mutual funds. Provides a universe of over 200,000 securities and over 2,000 market indexes; securities from over 100 U.S. exchanges; up to 20 years of equity, corporate bond, government debt and mutual fund pricing; current earnings, market capitalization, price/earnings ratio and shares outstanding figures; call and put option coverage. Users can screen for issues to meet investment criteria; design customized reports in either text or PRN formats; access snapshots that summarize security information; produce pricing or dividend history reports; and access data adjusted for all capital changes. Tradeline is also available on-line for a fixed monthly fee through Dow Jones News/Retrieval and Dow Jones Market Monitor.

TRADELINE ELECTRONIC STOCK GUIDE

Provides: charting, technical studies/indicators, fundamental stock screening, technical screening, stock quotes, index quotes
Transmission: diskette, CD-ROM
Access Fees: $159.95/year monthly updates; $74.95/year quarterly updates; $24.95 a la carte. AAII membership: $119.00/year monthly updates; $59.59/year quarterly updates; $19.95 a la carte.
Computer Systems: Win
System Requirements: 386 PC; Windows 3.1 or higher; 9M free disk space
Description: Windows-based product that provides user with a security performance "snapshot" for each of the 7,000 publicly traded stocks on the NYSE, Amex, and Nasdaq exchanges. Each printable snapshot includes average daily stock price/volume, P/E ratio, yield, payout ratio, annual dividend, total returns, 52-week high/low price and more. Also delivers a 52-week price and volume chart and a stock performance vs. the S&P 500 chart. Available to subscribers on diskette updated monthly or quarterly through an annual subscription program. Also available on Intuit's Quicken CD-ROM.

TRADELINE INTERNATIONAL
Provides: technical studies/indicators, fundamental stock screening, technical screening, mutual fund screening, stock quotes, index quotes
Transmission: modem
Access Fees: varies
Historical Quote Fees: varies
Computer Systems: any computer, modem, communications software
Description: Provides financial information for company analysis, price/performance analysis, technical analysis, industry/geographic evaluation, client reporting and much more. Updated daily providing international security information. Provides a universe of over 40,000 securities and over 2,000 market indexes; securities from over 98 international exchanges; equity, index and unit investment trust pricing; dividend and stock split event details back to 1986. Users can screen for issues to meet investment criteria; design customized reports in either text or PRN formats; access snapshots that summarize security information; produce pricing or dividend history reports; and access data adjusted for all capital changes. Tradeline International is also available on-line for a fixed monthly fee through Dow Jones News/Retrieval and Dialog.

TRADELINE POCKET STOCK GUIDE
Provides: charting, technical studies/indicators, fundamental stock screening, technical screening, stock quotes, index quotes
Transmission: flash ROM memory chip
Start-Up Fees: $199.95 for the reader and one quarter of information
Access Fees: $69.95/for 1 quarter; $199.95/year for quarterly updates
System Requirements: Franklin Personal Digital Book System
Description: Pocket-sized, electronic source for historical information on stocks traded on the NYSE, Amex, and Nasdaq (almost 6,000 stocks total), including market indexes. Charts stock and market performance, screens for stocks based on personal investment criteria, reviews important fundamental and pricing information and more. Updates are available on a subscription basis directly from IDD.

INTEGRATED FINANCIAL SOLUTIONS, INC.

1049 S.W. Baseline	(800) 729-5037
Suite B-200	(503) 640-5303
Hillsboro, OR 97123	fax: (503) 693-7487

DIAL UP/HISTORICAL DATA RETRIEVER

Provides: stock quotes, index quotes, futures quotes, mutual fund quotes, closed-end fund quotes

Transmission: modem

Access Fees: varies

Computer Systems: DOS, Win, Win NT, OS/2

Description: Provides historical data for gaining a perspective on price pattern discovery or analytic backtesting. Data can be purchased in different packages. To replace missing or incorrect quoters, a dial-up software program is within our on-line data service. Data is available on up to 10,000 stocks, mutual funds, indexes, and commodities going back 20 years.

FINANCIAL BULLETIN BOARD

Provides: message/mail areas

Transmission: modem

Access Fees: varies

Computer Systems: DOS, Win, Win NT, OS/2

Description: BBS system that allows investors to exchange information, software, ideas, and techniques with investors all across America and Canada. Provides technical support for QuoteExpress, Q-Net, Connect users, exchange of e-mail, sharing of tips and ideas for trading, and investment newsletters with stock recommendations.

INTERACTIVE DATA CORPORATION

Mail Location LI-AI	(617) 863-8100
95 Hayden Avenue	(617) 860-8181
Lexington, MA 02173-9144	fax: (617) 860-8289

DATAFEED FOR AIQ SYSTEMS TRADINGEXPERT

Provides: stock quotes, index quotes, options quotes, futures quotes, mutual fund quotes

Transmission: modem, diskette

Start-Up Fees: $100 deposit includes a one-time $25 fee for account set-up and $75 deposit for data charges

Access Fees: Two pricing plans: prime-time based on number of security prices accessed and communications time incurred ($10 monthly minimum fee); non-prime offers 3 monthly flat fee arrangements ($25, $40, and $50) with no communications charges and no monthly minimum fee

Computer Systems: DOS
Description: Securities market communications interface that links database to AIQ Systems TradingExpert. Contains both current and historical information. Financial data currently available includes: daily, weekly, and monthly high/low/close or bid/asked prices and volume for over 56,000 North American stocks, market indexes and market indicators; historical daily, weekly, and monthly listed stock prices and market indexes as early as 1968; market indicators as early as 1981; historical high/low/close or bid/asked/listed; Nasdaq and regional stock prices as early as 1973; daily, weekly, and monthly (current and historical prices, volume and open interest for options); stock splits, dividends; volatility data for listed equity securities; and daily, weekly and monthly (current and historical high/low/close or bid/asked prices and volume for international securities). Market Guide fundamental data is available for Trading Expert and Market Expert.

DATAFEED FOR METASTOCK
Provides: stock quotes, index quotes, options quotes, futures quotes, mutual fund quotes
Transmission: modem
Start-Up Fees: $25 set-up fee and $75 deposit for data charges
Access Fees: $10/monthly minimum
Current Quote Fees: between $0.01/security to $0.22/security
Historical Quote Fees: between $0.03/security to $0.25/security
Computer Systems: DOS
Description: Identifies, creates, and maintains price security files for international and North American securities data. Contains current and historical equity, commodity, index prices, and other related data on over 155,000 active (and 365,000 inactive) international and North American issues and options. Also contains North American dividend/stock split information on 56,000 securities. Creates files in MetaStock format (also used by The Pulse Portfolio Management System). Allows user to retrieve pricing information on individual securities daily, weekly, or monthly.

INVESTABILITY CORPORATION

P.O. Box 43307   (502) 722-5700
Louisville, KY 40253

INVESTABILITY MUTUAL FUND DATABASE
Provides: mutual fund screening
Transmission: diskette
Access Fees: $29/quarter; $99/year for quarterly updates
Computer Systems: DOS
Description: Provides information on over 5,300 mutual funds including: total assets; year started; address and phone number; investment objective; minimum and maximum loads; most-recently reported expense ratio; minimum purchase requirements; latest quarter, 1-, 3-, 5-, and 10-year returns on both a before- and after-load basis. Statistical measures include: beta, alpha, R-square, and standard deviation. Funds can be sorted and ranked by return as a whole or by investment objective. After-load rankings show how a $1,000 investment would have grown over the selected time period. Fund family sort tables list all the funds distributed by each of more than 400 companies. User can find individual funds or distribution companies. Help is provided through on-line screens and disk-resident documentation. Provides hypothetical performance examination and side-by-side comparisons.

INVESTMENT COMPANY DATA, INC.

2600 72nd Street #A
Des Moines, IA 50322-4724

(800) 426-4234
(515) 270-8600
fax: (515) 270-9022

ICDI MUTUAL FUND DATABASE
Provides: charting, technical studies/indicators, technical screening, mutual fund screening, mutual fund quotes
Transmission: modem, diskette
Start-Up Fees: $50
Current Quote Fees: non-prime: $0.35/fund; $0.02/NAV (daily and monthly); $0.12/distribution
Min. Usage per Month: $10
Computer Systems: any computer, modem, communications software
Description: Provides a mutual fund database and analysis software. Database includes total returns, statistics, total net assets, net asset values, distributions, asset compositions, cash flow analysis, loads and much more for over 4,700 mutual funds and index. The monthly database dates back to 1962 or the fund's inception date. The daily database begins in 1971 for 200 funds and as early as 1985 for the remainder. Software packages available for subscribers include a

spreadsheet produced monthly and Hypothetical, Asset Allocation, and on-line systems. Hypothetical system provides performance reports and graphs of user's hypothetical investments in a fund or portfolio. Asset Allocation system determines how to allocate assets to receive the optimal return. On-line System provides a direct link to the daily database of performance, statistical and fund profile information which can be calculated between any 2 dates. A second on-line service, the Interface, allows user to download daily NAVs and distributions.

IVERSON FINANCIAL SYSTEMS, INC.

111 W. Evelyn Avenue   (408) 522-9900
Suite 206   fax: (408) 522-9911
Sunnyvale, CA 94086-6140

SECURITIES HISTORY DATA
Provides: technical studies/indicators, technical screening, stock quotes, index quotes, options quotes, futures quotes, mutual fund quotes, closed-end fund quotes
Transmission: modem, diskette
Historical Quote Fees: daily: $0.0025/data point; weekly: $0.01/data point; monthly: $0.03/data point; special packages available at discounted prices; $1.50/contract year for futures
AAII Discount: 10%; applies to historical quote fees
Computer Systems: any computer, modem, communications software
Description: Covers end-of-day data for all equity issues and indicators for the NYSE, Amex, Nasdaq, Toronto, and Montreal exchanges from 1980 to present (data on some issues dates back to 1972). Also covers data on all domestic and some foreign futures issues. Futures data includes open, high, low, close, volume and open interest in individual or continuous contract form. End-of-day data for mutual funds and money markets available back to 1986. Available equity data includes: open, high, low, close and volume; dividends and splits; earnings; shares outstanding; rating; and corporate actions. Data may be received in ASCII, Lotus 1-2-3, MetaStock or Compu Trac file format; transmitted at up to 9600 baud; or 9 track, 1,600 bpi, standard 1/2 inch magnetic tape or UNIX compatible tape cartridge.

KNIGHT-RIDDER FINANCIAL

30 S. Wacker Drive
18th Floor
Chicago, IL 60606

(800) 526-3282
(312) 454-1801
fax: (312) 454-0239

ELECTRONIC FUTURES TREND ANALYZER
Provides: options quotes, futures quotes
Transmission: modem, fax (printed copy)
Start-Up Fees: packages start at $50/month
Historical Quote Fees: 1-50,000/day order—$0.01/day; over 50,000/day order—$0.005/day
Computer Systems: DOS
Description: A medium- to long-term trading system.

FINAL MARKETS END-OF-DAY PRICE SERVICE
Provides: options quotes, futures quotes
Transmission: modem
Start-Up Fees: free 5-day trial
Historical Quote Fees: 1-50,000/day order—$0.01/day; over 50,000/day order—$0.005/day
Computer Systems: DOS
Description: Access to end-of-day prices for over 360 futures markets. Data includes: open/high/low/settle prices and total volume/open interest. Packages start at $20/month.

HISTORICAL DATA
Provides: options quotes, futures quotes
Transmission: modem
Historical Quote Fees: 1-50,000/day order—$0.01/day; over 50,000/day order—$0.005/day
Computer Systems: DOS
Description: Provides historical price information on over 350 futures, options and cash markets. Daily prices available back 50 years in some markets.

KNIGHT-RIDDER END-OF-DAY NEWS REPORTS
Provides: general/business news, economic news/data, options quotes, futures quotes
Transmission: modem
Start-Up Fees: free 5-day trial

Historical Quote Fees: 1-50,000/day order—$0.01/day; over 50,000/day order—$0.005/day

Computer Systems: DOS

Description: Reports cover major events of the day affecting the futures markets. Downloading usually takes 1-2 minutes.

LOWRY'S REPORTS, INC.

631 U.S. Highway One   **(407) 842-3514**
Suite 305   **fax: (407) 842-1523**
North Palm Beach, FL 33408

LOWRY'S MARKET TREND ANALYSIS DATABASE ON DISKETTE

Provides: technical studies/indicators, index quotes

Transmission: diskette

Access Fees: $25/year plus $2.50/month for periods less than one year

AAII Discount: 15%; applies to access fees

Computer Systems: DOS

Description: Daily information provided from 1/1/40 for DJIA high, low and close; Lowry's Buying Power Index, Selling Pressure Index and Short-Term Index; NYSE advances, declines, unchanged issues; NYSE upside volume, downside volume, unchanged volume; NYSE points gained and points lost; NYSE new highs and lows (from 1962+); and Lowry's average power rating (weekly from 1950+). Points, volume and issues measure internal strength of the market. Calculate 6-, 12-, 30-, 60-, 90-, 120-, and 200-day moving averages. Can use trend and relationship of the 30-day figures to confirm the buying power and selling pressure indexes. Points, issues, and volumes can be displayed as cumulative indexes or as a difference of values plotted as an oscillator. Cumulative index of net points is an unweighted index of the broad market derived from the net gains and losses of all issues traded daily on the NYSE. Delivered on disk in ASCII, MetaStock, or Compu Trac format.

MARKET GUIDE, INC.

49 Glen Head Road   **(516) 759-1253**
Glen Head, NY 11545   **fax: (516) 676-9240**

MARKET GUIDE DATABASE

Provides: company news, financial statement data, fundamental stock screening, stock quotes

Transmission: modem, diskette, CD-ROM

Start-Up Fees: varies

Computer Systems: DOS

Description: Provides financial and narrative information on over 6,700 U.S. and foreign public companies traded on the NYSE, Amex, and Nasdaq exhanges, as well as many OTC companies. Database contains company financial statements (6 years of annual data and 5 years of quarterly data) in the same "as reported line item description" format as was used by the company when it filed with the SEC. The database contains business and product descriptions; SIC codes; stock symbols; recent bid price and price range; volume; 250 precalculated ratios and statistics; growth rates; company-to-industry comparisons; institutional ownership; trading statistics; company officers; company contact; address; phone and fax number; underwriter and latest stock offering; transfer agent; state and date of incorporation; equity and debt composition; market makers and exchanges; short interest information and quarterly per share history. The database is available on diskette, on-line through Market Guide's own dial-up service; on CD/ROM through the various One Source Products; and through various information providers such as AIQ, CDA Investment Technologies, Dial/Data, Dow Jones Telerate, Interactive Data Corp., Instinet, InvesText, PC Quote, Charles Schwab, Telemet America, Telescan, Track Data, and others.

MARKET SCREEN

Provides: stock quotes

Transmission:

Start-Up Fees: $3,599, includes the software and weekly updates on diskette

AAII Discount: 20%; applies to start-up fees

Computer Systems: DOS

Description: Searchs the Market Guide database of 6,700 public companies traded on the NYSE, Amex, and Nasdaq for companies that fit a given profile. Users can design the screening criteria for stock selection, then create reports for printing or downloading to popular spreadsheets. Company financial statements are displayed in SEC filing format. The reports include four years of quarterly per share history, full income statements for the past four years, and two years of balance sheet data. Some of the features of the Market Screen software product include: company's business description, products and recent operation results, sources of income and equity and debt distribution; description of common stock and other outstanding securities, including par value, outstanding shares, latest stock offering, transfer agent insider ownership, institutional ownership, underwriters, and market makers; company information such as the address, telephone number, SIC codes, stock symbol and exchange it is traded on, company officers, company contact, and state and date of incorporation; pricing information such as recent bid price and price range, volume and 12-month earnings; and ratios such as revenue per share, book value per share, EPS, financial ratios such as price earnings, yield, price-to-book, ROE, ROA, current ratio and long-term debt to equity, and growth rates.

MARKET SCREEN ONLINE

Provides: general/business news, financial statement data, fundamental stock screening, stock quotes
Transmission: modem
Start-Up Fees: $500 includes software
Access Fees: $1/minute
Min. Usage per Month: $20
AAII Discount: 20%; applies to start-up fees
Computer Systems: DOS
Description: Searches Market Guide database of 6,700 publicly traded companies on the NYSE, Amex, and Nasdaq for companies that fit a given profile. Users can design the screening criteria for stock selection, then create reports for printing or downloading to popular spreadsheets. Company financial statements are displayed in SEC filing format. The reports include four years of quarterly per share history, full income statements for the past four years, and two years of balance sheet data. Some of the features of the Market Screen software product include: company's business description, products and recent operation results, sources of income and equity and debt distribution; description of common stock and other outstanding securities, including par-value, outstanding shares, latest stock offering, transfer agent, insider ownership, institutional ownership, underwriters, and market makers; company information such as the address, telephone numbers, SIC codes, stock symbol and exchange it is traded on, company officers, company contact, and state and date of incorporation; pricing information such as recent bid price and price

range, volume and 12-month earnings; and ratios such as revenue per share, book value per share, EPS, financial ratios such as price earnings, yield, price-to-book, ROE, ROA, current ratio and long-term debt to equity and growth rates.

MEAD DATA CENTRAL, INC.

9443 Springboro Pike	(800) 227-4809
P.O. Box 933	(513) 859-1608
Dayton, OH 45401-9964	fax: (513) 865-1666

LEXIS FINANCIAL INFORMATION SERVICE

Provides: general/business news, economic news/data, company news, financial statement data, SEC filings, analyst reports, earnings estimates, stock quotes, index quotes, bond quotes, mutual fund quotes, closed-end fund quotes

Transmission: modem

Start-Up Fees: $50

Access Fees: $50/month

Current Quote Fees: $1.00/quote plus connect time

Historical Quote Fees: $0.15/price observation, $0.25/dividend observation plus connect time

System Requirements: MDC Session Manager required

Description: In addition to stock quotes, contains international news and country analysis reports by country, region, and topic. Also offers the ALERT library, which carries news updated every 3 hours. International files can be searched all at once, individually, or by region. Part of the NEXIS service of Mead Data Central, a computer-assisted electronic information service offering full-text articles from hundreds of the world's leading news and business sources.

MEDIA GENERAL FINANCIAL SERVICES

301 E. Grace Street	(800) 446-7922
Richmond, VA 23219	(804) 649-6587
	fax: (804) 649-6097

MEDIA GENERAL DATABASE SERVICE

Provides: financial statement data, technical studies/indicators, fundamental stock screening, technical screening, mutual fund screening, stock quotes, index quotes, mutual fund quotes, closed-end fund quotes

Transmission: modem, diskette, CD-ROM

Start-Up Fees: varies with service

Current Quote Fees: varies with service

Historical Quote Fees: varies with service

System Requirements: IBM for disk updates; any computer, modem, communications software for on-line access

Description: Provides statistical information on 7,000 NYSE and Amex-listed common stocks and Nasdaq National Market issues. Includes detailed income statement and balance sheet data, historical price and volume statistics and a variety of calculated fundamental and technical ratios. Also maintains large databases that track mutual funds, industries, and the financial markets. All or selected parts of Media General data are available on-line through Dialog and DJN/R. Lotus One Source provides the common stock database on CD-ROM. Customized IBM PC diskettes, custom screenings, hard copy reports, magnetic tapes and electronic data transfer are available from Media General.

MEDIA GENERAL PRICE AND VOLUME HISTORY

Provides: technical studies/indicators, technical screening, stock quotes, index quotes

Transmission: diskette

Historical Quote Fees: varies

Computer Systems: DOS, Win, Win NT, OS/2

Description: Fully-adjusted price history available on 7,000 stocks, 60 industry groups and 32 major market indexes. Data available daily, weekly, monthly, or quarterly.

MEDIA GENERAL SCREEN & SELECT

Provides: financial statement data, technical studies/indicators, fundamental stock screening, technical screening

Transmission: diskette

Access Fees: varies

Computer Systems: DOS, Win, Win NT, OS/2

Description: User can develop customized data service by selecting desired data, desired population of companies, and any data-screening criteria.

MEDIA GENERAL STANDARD DATA DISKETTE

Provides: financial statement data, technical studies/indicators, fundamental stock screening

Transmission: diskette

Access Fees: annual contract required @ $65/month; diskette updated monthly.

Computer Systems: DOS, Win, Win NT, OS/2, Mac

Description: A standard monthly diskette of vital financial data and performance statistics on approximately 8,000 publicly-held companies. Contains basic data and broad company coverage for many types of quantitative analyses. Provides a current file of 35 key data items including: company name, exchange indicator, ticker symbol, Media General industry group code and sequence number, month-end close price, 52-week high/low price and percentage price change on current month.

MICRO CODE TECHNOLOGIES

220 E. 54th Street   (212) 838-6324
#12-J   fax: (212) 595-1590
New York, NY 10022

FREE FINANCIAL NETWORK (FFN) *(formerly Financial Software Exchange)*

Provides: general/business news, economic news/data, analyst reports, charting, technical studies/indicators, message/mail areas, software library for downloading, stock quotes, index quotes, futures quotes, mutual fund quotes, closed-end fund quotes

Transmission: modem

Start-Up Fees: free to end-users

Access Fees: free to end-users

Current Quote Fees: $49.95/six month; $79.95/year

Historical Quote Fees: $.01/K (one cent); 1 kilobyte=33 days of data=one cent

Computer Systems: any computer, modem, communications software

Description: A 64-line BBS geared to financial computing. On-line information includes: closing stock quotes, financial magazines, professional associations, investment newsletters, recommendations, investment and financial computing roundtables and forums. Third-party vendors can rent private sections to distribute financial information to customers. Up to 14400 baud capability on-line 24 hours a day. Set up free account by typing NEW when asked for user ID. BBS number: (212) 752-8660; 8 data/no parity/1 stop bit.

MICROPAL

31 Milk Street	(617) 451-1585
Suite 1002	fax: (617) 451-9565
Boston, MA 02109	

MICROPAL
Provides: mutual fund screening, mutual fund quotes
Transmission: modem
Start-Up Fees: contact vendor for pricing
Computer Systems: DOS, Win
Description: An on-line mutual fund screening and fundamental data service. Features total return data, NAV, dividend and capital gains distributions, expense ratio, net income to assets, portfolio turnover, total assets, principal return with/without loads, annualized returns, beta, alpha, r-squared, mean, Sharpe ratio, Treynor ratio, portfolio manager, composition, and percentage invested in foreign securities. Also includes ability to screen on any data field including performance, load, asset size, 12-b1, expense ratio, yield, standard deviation, etc.

MOMENTUM

7516 Castlebar Road	(800) 735-0565
Charlotte, NC 28270	(704) 376-0206
	fax: (704) 376-0206

MOMENTUM
Provides: stock quotes
Transmission: CD-ROM
Historical Quote Fees: $99
Computer Systems: DOS, Win
Description: CD-ROM disk containing stock market historical data. Includes five years of daily open, high, low, close, and volume data on over 8,000 stocks on the New York American and over-the-counter

stock exchanges. Daily data on the Dow Jones averages (industrial and transportation since 1897, bonds since 1923, and utilities since 1934) is also included. The data is available in both ASCII and MetaStock formats on one CD-ROM disk.

MORNINGSTAR

225 West Wacker Drive   (800) 876-5005
Chicago, Il 60606-1224   (312) 427-1985
                                                                      fax: (312) 427-9215

MORNINGSTAR MUTUAL FUNDS ONDISC

Provides: general/business news, analyst reports, fundamental stock screening, mutual fund screening, index quotes, mutual fund quotes

Transmission: CD-ROM

Access Fees: $295/year for annual update, $495/year for quarterly updates, $795/year for monthly updates

Computer Systems: DOS

Description: CD-ROM based software program/information service to compare, analyze, and track over 3,100 mutual funds and produce customized reports and graphs. Provides over 160 fields of information for each mutual fund with coverage beginning in 1976. Menu-driven software lets user search, rank, average, graph and print all mutual fund information within seconds. Features include the ability to search for and sort the funds that match investment needs using the 66 screening fields. User can build customized, hypothetical portfolios by specifying investment amounts and frequency, reinvestment plans, sales loads, taxes and more. Allows user to identify the funds that hold a specific stock; generate detailed line, bar, and pie graphs to present findings; compare total returns for a single fund or for a group of funds over multiple time periods; evaluate results—numerically or graphically—against any of 25 benchmarks including the S&P 500, Lehman Brothers government/corporate bond index and the Wilshire 4500. It can also print directly from the program or export the data, reports, or graphs for use in other software programs.

MORNINGSTAR MUTUAL FUNDS ONFLOPPY

Provides: general/business news, mutual fund screening, mutual fund quotes

Transmission: diskette

Access Fees: $45/one-time diskette, $95/year for quarterly updates, $185/year for monthly updates
Computer Systems: DOS
Description: Provides fundamental data on more than 3,000 mutual funds. Users can screen and rank on more than 90 fields of information including Morningstar ratings, risk and return scores, investment style box, total returns, sales charges, fees and expenses, sector weightings, portfolio composition and more. OnFloppy also allows users to produce customized mutual fund reports and performance graphs. On-line help is available and technical support is free.

U.S. EQUITIES ONFLOPPY *(formerly Market Base)*
Provides: financial statement data, charting, fundamental stock screening, stock quotes
Transmission: diskette
Access Fees: $995/year weekly updates, $295/year monthly updates, $145/year quarterly updates; $55 trial issue includes complete system
Computer Systems: DOS
Description: A data-on-disk fundamental analysis system. Covers over 6,000 companies whose common stock trades on the NYSE, Amex and Nasdaq exchanges. Provides immediate access to companies' interim and 5-year financial histories, income statements, balance sheets, cash flow reports, recent 52-week and 60-month high/low prices, various fundamental ratios, yields, returns, growth rates, institutional and closely-held shares, SIC codes (industry), footnotes on important company events, and company descriptions and telephone numbers. Features include screening capabilities using over 100 fields, exporting data to other programs such as spreadsheets, sorting by any field or combination of fields, user/defined data fields with 67 character-long mathematical formula and weighted scoring. Also includes a custom report generator, creation and analysis of ticker portfolios, and 52-week and 60-month closing price trend graphs. Includes 110-page manual/tutorial.

MULTI SOLUTIONS, INC.

PO Box 5327   (800) 367-7080
Hilton Head Island, SC 29938   (203) 854-1700

BIOTECH ON DISK

Provides: general/business news, financial statement data, fundamental stock screening
Transmission: diskette
Start-Up Fees: $100/yr
Access Fees: $95/yr for quarterly updates
AAII Discount: 15%; applies to start-up fees
Computer Systems: Win
System Requirements: 386+
Description: BioTech is a Windows-based database containing background information on over 200 U.S. publicly-traded biotechnology companies. Information can be retrieved by several approaches, including the user's own topic of interest, the companies that relate to that topic, the companies' products, and the administrators in charge. BioTech also features several analytical tools to aid in performing stock evaluations, including 14 stock calculations (such as P/E ratio and net worth) and 6 industry specific biotechnology analyzers (such as burn rate and EPS prognosticator).

MUTUAL FUND ON-LINE DATA, INC.

405 El Camino Real, Suite 418   (800) 831-7777
Menlo Park, CA 94025   (415) 664-7777

FUNDS-ON-LINE

Provides: technical studies/indicators, technical screening, mutual fund screening, mutual fund quotes
Transmission: modem
Start-Up Fees: $75
Access Fees: $20/month for weekly updates
AAII Discount: 20%; applies to start-up fees
Computer Systems: DOS
Description: A combination software and on-line database focusing on comparing mutual funds and analyzing the optimal time to buy and sell. Data is acquired automatically via modem within 24 hours after the close of the market each week. Covers 308 funds. Data, adjusted for dividends and distributions, includes current market price, exponential moving averages, percent change in NAV, modified momentum, load-adjusted percent and beta-adjusted percent gain (loss) calculated on 4-, 13-, 26-, 39-, and 52-week basis. Menu-driven sorting system allows relative performance of any fund to be viewed readily and in any

desired parameters. Color graphs allow the choice of the NAV plus any 2 exponential moving averages or a market index or a 2nd fund for viewing comparative performance. Investment guidelines for using the data are offered plus model portfolios are displayed including their performance year-to-date.

ONESOURCE INFORMATION SERVICES, INC.

150 Cambridge Park Drive
Cambridge, MA 02140

(800) 554-5501
(617) 441-7000
fax: (617) 441-7058

ONESOURCE

Provides: general/business news, economic news/data, company news, financial statement data, SEC filings, analyst reports, earnings estimates, charting, fundamental stock screening, stock quotes, index quotes, bond quotes, options quotes, futures quotes

Transmission: CD-ROM

Access Fees: call for information

Computer Systems: Win

System Requirements: 386 or higher, Windows 3.1 for Notes

Description: System of business and financial information products delivered on CD-ROM. These integrated systems enable user to organize, analyze, and disseminate information. The CD/Investment product line (U.S. Equities, U.S. Research, International Equities) provides U.S. and international financial information on companies, stocks, and financial issues. Full integration with Lotus 1-2-3 and Microsoft Excel. Includes: Standard & Poor's, McGraw Hill's Compustat, Muller, Ford, I/B/E/S, Interactive Data, Media General and Value Line. The CD/Corporate product line (U.S. Public Companies, U.S. Private+, U.K. Private Companies, International Public Companies) contains a range of U.S. and international company financial and textual information. Data providers include: UMI/Data Courier, Thomson, Moody's, Market Guide, MacMillan, Predicasts, ICC and Extel. The CD/Banking product line (commercial banks, bank holding companies, savings banks, savings and loans) contains U.S. bank data for users specializing in correspondent banking, bank acquisition and credit analysis, branches, and includes deposit and demographic data on over 100,000 commercial banks, savings banks, S&Ls and credit union branches. Data supplier is Sheshunoff data services. Transfers data to Lotus 1-2-3 and Microsoft Excel.

ONLINE INTELLIGENCE

(formerly Investa, Inc.)

1400 Post Oak Boulevard
Suite 800
Houston, TX 77056

(800) 359-9359
(713) 877-1206
fax: (713) 877-1650

INVESTMENT WIZARD

Provides: economic news/data, analyst reports, charting, message/mail areas

Transmission: modem

Start-Up Fees: $49

Access Fees: $15/hour

AAII Discount: $10 free on-line time

Computer Systems: DOS

Description: An on-line database of current Wall Street opinions and predictions on U.S. and foreign stocks, industry groups, stock and bond markets, mutual funds, the U.S. and world economy, and interest rates. Updated daily. Opinions and predictions from leading periodicals, magazines, newsletters and research reports are read, summarized and cross-referenced by analyst, investment subject, industry group, individual stock or mutual fund. A bullish or bearish, positive or negative bias is assigned to each opinion or prediction. Analysts' prior predictions can be retrieved to help judge the credibility of their current opinions. Displays charts for 10,000 stocks.

OPTIMA INVESTMENT RESEARCH, INC.

111 W. Jackson
15th floor
Chicago, IL 60604

(800) 344-4403
(312) 427-3616
fax: (312) 427-9840

DAILY FINANCIAL MARKET RESEARCH

Provides: economic news/data, charting, technical studies/indicators, index quotes, bond quotes, options quotes, futures quotes

Transmission: modem, fax, electronic mail, wire services: FutureSource, TrackData and Bloomberg

Current Quote Fees: from $195/month

Computer Systems: any computer, modem, communications software

Description: Provides daily fundamental and technical research on the financial cash and futures markets. Includes the International Morningstar Report which contains the morning calls and also reports overnight developments in the Asian and European markets. The fundamental analysis includes economic analysis of events in the U.S. and international financial markets. Also includes a world economic calendar with market expectations for the major reports. The various technical sections cover interest rates, currencies, and equities. The technical analysis includes commentary and lists the support/resistance levels that are widely followed on the Chicago trading floors.

PC QUOTE, INC.

401 S. LaSalle Street
Suite 1600
Chicago, IL 60605

(800) 225-5657
(312) 786-5400
fax: (312) 427-8607

PC QUOTE

Provides: general/business news, economic news/data, company news, financial statement data, analyst reports, earnings estimates, charting, technical studies/indicators, fundamental stock screening, technical screening, stock quotes, index quotes, bond quotes, options quotes, futures quotes, mutual fund quotes, closed-end fund quotes

Transmission: modem, satellite

Start-Up Fees: $250 for self-installation

Access Fees: $195/month and up depending on configuration and number of workstations plus exchange fees

Computer Systems: DOS, Win NT, OS/2

System Requirements: 386, 25MHz or greater

Description: Delivers last-sale, bid/ask, open, high, low and volume quotations via satellite and modem from U.S. stock, option and commodity exchanges and Canadian stock exchanges. Delivers dividends, P/E ratios, yields, 52-week high/low and mutual fund data. Features include limit minders and alerts, financial news, block (basket) tickers, option page, top 10-page, option theoretical values, charting and timing sales.

PRODIGY SERVICES COMPANY

445 Hamilton Avenue
White Plains, NY 10601

(800) 776-3449
(914) 993-8000
fax: (914) 684-0278

PRODIGY

Provides: general/business news, economic news/data, company news, financial statement data, analyst reports, charting, technical studies/indicators, on-line brokerage, message/mail areas, software library for downloading, fundamental stock screening, mutual fund screening, stock quotes, index quotes, bond quotes, mutual fund quotes, closed-end fund quotes

Transmission: modem

Start-Up Fees: $49.95

Access Fees: $14.95/mo. for core service; $14.95/mo. Strategic Investor

Current Quote Fees: daytime: $4.80-$3.60/hr; evening: no hourly fee after market close

Computer Systems: DOS, Mac

Description: Provides national and international news, weather, travel information, entertainment, features, BBS facilities, games, computer news, and shopping. Finance-related services include economic, market, industry and company news; stock, bond, and mutual fund quotes; financial columns, on-line brokerage and banking; and finance-related BBS sections. Strategic Investor, an optional service, provides data and screening on more than 5,000 stocks and 2,500 mutual funds. This data can be veiwed on-line, printed or downloaded for use in other programs. Reports include investment strategies and economic, industry and company analyses and news.

STRATEGIC INVESTOR

Provides: financial statement data, earnings estimates

Transmission: modem

Start-Up Fees: $14.95

Description: Fundamental screening program containing information on 6,000 stocks covered in the NYSE, Nasdaq, and Amex exchanges. Includes balance sheet, income statement, and cash flow data. Also has earnings estimates, precalculated growth rates, annual and 5-year high and low prices, beta, relative strength, institutional holdings, etc. Screening can be done against any constant field, and has the ability to search by both company and ticker.

PROPHET INFORMATION SERVICES, INC.

(formerly Prophet Software Corporation)

3350 West Bayshore
#106
Palo Alto, CA 94303

(800) 772-8040
(415) 856-1142
fax: (415) 856-1143

PROPHET DATA SERVICE (*formerly Access Custom Financial System*)
Provides: stock quotes, index quotes, options quotes
Transmission: modem, diskette
Start-Up Fees: $49.95
Access Fees: No fees for on-line time
Current Quote Fees: $0.10/futures market/day; $0.01/stock/day;
    $0.03 per index/day; special rates for packages
Historical Quote Fees: $0.75/futures market/month; $0.10/stock/
    month; $0.30 index/month; special rates for packages
Min. Usage per Month: $10/month if system accessed
AAII Discount: 50%; applies to start-up fees
Computer Systems: DOS, Win, Win NT, OS/2, Mac
System Requirements: 5M free disk space
Description: Provides historical financial data and daily updates customized to individual specifications. Stock and index databases
contain open, high, low, close and volume on all U.S. equity markets
for over a decade. Futures database contains all North American futures and many foreign futures going back as far as a quarter century.
Daily updates for both stocks and futures are available. Users can
download both histories and daily updates. Extended histories can be
shipped to users on disk. Performs all data management functions and
automatically discovers and corrects errors in the user's database.

QUICK & REILLY, INC.

460 California Avenue
Suite 302
Palo Alto, CA 94306

(800) 634-6214
(415) 326-4200
fax: (415) 326-2432

QUICKWAY

Provides: general/business news, economic news/data, company news, financial statement data, analyst reports, on-line brokerage, stock quotes, index quotes, options quotes, futures quotes, mutual fund quotes, closed-end fund quotes

Transmission: modem

Access Fees: $0.44/minute prime-time; $0.10/minute non-prime; $12/hour

Current Quote Fees: $30/mo.

Historical Quote Fees: $0.04/quote

Computer Systems: any computer, modem, communications software

Description: Service to buy and sell securities 24 hours a day, receive real-time, delayed or historical security prices, automatically maintain tax records and manage a portfolio on-line. User can specify price ranges (and system flags price breakouts) and establish as many accounts as needed to handle a variety of securities. Can handle individual or joint accounts, IRA, Keogh, pension, profit sharing, custodial, trust, estate, corporate, partnership and investment club.

QUOTE.COM

1005 Terminal Way
Suite 110
Reno, NV 89502

(800) 261-7740
(702) 324-4325

QUOTE.COM

Provides: general/business news, economic news/data, company news, financial statement data, analyst reports, earnings estimates, charting, technical studies/indicators, stock quotes, index quotes, bond quotes, options quotes, futures quotes, mutual fund quotes, closed-end fund quotes

Transmission: modem

Start-Up Fees: $9.95/mo.

Current Quote Fees: European exchanges $19.95/mo.; London exchanges $19.95/mo.; Canadian exchanges $9.95/mo.

Historical Quote Fees: $1.95/file

Computer Systems: any computer, modem, communications software

Computer Systems: Unix

System Requirements: E-mail and/or Internet access

Description: An Internet service that allows users to access quotes, charting, S&P Marketscope, S&P Stock Guide, Hoover's reference report, Business Wire, investment newsletters, and historical data. Provides quotes on over 10,000 stocks, mutual funds, commodities, metals and futures both U.S. and international. Exchanges supported include NYSE, Nasdaq, Amex, Chicago Mercantile Exchange, CBOT, Commodities Exchange Center, New York Mercantile, Kansas City Board of Trade, Toronto Stock Exchange, Montreal Exchange, Vancouver Exchange, Alberta Exchange, Canadian Over-The-Counter, International Stock Exchange of London, London International Financial Futures, International Petroleum Exchange, London Commodity Exchange, London Metals Exchange, Frankfurt Stock Exchange, Amsterdam Stock Exchange, Deutsche Terminborse, Marche a Terme Internationale de France, Paris Stock Exchange.

REALITY TECHNOLOGIES, INC.

2200 Renaissance Boulevard
King of Prussia, PA 19406

(800) 346-2024
(215) 277-7600
fax: (215) 278-6115

REUTERS MONEY NETWORK
Provides: general/business news, economic news/data, company news, financial statement data, earnings estimates, charting, on-line brokerage, message/mail areas, fundamental stock screening, technical screening, mutual fund screening, stock quotes, index quotes, options quotes, mutual fund quotes, closed-end fund quotes
Transmission: modem
Start-Up Fees: $49.99
Access Fees: flat fee of $9.95-$25/month
Computer Systems: DOS, Win, Mac
Description: An on-line personal investing service. Provides financial information, analysis and management tools, investment guidance, and on-line trading. Develops optimal investment mix and provides specific suggestions on mutual funds, CDs, and money markets. Information is obtained on-line from an assortment of investment publications and financial data companies including Reuters, Dow Jones, Money, The Wall Street Journal, CNBC, S&P, Morningstar and top investment newsletters. Features include market highlights and briefs, fundamental research on over 18,500 investment options, the personal news clipping service (an additional $6.95/month), personal and product alerts, historical pricing charts (52 week, 100-day with 50-day moving average for over 12,000 stocks and 70 indexes), portfolio

analysis based upon latest analysts reviews, and performance graphs over time.

REUTERS MONEY NETWORK FOR QUICKEN

Provides: general/business news, economic news/data, company news, financial statement data, analyst reports, technical studies/indicators, stock quotes, index quotes, bond quotes

Transmission: modem

Start-Up Fees: $24.95 for program

Access Fees: starts at $9.95/month

Computer Systems: Win

System Requirements: 4M RAM, Quicken

Description: This Windows-based product allows Quicken users to obtain the latest news, quotes, and financial information on their portfolio of investments. Information is obtained on-line from an assortment of investment publications and financial data companies including Reuters, Dow Jones, Money, The Wall Street Journal, CNBC, S&P, Morningstar and top investment newsletters. Features include market highlights and briefs, fundamental research on over 18,500 investment options, the personal news clipping service (an additional $6.95/month), personal and product alerts, historical pricing charts (52-week, 100-day with 50-day moving average for over 12,000 stocks and 70 indexes), portfolio analysis based upon latest analysts reviews, and performance graphs over time.

S&P COMSTOCK

600 Mamaroneck Avenue

Harrison, NY 10528

(800) 431-5019

(914) 381-7000

fax: (914) 381-7021

S&P COMSTOCK

Provides: general/business news, company news, financial statement data, analyst reports, technical studies/indicators, stock quotes, index quotes, bond quotes, options quotes, futures quotes, mutual fund quotes

Transmission: modem, satellite

Access Fees: $345/month and higher

Computer Systems: any computer, modem, communications software

Description: Provides real-time information from over 50 markets and exchanges—both domestic and international. Includes equities, options, futures, commodities, foreign exchange, currency analysis and news. Provides instantaneous retrieval on any issue from exchanges; system may be programmed for 10 user-defined pages holding 22 through 66 symbols. Offers Dow Jones Broadtape News, Dow Jones Corporate Report, Platt's Global Alert, MMS International's Currency Market Analysis and S&P MarketScope Alert for extra fees. Provides direct interface with many analytical software programs. Real-time software is available for charting and analysis, options evaluation, portfolio management and spreadsheet interface capabilities. Information is provided via satellite or dedicated phone line. Uses a receiver with its own memory and processor allowing PC to be turned off or applied to other uses while quotes are being continousely updated. OpenArc, full-featured Windows-based program also available.

SAVANT SOFTWARE, INC.

120 Bedford Center Road (800) 231-9900
Bedford, NH 03110 (603) 471-0400
fax: (603) 472-5981

DISCLOSURE DATA FOR THE FUNDAMENTAL INVESTOR
Provides: financial statement data
Transmission: diskette
Access Fees: $185 to $1,800 depending on coverage and update frequency
Computer Systems: DOS
System Requirements: IBM PC
Description: Covers over 10,000 major companies traded on the national exchanges and OTC markets as well as several thousand smaller companies. Service is available through 6 different subscription series. Information includes income statement and balance sheet items (e.g., assets and earnings); sales, net income and earnings per share growth rates; dividend yield; price/earnings and price/sales ratios; price as percent of book value; percent institutional and insider ownership.

SILVERPLATTER INFORMATION, INC.

100 River Ridge Drive (800) 343-0064
Norwood, MA 02062-5043 (617) 769-2599
fax: (617) 769-8763

COMLINE

Provides: general/business news, company news
Transmission: CD-ROM
Access Fees: $995/year for bimonthly updates
Computer Systems: DOS, Win, Mac
Description: Contains over 75,000 English-language summaries abstracted from over 130 Japanese publications. Each item is edited by American and British editors. Most records contain a source contact telephone for further research. Covers 1986 to the present.

CORPORATE & INDUSTRIAL NEWS FROM REUTERS

Provides: general/business news, economic news/data, company
  news, earnings estimates
Transmission: CD-ROM
Start-Up Fees: $3,000/annual subscription for stand-alone user with
  monthly updates
Computer Systems: DOS, Win, Mac
Description: Worldwide company and industry information including strategy/plans, earnings, credit ratings, marketing, and competition. Includes over 150,000 records.

FINDEX

Provides: general/business news, company news, financial statement
  data
Transmission: CD-ROM
Start-Up Fees: $995/annual subscripton for stand-alone user with
  quarterly updates
Computer Systems: DOS, Win
Description: Contains market research reports, studies and surveys in virtually every type of industry. Each report includes a 50-100 word summary. Company profile gives researchers and potential investors access to detailed information about companies.

ICC KEY NOTES

Provides: general/business news, company news, analyst reports
Transmission: CD-ROM
Access Fees: $13,900/year bimonthly updates; $10,425/year annual
  updates; $5,250/each individual sector—consumer, industrial or
  services
Computer Systems: DOS
Description: Features the full text of over 220 detailed market research

reports covering 130 UK markets. Information includes reports on market size and trends, recent developments, major players and more. Available separately are: consumer sector reports, industrial sector reports, and service sector reports.

INVESTEXT: U.S. COMPANIES

Provides: general/business news, economic news/data, company news, financial statement data, analyst reports
Transmission: CD-ROM
Start-Up Fees: $3,495/annual subscription for stand-alone user with monthly updates
Computer Systems: DOS
Description: Provides analysis and data on approximately 12,000 publicly traded corporations. Objecive financial data is coupled with in-depth analysis of current strategy, financial outlook, and long-term competitive stature.

PREDICAST F&S INDEX PLUS TEXT

Provides: general/business news, company news
Transmission: CD-ROM
Start-Up Fees: international coverage: 1990-present $6,000, 1992-present-$3,500; U.S. coverage: 1990-present $4,000; 1992-present $3,500; annual subscription for stand-alone user with monthly updates
Description: Business reference research about companies products, markets and applied technology worldwide. Sources include over 2,400 trade and business journals, periodicals, and government publications.

SEC ONLINE-10K

Provides: company news, financial statement data, SEC filings
Transmission: CD-ROM
Access Fees: $2,900/year corporate (full set) quarterly updates
Computer Systems: DOS
Description: Contains the 10K portion of SEC Online on SilverPlatter including financial statements from 1990 to present.

SEC ONLINE ON SILVERPLATTER

Provides: company news, financial statement data, SEC filings
Transmission: CD-ROM
Access Fees: $6,950/year for monthly updates
Computer Systems: DOS

Description: Contains the forms 10K, 10Q, annual reports, proxy statements, and 20F for all NYSE, Amex and selected Nasdaq NMS companies. Documents are provided "as reported" from 1990 to present.

SEC: HEALTHCARE, PHARMACEUTICALS & BIOTECH

Provides: company news, financial statement data, SEC filings
Transmission: CD-ROM
Access Fees: $1,750/annual subscription for stand-alone user with bi-monthly updates
Description: Contains company information as reported ot the U.S. Securities and Exchange Commission for over 360 companies in the healthcare, pharmaceuticals and biotechnology.

UK CORPORATIONS CD

Provides: general/business news, company news, financial statement data
Transmission: CD-ROM
Access Fees: $4,200/year monthly updates
Computer Systems: DOS
Description: Contains over 3,000 annual reports (including financial statements) for every company listed on the International Stock Exchange in London and for 500 of the largest quoted companies in Europe. All foreign language annual reports are translated into English.

SMALL INVESTOR'S SOFTWARE COMPANY

138 Ocean Avenue   (800) 829-9368
Amityville, NY 11701   (516) 789-9368

PERSONAL INVESTING ONLINE SERVICE

Provides: general/business news, economic news/data, company news, financial statement data, analyst reports, message/mail areas
Transmission: modem
Computer Systems: any computer, modem, communications software
Description: Free on-line service 24 hours a day, 7 days a week. No monthly fees, access charges, downloading fees or obligation to purchase. User has access to research and analysis on over 7,300 stocks, 2,100 mutual funds, 40 futures markets, and 30 options. These analyses include relative strength rankings, volume analyses, and price-volatil-

ity analyses. Also accesses daily market news summary reports, weekly worry lists, and the earnings reports. User can also research database by date, news item, or key phrase. There is even an investor forum that includes the top 10 list for each investment class each week. Electronic mail system is also available.

STANDARD & POOR'S CORPORATION

26 Broadway
New York, NY 10004

(800) 289-8000 x56
(212) 208-8581

S&P STOCK GUIDE ON DISK
Provides: financial statement data, stock quotes
Transmission: diskette
Access Fees: $139.95/year for monthly updates
Computer Systems: DOS
Description: Monthly updated database providing 44 financial facts on 7,200 common and preferred stocks. Runs exclusively with INSTIN software. Can search by industry, S&P earnings and dividend rankings for common stocks, price, long-term debt, EPS, current yield and more. Includes ratios such as price percentage change from year end, market capital, long-term debt percentage of market capital, growth rate, cash as a percentage of price, sales-to-equity ratio, price-to-book ratio, institutional holdings, etc. Also includes description of company's principal business, financial position, and capitalization; historical price ranges for the past 20 years, last year, and current year; earnings per share for up to 5 years; dividend record—past, present, and future; and date on earnings, convertible stocks and warrants, trading column and details of stock splits.

STOCK DATA CORP.

905 Bywater Road
Annapolis, MD 21401

(410) 280-5533
fax: (410) 280-6664

STOCK MARKET DATA
Provides: technical screening, stock quotes, index quotes
Transmission: modem, diskette

Current Quote Fees: $500/yr. for weekly updates by mail or daily updates by modem for all 3 markets

Historical Quote Fees: for all 3 U.S. markets $1.00/day; for all stocks $250/year; historical data on CD-ROM 5 year minimum $500

Computer Systems: DOS, Win, Win NT

Description: Provides stock market information for the NYSE, Amex, and Nasdaq markets collected daily and mailed weekly on diskette or downloaded via modem. Historical data is available from fall 1987 and is stored in the most common formats. Some customization can be done free of charge, and "C" source code for direct data access can be provided. Several utility programs are included with any purchase: lookup routine to view any issue instantly; a stock screening program that can screen the entire market or any portion of the market for issues that meet specifications; a daily volume analysis program that tests for accumulation or distribution of an issue; and a stock symbol-company name lookup program with over 9,000 company names.

STREET SOFTWARE TECHNOLOGY, INC.

230 Park Avenue (212) 922-0500
Suite 857 fax: (212) 922-0588
New York, NY 10169

CMO/REMIC PRICING SERVICE
Provides: bond quotes
Transmission: modem, diskette
Access Fees: varies
Computer Systems: any computer, modem, communications software
Description: Covers over 22,000 CMO/REMIC pricing on a daily, weekly or monthly basis. Also contains analytic information such as speed, average life, Treasury spread, coupon, maturity, and agency ratings. Prices are obtained from the trading floor of a major primary dealer. Database is accessed via modem or by 3780 bisync transmission.

DAILY PRICING SERVICE
Provides: bond quotes, options quotes, futures quotes
Transmission: modem
Access Fees: $450/month
Computer Systems: any computer, modem, communications software
Description: Provides closing bid and asked quotes for a list of U.S.

Treasury notes, bonds, bills, agencies, STRIPS, mortgage-backed securities, CMO/REMIC and interest rate futures/options. Includes CU.S.IP numbers for easy integration with user's system. Pricing files available by 5 pm. Dial-up at 1200-/9600-baud or 3780 bisync.

FIXED-INCOME PRICING SERVICES

Provides: bond quotes, options quotes, futures quotes
Transmission: modem, diskette
Start-Up Fees: $300
Access Fees: varies
Computer Systems: any computer, modem, communications software
Description: Provides prices for Treasury notes, bonds and bills; Treasury STRIPS; CMO/REMICs; mortgage-backed securities; U.S. agencies; REFCO STRIPS; interest rate futures and options. Provides intraday Treasury, agency and mortgage-backed security pricing. Prices are obtained from the trading floor of a major primary dealer.

TRADER'S SPREAD SYSTEM (TSS)

Provides: analyst reports, bond quotes, options quotes, futures quotes
Transmission: modem
Access Fees: $600/month
Computer Systems: any computer, modem, communications software
Description: A menu-driven package that accesses the manufacturer's 6-month database of prices and yields for U.S. Treasury and agency securities, financial futures and options and money market instruments. Includes 10 different quote sheets that are updated by 5:00 pm. U.S. Treasury note/bond quote sheet includes weekend yield calculations.

TREASURY HISTORICAL DATA

Provides: bond quotes
Transmission: modem, diskette
Access Fees: varies
Computer Systems: any computer, modem, communications software
Description: Each data file contains an entire month of prices or yields; historical data from 1975. The source of data is the trading floor of a primary dealer. Contains Treasury notes, bonds, bills, agencies, STRIPS, money market, mortgage-backed and fixed maturity Treasuries/agencies. Individual categories also available.

TELEMET AMERICA, INC.

325 First Street   (800) 368-2078
Alexandria, VA 22314   (703) 548-2042

POCKET QUOTE PRO

Provides: company news, stock quotes, index quotes, options quotes, futures quotes, mutual fund quotes, closed-end fund quotes
Transmission: FM
Start-Up Fees: $395
Current Quote Fees: $27.50/month
System Requirements: No computer required
Description: A hand-held, calculator-size quote monitor. Gives direct access to real-time stock, option, index and futures prices within about 50 miles of almost 2 dozen major metropolitan areas in the U.S. User can key in ticker symbols of favorite issues and stay in touch with all the markets. Features: monitoring of 160 issues; programmable limit alerts notify user when specific price or volume points are reached; flexible services (real-time and delayed quotes can be mixed); business headlines from Dow Jones News; and computer interface capabilities.

RADIO EXCHANGE

Provides: general/business news, economic news/data, company news, SEC filings, technical studies/indicators, stock quotes, index quotes, options quotes, futures quotes, mutual fund quotes, closed-end fund quotes
Transmission: FM, satellite
Start-Up Fees: $394
Current Quote Fees: $33/month
Computer Systems: DOS
Description: Digital radio interface offers up-to-the-second market prices. Screen shows real-time stock, option, index and futures prices. Tracks up to 328 issues and charts intraday and/or end-of-day prices. Price and volume limits on any issue can be programmed for immediate notice when limits are reached. Can export prices on up to 300 issues to other PC applications through a file utility. Other features include: flexible services (real-time and delayed quotes on all exchanges in the U.S. can be selected and mixed); FM quote system with business news from Dow Jones News; integrated charting capability.

TELEMET ENCORE
Provides: general/business news, economic news/data, company news, charting, technical studies/indicators, software library for downloading, stock quotes, index quotes, options quotes, futures quotes, mutual fund quotes, closed-end fund quotes
Transmission: FM, satellite
Start-Up Fees: $600 deposit
Access Fees: $139/month
Current Quote Fees: $27.50/month
Computer Systems: Win
Description: Offers up-to-the-second market prices and tracks almost 10,000 issues that can be exported to other PC applications with a file export utility. Real-time stock, option, index, and futures prices are available within about 50 miles of almost 24 metropolitan areas by FM. Quotes, charts, and news system using the Microsoft Windows environment offers subscribers multiple views of the markets. Program price and volume limits on any issues for instant alert when limits are reached. Features: flexible service options (real-time or delayed quotes can be selected and mixed); business news from Dow Jones News; integrated real-time 2-minute and/or end-of-day price charting; link to the Microsoft Excel spreadsheet in real-time for real-time analysis and specialized computations; programmable price and volume points that trigger alerts.

TELEMET ORION SYSTEM
Provides: general/business news, economic news/data, company news, financial statement data, SEC filings, charting, technical studies/indicators, fundamental stock screening, stock quotes, index quotes, bond quotes, options quotes, futures quotes, mutual fund quotes, closed-end fund quotes
Transmission: satellite
Access Fees: $330/month
Current Quote Fees: $27.50/month
Computer Systems: Win
Description: Satellite delivered market quotation and news system that gives instant stock, option, index and futures quotes, real-time and historical charts and business news using Microsoft Windows. Features include: flexible service options (real-time delay services can be mixed); a hypertext interface to financial stories from Dow Jones News (headlines and in-depth stories); a link to the Microsoft Excel spreadsheet in real-time for analysis; programmable price and volume

points that trigger alerts; ability to export quotes on 20,000 issues to other PC applications with a file export utility. Also available: Market Guide database of fundamental data and screening of database.

TELESCAN, INC.

10550 Richmond Avenue (800) 324-8246
Suite 250 (713) 952-1060
Houston, TX 77042 fax: (713) 952-7138

TELESCAN ANALYZER

Provides: general/business news, economic news/data, company news, financial statement data, SEC filings, analyst reports, earnings estimates, charting, technical studies/indicators, message/mail areas, fundamental stock screening, technical screening, mutual fund screening, stock quotes, index quotes, bond quotes, options quotes, futures quotes, mutual fund quotes, closed-end fund quotes

Transmission: modem

Start-Up Fees: $199

Access Fees: $45/month for unlimited non-prime time; standard database—$0.75/minute prime time, $0.33/minute non-prime time, 25% surchage for 2400-/9600-baud access. In Alaska or Hawaii, $0.75/min. both prime and non-prime time

AAII Discount: 10%; applies to start-up fees

Computer Systems: DOS

Description: Combination software program and on-line database that allows user to perform technical and fundamental analysis on more than 74,000 stocks (NYSE, Amex, and Nasdaq), mutual funds, industry groups, options, and market indexes. Updated approximately every 15 minutes. Information dates back 20 years. Users can access more than 80 popular technical and fundamental indicators; read and plot insider trading information; access quarterly earnings reports and Zack's Estimate Service of analysts' projections for future earnings; read late-breaking and historical news, company fact sheets and money-making investment newsletters; view intraday graphs, and up to 4 graphs on a single screen; and use profit tester and stock optimizer to test buy/sell signals of technical indicators and find optimal parameters. Access S&P MarketScope, Morningstar, MarketGuide Reports, and SEC Online.

TELESCAN EDGE

Provides: general/business news, company news, financial statement data, SEC filings, earnings estimates, charting, technical studies/indicators, fundamental stock screening, technical screening, mutual fund screening

Transmission: modem

Start-Up Fees: $249

Access Fees: $2/search prime time, $1/search non-prime or $15/month unlimited non-prime time searches; additional on-line access of $0.60/minute prime time (25% surcharge for 2400 baud), $0.30/minute non-prime (25% surchage for 2400 baud)

AAII Discount: 10%; applies to start-up fees

System Requirements: IBM PC or compatible with 384K, 2 disk drives or hard disk, CGA, EGA, VGA or Hercules graphics, Hayes 1200- or 2400-baud modem and Telescan Analyzer

Description: A security search program that works with the Telescan Analyzer. Searches more than 11,000 stocks listed in the NYSE, Amex, and Nasdaq using up to 15 criteria out of 50 fundamental and technical factors in less than 15 seconds to find stocks or industry groups that fits the user's goals. Features: daily updates, scoring of every stock for each 50 technical and fundamental indicators, weighting to emphasize more important criteria while still considering less important criteria, ability to specify which industry groups to include or exclude, scrolling lists and on-screen help menus, off-line compilation of search requests and integration with Telescan Analyzer.

TELESCAN MUTUAL FUND EDGE

Provides: general/business news, economic news/data, company news, financial statement data, SEC filings, earnings estimates, charting, technical studies/indicators, message/mail areas, fundamental stock screening, technical screening, mutual fund screening, index quotes, mutual fund quotes

Transmission: modem

Start-Up Fees: $100

Access Fees: $2/search prime time, $1/search non-prime time or $15/month unlimited non-prime time searches; additional on-line access of $0.75/minute prime time, $0.33/minute non-prime time (25% surchage for 2400-/9600-baud). In Alaska or Hawaii, $0.75/minute both prime and non-prime

AAII Discount: 10%; applies to start-up fees

Computer Systems: DOS

System Requirements: Must have Telescan Analyzer/ProSearch software to run Mutual Fund Edge

Description: A search program that works in conjunction with Telescan Analyzer. Searches through more than 3,000 mutual funds in 24 categories. Users can search all funds or restrict the search to one or more categories in up to 20 out of 80 different criteria. Features include: scoring of every fund for each of 80 factors; weighting to emphasize important criteria while still considering less important criteria; and off-line compiling of search requests.

TELESCAN PROSEARCH 4.0

Provides: general/business news, economic news/data, company news, financial statement data, SEC filings, analyst reports, earnings estimates, charting, technical studies/indicators, message/mail areas, fundamental stock screening, technical screening, mutual fund screening, stock quotes, index quotes, bond quotes, options quotes, futures quotes, mutual fund quotes, closed-end fund quotes

Transmission: modem

Start-Up Fees: $395 plus $100 for optional forecasting module, includes Telescan Analyzer (10% discount for AAII members)

Access Fees: $2/search prime time, $1/search non-prime or $15/month unlimited non-prime time searches, $50/month unlimited prime time searches; additional on-line access of $0.75/minute prime time, $0.33/minute non-prime (25% surcharge for 2400-/9600-baud.) If Alaska or Hawaii $0.75/minute both prime and non-prime.

AAII Discount: 10%; applies to start-up fees

Computer Systems: DOS

System Requirements: Must have Telescan Analyzer to run ProSearch

Description: A stock search program that works in conjunction with Telescan Analyzer. Searches more than 8,000 stocks listed on the NYSE, Amex, and Nasdaq using as many as 40 of the 207 fundamental, technical and forecasting criteria. Returns up to 200 securities in less than 15 seconds to find stocks or industry groups that fit the user's goals. Features include: daily updates; ability to exclude specific industry groups; scrolling lists and on-line help screens; backtesting to see how user searches performed historically; weighting individual criteria; scoring to search for the highest and lowest values for any given indicator, as well as to screen out stocks above/below desired minimum and maximum values; and the ability to compile searches off-line.

TICK DATA, INC.

720 Kipling Street (800) 822-8425
Suite 115 (303) 232-3701
Lakewood, CO 80215 fax: (303) 232-0329

TICK-BY-TICK HISTORICAL PRICE DATA
Provides: technical studies/indicators, stock quotes, index quotes, options quotes, futures quotes
Transmission: modem, diskette
Start-Up Fees: $49
Historical Quote Fees: $10/month/commodity
Computer Systems: DOS, Mac
Description: Supplies historical time and sales data on futures and options contracts. Software converts data to Compu Trac, CSI, Lotus 1-2-3, MetaStock or ASCII formats; connects to Tick Data for dial-up service and displays and prints graphs. Diskette data from 1977; on-line data stores information for the last 45 trading days.

TOOLS FOR TIMING

11345 Highway 7 (800) 325-1344
#499 (612) 939-0076
Minnetonka, MN 55305 fax: (612) 938-1275

HOURLY DJIA
Provides: charting, technical studies/indicators, index quotes
Transmission: diskette
Start-Up Fees: $50
Computer Systems: DOS
Description: Shows the Dow Jones industrial average on an hourly basis along with the last indicator and several popular momentum indictors calculated from hourly parameter. Indicators provided include: last hour indicator, trading bands, Bollinger bands, relative strength index, stochastics, and MACD. Supplies hourly data on the DJIA starting from 1986.

TRACK/ONLINE DIVISION OF GLOBAL MARKET INFORMATION

(formerly Track Data Corp.)

56 Pine Street
New York, NY 10005

(800) 935-7788
(212) 248-0300
fax: (212) 248-9162

TRACK/ON LINE
Provides: general/business news, economic news/data, company news, financial statement data, SEC filings, analyst reports, earnings estimates, stock quotes, index quotes, bond quotes, options quotes, futures quotes, mutual fund quotes, closed-end fund quotes
Transmission: modem
Start-Up Fees: $175
Access Fees: $145/month basic service, includes quotes, news, and historical quotes; no hourly charges
Min. Usage per Month: flat fee
Computer Systems: any computer, modem, communications software
Description: Business and financial information and quotes. Users can receive delayed and real-time quotes from all major exchanges, including Canadian and London exchanges, on stock, options and futures. News database provides current and historical news. Includes: risk arbitrage; institutional holdings and 144 filings; earnings estimates; and equity analysis, technical indicators, economic and monetary projections, bond data, etc. from S&P MarketScope. Provides analysis on put/call option series, volatility analysis, market pulse and option scanning.

TRENDPOINT SOFTWARE

9709 Elrod Road
Kensington, MD 20895

(301) 949-8131

TRENDPOINT DATA LIBRARY
Provides: economic news/data, technical studies/indicators, index quotes, bond quotes, options quotes, futures quotes
Transmission: diskette
Historical Quote Fees: $1.25/calendar year daily data; $3/file weekly data (approx. 10 years/file); minimum order $25

AAII Discount: 20%; applies to current quote fees, historical quote fees
Computer Systems: DOS
Description: Historical daily, weekly, and monthly data for technical analysis. Provided on disk, in ASCII or MetaStock format. Includes most major stock and bond indexes, NYSE and Nasdaq daily market breadth data, new high and lows, trading volume, TRIN (Arms) index, interest rates, yields, S&P futures, gold prices and the Wilbur timing index. Most data goes back to the 1970s, some goes back to 1928. Also available: "Stock Market Timing Using the Personal Computer," approximately 50 pages (hard copy) of notes on using historical and current data for market timing.

VALUE LINE PUBLISHING

220 E. 42nd Street
New York, NY 10017-5891

(800) 654-0508
(212) 687-3965
fax: (212) 661-2807

VALUE/SCREEN III
Provides: financial statement data, earnings estimates, fundamental stock screening, technical screening
Transmission: modem, diskette
Access Fees: $325/year quarterly updates; $465/year monthly updates; $1,995/year weekly updates
Computer Systems: DOS, Mac
Description: Stock screening program based on information from Value Line. Supplies over 50 fundamental and technical data items on approximately 1,600 stocks. The user can simultaneously conduct stock screens based on up to 25 different criteria. All data can be downloaded to a spreadsheet program such as Lotus 1-2-3, Symphony, or Excel.

WORDEN BROTHERS, INC.

4905 Pine Cone Drive
Suite 12
Durham Hill, NC 27707

(800) 776-4940
(919) 408-0542
fax: (919) 408-0545

TELECHART 2000 SYSTEM

Provides: charting, technical studies/indicators, technical screening, stock quotes, index quotes, closed-end fund quotes
Transmission: modem
Start-Up Fees: $29 (50% discount for AAII members)
Access Fees: $0.69 minimum charge per access (includes price of data if less than $0.69)
Current Quote Fees: $0.005/quote
Historical Quote Fees: $1.50 for 1st yr. of historical data/stock; $0.50 each additional yr./stock
AAII Discount: 50%; applies to start-up fees
Computer Systems: DOS
Description: A stock charting and analysis service. Provides charts and downloads data through a toll-free number. Service includes a charting package for technical analysis. Data can be exported for use with most popular stock and analysis software programs.

X*PRESS INFORMATION SERVICES, LTD.

4700 S. Syracuse Parkway   (800) 772-6397
Suite 1050   (303) 721-1062
Denver, CO 80237   fax: (303) 267-4172

X*PRESS EXECUTIVE

Provides: general/business news, economic news/data, company news, financial statement data, SEC filings, earnings estimates, charting, stock quotes, index quotes, options quotes, futures quotes, mutual fund quotes, closed-end fund quotes
Transmission: cable TV, satellite
Start-Up Fees: $250 for satellite; $150 for cable
Current Quote Fees: $20.95-$25.95/month for unlimited use
AAII Discount: 50% for 1st 3 mo.; applies to current quote fees
Computer Systems: DOS, Mac
Description: Delivers a steady flow of market quotes on over 30,000 stocks, indexes, funds, rights and warrants, commodities, futures and options from the major North American exchanges on a 15-minute delayed basis. Also contains interest and money rates, exchange rates, precious metals reports, market statistics, mergers and acquisitions filings, S&P MarketMovers, Business Wire and PR Newswire. Carries business and financial news from Knight-Ridder and up-to-the-minute national and international news from major news wires around the

world provided by ITAR-TASS (former Soviet Union), Kyodo (Japan), Xinjua (China), Deutsche Presse-Agentur (West Germany), Central News Agency (Taiwan), Agence France Presse (France) and more. Contains consumer news, sports scores and reports, weather information from all 50 states, personal computer news, movie and book reviews and special interest topics.

ZACKS INVESTMENT RESEARCH

155 N. Wacker
Chicago, IL 60606

(800) 767-3771
(312) 630-9880
fax: (312) 630-9898

ZACKS CONSENSUS SUMMARY DISKETTE
Provides: earnings estimates
Transmission: diskette
Start-Up Fees: weekly $7,500; semimonthly $5,000; monthly $3,000
Computer Systems: DOS
Description: Includes over 300 earnings estimate data items for 6 fiscal-year periods. Available monthly, semimonthly and weekly.

ZACKS ON-LINE
Provides: earnings estimates
Transmission: modem
Start-Up Fees: access directly from Zacks: $7,500 weekly, $3,600 semimonthly, $3,000 monthly; individual company reports are also available through DJN/R and Telescan at varying prices
Computer Systems: any computer, modem, communications software
Description: Provides history of analysts' ratings (expectations) for a given analyst on a given company. Includes EPS estimates and stock recommendations and analysts revisions; monitors the number of analysts following a given company during the current quarter; surprise reports; histograms on earnings; earnings reports and dates expected.

Appendix A

Stock Market and Business Related BBSs

The following BBSs are either devoted exclusively to investment topics or maintain stock market, general business or real estate sections along with non-investment areas of interest to investors. Some of the systems require a registration or subscription fee before access is granted to all features of the BBS.

Please contact our free *Computerized Investing* BBS in Chicago at (312) 280-8565, -8764, -9043, or -9623 to add to or update this listing.

Name	Number
The Market	(201) 467-3269
Investors On-Line	(206) 285-5359
Free Financial Network (Microcode)	(212) 752-8660
Wall Street BBS	(214) 349-0241
The Market	(301) 299-8667
Real Estate Board	(301) 384-9302
Computerized Investing	(312) 280-8565
Computerized Investing	(312) 280-8764
Computerized Investing	(312) 280-9043
Computerized Investing	(312) 280-9623
Pisces Financial	(312) 281-6046
Chicago Megaphile	(312) 283-7967
NEBLink—Wayne State College BBS	(402) 375-7535
McAffee	(408) 998-4004
PK Ware	(414) 354-8670
Quant IX Software	(414) 961-2592
Telestock One	(512) 338-4591
The List (PDSLO)	(516) 938-6722
E. KY College (Prof BBS)	(606) 269-1565
Dollars & Bytes	(619) 483-5477
Jack's Emporium	(703) 373-8215
Chelsea Systems (Don Rosenberger)	(703) 922-4077
The CPA—Pro Forum	(813) 355-3226
Executive Network	(914) 667-4567

Bulletin Boards Sponsored by the U.S. Government

Name	Number
Economic BBS	(202) 482-2584
Economic BBS	(202) 482-3870
Census Bureau	(301) 763-7554
Census Bureau—9600-baud	(301) 763-1568
Federal Reserve Bank of St. Louis	(314) 621-1824
Federal Reserve Bank of Minneapolis	(612) 340-2489
NIST "Fedworld," Dept. of Commerce	(703) 321-8020

Appendix B

Computer Special Interest Groups (SIGs)

The following is a listing of the currently active AAII and other computer subgroups throughout the country, along with the name and phone number of the person to contact if you are interested in becoming a member of the group. Computer-user groups offer a way of exchanging ideas and knowledge of investment theory and computer programs with other people in your area. Meetings often feature hands-on demonstrations of investment software and computer systems. AAII computer subgroups are composed of subscribers to *Computerized Investing*, a bimonthly newsletter published by the American Association of Individual Investors. Subscription rate is $60.00 per year, or $30.00 per year to members of AAII.

AAII COMPUTER SPECIAL INTEREST GROUPS

Arizona

Phoenix
James O. Seamans
4136 E. Solano Drive
Phoenix, AZ 85018-1145
(602) 952-0905

Tucson
Brad Becker
2970 N. Swan
Suite 221
Tucson, AZ 85712
(602) 881-7999

California

Los Angeles
Don Gimpel
1840 San Ysidro Drive
Los Angeles, CA 90210
(310) 276-9875

Orange County
Phil Ross
2516 Monterey Place
Fullerton, CA 92633
(714) 738-1419

Sacramento
Seth Hall
412 Lagomarsino Way
Sacramento, CA 95819
(916) 485-6117

San Diego
Dennis Costarakis
12926 Candela Place
San Diego, CA 92130-1855
(619) 625-4059

San Francisco
Dr. Arturo Maimoni
134 Crestview Drive
Orinda, CA 94563
(415) 254-1708

Silicon Valley
Charles Pack
25303 La Loma Drive
Los Altos Hills, CA 94022
(415) 949-0887

South Bay
Frank Lyons
2018 West 149th Street
Gardena, CA 90249
(310) 323-4430

Colorado

Denver
Dan Furman
P.O. Box 110543
Aurora, CO 80042
(303) 366-4001

Connecticut
James Darkey
43 Arnold Drive
Tolland, CT 06084
(203) 875-1295

Florida

Boca Raton
Robert Lewison
23265 Boca Club
Colony Circle
Boca Raton, FL 33433
(407) 750-9529

Orlando
Robert E. Hilton Jr.
3801 Appleton Way
Orlando, FL 32806
(407) 856-1576

The Palm Beaches
Drew Mayer
P.O. Box 32472
Palm Beach Gardens, FL 33420
(407) 655-7170

Tampa
Jim Anderson
1200 W. Mlk Blvd.
Plant City, FL 33564
(813) 752-1155

Georgia

Atlanta
Henry R. Dunlap
1141 Oxford Crescent
Atlanta, GA 30319
(404) 255-1141

Hawaii

Honolulu
Anthony Lojac
1778 Ala Moana Blvd., #2120
Honolulu, HI 96815-1623
(808) 521-3520

Indiana

Indianapolis
Joe Huff
10651 Vandergriff Road
Indianapolis, IN 46239
(317) 862-4433

Louisiana

Baton Rouge
Mack Ingle
11549 Sheraton Drive
Baton Rouge, LA 70815
(504) 275-8845

New Orleans
Charles Deinken
4709 Bissonet
Metairie, LA 70003
(504) 889-0592

Massachusetts

Boston
Jim Yoshizawa
100 Federal Street
26th Floor
Boston, MA 02101
(617) 261-2634

Michigan

Detroit
Monica Lowden
288 E. Maple, #316
Birmingham, MI 48009
(313) 737-7300

Grand Rapids
Charles McInturff
1510 Southlawn Drive S.W.
Grand Rapids, MI 49509
(616) 532-7283

Minnesota

Minneapolis
Mark Madl
4041 Stonebridge Drive South
Eagan, MN 55123
(612) 683-9150

Missouri

Kansas City
Thomas Lance
11908 West 82nd Terrace
Lenexa, KS 66215
(913) 888-7412

St. Louis
W.R. Stephens
13002 Hunter Creek Road
Des Pares, MO 63131
(314) 821-6115

Nebraska/Iowa

Jean Hunter
1518 N. 76th Street
Omaha, NE 68114
(404) 391-4383

New Mexico

Albuquerque
John Emerson
1416 La Meseta NE
Albuquerque, NM 87112
(505) 275-7026

New York

Buffalo
Michael Hart
P.O. Box 32
East Aurora, NY 14052
(716) 652-0697

Long Island
Albert Golly Jr.
P.O. Box 381
Medford, NY 11763
(212) 541-3955

New York City
Scott Martin
353 West 56th Street
Suite 7A
New York, NY 10019
(212) 246-5060

Rochester
Don Bay
770 Victor Road
Macedon, NY 14502
(315) 956-4580

North Carolina

Research Triangle
David Johnson
2213 Oxford Hills Drive
Raleigh, NC 27608
(913) 828-0691

Ohio

Cincinnati
Dr. Richard Allnutt
112 Wallace Avenue
Covington, KY 41014
(606) 581-7719

Cleveland
Bob Watson
822 Stuart
South Euclid, OH 44121
(216) 382-1481

Columbus
Carl Crawford
290 Beckley Lane
Dublin, OH 43017
(614) 761-0967

Oregon

Portland
Lyle Remington
1809 N.W. Johnson Street, #12
Portland, OR 97209-1306
(503) 222-3055

Pennsylvania

Philadelphia
Donald Lee
2033 Parkview Avenue
Abington, PA 19001
(215) 659-5594

Pittsburgh
R. Buck Gray
203 Hibiscus Drive
Pittsburgh, PA 15235
(412) 241-5634

Texas

Austin
Archie McNeill
4504 Chiappero Trail
Austin, TX 78731
(512) 458-3466

Dallas/Ft. Worth
Bud Liles
3916 Hillwood Way
Bedford, TX 76021
(817) 283-5977

Houston
C.J. Leleux
7603 Braesglen
Houston, TX 77071
(713) 771-4728

San Antonio
Norman Black
9002 Swinburne Court
San Antonio, TX 78240-3636
(512) 681-0491

Virginia

Hampton Roads
Bill Kelly
461 Ashton Green Boulevard
Newport News, VA 23602
(804) 887-5958

Washington

Seattle
Barry Griffiths
11312 83 Place N.E.
Kirkland, WA 98034
(206) 823-8459

Wisconsin

Milwaukee
Rich Scott
300 Mandan Drive
Waukesha, WI 53188

Club 3000

4550 North 38th Street
Augusta, MI 49012

This special interest group is not devoted exclusively to computers but to commodity trading in general (70% of the members use computers). The purpose of its formation in 1982 was simply to allow persons interested in commodity trading to be able to communicate and share ideas with others having similar interests.

Their newsletter, *Club 3000 News*, is not a monthly; the number of issues per year depends on the amount of material received from members and vendors. In this way, there is an exchange of comments and opinions on the various commodity trading systems and strategies. A number of trading advisers submit their results for publication as well. This enables members to follow their performance and possibly pick someone to manage their commodity funds.

The other feature of Club 3000 is its database, which contains cross references between subjects and newsletter issues as well as member profiles and general information. Members who paid the full subscription rate and who contribute knowledge published in the newsletter get a one-time 100% extention of their subscription term. In addition, any member who submits his letter on a word processor (ASCII) disk or via E-mail gets an additional month for each submission.

Articles from the newsletters are compiled into annual yearbooks at a cost of $0.15 per page. The current subscription rate for the upcomming year is $80, $41 for six months, and $21 for three months.

Market Technicians Association, Inc.

1 World Trade Center
Suite 4447
New York, NY 10048
(212) 912-0995
fax: (212) 912-1064

MTA, founded in 1972, is the national organization of the market analysis professionals in the United States. Consisting of about 250 practicing technicians, this not-for-profit association has three main goals: to encourage the exchange of technical information and collectively explore new frontiers in the area of technical research, to educate the public and investment community about the use, value, and limitations of technical research, and to uphold a code of ethics and the professional standards among technical analysts.

These goals of the MTA are accomplished through a wide variety of activities and publications, such as: the annual 4-day seminar, monthly educational meetings, monthly newsletters, the biannual journal, the Chartered Market Technician Program, a comprehensive lending library devoted to the field of technical analysis, an informal clearing house for technical analysis job openings and those seeking employment in the field, and a computer bulletin board system. Annual dues in the MTA are $150, while subscription to the journal only (provides none of the other benefits listed) is available at $50 for two issues. Back issues of the journal are available for $30 each.

Houston Computer Investors' Association

820 Gessner, Suite 220
Houston, TX 77024

HCIA is a non-profit association of active personal investors. Founded in 1981, the group shares a mutual interest in sharing knowledge in using computers with their investment activities.

Membership splits into smaller groups of individuals that share a similar investment topic, such as stocks, bonds, mutual funds . . . are organized into "Super Special Interest Groups" (SUPER SIGS). Chairpersons typically volunteer for and organize these individual SUPER SIGS, which usually get together at each HCIA monthly meeting.

HCIA holds monthly meetings, publishes a monthly newsletter, and also maintains a computer bulletin board system where investors can communicate with other investors.

The membership dues are $60 for the first year, which includes a one-time $10 application fee. Thereafter, the yearly dues are $50. New members can prepay for a three-year term at a cost of $110 ($100 for current members).

The MicroComputer Investors Association (MCIA)

Dr. Jack M. Williams
902 Anderson Drive
Fredericksburg, VA 22405
(703) 371-5474
BBS: (703) 373-8215

MCIA is a professional, non-profit association of persons who utilize computers to make and manage investments. Information, ideas, programs, and data are shared among members via the association's journal, The MicroComputer Investor (MCI). There is a current target to compose at least two issues of the journal each year. There are two requirements for membership: The first is the acceptance of an obligation to furnish at least one article per year that is suitable for publishing in the association's journal, MCI. The second is payment of $50 in dues each year, which entitles each member to two issues of MCI, whenever published. Such issues may be downloaded from the bulletin board when, and as, available. No charge will be made to any member for using this bulletin board, however, if members desire to download back issues or copies of articles published before they became members (or while they were in an inactive status) there will be a charge for such services. Normal operating hours for the MCIA Bulletin Board are 24 hours a day, 7 days a week. The cost of each article is $0.10 per page. There is a minimum charge of $5.00 for each order. The articles and programs on the MCIA bulletin board are neither shareware or freeware. The articles purchased are for personal use only.

Boston Computer Society

101 A First Avenue
Suite 2
Waltham, MA 02154
(617) 290-5700

BBS:
IBM: (617) 466-8730
members-only IBM: (617) 466-8740
Mac: (617) 864-3375

The BCS Investment Group is dedicated to the improvement of its member's investing practices through the use of computer technology. The investment group meets monthly to discuss investments, manage hypothetical portfolios, and listen to speakers. Members also present forecasts based on technical and fundamental analysis. The BCS Investment Group also sponsors an annual seminar. The membership fee is $49 per year.

Connecticut PC Wall Street

Dick Orenstein
P.O. Box 512
Westport, CT 06881-0512
(203) 226-5251

The Wall Street SIG of the Connecticut IBM PC Users Group meets on the second Thursday of the odd numbered months at Manero's, 556 Steamboat Road, Greenwich, CT. The meeting commences at 6:30 p.m. with a cash bar, followed by dinner. During dinner there are general roundtable discussions and introductions of new members. A presentation follows dinner, highlighting investment strategies, software, books, or some other subject related to computerized investing. The group is informal; member experience levels range from novice to professional money manager.

Index

A

AAII Fundamental Stock Analysis Disk, 102, 168

AAII Online, 144, 436

@Bonds XL U.S. Series and International Series, 46, 102, 322

ADS Associates, Inc., 163

Advanced Analysis, Inc., 163-164

Advanced Business Valuation, 102, 248

Advanced G.E.T., 76, 102, 414

Advanced Total Investor (ATI), 46, 62, 76, 102, 277

Advanced Wireless, Inc., 433-434

Advent Software, Inc., 165

@Exotics XL, 46, 102, 323

Affiliated Computer Services, Inc., 165-166

AIQ Inc., 166-168

AI Research Corporation, 434

Alexander Steele Systems Technologies, Inc., 434-435

Alliance 5.0, 76, 326

All-Quotes, 144, 436

All-Quotes, Inc., 436

American Association of Individual Investors, 168 - 169, 436-438

American Institute of Small Business, 169

American River Software, 169-170, 438-439

American Venture Capital Exchange, 144, 439

America Online, 144, 440

AmortizeIt!, 46, 102, 352

Amortizer Plus, 46, 269

@nalyst, 46, 62, 102, 396

Analytic Associates, 170-171

Andrew Tobias' Tax Cut, 46, 311

@Options XL Pro, Premium, and Extended Binomial Series, 46, 102, 323

Applied Artificial Intelligence Corporation, 171- 172

Asset Allocation Expert, 46, 391

Asset Allocator, 46, 62, 102, 354

AVCO Financial, Corp., 172

Axys Advantage, 62, 165

B

Baarns Publishing, 172-174, 441-442

Basic Cycle Analysis, 76, 102, 263

Behold!, 76, 297

Binomial Market Model, 102, 308

BioTech On Disk, 144, 492

BMI, 442-444

BMW, 102, 355

BNA Estate Tax Spreadsheet, 46, 175

BNA Fixed Asset Management System, 46, 175

BNA Income Tax Spreadsheet with Fifty State Planner, 46, 176

BNA Real Estate Investment Spreadsheet, 46, 104, 176

BNA Software, 175-176

Bond Buyer Full Text, 144, 459

BondCalc, 46, 62, 104, 176

BondCalc Corporation, 176-177

Bond Portfolio, 46, 104, 172

Bond Portfolio Manager, 48, 62, 104, 298

Bond Pricing, 48, 104, 173

Bonds and Interest Rates Software, 104, 356

Bondseye, 104, 246

Bondsheet, 104, 341

BOND$MART, 104, 356

Bond-Tech's Bond Calculator, 104, 177

Bond-Tech, Inc., 177-178

Borland International, 178-179

BrainMaker, 104, 180

BrainMaker Professional, 104, 180

Budget Model Analyzer, 48, 212

Business Connection, 144, 460

Business DateLine, 144, 460

Business Forecast Systems, 179

Business Pack, 48, 104, 212

Business Week Mutual Fund Scoreboard, 144, 445

Buysel, 76, 104, 213

Buy-Write Model, 104, 329

C

Calcugram Stock Options System, 104, 213

California Scientific Software, 179-180

Cambridge Planning & Analytics, Inc., 445-446

Canadian Quotes Module for Quote Express, 283

Candlestick Forecaster, 76, 106, 285

Candlestick Forecaster Master Edition, 76, 106, 286

Candlestick Forecaster Real Time, 62, 76, 106, 286

CAPTOOL, 48, 62, 76, 106, 397

CAPTOOL Global Investor, 48, 62, 76, 106, 398

CAPTOOL Professional Investor, 48, 62, 78, 106, 399

CAPTOOL Real Time, 48, 64, 78, 106, 399

Capture, 186

Caribou Codeworks, 181

CDA/INVESTNET, 446

Centerpiece, 64, 106, 350

Centerpiece Performance Monitor, 64, 351

Charles L. Pack, 181-182

Charles Schwab & Company, Inc., 183-184, 447-448

Charlton Woolard, 184-185

ChartistAlert, 78, 106, 379

Chartmaster, 78, 377

ChartPro, 78, 375

CheckFree, 144, 449

Checkfree Corp., 449

Clarks Ridge Associates, 185

CMO/REMIC Pricing Service, 144, 506

Coast Investment Software, Inc., 186-187

Coherent Software Systems, 187-189

Coindata, 214

Coins, 214

Collectors Paradise, 214

COMEX, The Game, 108, 190

Comfuture Software Systems, 189

COMLINE, 144, 502

Commercial/Industrial Real Estate Applications, 108, 366

Commission Comparisons, 328

FirstAlert, 66, 82, 114, 380
First Financial Software, 261-262
First Release, 148, 461
Fixed-Income Pricing Services, 148, 507
Flexsoft, 262-263
Folioman, 50, 66, 82, 114, 246
Folioman+, 50, 66, 82, 114, 247
Ford Data Base, 148, 471
Ford Investor Services, 471-472
Forecast!, 114, 288
The Forecasting Edge, 114, 219
Forecast Pro, 114, 179
Foreign Exchange Software Package, 82, 114, 357
Fortune 500 on Disk, 114, 205
Foundation for the Study of Cycles, 263-264
Fourcast, 82, 114, 240
Fourier Analysis Forecaster, 82, 114, 220
401(k) Forecaster, 50, 114, 422
FPLAN-KWIK Financial & Retirement Planner, 50, 261
FPLAN-Personal Financial Planner, 52, 261
FPLAN-Professional Financial Planner, 52, 262
Free Financial Network (FFN), 148, 488
F2S Enterprises, 264-265
Fundamental Investor, 114, 383
Fundgraf, 82, 347
Fundgraf Downloader, 347
Fundgraf Supplemental Programs, Disk 1, 66, 82, 348
Fund Master TC, 66, 82, 407
Fund Pro, 66, 82, 408
FundScope, 148, 438
Funds-On-Line, 148, 492
Fundwatch, 82, 220

Fundwatch Online by Money Magazine, 148, 452
Fundwatch Plus, 82, 272
Futures Markets Analyzer, 114, 296
Futures Pro, 84, 114, 249
Futures Truth Co., 265
Future Wave Software, 266

G

Gannsoft Publishing Co., 266-267
GannTrader 2, 84, 266
G.C.P.I., 267-268
GE Information Services, 472-473
GEnie, 148, 472
Glendale, 84, 199
Global Trader Calculator, 114, 163
Goldspread Statistical, 114, 221
Good Software, Corp., 268-270
Greenstone Software, Inc., 270
Guru Systems, Ltd., 270-271

H

Hamilton Software, Inc., 271-274
H & H Scientific, 274-276
Hansen-Predict, 84, 114, 221
Harvest-Time Retirement Planning Software, 52, 197
Hedgemaster, 116, 190
Historical ADL, 84, 116, 409
Historical Data, 148, 482
Home Appraiser, 116, 222
Home Purchase, 116, 370
Hourly DJIA, 84, 148, 409, 513
How to Write a Business Plan, 52, 116, 169
Howardsoft, 276-277

P

Q

Retirement Planner, 58, 427

Retirement Solutions, 58, 132, 322

Retirement Trio, 58, 132, 427

Ret-Tech Software, Inc., 375-376

Reuters Money Network, 154, 499

Reuters Money Network for Quicken, 154, 500

Revenge Software, 376-377

Rich & Retired, 58, 201

RiskAlert, 94, 132, 381

RJT Systems, 377-378

RMC, 378-379

Roberts-Slade, Inc., 379-381

Roll Model, 132, 331

Rory Tycoon Options Trader, 132, 187

Rory Tycoon Portfolio Analyst, 58, 72, 94, 132, 188

Rory Tycoon Portfolio Manager, 58, 72, 132, 188

RTR Software, Inc., 382

S

S&P 1957-1991 Monthly, 154, 442

S&P ComStock, 154, 500-501

S&P Daily 1953-1991, 154, 442

S&P Daily 1980-1990, 154, 442

S&P Stock Guide Database by DTN, 154, 457

S&P Stock Guide on Disk, 154, 505

SASI Software, Corp., 382-383

Savant Software, Inc., 383-386, 501

Schwab Brokerage Services on GEnie, 154, 447

Scientific Consultant Services, Inc., 386-387

SEC: Healthcare, Pharmaceuticals & Biotech, 154, 504

SEC Online, 154, 462

SEC Online on SilverPlatter, 154, 503

SEC OnLine-10K, 154, 503

Securities History Data, 154, 481

Serenson Consulting Service, 387

SIBYL/RUNNER Interactive Forecasting, 132, 303

Signal, 154, 455

Silverplatter Information, Inc., 501-504

Small Investor's Software Company, 387-388, 504 - 505

Smartbroker, 72, 94, 132, 184

SMARTrader, 72, 94, 132, 393

SMARTrader Professional, 72, 94, 132, 394

Software Advantage Consulting Corporation, 389-390

SolveIt!, 58, 132, 353

Sophisticated Investor, 58, 72, 94, 132, 320

SORITEC, 132, 390

Sorites Group, Inc., 390

Sponsor-Software Systems, Inc., 391

Spread Maker, 132, 332

SPSS for Windows, 58, 94, 132, 391

SPSS, Inc., 391-393

SPSS/PC+, 94, 132, 392

SPSS/PC+ Trends, 94, 132, 392

Stable—Technical Graphs, 94, 430

Stampdata, 234

Stamps, 235

Standard & Poor's Corporation, 505

U.S. Equities OnFloppy, 158, 491

V

V.A. Denslow & Associates, 419-421
Value Line Publishing, 515
Value/Screen III, 158, 515
VantagePoint Intermarket Analysis Program, 100, 138, 312
VenCap Data Quest/Portfolio Companies 1.0, 158, 434
Vertical Spread Model, 138, 333
Vertigo Development Group, 421
Village Software, Inc., 421-428
Volume Dynamics, Inc., 428-429

W

Wall Street Journal Personal Finance Library, 60, 211
Wall Street Trainer, 138, 236
Wall Street Watcher, 100, 319
Wave Wise Spreadsheet for Windows, 100, 138, 297
WealthBuilder by Money Magazine, 60, 74, 138, 369
Wealth Creator, 60, 138, 362
What'sBest!, 60, 138, 303

Wilson Associates, 429
Windows on Wall Street Pro, 100, 138, 310
Winterra Software Group, 430
Worden Brothers, Inc., 515-516
Worldscope EMERGING MARKETS, 158, 466
Worldscope GLOBAL, 158, 466

X

X*Press Executive, 158, 516
X*Press Information Services, Ltd., 516-517
Xtrapolator Time Series Forecasts, 138, 237

Y

The Yellow Pad, 60, 345
Yield Curve, 138, 428

Z

Zacks Consensus Summary Diskette, 158, 517
Zacks Investment Research, 517
Zacks On-Line, 158, 517
Zenterprise Real Estate Investor, 138, 237

STOCK
INVESTOR

AAII's *Stock Investor* software program provides an easy and convenient way to screen stocks. *Stock Investor* enables you to screen through data on over 8,000 stocks, using a menu-driven program. You can research stocks by using over 250 financial variables including those you have created. You can design custom reports or use the standard report formats supplied by the program. *Stock Investor* is updated quarterly and covers all stocks on the New York Stock Exchange, American Stock Exchange, Nasdaq National Market System and Nasdaq Small-Cap.

***Stock Investor* features:**
- Over 8,000 stocks
- More than 250 financial variables for each stock
- Industry averages for comparisons
- Earnings estimates
- Ranking of stocks on any variable
- Information on dividend reinvestment plans
- User's guide with tutorial and on-line help

User options available:
- Custom screening on 50 predetermined and/or created variables
- Ability to create financial variables for screening
- Ability to create your own financial reports
- Nine full-page financial statements per company
- Export data in a number of popular file formats

System Requirements: IBM 386 equivalent or better with 30M of hard drive space available to install and at least 3M of available RAM. **Price:** $99.00 for annual subscription ($150 for non-members); price includes quarterly updates (Feb, May, Aug, Nov). For more information, contact the American Association of Individual Investors, 625 N. Michigan Avenue, Suite 1900, Chicago, IL 60611; (312) 280-0170.

AAII
AMERICAN
ASSOCIATION OF
INDIVIDUAL
INVESTORS®

—————————————————[Company Summary]—————————————————

Intel Cp	Ticker: INTC	Price: $58.50
P.O. Box 58065	Mailstop GR1-58	
Santa Clara, CA 95052-8065		(800) 548-4725

Description: Des/dev/mfr/sell semicond components & systems

Exchange: NASDAQ Nat'l Market	Industry# 17	Industry# 171
	Electronics	Electronic: Equipment
	Company		Manufacturers

Multiples

	Company	Electronics	Electronic: Equipment Manufacturers
Price/Earnings..........	10.9	28.7	19.3
Price/Earnings-5yr Avg..	12.9	27.2	18.1
Price/Book..............	3.18	3.38	3.47
Price/Sales.............	2.7	1.0	1.0
Dividend Yield (%).......	0.4	0.0	0.0
PE to Growth Ratio.......	0.2	0.9	0.9

Annual Growth Rates

	Company	Electronics	Electronic: Equipment Manufacturers
Sales (%)...............	29.5	10.6	6.9
Net Income (%)..........	55.7	12.0	20.2
EPS-Total (%)...........	49.5	19.1	13.6
EPS-Continuing (%)......	49.5	18.8	13.6
Dividend (%)............	G	0.0	0.0

< ELP > < Find > <rowse> <rint > < Back > < Next > < Pg p > <Pg own> < lose>

SAMPLE

—————————[Income Statement - Annual]—————————

| Intel Cp | Ticker: INTC | Price: $58.50 |

	Last Mos.	93/12	92/12	91/12	90/12	89/12
			Annual, Ending			
Sales ($M).....	9,418.4	8,782.0	5,844.0	4,778.6	3,921.3	3,126.8
CoGS ($M).......	2,861.4	2,518.0	2,023.8	1,897.3	1,637.9	1,483.8
Gross Inc ($M)..	6,557.0	6,264.0	3,820.2	2,881.3	2,283.4	1,643.0
Net Inc ($M)....	2,364.0	2,295.0	1,066.5	818.6	650.3	391.0
Gross Margin (%)	69.6	71.3	65.4	60.3	58.2	52.5
Net Margin (%)..	25.1	26.1	18.2	17.1	16.6	12.5
EPS-Total ($)...	5.38	5.20	2.49	1.96	1.60	1.04
EPS-Cont ($)....	5.38	5.20	2.49	1.96	1.60	1.04
Cash Flow ($)...	7.17	6.87	3.82	3.03	2.36	1.70
Dividend ($)....	0.20	0.20	0.05	0.00	0.00	0.00
Payout Ratio (%)	3.7	3.8	2.0	0.0	0.0	0.0
Shares (Mil)....	442.0	441.0	418.6	407.8	399.3	369.0

< ELP > < ind > < rowse> < rint > < B ck > < ext > < Pg p > <Pg own> < lose>

Quarterly Low-Load Mutual Fund Update®

Keep up-to-date on all the funds you've read about with the *Quarterly Low-Load Mutual Fund Update*.

This quarterly newsletter covers over 900 no-load and low-load mutual funds. Information reported for each fund includes:

• performance by quarter over the last year and annual total return for the last year, three years and five years
• difference between a fund's performance and that of an average of funds of the same category
• risk index
• yield
• expense ratio
• lists of top-performing funds and the performance of major indexes
• recent fund developments

The Quarterly Update is also available for IBM-compatible and Macintosh computers with a computerized menu-driven program that provides fund returns and investment category comparisons of these returns by quarter over the last year, last three years and last five years. Returns are also provided for each of the last 10 years and over the most recent bull and bear market periods. Risk statistics provided include standard deviation, investment category risk index, beta for stock funds and average maturity for bond funds. The IBM version requires a 386 IBM PC or compatible with 3M free RAM and 5M hard drive storage space. The Mac version requires a Mac S130 or higher with 3M hard disk storage.

Annual subscription to *The Quarterly Update,* $24 (non-members, $30); newsletter plus computer program, $39 (non-members, $50). For more information, contact the American Association of Individual Investors, 625 N. Michigan Avenue, Suite 1900, Chicago, IL 60611; (312) 280-0170.

		Total Return (%)						Annual Total Return (%)						Risk Index	Yield (%)	Exp. Ratio (%)	Max. Load (%)	Max. 12b-1 (%)	Phone
		Last Qtr.	Cat. +/-	Last 2 Qtrs.	Cat. +/-	Last 3 Qtrs.	Cat. +/-	Last Year	Cat. +/-	Last 3 Years	Cat. +/-	Last 5 Years	Cat. +/-						

Balanced Funds

Fund		Last Qtr.	Cat. +/-	Last 2 Qtrs.	Cat. +/-	Last 3 Qtrs.	Cat. +/-	Last Year	Cat. +/-	Last 3 Years	Cat. +/-	Last 5 Years	Cat. +/-	Risk Index	Yield	Exp.	Load	12b-1	Phone
T. Rowe Price Spectrum Income	∎	1.7	0.0	4.4	(1.1)	7.4	(0.2)	12.4	(0.9)	13.1	(2.1)	na	na	0.48	6.2	0.00	—	—	(800) 638-5660
Twentieth Century Balanced		(0.8)	(2.5)	3.4	(2.1)	6.2	(1.5)	7.2	(5.1)	13.9	(1.3)	13.6	1.4	1.85	2.3	1.00	—	—	(800) 345-2021
USAA Balanced		2.3	0.6	4.7	(0.8)	9.0	1.3	13.7	0.4	11.0	(4.2)	na	na	0.82	3.5	0.92	—	—	(800) 382-8722
USAA Cornerstone	aa	3.9	2.2	8.6	3.1	12.4	4.7	23.7	10.4	15.2	0.0	11.1	(1.1)	1.19	2.5	1.18	—	—	(800) 382-8722
USAA Income		(0.2)	(1.9)	1.9	(3.6)	4.9	(2.8)	9.9	(3.4)	12.4	(2.8)	12.2	0.0	0.86	6.9	0.42	—	—	(800) 382-8722
Value Line Income	aa	0.0	(1.7)	1.0	(4.5)	4.4	(3.3)	8.2	(5.1)	12.2	(3.0)	12.0	(0.2)	1.40	3.1	0.89	—	—	(800) 223-0818
Vanguard Asset Allocation	aa	1.2	(0.5)	5.2	(0.3)	7.4	(0.2)	13.4	0.1	15.2	0.0	13.9	1.7	1.21	3.3	0.52	—	—	(800) 662-7447
Vanguard Balanced Index	da	0.9	(0.8)	4.4	(1.1)	5.8	(1.8)	9.9	(3.4)	na	na	na	na	na	3.5	na	—	—	(800) 662-7447
Vanguard Star	∎	0.6	(1.1)	4.6	(0.9)	5.9	(1.8)	10.8	(2.5)	15.0	(0.2)	11.7	(0.5)	1.08	3.5	0.00	—	—	(800) 662-7447
Vanguard Wellesley Income		(0.8)	(2.5)	4.1	(1.4)	7.3	(0.4)	14.6	1.3	14.8	(0.4)	13.7	1.5	0.90	5.9	0.35	—	—	(800) 662-7447
Vanguard Wellington		2.0	0.3	4.9	(0.6)	7.9	0.2	13.5	0.2	14.8	(0.4)	12.3	0.1	1.21	4.5	0.33	—	—	(800) 662-7447
BALANCED FUND AVERAGE		1.7	0.0	5.5	0.0	7.7	0.0	13.3	0.0	15.2	0.0	12.2	0.0	1.80	3.3	1.04	—	—	SD 6.2%

Corporate Bond Funds

Fund		Last Qtr.	Cat. +/-	Last 2 Qtrs.	Cat. +/-	Last 3 Qtrs.	Cat. +/-	Last Year	Cat. +/-	Last 3 Years	Cat. +/-	Last 5 Years	Cat. +/-	Risk Index	Yield	Exp.	Load	12b-1	Phone
⬅ CGM Fixed Income		2.7	1.8	6.5	2.7	10.8	4.3	18.9	7.5	na	na	na	na	na	6.0	0.85	—	—	(800) 345-4048
Fidelity Short-Term Bond		1.6	0.7	3.6	(0.2)	5.5	(1.0)	9.1	(2.3)	10.1	(1.9)	9.3	(0.8)	0.57	6.9	0.77	—	—	(800) 544-8888
Fidelity Spartan Investment Grade Bond		(0.6)	(1.5)	4.5	1.2	8.8	2.3	15.7	4.3	na	na	na	na	na	7.3	0.65	—	—	(800) 544-8888
Fidelity Spartan Short-Term Bond		1.5	0.6	3.5	(0.3)	5.5	(1.0)	9.0	(2.4)	na	na	na	na	na	7.2	0.00	—	—	(800) 544-8888
⬅ Homestead Short-Term Bond		0.5	(0.4)	2.1	(1.7)	3.4	(3.1)	6.6	(4.8)	na	na	na	na	na	6.5	0.75	—	—	(800) 258-3030
INVESCO Income—Sel Income		1.4	0.5	3.1	(0.7)	6.1	(0.4)	11.3	(0.1)	13.3	1.3	10.5	0.4	na	7.5	1.14	—	0.250	(800) 525-8085
Janus Flexible Income		1.7	0.8	5.8	2.0	8.8	3.3	15.8	4.2	17.5	5.8	10.1	0.0	na	7.7	1.00	—	—	(800) 525-3713
Janus Short-Term Bond		0.6	(0.3)	2.4	(1.4)	3.7	(2.8)	6.1	(5.3)	na	na	na	na	na	5.9	1.00	—	—	(800) 525-3713
Loomis Sayles Bond		3.2	2.3	7.7	3.9	13.5	7.0	22.2	10.8	na	na	na	na	na	8.0	1.00	—	—	(800) 633-3330
Merrill Lynch Corp Interm "A"		(0.3)	(1.2)	3.4	(0.4)	6.0	(0.5)	11.8	0.4	11.		11.	0.9	1.70			2.00†	—	(609) 282-2800
⬅ Paine Webber Investment Gr Inc "D"		0.1	(0.8)	4.0	0.2	7.0	0.5	12.7	1.3	na	na	na	na	na	6.	na	—	0.750	(800) 647-1568
Permanent Port—Versatile Bond		0.5	(0.4)	1.4	(2.4)	2.0	(4.5)	3.7	(7.7)	na	na	na	na	0.89	2	0.89	—	0.250	(800) 531-5142
StanRoe Income		0.5	(0.4)	3.8	0.0	7.4	0.9			na	na	10.4		1.48	6.8	0.82	—	—	(800) 338-2550
Strong Advantage		1.8	0.9	3.4	(0.4)	5.2	(1.3)			8.	(3.1)	8.5	(1.6)	0.37	5.7	1.00	—	—	(800) 368-1030
Strong Short-Term Bond		1.6	0.7	3.4	(0.4)					10.1		8.7	(1.4)	0.70	6.5	0.60	—	—	(800) 368-1030
Vanguard Long Term Corp Bond		(0.6)	(1.5)	3.7	(0.1)	7.	1.1		2.9	9	2.	13.1	3.0	1.96	6.8	0.31	—	—	(800) 662-7447
Vanguard Short-Term Corporate		0.6	(0.3)		(1.5)	3.8		7.0	(4.4)	0	(3.0)	9.5	(0.5)	0.81	5.6	0.27	—	—	(800) 662-7447
CORPORATE BOND FUND AVERAGE		0.9	0.0			5.5	0.0	11.4	0.0	12.0	0.0	10.1	0.0	1.80	6.1	0.72	—	—	SD 2.7%

Corporate High-Yield Bond Funds

Fund		Last Qtr.	Cat. +/-	Last 2 Qtrs.	Cat. +/-	Last 3 Qtrs.	Cat. +/-	Last Year	Cat. +/-	Last 3 Years	Cat. +/-	Last 5 Years	Cat. +/-	Risk Index	Yield	Exp.	Load	12b-1	Phone
Fidelity Capital & Income			0.5	14.2	3.5	24.8	6.4	27.5	7.0	14.8	3.5	1.47	8.4	0.91	1.50†	—	(800) 544-8888
Fidelity Spartan High Income		5.2	1.	7.	1.5	13.5	2.7	21.8	3.4	25.7	5.2	na	na	1.36	9.2	0.70	1.00†	—	(800) 544-8888
GIT Income—Maximum		4.6		6.0	(0.4)	9.1	(1.8)	15.0	(3.4)	17.4	(3.1)	9.0	(1.5)	1.14	8.0	1.54	—	—	(800) 336-3063
INVESCO Income—High Yield			(0.5)	5.2	(1.2)	9.2	(1.7)	15.6	(2.8)	17.8	(2.7)	10.1	(0.4)	0.92	8.0	1.00	—	0.250	(800) 525-8085
Nicholas Income		2.4	(1.8)	4.7	(1.7)	7.5	(3.4)	12.9	(5.5)	15.3	(5.2)	9.5	(1.0)	0.89	8.2	0.68	—	—	(800) 227-5987
Northeast Investors Trust		6.0	1.8	8.5	2.1	13.9	3.0	23.5	5.1	22.4	1.9	10.7	0.2	1.25	9.7	0.79	—	—	(800) 225-6704
⬅ Paine Webber High Income "D"		3.3	(0.0)	6.3	(0.1)	8.1	(2.8)	13.6	(4.8)	na	na	na	na	na	6.7	na	—	0.750	(800) 647-1568
⬅ Safeco High Yield Bond		3.0	(1.2)	5.3	(1.1)	9.7	(1.2)	16.9	(1.5)	18.2	(2.3)	10.2	(0.3)	1.03	9.2	1.05	—	—	(800) 426-6730
T. Rowe Price High Yield		4.7	0.5	6.5	0.1	12.6	1.7	21.7	3.3	22.2	1.7	9.9	(0.6)	1.25	8.8	0.97	1.00†	—	(800) 638-5860
Value Line Aggressive Income		5.4	1.2	7.6	1.2	11.6	0.7	19.0	0.6	19.1	(1.4)	10.7	0.2	1.25	8.4	1.15	—	—	(800) 223-0818
Vanguard High Yield Corporate		3.5	(0.7)	6.0	(0.4)	10.7	(0.2)	18.2	(0.2)	20.3	(0.2)	10.8	0.3	1.14	8.6	0.34	1.80†	—	(800) 662-7447
CORPORATE HIGH-YIELD FUND AVERAGE		4.2	0.0	6.4	0.0	10.9	0.0	16.4	0.0	20.5	0.0	9.9	0.0	1.80	8.4	0.91	—	—	SD 3.6%

Government Bond Funds

Fund		Last Qtr.	Cat. +/-	Last 2 Qtrs.	Cat. +/-	Last 3 Qtrs.	Cat. +/-	Last Year	Cat. +/-	Last 3 Years	Cat. +/-	Last 5 Years	Cat. +/-	Risk Index	Yield	Exp.	Load	12b-1	Phone
⬅ 1784 U.S. Gov't Med-Term Income		0.0	0.5	2.0	(0.7)	na	na	na	na	na	na	na	na	na	na	na	—	0.250	(800) 252-1784
⬅ Alliance Bond—U.S. Gov't "C"		(0.2)	0.3	2.2	(0.5)	na	na	na	na	na	na	na	na	na	na	na	—	1.000	(800) 221-5672
BNY Hamilton Interm Gov't		(0.6)	(0.1)	1.8	(0.9)	4.2	(1.5)	8.0	(2.4)	na	na	na	na	na	5.0	0.75	—	0.250	(800) 426-9363
⬅ Benham Long Term Treasury and Agency		(1.8)	(1.3)	5.0	2.3	10.4	4.7	17.6	7.2	na	na	na	na	na	6.4	0.00	—	—	(800) 321-8321
Benham Short-Term Treasury & Agency		0.4	0.9	1.7	(1.0)	2.7	(3.0)	5.4	(5.0)	na	na	na	na	na	3.9	0.00	—	—	(800) 321-8321
Benham Target Mat Trust—1995		0.4	0.9	1.9	(0.8)	3.2	(2.5)	6.9	(3.5)	10.0	(0.8)	10.9	0.5	0.86	0.0	0.82	—	—	(800) 321-8321
Benham Target Mat Trust—2000		(1.1)	(0.6)	2.6	0.1	7.5	1.8	15.4	5.0	14.7	3.9	13.9	3.5	1.67	0.0	0.85	—	—	(800) 321-8321
Benham Target Mat Trust—2005		(2.4)	(1.9)	4.6	1.3	12.0	6.3	21.5	11.1	17.3	6.5	15.7	5.3	2.21	0.0	0.83	—	—	(800) 321-8321
Benham Target Mat Trust—2010		(2.1)	(1.6)	6.3	3.6	16.3	10.6	26.2	15.8	19.8	8.0	16.5	6.1	2.55	0.0	0.70	—	—	(800) 321-8321

SAMPLE